Eastward Flows the Great River

Eastward Flows the Great River

Festschrift in Honor of Professor William S-Y. Wang on his 80th Birthday

Edited by
PENG Gang, SHI Feng

City University of Hong Kong Press

ISBN: 978-962-937-216-3

Published by
        City University of Hong Kong Press
        Tat Chee Avenue
        Kowloon, Hong Kong
        Website: www.cityu.edu.hk/upress
        E-mail: upress@cityu.edu.hk

Printed in Hong Kong

Contents

17. Northern-Min Glottalized Onsets and the Principles of Tonal Split and Tonal Merger
Weera OSTAPIRAT

18. Different Semantic Nature of Homonym, Metaphor and Polysemy in Mandarin Chinese: Evidence from Behavioral and Functional Magnetic Resonance Imaging Experiments
Fan-pei YANG, Dai-lin WU

19. A Few Morphological Functions of the Suffix *-s in Shang Chinese
Ken-ichi TAKASHIMA

20. Computer Simulation of Language Convergence
Tao GONG, Lan SHUAI, Umberto ANSALDO

W. S-Y. Wang and parents in Shanghai, around 1940

Matthew Chen（陳淵泉）and W. S-Y. Wang in La Jolla, California, 1981

W. S-Y. W, Mason Yang, Yang Chenning（楊振寧）, Yang Chenping（楊振平）, Barbara Shih（史美）, at Gui Gen Ju（歸根居）at Tsinghua University in Beijing, 2004.

W. S-Y. Wang, Tsai Yaching（蔡雅菁）and Mr. & Mrs. Shibatani Masayoshi（柴谷方良）in Rokkomichi, Kobe, 2006

W. S-Y. Wang with five children and son-in-law David Turell in USA, 2006

Yusi Wang（王友思）and W. S-Y. Wang in USA, 2006

W. S-Y. Wang, Kong Jiangping（孔江平）and Fujimura Osamu（藤村靖）in Hong Kong, 2006

Ikegami Takashi（池上高志）, Ciro Cattuto, James Minett, Francis Wong（黃俊傑）, Tan Lihai（譚力海）, Ovid J. Tzeng（曾志朗）(front), James Hurford (behind), Ogura Mieko（小倉美惠子）, Mike Dowman, W. S-Y. Wang, Thomas Schoenemann, Vittoro Loreto, Jean-Julien Aucouturier, Paul Kay, Shibatani Masayoshi（柴谷方良）, Erhan Oztop, Salikoko Mufwene, Kanamori Junjiro（金森順次郎）and Fujimura Osamu（藤村靖）in Kyoto, 2007

W. S-Y. Wang in Venice, 2007

Paul Kay and W. S-Y. Wang in Hong Kong, 2007

Zheng Hongying（鄭洪英）, Gong Tao（龔濤）, Ogura Mieko（小倉美惠子）, Seana Coulson, Kanamori Junjiro（金森順次郎）, Richard Ivry, Asada Minoru（淺田稔）, James Minett, Francis Wong（黃俊傑）, W. S-Y. Wang, Okanoya Kazuo（岡ノ谷一夫）and Hashimoto Takashi（橋本敬）in Kyoto, 2008

Benjamin K. Tsou（鄒嘉彥）, Sydney Lamb and W. S-Y. Wang at City University of Hong Kong, 2009

W. S-Y. Wang with grandson Niko Turell and daughter Yusi Wang（王友思）in USA, 2009

W. S-Y. Wang and Yumei Wang（王友梅）in USA, 2009

Lu Jianming（陸儉明）, W. S-Y. Wang, Redouane Djamouri and Marjorie K. M. Chan（陳潔雯）in Paris, 2009

Gene Wang（王友進）and W. S-Y. Wang at Hong Kong Science Park, 2010

W. S-Y. Wang and Charles K. Kao（高錕）at The Chinese University of Hong Kong, 2010

W. S-Y. Wang in Singapore, 2011

W. S-Y. Wang and Jack Gandour in Hong Kong, 2011

W. S-Y. Wang and Mr. & Mrs. Yulun Wang（王友倫）in Washington, 2011

William Labov and W. S-Y. Wang at The Chinese University of Hong Kong, 2012

Shi Feng (石鋒), Ogura Mieko (小倉美惠子), Peng Gang (彭剛), Thomas Lee (李行德), W. S-Y. Wang, Benjamin K. Tsou (鄒嘉彥), Lien Chin-fa (連金發) and James Minett at The Chinese University of Hong Kong, 2012

W. S-Y. Wang, Tsai Yaching（蔡雅菁）, Elena Valussi and Edward Shaughnessy at The Chinese University of Hong Kong, 2013

Gloria Zhang（張燕輝）, Audrey Li（李豔惠）, Lawrence Cheung（張欽良）, Patrick Wong（黃俊文）, Virginia Yip（葉彩燕）, W. S-Y. Wang, Tsai Yaching（蔡雅菁）, Ovid Tzeng（曾志朗）, Peng Gang（彭剛）and Janet Hsiao（蕭惠文）at The Chinese University of Hong Kong, 2013

James H.-Y. Tai（戴浩一）, Ovid Tzeng（曾志朗）, W S-Y. Wang, Cheng Chin-Chuan（鄭錦全） at IACL 2013 in Taiwan. Note: W S-Y. Wang was elected President of the International Association of Chinese Linguistics (IACL) when it was first founded in 1992.

Tan Lihai（譚力海）and W. S-Y. Wang at The Chinese University of Hong Kong, 2013.

Wing Wong（黃詠）Peng Gang（彭剛）, Lee Junren（李俊仁）, Kong Jiangping （孔江平）, W. S-Y. Wang （王士元）, Daisy Hung （洪蘭）, Joseph J. Y. Sung（沈祖堯）, Ovid Tzeng（曾志朗）, Virginia Yip （葉彩燕）, Leung Yuen Sang（梁元生）, Chen Baoya（陳保亞）, Wang Feng （汪鋒）, Rose Lee（李如蕙）, Denise Wu（吳嫺）at The Chinese University of Hong Kong, 2013

Foreword

William S-Y. Wang: Epoch-Making Linguist

Eastward flows the Great River;
With gushing waves it carries away
Gallant souls from days of yore.
— (Song dynasty) Su Shi

Browsing through volumes of the long history of linguistics, the pages glitter with familiar names. Many linguists have dedicated their lives and wisdom to the research of languages, the young talents taking up the works of the old ones and marching forward with force and energy on the path to explore the mysteries of languages. Among the linguists of the 20th century, an eminent name stands out: William S-Y. Wang.

Prof. William Wang is a pioneer in interdisciplinary linguistic studies and a distinguished scholar of evolutionary linguistics. He is a worldwide acclaimed master of linguistics and an epoch-making linguist.

The compilation of the *Festschrift in Honor of William S-Y. Wang on his Eightieth Birthday* has gained enthusiastic support from numerous linguists in Mainland China, Hong Kong, Taiwan, East Asia as well as in Europe and the United States. With a total of over sixty excellent contributions covering the major fields of contemporary linguistics, the *Festschrift* is divided into the Chinese and English volumes and is scheduled to be published on Prof. Wang's 80th birthday. This is an important event not only in the community of Chinese scholarship, but also in international linguistics. It is indeed a great honor to experience this historical event! Living in the present while evoking memories of the past, we cannot but feel an upsurge of excitement.

The title of the *Festschrift*, "*Eastward Flows the Great River*", has two implications: one is a metaphoric depiction of Prof. Wang's attitude in linguistic research, which resembles the rolling waves of the Yangtze rushing eastward, with its waters always flowing forward to finally empty into the ocean of knowledge. The other is to describe the boundless currents of contemporary linguistic studies which started in the West and continue towards the East with booming and innovative vitality. The verse "Eastward flows the Great River" by the Song dynasty poet Su Shi is both succinct and unadorned, but evokes an image of powerful grandeur. With these words the poet expressed his nostalgic sentiments towards the historic heroes, revealing a philosophical insight on the rise and fall of the ages. The power of his writing remains unexcelled to this day.

Our celebration of Prof. Wang's 80th birthday is not merely about recognizing his seminal contributions to linguistic studies, but also about identifying the goal and direction which he represents in contemporary linguistics. Whether viewed from the current global situation of international linguistics, or considered from the historical development of modern linguistics,

Prof. Wang's research works on linguistics over the past fifty some years have given us precious inspirations. They also reflect the stride linguistics has made in more than half a century.

1.   Starting from Jakobson

Ferdinand de Saussure (1857–1913) and Roman Jakobson (1896–1982) are two summits in the 20th century linguistics. However the situations they went through in China are utterly different. Jakobson even seems hardly known. This is an aberrant phenomenon in the academic circles that came to assume shape under abnormal historical and social circumstances, which requires an urgent change.

Saussure was able to overcome the extreme historicist tendency of the 19th century linguistics and is therefore esteemed as the father of modern linguistics. Nonetheless, one tendency covered over another, and Saussure's emphasis on synchrony went to the other extreme. He studied language for the sake of language, excluding all that is external to linguistics (1980: 20), advocating a closed atmosphere of lesser linguistics. The study of language thereafter stepped into an ever narrowing alley to enter finally the ivory tower. The discipline has become hypercorrected in its rectifying behavior.

Jakobson was one of the most talented and creative linguists and literary theorists of the 20th century. Influenced by Saussure, he was among the first to propose a structural-functional analysis of language, laying the theoretical foundations for the Prague School and thus praised as the father of structuralism. He regarded structure as the approach of analysis rather than the goal of research. He introduced anthropology into linguistics, integrated poetics with linguistics, investigated aphasics in hospitals (1941), and wrote papers in collaboration with engineers (1951). He promoted an open atmosphere of greater linguistics. Jakobson did more than simply repeat and continue the words of Saussure, but truly inherited and developed the Saussurean essence of innovation. He was an open-minded pioneer in linguistic research across disciplines, across fields and across schools.

The position Prof. Wang takes in linguistic research is a succession of the Jakobsonian ideas. From the elevated viewpoint of language evolution, he sees archaeology, genetics and linguistics as the three windows on prehistory (Wang 1998), expanding the breadth and depth of language studies. His comprehensive interdisciplinary perspective is reflected in two respects: he is the first one to combine linguistics with computer science, so that linguistics is greatly assisted with the wings of modern technology. He also applies the progress in neuroscience to the study of language evolution, and his explorations remain all the time on the cutting edge of linguistic studies.

Early in the 1960s, Prof. Wang, Cheng Chin-Chuan and colleagues took the lead to make the first computer dictionary of Chinese dialects, the earliest database of linguistic corpus. The establishment of his theory of lexical diffusion was based on such a corpus, the earliest result from the marriage of computer and linguistics. He once collaborated with the mathematician D. A. Freedman, applying a probabilistic model to resolve the problem of monogenesis or polygenesis of language emergence (Freedman and Wang 1996). In recent years he modeled the conventionalization process of language emergence by computer simulation (Wang and Ke 2001), and successfully applied computer modeling to study horizontal and vertical transmission of language evolution (Wang and Minett 2005). Working closely with John H. Holland, the father of genetic algorithm, they promoted modeling and simulation research on language as a complex adaptive system.

Starting from the 1960s, Prof. Wang began to conduct perception experiments of Chinese tones (Wang and Li 1967). He also explored the connection between language and the brain with colleagues like Ovid J. L. Tzeng (Tzeng, Hung, and Wang 1977), opening up psycholinguistics and neurolinguistics research of the Chinese language and sinograms. He co-taught the course "Biological Foundations of Language" at the University of California at Berkeley with Prof. Tzeng in the 1970s. Although decades have passed, Prof. Tzeng still remembers those happy moments of mutual interaction which brought "overwhelmingly thrilling satisfaction." (Tzeng 2004) Prof. Wang has never ceased to march forward. His *Language, Evolution and the Brain* (Wang 2011), *Essays on Evolutionary Linguistics* (Wang 2013) and a series of publications on similar themes reflect his latest advancements in research.

With his rich and original research achievements Prof. Wang actively engages in interdisciplinary pursuits and leads a new avenue of language studies. Contemporary language research has thus taken on a new look, enabling linguistics to be in synchronous development with human sciences. The subsequent profound transformation of the overall linguistics theory and of methodology will become all the more obvious with the passing of time. Prof. Wang raises the flag to lead the way. He is the quintessential interdisciplinarian of linguistic research and another summit after Jakobson.

2.　Colleague with Y. R. Chao

Chao Yuen Ren (1892–1982) was a trailblazer of modern Chinese linguistics. His research was multifaceted. Chao and Jakobson were quite similar in their versatility. Jakobson was both a linguist and a poet, while Chao was both a linguist and a musician. He studied dialects during field trips and with empirical methods. He recorded the standard Chinese pronunciation gramophone records and designed the Gwoyeu Romatzyh, a Chinese romanization scheme. He also invented a five-scale notation for transcribing tonal pitch variation in spoken languages and proposed the multifunctionality of phonemic analysis (Chao 1934). He published *Grammar of Spoken Chinese*. Chao is credited as the father of Chinese linguistics.

At the invitation of Chao, Prof. Wang relocated to Berkeley from Ohio and became both a colleague and a good friend to Chao despite a difference of age. They were both originally from China: one from Changzhou and the other from Shanghai; they both majored in science in university: one in mathematics and the other in electronic engineering; above all, they have a common love for their native heritage, taking as their own responsibility the vision to revive Chinese linguistics.

Prof. Wang is keen in promoting and moving forward the research on Chinese linguistics. When at the Ohio State University he helped found the Department of Linguistics and the Department of Asian Languages and Cultures. The Phonology Laboratory he founded at the University of California at Berkeley is one of the earliest phonetics labs in the United States. The *Journal of Chinese Linguistics* (JCL) he founded is the first international publication in the field of Chinese linguistics. The inaugural issue was dedicated to Chao and a classic article by Prof. Li Fang-kuei, father of non-Chinese linguistics, on the genealogy of Sino-Tibetan languages was published in this issue. Prof. Wang led the Project on Linguistic Analysis (POLA) for more than thirty years, making POLA a landmark in Chinese linguistics. Many scholars of the older generation still have fond memories of the POLA Forever (Ho and Tzeng 2005). Prof. Wang was the inaugural president of International Association of Chinese Linguistics (IACL). He taught several times in the summer schools organized by the Linguistic Society of America and in those sponsored by Santa Fe Institute. He also helped to organize the first summer school on Chinese linguistics in China and came all the way to Nankai University in Tianjin for delivering lectures.

Prof. Wang went to Kyrgyzstan to investigate the relationship between the Donggan language and Northwestern Chinese dialects. He also went to such places as northern Thailand and southern China to examine languages of the ethnic minorities, completing the computational population analysis of the Sino-Tibetan language. Earlier we also mentioned his exploration of the psycho-cognitive and brain processing mechanisms of Chinese lexical tones and sinograms, as well as his computer simulation and modeling works on language evolution based on Chinese lexicon and syntax which have obtained fruitful results, bringing studies of the Chinese language onto the stage of international linguistics.

Prof. Wang has helped nurture numerous scholars in Chinese linguistics: Hashimoto Mantaro, Anne Yue-Hashimoto, Matthew Chen, Hsieh Hsin-I, Shibatani Masayoshi, Liao Chiu-chung, Benjamin K. Tsou, Lien Chin-fa, Shen Zhongwei, Ogura Mieko, Kong Jiangping, Peng Gang, Wang Feng, Gong Tao, Francis Wong, sand so on, are all his pupils. Prof. Wang is modest and sincere towards people and broad-minded. Many students have been directly or indirectly inspired and influenced by him to embark on their journey of linguistics.

Based on the phonetic data of Chinese dialects Chao proposed a multifunctionlaity account of phonemic analysis in the 1930s. Likewise Prof. Wang made use of the computer dictionary of Chinese dialects to establish his theory of lexical diffusion in the 1960s, completing another significant innovation where Chinese linguistics has contributed to the international circle of linguistics. The essence of lexical diffusion is that phonetic change not merely involves the change of sound classes, but also has an interactive relation with the lexicon. A certain sound change is actually the process of diffusion across time of words governed by this class of sound. Lexical diffusion offers an innovative methodology and theoretical framework for studying the microhistory and macrohistory of language evolution.

Geneticist L. L. Cavalla-Sforza of Stanford University once remarked, "The theory of lexical diffusion has been recognized as the most important innovation in the study of linguistic change." (Cavalli-Sforza 1994). Fruits from Chinese linguistics have gained recognition by world-renowned scholars and have been written into various monographs and encyclopedias on theoretical linguistics.

The late Harvard University professor and anthropologist Chang Kuang-Chih once reviewed the contributions and influences the discipline of Chinese humanities and social sciences of the 20th century has offered to the international academics, "It is only in the field of linguistics that works of Chinese linguists such as Y. R. Chao, F. K. Li and W. S-Y. Wang are quoted in publications of general linguistics." (Chang 1994). In this respect, Prof. Wang and Prof. Chang share a common goal: "We strive to be the main stream, and this can be seen as the responsibility of Chinese scholars of humanities and social sciences to the world."

If the center of the 19th century linguistics was in Europe, while the 20th century linguistics switched its focus to the United States, then 21st century linguistics will begin to look towards China. In such a tendency Prof. Wang's efforts are definitely to be credited. He ushered in new ideas and new methods for Chinese linguistics, instilling immense energy for the multi-disciplinary development of Chinese linguistics. Prof. Wang is the trailblazer of contemporary Chinese linguistics. He is a great mind in Chinese linguistics after Y. R. Chao and F. K. Li and an epoch-making linguist.

3.　Dialog with Labov

A refreshing academic event of the century took place in The Chinese University of Hong Kong in May, 2012. Two outstanding linguists, William Labov and William Wang, engaged in an in-depth dialogue in a forum with the theme on "Sound Change: Past, Present and Future." During their several decades of academic career, both started from different points of departure towards an identical direction to construct an evolutionary view of linguistic variation. Now they were reunited.

Prof. Labov studies language change in societies, maintaining that language study should not be limited to language-internal factors, but that it is necessary to examine how various social factors may influence language change, switching the direction of linguistic research since Saussure. Prof. Labov investigates languages not only in fields, but also on streets, in shops, collecting hundreds and thousands of samples for experiments and statistical analysis. With the aid of large databases he exemplifies language as a heterogeneous but ordered macro-system. Prof. Labov has opened up a new avenue of research for studies on language change.

Prof. Wang's proposal of the theory of lexical diffusion (1969) and the publication of an article on language change by Weinriech, Labov et al. (1968) were almost contemporaneous. When delivering the inauguration speech as President of the Linguistic Society of America in 1971, Prof. Labov gave lexical diffusion the earliest constructive and insightful evaluation. In the beginning Acknowledgements of his three big volumes of *Principles of Linguistic Change*, Prof. Labov wrote, "Many of the inquiries, investigations, and assessments in this volume are in response to the innovative and insightful work of William S-Y. Wang on competing sound change, lexical diffusion, and dialect mixture... Though my own alignment on all issues is not identical with theirs, I have never failed to be impressed by the force of their arguments and the relevance of their data." (1994: xvi)

Indeed, Prof. Labov's *Principles of Linguistic Change* makes use of the analysis of word class, investigating the sound change of a certain class of words which share the same phoneme. Although not entirely identical in methodology, his way of reasoning in a broad sense converges with the theory of lexical diffusion. Prof. Wang once remarked that lexical diffusion predicts that all living languages would present a large quantity of orderly heterogeneity. This remark not only recognizes that what Prof. Labov proposed is appropriate, but elucidates the close connections between lexical diffusion and language change. Prof. Wang's and Prof. Labov's thinking represent a whole new perspective on language and language evolution. In light of this, both Prof. Wang and Prof. Labov symbolize innovations and new horizons for linguistics.

Prof. Wang's lexical diffusion makes use of the notion of variation-selection in biological evolution to explain sound change. Prof. Wang has since then embarked on his exploration of evolutionary linguistics. He maintains that there are important similarities between language evolution and biological evolution. It is therefore plausible that there also exist many similarities between the evolution of the biological world and that of the social system. Language is in itself a complex adaptive system. Along this line of thought Prof. Wang's team has conducted computational modeling and multi-agent simulation analyses on such significant linguistic questions of language origin, lexical emergence, tone development, co-evolution of lexicon and syntax, language death, and has made much progress in these areas to broaden a new horizon.

Ranging from language emergence of antiquity to the most modern advances of the brain mechanisms, studies of these various domains have converged into the research of evolutionary linguistics. Towards this direction the systematic and social nature of language integrate perfectly, and synchrony and diachrony of language research are highly united. The calling of linguistics scholars is to disclose the enigma of language, and to reveal the mystery of language evolution. The mystery of language is also the mystery of mankind. In view of this definition the study of language is also the study of our species *Homo sapiens*. It is no wonder that Prof. Wang once lamented, "We can hardly recognize the true face of language because we are all the times immersed in speech," paraphrasing another famous poem by Su Shi who is quoted in the beginning of the foreword.

The founder of quantum theory Max Planck once said, "Science is an internal whole. The fact that it is dissected into separate departments is not determined by the nature of things, but by the limitation of the human ability for knowledge. There exists in reality a chain that links physics to chemistry through biology and anthropology to sociology. This is a chain in nowhere of which can it be broken." Viewed as a whole, the different domains of language research are nothing but a link within this entire chain from anthropology to sociology.

Prof. Wang once remarked that the boundaries between different disciplines are like the lines we draw on the beach. With the new tide of advanced knowledge coming onshore, boundaries are slightly altered or even entirely erased. Human knowledge, especially knowledge on language study, should be interconnected and eventually integrated. Cross-disciplinary and pan-disciplinary open research should be the important trait that characterizes contemporary science.

Winning recognition and support from the most eminent scholars in anthropology, genetics, mathematics and psychology is a distinctive characteristic of Prof. Wang's research. For decades he has been committed to the study of language from a multidisciplinary perspective. This is the source of his enormous academic charisma: he always stands with plenty of energy in the forefront of the latest research.

Let us extend our most sincere regards to Prof. Wang. Wish him many happy returns of the day in his never-ending intellectual pursuits.

Shi Feng & Peng Gang
Translated by Tsai Yaching
First draft on Nov. 18, 2012
Modified on March 27, 2013

REFERENCES

Cavalli-Sforza, L. Luca. 1994. An evolutionary view in linguistics. In *Interdisciplinary Studies on Language and Language Change*, eds. by Matthew Chen, and Ovid Tzeng, 17–28. Taipei: Pyramid Press.

Chang（張光直）。1994。〈中國人文社會科學該躋身世界主流〉，《亞洲週刊》，7月10日。64頁。

Chao, Yuen Ren. 1934. The non-uniqueness of phonemic solutions of phonetic systems. *Bulletin of the Institute of History and Philology, Academia Sinica* 4:363–397.

Ho, D.-A., and O. J. L. Tzeng, eds. 2005. *POLA Forever: Festschrift in Honor of Professor William S-Y. Wang on His 70th Birthday*. Taipei: Institute of Linguistics, Academia Sinica.

Freedman, D. A., and W. S-Y. Wang. 1996. Language polygenesis: A probabilistic model. *Anthropological Science* 104 (2): 131–138.

Jakobson, Roman. 1941. *Kindersprache, Aphasie, und Allgemeine Lautgesetze*. Uppsala: Almqvist & Wiksell. Allan. R. Keiler, trans. 1968. *Child Language, Aphasia, and Phonological Universals*. The Hague.

Jakobson, Roman, Gunnar M. Fant, and Morris Halle. 1951. *Preliminaries to Speech Analysis*. M. I. T. Press. 王力譯：〈語音分析初探：區別性特徵及其相互關係〉，《國外語言學》，1981。

Labov, William 1994. *Principles of Linguistic Change*, Vol. 1: Internal Factors, Blackwell Publishing Ltd.

Saussure（索緒爾）。1980。《普通語言學教程》。高名凱譯，商務印書館。

Tzeng（曾志朗）。2004。《人人都是科學人》。台北遠流出版公司。

Tzeng, Ovid J. L., D. L. Hung, and William S-Y. Wang. 1977. Speech recording in Chinese characters. *Journal of Experimental Psychology: Human Learning and Language* 3 (6): 621–630. Reprinted in Wang 1991, 249–262.

Wang, William S-Y. 1969. Competing changes as a cause of residue. *Language* 45 (1): 9–25. Reprinted with postscript in *Readings in Historical Phonology: Chapters in the Theory of Sound Change*, eds. P. Baldi, and R. N. Werth, 236–257. Pennsylvania University Press, 1978. Reprinted in Wang 1991, 3–19. Also in Wang 2010, 132–153.

Wang, William S-Y. 1970. Project DOC: Its methodological basis. *Journal of American Oriental Society* 90 (1): 57–66. Reprinted in Wang 2010, 163–77.

Wang, William S-Y. 1991. *Explorations in Language*. Taipei: Pyramid Press.

Wang, William S-Y. 1998. Three windows on the past. In *The Bronze Age and Early Iron Age Peoples of Eastern Central Asia*, ed. V. Mair, 508–534. University of Pennsylvania.

Wang（王士元）。2010。《王士元語音學論文集》。北京：世界圖書出版公司。

Wang（王士元）。2011。《語言、演化與大腦》。商務印書館。

Wang（王士元）。2013。《演化語言學論集》。商務印書館。

Wang, and Ke（王士元、柯津雲）。2001。〈語言的起源及建模仿真初探〉。《中國語文》，第282期，195–200頁。Also in《王士元語言學論文集》，280–298頁。2002。

Wang, W. S-Y., and Kung-Pu Li. 1967. Tone 3 in Pekinese. *Journal of Speech and Hearing Research* 10 (3): 629–36. Reprinted in Wang 1991, 186–92. Also in Wang 2010, 90–98. 焦立為譯，北京話的第三調，《語言的探索——王士元語言學論文選譯》，244–252頁。北京語言大學出版社，2000。

Wang, W. S-Y., and J. W. Minett. 2005. Vertical and horizontal transmission in language evolution. *Transactions of the Philological Society* 103 (2): 121–146. 張靜芬譯：語言演變中的橫向傳遞與縱向傳遞，《演化語言學論集》，184–209頁。商務印書館，2013。

Weinriech, Uriel, W. Labov, and M. Herzog. 1968. Empirical foundations for a theory of language change. 184–209頁。In *Directions for Historical Linguistics*, eds. W. P. Lehmann, and Y. Malkiel, 97–195. University of Texas Press.

List of Illustrations

Tables

Figures

1

How Many Chinese Words Have Elastic Length?[1]

San DUANMU（端木三）
University of Michigan

Abstract

A word has elastic length when it has both a short form and a long form, such as 煤–煤炭 'coal' and 種–種植 'to plant'. The goal of this study is to find out how many Chinese words have this property. We sample 1/50 of all monomorphemic Chinese words, selected from those represented by the top 3,000 most common characters. It is found that 80%–90% of all Chinese words have elastic length. In addition, the percentage for verbs is higher than the average, and the percentage for nouns is higher still.

---

1. This paper was written in 2011 and was probably the first quantitative study of elastic word length in Chinese. Since then two related papers have been published: Duanmu (2012), a corpus study of word length patterns in modern written Chinese, and 黃麗君、端木三 (2013), a study of elastic word length in the Chinese lexicon, with an improved method and a larger sample size.

1.   Introduction

An unusual property of Chinese is that many of its words have elastic length, such as 煤–煤炭 'coal', 麥–小麥 'wheat', 種–種植 'to plant', and 學–學習 'to study'. Some English words also do, such as John–Johnny and lab–laboratory, but the scope is more limited in English than in Chinese. The property has been observed for a long time (see 郭紹虞 1938 for early references), but it remains unclear how many Chinese words have elastic length. 潘文國 (1997, 141) suggests that 'nearly all Chinese words' have elastic word length, but he provides no evidence. This study takes a close look at the issue through a quantitative analysis of the Chinese lexicon.

2.   What Is Elastic Word Length?

Many Chinese words can be long (two syllables) or short (one syllable), with more or less the same meaning. 郭紹虞 (1938) uses the term 'elastic word length' to refer to this property. Duanmu (2007) uses the term 'dual vocabulary' to refer to the same thing. Some examples are shown in Table 1.1.

Table 1.1   Elastic word length in Chinese

2 syllables	1 syllable	
學習	學	'to study'
種植	種	'to plant'
煤炭	煤	'coal'
工人	工	'worker'
商店	店	'store'
老虎	虎	'tiger'
印度	印	'India'

The two forms of each pair are interchangeable in at least some context. For example: 'coal store' can be 煤炭店 or 煤店 and 'skill worker' can be 技術工人 or 技術工. The two forms of a pair need not be interchangeable in all contexts. For example, 'coal mine' is 煤礦 and not 煤炭礦, and 'worker union' is 工會 and not 工人會. This shows that the actual usage may be partly influenced by convention.

The long form may look like a compound, but it is not. For example, the long form of 虎 'tiger' is 老虎, which literally means 'old tiger'. However, 老虎 simply means 'tiger' and not 'old tiger', because even a baby tiger can be called 老虎. Similarly, the long form of 煤 'coal' is 煤炭, which literally means 'coal–charcoal' but actually means 'coal', not 'coal and charcoal'. Therefore, we can call the long forms 'pseudo-compounds' (Duanmu 2007).

Word-length alternation is not limited to 2–1 pairs. For example, 'Canada' has a 3–1 pair 加拿大 and 加, and 'California' has a 5–1 pair 加利福尼亞 and 加. However, 2–1 pairs are clearly the most common.

Word-length alternation in Chinese has been observed for a long time (see 郭紹虞 1938 for early references and Duanmu 2007, Chapter 7, for recent ones). However, it remains unclear how many Chinese words have elastic length. 潘文國 (1997) suggests that nearly all Chinese words do, but he offers no evidence. In this study I address this question in detail through a quantitative analysis of the Chinese lexicon.

3.   Words and The Lexicon

To find out how many words have elastic length, it is necessary to ask how many words there are in the lexicon. The latter question in turn invites another question: What is a word?

In English, words are usually separated by space, although some complications exist. For example, should compounds be included in the lexicon? What kinds of compounds should be included? How do we define compounds? Hockett (1958, 167) argues that out- in *outside* is a word and so *outside* is a compound, but in the CELEX lexicon (Baayan et al. 1995), *out-* in *outside* is a prefix and *outside* is not a compound. Even if we can set such cases aside, there are still different ways to define the lexicon. For example, CELEX offers three lexicons for English, shown in Table 1.2.

Table 1.2   Different definitions of the English lexicon by CELEX

Definition	Size (words)
Word shape, including inflection	160,595
Lemmas, excluding inflection	52,447
Monomorphemic words	7,401

If words are defined by their orthographic shapes (e.g., counting *cat, cats, cat's,* and *cats'* as different words), English has 160,595 words. If inflection is excluded (e.g., counting *cat* but not *cats, cat's,* or *cats'*), English has 52,447 words (or 'lemmas'). We can even limit words to single morphemes, in which case there are 7,401 words.

The issue in Chinese is also problematic. Bloomfield (1926) defines a (minimal) word as a free morpheme, but the distinction is not always clear (e.g., 呂叔湘 1959, 1962, 1979; Xia 2000; and 王洪君 2001). In particular, monosyllabic forms, such as 虎 'tiger', are not always free, but they are not affixes either. According to Sproat and Shih (1996), most Chinese monosyllables are bound roots and the disyllabic forms are root compounds. But a Chinese monosyllable differs from a bound root or affix in English in an important way: the latter requires a (certain kind of) morpheme on a particular side, but the former does not. For example, theo- requires a morpheme to its right and –ology requires a morpheme to its left. In contrast, a Chinese root simply needs another syllable, on either side. For example, 猛虎 'fierce tiger' and 虎山 'tiger mountain' are both fine. Thus, the lack of freedom for Chinese monosyllables is not morphological but phonological, i.e., the need for a minimal word to be disyllabic. Therefore, we can continue to treat them as words.

As in English, the size of the Chinese lexicon depends on the definition. One difficulty is the lack of distinction between a word and a compound or phrase. For example, 雞 'chicken' is a free word but 鴨 'duck' is not quite so, because it is often used in a disyllabic form 鴨子. If we treat 雞蛋 'chicken egg' as a compound and 鴨蛋 'duck egg' as a single word, we lose a structural parallel. Similarly, it is controversial whether 有錢 'have money (rich)' is a word, a phrase, or sometimes a word and sometimes a phrase.

Modern compilers of the Chinese lexicon often follow a practice in which an expression is treated as a word if it occurs frequently, even if its constituents are free and the meaning is transparent (e.g., Xia 2000 and 王洪君 2001). For example, in 《現代漢語常用詞表》 (現代漢語常用詞表課題組 2008) and the Lancaster Corpus of Mandarin Chinese (McEnery and Xiao 2004), 雞蛋 'chicken egg' is a word, so is 有錢 'have money (rich)'. According to this method, the size of the Chinese lexicon is similar to that in English, excluding inflections. This is shown in Table 1.3.

Table 1.3　The size of the Chinese lexicon

Size (words)	Source
56,064	《現代漢語常用詞表》
45,429	Lancaster Corpus of Mandarin Chinese

According to 《現代漢語常用詞表》 and the Lancaster Corpus of Mandarin Chinese, Chinese has about 50,000 words, a size comparable to that of the English lexicon (e.g., 52,447 in the 'lemma' lexicon of CELEX). The Lancaster Corpus of Mandarin Chinese has a smaller lexicon because it is based on a smaller corpus.

4.　Words, Entries, and Senses

Traditional dictionaries distinguish 'entries' (詞條) and 'senses' (詞義). An entry can be made of one or more words. For example, in the dictionary 《現代漢語詞典》 (中國社會科學院語言研究所詞典編輯室 2002), some entries headed by 煤 'coal' are shown in Table 1.4, where coal balls are made from coal powder for easy use in stoves. It can be seen that the entries 煤 and 煤炭 have the same meaning. They are the short and long forms of the same word.

Table 1.4   Some entries (詞條) headed by 煤 in《現代漢語詞典》

Entries headed by 煤	
煤	'coal'
煤層	'coal layer'
煤末	'coal powder'
煤氣	'coal gas (natural gas)'
煤球	'coal ball'
煤炭	'coal'
煤田	'coal field'

Sometimes an entry has several related meanings or represents different word categories. These are called senses (詞義) and are grouped under the same entry. For example, in《現代漢語詞典》, the entry 青 has six senses, shown in Table 1.5, and the entry 俘 has two, shown in Table 1.6.

Table 1.5   Senses (詞義) of the entry 青 in《現代漢語詞典》

a. blue or green
b. black
c. green grass
d. young age
e. young person
f. a family name

Table 1.6   Senses (詞義) of the entry 俘 in《現代漢語詞典》

a. to take prisoner of war
b. prisoner of war

An entry made of two (or more) words can also have more than one sense. For example, the compound 青年 has two senses, shown in Table 1.7.

Table 1.7   Senses (詞義) of the entry 青年 in《現代漢語詞典》

a. young age (between fifteen and thirty)
b. people in this age range

In this study, we focus on word entries, rather than word senses. Sometimes, we shall divide the senses of a word into two (or more), if they seem different enough. For example, ignoring the family name, the five senses of 青 can be divided into 'color' and 'age', where the former has a disyllabic form 青色 'blue/green/black color' and the latter a disyllabic form 青年 'young age'. Similarly, the senses of 俘 have the disyllabic forms 俘虜 (a noun) and 俘獲 (a verb).

5. Procedure

Since we are interested in the elastic length of single words, we can focus on monosyllabic words, or 字 'characters'. The reason is that most polysyllabic words in Chinese are compounds or phrases, such as 雞蛋 'chicken egg', 有錢 'have money (rich)', and 煤田 'coal field'. Their components are already represented by other words. Some disyllabic words are not true compounds but monomorphemic in nature, such as 煤炭 'coal', 大蒜 'garlic', and 學習 'study', which are also represented by their monosyllabic counter parts, i.e., 煤, 蒜, and 學 respectively. Therefore, excluding polysyllabic words will not affect the accuracy of our study. Finally, true polysyllabic words, such as 瑪瑙 'amber' and 尷尬 'embarrassed', which are quite rare in Chinese, are listed under both characters and will not be missed (as long as we do not double-count them).

According to Da (2004), in a corpus of over 190 million character tokens in modern Chinese, there are 9,933 different characters, but 99% of the texts are covered by the top 3,000 most frequent ones. This is shown in Table 1.8.

Table 1.8 Coverage of Chinese characters (字) in modern texts (Da 2004)

Number of characters	Text coverage
First 500	75.81%
First 1,000	89.14%
First 1,500	94.55%
First 2,000	97.13%
First 2,500	98.45%
First 3,000	99.18%
First 4,000	99.74%
First 5,000	99.92%
First 6,000	99.98%
All 9,933	100.00%

Let us focus on the top 3,000 characters, some of which represent more than one word each. To determine how many of the words have elastic length, we use the procedure in Table 1.9.

Table 1.9 Procedure on determining the elastic length

Procedure
a. Select the top 3,000 most frequent characters from Da (2004)
b. Randomize the 3,000 characters
c. Select every 50th character, yielding 60 characters in all
d. List all the words each selected character represents
e. Determine how many of the words have elastic length

First, each character was assigned a random number by the Excel function 'randbetween (1, 3000)'. Then the characters were sorted by the random number, and every 50th was selected. For each selected character, the dictionary 《現代漢語詞典》 was used to determine the word(s) it represents.

6. Result

The result of our analysis is shown in Table 1.10. The columns provide information on each selected character, its frequency rank among all characters (smaller numbers indicate higher ranks, based on Da 2004), the gloss of each word a character represents, the short and long forms of each word, and whether the word can be a noun, a verb, or both (part of speech).

Table 1.10 Result

Char	Rank	Gloss	Short	Long	POS
安	232	peace	安	安全	N
			[W 書] how can	安	
		amp	安	安培	N
俺	2,749	[D 方] I/we	俺	俺們	
斃	2,534	die violently	斃	斃命, 槍斃	V
測	861	measure	測	測量	N, V
朝	593	court, face	朝	朝代, 朝着	N, V
		morning, day	朝		N
吵	2,040	shout	吵	爭吵	V

continued on next page

Table 1.10—*continued*

Char	Rank	Gloss	Short	Long	POS
		[D 方] noisy	吵	吵吵	
呈	1,563	display	呈	呈現, 呈上	V
池	1,709	pond	池	池子, 水池	N
雌	2,382	female	雌	雌性	N
賜	2,072	bestow	賜	賜予	V
摧	2,166	destroy	摧	摧毀	V
俄	975	[W 書] a while	俄	俄頃	
		Russia	俄	俄羅斯	N
俘	2,057	prisoner of war	俘	俘虜, 俘獲	N, V
尬	2,729	embarrassed		尷尬	
該	19	should	該	應該	
		owe	該		V
		that	該	該個	
		[W 書] include	該	賅括	
肝	1,760	liver	肝	肝臟	N
閣	1,682	chamber	閣	樓閣	N
詭	2,578	tricky	詭	詭詐	
涵	2,330	contain	涵	涵蓋	V
話	170	speak, speech	話	説話, 話語	N, V
及	198	reach	及		V
		and	及	以及	
獎	1,233	award	獎	獎勵, 獎品	N, V
楳	2,108	[M 量]	楳		
坑	2,242	pit	坑	土坑, 坑害	N, V
哭	1,210	weep, cry	哭	哭泣	V
爛	1,754	rotten, broken	爛		
力	106	force, power	力	力量, 能力	N
蓮	1,837	lotus	蓮	荷蓮, 蓮子	N
鹿	2,056	deer	鹿	鹿子	N
侖	2,139	[W 書] order	侖	倫次	
蜜	2,014	honey	蜜	蜂蜜	N

continued on next page

Table 1.10—*continued*

Char	Rank	Gloss	Short	Long	POS
寞	2,601	lonesome	寞	寂寞	
納	684	collect	納	納入	V
		sew (shoe)	納		V
偶	1,361	image	偶	偶像	N
		even (number)	偶	偶數	N
		accidental	偶	偶然	
擒	2,850	capture	擒	擒獲	V
青	497	green/blue, young	青	青色, 青年	N
卻	287	retreat	卻	退卻	V
		but	卻	卻是	
曬	2,630	sun bathe	曬	日曬	V
師	333	master	師	老師, 師傅	N
		division (military)	師		N
授	968	give, award	授	授予	V
蜀	2,602	Sichuan	蜀	蜀漢	N
司	278	administer, office	司		N, V
套	1,091	cover, sheath, set	套	套子, 套住	N, V
條	214	strip, item	條	條子, 條目	N
帖	2,892	fit snugly	帖	服帖	V
		card	帖	帖子	N
		model example	帖	帖模	N
		[D 方] prescription	帖		
惟	1,856	only	惟	惟一	
		[W 書] 助詞	惟		
		thought	惟	思維	N
嗡	2,783	humming	嗡	嗡嗡	
窩	1,962	nest	窩	鳥窩, 窩窩	N
昔	2,388	past	昔		
閑	1,529	leisure, idle	閑	閑空, 空閑	N
限	613	limit	限	限度, 限制	N, V
新	161	new	新		

continued on next page

Table 1.10—*continued*

Char	Rank	Gloss	Short	Long	POS
徐	1,313	slow	徐	徐徐	
選	499	choose	選	挑選	V
陽	650	sun, yang	陽	太陽, 陽性	N
頤	2,999	[W 書] chin	頤		
		[W 書] nourish	頤	頤養	
鷹	1,927	eagle	鷹	老鷹	N
志	542	will	志	志向	N
		[D 方] weigh	志		
		gazette, mark	志	志記, 標誌	N
注	492	inject	注	注入, 注射	V
		comment	注	批注	N, V
鑽	1,724	make/enter (a whole)	鑽		V
		drill, diamond	鑽	鑽子, 鑽石	N

The characters are listed alphabetically by Pinyin. When a character represents two or more words (entries), each is shown on a separate line. For example, 安 represents three words, shown on three lines. In the Gloss column, one or more senses are listed for each word. In the Gloss column, the label [W 書] indicates whether the word is for written language only, [D 方] indicates whether it is a dialectal term, and [M 量] indicates whether it is a measure word only. For each word, a short form is given if available, and one or more long forms are given if available. Finally, the part of speech (POS) column indicates whether a word is usually a noun, a verb, or both, excluding words that are dialectal or written only.

The percentage of words that have elastic length is shown in Table 1.11. It can be seen that about 80% of all words have elastic length, i.e., having both a short and a long form.

Table 1.11 Statistical result on elastic word length

	Count	Percent
Long form only	1	1.2%
Short form only	17	20.2%
Both forms available	66	78.6%
Total	84	100%

If we focus on nouns and verbs, the result is shown in Table 1.12, excluding words that are dialectal or for written language only.

Table 1.12   Elastic word-length in nouns and verbs

	Total	Elastic	% elastic
N	39	36	92%
V	29	24	83%

The result shows that there is a higher than average percentage of word with elastic length in nouns and verbs. The nouns and verbs without elastic length are shown in Table 1.13.

Table 1.13   Nouns and verbs without elastic word-length

N	朝	morning, day
N	師	division (military)
N	司	office
V	司	administer
V	該	owe
V	及	reach
V	納	sew (shoe)
V	鑽	make/enter (a whole)

Most of the words seem to have restricted usage. For example, 朝 is a less common word for morning (早上, 上午) or day (天, 日), 師 is a specific rank of military units, and 司 is a specific level of government office. Among verbs, 司 is rarely used in modern Chinese, 該 is a less common (and probably dialectal) word for 欠, 及 is mainly used in 不及 'not as much as' and 及格 'pass (exam)', and 納 is used for sewing the sole of a shoe. This means that, among commonly uses nouns and verbs, the percentage of words with elastic length would likely be still higher.

7.   Concluding Remarks

In our study, 1/50 of the 3,000 most frequent Chinese characters were examined and the words they represent were determined. Based on the sample, it is found that 80% to 90% of Chinese words (monomorphemic entries in a dictionary) have elastic length, i.e., a monosyllabic form and a disyllabic (or longer) form. In addition, the percentage for verbs is higher than the average, and the percentage for nouns is higher still.

Our study has some theoretical implications. First, a word should not be equated to a character (字), as is sometimes done (e.g., 馬建忠 1898). The reason is that most words have both a short form and a long form, and a character (字) only represents the short form.

Second, our study can help explain some problems in defining words in Chinese. In particular, 呂叔湘 (1979, 491–492) notes two problems in applying Bloomfield's (1926) definition of words to Chinese. The first is a lack of distinction between free and bound morphemes. The second is a lack of distinction between a word and a compound. Our study provides an explanation for both problems. Because Chinese requires a minimal expression to be disyllabic, the monosyllabic form of a word, such as 虎 'tiger', is often not free. However, the disyllabic form of a word, such as 'tiger' 老虎, is free. This means that most Chinese words have a free (disyllabic) form and a non-free (monosyllabic) form, hence the lack of distinction between free and bound morphemes. In addition, the long form of a word often looks like a compound, such as 老虎 (literally 'old tiger') and 商店 (literally 'business store'). However, such compounds, or pseudo-compounds, are semantically equivalent to single words (their monosyllabic counterpart), hence the lack of distinction between words and compounds.

Elastic word length can also explain apparent meaning changes in translation. For example, Tamil Tiger (an anti-government organization in Sri Lanka) is translated as 泰米爾猛虎, literally 'Tamil Fierce Tiger'. Although 'fierce' may better describe what the rebels were, tigers are already fierce, and therefore the adjective is largely redundant. A better explanation for the extra word in Chinese, it seems, is the need for a disyllabic form of 'tiger' in this prosodic context.

Finally, our study provides a basis for more accurate studies of length patterns, and for the analysis of linguistic constraints. For example, given the percentage of nouns that have elastic length, we can predict the probabilities of 2+2, 2+1, 1+2, and 1+1 in noun-noun compounds (where 1 is a monosyllabic form and 2 a disyllabic one). Then we can compare the predictions against the actual frequencies. If the actual frequency of a pattern is lower than the prediction, there is likely a constraint against the pattern.

Our study has focused on elastic length in Chinese words (詞條). It would be interesting to examine elastic length in different senses (詞義) of a word. For example, 力 has four senses (excluding the use as a family name): 'force', 'bodily strength', 'ability', and 'effort', all of which seem to have a long form: 力量, 力氣, 能力, and 努力 respectively. Similarly, 條 has six senses, 'a twig', 'a strip', 'a strip shape', 'an item or entry', 'orderliness', and a measure word, all of which except the last seem to have a long form: 枝條, 條子, 條形, 條目, and 條理. This topic is left for a separate future study.

REFERENCES

Baayen, R. H., R. Piepenbrock, and L. Gulikers. 1995. The CELEX Lexical Database: Release 2 (CD-ROM). Philadelphia: Linguistic Data Consortium, University of Pennsylvania.

Bloomfield, L. 1926. A set of postulates for the science of language. *Language* 2 (3): 153–164.

Da, J. 2004. Chinese text computing. Murfreesboro: Department of Foreign Languages and Literatures, Middle Tennessee State University. http://lingua.mtsu.edu/chinese-computing/ (accessed September 14, 2011).

Duanmu, S. 2007. *The Phonology of Standard Chinese*. 2nd Edition, Oxford: Oxford University Press.

Duanmu, S. 2012. Word-length preferences in Chinese: A corpus study. *Journal of East Asian Linguistics* 21 (1): 89–114.

Hockett, C. F. 1958. *A Course in Modern Linguistics*. New York: Macmillan.

Mcenery, T., and R. Xiao. 2004. The Lancaster corpus of Mandarin Chinese: A corpus for monolingual and contrastive language study. In *Proceedings of the Fourth International Conference on Language Resources and Evaluation (LREC) 2004,* eds. M. T. Lino, M. F. Xavier, F. Ferreire, R. Costa, and R. Silva, 1175–1178. Lisbon, May 24–30, 2004.

Sproat, R., and C. Shih. 1996. A corpus-based analysis of Mandarin nominal root compound. *Journal of East Asian Linguistics* 5 (1): 49–71.

Xia, F. 2000. The segmentation guidelines for the Penn Chinese Treebank (3.0). http://www.cis.upenn.edu/~chinese/ctb.html (accessed April 3, 2011).

郭紹虞 1938。〈中國詞語之彈性作用〉。《燕京學報》。第24期，1–34頁。

黃麗君、端木三 2013。〈現代漢語詞長彈性的量化研究〉。《語言科學》。第12卷，第1期（總第62期），8–16頁。

呂叔湘 1959。〈漢語裏「詞」的概述〉。《語言學問題》（俄羅斯雜志*Вопросы Языкознания*），1959年第5期。Chinese version reprinted in 1990 in《呂叔湘文集第二卷：漢語語法論文集》，359–369頁。北京：商務印書館。

呂叔湘 1962。〈説「自由」和「粘著」〉。《中國語文》。第1期，1–6頁。Reprinted in 1990 in《呂叔湘文集第二卷：漢語語法論文集》，370–384頁。北京：商務印書館。

呂叔湘 1979。《漢語語法分析問題》。北京：商務印書館。

馬建忠 1898。《馬氏文通》。上海：商務印書館。

潘文國 1997。《漢英語對比綱要》。北京：北京語言文化大學出版社。

王洪君 2001。〈「信息處理用現代漢語分詞詞表」的內部構造和漢語的結構特點〉。《語言文字應用》。2001年11月，第4期，90 97頁。

現代漢語常用詞表課題組 2008。《現代漢語常用詞表》（草案）。北京：商務印書館。

中國社會科學院語言研究所詞典編輯室 2002。《現代漢語詞典》（2002年增補本）。北京：商務印書館。

2

More Gradual than Abrupt

Umberto ANSALDO

The University of Hong Kong

Foreword

Until the 1980s, a general consensus in creole studies taught that creoles developed out of pidgins (Hall 1966). This process of nativization, it was claimed, would be rather rapid, reaching completion within two generations (Bickerton 1981, 1984). Today we know that the picture is not that simple. Theories, it appears, are ultimately philosophical ideas and, as such, are dependent on the time and place in which they evolve. It was thus that in the late 1980s, with the advent of serious historical research in creole studies, based on documentary and demographic evidence, a competing view emerged, often referred to as 'gradualist' (Baker 1982; Arends 1989, 1993). In this view, nativization (or creolization) could not be seen as happening instantaneously and, though perhaps still somewhat 'rapid', a new grammar would be expected to take a fairly long time to stabilize. In a gradualist view of creolization, moreover, the types of change that occur in creole genesis are not categorically different from other types of contact-induced change, and the typological distance between input languages and emerging grammar is so significant that gradual transfer has to be factored into the explanation (Thomason and Kaufman 1988). Abruptness, on the other hand, also resurfaces in related studies, i.e., in the literature on mixed languages, of which at least one subset, the vaguely defined 'intertwined languages', supposedly emerges in a very short time-frame (Matras and Bakker 2003).

In order for us to understand the rationale behind these apparently contrasting positions, we need to clarify the following points:

- When we talk about the time it takes for a language to emerge, are we talking about psychological or historical time?
- Is rate of change an inherent feature of specific mechanisms of change or is it an epiphenomenon?
- Is there a 'normal' rate of change?

It is to these questions that I turn in the following sections.

1.   Introduction

In a number of works so far, I have claimed that (a) dichotomies result from our philosophical ideas about the state of the world and are best dissolved (Ansaldo and Matthews 2001); and (b) that exceptionalist explanations should only be invoked when everything else fails and not constitute a priori positions from which we construct our theories (Ansaldo and Matthews 2007; Ansaldo 2009). This chapter develops along the same lines and argues that:

- Abruptness and graduality are two complementary views of reality. They are consequences of the analysis and not explanatory principles.

- Rate of change depends on environmental factors.

- In historical linguistics (of which Creoles are part), change must be gradual.

This short chapter is organized as follows: section 2 presents some philosophical ideas relating to our understanding of terms such as 'abrupt' and 'gradual'. In the same section I also explore the difference between psychological and historical time and, related to this, introduce the difference between exaptation and propagation from an evolutionary perspective. In section 3, I give two brief examples of how, by not making these distinctions clear at the outset, we produce erroneous (or vacuous) readings of a given contact environment. In section 4, I draw my conclusions.

2.   Philosophies of Continuity

> A map is a discrete translation of the terrain, which is homogeneous and ever pervasive. There is no empty space between A and B; one always encounters something, a tree, a city, a road, a fountain where nobody stops. On maps, however, one often encounters empty paper, one crosses spaces that are nothing but pure distance. (Pierantoni 1981)

The quote above is an apt illustration of the way in which we perceive of space or, for that matter, the way we experience the world around us. Continuity and discontinuity can be seen as two opposites between which we oscillate. The former is related to our need for conflating our observations into a dimension of a higher order, one, single and comprehensive model. The latter derives from our ability of isolating objects in order to evaluate their single features.

2.1   Abruptness and graduality as complementary

The debate surrounding the abrupt vs. gradual development in language change has striking similarities with debates that span classic Western philosophy to contemporary evolutionary biology. In early Greek thought, we find a number of claims in support of gradualism: Aristoteles claimed that no surface nor any other continuous entity can be segmentable, and Parmenides clearly denied the existence of discontinuity. In his famous paradox, Zeno proved that, if we accepted the infinite segmentability of space, we would live in a world where Achilles would be outrun by the turtle. Much later Descartes claimed that there are no atoms because, if there were any, we would—at least in thought—be able to divide them up. The general idea that *natura non facit saltus* is often see as central in Darwinian thought but with Eldredge and Gould (1972) the notion of abruptness arises as a complementary explanatory tool. In a series of works starting in the early seventies, Gould and Eldredge developed the concept of punctuated equilibrium in evolution. This can be seen as a departure from a strong claim of the gradual nature of evolution put forward by Darwin, which relegated gaps and missing links in evolution to the limits of our own knowledge. Eldredge and Gould (1972), based on Mayr's theory of speciation, claim that speciation follows a rhythm of long periods of stability, interrupted by relatively rapid ones in which change occurs. According to this theory, innovation takes place in these macroscopically rapid, creative phases. Clearly, in this view, discontinuity is reinstated in the Darwinian tradition of evolution, and continuity and discontinuity appear as complementary. Does this apply to evolution of languages?

2.2   On exaptation and propagation

A basic distinction between the individual and the community as clearly different levels of linguistic analysis can already be found in Weinreich, Labov and Herzog (1968). Elaborating on this, in a biological view of language change, one can distinguish between grammar as an individual entity that exists in people (generative principles), and language as a population of grammars or idiolects (Paul 1880; Lass 1999; Lightfoot 1999; Croft 2000). Following this distinction, we identify two different levels of analysis: (a) the psychological, and (b) the social. As already pointed out in Lass (1999, 370), in order to talk sensibly about change, it is necessary to understand what we are really talking about. In discussing the nature of language change, much confusion is created if we do not keep the different levels of analysis apart. Though there may be a relation between what goes on the minds of speakers and the verbal interaction in which they engage, it is difficult to imagine that the principles that underlie I-language would be identical to those underlying E-languages. The former, however defined, would pertain to the realm of the psychological, or the cognitive (biological grammars in Lightfoot 1999, 101), while the latter would be defined by social and historical necessities.

If we talk about structural changes occurring in the idiolect of an individual—due to multilingual grammars interacting within one another—we are really looking at structural *innovation*. In a contact environment, innovation typically means adoption of a new (set of) structural feature(s); Lightfoot argues that, when we view grammar as a mental 'entity' rather than a social one, any change must be viewed as a resetting of parameters and is, as such, abrupt (Lightfoot 1999, 107; Ansaldo 2009). In this view, in the study of I-language, there is no place for gradualism. There is however disagreement among generativists on this issue, e.g., Newmeyer's (1998) more gradualist position, but this is related to which generative theory is being advocated (Botha 2003); in any event, let us assume that abrupt change may exists in I-language. When we turn to changes that affect a language as a social construct, on the other hand, we are really talking about *propagation* of variables. Propagation is by definition a gradual phenomenon, and whether it occurs more or less rapidly depends on the size and nature of the community we are talking about (Milroy and Milroy 1985; Trudgill 2001). In other words, a given change can register and stabilize in a small group of close-knit individuals within a generation. On the other hand, for a change to spread and be registered in a large, diffuse population, several hundred years will be necessary. Since it is important to fully appreciate this difference, I offer two brief examples. The French double-negation *ne...pas* is a particular development within Romance that has received a certain amount of attention. We know that the noun *pas* 'step' started being used as an emphatic form and was probably also used to reinforce verbs of motion around the twelfth century (Price 1984). The texts from this period show a behavior that is not particularly emphatic but simply negative in function; at this time *pas* was in competition with other negative particles but, because of social prestige, by the end of the 15th century it had 'won' over the competition. In modern French, not only is *pas* an obligatory negative marker, it can function as the sole negative marker in constructions where *ne* is omitted (McMahon 1994). Several stages can be postulated to account for this change; for the sake of discussion let us assume the following:[1]

(1) *Je ne vais un pas* ➤ *Je ne vais pas*
    'I'm not going a step' ➤ 'I'm not going'

(2) *Blet n'i poet pas creistre* ➤ *Je ne peux pas le faire*
    'Wheat cannot grow there'[2] ➤ 'I can't do it'

(3) *Je ne suis pas allée* ➤ *Je suis pas allée*
    'I didn't go'

What these stages indicate is that at least three reanalyses occur in this change: each reanalysis produces an innovative feature that requires a certain amount of time to spread and stabilize in usage, i.e., to be fully accepted by the speech community. Each reanalysis may be abrupt in the I-language of the speaker if Lightfoot (1999) is right. We would probably not want to interpret these reanalyses as indicating that it took a speaker of French several hundred years to reanalyze a noun into an emphatic construction or an emphatic construction into a negative particle or a double-negative construction into a single-negative one; it would be nonsensical. Likewise, the grammaticalization of a noun into a negative marker as an abstract process of change with internal characteristics cannot exist. It can only exist in the external history of a language. It is this very social history, which covers varieties spoken and written in different regions of France over several hundred years, that illustrates that it took us six to seven centuries of textual evidence to observe the stabilization of a new pattern (and that we are observing the continuation of the change in progress as we speak). Therefore the history of a given change can be long or

---

1. The historical accuracy of the steps presented here is not relevant for my general claim; the same holds for the Tok Pisin data below.

2. From the *Chanson de Roland*

short, depending on the size and nature of the speech community that we are assessing, and also the type of evidence we have available to us.[3]

In a related manner, let us consider the development of Tok Pisin habitual aspect marker *sa* from a verb *save* 'to know'. These changes can be captured in a series of steps (Aitchinson 1989 in McMahon 1994, 165–6):

(4) *God i save olgeta samting → Colgate i save strongim tit belong yu*
'God knows everything' → 'Colgate knows how/ can strengthen your teeth'

(5) *Colgate i save strongim tit belong yu → Yu save smok?*
'Colgate knows how/can strengthen your teeth' → Do you (know how to) smoke?
(know how > be accustomed to > be used to)

(6) *Mi sa kirap long moning long hapas siks → Mi bin sa long skul*
'I usually get up at half past six in the morning' → 'I used to go to school'

Again, we can say that it takes three steps of reanalysis in order for a verb to be reanalyzed as a habitual marker. What this means is that we can identify three discrete transitions in the history of Tok Pisin; there could be fewer or more but let us assume this to be the current state of our knowledge. If we think of I-language, each step of functional adaptation may involve abrupt change in the mind of a speaker: (4) from 'know' to 'know how'; (5) from 'know how' to 'to be used to'; (6) from 'to be used to' to a habitual action. If, on the other hand, we consider the time it takes for *sa* to emerge, we are reflecting on the social history on Tok Pisin: this will depend on the evidence available (or often *not* available in creole studies) and on the size and nature of the community. The history of Tok Pisin is not so long and, until recently, the community of users was relatively limited; what else would we expect but for *sa* to have 'developed' and established itself over a relatively short time span, creating perhaps a feeling of speed? In other cases of creole formation, where most historical evidence is lacking, would we expect anything but abruptness to emerge from the picture?

Obviously, in the study of language histories, abruptness is but a reflection of the lack of gradual evidence, i.e., as early Darwinism suggested, a measure of our ignorance. In other words, E-change must always be more or less gradual, since a new feature needs to pass from user to user until all or most have accepted it; this will be quick if few and close speakers are involved (say, a family), slow if we track the propagation of an innovative feature across generations and countries (say, a language family). When looking at change in I-language, on the other hand, abruptness may indeed be there.[4]

---

3. Similarly, it makes no sense at all to say that the development [N → double negative → single negative] is typical of, say, 'romanization'; in fact this would be incorrect, as we do not find this development in other Romance languages.

4. The new function may replace or coexist with the old one but this does not detract from the instantaneousness of the change itself. Related effects, such as phonological reduction or sound change, belong to the social dimension and are therefore gradual.

2.3   Evolution and ecology

In reflecting on the relationship between population type and rate of change, the relevant literature offers at least two somewhat diverging claims. It is an accepted fact of population genetics that random drift affects smaller populations more than larger ones. This is because the former are more prone to random changes in gene frequency. Applying this to language, Nettle (1999) suggests that in small communities, adoption of a marked pattern will be easier, therefore we can find more of them and we expect these to arise more frequently. However, Trudgill (2004), thinking along the same lines, offers a different explanation in recent work: small—and tight-knit—communities, in his view, are more conservative, change more slowly and are therefore more prone to maintain marked structure; note that for him marked structure can be characterized by structural redundancy (surface complexity) or oversimplification, i.e., very small phoneme inventories (e.g., Austronesian). In this view, small, tight communities are more conservative and can rely more on shared information; this is why we find both very 'simple' and very 'complex' structural features. Larger populations will fall in between these extremes.

Can these two views be reconciled? I think so, but we need to realize the following:

- Diversity arises out of the splitting and occupation of different ecological niches, i.e., geographic variation and isolation, very much like the actual process of speciation.

- Speciation, as pointed out in Eldredge and Gould's (1972) work, is gradual: 'most species' history are marked by stability over time'. This means that rate of change is relative: speciation is a very slow process to a biologist but would seem extremely quick to a palaeontologist.

- Punctuation, i.e., the claim that most speciation occurs in rapid bursts which punctuate long stretches of relative stability, *is fast only in geological time*, where 10,000 years are an instant: Eldredge and Gould (1972) never supported a theory of saltation, and Gould (1987) is very clear on this point, stating that the notion of punctuation should *not* be used as a synonym for any theory of rapid evolutionary change on any other scale.

The notion of punctuation in linguistics is perhaps the number one casualty of biological metaphors applied to historical linguistics: the notion of punctuated equilibrium is used by various linguists, such as Bickerton (1984), Labov (1994), Dixon (1997), Lightfoot (1999) etc., to suggest that one can distinguish between rapid and not-so-rapid (or perhaps normal) language change. However there is no support for this view in the original theory, and the fields of sociolinguistics and historical linguistics clearly argue in favor of a gradual view of propagation and stabilization of new variables.

I believe that the views on rapidity mentioned above, including Nettle's and Trudgill's, are misled by the view of change as something that can vary *qualitatively* within populations. In Nettle, the implication would be that change is faster in small communities, therefore more markedness. In Trudgill, the clear implication is that change is slower, therefore more markedness. But if markedness can arise both from slow and fast change, then the obvious conclusion is that *there is no relation between the types or mechanisms of change and the rate at which they are observed to occur.*

Crucially, it takes the creolist one to three generations of documents (when available) to track down the propagation of a given change in a creole community, therefore the change appears somewhat rapid. Any change ascribed to 'creolization' can only take, at best, three centuries because this is all there is in terms of the E-histories of such languages. It takes the historical linguist half a century of documents to establish the successful diffusion of a change in, say, Germanic; thus, such a change appears to us as slower and, since we have plenty of documentary sources available, we can observe its regularity (see e.g., Dahl 2004). These are reflections of the linguistic history of a community and have nothing to say about the qualitative difference of mechanisms of change. Claiming that there is an abstract 'Creolization' process of change with peculiar principles, such as abruptness, is like claiming that there is a process of 'Germanization' with inherent principles not found in other types of language change, e.g., graduality. We can therefore say that there is no objective, universal notion of normal rate of change: if we talk about innovations in I-language, these may be abrupt or not depending on which version of generative grammar one subscribes to. If we talk about rate of propagation and stabilization of certain variables, this will be relative to a number of factors including (a) size of population, (b) type of network and, last but not least, (c) availability of documentary evidence. Moreover, there is no abstract process of change such as 'creolization'. Processes of change are manifestations of E-language and can only properly be treated in social and historical terms.

3.   When Rapidity Gets (us) Into Trouble

Two examples of the problems that arise when exaptation and propagation are not kept apart come to mind. The first one is obviously Bickerton's claim of abrupt creolization (Bickerton 1981, 1984) in the formation of Hawai'i Creole English (HCE), I will not deal with this claim in detail because much time has passed since Bickerton's Language Bioprogram Hypothesis (LBH), and, in the meantime, it has been shown that the hypothesis of pidginization does not hold when tested on many creole languages we know of. In a series of studies on HCE by Roberts (1998, 1999, 2000), it has been shown that it took the creole at least two generations to emerge. Moreover, Siegel (2007) convincingly argues that the origins of many HCE features can be found in their substrates and that such features were readily available to speakers in the form of an expanded pidgin. Clearly, Bickerton's rapid creation idea needs no further entertainment. The mistake was to attribute an aspect of language history, namely rate of propagation and stabilization, to abstract mechanisms of change happening in the minds of speakers; E-language and I-language were not kept apart.

This interpretation of rapidity in language creation is still often evoked: we can find it in the treatment of creolization (see e.g., Thomason and Kaufmann 1988) as well as in the literature on mixed-language genesis (Bakker 2000; Matras and Bakker 2003). In a specific proposal for rapid types of language change, Bakker (2000) importantly identifies the relation between the rate in which admixture occurs and the size of the community it takes place in. In small communities, and in particular during periods of social instability, change happens readily and spreads fast; it is therefore not surprising that we find mixed languages that have *stabilized* over a few decades. I stress the word 'stabilized' since we do not always know for how long widespread (partial or full) bilingualism may have existed and it is often extremely difficult to identify when a code-switching practice becomes truly a new variety of a community. As we have already seen, the problem lies in the construction of an abstract process of change, in this case defined by rapidity. It is problematic because we might unconsciously move from *describing aspects of an E-language*, i.e., its linguistic history, to suggesting *specific patterns of restructuring of an I-language*. And indeed—and this is where the problem arises—Bakker (2000), based on the assumption that intertwining is a rapid process of change, reasons that because a language like Sri Lanka Malay (SLM) looks structurally intertwined (through convergence), it must have arisen rapidly. In order to validate this claim, a scenario is constructed that justifies a rapid change, i.e., a situation in which speakers of SLM totally change their grammars in a few decades.[5] The best way to prove rapidity in such a case is to postulate a pidgin-like older stage, which is then revolutionized into an inflected language, i.e., contemporary SLM (Bakker 2000, 606–7). The problems with this account are several:

(i)   A pidgin is not at all attested in the history of SLM.

(ii)   There is evidence of inflectional morphology in the past history of the language (Hussainmiya 1989; Smith et al. 2004; Ansaldo 2005a, 2007).

(iii) As argued in Ansaldo (2007) and Ansaldo and Nordhoff (2008), an explanation based on rapidity is in fact unnecessary in the genesis of SLM. SLM has a history of multilingualism in and convergence with its Lankan adstrates, Sinhala and Tamil, spanning roughly three and a half centuries.

Considering that we are looking at innovations that lead us from an analytical Austronesian type to a typical, inflected Lankan type of language, any account of the grammaticalization will require a series of steps in which constituency and categorial status shift from colloquial Malay—the lexifier of SLM—to Lankan grammar. Specifically, the development of case markers in SLM requires at least the following steps: (i) a functional transfer occurs whereby nouns start requiring overt marking of thematic roles in discourse;[6] (ii) as a consequence of (i), an adposition is reanalyzed as a post-nominal marker of grammatical relation; and (iii) a word-order shift occurs that turns the basic sentence from verb-medial to verb-final.

These steps clearly require gradual, successive stages of propagation and will take time to stabilize throughout a community. That each step may spread *relatively* fast is simply explained

---

5. In particular, in a period of roughly thirty years according to Bakker's scenario, a case system would have emerged in which distinct nominal suffixes encode the core functions of Dative and Accusative as well as other cases (see also Ansaldo 2005b; 2007).

6. See Aboh and Ansaldo 2007.

by the relatively small population of Malays in Sri Lanka and by a relatively tight network, coupled with the typological ecology within which the new grammar develops (Ansaldo 2007).

In a general sense, one can indeed say that the development of case in SLM appears quicker than in some other languages we know of, where it can take five to six centuries, but this is just a reflection of the language histories of the communities in question, and not a consequence of different process of change, such as 'normal' vs. 'creolization' or 'intertwining' (Mufwene 2005; Ansaldo, Lim, and Mufwene 2007). Bakker (2000) is right in thinking of intertwining as a relatively fast process, because it occurs in the type of small and tight community where it spreads efficiently, not because there is an abstract process of change called intertwining that is, in an abstract dimension—be that internal, cognitive or else—faster than other types of change.

What is important for the SLM case presented above is that case systems emerge over a series of relatively complex steps and thus require time (Dahl 2004); moreover, the steps that characterize such changes are quite likely to be similar across language histories (Ansaldo 2005b) as patterns of grammaticalization follow certain predictable (possibly universal) paths. Therefore, each step, if considered as occurring in the mind of a speaker, *may be* abrupt, depending on the generative theory of choice. But for the history of the language, as argued above, whatever is rapid is but a function of society and history; we should be very careful in attributing differential types of abstract language change to different populations as they are merely epiphenomena of the linguistic history of a community.

4. Final Remarks

In light of the discussion above, the answers to the questions asked at the outset are summarized below:

- In researching language change, we need to distinguish the locus of change that we are investigating, as 'biological' and social grammars require different explanatory dimensions.

- Rate of change is not a feature of types of change but of types of society.

- There is no objectively normal rate of linguistic change.

However, though in the opening of this chapter I suggest that this may be a matter of perspective, the picture that emerges is not so relativistic. More specifically, what we have established so far is the following:

- If all processes of innovation are abrupt in I-language, then language change in both creole and non-creole speakers is abrupt. From the point of view of I-language, creolization *is* acquisition as there can be no difference between the biological grammar of a creole speaker and that of a non-creole speaker (DeGraff 2001, 2003, 2005).

- Creole language histories are usually two to three hundred years old, and they contain many gaps in documentary evidence. They thus create the illusion of change having happened fast, because in the histories of languages with longer and better documentation, average cycles of change may take up to six hundred years (Dahl 2004). This happens when we turn a historical pattern into an abstract (perhaps 'internal') pattern of change.

- Creole languages develop in relatively small communities, therefore innovations would have diffused and stabilized very efficiently. This creates the illusion that creoles developed faster than other languages.

From the point of view of E-language, change is always gradual, and new features spread differentially across populations depending on size and density. There are no intrinsically different types of change at an abstract (or internal) level. It seems that gradualism is right.

REFERENCES

Aboh, E. O., and U. Ansaldo. 2007. The role of typology in language creation. In *Deconstructing Creole: New Horizons in Language Creation,* eds. U. Ansaldo, and S. J. Matthews. Amsterdam/Philadelphia: John Benjamins.

Ansaldo, U. 2005a. Typological admixture in Sri Lanka Malay. The case of Kirinda Java. (ms) University of Amsterdam.

Ansaldo, U. 2005b. Contact-induced morphologization: Motivations for emergence of case in Kirinda Java. Paper presented at *New Reflections on Grammaticalization 3*, Santiago de Compostela, 17–20 July 2005.

Ansaldo, U. 2007. Revisiting Sri Lanka Malay: Genesis and classification. In *Lessons from Documented Endangered Languages: A World of Many Voices*, eds. A. Dwyer, D. Harrison, and D. Rood. Amsterdam/Philadelphia: John Benjamins.

Ansaldo, U. 2009. *Contact Languages: Ecology and Evolution in Asia*. Cambridge: Cambridge University Press.

Ansaldo, U., L. Lim, and S. Mufwene. 2007. The sociolinguistic history of the Peranakans: What it tells us about 'creolization'. In *Deconstructing Creole: New Horizons in Language Creation*, eds. U. Ansaldo, and S. Matthews. Amsterdam/ Philadelphia: John Benjamins.

Ansaldo, U., and S. J. Matthews. 2001. Typical creoles and simple languages. *Linguistic Typology 5* (2–3): 311–324.

Ansaldo, U., and S. J. Matthews, eds. 2007. *Deconstructing Creole: New Horizons in Language Creation*. Amsterdam/ Philadelphia; John Benjamins.

Ansaldo,, U. and S. Nordhoff 2008. Complexity and the age of languages. In E.O. Aboh, and N. Smith (eds). *Complex Processes in New Languages*. (Creole Language Library). Amsterdam/Philadelphia: John Benjamins. 345–363.

Arends, J. 1989. Syntactic Developments in Sranan. Ph.D. University of Nijmegen.

Arends, J. 1993. Towards a gradualist model of creolization. In *Atlantic Meets Pacific,* eds. F. Byrne, and J. Holm, 371–380. Amsterdam/ Philadelphia: John Benjamins.

Baker, P. 1982. On the origins of the first Mauritians and of the creole languages of their descendants: A refutation of Chaudenson's 'Bourbounnais' theory. In *Isle de France Creole: Affinities and Origins,* eds. P. Baker, and C. Corne, 31–259. Ann Arbor: Karoma.

Baker, P. 2000. Rapid language change: Creolization, intertwining, convergence. In *Time Depth in Historical Linguistics* Vol. 2, eds. C. Renfrew, A. McMahon, and L. Trask, 585–620. Oxford: The McDonald Insitute for Archeological Research.

Bickerton, D. 1981. *Roots of Language*. Ann Arbor: Karoma.

Bickerton, D. 1984. The language bioprogram hypothesis. *Behavioral and Brain Sciences* 7:172–221.

Botha, R. 2003. *Unravelling the Evolution of Language*. Elsevier.

Croft, W. 2000. *Explaining Language Change: An Evolutionary Approach*. Longman.

Dahl, Ö. 2004. *The Growth and Maintenance of Linguistic Complexity*. Amsterdam/Philadelphia: John Benjamins.

DeGraff, M. 2001. On the origins of creoles: A Cartesian critique of neo-Darwinian linguistics. *Linguistic Typology* 5 (2–3): 213–311.

DeGraff, M. 2003. Against creole exceptionalism. *Language* 72 (2): 391–410.

DeGraff, M. 2005. Linguistis most dangerous myth: The fallacy of creole exceptionalism. *Language in Society* 34 (4): 533–591.

Dixon, W. 1997. *The Rise and Fall of Languages*. Cambridge University Press.

Eldredge, N., and S. J. Gould. 1972. Punctuated equilibria. An alternative to phyletic gradualism. In *Models in Paleobiology,* ed. T. J. M. Schopf. San Francisco: Freeman Cooper.

Gould, S. J. 1987. *Time's Arrow, Time's Cycle*. Harvard University Press.

Hall, R. A. 1966. *Pidgin and Creole Languages*. Ithaca: Cornell University Press.

Labov, W. 1994. *Principles of Linguistic Change*. Vol. 1, *Internal Factors*. Oxford: Basil Blackwell.

Lass, R. 1999. *Historical Linguistics and Language Change*. Cambridge University Press.

Lightfoot, D. 1999. *The Development of Language: Acquisition, Change and Evolution*. Oxford: Basil Blackwell.

McMahon, A. 1994. *Understanding Language Change*. Cambridge University Press.

Matras, Y., and P. Bakker, eds. 2003. *The Mixed Language Debate: Theoretical and Empirical Advances*. Berlin: Mouton de Gruyter.

Milroy, J., and L. Milroy. 1985. Linguistic change, social network and speaker innovation. *Journal of Linguistics* 21:339–84.

Mufwene, S. 2005. *Créoles, Écologie Sociale, Evolution Linguistique*. Paris: L'Harmattan.

Muysken, P. *Media Lengua*. Amsterdam/ Philadelphia: John Benjamins.

Nettle, D. 1999. *Linguistic Diversity*. Oxford University Press.

Newmeyer, F. 1988. On the supposed 'counterfactuality' of Universal Grammar: Some evolutionary implications. In *Approaches to the Evolution of Language*, eds. J. R. Hurford, M. Studdert-Kennedy, and C. Knight, 305–319. Cambridge: Cambridge University Press.

Paul, H. 1880. *Prinzipien der Sprachegeschichte*. Halle: Niemeyer.

Pierantoni, R. 1981. La discontinuità siamo noi. *Sfera* 25:8–15.

Price, G. 1984. *The French Language: Present and Past*. London: Grant and Cutler.

Roberts, S. 1998. The role of diffusion in the genesis of Hawaiian creole. *Language* 74:1–39.

Roberts, S. 1999. The TMA system of Hawaiian creole and diffusion. In *Creole Genesis, Attitudes and Discourse: Studies Celebrating Charlene J. Sato,* eds. J. R. Rickford, and S. Romaine, 45–70. Amsterdam/ Philadelphia: John Benjamins.

Roberts, S. 2000. Nativization and genesis of Hawaiian creole. In *Language Change and Language Contact in Pidgins and Creoles,* ed. J. McWhorter, 257–300. Amsterdam/ Philadelphia: John Benjamins.

Siegel, J. 2007. Recent evidence against the Language Bioprogram Hypothesis. *Studies in Language* 31(1): 51–88.

Smith, J., S. Pauuw, and B. A. Hussainmiya. 2004. Sri Lanka Malay: The state of the art. In *Yearbook of South Asian Languages 2004,* ed. R. Singh, 197–215. Berlin/New York: Mouton de Gruyter.

Thomason, S., and T. Kaufman. 1988. *Language Contact, Creolization and Genetic Linguistics*. Berkeley: University of California Press.

Trudgill, P. 2001. Linguistic and social typology. In *Handbook of Language Variation and Change,* eds. J. K. Chambers, P. Trdugill, and N. Schilling-Estes, 705–728. Oxford: Blackwell.

Trudgil, P. 2004. Linguistic and social typology: The Austronesian migrations and phoneme inventories. *Linguistic Typology* 8 (3): 305–320.

Weinreich, U., W. Labov, and M. I. Herzog. 1968. Empirical foundations for a theory of language change. In *Directions for Historical Linguistics,* eds. W. P. Lehman, and Y. Malkiel, 95–195. Austin: University of Texas Press.

3

Phonetic Features of Colloquial Cantonese

Robert S. BAUER
University of Hong Kong and Chinese University of Hong Kong

Abstract

Five phonetic features are identified as being associated with colloquial Cantonese morphosyllables: (i) phonetic shapes of certain rimes; (ii) long vowels instead of the expected short ones in morphosyllables carrying Upper Yin Ru tone; (iii) morphosyllables with sonorant initial consonants m-, n-, ng-, and l- co-occurring with upper register tones; (iv) initial consonant clusters with the lateral approximant -l- in some polysyllabic expressives and substantives in rapid, casual speech; and (v) changed tones, or the so-called bin3 jam1 變音, produced through tonal assimilation and used for word derivation.

1.   Introduction

> *"What's in a name? That which we call a rose by*
> *any other name would smell as sweet."*

From *ROMEO AND JULIET*
Act II, Scene 2, by William Shakespeare (1564–1616)

Indeed, what *is* in a name for a particular thing? Shakespeare, who is regarded as one of the greatest poets and playwrights in the history of the English-speaking world, so poetically and timelessly answered his own question four hundred years ago by recognizing that the connection between the sound shapes (pronunciations) of words and their meanings is largely arbitrary, as there is really nothing inherently better or more attractive about the sound of any one particular word and what it means over that of any other word. So why do speakers of different languages respond to this connection in the ways they do? Speakers' affective evaluations of the associations between sounds and meanings of words range from the sublime to the profane and to even the fearful; they judge some words as profound, uplifting, exciting, beautiful, while other word-pronunciations strike them as obscene, vulgar, disgusting, repulsive, or even tabooed and frightening, and to be avoided in the face of social censure. All of these attitudes about and connotations of words are based on the cultural values that have been instilled into speakers by the particular speech communities to which they belong. What I am leading up to here is that a speech community's identification of particular speech sounds and word pronunciations as being either refined, literary, and educated, on the one hand, or colloquial and so ordinary or even vulgar, on the other, is also essentially arbitrary. So, for example, why should the Cantonese rimes "ing" and "ik" be assigned to the category of literary pronunciation, that is, they are associated with the standard Chinese characters as their standard reading pronunciations, while the corresponding rimes into which they have historically developed, "eng" and "ek", are regarded as belonging to the colloquial category and typically used in daily speech? The short answer to this question is this just so happens to have been the direction of the two rimes' phonetic evolution, and not the other way around. We will return to this point later on.

As for the term *phonetic features* as used with respect to colloquial Cantonese, I am referring to those speech sounds, or more particularly, Cantonese rimes, morphosyllables, and tones, that can be specifically identified as belonging to the informal or casual speech register of daily conversation; that is, the pronunciations of these morphosyllables (that correspond to standard and non-standard Chinese characters and also unwritable word-forms if the speech were transcribed) signal to addressees the informality, casualness, or "slanginess" of Cantonese speakers' utterances. In contrast, if speakers were to switch to the literary pronunciations of the standard Chinese characters, and this includes adjusting the tones that had been changed in colloquial speech back to their basic tones, then such reading-style pronunciations shift the speech situation to the formal end of the sociolinguistic continuum. Although much of the linguistic data presented and discussed here have appeared in other publications, namely, Bauer (2006), Bauer and Benedict (1997), Bauer and Cheung (2005), Bauer and Wong (2010), in this paper I have explicitly focused my microscope on the phonetic features of colloquial Cantonese to produce this description and analysis. Five major phonetic features identify colloquial Cantonese, and these include the following: (1) phonetic shapes of particular rimes; (2) long vowels instead of short ones in morphosyllables belonging to the Upper Yin Ru tone category; (3) morphosyllables with sonorant initial consonants co-occurring with upper register tones in contrast to the predominant tendency for such initials in literary morphosyllables to co-occur with the lower register tones; (4) initial consonant clusters with the lateral approximant l in polysyllabic expressions in the rapid, casual speech of some speakers; and (5) the use of changed tones, or the so-called bin3 jam1 變音, in tonal assimilation and word derivation.

1.1 Stratification of the Cantonese lexicon and syllabary

In studying the Cantonese lexicon and the phonological system's syllabary from which morphosyllables are drawn to form lexical items, I (Bauer 2006) have previously proposed that we can recognize two main strata, namely, the literary and colloquial layers. On the basis of their phonetic shapes, some morphosyllables belong only to the literary layer (syllables associated with the standard Chinese characters as their standard reading pronunciations), some only to the colloquial layer (morphosyllables only occurring in colloquial words), while some morphosyllables occur in both strata because of homophony.

At the same time there is a third, relatively smaller stratum (in terms of its number of morphosyllables) which we may additionally distinguish, and it comprises those morphosyllables that only occur in the phonetic transliteration of English loanwords. As a result of its intimate contact with English over the past 300 years in South China, Cantonese has borrowed hundreds of English words, thus enriching its lexicon. In the process of phonetically-transliterating words borrowed from English speakers of Cantonese have been drawing upon syllables that already exist in the syllabary to do this, or they have even created new syllables by recombining existing syllable-initial consonants with existing rimes, or they have created new rimes by combining existing nuclear vowels with existing syllable endings. The important point to emphasize here is that while these loanword syllables are completely new innovations in the system, nonetheless, they still completely conform to Cantonese phonotactics, that is, they do not violate any constraints on what sound segments can combine together to form good syllables. The creation of such new syllables has had the effect of expanding the size of the Cantonese syllabary. However, there is no official body of experts assigned the task of standardizing the Cantonese pronunciations of English loanwords, and so some loanwords may have variant pronunciations and written forms. Some people may look down on English loanwords and criticize speakers who use them in their speech as speaking impure or corrupted Chinese. Some speakers may regard loanwords as a kind of informal language or their use as being more appropriate to the informal rather than formal style of speech. Although I have treated loanwords as belonging to a third stratum of the Cantonese lexicon, I believe we also may regard them as being a kind of subcategory within the colloquial layer.

Eastward Flows the Great River: Festschrift in Honor of Professor William S-Y. Wang on his 80th Birthday

1.2 Formation and evolution of Cantonese and the development of the colloquial stratum

The Yue dialects in general and Cantonese in particular were originally formed within their own unique set of historical, geographical, demographic, and linguistic circumstances; they have traveled down paths of development that have made them what they are today. Despite successive waves of northern Chinese influence brought about by immigration to Guangdong and Guangxi over the years, the Yue dialects and Cantonese itself have still managed to maintain to this day a substantial number of identifying phonological, lexical, morphological, and syntactic features that distinguish them from other dialect families. In the case of Cantonese these linguistic features make it mutually unintelligible with Putonghua and other regional Chinese varieties.

2. Phonetic Features of Colloquial Cantonese

In this chapter I have identified five major phonetic features that are associated with colloquial Cantonese as follows: (1) colloquial morphosyllables formed with rimes [i, e, ew, em, en, eng, ep, et, ek]; (2) long vowels occurring in colloquial morphosyllables belonging to the Upper Yin Ru tone category; (3) co-occurrence of colloquial morphosyllables with sonorant initial consonants (m-, n-, ng-, l-) and upper register tones; (4) consonant clusters with the lateral approximant -l- that have been formed through the contraction of two morphosyllables into one in some polysyllabic onomatopoeic expressions and colloquial words that occur in the rapid speech of some speakers; and (5) changed tones which result from tonal assimilation or are used for word-derivation.

2.1 Colloquial rimes

The Cantonese phonological system is here analyzed in terms of its initial consonants and rimes, and their corresponding combinations into syllables. The phonological system comprises the following categories of sounds: (1) 20 initial consonants: b, p, d, t, g, k, gw, kw, m, n, ng, f, s, h, z, c, w, l, j, O (zero-initial); (2) two vowel endings and six final consonants: i, u, m, n, ng, p, t, k; (3) nine nuclear vowels: i, yu, e, oe, eo, a, aa, u, o which combine the vowel endings and final consonants to form 60 rimes as indicated in Table 3.1; and (4) six tones: 1 High Level and High Stopped, 2 High Rising, 3 Mid Level and Mid Stopped, 4 Mid-low Falling, 5 Mid-low Rising, 6 Mid-low Level and Mid-low Stopped. (This chapter has employed the Jyut Ping system of romanization for transcribing the pronunciations of Cantonese syllables. Appendix 1 has listed the romanized initial and final consonants, vowels, and tones followed by their equivalent IPA counterparts that are enclosed within brackets).

Table 3.1 below lists the phonological system's complete inventory of 60 rimes which have been marked according to their stratification within the syllabary and the lexicon, that

32

is, unmarked syllables occur as the standard reading pronunciations of the standard Chinese characters, or in colloquial syllables, or in loanword syllables; the superscript "c" indicates syllables that only occur as or in colloquial words, and the superscript "+" indicates syllables that only occur in English loanwords (lexical stratification will be explained further below).

Table 3.1 System of Cantonese rimes

System of Cantonese rimes comprises 60 syllables that are the standard reading pronunciations of standard Chinese characters, syllables only occurring in colloquial syllables (marked with superscript "c"), and English loanword syllables (marked with superscript "+").

Nuclear	Final Vowel or Consonant								
Vowel	0	i	u	m	n	ng	p	t	k
i	i	□	iu	im	in	ing	ip	it	ik
yu	yu	□	□	□	yun	□	□	yut	□
e	e	ei	ᶜeu	ᶜem	en	eng	ᶜep	ᶜet	ek
oe	oe	□	□	⁺oem	□	oeng	□	ᶜoet	oek
eo	□	eoi	□	□	eon	□	□	eot	□
a	□	ai	au	am	an	ang	ap	at	ak
aa	aa	aai	aau	aam	aan	aang	aap	aat	aak
u	u	ui	□	□	un	ung	□	ut	uk
o	o	oi	ou	⁺om	on	ong	⁺op	ot	ok

It is worth noting here that a decade and a half ago Bauer and Benedict (1997, 49, 407) recognized a total of 56 rimes. However, since the publication of that volume on modern Cantonese phonology, four additional rimes have been identified and added into the rime system: three of these rimes, namely, *oem, om, op*, only occur in English loanwords at the present time, and the fourth rime *oet* only occurs in one colloquial Cantonese word; these "new" rimes thus demonstrate an important but rarely recognized feature of the Cantonese phonological system, viz., that it operates in a continuously dynamic state of ongoing change and expansion. With 20 initial consonants and 60 rimes the syllabary has the potential to comprise 1,200 syllables; however, as it turns out, not every consonant combines with every rime due to accidental and systematic gaps within the syllabary, and so the syllabary actually comprises a smaller number of syllables. As explained in detail in Bauer and Benedict (1997, Chapter 3), the Cantonese syllabary can be analyzed in terms of the stratification or distribution of syllables within the lexicon, that is, syllables can be classified into four categories:

(1)   syllables that occur as the standard reading (or literary) pronunciations of the standard Chinese characters, for example, 花 faa1 'flower', 你 nei5 'you', 我 ngo5 'I', 書 syu1 'book', etc.;

(2)   syllables that occur in the colloquial layer of the lexicon, including those that only occur in colloquial words (which are not etymologically associated with standard Chinese characters and so may be written with standard Chinese

characters that have been borrowed for their similar sounds or specially created dialectal characters, or they may have no written forms because of the obscure origins of such words), for example, 啲 di1 'plural marker for nouns; marker of comparative degree for stative verbs', 踔 pe5 'to stagger, walk haltingly', 嚡唎 keu4 leu1 'to be weird, strange, odd, unusual; to be finicky, picky', 餸 mam1 'to eat in baby talk', 扲 ngam4 'to feel with hand', 揼 dap6 'to beat, pound, thump', and the colloquial readings of the standard Chinese characters, for example, 餅 beng2 (bing2) 'round flat cake', 請 ceng2 (cing2) 'to invite, request', 頂 deng2 (ding2) 'crown, top', 聽 teng1 (ting1) 'to hear, listen', 名 meng4/2 (ming4) 'name', 尺 cek3 (cik3) 'ruler (for measurement)', 劈 pek3 (pik3) 'to chop', 踢 tek3 'to kick';

(3)   syllables that only occur in the phonetic transliteration of English loanwords, for example, ben1 < *band*, fek1 < *fax*, gek1 < *gag*, wom1 < *warm*; and

(4)   non-occurring syllables.

Over the past decade the author's research work on Cantonese phonology and English loanwords borrowed into Cantonese has yielded a number of syllables that belong to each of these four categories, and so the findings that were given in Bauer and Benedict (1997, 409–411) have now been superseded. According to the author's most recent tally (based on Bauer and Wong 2010), the Cantonese syllabary comprises a total of 807 different syllables (without taking into account their co-occurrence with tones; this is an increase from 750 in 1997); this number includes 555 standard Cantonese syllables; 172 colloquial syllables; 79 syllables that only occur in English loanwords (which is almost double the 40 syllables recognized in 1997); and 397 non-occurring syllables (as mentioned above, the rime system now includes 60 rimes as opposed to 56 in 1997; this accounts for the larger number of non-occurring syllables today, as opposed to the 372 non-occurring syllables that were recognized in 1997). As for the phonetic structures of loanwords, Bauer and Wong (2010) presented a detailed study which was based on s number of loanwords, so the reader is referred to the findings that were presented there.

Included in the inventory of colloquial Cantonese rimes are the following: [-i, -e, -eu, -em, -en, -eng, -ep, -et, -ek]. As for rimes with nuclear vowels [i] and [e], they occur in both literary and colloquial syllables, so they cannot be considered exclusively colloquial rimes. Let us now take a close look at the full set of syllables formed with the first rime [i]; 18 out of the 20 initial consonants combine with [i] to form syllables (the two non-occurring syllables are *kwi* and *i* with the so-called zero-initial, that is, glottal stop). In the following list the lexical items are in three groups and are marked as follows: (1) no symbol before the syllable indicates that it occurs in the standard reading pronunciations of standard Chinese characters; (2) symbol "c/" preceding the syllable indicates that it belongs to the colloquial stratum of the lexicon; and (3) the symbol "+/" indicates the syllable only occurs in the phonetic transliteration of English loanwords. (1) Four syllables are literary: zi in zi1 知 'to know', ci in ci4 詞 'word', si as in si4 gaan3 時 間 'time', and ji in ji1 sang1 醫生 'doctor'; (2) 13 colloquial syllables. c/bi in bi1 bi1 □□ 'whistle', c/pi in pi1 li1 paak1 laak1 嗶哩拍勒 'cracking, spluttering', c/di 啲 'plural marker; marker of comparative degree', c/gi in gi1 li1 gu1 lu1 嘰哩咕嚕 'gibberish', c/ki in ki1 ki1 seng1□□聲 'sound of laughing', c/gwi in gwi1 gwaa1 gwai2 giu3 □呱鬼叫 'gibberish', c/mi in mi1 maai4 ngaan5 咪埋眼 'close the eyes', c/ni in ni1 go3呢個 'this', c/ngi in ngi4 ngi4 ngaa4 ngaa4 □□ 呀呀 'squeaking, chirping (of animals)', c/fi in fi4 li1 fe4 le4 菲喱啡例 'to jabber', c/hi in hi1 hi1 haa1 haa1 嘻嘻哈哈 'sound of laughter', c/wi in wi1 waa1 gwai2 zan3 □嘩鬼震 'noisy and confused', c/li in fi4 li1 fe4 le4 菲喱啡例 'to jabber'; (3) And one loanword syllable: +/ti in ti1 seot1 T裇 'T-shirt'. As we see from the lexical items listed in these three categories, the large majority of the syllables (13 out of 18) are colloquial.

The rime [e] shows a somewhat similar distribution to [i] in the way it combines with the initial consonants; (1) Six syllables occur as the standard reading pronunciations of standard Chinese characters: de 爹, ke 茄, se 寫, ze 姐, ce 車, je 夜; (2) There are 12 colloquial syllables: c/ be '', c/pe '', c/ge '', c/gwe '', c/me '', c/ne '', c/nge '', c/fe '', c/he '', c/we '', c/le '', c/e ''; and (3) There are no loanword syllables (two initial consonants do not combine with [e], namely, t- and kw-).

The five rimes -eu, -em, -en, -ep, and -et only occur in colloquial morphosyllables and English loanword syllables; a few morphosyllables may have either standard or colloquial variant form with rimes –iu, im, in, ip, it, respectively. Lexical examples of these rimes include the following (data from Bauer (2006), Bauer and Benedict (1997) and Bauer and Wong (2010)): (1) -eu: c/beu6 (variants c/baau6, c/biu6) 髀 'jostle with the hips, c/deu6 掉 (standard Cantonese diu6) 'to throw away', c/keu4 and c/leu1 in keu4 leu1 嶠喇 (variant c/kiu4 c/liu1) 'to be weird, strange, odd, unusual; to be finicky, picky', c/zeu1 (variant c/ziu1) 'penis' (child's term); +/teu in di1 teu4 啲□ < *detail*, +/seu in seu1 si2 □□ < *sales*, +/zeu1 < *gel*. (2) -em: c/dem1 □ 'to taste, sip', c/kem4 in kem4 kem2 □□ 'sound of clearing one's throat', c/lem2 (variant c/lim2) in lei6 lem2 lem2 脷醶醶 'sticking out the tongue and licking the corners of the mouth'; +/kem1 < *chemistry*, +/gem □ < *game*, +/zem 占 < *jam*, +/em < M, as in *M*記 em1 gei3 'McDonald's (the fast-food restaurant chain)'. (3) –en: c/ken4 po4 虔婆 (standard Cantonese kin4) 'pious, sincere woman'; +/ben □ < *band*, +/den in kon6 den1 saa2 □□□ < *condenser*, +/ten in ten1 ni6 si2 □□□ < *tennis*, +/ken in ken1 saa2 □□ < *cancer*, +/men □ < *man*, +/wen1 軨 < *van*, +/ en1 in en1 zin2 安展 < *engine*. (4) –ep: c/dep1□ 'to taste' (cf. c/dem1), c/gep6 (variant c/gip6) 挾 'to clasp something under the arm by pressing the arm against the side of the body', c/ep3 □ 'to carry something under the arm'; +/kep1 in kep1 teon2 唫噸 < *captain*, +/nep1 in nep1 bo1 □波 < *net ball*, +/hep1 in hep1 pi2 □□ < *happy*, +/wep1 □ < *rap*, web. (5) -et: c/bet6 in nam4 bet6 bet6 腍□□ 'soft', c/pet6 'mass of soft stuff', c/det6 in jyun5 det6 det6 軟□□ 'soft', c/tet6 in 扁撻撻 bin2 tet6 tet6 'to be undesirably flat in shape', ket1□'sound of giggling', c/gwet1 in gwit1 gwit1 gwet1 gwet1 □□□□ 'shrill sound', c/nget6 in nget6 haa5 nget6 haa5 □吓□吓 'to work slowly', c/fet6 and c/let6 in fi4 li1 fet6 let6 菲喱□□ 'sound of crying', c/wet1 □ 'to go somewhere to have a good time', c/et6 in et6 haa5 et6 haa5 □吓□吓 'to work slowly'; +/det1 and +/ket6 in ket6 det1 zai2 < *CADET* 仔, +/ket1 in zek1 ket1 < *jacket*, +/met1 in met1 si6/2 吪士 < *maths*, +/het1 < *head*, +/set1 < *set* (hair), +/let2 in bi1 let2 □□ < *billiards*.

As for the development of colloquial rimes –eng and -ek from earlier literary –ing and –ik, respectively, with continued alternation in some instances, Bauer and Benedict (1997, 99–107) has already presented a quite thorough analysis, so I will not repeat the details given there. Examples demonstrating the literary/colloquial variation or shift in these rimes are the following (data based on Bauer and Benedict (1997) and Zhan and Zhang (1987)): (1) -eng: bing2 餅 'cake' => beng2, ping4 平 'flat' ~ peng4 'low (in price), cheap', ding1 釘 'nail' => deng1, ting1 聽 'to listen, hear' ~ teng1, ging1 驚 'afraid' ~ geng1, ming4 名 'name' ~ meng4/2, sing4 成 'whole' ~ seng4, hıng1 輕 'light (in weight)' ~ heng1, zing3 正 'exactly' ~ zeng3, cing2 請 'to invite' ~ ceng2, ling4 零 'zero' ~ leng4, jing4 贏 'profit, gain' => jeng4 'to wın'; (2) –ek: bik1 壁 'wall' ~ bek3, pik1 劈 'to chop' ~ pek3, dik6 笛 'flute' => dek6/2, tik3 踢 'to kick' => tek3, kik6 劇 'opera, drama' => kek6, sik3 錫 'tin' ~ sek3, zik3 脊 'backbone' ~ zek3, cik3 赤 'red; naked' => cek3. For some items only the colloquial pronunciation is now used, and the older literary form has become obsolete, for example, beng2 餅 'cake', beng6 病 'sick', deng1 釘 'nail', geng2 頸 'neck'; tek3 踢 'to kick', dek6 糴 'to buy (grain)', dek6/2 笛 'flute', kek6 劇 'opera, drama', cek3 尺 'ruler'. Colloquial forms can undergo semantic narrowing, for example, peng4 平 'cheap', jeng4 贏 'to win'.

2.2   Colloquial syllables with long vowels in upper Yin Ru

One very interesting and uniquely-Cantonese development in the tone system that distinguishes Cantonese from other Chinese dialects is the split of its Yin Ru category into upper Yin Ru (上陰入) with High Stopped contour N5, on the one hand, and lower Yin Ru (下陰入) with Mid Stopped contour 333, on the other. The conditioning factor for this split has been vowel length: As a general rule, those syllables with short vowels that are associated with the standard Chinese characters as their literary readings belong to upper Yin Ru, while syllables with long vowels that are the literary readings of the standard Chinese characters belong to lower Yin Ru. In examining the following paired examples, the reader can refer to Appendix 1 for the correspondence between the romanized vowels and their narrowly transcribed phonetic values as represented by IPA symbols: bat1 筆 'writing tool, pen, pencil' vs. baat3 八 'eight', bak1 北 'north' vs. baak3 百 'hundred', buk1 卜 'to consult an oracle' vs. bok3 膊 'shoulder', guk1 菊 'chrysanthemum' vs. gok3 覺 'to feel, perceive', sat1 失 'to lose' vs. saat3 殺 'to kill', sak1 塞 'to jam, block' vs. saak3 索 'to ask for', sik1 色 'color' vs. sek3 錫 'tin'. Generally speaking, this distribution of tones and vowels is quite regular and systematic, and in a few cases we observe the corresponding change in tone from High Stopped to Mid Stopped when there is variation between a standard reading pronunciation with a short vowel and a colloquial pronunciation with a long vowel; for example, bik1 壁 'wall' ~ bek3, pik1 劈 'to chop' ~ pek3. While the rule is relatively regular, we do find some exceptions, but they are not common; examples with short vowels and Mid Stopped tone: 鴿 gap3 'pigeon', 捉 zuk3 'to catch, arrest'; morphosyllables with Mid Stopped tone that have variation between short and long vowels but no tonal variation: sik3 錫 'tin' ~ sek3, cik3 赤 'red; naked' ~ cek3.

At the same time, however, in inspecting the colloquial layer of the lexicon that includes morphosyllables that are the colloquial pronunciations of the standard Chinese characters and colloquial morphosyllables which may not have Chinese characters as their written forms, we discover morphosyllables with long vowels co-occurring with the upper Yin Ru tone; some examples of colloquial morphosyllables include daap1 ~ dip1 ~ dep1 'to taste, sip, savor', kwaak1 in dam4 dam4 kwaak1 'to go around in a circle', 呃 ngaak1 'to cheat, trick', saap1 'to take a photo'; examples of colloquial readings of standard Chinese characters with long vowels include caak1 (vs. cak1) in 揼揼測 dam1 dam1 caak1 'for business to be slack', 黑 haak1 'black, dark' (vs. literary hak1), as in gam1 maan5/1 haak1 'this evening', 黑 je6 maan5 haak1 'night time'. English loanwords which are classified as belonging to the colloquial lexicon include morphosyllables in which rimes with long vowels co-occur with upper Yin Ru tone: kaat1 咭 'card', maat1 嘜 in si6 maat1 士嘜 'smart', paat1 naa2 啪嗱 'partner', saap3/1 雭 'sharp'.

2.3 Colloquial syllables with sonorant initials and upper register tones

One important development in the history of the Cantonese language over the past 1,500 years or so concerns the relationship between initial consonants and the ancient four-tone category system. Morphosyllables that had both voiced and voiceless initial consonants occurred in the same tone category, but the former were produced with slightly lower phonetic pitch; when these voiced initial consonants became devoiced, the formerly phonetic feature of lower pitch was rephonologized into tonemic differences, that is, the ancient four-tone category system neatly split into upper and lower tonal registers in Cantonese, with the former having tone contours with tone values that are comparatively higher than those associated with the lower register tone contours. This relatively neat correspondence between the historically voiced initial consonants, including the sonorant initials that still remain voiced in contemporary Cantonese, and lower register tones, on the one hand, and morphosyllables with voiceless initials and upper register tones, on the other, is the result of complex historical processes and can be seen to be the preponderant tendency as it applies to the vast majority of Chinese characters. However, there is nothing inherent in Cantonese phonotactics that prohibits the co-occurrence of upper register tones and sonorant initials in the same morphosyllables, since we do find a number of Chinese characters with such reading pronunciations that are exceptions to this general rule as will be demonstrated by sets of relevant examples; although we would like to offer an explanation for why upper register tones occur in place of the expected or predicted lower register tones, the best we can do at this time may be characterizing them as exceptional tonal developments. The following set of characters which historically had the voiced alveolar nasal [n-] 泥 nai4 in Ancient Chinese are all pronounced today as nau2 instead of the expected Mid-low Rising tone 5: 妞, 狃, 紐, 忸, 鈕, 扭, 朽 (LSHK 2002, 112); the following characters are all pronounced nik1 with High Stopped tone instead of the expected Mid-low Stopped tone: 匿, 暱, 搦, 昵, 嬺, 衵, 袡; all of the characters in the following set historically had the voiced lateral initial [l-] 來 loi4 of Ancient Chinese, but instead of having one of the expected lower register tones, they are pronounced with an upper register tone: 拉 laai1 'to pull', 癩 laai3 'leprosy; favus of the scalp', 裸 lo2 'naked'; 欖 laam2 'olive', 笠 lap1 'hat made from bamboo or grass', 轆 luk1 'wheel', 碌 luk1 'mediocre'; a series of Rusheng characters are pronounced lok3 with Mid Stopped tone, rather than with the expected Mid-low Stopped tone 6: 洛, 駱, 絡, 烙, 珞, 酪, 犖 (LSHK 2002, 102; ZBH 2002, 739); [however, 洛, 駱, and 絡 do have colloquial readings with tone 6, according to LSHK (2002, 102)]. For the moment I do not have a satisfactory reason to explain the exceptional tonal developments in the readings of the characters listed here.

We are particularly interested in how morphosyllables with sonorant intial consonants are distributed among the upper and lower-register tone categories, because, as we will see, this

Table 3.2   Modern Cantonese tone categories as derived from the historical four-category tone system of Ancient Chinese

	平聲 'Level Tone'	上聲 'Rising Tone'	去聲 'Going Tone'	入聲 'Entering Tone'
陰	High Level: 衣 [ji: ˥55] 'clothing' ji1	High Rising: 椅 [ji: ˊ25] 'chair' ji2	Mid Level: 意 [ji: ˧33] 'idea' ji3	High Stopped: 益 [jek ˥5] jek1 'benefit' 1
				Mid Stopped: 喫 [ja:k ˧33] 'eat' jaak3
	1	2	3	3
陽	Mid-Low Falling: 疑 [ji: ˩21] 'suspicious' ji4 4	Mid-Low Rising: 耳 [ji: ˩23] 'ear' ji5 5	Mid-Low Level: 二 [ji: ˩22] 'two' ji6 6	Mid-Low Stopped: 亦 [jek ˩2] 'also' jik6 6

distribution appears to be closely correlated with the literary-colloquial stratification of the lexicon. As for morphosyllables that are the reading pronunciations of the standard Chinese characters and have the four sonorant initials m-, n-, ng-, and l-, they typically carry the four lower register tones of Mid-low Falling (4), Mid-low Rising (5), Mid-low Level (6), and Mid-low Stopped (6); for example, 明 ming4 'bright', 物 mat6 'material', 你 nei5 'you', 諾 nok6 'promise', 眼 ngaan5 'eye', 樂 ngok6 'music', 爛 laan6 'soft, rotten, worn-out', 力 lik6 'strength'. In contrast, morphosyllables that are the reading pronunciations of the standard Chinese characters and that have voiceless initials typically carry the upper register tones of High Level (1), High Rising (2), Mid Level (3), High Stopped (1), and Low Stopped (6). Close examination of the colloquial lexicon turns up many morphosyllables in which sonorant initials co-occur with the upper register tones (McCoy (1980, 208–212) listed over 200 such lexical items), and so they contradict the generalization that was made for the reading pronunciations of the standard Chinese characters. It is very likely that the existence of these anomalous lexical items constitutes evidence in support of the very complex origin and development of the Cantonese lexicon; at the same time they also justify recognizing the Cantonese lexicon as comprising multiple layers.

Examples of morphosyllables with the sonorant initial consonants m-, n-, ng-, l- co-occurring with upper register tones include the following items (completely homophonous morphosyllables, i.e., tones are also identical, have been excluded):

(1)   m-initial: maa1 孖 'twin, double, pair', maan1 擾 'to hold on to, cling to; to save, remedy', maang1 掹 'to pull tight', mai1 咪 'pinch, nip, press with fingernails',

mam1 餂 'soft food for baby', mang1 擝 'to pull something out of a pocket, bag, etc.', mat1 乜 'what', mau1 跕 'to squat', me1 孭 'to carry something on one's back', mei1 瞇 'to close (eyes)', mit1 搣 'to tear, twist with finers';

(2)   n-initial: naa1 撐 'and, with', naa2 嬤 'mother; female suffix for animal names', naam3 蹃 'to step across', naan3 攣 'to sew with long interval stitches when making a cotton-padded quilt or garment so as to hold cotton and cloth together', naat3 炳 'to be hot; to burn', nam2 諗 'to think, consider', nau1 嬲 'to be angry', 閳 nei1 'to hide oneself', ni1 呢 'this', nin1 羋 'female breast; milk', nip1 啊 'to be concave, sunken in', niu1 杽 'to be slender, thin, slim', nung1 燶 'to be burned, scorched';

(3)   ng-initial: ngaak1 詏 'to cheat'; ngaam1 喺 'to be correct, suitable', ngaau1 捎 'to scratch', ngai1 哓 'to beg, implore', ngam2 揞 'to cover up, block', ngap1 噏 'to talk, say, tell', nge1□ 'to speak up, utter a word';

(4)   l-initial: laai1 蘱 'last (as in a series); youngest (child)', laai2 䑛 'to lick', laan1 躝 'to crawl, sneak off, slip away', laap3 𥄫 'to glance at something', lam1 萪 'bud (of a flower)', lam3 冧 'to fall down, cave in, collapse', lang1 in liu1 lang1 叻嘥 'to be uncommon, rare, unusual and highly specialized', lap1笠 'to put on a garment by putting one's head through the neck hole', lak1 in lak1 kak1 躑搩 'to be stuttering speaking haltingly or unclearly', lat1 甩 'to come off, slip off', leoi1 跺 'to fall or drop down suddenly; to curl up one's body', lek1叻 'to be smart, clever', lem2 舔 'to lick', leng1 嚦 'members of a triad society', leon1 嶙 'gnaw and suck on (bones)', leu1 in keu4 leu1 嶠啤 'to be weird, strange, odd, unusual; to be finicky, picky', liu1 in liu1 lang1 叻嘥 'to be uncommon, rare, unusual and highly specialized', lo1 in lo1 jau6/2 𦟌柚 'buttocks', lo2 攞 'to collect, get, bring, take, use', loe1 碌 'to spit out', long1 嘲 in faat3 long1 lai2 發嘲嘱 'to lose one's temper', long2 哴 'to rinse (one's mouth)', lou2 佬 'guy, fellow', luk1 摝 'to roll', lung1 窿 'hole'.

As shown by the above list, numerous morphosyllables of this kind are to be found in the colloquial layer. The anomaly of the sonorant initials co-occurring with the upper register tones raises the question about their ultimate origin, and it is quite likely that they have come into Yue from the non-Han languages with which Yue has been in contact in South China over the course of its evolution. At the same time, however, we must recognize that some colloquial morphosyllables with sonorant initials do co-occur with lower register tones, because we do in fact find such items, although these seem to be fewer in number; for example, (1) m-initial: m4 唔 'no, not', mai5 咪 'don't', mou5 冇 'not have, none'; (2) n-initial: naam5 腩 'fatty meat on belly of pig or cow', nam4 腍 'soft', nam6 淰 'to be soaked through; to be in deep or sound sleep', nap6 㲃 'to be sticky, slow'; (3) ng-initial: ngaa6 zaa6 掗拃 'to obstruct, bar the way', ngam4 扲 'to pull out (as from a bag)', ngok6 'to raise (the head)'; (4) l-initial: lai4 嚟 'to come', lam6 淋 'to pile up, stack up', luk6 渌 'to scald'.

2.4 Colloquial syllables with consonant clusters formed with lateral approximant [l]

Consonant clusters are found in certain types of polysyllabic lexical items that occur in the rapid, casual speech of some speakers, and they are the result of the contraction of two syllables into one. These items belong mainly to the following three lexico-syntactic categories: (1) onomatopoeic expressions, such as plik1 plak1 from 霹叻啪嘞 pik1 lik1 pak1 lak1 'sound of crackling firecrackers', kling1 klaang1 from 傾鈴哽哈king1 ling1 kaang1 laang1 'sound of banging and clanging (as from pots and pans hitting against each other)', etc.; (2) vivid expressives, such as ham6 blaang6 from 冚嘩唥 ham6 baang6 laang6 'all, completely', zik6 blat1 from 直嗶甩 zik6 bat1 lat1 'ramrod straight'; and (3) substantives, such as glok3 tau4/2 from 角落頭 gok3 lok6/1 tau4/2 'corner', glaak3 dai2 from 胳肋底 gaak3 laak1 dai2 'armpit', etc. We may also note that some speakers who do not have the consonant clusters may still reduce the first syllable to an unstressed short vowel, for example, ga laak1 dai2, ga lok6/1 tau4/2, ham6 ba laang6, ka ling1 ka laang1.

2.5 Morphosyllables in colloquial words can carry changed tones

In addition to marking colloquial pronunciation with certain sound segments as demonstrated above, Cantonese employs changes in the contours of the basic tones of morphosyllables that also indicate colloquial pronunciation. There are two main types of the so-called "changed" tones or bin3 jam1 變音 in Cantonese: the first type is associated with the phonetic environment and is the product of tonal assimilation (motivated by ease of articulation), that is, the basic tone of a morphosyllable may change to High Level due to the proximity of a morphosyllable carrying the High Level tone; so, for example, a High Level tone causes a neighboring low tone (Mid-low Falling, Mid-low Rising, Mid-low Level) to change to High Level. The High Level changed tone is identical to the regular High Level tone, but the pronunciations of morphosyllables that undergo such tone change are regarded as belonging to the colloquial register. Some examples of tone change in which a usually low tone on a morphosyllable assimilates to a neighboring High Level tone include the following lexical items (the representation of the basic and changed tones in all examples is for the basic tone to appear first after the romanized morphosyllable and it is then followed by / (slash) and the changed tone): maan5 晚 => maan5/1 in aaj1 maan5/1 挨晚 'towards evening', gam1 maan5/1 今晚 'this evening', ting1 maan5/1 聽晚 'tomorrow evening'; mei5 尾 => mei5/1 in laai1 mei5/1 孻尾 'finally, later' (also written with colloquial Chinese character as 孻屘 laai1 mei1), sau1 mei5/1 收尾 'finally, in the end' (also written as sau1 mei1 收屘); lau4 留 => lau4/1 in bat1 lau4/1 不留 'until now, always', ji4 而 => ji4/1 in ji4/1 gaa1 而家 'now' (also written as ji1 gaa1 依家). The change of the High Rising tone on the second syllable of gaa1 ze2/1 家姐 'older sister' may be due to the assimilation of the second tone to the first one. The pronunciations of these common words are typically used in daily conversational speech.

The second main type of bin3 jam1 變音 is based in morphology, and as Y. R. Chao (1947, 34) cogently observed sixty-odd years ago, it carries "a morphological meaning, namely, that familiar thing (or person, less frequently action) one often speaks of." We can recognize two subtypes of morphological bin3 jam1 變音 depending on the shape of the contours of the changed tones. The first subtype is associated with reduplicated morphosyllables in kinship terms: the basic tone changes to Mid-low Falling followed by High Rising, with these changes conveying the feeling of familial intimacy; for example, mui6 妹 in its reduplicated form is most often pronounced as mui6/4 mui6/2 妹妹; other examples include kau5 舅 => kau5/4 kau5/2 'uncle (mother's brother)', naai5 奶 => naai5/4 naai5/2 奶奶 'granny, i.e. maternal grandmother', neoi5 女 => neoi5/4 neoi5/2 女女 'daughter'. This general rule applies to those morphosyllables carrying any tone except High Level, as this tone does not change on the second morphosylable of the reduplicated form, for example, baa1爸 => baa4/1 baa1 爸爸 'father', maa1 媽 => maa1/4 maa1 媽媽 'mother', go1 哥 => go1/4 go1 哥哥 'older brother'. As for the above-stated general rule, a few exceptions can be found, for example, ze2 姐 => ze2/4 ze2/1 姐姐 with the original High Rising tone on the second morphosyllable becoming High Level; for reduplicated taai3 太 there is no tone change on the first morphosyllable, i.e. taai3 taai3/2 太太 'wife' (for additional examples, see Table 2.46 in Bauer and Benedict (1997, 207)).

A few monosyllabic kinship terms undergo tone change to High Rising, that is, the changed tone is phonetically identical to the regular High Rising tone: mui6/2 妹 'younger sister', neoi5/2 女 'daughter', zat6/2 侄 'nephew'. In some polysyllabic kinship terms which do not involve reduplication the last syllable can take either High Rising or High Level bin3 jam1 變音, as in the following examples: gaa1 ze2/1 家姐 'older sister', gu1 naai5/1姑奶 'aunt (father's younger sister)', san1 noeng4/2 新娘 'bride', san1 long4/2 新郎 'groom', sai3 mui6/2 細妹 'younger sister', lou5 mou5/2 老母 'mother', ji6 gaa1 ze2/1 二家姐 'second oldest sister', aa3 ji4/2 阿姨 'aunt (mother's younger sister)'.

The second subtype of changed tone functions as a morphological device for deriving new words by changing the morphosyllable's basic tone to either High Level or High Rising (that is, the changed tones are phonetically identical to these two tones), with this latter changed tone being the more frequently-occurring one. Such derived words are regarded as belonging to the colloquial stratum of the lexicon. As noted in Bauer and Benedict (1997, 235–236), these two changed tones generally correspond in Putonghua to the two nominalizing suffixes of er2兒 (non-syllabic retroflexion) and zi 子 (which carries the neutral tone). Derivational tone change is widespread throughout the Cantonese lexicon, and numerous syntactic categories with corresponding lexical examples could be cited as has been done in Chapter 2 of Bauer and Benedict (1997). For example, bin3 jam1 變音 is used to derive nouns from verbs: baan6 辦 'to manage (business) => baan6/2 'sample of goods', bong6 磅'to weigh' => bong6/2 'a scale', paaw4 刨 'to plane' => paaw4/2 'a plane (tool), doi6 袋 'to put in a bag => doi6/2 'a bag', kim4 鉗 'to pinch, grip with (pincers)' => kim4/2 'pliers, pincers, tweezers', waa6 話 'to speak, say' => waa6/2 'speech, words'. We can observe that the tone on monosyllabic names for some animals and plants typically changes to High Rising: aap3/2 鴨 'duck', hok6/2 鶴 'crane (kind of bird), jyu4/2魚 'fish', lo4/2 螺 'snail', luk6/2鹿 'deer', maang5/2 蜢 'grasshopper', ngo4/2 鵝 'goose', sim4/2 蟬 'cicada', zoek3/2 雀 'bird'; dau6/2 豆 'bean, pea', laam5/2 欖 'olive', lei4/2

梨 'pear', lei5/2 李 'plum', mui4/2 梅 'plum', tou4/2 桃 'peach'. The same change is observed for the tone on the last syllable in many polysyllabic animal and plant names: hung4 jan4/2 熊人 'bear', wong4 ngau4/2 黃牛 'ox', wu1 jyu4/2 烏魚 'black fish', zyu1 mou5/2 豬母 'sow'; gaai3 laan4/2 芥蘭 'Chinese kale', kam2 laam5/2 橄欖 'olive', mat6 tong4 dau6/2 蜜熨豆 'sweet snap peas', mou4 ke4/2 毛茄 'okra', mut6 lei6/2 茉莉 'jasmine', nam4 ci5/2 脸柿 'persimmon', faan1 ke4/2 番茄 'tomato', faan1 syu4/2 番薯 'sweet potato', luk1 jau6/2 碌柚 'pomelo', joeng4 tou4/2 楊桃 'star fruit'.

3. Conclusion

In this paper we have examined the following five phonetic features that are associated with the colloquial form of Cantonese: (1) Rimes i.e., eu, em, en, eng, ep, et, ek as they are distributed in the lexicon; (2) Long vowels occurring in morphosyllables belonging to the upper Yin Ru tone category as opposed to short vowels in the literary or standard pronunciations of the standard Chinese characters; (3) Morphosyllables with sonorant initial consonants co-occurring with upper register tones when standard morphosyllables with such initials typically carry lower register tones ; (4) Initial consonant clusters with the lateral approximant l occurring in some polysyllabic substantives and expressives in the rapid, casual speech of some speakers; and (5) Changed tones or the so-called bin3 jam1 變音 which occur as the result of tonal assimilation or are used for word derivation.

In addition, as exemplified above, we have identified a so-called colloquial layer of the lexicon which comprises lexical items that do not appear to be etymologically related to (i.e., historically-cognate with) semantically-equivalent items in standard Chinese; these items very likely have come into Cantonese through its contact with non-Chinese languages. Another interesting aspect of these colloquial lexical items that suggests they are not Chinese in origin is that they have an unusual phonetic feature, namely, the co-occurrence of sonorant initial consonants with upper register tones; this feature conflicts with the general tendency for morphosyllables associated with the standard Chinese characters as their standard reading pronunciations and having sonorant initials to carry the lower register tones. The next step in verifying that these colloquial items have been borrowed from non-Chinese languages is to undertake a study that compares them with phonosemantically-similar items in non-Chinese languages of the region, such as Zhuang-Dong and Mon-Khmer languages.

APPENDIX 1

Jyut Ping Romanization（粵語拼音）with Corresponding IPA Symbols [enclosed in brackets]:

Initial Consonants	b = [p], p = [pʰ], d = [t], t = [tʰ], g = [k], k = [kʰ], gw = [kʷ], kw = [kʰʷ], m = [m], n = [n], ng = [ŋ], f = [f], s = [s], h = [h], dz = [ts, tɕ], c = [tsʰ, tɕʰ], w = [w], l = [l], j = [j], ø = [ʔ]
Final Consonants	m = [m], n = [n], ng = [ŋ], p = [p̚], t = [t̚], k = [k̚]
Vowels	i = [iː], ing = [eⁱŋ], ik = [eⁱk]
	yu = [yː], yun = [yːn], yut = [yːt]
	e = [ɛː], ei = [eⁱj], eu = [ɛːw], em = [ɛːm], en = [ɛːn], eng = [ɛːŋ], ek = [ɛːk]
	oe = [œː], oem = [œːm], oeng = [œːŋ], oek = [œːk]
	eo = eoi = [ɵʉ], eon = [ɵn], eot [ɵt]
	ai = [ɐj], au = [ɐw], am = [ɐm], an = [ɐn], ang = [ɐŋ], ak = [ɐk]
	aa = [aː], aai = [aːj], aau = [aːw], aam = [aːm], aan = [aːn], aang = [aːŋ], aap = [aːp], aat = [aːt], aak = [aːk]
	u = [u], ui = [uːj], un = [uːn], ung = [oŋ], ut = [uːt], uk = [ok],
	o = [ɔː], oi = [ɔːj], ou = [ow], om = [ɔːm], on = [ɔːn], ong = [ɔːŋ], op = [ɔːp], ot = [ɔːt], ok = [ɔːk]
Tones	1 陰平 = [˥55] and 上陰入 [˥5];
	2 陰上 = [˧˥25];
	3 陰去 = [˧33] and 下陰入 [˧33];
	4 陽平 = [˨˩21];
	5 陽上 = [˨˧23];
	6 陽去 = [˨22] and 陽入 [˨2], [˨22]

REFERENCES

Bauer, R. S. 2006. The stratificaton of English loanwords in Cantonese. *Journal of Chinese Linguistics*. 34 (2): 172–191.

Bauer, R. S., and P. K. Benedict. 1997. *Modern Cantonese Phonology*（摩登廣州話語音學）Berlin: Mouton de Gruyter.

Bauer, R. S.（包睿舜）, and K. H. Cheung（張群顯）. 2005. *Database of Cantonese Words Derived Through Diminutive Bianyin*（粵語小稱變音詞語派生的詞彙）, 載鄧景濱主編 [Jingbin, Deng. ed.],《第九屆國際粵方言研討會論文集》*Proceedings from the 9th International Yue Dialects Conference* (Macau, 2003). 澳門：澳門中國語文學會 [Macau: Macau Chinese Language Association]. 174–179.

Bauer, R. S.（包睿舜）, and Cathy S. P. Wong（黃倩萍）. 2010. New loanword rimes and syllables in Hong Kong Cantonese. In *The Joy of Research II, A Festschrift in Honor of Professor William S-Y. Wang on His Seventy-fifth Birthday*《研究之樂，慶祝王士元先生75壽辰學術論文集》, eds. PAN Wuyun 潘悟云 and SHEN Zhongwei 沈鐘偉, 1–24. Shanghai: Shanghai Education Publishing（上海：上海教育出版社）.

McCoy, J. 1980. The reconstruction of upper register nasals and laterals in proto-Cantonese. In *Contributions to Historical Linguistics, Issues and Materials,* eds. Frans van Coetsem and Linda R. Waugh, 200–213. Leiden: E. J. Brill.

Xianggang Yuanxue Xuehui 香港語言學學會（Linguistic Society of Hong Kong）. 2002. *Guide to LSHK Cantonese Romanization of Chinese Characters*《粵語拼音自表》. 香港：香港語言學學會.

Zhan Bohui（詹伯慧）, and Risheng Zhang（張日昇）. 1987. *A Survey of Dialects in the Pearl River Delta, Volume 1, Comparative Morpheme-Syllabary*《珠江三角洲方言字音對照》. Hong Kong: New Century Publishing House（香港：新世紀出版社）.

4

Linguistic Adaptation:
The Trade-Off between Case Marking
and Fixed Word Orders
in Germanic and Romance Languages

Christian BENTZ

Department of Theoretical and Applied Linguistics, University of Cambridge

Morten H. CHRISTIANSEN

Department of Psychology, Cornell University

Foreword

Understanding language evolution in terms of cultural transmission across generations of language users raises the possibility that some of the processes that have shaped language evolution can also be observed in historical language change. In this paper, we explore how constraints on production may affect the cultural evolution of language by analyzing the emergence of the Germanic and Romance languages from their proto-languages. Specifically, we focus on the change from flexible but OV (Object-Verb) dominant word orders with complex case marking to fixed SVO (Subject-Verb-Object) word order with little or no noun inflection in modern Romance and Germanic languages. We suggest that constraints on second language learners' ability to produce sentences may help explain this trade-off between nominal case marking and fixed word orders. Furthermore we assume that this scenario might not only hold for the Germanic and Romance branches of the Indo-European languages but could perhaps be extended to a variety of language families and areas. We conclude that historical data on linguistic change can provide a useful source of information relevant to investigating the cognitive constraints that affect the cultural evolution of language.

1.   Introduction

If language has evolved primarily through cultural transmission (e.g., Christiansen and Chater 2008), then language evolution and language change may not be clearly distinct in a theoretical sense (Christiansen, in press). Rather, it may be expected that the processes proposed to underlie patterns of historical language change (e.g., grammaticalization) also have been at play across the longer timescale of language evolution (Heine and Kuteva 2009). Thus, diachronic change may be construed as a microcosm of language evolution and potentially provide a rich source of data to illuminate potential constraints on linguistic adaptation.

In this chapter we want to address the following question: Are there diachronic data on language change that indicate that constraints on human cognition have shaped language on a historical time scale? To answer this question, we consider as a case study the pathways from a reconstructed Indo-European proto-language to the Germanic and Romance languages of today, focusing on how limitations on production may affect linguistic adaptation. We sketch an account that offers production as one of the multiple cognitive constraints explaining historical language change. This account highlights the sequencing problems that a second language (L2) learner faces when producing a sentence. Together, these observations corroborate our suggestion that historical language change may be construed as *linguistic adaptation*, i.e., language structures adapt to domain-general constraints deriving from the human brain, rather than vice versa.

2.   The Diachronic Pathways

2.1   From Proto-Indo-European to Proto-Germanic and Classical Latin

There are mainly two tendencies prominent in diachronic accounts of the change from the reconstructed Indo-European proto-language to Modern Romance and Germanic languages. First, the canonical word order of transitive sentences seems to have changed from free word order (perhaps with slight OV dominance) to fixed SVO patterns. Second, while Proto-Indo-European used a complex set of nominal case marking paradigms to indicate who-did-what-to-whom, most of its modern linguistic descendants no longer adopt this strategy. We can follow this pathway of case marking decline in Romance and Germanic languages as far back as to the period of roughly 2000 BC. By comparing case marking systems in attested languages such as Classical Latin, Old Greek, Hittite and Sanskrit researchers have come to the conclusion that Proto-Indo-European had a fully-fledged system of nominal case affixation with eight (Behaghel 1923; Meier-Brügger and Krahe 2002; Hutterer 2002) or even nine paradigms (Speyer 2007): Nominative, Genitive, Dative, Accusative, Vocative, Instrumental, Locative, Ablative and Allative. The issue of a canonical versus flexible word order, however, is a rather controversial one. Ebert (1978) and Speyer (2007) argue that the main clause in Proto-Indo-European must have been dominated by the SOV type, whereas Admoni (1990) highlights the general flexibility of the word order, which goes hand in hand with the nominal marking strategy. As we will see below, the issue of a prevailing word order is hard to settle even when corpora are available. Therefore we do not dwell on this issue here but adopt the compromise assumption that the Indo-European proto-language most likely displayed flexible word order patterns, perhaps with the tendency towards prevailing SOV patterns. Henceforth, we categorize word orders by using a notation similar to the one introduced by Van Everbroeck (2003). According to this notation the Proto-Indo-European type would be XXX in reference to Admoni (1990) or SOV in reference to Speyer (2007) and Ebert (1978). The three letters indicate the assumed word order (SOV, SVO, etc., or XXX for flexible word order). Using these definitions, we categorize the Proto-Indo-European language as XXX (SOV). The SOV in parentheses indicates that there might have been a distributional tendency towards using SOV structures, albeit in a generally very flexible system.

The change from Proto-Indo-European towards Germanic, and Westgermanic in particular (spoken in northern Germany and Scandinavia), on the one hand, and from Proto-Indo-European to Classical Latin, on the other hand, took about 2000 years from ~3000BC to ~1000BC/500BC (Speyer 2007, 13). In this time span a simplification of the nominal marking system has already taken place in both language families. For Germanic, Behagel (1923, 477) argues that only the ablative case was lost in Proto-Germanic and replaced by dative markers. However, it seems likely that the locative functions also started to get covered by the dative paradigm (Hutterer 2002, 54). In this context, Speyer (2007, 72) concludes that the reduction from eight or nine cases in Indo-European to six in Proto-Germanic is an essential part of the so-called 'simplification of the Proto-Germanic nominal system'. For Latin it is clear that the Allative and Instrumental cases were lost, which leaves at least five and at most seven paradigms: Nominative, Accusative, Dative, Genitive, Ablative as well as Vocative and Locative (which were also already in decline).

What about the canonical word order of these periods? With reference to Gothic rune inscriptions and the Old English text *Beowulf*, Ebert (1978, 35) assumes that verb final structures must have gained dominance already in Germanic times. Again, because of the lack of direct corpora this is a controversial issue. The use of six distinct case marking paradigms in Germanic would have allowed speakers to change word orders without risking the loss of relevant information (Hutterer 2002, 64). All in all, the available evidence suggests that the trend towards a SOV dominated system was realized more strongly in Proto-Germanic than in Proto-Indo-European, although using flexible word order patterns was still possible because of the six productive case paradigms. Therefore, we would categorize Germanic as SOV (XXX) language.

For Classical Latin, there is a fair amount of corpora available. As will be shown in the next section in more detail, the Classical Latin system can also be categorized as SOV (XXX), since the SOV pattern was used on a regular basis, although the case system was still productive enough to allow flexible use of word order patterns. Thus, the changes in the branches from Proto-Indo-European to Proto-Germanic as well as to Classical Latin seem to follow similar pathways. In the roughly two thousand years between these stages both the Germanic and the Latin language seemingly strengthened SOV as canonical word order and both lost two or three productive case-paradigms (Allative, Locative and Ablative in the Germanic case; Allative and Instrumental in the Latin case). But from this point (~500BC) onwards, Germanic and Latin, as well as the languages splitting off from these, started to take different paths in terms of their strategies for encoding thematic information. In the following, we propose that one key factor in determining the paths toward further case loss and canonical word order was the strength of influence of production constraints from L2 speakers. Therefore, we are concentrating on the developments from Classical Latin to the Romance languages and from Germanic to Modern High German and Modern English as examples of *linguistic adaptation*: here, the shaping of grammatical structures by the cognitive constraints of the speaker population.

2.2   Latin to the Romance languages

Taking the development of Latin towards modern Romance languages as an example of linguistic adaptation, we concentrate on simple transitive sentences because they can be considered the neutral prototype of other more complicated constructions (Slobin and Bever 1982). There are two interesting changes to this sentence type occurring in the time span between Latin (~500 BC – AD 500) and recent Romance languages:

(i)   While Latin had a five to seven case system (i.e., Nominative, Accusative, Dative, Genitive, Ablative, (Locative), (Vocative)) all subsequent Romance languages use fewer cases.

(ii)   The word order in simple transitive sentences has changed from OV (foremost realized in SOV and OSV) to SVO.

Consider for example the following aphorism by Vergil:

(1)   *Fata*　　　　*viam*　　　　　*invenient*
　　　fate-NOM-PL　way-ACC-SG　find-3P-PL-PRE-ACT

(2)   *I fati trovano una via* (direct Italian translation)

(3)   *The fates find their way* (direct English translation)

Latin makes use of the accusative marker to indicate who finds whom: fata via-m, but in Italian (as in English) the marker has vanished and the problem of assigning thematic roles is solved by using a strict SVO word order. The nature of the change in word order has been the subject of some debate among specialists of Romance languages (Pinkster 1991; Lee 2002; Salvi 2004). We therefore tabulated the number of sentences with different {S,O,V} ordering in simple declarative sentences. Using the two complete sets of counts from the classical period (Caesar and Petronius) and the later *Peregrinatio* (AD 400) from Pinkster (1991), we obtained the distribution shown in Figure 4.1. As Pinkster notes, S preferably takes initial position and O precedes V more often than the other way around. This displays the OV pattern as predominant, albeit in a flexible system.

In contrast, Modern Romance languages are widely assumed to have a clear predominance of SVO word order (Harris 1988; Lee 2000; Salvi 2004). For example, Slobin and Bever (1982) report word order frequency data for Italian indicating a clear predominance of SVO sentences

Figure 4.1   The frequencies of different word orders in Latin (based on Pinkster 1991, 72)

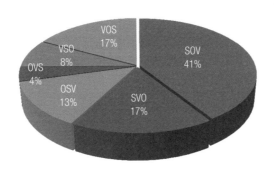

(adults: 82% SVO, 2% SOV, 0 % OSV; children: 72% SVO, 1% SOV, 1 % OSV). Thus, usage of the OV patterns has declined to a minimum in Romance languages, such as Italian.

To summarize, while Classical Latin is an example of a SOV (XXX) system, displaying a strong tendency to use SOV patterns and additional nominal affixes, the modern Romance languages can be categorized as SVO languages, i.e., fixed SVO word order systems without nominal case marking (except Romanian, which preserved nominal markers for the opposition Nominative/Accusative and Genitive/Dative). As outlined by Herman and Wright (2000), the Vulgar Latin period (~100BC–~500AD) can be seen as a gradual transition from Classical Latin to the modern Romance type. Vulgar Latin can be defined as SOV (SVO), because SOV was still predominant although SVO patterns already started to become more frequent while nominal case marking started to decline. The nominative, accusative and ablative merged into one category because of semantic confusions and phonological leveling. Likewise, the genitive and dative merged to become an oblique case with a separate marker in contrast to the nominative (Herman and Wright 2000, 57). Depending on regional differences, this two-way distinction was either further weakened, as in Italian, Spanish and French, or preserved as in the Romanian case (Herman and Wright 2000, 58). However, the overall tendency from Classical Latin towards the Romance languages is relatively clear: While case declensions started to become eroded, the SOV dominant pattern changed into a fixed SVO order. As will be shown in the next section, these tendencies are also reflected to different degrees in the development from Proto-Germanic to Modern English and Modern High German.

2.3   Germanic and the contrast between Modern English and Modern High German

The changes in the Germanic branch are quite similar to the ones observed in the Romance example. Deriving from Proto-Germanic, the split-off point between the German and English branches directly precedes the Old English (~450–1150 AD) and Old High German (~750–1050 AD) stages (Baugh and Cable 2006, 52). Thus, it is not surprising that OE and OHG were still quite similar in terms of word order and number of case marking paradigms. Analyzing the available corpora we find the early tendency to use the so-called *Verbzweitstellung*, i.e., the verb in second position in declarative main clauses in both OHG (Admoni 1990; Ebert 1978; Speyer 2007; Braune et al. 2004) and in OE (Baugh and Cable 2006; Speyer 2007; Hogg and Blake 1992). This gradual change of word order towards the *Verbzweitstellung* seems to go hand in hand with further loss of productive case marking paradigms. The replacement of the vocative by the nominative and the instrumental by the dative means that both OE and OHG are left with the same four case paradigms: Nominative, Genitive, Accusative, and Dative (Admoni 1990; Behaghel 1923; Hutterer 2002; Campbell 1959; Baugh and Cable 2006).

However, from this point onwards the changes in the English branch are very different from the ones in the German line. While the Middle English period (~1150–1500AD) is known as the period of 'leveled inflections' (Baugh and Cable 2006, 52), the German nominal system of affixes has been more strongly preserved until today (Dal 1962, 4). A closer look at the changes in the case marking paradigms reveals that the pathway from Old High German to Middle High German and to Modern High German is as well characterized by analogical leveling of formerly differentiated case declensions, which is, however, not nearly as radical as in the Middle English case. Except for some personal pronouns like *him* or *whom* in Modern English there is no trace left of the Old English four case paradigms, which are still reflected in German nominal affixes, pronouns and articles. Although Allen (1997, 2005) argues that if different writing habits of OE and ME scribes are taken into account, the transition from OE to ME seems less abrupt, this does not change the big picture that loss of case inflections was noticeably intensified in the few hundred years between ~1150 and ~1500. In Section 4, we seek to explain this phenomenon with reference to L2 production constraints. But for now it is important to note that the Middle English period might be categorized as SVO (SOV) type, and the Modern English period as fixed SVO. In Modern High German the second position of the verb is dominant in simple transitive main clauses, whereas subordinate clauses still regularly display the 'old' verb final (VF) pattern, which was still grammatical in main clauses of Middle High German. Therefore the German categories are SVO (SOV) for both Middle High German and Modern High German.

In summary, we have briefly outlined the emergence of the Romance languages as well as Modern English and Modern High German from their Classical Latin and Proto-Germanic predecessors. Figure 4.2 provides an overview of all the changes in the different branches discussed here. Note that all the categories reflecting number of nominal case marking paradigms, word orders and dependent marking are still crude. But we submit that the general trends from Proto-Indo-European to Germanic and Latin as well as their modern descendants are captured in this outline. If a free word order (XXX) with SOV tendencies is assumed for the putative Indo-European proto-language, then it is remarkable that the Germanic and Romance languages all tend to shift this word order towards a fixed SVO pattern. A second trend that can be deduced from this illustration is the loss of nominal case marking paradigms throughout the course of historical language change. More precisely, it is interesting that the rate of case loss seems to differ quite substantially between different periods and languages. While only 2–3 paradigms were lost during the about 2000 years between Proto-Indo-European and Proto-Germanic as well as Classical Latin, some 4–5 case paradigms almost completely vanished within just a few hundred years during the periods of Vulgar Latin and Middle English. This suggests that either the crucial factor governing case loss was strongest in these periods, or that

Figure 4.2   The diachronic pathways of nominal case marking paradigms and word order in German, English and the Romance languages

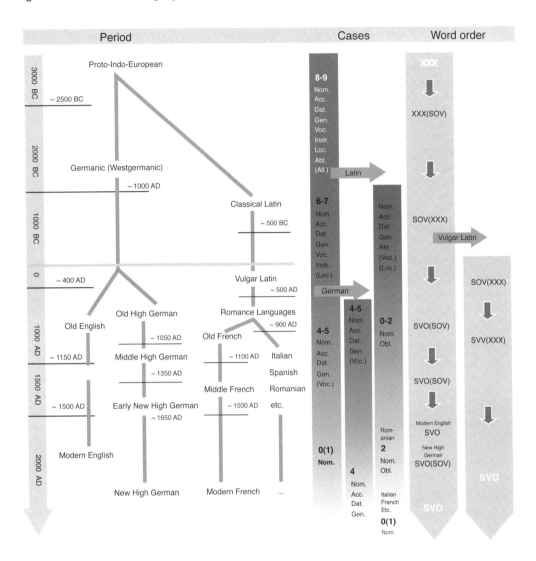

there are various factors accounting for a 'baseline' of case erosion, which were reinforced by an additional factor in Middle English and Vulgar Latin. We propose that the impact of L2 learners on nominal paradigms is one of these relevant driving forces. In Section 4, we provide more detailed information about the social backgrounds of Vulgar Latin and Middle English to corroborate this view.

However, we are not suggesting that L2 learning constraints are the only factor relevant for the loss of case paradigms. There are likely to be a multitude of intertwined social, cognitive and linguistic factors accounting for these tendencies in general. For both the Romance and Germanic branches, it has been argued that different writing styles of scribes in earlier times complicate the picture of the correct usage of nominal affixes and canonical word orders, let alone the differences between written and spoken language in the same period (Pinkster 1991; Allen 1997). Still, we contend that the overall tendencies must be connected to an additional factor, since writing habits might give a distorted picture of case use in actual speech but they do not account for the functional preservation or loss of case categories per se (for a more detailed discussion of 'linguistic' and 'extra-linguistic' factors, see Bentz and Winter, in press). The factors we focus on here are the production constraints facing non-native speakers of a language, i.e., the difficulties in determining the appropriate nominal affixes that late learners of Vulgar Latin and Middle English would have experienced when producing even simple transitive sentences. These constraints are discussed in the next section using examples from Classical Latin and Italian.

3.   Production Constraints as a Source of Language Change

Past work investigating how cognitive constraints may shape language change has primarily focused either on limitations on learning (Polinksy and Van Everbroeck 2003) or parsing (Hawkins 2004). Because comprehension can be managed by integrating partial information, whereas production means specifying the complete sequence, we suggest that the latter may cause more problems for L2 learners and therefore provide a strong pressure toward linguistic adaptation. Consider the diagram in Figure 4.3, illustrating the complex dependency relationships within the previous Latin sentence in (1).

Subject agreement information has to 'bypass' the direct object to get to the verb. This is likely to complicate processing further in sentences with embedded structures due to memory limitations (Hawkins, 2004). Moreover, the information required to inflect the direct object correctly, namely the thematic role assigned by the verb, is not provided until the end of the sentence. Thus, thematic role assignment has to be 'back-projected' from the verb to the subject and object, complicating the left-to-right sequencing of words in language production. The more complex the sentence, the more complex the role assignment becomes. In the example of a ditransitive sentence in (4), the speaker has to assign three roles and therefore inflect two nouns:

(4)   *Magister*   *puell-ae*   *libr-um*   *dat*
      teacher-NOM-SG   girl-DAT-SG   book-ACC-SG   give-3P-PRE

This complexity contrasts with the much simpler set of dependency relationships shown in Figure 4.4 for the Italian transitive sentence in (2) (which would also hold for the English sentence in (3)). Crucially, all arrows proceed from left to right, except the one assigning the thematic role of agent to the subject (mapped onto the voice character of the verb). But as the subject does not inflect according to the thematic role in Italian (at least for proper nouns) this is not a problem.

Thus, Italian (and English) SVO word orders fit well with a simple left-to-right sequence production mechanism. Obviously there is a trade-off between two constraints within such

Figure 4.3   SOV with case marking in the Latin sentence Fata viam invenient

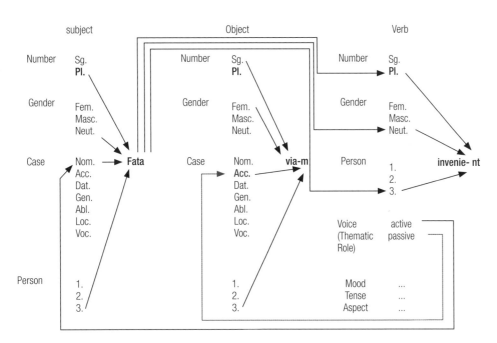

Figure 4.4   SVO without case marking in the Italian sentence *I fati trovano una via*

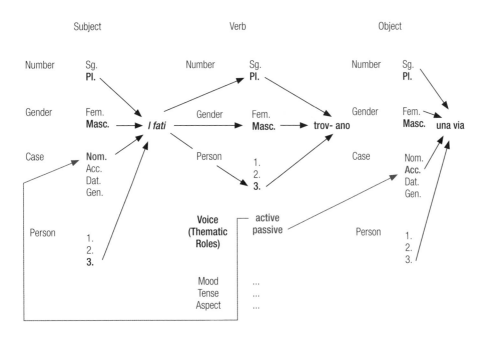

simple transitive sentences. On the one hand, the verb should follow the subject because then the information regarding agreement of person and number is available when the verb has to be inflected. On the other hand, the verb should precede both subject and object to facilitate case marking. Given these constraints, the change from Latin OV and case marking of proper nouns to Italian SVO and no case marking makes sense given a production system that generates left-to-right sequences. Note, however, that based on the historical texts of Vulgar Latin it is difficult to determine whether the change of word order preceded or succeeded the loss of case paradigms, since both phenomena are intertwined and gradual in nature.

The production constraints outlined here are, in principle, the same for Middle English and Middle High German. There seems to be a trade-off between systems in which thematic information about the participants of a scene is reflected by nominal affixes—allowing a free word order—and systems in which this information is encoded using a canonical fixed word order as in the Italian example in Figure 4.4. The templates in Figure 4.3 and 4.4 illustrate how a fixed SVO word order without nominal case affixes is easier to handle from the perspective of left-to-right production because a) the subject precedes the verb which then can be inflected according to person and number, and b) there is no relevant information that has to be 'back-projected' by way of a nominal marker preceding the verb. This is in line with the assumption that word order and case marking are not independent structural features of languages but are rather intertwined from a typological perspective (Greenberg 1966, Universal 41). We will get back to this point in section 5. In the next section we first want to consider the social setting in which production constraints on case marking may come into play.

4.   Meeting the Needs of Adult L2 Learners

Native speakers of Latin and Germanic would, of course, have been able to learn, process, and produce constructions such as (1) and (4) despite their complex dependency relationships, just as children are able to understand *who-did-what-to-whom* in Turkish, another heavily case-marked language with flexible but OV-biased word order (Slobin and Bever 1982). Therefore we suggest that an important pressure toward the simpler dependency relationships found in the Romance and Germanic languages came primarily from adult L2 learners, and only to a smaller extent from L1 acquisition.

As the Roman Empire grew, (Vulgar) Latin became its *lingua franca* and thus 'recruited' large numbers of non-native speakers. In a similar fashion, the English branch of the Germanic family was influenced by the presence of Scandinavian and Norman conquerors during several centuries of the Late Old English and Middle English period. These situations of intergroup contact may be seen as a large-scale historical parallel to the change from *esoteric* to *exoteric* communication, described by Wray and Grace (2007): Whereas the former is shaped by children's learning abilities, allowing the existence of idiosyncratic regularities that are hard for adult learners to master, the latter is tailored to the need for cross-group interactions, oftentimes by adult L2 learners. Thus, having to produce sentences with SOV word order and complex case markings as sequential *output* would have created considerable difficulties for adult L2 learners of Latin and Old English. These difficulties provided an important pressure towards the SVO without case marking system in Modern Romance languages and Modern English.

But is there historical evidence that the 'recruitment' of non-native speakers might have impacted the structure of these languages? For the Vulgar Latin case, Herman and Wright (2000) describe the speech community between 100 BC and 500 AD, suggesting that speakers of other languages (e.g., slaves, merchants, inhabitants of the Romanized provinces) were continuously integrated into the wider Latin speech community on a large scale. This led to the atypical situation in which non-native L2 learners in many geographical areas outnumbered native speakers of Latin. Based on a detailed analysis of changes to Latin's formerly rich case system, Herman and Wright argue that the large amount of L2 speakers is likely to have shaped Vulgar Latin both in terms of morphology and syntax. The overall result would have been an increasing number of semantic and functional confusions between cases that previously had been distinctive: Ablative constructions were replaced by nouns with accusative markers and dative was used with prepositions to indicate possession instead of the classical genitive. Importantly, for our purposes, Herman and Wright note that (2000, 54), 'The accusative was originally used for the direct object of a transitive verb, and transitivity itself increased. Many verbs in Classical Latin were followed by a noun in the genitive, dative, or ablative case, but in Vulgar texts these verbs tend to take an accusative.' Because the word order in the period of Vulgar Latin still displayed mainly OV patterns, the tendency to over-generalize accusative case may be seen as a consequence of the difficulty of 'back projecting' thematic roles outlined in Figure 4.2. As a consequence of this ambiguous use of the case markers, the full system could no longer be maintained, and it shrank to a minimum. Therefore another strategy for solving who-did-what-to-whom dependencies was needed and emerged in the form of a fixed SVO word order.

In the Middle English period we find similar evidence for 'recruitment' of large amounts of non-native speakers. The first event of relevance in this context is the ongoing spreading of Danish and Scandinavian tribes to the English mainland between ~800 and ~1100 AD, i.e., in the Late Old English and Early Middle English period. After invasions and plundering of smaller villages, these foreign groups started to settle down extensively when Danish and Norwegian troops formed an alliance and gained the upper hand on the island. From 1014 to ~1029 England was reigned by kings of Danish descent. Even today the large-scale settlement of Scandinavian tribes is reflected in more than 1,400 Scandinavian place names in the United Kingdom (Baugh and Cable 2000, 95). A second and even more important phase of language contact started with the Norman Conquest in 1066. Baugh and Cable (2006, 108) consider this invasion as the immediate starting point of the inflectional erosion in Middle English. Although there are no concrete numbers of French people learning English as their L2 given for this period, we can get an impression of the extent of foreign speakers by the following quote: 'Among those of lower rank, whose position brought them into contact with both the upper and the lower class—stewards and bailiffs, for example—[…], the ability to speak English as well as French must have been quite general. […] The conclusion that seems to be justified by the somewhat scanty facts we have to go on in this period is that a knowledge of English was not uncommon at the end of the twelfth century among those who habitually used French; […]' (Baugh and Cable 2006, 123).

In short, both Vulgar Latin and Middle English seem to have recruited large numbers of L2 speakers by means of geographical spreading in the former case and invasion to the mainland in the latter. We suggest that these social factors led to substantial confusion between formerly distinctive case declensions and consequently to a stronger trade-off between SOV (XXX) and nominal case marking systems and the fixed SVO type without marking, when compared to other languages in the same branches such as German.

5. Possible Effects of L2 Acquisition beyond the Romance Languages

The claim that fixed SVO word order without case marking should be easier to use by L2 learners than flexible OV word order with case marking may appear problematic when compared to the typological frequencies of the world's languages. Standard typological analyses in terms of number of languages associated with certain word orders indicate that SOV word order is predominant: SOV 497; SVO 435; VSO 85; VOS 26; OVS 9; OSV 4 (Haspelmath et al. 2005, 330). However, if we look at the number of speakers that each language has, then a different picture emerges. Figure 4.5 shows the number of speakers for the twenty most frequently spoken languages in the world (*SIL Ethnologue online version*) and their respective word order according to the online version of WALS (World Atlas of Language Structures, Haspelmath et al. 2005). Adding up the numbers of speakers of these languages, a different pattern emerges: roughly 2,390 million speakers of SVO languages against 894 million of SOV languages. Even when taking statistical error into account (+/- 25%) SVO still outnumbers SOV by far in terms of number of speakers.

Strikingly, this predominance of SVO patterns is mainly due to the fact that the three most widespread languages: Chinese, English and Spanish are SVO languages. Perhaps Chinese has also been subject to pressures from L2 learners? In the case of Modern and Old Chinese, Xu (2006) argues that in earlier periods, Mandarin was a typological 'mixed language' because it oscillated between verb-object (VO) and object-verb (OV) word orders. However, in a text-count study of written and spoken Modern Mandarin, Sun (1996) found that 90% of the syntactic objects followed the verb (VO), whereas OV with grammaticalized verb-constructions marking agent/patient dependencies only occur in 10% of the sentences, pointing to SVO as the dominant word order. When these observations are combined with our analysis of Classical Latin and Germanic, we may speculate that production pressures from L2 learners can push OV languages with complex systems of solving *who-did-what-to-whom* ambiguities toward a fixed SVO word order with little or no additional case marking. This is consistent with Lupyan and Dale's (2010) statistical analyses indicating that languages with large numbers of users tend to have highly simplified systems of morphology and case.

A second interesting fact about the general trade-off between case marking systems and word order systems was partly anticipated by Greenberg (1966) in his *Universal 41*: 'If in a language the verb follows both the nominal subject and the nominal object as the dominant order, the language almost always has a case system.' Or, expressed in WALS terms: If a language can

Figure 4.5   WALS distribution of word order patterns mapped onto the number of speakers

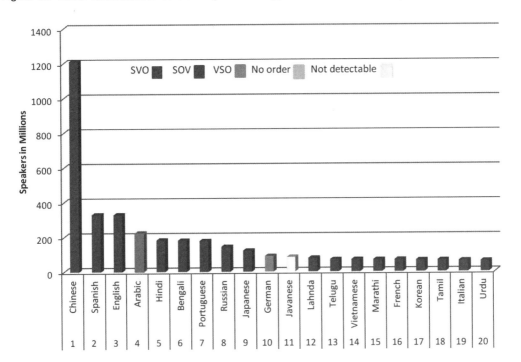

Figure 4.6   Mapping the number of SOV and SVO languages onto the number of case categories attested in the World Atlas of Language Structures (Haspelmath et al. 2005)

The category "borderline case marking" was left out because Iggesen (2011) argued that these are not genuine case markers. For the 4 languages with OSV order in the WALS there is no information on case marking available.

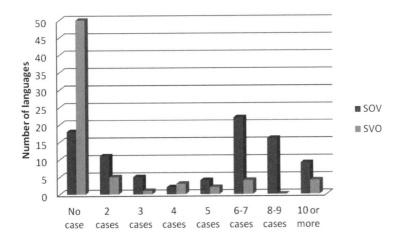

be categorized as either SOV or OSV type, than it should display case marking. This assumption can be tested by crossing the features (49A) 'Number of Cases' and 'Order of Subject, Object and Verb' of the WALS, yielding the distribution shown in Figure 4.6.

There are two interesting trends to be observed in this crossover of word order and case marking. 1) Indeed, there are 98 SOV type languages for which case marking information is available, 70 of these languages (80%) confirm Greenberg's universal, because they display 2 or more cases, whereas only 18 of these languages (20%) do not have case marking at all (contradicting Greenberg's universal). Moreover, especially abundant case marking systems of more than 6 cases seem to be associated with SOV word order (47 languages, 53% of the total). 2) The opposite pattern is true for the 69 SVO languages, 50 of these (72%) are associated with the category 'no morphological case marking', versus 19 (28%) with more or less abundant case marking.

Summarizing these statistical trends, we observe that the association of SOV word order with case marking and the dissociation of SVO languages with case marking are general trends that hold for a wide sample of languages across the world. This is in line with another quantitative study by Bentz and Winter (in press) who aim to show that the impact of L2 learning constraints on case marking paradigms is not restricted to the Romance and Germanic branches of Indo-European languages but rather holds for a wider variety of languages in different families and areas.

6.   Conclusion

In this chapter we have argued that the pattern of SVO with no case marking in Modern Romance and Modern Germanic languages has been preceded by stages in proto-languages such as Latin, Proto-Germanic and Proto-Indo-European that still maintained flexible SOV systems with fully fledged case marking paradigms. These nominal marking strategies gradually eroded away because of language internal and external factors such as production constraints of L2 learners, up to a point where the case marking strategy could no longer be maintained. At this point, an alternative strategy—the encoding of who-did-what-to-whom information by a fixed SVO word order—started to dominate sentence structures.

Because there seems to be a trade-off between strict SVO word order without case marking and flexible OV word order with additional morphological markers (Greenberg 1966, Universal 41), it is an interesting fact that both Romance and Germanic languages 'chose' the first strategy. In this paper, we have suggested that this change may be an example of how language adapts to the human brain. In particular, the difficulties in determining the relevant dependency relationships and generating the appropriate sequence of case-marked words would make L2 Latin learners and non-native Middle English speakers prone to errors. L2 production pressures may furthermore have played a role in the similar shift from a relatively flexible word order to fixed SVO in Chinese, which has historically recruited a large number of L2 speakers. The degree to which similar pressures have played a role in the development of a wider sample of languages from different language families and areas needs to be answered in future research. A first promising attempt has shown that the number of L2 speakers in relation to the L1 speakers of a population can be used as a predictor for the number of case marking paradigms in statistical analysis (Bentz and Winter, in press).

Besides these purely quantitative arguments, it should be noted that pressures from L2 speakers' learning constraints may not only provide an explanation for case loss but may also hint at an explanation for case evolution. In connection to the distinction between exoteric and endoteric languages (Wray and Grace 2007), it seems reasonable to speculate that more closed societies and their languages should be more likely to develop opaque morphological forms such as case markers due to L1 learning constraints, whereas open societies would tend to lose these forms as a result of a shift in the speaker population. Such tendencies would change the cognitive 'niche' within which language is adapting (Lupyan and Dale 2010). This additional explanatory power could be an advantage over traditional accounts of case loss, which do not answer the question of why case marking came into being in the first place.

From a more general point of view, our analyses suggest that historical language change can be used as a source of data for understanding the kind of constraints that may have shaped linguistic adaptation over historical and perhaps even evolutionary timescales. From this point of view, the distinction between language evolution as a biological adaptation of the human language competence on the on hand, and historical language change as a side effect of language performance on the other hand, is misleading in the sense that it disguises the complex diachronic interplay between human learning constraints and language structures.

REFERENCES

Admoni, V. G. 1990. *Historische Syntax des Deutschen*. Tübingen: Niemeyer.

Baugh, A. C., and T. Cable. 2006. *A History of the English Language*. London: Routledge.

Behaghel, O. 1923. *Deutsche Syntax: Eine Geschichtliche Darstellung,* Band I, *Nomen, Pronomen*. Heidelberg: Winter.

Bentz, C., and B. Winter. in press. Languages with more second language learners tend to lose nominal case. *Language Dynamics and Change*.

Braune, W., I. Reiffenstein, and R. Schrodt. 2004. *Althochdeutsche Grammatik* (15. Aufl). Tübingen: Niemeyer.

Campbell, A. 2003. *Old English Grammar* (Repr.). Oxford: Clarendon Press.

Christiansen, M. H. in press. Language has evolved to depend on multiple-cue integration. In *The Evolutionary Emergence of Human Language,* eds. R. Botha, and M. Everaert. Oxford: Oxford University Press.

Christiansen, M. H., and N. Chater. 2008. Language as shaped by the brain. *Behavioral and Brain Sciences* 31:489–509.

Dal, I. 1962. *Kurze deutsche Syntax. Auf Historischer Grundlage* (2., verb. Aufl). Tübingen: Niemeyer.

Ebert, R. P., O. Reichmann, and K.-P. Wegera. 1993. *Frühneuhochdeutsche Grammatik.* Tübingen: Niemeyer.

Ebert, R. P. 1978. *Historische Syntax des Deutschen.* Stuttgart: Metzler.

Greenberg, J. H., ed. 1966. *Universals of Language: Report of a Conference held at Dobbs Ferry, New York, April 13–15, 1961* (2nd Ed.). Cambridge, MA: MIT Press.

Herman, J., and R. Wright. 2000. *Vulgar Latin.* University Park, PA: The Pennsylvania State University Press.

Harris, M. 1988. *The Romance Languages.* London: Routledge.

Haspelmath, M., M. S. Dryer, D. Gil, and B. Comrie, eds. 2005. *The World Atlas of Language Structures.* Oxford: Oxford University Press.

Hawkins, J. A. 2004. *Efficiency and Complexity in Grammars.* New York: Oxford University Press.

Heine, B., and T. Kuteva. 2009. *The Genesis of Grammar. A Reconstruction.* Oxford: Oxford University Press.

Hogg, R. M., and R. Lass. 1999. *The Cambridge History of the English Language.* Vol. III: 1476–1776. Cambridge: Cambridge University Press.

Hutterer, C. J. 2002. *Die germanischen Sprachen. Ihre Geschichte in Grundzügen.* (Nachdr. der 4., erg. Aufl.). Wiesbaden: VMA-Verlag (Albus).

Lee, C. 2000. *Linguistica Romanza.* Rome: Carocci.

Lupyan, G., and R. Dale. 2010. Language structure is partly determined by social structure. *PLoS ONE* 5(1), e8559. doi:10.1371/journal.pone. 0008559

Meier-Brügger, M., M. Fritz, and H. Krahe. 2002. *Indogermanische Sprachwissenschaft.* (8., überarb. und erg. Aufl. der früheren Darstellung von Hans Krahe). Berlin: de Gruyter.

Meillet, A. 1934. *Introduction à l'étude Comparative des Langues Indo-européennes.* Paris: Hachette.

Paul, H., T. Klein, I. Schöbler, and H.-P. Prell. 2007. *Mittelhochdeutsche Grammatik* (25. Aufl.). Tübingen: Niemeyer.

Pinkster, H. 1991. Evidence for SVO in Latin? In *Latin and the Romance Languages in the Early Middle Ages*, ed. R. Wright, 69–82. London: Routledge.

Pintzuk, S. 1999. *Phrase Structures in Competition: Variation and Change in Old English Word Order*. New York: Garland.

Polinksy, M., and E. van Everbroeck. 2003. Development of gender classifications: Modeling the historical change from Latin to French. *Language* 79:356–390.

Slobin, D. I., and T. G. Bever. 1982. Children use canonical sentence schemas. A crosslinguistic study of word order and inflections. *Cognition*, 12:229–265.

Speyer, A. 2007. *Germanische Sprachen. Ein historischer Vergleich*. Göttingen: Vandenhoeck und Ruprecht.

Sun, C. 1996. *Word-order Change and Grammaticalization in the History of Chinese*. Stanford, CA: Stanford University Press.

Wray, A., and G. W. Grace. 2007. The consequences of talking to strangers. Evolutionary corollaries of socio-cultural influences on linguistic form. *Lingua* 117:543–578.

Xu, D. 2006. *Typological Change in Chinese Syntax*. Oxford: Oxford University Press.

5

On the Value of the Han'gul Letter E in Certain Korean Transcriptions of Ming-Time Chinese

W. South COBLIN
University of Lowa

Abstract

In earlier studies it has generally been assumed that the Late Middle Korean vowel {e} as a transcriptional letter represented an unrounded vowel in Chinese, probably similar to or identical with Late Middle Korean [ə]. However, in two unpublished doctoral dissertations, i.e., Y. Kim (1989) and K. Kim (1991), two coinciding alternate views were presented, both of which held that Korean {e} stood for the rounded Chinese vowel [ɔ] in many environments. In the present paper, this question is examined in detail and new evidence of various kinds is brought to bear on it. Our conclusion is the position of Drs. Y. Kim and K. Kim is in fact the correct one and that the older view reading the nature of {e} should be set aside.

1.   Introduction

During the Míng Dynasty Korean scholars were actively involved in the study of Guānhuà 官話 ("The Language of the Officials"), which was the current national koine of China. For this purpose they adapted their newly invented alphabet, now called Han'gûl, to serve as an accurate transcriptional medium for spoken Chinese. In general, the way this transcriptional version of Han'gûl was used is clear and uncontroversial. But in the case of the Han'gûl letter e, there are problematic points. The present paper will examine these.

In our work it will be useful to distinguish paleographic transliterations of the Korean transcriptional forms from their phonetic interpretations. Accordingly, orthographic forms will be enclosed in curly brackets, while phonetic interpretations of the written forms will be placed in square brackets. In the case of the consonants, which are not at issue here, we shall accept the phonetic interpretations of K. Kim (1991) and use them concurrently as orthographic transliterations. For the vowels, we must maintain a stricter delineation. The vowel system of Late Middle Korean, the language which the Han'gûl alphabet was originally designed to write, is generally thought to have been as follows (Lee and Ramsey 2011, 156):[1]

｜ {i} [i]	— {ɨ} [ɨ]	ㅜ {u} [u]
ㅓ {e} [ə]	ㅗ {o} [o]	
ㅏ {a} [a]	．{ʌ} [ʌ]	

The phonetic value of the native Korean vowel written with orthographic {e} was probably [ə]. In Korean transcriptions of fifteenth and sixteenth century Chinese, orthographic {je} [jə] is generally thought to have stood for Chinese [je] or [jɛ]. This interpretation is uncontroversial and will not concern us here. Instead, we shall focus on orthographic {e} as used elsewhere in the Korean-Chinese transcriptions.

2.   Discussion

The earliest Korean transcriptions of Chinese were made by Sin Sukchu 申叔舟 (1417–1475), a Korean Sinologist and linguist who compiled a number of philological works dealing with Guānhuà pronunciation. These are generally thought to date from ca. 1450, and the readings they record are of two types: i) formal or dictionary forms, called Standard Readings (zhèngyīn 正音), and ii) actual spoken Guānhuà forms, preserved in various sources as Popular Readings (súyīn 俗音) or Left Readings (zuǒyīn 左音).[2] We shall be concerned here with the Standard and Left Readings.

---

1. Compare also Lee (1977, 134–36) and Sohn (1999, 45–6).

2. For detailed discussions of the various reading types and their text sources, see K. Kim (1991, Chaps. 1 and 3) and Yùchí (1990).

From the early sixteenth century we have another set of transcriptions, framed by Ch'we Sejin 崔世珍 (1467–1542).[3] Like Sin, Ch'we was a talented phonetician and Chinese language specialist. It is his Right Readings (yòuyīn 右音), recorded in the early 1500s, which will concern us here.[4] The transcriptional practices and preferences of Sin and Ch'we were not identical, and the types of Guānhuà they recorded were also clearly different. For it is likely that Sin worked with Yangtze watershed-based pronunciation varieties, known by the Chinese of Míng and Qīng times as Nányīn 南音. Ch'we, on the other hand, recorded a northern-based pronunciation type which was called Běiyīn 北音.

In earlier studies it has generally been assumed that Korean {e} as a transcriptional letter represented an unrounded vowel in Chinese, probably similar to or identical with Late Middle Korean [ə]. However, in two unpublished doctoral dissertations, i.e., Y. Kim (1989) and K. Kim (1991), this view was not adopted. Instead, these individuals, apparently working entirely independently and using rather different approaches, both concluded that {e} stood for the rounded Chinese vowel [ɔ] in many environments. In the case of Y. Kim, this position was the result of certain theoretical and structural considerations (see, for example, 1989, 154–5, 205). K. Kim, on the other hand, uncovered a set of special notes by Sin Sukchu on the transcriptional value of {e} (1991, 43). These occur in the Hongmu chông'un yôkhun 洪武正韻譯訓 (completed 1455) and deal with the gē 歌 rime and its shǎng 上 and qù 去 tone counterparts. The note for the gē rime is as follows (Sin 1455/1974, 43):

韻內諸字中聲，若直讀以ㅓ，則不合於時音。特以口不變而讀如ㅓㅡ之間。故其聲近於ㅗ。ㅞ之字亦同。

"For the vowel of all the characters in [this] rime, if one reads it directly as {e} [ə],[5] then it will not accord with contemporary [Chinese] pronunciation. One merely reads it as if [it lay] between {e} [ə] and {ɨ} [ɨ], in such a way that the mouth does not change. Therefore, its sound is close to {o} [o]. The digraph {ue} is to be treated in the same way."

This explanation is repeated verbatim for the corresponding shǎng and qù tone rimes (149, 245). For the pertinent rù tone entry Sin merely states that the vowel should be read as in the word hé 何, which itself belongs to the gē rime (295). On the basis of these passages, K. Kim reads {e} as [ɔ] and {ue} as [wɔ], yielding an interpretation whose result agrees perfectly with the conclusions of Y. Kim. K. Kim then extends this by analogy to other finals, such as {en} [ɔn] and {uen} [wɔn], where, again, the two investigators concur in their interpretations. Now, as indicated above it seems very likely that the several types of Chinese recorded by Sin Sukchu represent the southern or Nányīn variety of Guānhuà pronunciation. And it is

---

3. Ch'we Sejin's dates, particularly that of his birth, have hitherto posed difficulties for historians. These were recently resolved by the discovery in 1999 of Ch'we's mortuary stele. For a full discussion, see J. Kim (1999). I should like to express my gratitude to Professor Akihiro Furuya, through whose kindness I gained access to Kim's article.

4. On these, see again K. Kim (1991, loc. cit.) and Yùchí (1990).

5. That is to say, if one uses the normal Korean value of the letter.

therefore interesting to compare some of his orthographic forms, together with their phonetic interpretations (as propounded by Y. Kim and K. Kim), with Nányīn spellings recorded in Latin script several centuries later by European missionaries. In the following examples, the Korean transcriptions are taken from Sin's Standard Reading system. The European forms are from Francisco Varo's 1703 grammar of Guānhuà (Coblin and Levi 2000).

		Sin			Ch'we
gè	個	{ke}	(去)	[kɔ]	kó [kɔ]
gē	割	{ke}	(入)	[kɔʔ]	kɛ [kɔʔ]
duō	多	{te}	(陰平)	[tɔ]	tō [tɔ]
duān	端	{tuen}	(陰平)	[twɔn]	tuōn [tuɔn]
pàn	判	{p'uen}	(去)	[p'wɔn]	p'uón [p'uɔn]

The agreement of vowel correspondences between the two sets of forms is striking and confirms the conclusions of Y. Kim and K. Kim, at least as regards the use of {e} in Sin Sukchu's transcriptions. Here, {e} almost certainly stood for a rounded vowel. And, since Sin refrained from using Korean {o} [o] in his transcriptions, we can assume that the Chinese vowel was phonetically somehow different from the Korean sound represented by {o}. Thus, a different value, such as [ɔ], would seem to have been the underlying sound here.

Y. Kim does not specifically refer to the transcriptions of Ch'we Sejin. Instead, he seems to be primarily concerned with those of Sin. K. Kim, on the other hand, deals extensively with Ch'we's forms. As noted earlier, Ch'we's transcriptions are thought to reflect the Běiyīn or northern system of Guānhuà pronunciation. And, unlike Sin, he makes active use of Korean {o}. In K. Kim's view, Ch'we intended {o} to stand for underlying Chinese [wɔ]. The following examples illustrate the differences in usage between Sin and Ch'we here:[6]

		Sin			Varo	
duō	多	{te}	(陰平)	[tɔ]	{.to}	[twɔ]
bō	波	{pue}	(陰平)	[pwɔ]	{.po}	[pwɔ]
huō	火	{xue}	(上)	[xwɔ]	{xo}	[xwɔ]

In the case of duō 多, there was probably a minor difference in pronunciation between the two koiné types. In the second and third examples, essentially the same phonetic forms were being transcribed, but in different ways. In our view it seems likely that Kim is correct in his assessment of the underlying sounds here.

---

6. In Ch'we's notation, tones are indicated by left-side dots as follows: no dot = shǎng 上, one dot = yīnpíng 陰平 or qù 去, two dots = yángpíng 陽平. The significance of single and double dots on traditional rùshēng syllables is disputed. Some authorities believe such syllables had merged into the qù and yángpíng tones classes respectively. Others hold that they still retained a separate rù tone but were phonetically similar to the qù and yángpíng tones. For a discussion, see Kim (1991, 106–123).

Ch'we also uses orthographic {e} in his transcriptions, but he makes no comment on what underlying Chinese sound this letter should represent. K. Kim nonetheless assumes that Ch'we's usage is the same as Sin's and that the underlying vowel should be [ɔ]. The following are examples of forms from Ch'we's Right Reading corpus, accompanied by Kim's interpretations:

gē 哥 {.ke} [kɔ]   kě 可 {k'e} [k'ɔ]   hé 何 {:xe} [xɔ]

Now, in many modern north Chinese dialects, and also in modern standard Chinese, syllables of this type have unrounded vowels, i.e., [ɤ] or [ə]; and, contra Kim, one might therefore suggest here that Ch'we, unlike Sin, had chosen to use {e} to represent such an unrounded vowel. However, Kim's interpretation gains support from a very different quarter. From about one hundred years after Ch'we's time we have two traditional style phonological works which are believed to reflect the Běiyīn system as it existed in late Míng Peking. They are the Chóngdìng *Sīmǎ Wēn gōng děngyùn tújīng* 重訂司馬溫公等韻圖經 and the *Hébìng zìxué piānyùn biànlǎn* 合併字學篇韻便覽 of Xú Xiào 徐孝 (fl. late 1500's). The first of these is a rime table, while the second is a rime book. They are complementary and represent the same underlying system. Today they appear in a composite work entitled *Hébìng zìxué jíyùn* 合併字學集韻, dating from 1606. They are cited here according to a microfilm copy of an edition of the *Hébìng zìxué jíyùn* held by the Library of Congress. In Xú's table, words such as those in the preceding two sets of examples are all placed in the same combinatory rime set (Chinese: shè 攝), called Guǒshè 果攝 in the text. Duō 多, bō 波, and huǒ 火 are in the labialized or hékǒu 合口 section of the table, while gē 哥, kě 可, and hé 何 are in the unlabialized or kāikǒu 開口 section. Now, if we assume with Kim that duō 多, bō 波, and huǒ 火 ended in -wɔ in Xú's time, which seems reasonable, then, given the way rime tables are normally set up, gē 哥, kě 可, and hé 何 should end in -ɔ. This would seem to confirm Kim's position.

There is, however, a further and rather serious difficulty with this assumption. This problem involves another set of syllable types, all of which are placed by Xú in a separate rime set called the Zhuóshè 拙攝. The following are examples from this set, with Ch'we's forms and Kim's interpretations added:

Zhuóshè kāikǒu Level 1   拙攝開口一等

kè 克   {:k'e} [k'ɔ] hé 核 {:xe} [xɔ] zé 則 {:tse} [tsɔ] dé 德 {:te} [tɔ]

Zhuóshè hékǒu Level 1   拙攝合口一等

guó 國   {:kue} [kwɔ]   bó 伯 {:pe} [pɔ]

In Ch'we's transcriptions the finals of this set have the same final types (i.e., -ɔ, -wɔ) found in the Guǒshè examples. But the very separation by Xú into separate sets points to different nuclear vowels in the two types of examples. Were Xú's materials older than Ch'we's we would surely conclude here that a merger had occurred in the underlying language after Xú's time but before Ch'we's. However, since Xú's text is later, no such explanation is possible. One could of course suppose that Xú's tables were excessively conservative and preserved a distinction which had already been lost in actual speech by Ch'we's time. This, however, cannot have been the case. For we have convincing transcriptional evidence that Xú's division was based on linguistic reality. This testimony comes from pre-conquest (i.e., pre-1644) Manchu transcriptions, as found in Old Manchu archival material and in translations of novels.[7] Let us now consider the following early Manchu transcriptional forms, arranged according to Xú's Guǒ and Zhuó rime sets:

Guǒshè kāikǒu Level 1 果攝開口一等

可 k'o　河 ho　阿 o

Guǒshè hékǒu Level 1　果攝合口一等

郭 g'o　薄 bo

Zhuóshè kāikǒu Level 1 拙攝開口一等

則 dze　德 de

Zhuóshè hékǒu Level 1　拙攝合口一等

國 guwe 伯 be

In these examples the Manchu forms exhibit a vowel distinction, realized as Manchu o versus e, which corresponds perfectly to Xú Xiào's division of the pertinent syllables into Guǒ and Zhuó sets respectively. It therefore seems likely that Xú's arrangement represented what he actually heard.

Another possible rationalization here would be that a final distinction was indeed present in Ch'we's time but that he either missed it entirely, or, if he did hear it, that he was unable to represent it adequately in transcription. This, while a conceivable explanation, flies in the face of everything we know about Ch'we and his work. For all indications, both in historical accounts and in his surviving œuvre, are that he had a superb ear and pursued his linguistic research with infinite care and precision.[8] To simply set these facts aside would be a desperate recourse.

Finally, we might suppose that the type of Běiyīn system Ch'we recorded was, for unknown reasons, simply different from that represented in Xú's books some 75 to 100 years later. There is no real evidence of any kind for such an assumption. It would be totally ad hoc and, if anything, more desperate than the one suggested in the preceding paragraph.

In attacking this conundrum, it is useful to consider again its salient points. As we have observed, there seems to be no historical reason for assuming a sharp interruption in the history of the Běiyīn between 1500 and 1600. Nothing in political or demographic history supports such a view. And, under the assumption that sound change is regular, if we are dealing here with linear phonological development between an earlier and later stage in a single language, then we are at a loss to account for the unconditioned appearance of a distinction which had not existed earlier. But at this point we may well ask, what was the Běiyīn? Was it really simply the sound system of a "language" or "dialect" as we normally understand these terms? The answer

---

7. Old Manchu archival forms are cited from Kanda, et al (1972–75) and Guǎng and Lǐ (1970). Novel material is taken from the *llan-gurun-i bithe*, a translation of the Chinese work, *Sānguózhì yǎnyì* 三國志演義. The received edition of this translation is dated 1650, but significant parts of it may date from the 1630s. For a full discussion of the text and its history, see Gimm (1988, 105–105). We cite it after the Chinese Materials Center reprint of 1979.

8. See Ledyard (1966, 323–30) and K. Kim (1991, 12–13).

is, of course, that it was not. It was instead a koiné pronunciation system. What, then, was its origin? The traditional view has been that it was simply the sound system of Peking dialect. But our position, recently introduced elsewhere (2007, 2009) and now adopted here as a working hypothesis, is that it was nothing of the sort. It was instead an effort by northerners to pronounce standard southern Guānhuà by replicating as best they could the Nányīn system of pronunciation. In brief, when the seat of government was moved from Nanking to Peking in 1421, the Nányīn system was introduced into the northern capital by courtiers and government officials who had relocated there. The northerners heard this now prestigious "Language of the Officials" and tried to copy its pronunciation to the extent that this was feasible within the framework of their own native sound system. The result was the Běiyīn. Here and there they did import patently northern dialectal forms into their spoken Guānhuà, but for the most part what they used was the southern system in a northern garb. It was, in other words, a unique, hybrid construct, which had not existed before 1421. And a particularly interesting aspect of it, as demonstrated in a recent study (Gāo 2002), is that it did not remain fixed after its initial formation. Instead, in addition to "normal" sound change, it later underwent other, essentially ad hoc, modifications occasioned by reinterpretation of particular aspects of contemporary Nányīn pronunciation. As an illustration of this, we may cite the word sè 色 "color; sex". The early spoken Nányīn form for this etymon was recorded by Sin Sukchu as Left Reading {ṣɨjʔ}. The corresponding Běiyīn form, as given by Ch'we Sejin is {:ṣe} [ṣɔ]. This older Běiyīn form survives today as shè in the rare variant pronunciations of the compounds shèguǐ 色鬼 "lecher" and shèmí 色迷 "lechery", for which the more common current readings are sèguǐ and sèmí respectively. The northern vernacular or dialect pronunciation of this etymon is believed to have been *ṣai, which was never accepted into the formal Běiyīn pronunciation system but survives as modern shǎi in such forms as Pekingese colloquial yánshai 顏色 "color". The common modern reading sè has yet another origin. It is in fact descended from a later Běiyīn form, which was itself an attempt to render later Nányīn [sɛʔ] (compare, for example, Varo's reading: sě). In earlier practice, forms like shǎi have been characterized by Chinese linguists as báidú 白讀 "popular readings", while sè would be labeled wéndú 文讀 "literary reading". In the present case, however, we have two different wéndú, i.e., an earlier shè and a later sè. Gāo (2002, 236) proposes that they be called "literary type 1" (文讀1) and "literary type 2" (文讀2). The importance of his observation for us lies in its confirmation of the fact that the Běiyīn could in later periods reinterpret and re-borrow Nányīn forms which had already been imported earlier.

The question now is, can this information aid us in solving our original problem? Let us begin with words like gē 哥 and kě 可. In the Nányīn system of ca. 1450 these were pronounced [kɔ] and [k'ɔ] respectively. And this was apparently also their pronunciation in North China. Therefore, northerners need do no more than substitute their own pronunciations here in order to arrive at satisfactory Běiyīn readings. The same would have been true for words like bō 波 and huǒ 火 where northern [pwɔ] and [xwɔ] were essentially perfect renderings of their Nányīn equivalents. For Nányīn duō 多 [tɔ] the northerners said [twɔ], and this was apparently felt to be an adequate, if imperfect, substitution. All of this would have been plain sailing. But what was to be done with forms like the following, which occur in Xú Xiào's Zhuóshè and for which we add here Sin's Left Reading forms:

    kè 克 {k'ɨjʔ}   hēi 黑 {xɨjʔ}   bó 伯 {pɨjʔ}   dé 德 {tɨjʔ}   zé 則 {tsɨjʔ}

To begin, we note that Sin's forms are written with the diphthong {ij}. As we have noted, Sin's transcriptions are generally believed to represent a Nányīn-type system. And later representatives of this system, whether modern or pre-modern, seem never to have had diphthongs in syllables of this sort. For example, for dé 德 and bó 伯 we find Varo's tĕ [tɛʔ] and pĕ [pɛʔ] respectively. And in Nányīn-connected modern dialects of the Yangtze watershed the corresponding finals are -əʔ, -eʔ, -ɛʔ, etc. Diphthongal finals such as -əjʔ, -ejʔ, and -ɛjʔ, are apparently foreign to currently known Yangtze watershed Mandarin speech types. We may therefore suspect that what Sin was transcribing here was really a final type which we may tentatively represent as -eʔ, i.e., a mid unrounded vowel of some sort plus glottal closure. But why would Sin have spelled such a final with a diphthong? The answer suggests itself if we recall the Late Middle Korean vowel inventory:

{i} [i]   {ɨ} [ɨ]   {u} [u]

{e} [ə]   {o} [o]

{a} [a]   {ʌ} [ʌ]

In this configuration there was no mid front vowel at all. And Sin expressly stated that he intended to use Korean {e} [ə] to represent a Chinese rounded vowel. This would have left him with no alternative but to represent a Chinese -eʔ in some other way. His choice was to use the Korean diphthong {ij} [ij]. This move is in fact quite understandable. In the spoken English of the present writer, there is no pure higher mid front vowel [e] in word final position. Consequently to me, the Taiwanese word [se⁵³] "to wash, bathe" sounds like [sej]; and, if pressed, I might well choose to spell it as English "say" [sej]. Sin's transcriptional strategy seems to have been analogous. Let us then assume, for the sake of argument, that the actual phonetic shapes of the early Nányīn forms for our sample syllables were as follows:[9]

kè 克 [k'eʔ]   hēi 黑 [xeʔ]   bó 伯 [peʔ]   dé 德 [teʔ]   zé 則 [tseʔ]

How would a north Chinese speaker of the 1400's have heard and reproduced these forms? Substitution of native readings would have been less than optimal, for it is virtually certain that all these syllables ended in unchecked diphthongs in the native vernaculars. "Black", "virtue", and "principle" must have had something like -əj or -ej, "elder paternal uncle" something like -aj, etc. For suitable Běiyīn equivalents one would have had to fashion new forms. How was this to be done? The optimal selection would have been made from available monophthongal or mono-vocalic finals of the native vernaculars. On the basis of Ch'we Sejin's recordings, we can now deduce that these were as follows:

-i   -ɨ   -u
                      -ɔ
            -a

---

9. The actual realization of [e] here may have been shwa-like for some Nányīn speakers, and more fronted for others, mirroring the spread of realizations, such as -əʔ, -ɛʔ, etc., found in the modern Yangtze watershed dialects.

We should note that this is not a full northern vowel inventory. It merely represents finals ending in a single vowel. For example, the language is thought to have had the vowel [e]; but this was found only in complex finals such as -je, -jej, and -jen. There was no simple final -e. And it would have been beyond the competence of most native speakers to extract [e] from its conditioning environments and then manipulate it in the abstract. Consequently, in representing Nányīn syllables such as [xeʔ] and [teʔ], the only northern mid vowel available for placement in final position immediately after a syllable initial would have been [ɔ]. The result was Běiyīn forms such as xɔ 黑 and tɔ 德. It was these forms that Ch'we heard and recorded.

Our next question is, then, what happened between the time of Ch'we Sejin (ca. 1500) and Xú Xiào (ca. 1600)? Here we must consider syllables of the following type, for which we supply Ch'we Sejin's spellings. Orthographic and phonetic forms are assumed to have been essentially identical here.

        zhě 者 {tʂje} [tʂje]   chē 車 {.tʂ'je} [tʂ'je]   shè 舍 {.ʂje} [ʂje]

In Ch'we's day syllables of this type had medial -j-. But there is good evidence that by Xú Xiào's time this medial -j- had been lost, yielding simple final -e, hence: zhě 者 [tʂe], chē 車 [tʂ'e], shè 舍 [ʂe]. This evidence comes from Xú's own tables. For example, in his Zhuóshè table he places zhě 者 in the same level (i.e., děng 等) and segmental homophone column with zhái 宅 (Ch'we: {tʂe} [tʂɔ]), and shè 舍 in the same homophone column with sè 色 (Ch'we: {ʂe} [ʂɔ]). Such words should share the same segmental sounds respectively and would have differed only by tone. And, most significantly for us, zhái 宅 and sè 色 did not have medial -j- at all during the period in question. Consequently, we can be confident that words such as zhě 者, chē 車, and shè 舍 had lost medial -j- in Xú Xiào's pronunciation.

The disappearance of medial -j- after retroflexes resulted in the emergence of a totally new final, -e. Our suggestion here is that this enabled northerners to revise their Běiyīn pronunciation of Nányīn syllables like 克 [k'eʔ], 黑 [xeʔ], 伯 [peʔ], 德 [teʔ], and 則 [tseʔ]. These could now be pronounced as 克 [k'e], 黑 [xe], 伯 [pe], 德 [te], and 則 [tse] rather than 克 [k'ɔ], 黑 [xɔ], 伯 [pɔ], 德 [tɔ], and 則 [tsɔ]. This was clearly an improvement in that (i) it more accurately reproduced the Nányīn target sounds and (ii) it enabled northerners to restore an important final distinction of the Nányīn system. This can be illustrated as follows:

	哥	可	克	德
Nányīn forms	kɔ	k'ɔ	k'eʔ	teʔ
Old Běiyīn forms	kɔ	k'ɔ	k'ɔ	tɔ
New Běiyīn forms	kɔ	k'ɔ	k'e	te

It is interesting to note at this point that forms like [tɔ] in the Old Běiyīn system and [k'e] and [te] in the new one represented entirely new syllable types for northern speakers. For, though created from currently available initials and finals, they had not existed as combinations in northern syllabic inventories before the northern effort to replicate Nányīn pronunciation. Today they have been completely nativized, though their currency varies from etymon to etymon. In some cases they ultimately became the common pronunciations of the etyma in question. For example, in the case of the word for "virtue" modern dé, which is the direct reflex of New Běiyīn [te], is the accepted current pronunciation. The true native form, děi, is preserved in Peking only among professional storytellers (Yú 1983, 36). For the syllabically parallel word "to get", both the Běiyīn and native forms survive, as dé and děi, but their lexical incidence is different and complementary in the modern standard language. In the word for "black", the colloquial northern dialect form hēi reigns supreme, while the New Běiyīn-derived form hè (< [xe]) is virtually unknown except among persons who recite poetry in the traditional style.

What of the Old Běiyīn forms in -ɔ? In fact, though they are gone today, there are hints that they may have survived at least into the nineteenth century among some speakers of northern Guānhuà. The *Lǐshì yīnjiàn* 李氏音鑒 (1805) of Lǐ Rǔzhēn 李汝珍 (1763–1830) contains a chapter (i.e., Juàn 卷4, Chapter 25)[10] devoted to the proper Běiyīn pronunciation of traditional rùshēng words. In this material the word duó 奪 is glossed as 董娥切. Duó is thought to have had a rounded nucleus (i.e., Old Běiyīn and New Běiyīn [twɔ]) throughout the Míng and Qīng periods. Now, the next entry in Lǐ's text is for dé 得 and dé 德. The gloss on them is as follows: 等娥切。或讀斗美切. The second fǎnqiè 反切 spelling is clearly for the form we would today read as děi, but the first must correspond to our dé. Nevertheless, it in fact yields for Lǐ the same syllable type as that given for duó 奪. Hence, it may represent a survival of the old Běiyīn reading. Oddly reminiscent of this is Joseph Edkins' transcriptional practice in his northern Guānhuà grammar of 1864. In this work the words dé 得 and dé 德 are in one place (1864, 62) romanized as te[2], while duó 奪 is written as to[2] (1864, 63). Later, however, Edkins writes dé 得 as to[2] (1864, 68), with the added note (1864, 69) thats this to[2] is the pronunciation found inside the city of Peking. Finally, we have Thomas Wade's grammar of 1867. In the appendix to his Peking Syllabary, alternate northern Guānhuà readings of the same etymon are collected and listed. And for hēi 黑 we are given the following selection of these (Appendix, p. 9): hei[1], hei[3], ho[4], hê (no tone). Here, the reading hê is the expected reflex of New Běiyīn [xe], already mentioned above. But Wade's ho4 must derive from the Old Běiyīn form [xɔ]. Apparently, such things could still be heard in the Peking area in the 1860's.

3.   Conclusions

This study was undertaken to assess the shared theory of Youngman Kim and Kwangjo Kim, propounded independently and on rather different grounds, that Han'gûl orthographic {e} (= Late Middle Korean [ə]) was used in the fifteenth and early sixteenth centuries to write a Chinese rounded vowel, posited by both of these investigators as [ɔ]. This theory, which departed from earlier interpretations, appeared on various grounds to be problematic. Indeed, our initial expectation was that it would prove untenable. However, a full consideration of the evidence has led to the conclusion that it is in fact the correct interpretation, a fact which throws interesting light on the early history of northern Chinese standard pronunciation.

---

10. Edition of the *Xùxiū Sìkù quánshū* 續修四庫全書, Shanghai: Shanghai Guji, 1995. vol. 260.

REFERENCES

A Manchu Edition of Ilan-gurun-i bithe. 1979. A limited edition reprint by Chinese Materials Center, Inc. San Francisco: Chinese Materials Center.

Coblin, W. S. 2007. Modern Chinese phonology: From Guānhuà to Mandarin. *Collection des Cahiers Linguistique Asie Orientale* 11. Paris: Ècole des Hautes Études in Sciences Sociales.

Coblin, W. S. 2009. Retroflex initials in the history of southern Guanhua phonology. *Cahiers de Linguistique Asie Orientale* 38 (1): 125–162.

Coblin, W. S., and A. L. Joseph. 2000. *Francisco Varo's Grammar of the Mandarin Language (1703): An English Translation of the 'Arte de la Lengua Mandarina'.* Amsterdam/ Philadelphia: John Benjamins.

Edkins, J. 1864. *A Grammar of the Chinese Colloquial Language Commonly called the Mandarin Dialect.* Shanghai: Presbyterian Mission Press.

Gao, Xiǎohóng（高曉虹）. 2002. Běijīnghuà zhuāngzŭzì fēnhuà xiànxiàng shìxī 北京話莊組字分化現象試析. *Zhōngguó Yǔwén* 中國語文 2002, 3:234–238.

Gimm, M. 1988. Manchu translations of Chinese novels and short stories: An attempt at an inventory. *Asia Major,* Third Series 1 (2): 77–114.

Guang Lù（廣祿）and Lǐ Xuézhì（李學智）. 1970. *Qīng Tàizǔ Cháo Lǎo Mǎnwén Yuándǎng* 清太祖朝老滿文原檔. *Academia Sinica Special Publication* no. 58. Nankang: Academia Sinica.

Kanda, Nobuo（神田信夫）, et al. 1972–75. *Kyū Manshūtō* 舊滿洲檔. Two vols. Tokyo: Tōyō Bunko.

Kim, Joonheon（金俊憲）. 1999. Sai Sechin no shōgai ni kansuru shin shiryō no hakken 崔世珍の生涯に關する新資料の發見. *Kaipian* 開篇 19:24–30.

Kim, Kwangjo. 1991. *A Phonological Study of Middle Mandarin: Reflected in Korean Sources of the Mid-15th and Early 16th Centuries.* University of Washington Doctoral Dissertation. Ann Arbor: University Microfilms.

Kim, Youngman. 1989. *Middle Mandarin Phonology: A Study Based on Korean Data.* Ohio State University Doctoral Dissertation. Ann Arbor: University Microfilms.

Ledyard, G. 1966. *The Korean Language Reform of 1446: The Origin, Background, and Early History of the Korean Alphabet.* University of California, Berkeley Dissertation.

LEE, Ki-moon. 1977. *Geschichte der Koreanischen Sprache* (Deutsche Übersetzung). Wiesbaden: Ludwig Reichert Verlag.

Lee, Iksop, and S. R. Ramsey. 2011. *A History of the Korean Language.* Cambridge: Cambridge University Press.

Sin, Sukchu（申叔舟）. 1455/1974. *Hongmu Chông'un Yôkhun* 洪武正韻譯訓. Reprint: 1974. Seoul: Koryô University Press.

Sohn, Ho-min. 1999. *The Korean Language.* Cambridge: Cambridge University Press.

Wade, T. F. 1867. *A Progressive Course Designed to Assist the Student of Colloquial Chinese as Spoken in the Capital and the Metropolitan Department.* London: Trübner & Co.

Yu, Mǐn（俞敏）. 1983. Lǐ Rūzhēn Yīnjiàn lǐ de rùshēng zì 李汝珍《音鑒》裏的入聲字. *Běijīng Shīfàn Dàxué Xuébào* 北京師範大學學報 1980, 4:30–40.

Yuchi, Zhìpíng（尉遲治平）. 1990. Lǎo Qǐdà Piáo tōngshì yànjiě Hànzìyīn de yǔyīn jīchǔ 老乞大、朴通事諺解漢字音的語音基楚. *Yǔyán Yánjiù* 語言研究 1990, 1:11–24.

6

Investigations into Determinants of the Diversity of the World's Languages

Christophe COUPÉ, Jean-Marie HOMBERT,
Egidio MARSICO, François PELLEGRINO
Laboratoire Dynamique du Langage
(CNRS – University of Lyon)

Foreword

During 2011, we had the occasion to meet Professor William Wang in different meetings in Lyon, Hong Kong and Shanghai. During these encounters, results obtained by Quentin Atkinson and published earlier in the year (Atkinson 2011a) were a topic of hot discussion. Prof. Wang published a short paper in one of Southern China's main newspapers, where he defended the possibility of multi-regional evolution of languages, and more generally suggested not to pay only attention to the global at the expense of local phenomena. With this idea in mind, we decided to adapt the statistical approach employed by Atkinson in order to consider local ecological contexts as potential determinants of linguistic and sociolinguistic phenomena. We hope that the results we present will be seen as a step towards a better acknowledgment of the richness and complexity of language, both aspects Prof. Wang especially led us to study and value.

1. Introduction: Identifying Determinants of Linguistic Phenomena

1.1 Phonemic diversity and the Out of Africa model

In a recent and heavily debated paper, Atkinson (2011a) put forward what he called a 'serial founder effect' in the distribution of the phonemic diversity of the world's languages. Relying on data from the WALS database (Dryer and Haspelmath 2011) and statistical analysis, he concluded that the size of the phonemic inventories of languages declined with distance from Africa, in the same way human genetic and phenotypic diversities do.

The concept of founder effect was borrowed from genetics, where a small group leaving a larger one only carries a portion of the genetic diversity of the latter. The relevance of this concept in linguistics has been attacked by linguists stating that no speakers were ever leaving a larger population with only a subset of the phonemes of its language (e.g., Maddieson, Bhattacharya, Smith and Croft 2011). Atkinson's core assumption was however different and perhaps not very convincingly described by the notion of founder effect. In fact, Atkinson relied on a previous study which found a correlation between the number of speakers of a language and the number of phonemes of this language (Hay and Bauer 2007). The reasoning, as we understood it, is as follows: if the Out of Africa mainly took place through the repetition of small groups leaving larger ones to go further away from the origin point of the migration, then these small groups, although initially leaving with the complete phonemic inventory of their language, could have later and gradually lost some of their phonemes. A gradual impoverishment would have thus resulted from the repetition of scissions of small populations from larger ones, with a spread from the origin point to the most recently colonized areas.

Atkinson's results were obtained on the basis of compiled quantitative data and statistical models. While some typologists have acknowledged that the approach was innovative with respect to typological issues (Jaeger, Graff, Croft and Pontillo 2011), many of its aspects came under criticism (Bybee 2011).[1] The use of a single quantitative measure of phonemic diversity was first contested (Maddieson et al. 2011), as well as the assimilation between the concepts of diversity and complexity (Ross and Donohue 2011). The positive correlation between the number of speakers and the size of the phoneme inventory of a language was rebutted on the basis of either specific examples of linguistic families (Rice 2011; Dahl 2011) or analyses of larger datasets of languages (Wichmann, Rama and Holman 2011; Donohue and Nichols 2011; Pericliev 2011). Its relevance during pre-Holocene times—when human populations were small and sparse—was also questioned (Sproat 2011). Ringe (2011) more specifically investigated the processes by which phonemes are lost or created in languages, and Trudgill (2011) insisted that, in general, migration does not lead to inventory reduction. Finally, specific assumptions behind the statistical models used by Atkinson were questioned, and the large number of small-sized linguistic families was identified as a limit preventing from investigating the potential weight of genetic groupings (Jaeger et al. 2011).

---

1. In the fall of 2011, a half special issue of the journal Linguistic Typology dealt with Atkinson's proposal.

The considerable amount of attention received by Atkinson's study showed that today's typology is not yet at ease with the use of quantitative and statistical approaches. It also highlighted the need for a better understanding of the relationship between social factors and linguistic ones.

Atkinson's study followed other works which focused on the relationship between the phonemic diversity of a language and its number of speakers. Trudgill stressed the contradicting hypotheses regarding the possible interaction between these two elements: on the one hand, a smaller population may have a smaller phonemic inventory, since a higher degree of interpersonal knowledge in tight social networks might result in a weaker need for phonological differentiation between words (Trudgill 2002). On the other hand, a smaller population size may imply easier adherence to linguistic norms, and therefore larger inventories (Trudgill 2004). Hay and Bauer (2007)'s study suggested a positive correlation between the number of speakers and the number of phonemes. However, the authors didn't propose any convincing explanation for it. Their results diverged from Pericliev (2004)'s statement of a lack of correlation between the number of speakers and the size of the consonantal inventory. Finally, a strong relationship was recently suggested between a range of sociolinguistic factors and the degree of complexity of morphological and syntactic structures (Lupyan and Dale 2010). Walker and Hamilton (2010) also stressed a link between social complexity and linguistic diversity during Austronesian and Bantu population expansions.[2]

In this context, we wish to stress the relevance of environmental factors to understand linguistic and sociolinguistic phenomena. In other words, we propose to go 'upstream' in the investigation of the cascade of factors that influence the current global linguistic situation. At the methodological level, we conduct statistical analyses on linguistic data and high-resolution biophysical and demographic datasets, which accurately describe the 'ecology' of today's languages.

In the remaining of this introductory section, we report studies which previously highlighted the impact of environmental factors. In the rest of this contribution, we introduce our sources of data and our statistical approach, before presenting and discussing the results.

1.2   Environmental factors and linguistic situations

Several of Atkinson's critics mentioned Nettle's pioneering works with respect to linguistic diversity across large geographic areas (Nettle 1999a). Nettle especially brought to light the role that ecological factors could play in influencing social aspects of language; he focused on

---

2. Such studies often define linguistic complexity by counting elements, or by considering the occurrence of specific features. Finer-grained approaches exist—e.g., (Coupé, Marsico and Pellegrino 2009; Maddieson 2009) regarding phonological complexity, but they require data difficult to collect for a large number of languages.

the concepts of ecological risk and growing season to explain the geographic extension and population size of linguistic groups in tropical regions (Nettle 1996, 1998). His arguments can be summarized as follows: i) the yearly duration of the growing season of plants is related to the risk faced by people of suffering from difficulties of getting the resources they need for their subsistence—the ecological risk; ii) the greater this risk, the stronger the need for a geographically wide social network, that is for solid relationships with distant people who can help in case of local problems; iii) the wider the social network, the higher the degree of linguistic convergence, and therefore the larger the linguistic groups (both in size and spread).

Nettle also investigated the relationship between the social structure of a population and its linguistic features. He tried to model how social factors impact language evolution (Nettle 1999b), and more specifically how the size of a population influences the rate of linguistic change (Nettle 1999c; see also Ringe 2011). In doing so, he paved the way for further studies on the relationship between ecological, social and linguistic factors. In the last decade, several authors have indeed built on Nettle's original geographic and age-divided social structure, relying for example on tools from graph theory (Ke, Gong and Wang 2008).

Jacquesson's advocacy for a 'linguistics of the quasi-desert' provides another example of how a specific living place—deserts—may result in particular linguistic dynamics because of the social relationships between the inhabitants (Jacquesson 2001; 2003). Though based on different approaches, these studies highlight that environmental factors may impact the social structure of speakers, which may in turn weigh on their linguistic structures.

It makes good sense to postulate indirect relationships between the environment and linguistic structures through the mediation of social factors. The alternative of direct relationships is also worth considering and some proposals do exist, such as the acoustic adaptation hypothesis. It states that languages, as other animal vocal communication systems, are adapted to the ecological environment in which they operate. Quoting Maddieson (2011d), 'temperate environments with open vegetation would facilitate transmission of higher frequency signals better than warmer more densely vegetated environments. Hence, languages in the first setting will tend to be more consonant-heavy (more consonant contrasts, more consonant-heavy syllables), whereas those in the second are likely to be more vocalic and to have simpler syllable structures (and perhaps longer words)'. Maddieson (ibid) tested this hypothesis and found a significant correlation between a combined phonological measure of consonant inventory size and complexity of the syllable system, and the proximity to the temperate zones around 45° of latitude north or south.

All these studies call for further investigation of the influence of the environment, whether direct or indirect, on linguistic variables. In the next section, we introduce the material we considered to this end, and explain how we assembled different sources of data into a proper dataset.

2. Material and Methods

Current studies on linguistic diversity at global scales take advantage of recent scientific advances: i) the availability of high-resolution global maps of biophysical, social, and linguistic data, ii) the development of computational and statistical tools to explore the structure of these data, iii) interdisciplinary efforts to bridge theories and tools from fields such as climatology, ecology, anthropology, geography, or linguistics. Following this trend, we gathered data from a variety of sources and disciplines. We first describe linguistic, then ecological and demographic data. We then report the procedures applied to them in the perspective of statistical tests.

2.1 Linguistic and sociolinguistic data

We started from Atkinson (2011a)'s data as they were available in the supplementary material of his publication. These data were extracted from the World Atlas of Linguistic Structure (WALS) (Dryer and Haspelmath 2011) and the Ethnologue (Lewis 2009). The dataset consisted in 504 languages, each of them being provided with geographic coordinates (latitude and longitude), a linguistic classification (at the family and gender levels), its estimated number of speakers and measures of vocalic, tonal and consonantal diversity in terms of numbers of phonemes. These phonological data were compiled by Maddieson in line with his efforts on the UPSID database (Maddieson 1984, 2011a, 2011b, 2011c; Maddieson and Precoda 1990). The three measures of diversity were standardized by Atkinson in order to take their average as a unified measure of phonemic diversity.

Additionally, we relied on the World Language Mapping System (WLMS). This digital dataset provided by Global Mapping International and SIL International (2012) contains geographic areas for the languages described in the Ethnologue at country-level, along with information such as the estimated number of speakers, linguistic family, etc. Such a dataset improves significantly over descriptions of languages as single geographic locations, and is useful to compute average values of environmental variables for the area where a language is spoken.

We merged data to shift from country-level to country-independent descriptions, deleted languages with no speakers, and obtained a dataset of 6,270 languages. In this dataset, we attempted at identifying the 504 previous languages. Most languages were readily found; a dozen corresponded to two languages in the WLMS, and were therefore split. Remaining languages could not be identified, and were therefore removed from the dataset. We furthermore discarded languages with more than 10 million speakers or less than 10 in order to minimize linguistic evolutions—expansions or language deaths—due to recent demographic and economic changes.

The previous processing led to a dataset of 460 languages. For each of them, we relied on the linguistic classification and measures of phonological diversity provided by Atkinson. From the WLMS dataset, we retained the numbers of speakers, and computed language areas with Quantum GIS (version 1.8). With the same software, a measure of linguistic density was

Figure 6.1   Geographic distribution of the 460 languages initially considered in the study

estimated by counting for each language how many other languages were overlapping or spoken less than 50 km from its area.

In the statistical models, the previous variables are described respectively with the codes Family, PhonemeDiv, NbSpeakers, LgArea and LgContact.

Figure 6.1 illustrates the areas of the 460 languages.

2.2   Environmental and demographic data

We took advantage of a number of freely available high-resolution datasets to obtain relevant data for our study.

We considered the WorldClim 1km global climate dataset (version 1.4, release 3) as a source of **climatic data** (Hijmans, Cameron, Parra, Jones and Jarvis 2005). Various variables were available and reminiscent of studies in ecology focusing on the determination of biomes from climatic factors (Holdrige 1947; Whittaker 1975; Kottek, Griser, Beck, Rudolf and Rubel 2006). For the sake of simplicity, we however only extracted the yearly average precipitations and temperatures.

Regarding **elevation**, we relied on the ETOPO 1' global elevation model (Amante and Eakins 2009), and used Quantum GIS to derive a surface rugosity index from elevation data.

Figure 6.2 Percentage of tree cover (light grey: 0% – black: 100%)

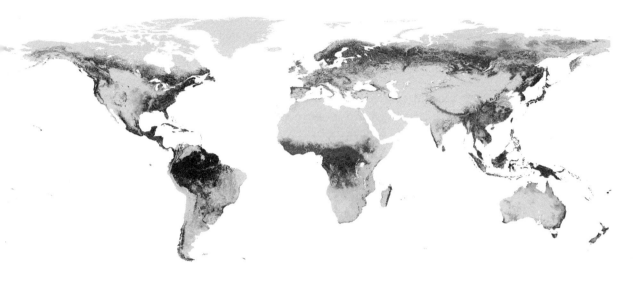

Figure 6.3 Population count (light grey: 1 pers./pixel – black: 36,455 pers./pixel; logarithmic scale)

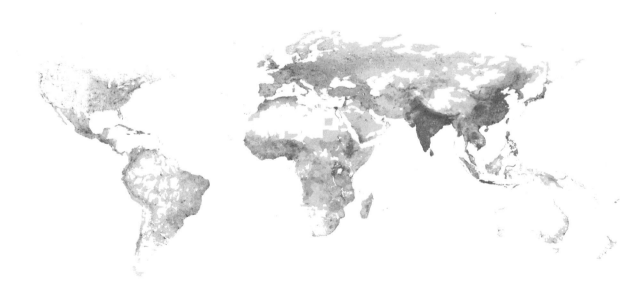

Two variables related to **vegetation** were considered. The length of growing period (LGP) was obtained as an average 16-class value for the period 1901–1996, at a 5' resolution from the Food and Agriculture Organization and International Institute for Applied Systems Analysis (2000). Tree coverage was obtained as a percentage of ground coverage at a 1km resolution from the Global Map (version 1) dataset (Geospatial Information Authority of Japan, Chiba University and collaborating organizations 2008).

The Global Rural-Urban Mapping Project (version 1) finally provided us with figures of **human population**—number of persons per pixel of dataset—at a 1km resolution for the year 2000 (CIESIN, IFPRI, World Bank and CIAT 2011).

For each language of the dataset described in 2.1, we computed the average values of this set of variables over the area where it is spoken (for population density, we divided the total number of persons by the surface of the linguistic area). Due to lack of data, this was not possible for three languages located on small islands (Fijian, Kiribati, and Rapanui); we therefore removed these three languages from the dataset.

Figure 6.2 depicts the percentage of tree cover at a global scale, and figure 6.3 the logged population count.

In the statistical models, the previous variables are described respectively with the codes Prec, Tmp, Elv, Rug, LGP, Tree, PopDens.

2.3   A priori model of the interactions

A number of studies introduced in section 1 relied on detecting statistically significant correlations and relationships between variables in large sets of numerical or categorical data. Within such a methodological framework, two important issues need to be addressed. The first one is the well-known difference between correlation and causation. A correlation between two phenomena A and B in no way necessarily means a direct causal relationship between them. Alternative options are a third phenomenon C causing both A and B, multiple causal interactions between A, B and other phenomena, or chance. Conclusions regarding causality therefore need to be cautious. The second issue is related to spurious correlations occurring by chance, and so-called Type II errors when crossing many variables with each other in regression models in the hope of detecting significant correlations.

To prevent the previous traps, we defined an a priori model of the possible causal interactions underlying the relationships between our variables. This model divides the variables into four levels, with the key assumption that factors at a given level may influence factors at a higher level, but not vice-versa.

The first level comprises environmental factors, such as Elv, Rug, Tmp, Prec, LGP and Tree in our study, and could include additional ones such as distance to freshwater, biomes, etc.

The second level contains phenomena related to human activities yet independent from the spoken languages. We only considered PopDens in this study, but age distribution, kin systems, etc. would fall into this category. The Out of Africa migration and its consequences also do.

The third level refers to languages with respect to their social aspects, but not their internal structures. It includes their geographical distribution, the social organization or history of speakers, but not features—whether phonological, morphological, syntactic, etc. NbSpeakers, LgArea and LgContact fall into this level.

Finally, the fourth level consists of variables describing the internal states of the language, its structures, and intrinsic complexity. Here we considered PhonemeDiv and Family, but any measure of complexity, the absence or presence of specific linguistic devices etc. could be considered.

Our assumption is that environmental variables (Level 1) are not determined by either social (Level 2), sociolinguistic (Level 3) or purely linguistic (Level 4) variables; non-linguistic social variables (Level 2) are not determined by sociolinguistic (Level 3) or purely linguistic (Level 4) variables. Importantly, we assume numbers of speakers, linguistic contacts and language areas (Level 3) to be independent of genetic relationships between languages (Level 4).

Table 6.1 summarizes the four levels and how the variables of our study fall into them.

This model can be contested on the basis that nowadays, human activities bear an impact on climate and other environmental phenomena; in some cases, linguistic facts weigh on social facts, such as in case of conflicts when spoken languages are politically utilized to displace populations, etc. However, in the vast arena of causal relationships to be unearthed, our approach reflects the assumption that some causal relationships are weaker than others, if not negligible, and can be discarded to better focus on the main phenomena.

Table 6.1   Categories of variables defined for statistical analysis

Level	Types of variables	Variables
1	Environmental	Elv, Rug, Tmp, Prec, LGP, Tree
2	Non-linguistic social	PopDens
3	Sociolinguistic	LgArea, LgContact, NbSpeakers, geographic locations of languages
4	Purely linguistic	PhonemeDiv, Family

2.4   Statistical processing of the data

We applied various statistical methods to our dataset of 457 languages, using the software R (version 3.0.0) and additional packages dedicated to statistical processing.

Some of the 12 variables (Prec, Tmp, Elv, Rug, LGP, Tree, PopDens, Family, PhonemeDiv, NbSpeakers, LgArea and LgContact) yielded distributions very distant from normality (PopDens,

NbSpeakers and LgArea), and none of them passed the Shapiro-Wilk normality test. For each variable, we therefore estimated the best parameters for a Box-Cox transformation (Box and Cox 1964), relying on the boxcoxfit function of the geoR package (Ribeiro and Diggle 2001) and the boxcox function of the MASS package (Venables and Ripley 2002). Normality tests were still significant at .05 after transformations for all variables but LgArea. However, all distributions except Tree and LGP were much closer to normality and therefore potentially better adapted to linear regression.

Our results are all based on the application of linear regression models to various subsets of variables. Given the nature of our data, we considered simple fixed effects regressions as well as random effects and spatial regression.

In each caes, we started with a standard linear regression of a predicted (dependent) variable against predictors (independent variables)—e.g., predicting NbSpeakers against the predictors PopDens, Tree, and Elv. We looked in the outputs of the model for outliers (normalized residuals, i.e. predictions errors, higher than 2.5 or 3 in absolute value) with high leverage thanks to influence plots (which simultaneously display for each entry of the model the value of the studentized residual, the hat value, and Cook's distance). When such entries were detected, they were removed from the dataset before running the model once again. As explained below, we relied in some cases on stepwise regression with the stepAIC function of the MASS package, which performed model selection by Akaike information criterion (AIC) to identify the 'best' set of predictors for a predicted variable.

Following among others (Jaeger, Graff, Croft and Pontillo 2011), we tested the assumptions behind the application and validity of such a model, namely:

- The linearity of the relationships between the dependent and independent variables—with Ceres plots
- The normality of the error distribution—with quantile-quantile plots and Shapiro-Wilk tests
- The homoscedasticity of the error distribution, i.e. the absence of correlation with predictors—with plots of residuals versus fitted values and Breusch-Pagan tests
- The absence of strong multicollinearity between the predictors—with Variance Inflation Factors (VIF) and condition indexes (VIF should be lower than 5 for all predictors, and the largest condition index below 30)

In our experiments, we did not often end with residuals satisfying tests like the Shapiro-Wilk or Breusch-Pagan tests. This was however not surprising since we had several hundreds of observations. The various graphics always suggested near normality and good homoscedasticity.

Another important assumption in linear regression is the assumption of independence of the observations from each other. In time-series for example, observations at time t partly influenced by earlier observations violate this assumption. This leads to autocorrelation in the residuals, and failure to take this issue into account weakens the predictive quality of the model.

In the case of languages, spatial proximities and their possible consequences as well as genetic relatedness violate the assumption of independence. Problems then lie in the possible differences between subgroups of languages, potentially generating artifacts such as Simpson's paradox (Simpson 1951). The issue was addressed by Hauer and Bauer (2007) by looking at the effect of the number of speakers at the family level, and also by considering family as a fixed effect. Atkinson also relied on a by-group approach, but replaced the former fixed effect by a more adapted random effect. Jaeger et al. (2011) stressed the relevance of mixed effects models for typological study, but also showed that the distribution of languages into families was too sparse to fully sort out the problem of genetic groupings in Atkinson's study.

In our analysis, we relied on two approaches to control for the spatial and genetic relationships between languages: in cases where we predicted variables of the 3rd level of our model—LgArea, LgContact, NbSpeakers—we assumed that genetic grouping was not significant, and only considered spatial relationships with spatial regression models. Two languages distant by less than 1,000 km were considered as neighbors in the definition of spatial weights. Following (Anselin 2005, 2007; Anselin, Syabri and Kho 2006), we applied Lagrange multiplier diagnostics for spatial dependence to our linear regressions to detect spatial autocorrelation and identify which model—spatial error or spatial lag model—could be applied to take it best into account.[3] The application of the correct model led to more robust regression coefficients and p-values. These p-values were computed, along with confidence intervals, with Markov Chain Monte Carlo (MCMC) approaches. More specifically, we used the pvalsfunc function of the spdep package.

In cases where we predicted the variable at the 4th level of our model—PhonemeDiv, we compared models with and without the categorical variable Family introduced as a random effect. This once again led to a better assessment of the various predictors.

As further explained in section 3, our analysis rested on the hierarchy between variables defined in our a priori model of interactions (see section 2.3). While we investigated predictions of variables at level 3 or 4 against variables of lower levels, we wished to consider the influence of factors at a given level while controlling for the influence of other factors. To this end, we inspected several definitions of 'sums of squares' in the regression (Myers, Montgomery, Vining and Robinson 2010), and the related Type I and Type III analyses. A Type III analysis evaluates the relationship between an independent variable and the dependent variable given that all other independent variables are included in the model. A Type I analysis is based on a hierarchical (or sequential) decomposition: whether an independent variable predicts a significant part of

---

3. Lagrange multiplier diagnostics are usually analyzed as follows: non-robust versions of the statistics—LMerr and LMlag—are considered first. If LMerr is not significant and LMLag is, a spatial lag model should be considered to account for spatial autocorrelation. If LMerr is significant but LMLag isn't, a spatial error model is recommended. If, and only if, both non-robust statistics are significant, robust versions—RLMerr and RLMlag—are analyzed in the same way as non-robust statistics. If both robust tests are significant, the spatial model is chosen according to the most significant one.

the variance is computed given that all the independent variables listed above in the model are included, but not the variables listed below. To refer to our specific variables, we could thus estimate the influence of environmental variables on sociolinguistic variables with or without controlling for population density in the model, or the potential impact of tree coverage on phonemic diversity controlling for sociolinguistic factors.

The following conventions were adopted to present the results:

- Regarding levels of significance, '***' stands for $p<0.001$, '**' for $p<0.01$, '*' for $p<0.05$, '.' for $p<0.1$, and 'n.s.' for non-significant
- S-W stands for the Shapiro-Wilk test, B-P for the Breusch-Pagan test, Cond. for the largest condition index, VIF for the largest variance inflation factor. LM test stands for the LM test for residual autocorrelation in the spatial regression model.
- For the Shapiro-Wilk test, the Breusch-Pagan tests, Lagrange multiplier diagnostics and LM tests, only p-values are given.

3.   Results

We summarize here the different models which were applied to our data, following the framework defined in section 2. Section 3.1 offers preliminary observations on the basis of graphical representations and coefficients of correlation between the variables. Section 3.2 revisits Nettle's proposal regarding LGP at a global scale, first without, then with, controlling for population density. Section 3.3 summarizes stepwise regressions for the three sociolinguistic variables NbSpeakers, LgArea and LgContact. Section 3.4 gives predictions of phonemic diversity against successively sociolinguistic variables, sociolinguistic variables and tree coverage, and sociolinguistic and environmental variables. Finally, section 3.5 reports investigations of Atkinson's hypothesis of a gradient of phonemic diversity from the origin of modern human populations.

3.1   Preliminary observations

In order to graphically illustrate data distribution, we propose to look at African languages. Figures 6.4, 6.5 and 6.6 respectively display normalized and standardized PopDens, NbSpeakers and LgContact variables for the African languages of our dataset. Language areas can easily be seen on each map. The maps allow large scale patterns to be detected, and similarities and differences between languages to be noticed. For example, Figure 6.6 illustrates the high number of contacts for languages in the sub-Saharan region.

In addition to maps, coefficients of correlation between the variables can be computed and analyzed. Tables 6.2, 6.3, 6.4 and 6.5 provide Pearson's product-moment correlations for the variables, grouped according to the levels of our model.

Figure 6.4   Density of population for the African languages of the dataset

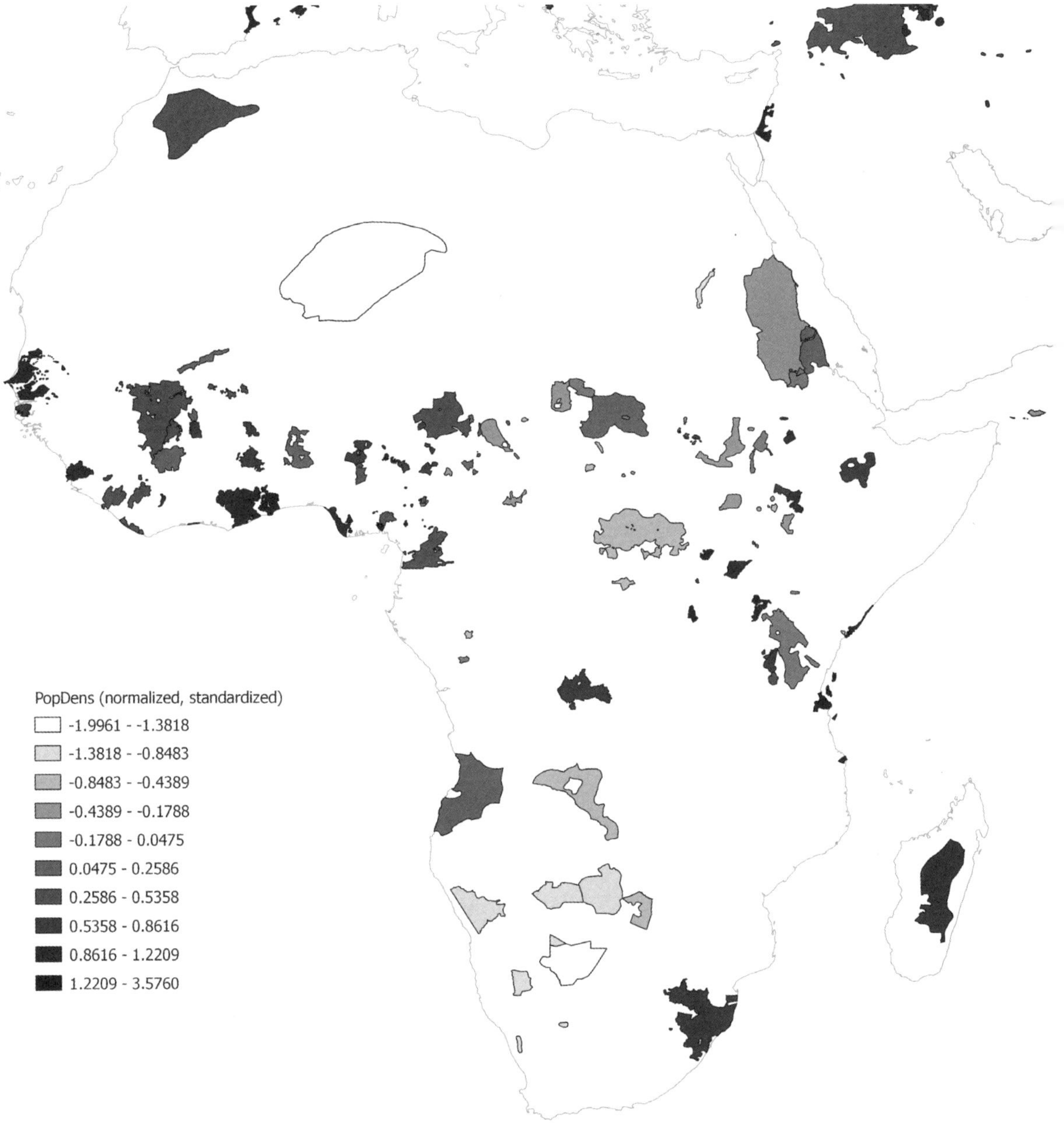

PopDens (normalized, standardized)
- [ ] -1.9961 - -1.3818
- -1.3818 - -0.8483
- -0.8483 - -0.4389
- -0.4389 - -0.1788
- -0.1788 - 0.0475
- 0.0475 - 0.2586
- 0.2586 - 0.5358
- 0.5358 - 0.8616
- 0.8616 - 1.2209
- 1.2209 - 3.5760

Figure 6.5   Number of speakers for the African languages of the dataset.

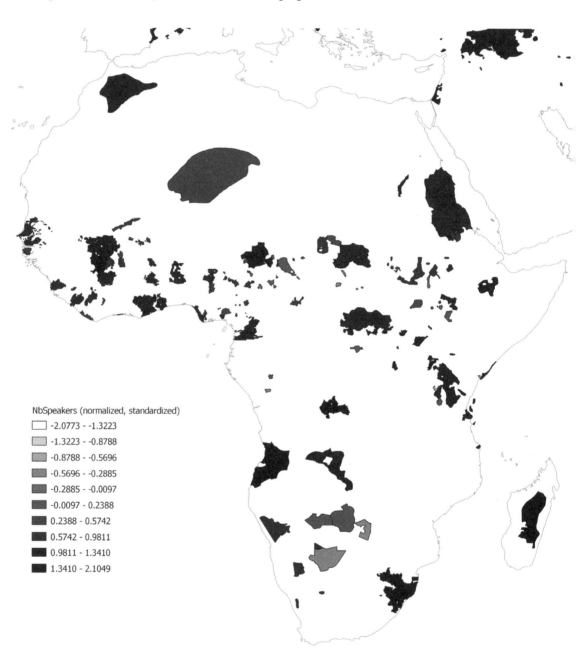

NbSpeakers (normalized, standardized)
- [ ] -2.0773 - -1.3223
- -1.3223 - -0.8788
- -0.8788 - -0.5696
- -0.5696 - -0.2885
- -0.2885 - -0.0097
- -0.0097 - 0.2388
- 0.2388 - 0.5742
- 0.5742 - 0.9811
- 0.9811 - 1.3410
- 1.3410 - 2.1049

Figure 6.6   Language contact for the African languages of the dataset.

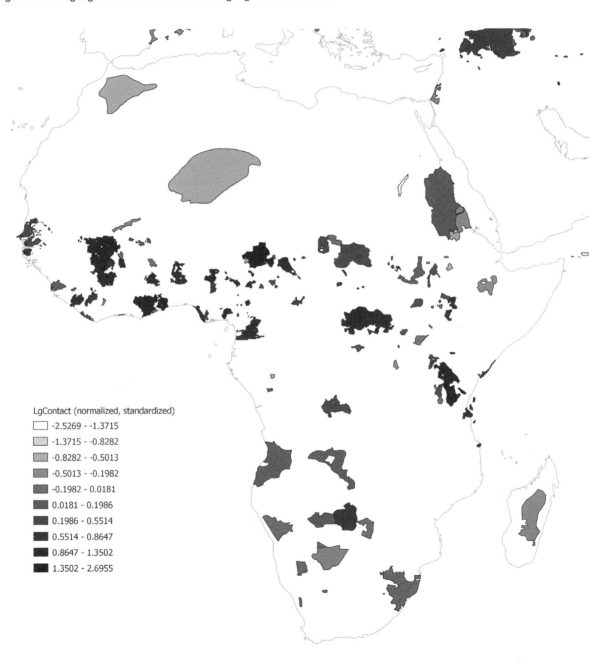

LgContact (normalized, standardized)
- -2.5269 - -1.3715
- -1.3715 - -0.8282
- -0.8282 - -0.5013
- -0.5013 - -0.1982
- -0.1982 - 0.0181
- 0.0181 - 0.1986
- 0.1986 - 0.5514
- 0.5514 - 0.8647
- 0.8647 - 1.3502
- 1.3502 - 2.6955

Table 6.2 indicates that environmental variables correlate with each other, positively or negatively, to a large extent. This was expected, as it is for example well known that rugosity increases and temperatures decrease as elevation increases. Prec, Tree and LGP correlate especially strongly and positively with each other; while this could also be expected—the more rain, the easier for plants to grow and the denser the tree coverage, correlations could have been weaker if one thinks of trees requiring only little water, or of heavy rains occurring yearly only during a few months. This suggests that Prec, Tree and LGP may play a similar role in a regression model, and should perhaps not be considered together to prevent strong multicollinearity.

In Table 6.3, PopDens correlates significantly and positively with Elv and Rug. This is surprising since we usually think of high and uneven lands as more difficult to inhabit, and since most of human population lives along the coast. However, since variables were normalized, the correlation may come from relationships primarily occurring at low altitudes. PopDens also correlates positively with Prec and LGP, which suggests higher densities of population in areas where plants grow easily, either for pastoralism, agriculture or gathering. NbSpeakers, LgArea and LgContact correlate with environmental factors, but one should wonder whether potential causal relationships are direct or indirect: if Rug for example causally impacts on LgContact, is it because rougher lands lead to denser populations, which in turn leads to more contacts, or because of another more direct causal mechanism?

Sociolinguistic variables also correlate with each other to a significant extent. Finally, PhonemeDiv correlates with most variables, suggesting a complex pattern of relationships and causal effects that require careful investigation.

Table 6.2 Pearson's correlations for environmental variables

	Tmp	Prec	Elv	Rug	Tree
Prec	.36***				
Elv	-.46***	-.22***			
Rug	-.46***	.15***	.67***		
Tree	.12*	.79***	-.15**	.21***	
LGP	.27***	.86***	-.16***	.18***	.79***

Table 6.3 Pearson's correlations between environmental variables and social and sociolinguistic variables

	PopDens	NbSpeakers	LgArea	LgContact
Tmp	.04 n.s.	-.02 n.s.	-.14**	.25***
Prec	.12*	-.15**	-.33***	.22***
Elv	.19***	.28***	.13**	.21***
Rug	.27***	.11*	-.16***	.13**
Tree	.01 n.s.	-.21***	-.30***	.16***
LGP	.14**	-.08.	-.30***	.25***

Table 6.4   Pearson's correlations for social and sociolinguistic variables

	PopDens	NbSpeakers	LgArea
NbSpeakers	.56***		
LgArea	-.17***	.52***	
LgContact	.28***	.41***	.08 n.s.

Table 6.5   Pearson's correlations between PhonemeDiv and other variables

	PhonemeDiv
Tmp	.04 n.s.
Prec	-.14**
Elv	.20***
Rug	-.02 n.s.
Tree	-.11*
LGP	-.12**
PopDens	.27***
NbSpeakers	.37***
LgArea	.08 n.s.
LgContact	.33***

3.2   Influence of the length of the growing period on sociolinguistic variables

In his approach to the linguistic diversity of Western Africa, Nettle (1996) considered the length of the growing period of plants (LGP) and the altitude to predict language areas and numbers of speakers.

We investigated whether Nettle's results could be reproduced at a global scale. We first ran regression models with Elv and LGP as predictors, and NbSpeakers, LgArea or LgContact as predicted variables.

From the three models, although the percentage of variance explained was low (around 7.5—12.5%), the following robust conclusions could be made:

- The higher, the more speakers, the larger the language areas and the more linguistic contacts;
- The longer the LGP, the smaller the language areas and the more linguistic contacts.

These results confirmed Nettle's hypothesis that when the ecological risk is high, language areas tend to grow. However, LGP did not have an impact on NbSpeakers as it had in Nettle's study. While this was potentially explained by different approaches to compute this figure, a positive correlation was nevertheless expected. Regarding language contacts, fewer contacts in case of higher ecological risk makes sense as a result of higher linguistic convergence.

The previous issue regarding LGP and NbSpeakers may be considered at the light of our a priori model and of the two levels of factors that may have an impact on sociolinguistic variables. In the former models as in Nettle's study, population density was not considered as a significant factor. It makes sense however to think of the impact of environmental factors with population density being taken into account, since significant correlations exist between PopDens and the sociolinguistic variables. Letting aside the effect of PopDens may thus prevent other effects to be visible.

To check this assumption, we ran three new regression models, with PopDens, Elv and LGP as predictors, and NbSpeakers, LgArea and LgContact as predicted variables. Tables 6.6, 6.7 and 6.8 provide the results.

Table 6.6   Regression of NbSpeakers against PopDens, Elv and LGP

Predicted variable: NbSpeakers								
	Type I Anova		Coefficients - standard regression			Coefficients - spatial regression		
	Sum Sq.	Pr(>F)	Estimate	Std. Error	Pr(>ltl)	Estimate	Std. Error	Pr(>lzl)
(Intercept)			4.95E-17	.038	1. n.s.	.007	.072	.921 n.s.
PopDens	142.64	4.56E-41 ***	.549	.039	9.07E-38 ***	.444	.046	<2.2E-16 ***
Elv	13.68	5.26E-06 ***	.151	.039	1.26E-04 ***	.132	.038	5.19E-04 ***
LGP	7.93	4.93E-04 ***	-.136	.039	4.93E-04 ***	-.146	.048	.002 **
Residuals	291.75							
Adj. R²	AIC	S-W	B-P	Cond.	VIF	Model: spatial error		
.356	1087	5.23E-04	2.26E-06	1.34	1.08	AIC: 992		
Lagrange multiplier diagnostics	LMerr	RLMerr	LMlag	RLMlag	B-P: 7.25E-04			
	<2.2e-16	2.58E-07	<2.2e-16	.002				
Deleted outliers: Squamish								

Table 6.7   Regression of LgArea against PopDens, Elv and LGP

Predicted variable: LgArea								
	Type I Anova		Coefficients - standard regression			Coefficients - spatial regression		
	Sum Sq.	Pr(>F)	Estimate	Std. Error	Pr(>|t|)	Estimate	Std. Error	Pr(>|z|)
(Intercept)			-3.73E-16	.044	1. n.s.	.075	.082	.361 n.s.
PopDens	13.38	1.17E-04 ***	-.158	.046	5.79E-04 ***	-.104	.054	.055 .
Elv	12.79	1.64E-04 ***	.122	.046	.008 **	.118	.045	.009 **
LGP	28.54	2.47E-08 ***	-.257	.045	2.47E-08 ***	-.281	.061	4.62E-06 ***
Residuals	401.29							
Adj. R²	AIC	S-W	B-P	Cond.	VIF	Model: spatial error		
.114	1233	.016	.159	1.361	1.089	AIC: 1146		
Lagrange multiplier diagnostics	LMerr	RLMerr	LMlag	RLMlag	B-P: .197			
	<2.2e-16	.002	<2.2e-16	.309				
Deleted outliers: Vanimo, Yapese								

Table 6.8   Regression of LgContact against PopDens, Elv and LGP

Predicted variable: LgContact								
	Type I Anova		Coefficients - standard regression			Coefficients - spatial regression		
	Sum Sq.	Pr(>F)	Estimate	Std. Error	Pr(>|t|)	Estimate	Std. Error	Pr(>|z|)
(Intercept)			3.94E-16	.043	1. n.s.	-.777	.121	1.14E-10 ***
PopDens	36.00	1.64E-10 ***	.205	.044	5.51E-06 ***	.026	.049	.593 n.s.
Elv	11.51	2.42E-04 ***	.21	.045	3.32E-06 ***	.177	.039	5.53E-06 ***
LGP	27.51	1.94E-08 ***	.253	.044	1.94E-08 ***	.15	.057	.008 **
Residuals	380.97							
Adj. R²	AIC	S-W	B-P	Cond.	VIF	Model: spatial error		
.159	1210	.279	.004	1.353	1.085	AIC: 1031		
Lagrange multiplier diagnostics	LMerr	RLMerr	LMlag	RLMlag	B-P: 8.37E-05			
	<2.2e-16	5.25E-04	<2.2e-16	.003				
Deleted outliers: Tibetan, Yapese								

Adding PopDens as a predictor increased the linearity of the relationships between the predictors and the predicted variable (not shown). The percentage of variance also increased in all three cases.

Even with PopDens included in the model, Elv and LGP explain a significant percentage of the variance in the standard regression. Additionally, they significantly predict all three predicted variables when spatial relationships between languages are accounted for. PopDens only predicts NbSpeakers when spatial relationships are accounted for.

The updated conclusions may therefore be suggested:

- The higher the population density, the more speakers
- The higher the elevation, the more speakers, the larger the language areas and the more linguistic contacts
- The longer the LGP, the less speakers, the smaller the language areas and the more contacts

Nettle's proposal regarding the role of ecological risk in sub-Saharan Africa therefore seems to be valid at a larger scale. The effect of PopDens on NbSpeakers also makes sense, while its independence from LgContact and LgArea is not surprising. The role of elevation is more difficult to explain. The relationship between LGP and LgContact suggests that an increase in ecological risk leads to reduced linguistic density and contacts, something which was not necessarily implied by an increase in numbers of speakers and language areas. More data on multilingualism would here be necessary to investigate the situation in more details.

3.3 Stepwise models for the regression of sociolinguistic variables against environmental and social factors

To further investigate the impact of environmental factors on sociolinguistic variables while controlling for population density, we ran stepwise regression models with PopDens as a fixed predictor in the regression. Tables 6.9, 6.10 and 6.11 give the results for NbSpeakers, LgArea and LgContact respectively.

We do not find LGP selected as a factor to predict NbSpeakers. However, Tree appears as a relevant factor and is highly positively correlated with LGP. It may thus stands for the previous effect of ecological risk. Both Elv and PopDens appear to have a strong impact on NbSpeakers, and rugosity is also selected in the model: other things being equal, the more rugosity the fewer speakers per language. It is interesting to note here that without controlling for other variables, rugosity was positively correlated, although not very strongly, with NbSpeakers. Once again, including other factors in the model modify the relationships between variables, which partially hinder analyses. The previous effect is complemented by the effect of rugosity as a predictor of LgArea: other things being equal, the rougher the ground, the smaller the areas of linguistic groups. We may postulate that on rough grounds, with increased difficulties to move across the land, linguistic groups are smaller both in terms of number of speakers and area.

Table 6.9   Stepwise regression of NbSpeakers against PopDens and environmental variables

Predicted variable: NbSpeakers								
	Type I Anova		Coefficients - standard regression			Coefficients - spatial regression		
	Sum Sq.	Pr(>F)	Estimate	Std. Error	Pr(>ltl)	Estimate	Std. Error	Pr(>lzl)
(Intercept)			7.23E-17	.036	1. n.s.	.024	.066	.718 n.s.
PopDens	142.64	6.10E-43 ***	.56	.038	1.61E-40 ***	.468	.045	<2.2.e-16***
Elv	13.68	2.83E-06 ***	.293	.054	9.49E-08 ***	.282	.059	1.83E-06 ***
Rug	19.2	3.38E-08 ***	-.21	.056	1.80E-04 ***	-.215	.062	5.49E-04 ***
Tree	5.56	.003 **	-.124	.041	.003 **	-.106	.044	.017 *
Residuals	274.93							
Adj. R²	AIC	S-W	B-P	Cond.	VIF	Model: spatial error		
.392	1042	.03	.006	2.772	2.332	AIC: 968		
Lagrange multiplier diagnostics	LMerr	RLMerr	LMlag	RLMlag		B-P: .005		
	<2.2e-16	1.67E-05	<2.2e-16	3.45E-04				
Deleted outliers: Comanche, Maricopa, Squamish								

Table 6.10   Stepwise regression of LgArea against PopDens and environmental variables

Predicted variable: LgArea								
	Type I Anova		Coefficients - standard regression			Coefficients - spatial regression		
	Sum Sq.	Pr(>F)	Estimate	Std. Error	Pr(>ltl)	Estimate	Std. Error	Pr(>lzl)
(Intercept)			-3.50E-16	.042	1. n.s.	.088	.08	.272 n.s.
PopDens	13.38	6.50E-05 ***	-.129	.045	.005 **	-.122	.052	.019 *
Elv	12.79	9.36E-05 ***	.31	.063	1.40E-06 ***	.392	.075	1.64E-07 ***
Rug	40.1	1.07E-11 ***	-.356	.068	2.97E-07 ***	-.383	.076	4.08E-07 ***
Tmp	9.07	9.75E-04 ***	-.133	.051	.009 **	-.058	.075	.441 n.s.
Tree	9.36	8.09E-04 ***	-.164	.049	8.09E-04 ***	-.109	.053	.039 *
Residuals	371.29							
Adj. R²	AIC	S-W	B-P	Cond.	VIF	Model: spatial error		
.177	1209	.015	.001	3.093	2.642	AIC: 1131		
Lagrange multiplier diagnostics	LMerr	RLMerr	LMlag	RLMlag		B-P: .141		
	<2.2e-16	8.72E-04	<2.2e-16	.136				
Deleted outliers: Ani								

Table 6.11   Stepwise regression of LgContact against PopDens and environmental variables

Predicted variable: Lgcontact								
	Type I Anova		Coefficients - standard regression			Coefficients - spatial regression		
	Sum Sq.	Pr(>F)	Estimate	Std. Error	Pr(>ItI)	Estimate	Std. Error	Pr(>IzI)
(Intercept)			4.41E-16	.04	1. n.s.	-.382	.099	1.18E-04 ***
PopDens	36.00	1.33E-11 ***	.169	.042	7.24E-05 ***	.047	.047	.316 n.s.
Tmp	25.16	1.21E-08 ***	.359	.047	1.33E-13 ***	.438	.077	1.39E-08 ***
Elv	43.09	1.75E-13 ***	.371	.047	2.22E-14 ***	.372	.051	3.89E-13 ***
LGP	14.32	1.48E-05 ***	.186	.043	1.48E-05 ***	.132	.055	.016 *
Residuals	337.42							
Adj. R²	AIC	S-W	B-P	Cond.	VIF	Model: spatial error		
.253	1144	.249	9.02E-04	1.812	1.343	AIC: 999		
Lagrange multiplier diagnostics	LMerr	RLMerr	LMlag	RLMlag	B-P: 1.99E-04			
	<2.2e-16	1.90E-09	<2.2e-16	.641				
Deleted outliers: Soqotri, Tibetan, Yapese								

A dense tree cover also negatively impacts on the area of languages. This once again may be related to ecological risk. PopDens also negatively impacts on LgArea: the higher the population density, the smaller the language areas.

Finally, as in 3.2, PopDens does not influence LgContact when spatial proximities between languages are taken into account, while Tmp, Elv and LGP all significantly predict the number of contacts with positive Type III coefficients.

Disentangling the various effects is difficult given the correlations between the selected variables. Exploring the data with stepwise regression is more hazardous than testing whether some models support hypotheses made a priori, like the role of ecological risk. All in all and on safe grounds, it may be noticed that nearly 40% of the variance of NbSpeakers is explained by PopDens, Elv, Rug and Tree. Although the two other models have weaker R^2, they also support the idea that local environmental factors should not be forgotten when considering sociolinguistic factors, even if these factors may be predominantly determined by non-linguistic social factors like population density.

3.4 Predictions of phonemic diversity by environmental, social and sociolinguistic factors

If we now turn to PhonemeDiv and the 4th level of our explanatory model, we may first investigate the effects of sociolinguistic variables. Table 6.12 summarizes a regression model with PhonemeDiv as predicted variable and NbSpeakers, LgArea and LgContact as predictors, while Table 6.13 gives the result of a non-spatial regression with Family as random effect.

Table 6.12 Regression of PhonemeDiv against sociolinguistic variables

Predicted variable: PhonemeDiv								
	Type I Anova		Coefficients - standard regression			Coefficients - spatial regression		
	Sum Sq.	Pr(>F)	Estimate	Std. Error	Pr(>ltl)	Estimate	Std. Error	Pr(>lzl)
(Intercept)			.014	.027	.619 n.s.	-.014	.023	.558 n.s.
NbSpeakers	26.08	4.23E-17 ***	.228	.035	3.37E-10 ***	.084	.031	.007 **
LgArea	3.53	.001 **	-.079	.032	.015 *	-.04	.028	.158 n.s.
LgContact	5.99	3.32E-05 ***	.128	.03	3.32E-05 ***	.091	.026	5.62E-04 ***
Residuals	154.31							
Adj. R²	AIC	S-W	B-P	Cond.	VIF	Model: spatial lag		
.182	806	.024	.037	2.132	1.689	AIC: 690		
Lagrange multiplier diagnostics	LMerr	RLMerr	LMlag	RLMlag	B-P: .714			
	<2.2e-16	.926	<2.2e-16	5.99E-09	LM test: 1.21E-06			
Deleted outliers: Usan								

Table 6.13 Regression of PhonemeDiv against sociolinguistic variables with Family as random effect

Predicted variable: PhonemeDiv			
	Estimate	Std. Error	Pr(>ltl)
(Intercept)	-.143	.050	.004 *
NbSpeakers	.034	.040	.392 n.s.
LgArea	-.042	.032	.194 n.s.
LgContact	-.074	.030	.013 *
		Std. Dev.	
Family		.357	
Residuals		.455	
cor(fitted, predicted)²: 0.573, AIC: 701			
Deleted outliers: Usan			

While spatial error models were predominant in earlier analyses, Lagrange multiplier diagnostics suggest a spatial lag model to account for the geographic proximities between languages. Including a Family random effect to account for the relationships between languages suggest that the effects of NbSpeakers and LgArea on phoneme diversity are rather problematic, since they lose their significance when Family is added. While LgArea is not a significant predictor in the spatial regression, NbSpeakers is; it is therefore difficult to conclude whether the random effect masks a real effect of NbSpeakers on PhonemeDiv, or whether this effect is an artifact when the groupings of languages into families are not considered. This incertitude is not surprising given the debates mentioned in section 1.1.

Interestingly, LgContact maintains a significant effect as predictor even when spatial or genetic relationships are considered. The idea that more linguistic contacts lead to higher phonemic diversity through borrowing from neighboring languages is therefore supported by our statistical tools.

Adding PopDens to sociolinguistic factors does not significantly increase the quality of the regression, and we therefore discard this factor in subsequent models.

Building on the previous conclusions regarding sociolinguistic and social variables, we also tested the acoustic adaptation hypothesis by considering the variable Tree as a predictor of both consonant diversity—ConsDiv – and vowel diversity—VowelDiv—, along with sociolinguistic variables.

ConsDiv and VowelDiv are defined by a limited range of values: five values for ConsDiv, which relate to the five categories 'Small', 'Moderately Small', 'Average', 'Moderately Large' and 'Large' for consonant inventories in the WALS, and three values for VowelDiv, which relate to the three categories 'Small', 'Average' and 'Large' used to classify vocalic inventories. Because of these specific distributions, linear regression is a rather poor choice of statistical model. To address this issue, we took advantage of the UPSID database, which contains the numbers of vowels and consonants of 451 languages overlapping the languages of our dataset. We identified the intersection between the two sets and built a new database of 319 languages, for which we not only had diversity figures but also and more accurately the numbers of consonants—ConsNb – and vowels—VowelNb. We then applied regression models to predict, on the one hand, ConsDiv and VowelDiv with our initial dataset of 457 languages and, on the other hand, ConsNb and VowelNb with our second dataset of 319 languages. Each time, the predictors were the sociolinguistic variables and Tree.

Predictions of vowel diversity are inconclusive with respect to the effect of Tree whatever the model or dataset used. Predictions of either ConsDiv or ConsNb prove more interesting, with a very significant effect of Tree in the different models. Tables 6.14 and 6.15 give the details of the regressions for the prediction of ConsNb. In this model, a barely significant positive effect of NbSpeakers is observed on the number of consonants (again, with other predictors included in the model) when Family is included as a random effect.

Table 6.14 Regression of ConsNb against NbSpeakers, LgArea, Lgcontact and Tree on the basis of a subset of 319 languages

Predicted variable: ConsNb								
	Type I Anova		Coefficients - standard regression			Coefficients - spatial regression		
	Sum Sq.	Pr(>F)	Estimate	Std. Error	Pr(>|t|)	Estimate	Std. Error	Pr(>|z|)
(Intercept)			-6.63E-13	.052	1. n.s.	-.02	.044	.65 n.s.
NbSpeakers	13.54	8.47E-05 ***	.276	.072	1.45E-04 ***	.17	.061	.006 **
LgArea	1.15	.246 n.s.	-.173	.063	.007 **	-.143	.054	.008 **
LgContact	10.18	6.29E-04 ***	-.118	.062	.057 .	-.056	.052	.278 n.s.
Tree	25.03	1.22E-07 ***	-.307	.057	1.22E-07 ***	-.198	.049	5.89E-05 ***
Residuals	268.09							
Adj. R²	AIC	S-W	B-P	Cond.	VIF	Model: spatial lag		
.146	831	.087	.002	2.364	1.912	AIC: 766		
Lagrange multiplier diagnostics	LMerr	RLMerr	LMlag	RLMlag	B-P: .003			
	<2.2e-16	.9	<2.2e-16	1.46E-04	LM test: .037			
Deleted outliers: Archi, Juhoan, NorthernHaida								

Table 6.15 Regression of ConsNb on the basis of a subset of 319 languages with Family as a random effect

Predicted variable: ConsNb			
	Estimate	Std. Error	Pr(>|t|)
(Intercept)	-.006	.108	.954 n.s.
NbSpeakers	.156	.078	.0454 *
LgArea	-.140	.059	.0189 *
LgContact	-.0121	.055	.823 n.s.
Tree	-0.148	.054	.0068 **
		Std. Dev.	
Family		.829	
Residuals		.637	
cor(fitted, predicted)²: 0.673, AIC: 768			
Deleted outliers: Archi, Juhoan, Northern Haida			

The following conclusions may be drawn from the previous regressions:

- The more contacts between languages, the higher the phonemic diversity;
- The less dense the tree coverage, the higher the number of consonants.

The first conclusion is in line with earlier comments on phonemic diversity. The second conclusion is in agreement with Maddieson (2011d)'s hypotheses and findings (see section 1.2). Our models support the idea that in densely vegetated environments, an impeded transmission of higher frequency acoustic signals leads to a reduced number of consonants in languages.

Finally, for explanatory purposes, we ran a stepwise regression of PhonemeDiv against sociolinguistic and environmental variables. Tables 6.16 and 6.17 summarize the results.

Table 6.16   Stepwise regression of PhonemeDiv against sociolinguistic and environmental variables

Predicted variable: PhonemeDiv								
	Type I Anova		Coefficients - standard regression			Coefficients - spatial regression		
	Sum Sq.	Pr(>F)	Estimate	Std. Error	Pr(>|t|)	Estimate	Std. Error	Pr(>|z|)
(Intercept)			.014	.026	.601 n.s.	-.015	.023	.509 n.s.
NbSpeakers	26.08	1.49E-18 ***	.25	.035	6.93E-12 ***	.107	.032	8.20E-04 ***
LgArea	3.53	7.87E-04 ***	-.161	.033	1.77E-06 ***	-.078	.03	.009 **
LgContact	5.99	1.34E-05 ***	.138	.031	1.07E-05 ***	.094	.027	5.36E-04 ***
LGP	7.45	1.26E-06 ***	-.174	.045	1.35E-04 ***	-.131	.039	8.79E-04 ***
Rug	1.49	.029 *	-.195	.041	2.40E-06 ***	-.103	.036	.004 **
Elv	4.6	1.31E-04 ***	.173	.041	3.12E-05 ***	.113	.036	.002 **
Tree	2.06	.01 *	.117	.045	.01 *	.108	.04	.006 **
Residuals	138.72							
Adj. R²	AIC	S-W	B-P	Cond.	VIF	Model: spatial lag		
.258	764	.12	.071	3.525	3.032	AIC: 671		
Lagrange multiplier diagnostics	LMerr	RLMerr	LMlag	RLMlag	B-P: .188			
	.	.451	.	1.56E-11	LM test: 5.57E-06			
Deleted outliers: Ndut								

Table 6.17 Stepwise regression of PhonemeDiv against sociolinguistic and environmental variables, with Family as a random effect

Predicted variable: PhonemeDiv			
	Estimate	Std. Error	Pr(>ltl)
(Intercept)	-.141	.048	.003 **
NbSpeakers	.055	.041	.178 n.s.
LgArea	-.063	.034	.064 .
LgContact	.076	.031	.014 *
LGP	-.108	.046	.018 *
Rug	-.081	.043	.059 .
Elv	.088	.041	.032 *
Tree	.104	.043	.016 *
		Std. Dev.	
Family		.334	
Residuals		.456	
cor(fitted, predicted)^2: 0.569, AIC: 718			
Deleted outliers: Ndut			

Several environmental variables significantly increase the quality of the model even with sociolinguistic variables included in the model. LGP, Elv and Tree preserve their effect both in the spatial regression and when Family is included, along with LgContact. One should not be surprised that the coefficient for Tree is positive in the three regressions, although this seems contradictory to the previous results regarding the acoustic adaptation hypothesis. The discrepancy can indeed be explained by the inclusion of LGP in the model, and the strong positive correlation between this factor and Tree. Once again, a Type III coefficient reflects the inclusion of all factors in the model, and the positive impact of Tree may be seen as a partial counterweight to the negative impact of LGP. This again stresses the difficulty of interpreting outputs of stepwise regressions.

While it is difficult to think of an explanation for the impact of LGP and Elv, we reach the more general conclusion that environmental factors play a role in phonetic/phonological processes; the acoustic adaptation hypothesis is one of possibly several causal patterns.

3.5 Phonemic diversity at the light of local factors and large-scale migrations

Our last attempt consisted in reconsidering Atkinson's global causal effect—the Out of Africa migration—on phonemic diversity at the light of our previous results. More specifically, we wondered whether the effect of the distance from a potential origin of the migrations would still be preserved once local factors had been included in a regression model. We therefore started from our last stepwise regression of PhonemeDiv, and added the distance from the most likely origin point found by Atkinson.

As illustrated by Tables 6.18 and 6.19, the distance from Atkinson's most likely origin point is a strongly significant factor. Its effect is preserved in spatial regression and with the inclusion of Family as random effect. The hypothesis that Atkinson's proposal regarding a phonemic gradient could have been explained by a coincidental distribution of local factors is therefore not supported by our models. We furthermore compared the distance from the most likely origin point to other distances from locations in the center of the various areas considered by Atkinson (Africa, Europe, Asia, North America, South America, and Oceania). We found that the distance from the best origin point was the best predictor when other local factors were considered. As a conclusion, the factors we considered in our study did not invalidate Atkinson's proposal.

Table 6.18 Regression of PhonemeDiv against sociolinguistic and environmental variables, with Atkinson's hypothesis included in the model

Predicted variable: PhonemeDiv								
	Type I Anova		Coefficients - standard regression			Coefficients - spatial regression		
	Sum Sq.	Pr(>F)	Estimate	Std. Error	Pr(>|t|)	Estimate	Std. Error	Pr(>|z|)
(Intercept)			.493	.059	4.90E-16 ***	.283	.063	8.42E-06 ***
NbSpeakers	26.08	2.81E-21 ***	.096	.037	.01 **	.055	.034	.113 n.s.
LgArea	3.53	2.74E-04 ***	-.091	.032	.004 **	-.062	.03	.037 *
LgContact	5.99	2.42E-06 ***	.054	.03	.075 .	.06	.028	.033 *
LGP	7.45	1.56E-07 ***	-.09	.043	.035 *	-.102	.04	.01 *
Rug	1.49	.018 *	-.158	.038	3.68E-05 ***	-.103	.035	.004 **
Elv	4.6	3.42E-05 ***	.185	.038	1.43E-06 ***	.13	.036	2.56E-04 ***
Tree	2.06	.005 **	.157	.042	2.06E-04 ***	.143	.039	2.86E-04 ***
Dist	21.16	7.50E-18 ***	-3.78E-05	4.21E-06	7.50E-18 ***	-2.29E-05	4.63E-06	7.50E-07 ***
Residuals	117.55							
Adj. R²	AIC	S-W	B-P	Cond.	VIF	Model: spatial lag		
.37	686	.562	.154	5.689	3.172	AIC: 648		
Lagrange multiplier diagnostics	LMerr	RLMerr	LMlag	RLMlag	B-P: .353			
	7.87E-11	.411	4.11E-14	8.25E-05	LM test:	9.37E-04		
Deleted outliers: late								

Table 6.19 Regression of PhonemeDiv against sociolinguistic and environmental variables, with Atkinson's hypothesis included in the model and Family as a random effect

Predicted variable: PhonemeDiv			
	Estimate	Std. Error	Pr(>ltl)
(Intercept)	-.408	.102	1.E-4 ***
NbSpeakers	.024	.040	.546n.s.
LgArea	-.047	.033	.151 n.s.
LgContact	.042	.030	.167 n.s.
LGP	-.082	.044	.063 .
Rug	-.099	.041	.015 *
Elv	.104	.040	.009**
Tree	.126	.042	.003 **
Dist	-3.40E-05	6.07E-06	<1E-04 ***
		Std. Dev.	
Family		.250	
Residuals		.455	
cor(fitted, predicted)^2: 0.557, AIC:715			
Deleted outliers: late			

4. Conclusion

We have investigated in this paper the effects and interactions of a number of non-linguistic and linguistic factors. To this end, we have put special care in the preparation of the dataset, and tried to apply meaningful statistical tests. The complexity and intricacies of the possible approaches make the exploratory analysis of the data difficult. However, we found statistical effects that, we believe, can be related to reasonable causal relationships:

- Nettle's hypothesis regarding the impact of ecological risk on sociolinguistic variables such as the number of speakers or the area of a language is supported by our models;
- Similarly, the acoustic adaptation hypothesis also finds support in our study of consonantal diversity;
- To some significant extent, elevation and rugosity also predict sociolinguistic and linguistic variables, although we did not find a simple explanation of these effects;

- More generally, it seems fair to assume that environmental factors do have causal effects on sociolinguistic and linguistic parameters, given the consistent effects repeatedly found in our models.

Additionally, that a higher degree of linguistic contact leads to a higher phonemic diversity suggests that one should look at Atkinson's so called founder effect in a reverse fashion: the gradient may not be the result of languages gradually losing their phonemes along migratory routes, but rather the consequence of languages staying behind the waves of migration gradually gaining phonemes with the increase in linguistic density - itself due to the slow increase in population density.[4] On the contrary, human groups at the front row of the migrations were much less exposed to other populations and languages. Given the small size of our ancestors' communities before farming, this reading seems more convincing to us, regardless of the statistical issues raised against Atkinson's proposal.

Various improvements can be brought to our approach: other factors could be considered, as well as other statistical models, such as ordinal logistic regressions to better fit the specific distributions of measures of diversity. The acoustic adaptation hypothesis could also be assessed more thoroughly with the testing of more specific aspects of phonetic systems, for example the presence or absence of specific classes of consonants or vowels. All in all, the recent availability of large sets of data providing a wealth of information on the environment of human populations calls for further explorations, and will likely both broaden and strengthen the field of linguistics.

REFERENCES

Amante, C., and B. W. Eakins. 2009. ETOPO1 1 arc-minute global relief model: Procedures, data sources and analysis. *NOAA Technical Memorandum NESDIS NGDC-24*.

Anselin, L. 2007. *Spatial Regression Analysis in R. A Workbook*. GeoDa Center for geospatial analysis and computation, https://geodacenter.asu.edu/learning/tutorials.

Anselin, L., I. Syabri, and Y. Kho. 2006. GeoDa: An introduction to spatial data analysis. *Geographical Analysis* 38 (1): 5–22.

Atkinson, Q. D. 2011a. Phonemic diversity supports serial founder effect model of language expansion from Africa. *Science* 332:346–349.

Atkinson, Q. D. 2011b. Linking spatial patterns of language variation to ancient demography and population migrations. *Linguistic Typology* 15 (2): 321–332.

---

4. Another factor influencing phonemic diversity may be the amount of within-population variability, although its relationship with population size is still debated (Trudgill 2004).

Baayen, R. H. 2008. *Analyzing Linguistic Data. A Practical Introduction to Statistics Using R.* Cambridge University Press.

Boë, L.-J., P. Bessière, and N. Vallée. 2003. When Ruhlen's 'mother tongue' theory meets the null hypothesis, *Proceedings of the XVth International Congress of Phonetic Sciences.* Spain, Barcelona.

Bowern, C. 2011. Out of Africa? The logic of phoneme inventories and founder effects. *Linguistic Typology* 15 (2): 207–216.

Box, G. E. P., and D. R. Cox. 1964. An analysis of transformations (with discussion). *Journal of the Royal Statistical Society B* 26:211–252.

Bybee, J. 2011. How plausible is the hypothesis that population size and dispersal are related to phoneme inventory size? Introducing and commenting on a debate. *Linguistic Typology* 15 (2): 147–153.

Center for International Earth Science Information Network (CIESIN), Columbia University, International Food Policy Research Institute (IFPRI), The World Bank and Centro Internacional de Agricultura Tropical (CIAT). 2011. *Global Rural-Urban Mapping Project, Version 1 (GRUMPv1): Population Count Grid.* Palisades, NY: NASA Socioeconomic Data and Applications Center (SEDAC). http://sedac.ciesin.columbia.edu/data/set/grump-v1-population-count. Accessed 24–01–2013.

Coupé, C., and J.-M. Hombert. 2005. Polygenesis of linguistic strategies: A scenario for the emergence of language. In Minett, J. & Wang, W.S. (eds), *Language Acquisition, Change and Emergence: Essays in Evolutionary Linguistics.* Hong Kong, City University of Hong Kong Press, 153–201.

Coupé, C., E. Marsico, and F. Pellegrino. 2009. Structural complexity of phonological systems. In Pellegrino, F., Marsico, E., Chitoran, I. & Coupé, C. (eds), *Approaches to Phonological Complexity*, Phonology & Phonetics Series Vol. 16. Berlin, New York: Mouton de Gruyter, 141–169.

Dahl, O. 2011. Are small languages more or less complex than big ones? *Linguistic Typology* 15 (2): 171–175.

Donohue, M., and J. Nichols. 2011. Does phoneme inventory size correlate with population size? *Linguistic Typology* 15 (2): 161–170.

Dryer, M. S., and M. Haspelmath. (eds.) 2011. The World Atlas of Language Structures Online. Munich: Max Planck Digital Library. Available online at http://wals.info/.

Fabrigar, L. R., D. T. Wegener, R.C. MacCallum, and E.J. Strahan. 1999. Evaluating the use of exploratory factor analysis in psychological research. *Psychological Methods* 4:272–299.

Food and Agriculture Organization (FAO) and International Institute for Applied Systems Analysis (IIASA). 2007. Length of growing period, 1901–1996. Global agro-ecological zones. In H. von Velthuizen et al. (eds.), *Mapping Biophysical Factors that Influence Agricultural Production and Rural Vulnerability*. FAO & IIASA.

Freedman, D. A., and W. S-Y. Wang. 1996. Language polygenesis: A probabilistic model. *Anthropological Science* 104:131–137.

Geospatial Information Authority of Japan, Chiba University and collaborating organizations 2008. *Global Map V.1 (Global version)*. http://www.iscgm.org/browse.html

Global Mapping International and SIL International. 2012. World Language Mapping System. Language area and point data for Geographic Information Systems (GIS). http://www.worldgeodatasets.com/language/.

Hay, J., and L. Bauer. 2007. Phoneme inventory size and population size. *Language* 83:388–400.

Hijmans, R. J., S. E. Cameron, J.L. Parra, P.G. Jones, and A. Jarvis. 2005. Very high resolution interpolated climate surfaces for global land areas. *International Journal of Climatology* 25:1965–1978.

Holdridge, L. R. 1947. Determination of world plant formations from simple climatic data. *Science* 105:367–368.

Jacquesson, F. 2001. Pour une linguistique des quasi-déserts. In A.M. Loffler-Laurian (ed.), *Etude de Linguistique Générale et Contrastive. Hommage à Jean Perrot*. Paris: Centre de Recherche sur les Langues et les Sociétés, 199–216.

Jacquesson, F. 2003. Linguistique, génétique et la vitesse d'évolution des langues. *Bulletin de la Société de Linguistique de Paris* 98 (1): 101–122.

Jaeger, T. F., P. Graff, W. Croft, and D. Pontillo. 2011. Mixed effects models for genetic and areal dependencies in linguistic typology. *Linguistic Typology* 15 (2): 281–320.

Ke, J., T. Gong, and W. S-Y. Wang. 2008. Language change and social networks. *Communications in Computational Physics* 3 (4): 935–949.

Kottek, M., J. Griser, C. Beck, B. Rudolf, and F. Rubel. 2006. World map of the Köppen-Geiger climate classification updated. *Meteorologische Zeitschrift* 15 (3): 259–263.

Lewis, M. P. (ed.). 2009. *Ethnologue: Languages of the World, Sixteenth Edition*. Dallas, Tex.: SIL International. Online version: http://www.ethnologue.com/.

Lupyan, G., and R. Dale. 2010. Language structure is partly determined by social structure. *PLoS ONE* 5 (1): 1–10.

Maddieson, I. 1984. *Patterns of Sounds*. Cambridge, MA: Cambridge University Press.

Maddieson, I. 2005. Issues of phonological complexity: Statistical analysis of the relationship between syllable structures, segment inventories and tone contrasts. *UC Berkeley Phonology Lab Annual Report*, 259–268.

Maddieson, I. 2009. Calculating phonological complexity. In Pellegrino, F., Marsico, E., Chitoran, I., and Coupé, C. (eds), *Approaches to Phonological Complexity*, Phonology & Phonetics Series vol. 16. Berlin, New York: Mouton de Gruyter, 85–109.

Maddieson, I. 2011a. Consonant Inventories. In: Dryer, Matthew S., and Haspelmath, Martin (eds.), *The World Atlas of Language Structures Online*. Munich: Max Planck Digital Library, chapter 1. Available online at http://wals.info/chapter/1. Accessed on 2011–12–03.

Maddieson, I. 2011b. Tone. In: Dryer, Matthew S., and Haspelmath, Martin (eds.), *The World Atlas of Language Structures Online*. Munich: Max Planck Digital Library, feature 13A. Available online at http://wals.info/feature/13A. Accessed on 2011–12–03.

Maddieson, I. 2011c. Vowel quality inventories. In: Dryer, Matthew S., and Haspelmath, Martin (eds.), *The World Atlas of Language Structures Online*. Munich: Max Planck Digital Library, feature 2A. Available online at http://wals.info/feature/2A. Accessed on 2011–12–03.

Maddieson, I. 2011d. Phonological complexity and linguistic patterning. *Proceedings of the 17th International Congress of Phonetic Sciences*. Hong Kong, China, 17–21 August 2011.

Maddieson, I., T. Bhattacharya, D.E. Smith and W. Croft. 2011. Geographical distribution of phonological complexity. *Linguistic Typology* 15 (2): 267–279.

Maddieson, I., and K. Precoda. 1990. Updating UPSID. *UCLA Working Papers in Phonetics* 74:104–111.

Myers, R. H., D. C. Montgomery, G. G. Vining, and T. J. Robinson. 2010. *Generalized Linear Models: With Applications in Engineering and the Sciences*. John Wiley & Sons Inc.

Nettle, D. 1996. Language diversity in West Africa: An ecological approach. *Journal of Anthropological Archaeology* 15:403–438.

Nettle, D. 1998. Explaining global patterns of language diversity. *Journal of Anthropological Archaeology* 17:354–74.

Nettle, D. 1999a. *Linguistic Diversity*. Oxford: Oxford University Press.

Nettle, D. 1999b. Using social impact theory to simulate language change. *Lingua* 108 (2–3): 95–117.

Nettle, D. 1999c. Is the rate of linguistic change constant? *Lingua* 108:119–36.

Pellegrino, F., C. Coupé, and E. Marsico. 2011. A cross-language perspective on speech information rate. *Language* 87 (3): 539–558.

Pericliev, V. 2004. There is no correlation between the size of a community speaking a language and the size of the phonological inventory of that language. *Linguistic Typology* 8:376–83.

Pericliev, V. 2011. On phonemic diversity and the origin of language in Africa. *Linguistic Typology* 15 (2): 217–221

Ribeiro Jr., P. J., and P. J. Diggle. 2001 geoR: A package for geostatistical analysis. *R-NEWS* 1 (2). ISSN 1609–3631.

Rice, K. 2011. Athabaskan languages and serial founder effects. *Linguistic Typology* 15 (2): 233–250.

Ringe, D. 2011. A pilot study for an investigation into Atkinson's hypothesis. *Linguistic Typology* 15 (2): 223–231.

Ross, B., and M. Donohue. 2011. The many origins of diversity and complexity in phonology. *Linguistic Typology* 15 (2): 251–266.

Ruhlen, M. 1994. *The Origin of Language: Tracing the Evolution of the Mother Tongue.* New York: John Wiley & Sons.

Simpson, E. H. 1951. The interpretation of interaction in contingency tables. *Journal of the Royal Statistical Society Ser. B* 13:238–241.

Sproat, R. 2011. Phonemic diversity and the out-of-Africa theory. *Linguistic Typology* 15 (2): 199–206.

Trudgill, P. 2002. Linguistic and social typology. In J. K. Chambers, Peter Trudgill, and Natalie Schilling-Estes (eds.), *The Handbook of Language Variation and Change.* Oxford: Blackwell, 707–28.

Trudgill, P. 2004. Linguistic and social typology: The Austronesian migrations and phoneme inventories. *Linguistic Typology* 8:305–20.

Trudgill, P. 2011. Social structure and phoneme inventories. *Linguistic Typology* 15 (2): 155–160.

Vautard, R., J. Cattiaux, P. Yiou, J.-N. Thépaut, and P. Ciais. 2010. Northern Hemisphere atmospheric stilling partly attributed to an increase in surface roughness. *Nature Geoscience* 3:756–761.

Venables, W. N., and B. D. Ripley. 2002. *Modern Applied Statistics with S.* 4th ed. Springer.

Walker, R. S., and M. J. Hamilton. 2010. Social complexity and linguistic diversity in the Austronesian and Bantu population expansions. *Proceedings of the Royal Society—Biological Sciences* 278:1399–1404.

Whittaker, R. H. 1975. *Communities and Ecosystems*, 2nded. New York: Macmillan.

Wichmann, S., T. Rama, and E.W. Holman. 2011. Phonological diversity, word length, and population sizes across languages: The ASJP evidence. *Linguistic Typology* 15 (2): 177–197.

Wang, William S-Y. 2011. Voices out of Africa? *Sunday Morning Post (South China Morning Post)*, May 29.

7

From Cognition to Language

Hsin-I HSIEH
University of Hawaii

Abstract

In mapping from cognition onto language, a sentence originates as an event composed of sub-events. This is first reduced in size in particular languages, then it is assigned a head-modifier relation, on which the x-bar composition operates to create an x-bar tree. This x-bar tree is then assigned a culture-induced conceptual relation, resulting in a structure of two parts: syntax and concept. The Chinese concept is an anterior-posterior relation, in contrast to the English concept, which is a thematic-role prominence relation. The indigenous Chinese grammar Bill Wang has envisioned with overdue enthusiastic responses could well be a grammar of this sort. If so, it may be time to start a serious exploration of an indigenous Chinese Grammar.

1.   Introduction

In the new perspective generated by the Complexity Theory, a system can be identified as in one of four states. It can be a 'simple' system, a 'complicated' system, a 'complex' system, or a 'chaos' (Mitchell 2009). Simple and complicated systems produce results that are predictable. But a complex system defies full prediction. Wang (1969) is one of the first few linguists who recognized that sound change can produce residues, which are results not predicted by the rules in the neo-grammarian hypothesis of predictable and regular sound change (see also Wang and Lien 1993). Wang's discovery is a very important historical step in changing our view of language as a complicated, predictable system to one as a complex, unpredictable system. Inspired by Wang's insight on the complexity of language, Hsieh (1989, 1991 and 2006) has proposed a theory of grammatical interaction. Two grammatical rules can be kept apart in a 'complementation', can be in a competition and produce a 'conflict', and can also be in a cooperation and produce a 'conspiracy'. Her (1991, 1994) refined Hsieh's initial proposal and injected Kiparsky's (1978) notions of feeding and bleeding between two adjacent rules. If rule A feeds to rule B, then A and B are in a conspiracy and jointly produce a single result. But if rule A bleeds rule B, then A and B are in competition, with A depriving B of a prospective input. As Her (1997) put it,

> Her (1994) further incorporates the more familiar terminology and concepts of 'feeding' and 'bleeding' (e.g., Kiparsky 1978) in historical phonology into Hsieh's taxonomy. Thus, two rules in 'complementation' are in a 'feeding' relation when the output of one rule expands, or 'feeds', the other rule's domain of application. Two rules in 'conflict' are in a 'bleeding' relation, for now the application of one deprives the other of (some of) its inputs (Kiparsky 1978). (1997, 16)

The point is that since we cannot foretell whether A and B are to be in a feeding or a bleeding relation, we cannot predict the outcome of the interaction of A and B. And we become aware that A and B are interacting in a complex system. This kind of unpredictability is now a key notion in any discussion of a complex phenomenon. Complexity is an emergent property, with no one in charge. As Mitchell (2009) puts it, when using the immune system to explain complexity:

> Like that of the brain and ant colonies, the immune system's behavior arises from the independent actions of myriad simple players with no one actually in charge... As yet many crucial aspects of this signal-processing system are not well understood. For example, it is still to be learned what, precisely, are the relevant signals, their specific functions, and how they work together to allow the system as a whole to 'learn' what threats are present in the environment and to produce long-term immunity to those threats. (2009, 9)

If we view language as a complex system, in which many individual items or groups or parts act independently and with no one in charge, then we begin to suspect that the pursuit of a formal or cognitive grammar of language as a *complicated* system could be misdirected.

Assuming that this misdirection is real and not imaginary, we wish to focus on a small corner of the grammar and explore its complex nature. To conduct this exploration, we wish to first build a perspective from which to understand how cognition is mapped onto language. Following the brilliant insight of Talmy (2000), we first assume that cognition is mapped onto language by universal principles. If we stop at this point, then complexity in language would be generated by units, groups, and portions of a grammar taken as a simplified copy, or a homomorphism, of cognition. In that view, if language A and language B express essentially the same thought slightly differently in a pair of translation-equivalent sentences, it is only the form, but not also the thought, that marks the two languages as different. The difference in the culture between the two languages would be left out of the picture. But we suggest that language is not only organized by logic and mathematics, but is also 'flavored', 'colored', 'informed', or 'interfered' by culture, as proponents (Boroditsky 2010, 2011) of the Whorfian hypothesis have argued. This interference can affect language on both a lower and a higher level. On the lower level, it can determine how a sentence is expressed variably in a supposedly universal 'formal pattern', as it is claimed in Chomsky's theory of Principles and Parameters (P&P) (Chomsky 1995). On the higher level, it can determine what regionally and culturally endorsed 'concept' is assigned to the sentence. Therefore, what we are proposing here is a hypothesis containing two transformations or functions. The first function maps cognition onto language, just as Talmy has suggested and demonstrated. The second function has two subparts. The first subpart involves a universal system of operations like the P&P, and the second subpart employs a mechanism that indicates the conceptual relation of a pair of words, phrases, or sentences in particular languages. If universal cognition maps by universal rules onto varying specific formal grammars, the result is largely predictable, as in a complicated system. However, since conceptual relations interfere with formal expressions in any particular grammar, producing results defying prediction, language is an unpredictable complex system. To show that language is a complex evolving system, we must first show that culture interferes with base syntax to create a full-fledged complex syntax.

2. Indigenous Chinese Grammar

Wang (1999) in his keynote speech at IsCLL-5 has reminded the audience that it is not enough for Chinese linguists to take English grammar as a template to produce a Chinese grammar as a variation of English grammar. Knowingly or unknowingly, Wang could be saying that a theory like P&P is not sufficiently well equipped to describe the Chinese language. After Wang finished his speech, an eminent scholar from Hawaii asked Wang: if there is an indigenous Chinese grammar, wouldn't there be also an indigenous Chinese physics? The presupposition in his question is that grammar is like physics, governed only by mathematics and logic. Wang was apparently tricked by the presupposition that does not hold, and hence he seemed unable to give a definite answer in terms of yes or no. If the eminent scholar from Hawaii had prior to his question asked Wang: Is the king of France bald? Wang would have quickly noticed the unwarranted presupposition. When queried, he would have answered that grammar, unlike physics, has its cultural layer, and therefore there can be an indigenous Chinese grammar, which is colored by Chinese culture. Apparently, this reasonable reply has evaded Wang in the unexpected exchange.

Before this exchange took place, Tai (1985, 2002) had already proposed that Chinese is different from English in habitually employing what he called the Principle of Temporal Sequence (PTS), by which words and phrases are ordered by the temporal sequencing of the events which they denote. Tai's claim is a reasonable and convincing one, although he has emphasized the *iconic* nature of the PTS rather than the *cultural* root of this iconic principle. It is as if Tai is saying that both English and Chinese follow Chomsky's universal rules but Chinese colors them in iconicity. Hence, Tai was not able to join the short exchange with a possible emphasis on the cultural source of PTS. I was also in the audience, and I was also perplexed amid this short but very stimulating conversation between Wang and the skeptical scholar.

Today, more than ten years after this unforgettable interchange of views regarding the indigenous nature or foreign-imported appearance of a Chinese grammar, I am able to see clearly that Wang is definitely right: there can be an indigenous Chinese Grammar, just as there is a Chinese language rooted in and natured by a Chinese culture. Wang often has a vision that evades other scholars. An important stimulation has prepared me for exploring Wang's vision. And that stimulation came from Jim Huang. In a recent paper of mine (Hsieh 2011), inspired by Huang (2005, 2006, 2007), I have begun to pay attention to the concept of macro-parameters, which Huang has originated. Huang used the pair of analytical pattern or 'analysis', as illustrated in (1a), and synthetic pattern or 'synthesis' as illustrated in (1b), to explain his theory of Macro-principle and Macro-parameters, or what I would term MP & MP:

(1)   a.   Zhang1san1 da3 dian4hua4 gei3 Li3si4.

Zhangsan-hit-telephone-give-Lisi.

'Zhangsan telephoned Lisi.'

張三打電話給李四。

   b.   John telephoned Bill.

(1a) in Chinese is an analysis, since it lays out all three elements of one complex notion; it shows the notion 'to telephone' as composed of da3 'hit' 打, dian4hua4 'telephone' 電話, and gei3 'give' 給. (1b) in English is a synthesis, because it combines these three elements into one single complex, or rather compressed, form: *telephone*. Huang shows that these two sentences are derived from one single source by the employment of two macro-parameters, or in the original terminology, two values of one macro-parameter. As we can see in (2a) and (2b), the x-bar trees underlying sentences (1a) and (1b) (from which the PP for (2a) and the NP for (2b) have been omitted) have the same configuration. However, they differ in the lexical status of the 'light verb', v. The v in (2a) is lexically filled by da3 'hit' 打, blocking the NP dian4hua4 電話 'telephone' from moving to take its place, but the v in (2b) is lexically empty, to which the NP *telephone* moves to assume the status of the verb.

When I became aware of Huang's innovative notion of macro-parameters, which Huang (2013) now ascribes to previous proposals by others, I became fascinated and inspired. And I began to ask myself this question: If a *syntactic* macro-principle can be deployed as two or more macro-parameters across different languages, can a concept related, or *'conceptual'*, macro-principle be also deployed as two or more macro-parameters across languages? If syntax is controlled by logic and mathematics, the cognition that maps onto syntax would be determined by logic and mathematics as one force or demand and by culture as another force or demand. And I began to look again at Tai's idea of a Principle of Temporal Sequence (PTS) to see how, instead of emphasizing the iconic nature of Chinese as opposed to the formal nature of English, I can begin to emphasize the fact that Chinese culture has made Chinese obey PTS, and likewise English culture has caused English to obey the Finite Verb Hierarchy. This is the rudimentary dichotomy that initially floats up to my mind, a preliminary division which we will gradually revise and refine as we proceed.

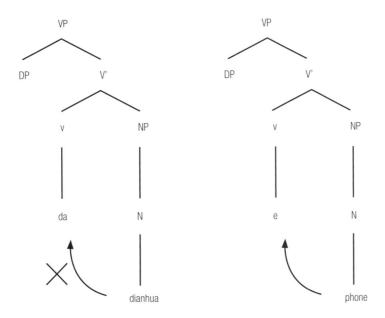

   (2)   a. Chinese analysis   b. English synthesis

Let us now look at Tai's well-known pair of sentences illustrating his PTS, as in (3):

(3)   a.   Zhang1san1zuo4 gong1gong4qi4che1 lai2 zhe4er0.

           Zhangsan-ride-bus-come-here.

           (i) 'Zhangsan came here by bus.'

           (ii) 'Zhangsan took the bus to come here.'

           張三坐公共汽車來這兒。

     b.   Zhang1san1 lai2 zhe4er0 zuo4 gong1gong4qi4che1.

           Zhangsan-come-here-ride-bus.

           'Zhangsan came here to take the bus.'

           張三來這兒坐公共汽車。

The Chinese sentence (3a), following Tai's Principle of Temporal Sequencing (PTS), which we may also call Frame of Temporal Sequence (FTS), puts the anterior sub-event *zuo4* 'ride' before the posterior sub-event *lai2* 'come'. By contrast, its English counterpart, as indicated by the two alternative translations, subscribes to the Frame of Finite-verb Hierarchy (FFH), and selects either *came* in (i) or *took* in (ii) as its finite verb. Similarly, the Chinese sentence (3b), in which the event sequence is reversed, places the anterior sub-event *lai2* 'come' 來 before the posterior sub-event *zuo4* 'ride' 坐. Thus, the pair (3a) and (3b) illustrates the PTS.

If we want to claim that Chinese relies mainly on FTS for word order, showing a contrastive pair like (3a) and (3b) is an important step, but it is not sufficient. We must also show that not only conceptually sequential events are represented as syntactically sequential clauses, but also that, within one simple event, the sub-parts or sub-events are also organized as temporally related. For example, we have to show that if Tai had recast (3a) as (4a), we could still see the operation of his PTS:

(4)　a.　Zhang1san1 *zuo4 shang4* gong1gong4qi4che1 *lai2 dao4* zhe4er0.

　　　　Zhangsan-*ride-on*-bus-*come-arrive*-here.

　　　　(i) 'Zhangsan came and arrive here by bus.'

　　　　(ii) 'Zhangsan got on the bus to come here.'

　　　　張三坐上公共汽車來到這兒。

(4) replaces the *lai2* 'come' 來 in (3a) with the sequence *lai2 dao4* 'come and arrive' 來到. Can we show that this sequence is a temporal sequence? Yes, we can, provided that we are willing to appeal to a culture-induced conceptual sequence of event unfolding. If Zhang-san had arrived here, he undertook two actions, which unfolded as two sequential events: first he *lai2* 'came toward' 來 here, then he *dao4* 'reached' 到 here. In addition, (4) substitutes *zuo4* 'ride' 坐 with *zuo4 shang4* 'ride and be on' 坐上. This latter is also a temporal sequence. First, Zhang-san *zuo4* 'rode' 坐, and then he was *shang4* 'on' 上 the bus. If a sentence is longer, having several parts reflecting several sub-events of one complex event, the PTS is still operative, as in (5a):

(5)　a.　Zhang1-san1 (a) ba3 Li3si4 (b) tui1 (c) dao3 (d) zai4 di4shang0.

　　　　Zhangsan-grab-Lisi-push-fall-on-the ground

　　　　'Zhangsan pushed Lisi down to the ground.'

　　　　張三(a)把李四(b)推(c)倒(d)在地上。

　　b.　John pushed Bill down to the ground.

The four sub-events in (5a)—labeled (a), (b), (c), and (d)—are ordered by Tai's PTS, which we have renamed as FTS. The *ba3* 把 is a co-verb and not a genuine verb, but it still attests to the fact that Zhangsan grabs or takes control of Lisi. The English counterpart of (5a) in (5b) obeys the Frame of Finite-verb Hierarchy (FFH). It has the finite verb *push*, the adverb *down*, and the preposition *to*. Their categories are ranked by FFH, with the verb *push* as the top ranked, the preposition *to* as the secondly ranked, and the adverb *down* as the bottom ranked. This ranking determines the constituent structure of the sentence in (5b). The constituent structures of (5a) and (5b) are analyzed as (6a) and (6b), respectively.

(6a)

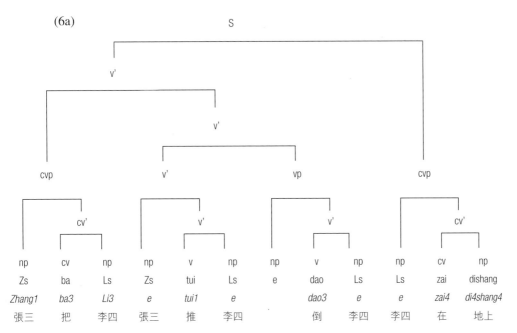

Note: We follow Huang, Li, and Li (2009) in drawing the x-bar tree. We made an adjustment: Of the two VPs, the first one is a transitive and 'stronger' and is rendered v', and the second one is an unaccusative and 'weaker' and is rendered VP.

(6b)

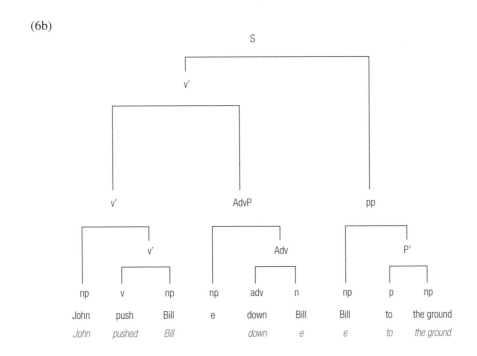

3.   Plain Sequence and Primacy Hierarchy

To compare (6a) and (6b), we need to characterize FTS and FFH more precisely. FTS is a particular mode of the general *Plain Sequence strategy* (PSs), and FFH is a particular variety of the general *Primacy Hierarchy strategy* (PHs). If the words of a sentence are treated as having the same rank, requiring little or no rank-markers, then the words are ordered sequentially according to some criterion, such as event time and thematic-role prominence, and a 'horizontal' Plain Sequence of words and word combinations is acquired. By contrast, if the individual words and word combinations are ranked and marked by their primacy in action, with primacy being defined by some such notion as the dynamic, forceful, and agile nature of an action, then 'vertical' Primacy Hierarchy is obtained.

Sentence (6a) for Chinese is organized primarily by the PSs. Its four sub-events (a), (b), (c), and (d) are temporally ordered. But it also employs the PHs, which recognizes the co-verb sub-event, (a), as secondary to the combined genuine-verb sub-events, (b) and (c). In addition, the PHs recognizes the co-verb sub-event, (d), as secondary to the event, composed of the sequence of sub-events (a), (b), and (c). Thus, we can see the intriguing interweaving of the PSs and the PHs in this particular sentence, which is typical of a Chinese sentence. By contrast, (6b) for English relies primarily on PHs, although to a lesser extent it also utilizes PSs. The *push* phrase is top-ranked, the *down* phrase is bottom-ranked, and the two combine into a V'. The node AdvP is unconventional, since it shows that the adverb *down* is reduced from a hypothetical un-accusative verb, 'to fall down'. The *to* phrase is a PP and is lower-ranked than the V', with which it composes into an S. The PP indicating a posterior event follows the V' showing an anterior event, and in doing so, the two obey the PSs. Thus, there is also an interweaving of the PHs and the PSs in English, apparently with the PHs, particularized as FFH, being more dominant, and the PSs as less dominant. When we say Chinese employs PSs and English utilizes PHs, we are emphasizing their contrast and disregarding their partial commonality. Perhaps we can look into how the PSs and the PHs are similarly or differently shaped in both languages to obtain a more accurate picture of their contrastive strategies. And we proceed to do that.

Comparing the PSs governing a Chinese sentence as (5a)—analyzed in (6a)—and the PHs governing an English sentence as (5b)—analyzed in (6b)—we reach the preliminary conclusion that PSs and PHs are system-wise or 'systemic' macro-parameters, which operate on an entire language rather than on just a large collection of sentence patterns in a language, on which Huang's 'syntactic' macro-parameters operate. If Huang accepts this view, he would probably use the term 'large scale trend', since to him a macro-parameter has two extremes or opposite values, such as analysis and synthesis.

The trees in (6a) and (6b) give us the coarse-grand pictures of the sentences (5a) and (5b). We need to provide their corresponding fine-grand pictures to make our comparison even more revealing of the culture-induced conceptual distinction between these two sentences. To do this, we re-formulate the PSs and PHs. The PHs operates on a pair of lexical, phrasal, or clausal units as a head and a modifier. By contrast, the PSs acts on it as an 'anterior' unit and a 'posterior' unit, as it does in Chinese, and as a more prominent and less prominent thematic role in English. And we obtain our fine-grand pictures, (7a) and (7b), from (6a) and (6b).

(7a)

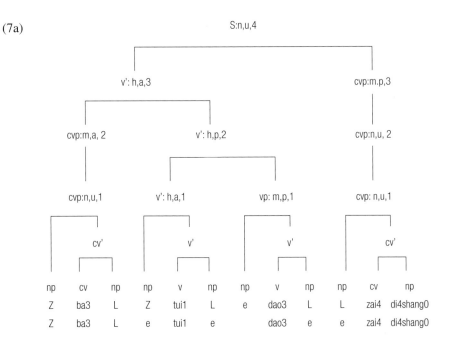

張生把李四推倒在地上

(5a)   Zhang1-san1 (a) ba3 Li3si4 (b) tui1 (c) dao3 (d) zai4 di4shang0.

'Zhangsan pushed Lisi down to the ground.'

(7b)

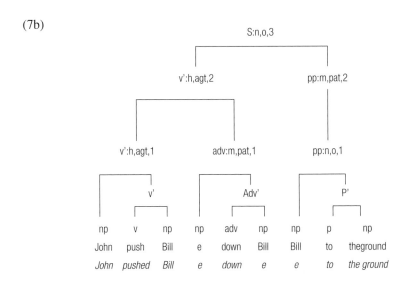

(5b)   John pushed Blll down to the ground.

We appeal to the X-bar theory, making use of the x-bar trees in (7a) and (7b). Each X' or YP has a degree of height or complexity k. The X' of degree k is composed with an YP also of degree k to form an X' of degree k+1, recursively. For example, in (7a), V' of degree 1 is composed with VP of degree 1 to form a V' of degree 1+1=2; in (7b), V' of degree 1 is composed with the AdvP of degree 1 to form a V' of degree 2. This standard procedure of combination is well known as a head-driven projection or an x-bar expansion. (7a) and (7b) shared this standard procedure. Where they differ is that, (7b) in English views X' and YP as simply a 'head' ('h') and its 'modifier' ('m'), (7a) in Chinese keeps this relation but adds another relation, in which, conceptually, X' holds a relation to YP. It is anterior ('a') to YP, which is posterior ('p') of it, or it is posterior ('p') of YP, which is 'anterior' ('a') to it. If a phrase of degree k is waiting for composition, its status is of course 'neutral' ('n') in a head-modifier relation, or 'undecided' ('u') in an anterior-posterior relation. To minimize the graphic complexity of the tree, we allow the two kinds of relation to be shown in one line. For example, in (7a) the 'CVP:n,u,1' as the left-most sub-tree of the tree indicates that it is a CVP, which is neutral in the head-modifier relation, and undecided in the anterior-posterior relation, and has complexity of degree 1. For another example, the sub-tree 'cvp:m,a,2' at the left-most of the tree indicates that it is CVP, which is a modifier, is an anterior, and has degree 2. We also make it clear that if phrase A and phrase B compose into phrase C, then A and B must have the same degree. Hence, when A and B are in composition, A or B must have its degree raised to equal that of B or A, respectively. In (7a), the right-most 'CVP: n,u,1' has its degree raised from 1 to 2, and then to 3, resulting in 'CVP: m,p,3', when it is composed with 'v':h,a,3' into 'S:n,u,4'.

Chinese has a syntactic head-modifier relation, in addition to the conceptual anterior-posterior relation in Chinese, which has been our focus so far, and similarly, English has the conceptual thematic-role prominence, in addition the head-modifier relation, which has pre-occupied our attention. We now focus on these two additional relations. Evidently, English employs a device for marking an NP as an agent ('agt'), patient ('pat'), or theme ('th'). The X' or YP in which the NP occurs is correspondingly interpreted as an agent phrase, patient phrase, or theme phrase. Thus, in (7b), we see 'v':h,agt,1', which denotes that the v' is a head, an agent, and has complexity of degree 1; 'advp:m,pat,1', which indicates that the AdvP is a modifier, a patient, and has complexity of degree 1; and 'pp:n,o,1', which signals that the PP is neutral, 'open' ('o'), and has complexity of degree 1. The notation 'open' ('o') indicates that a unit is open to later selection as an agent, patient, or theme.

So we now have Chinese (7a) and English (7b) on an equal footing. Chinese employs a syntactic head-modifier relation and a conceptual anterior-posterior relation. By contrast, English utilizes a syntactic head-modifier relation, but a conceptual thematic-role prominence relation. X-bar composition relies on the head-modifier relation, therefore X-bar composition and more broadly Chomsky's P&P applies to both Chinese and English.

Why does a language invest lavishly in two sorts of relations for its sentential configuration? One reason is perhaps to create redundancy. An operational system has to balance between processing cost and malfunction or break-down risk. Language, as an operational system, can rank efficiency over redundancy, and can also value redundancy over efficiency. Efficiency has the merit of a lower processing cost at the expanse of a higher risk of systemic break-down, and redundancy has the merit of a lower risk of systemic break-down at the expanse of a higher processing cost. The way Chinese has attempted a balance is that it uses the head-modifier relation for syntactic composition, and the temporal sequencing, or the anterior-posterior relation, for conceptual denotation. It adopts a redundancy-oriented grammar. English also opts for a redundancy-oriented grammar. It is equipped with a head-modifier relation for composition, and a thematic-role prominence relation for conceptual indication. Because of the difference in conceptual signification between English and Chinese, a pair of translation-equivalent sentences of Chinese and English can display a sharp contrast, especially with respect to the marking of words for their distinct lexical categories. For example, in (7b) the adverb *down* is clearly distinguished from the verb *push*, but in (7a), their counterparts *dao3* 'fall' 倒 and *tui1* 'push' 推 are both verbs of apparent equal status. One of these two verbs, the 'agent-initiated' transitive verb *tui1* 推 is ranked as the head, and the 'patient-receiving' un-accusative verb *dao3* 倒 is ranked as the modifier. But the two are not categorically or 'visibly' marked as their counterparts *push* and *down* in English are. As a result, it has become a dispute as to whether the first verb *tui1* 'push' 推 or the second verb *dao3* 'fall' 倒 is the 'main verb', in the sense that push in *pushed down* is a main verb in English. A sequence or combination of two verbs like *tui1 dao3* is a so-called Resultative Verbal Compound (RVC), which has the 'action' *tui1* 'push' 推 and the 'result' *dao3* 'fall' 倒. Given an RVC, of the form V_1–V_2, such as *tui1 dao3* 'push down' 推倒, *xie3 wan2* 'finish writing' 寫完, *chi1 bao3* 'eat to full' 吃飽, and *fu2 chu1* 'float out' 浮出, it is not easy to decide whether V_1 or V_2 is the main verb. Huang and Mangione (1985) suggested that V_2 is the main verb, but Huang (1988) argued that V_1 is the main verb. One possible reason for their disagreement could be that on the *conceptual* anterior-posterior layer, V_2, the 'result', is the main verb, but on the *syntactic* head-modifier layer, V_1, the 'action', is the main verb. If this is an acceptable explanation, then the syntactic and conceptual layers ensuring redundancy not only can conspire but can also conflict with each other.

4.   Mapping Cognition onto Language

We have now figured out how cognition could have mapped onto language. Assume that C is a set, whose elements are entities of cognition having different degrees of complexity, L is a set whose elements are ordered pairs of the form <s, m>, where 's' is the syntactic configuration obtained by applying the x-bar projection to a head and a modifier, and 'm' is the mental or conceptual relation forged by culture, which is the anterior-posterior relation in Chinese and the thematic-role prominence relation in English. Then the mapping of universal cognition onto a particular language is of the form f(C) =L, where L = {all x: x=<s, m>}, that is, where L contains elements which has the form <s, m>. In other words, universal cognition, C, is converted into a language, L, whose sentences have two layers: an x-bar tree layer, s, and a conceptual layer, m.

To elaborate a bit, a language has the head-modifier relation, which is universal, and also the conceptual relation, which is variable from language to language. The x-bar composition as a universal procedure works on the head-modifier relation to obtain an x-bar tree for a sentence in a particular language. The two x-bar trees in (7a) and (7b) can be made more sharply distinct if we recast them as two metaphoric bookshelves, shown as (8a) and (8b). There, we use the green color word or, failing to print the color, the word *green* to show the x-bar composition, the blue color word or the word *blue* to show the head-modifier relation, and the red color word or the word *red* to show the conceptual relation, which, as noted, is the anterior-posterior relation in Chinese, and the thematic-role prominence relation in English. Having added the color words, we can use a metaphor to bring out the clear distinction between a Chinese sentence and its English counterpart, in terms of the three colors indicated by the color words and their interconnection.

(8a)

S:n,u,4							
							green
V':h,a,3						blue	CVP:m,p,3
						red	
	green						
CVP:m,a,2	blue	V':h,p,2			black	CVP:n,u,2	
	red						
		green					
CVP:n,u,1 張三 - 把 - 李四	black	V':h,a,1 張三 - 推 - 李四	blue	VP:m,p,1 倒 - 李四	black	CVP:n,u,1 李四 - 在 - 地上	
			red				

(5a) 張三(a)把李四(b)推(c)倒(d)在地上.

Symbols: 'green' is for composition; 'blue' is for head-modifier relation; 'red' is for anterior-posterior relation. 'Black' indicates a lack of composition, and a neutral, or an indecisive relation.

(8b)

S:n,3			
green			
V':h,agt,2		blue	PP:m,pat,2
		red	
green		·	
V':h,agt,1 John- pushed- Bill	blue	AdvP:m,pat,1 e - down- Bill	black	PP:n,pat,1 Bill-to-the ground
	red			

(5b) John pushed Bill down to the ground.

Symbols: 'green' is for composition; 'blue' is for head-modifier relation; 'red' is for thematic-role prominence relation. 'Black' indicates a lack of composition, and a neutral, or open relation.

We are metaphorically viewing the tables, or graphs, of (8a) and (8b) as two bookshelves, which have the same overall plan but different internal frames, composed of front-open cases formed by horizontal plates and vertical plates. The horizontal plates extending from wall to wall of the frame are of a green color, which signals an x-bar composition. The vertical plates connecting two horizontal plates are of two parts. The top part is of a blue color, indicating a head-modifier relation, and the bottom part is of a red color, indicating a conceptual relation, which is an anterior-posterior relation in (8a), and a thematic-role prominence relation in (8b). A vertical plate may be of a black color, in which case it indicates a lack of any relation, and implies a non-application of the x-bar composition, which depends on the head-modifier relation. As (8a) and (8b) vividly convey, (5a) and (5b), analyzed as in (7a) and (7b), are nested in two quite different frames. The implication is that for proper arrangement of the event entries, one should not fit (5a) into (7b), nor (5b) into (7a).

We assume that (7a), yielding its surface form (5a), and (7b), yielding its surface form (5b), originate from the same universal cognition source, called the 'cognition of (7a), (7b), and additional translation-equivalent sentences in other languages', or for short 'cog (7a, 7b, etc.)'. Cog (7a,7b, etc.) is an event that has at least four parts or four sub-events. From cognition to language, the first step of transformation is called Reduction. Through reduction cog (7a,7b, etc.) is simplified as the four sub-events in (7a) and the three sub-events in (7b), where the sub-event matching the ba3 'control' 把 sub-event in (7a) is not preserved. In the second step of transformation, these two sets of sub-events obtained by reduction are analyzed as sentences having the x-bar tree structures in (7a) and (7b).

We have finally figured out a series of transformations that map cognition, or a cognitive entity, onto language, or its linguistic reflection, and the result is summed up in (9). As we can see in (9), the cognition reflected in (7a) and (7b) is labeled Cognition: $\{e_1, e_2, e_3, e_4, ..., en\}$. This universal cognition or cognitive entity is reduced or simplified to a Chinese cognition, labeled CH:$\{e_1, e_2, e_3, e_4\}$ and an English cognition, labeled EN: $\{e_1, e_2, e_3\}$. This reduction is step 1 of the entire transformation procedure. In step 2, universal syntax comes in and gives CH and EN their variable head-modifier relations. Apparently, this variation could have been caused by an interference of the varying conceptual relations. In step 3, universal x-bar composition applies and gives CH and EN their x-bar trees, which are similar in form but different in details. In step 4, culture brings concept in and invests CH and EN with their distinct conceptual relations, which are the anterior-posterior relation in CH and the thematic-role prominence relation in EN. Steps 3 and 4 could have occurred simultaneously in the following way: first the language-specific conceptual relation groups the sub-events, then the universal head-modifier relation permits the x-bar composition to apply, and third the conceptual relation is laid out. For graphic concision, we temporally disregard this complication, and put step 3 and step 4 in a sequence. In step 5, the eventual CH frame (7a) and EN frame (7b) emerge, and this is the linguistic reflections or the languages derived from a shared cognitive entity or cognition.

(9)

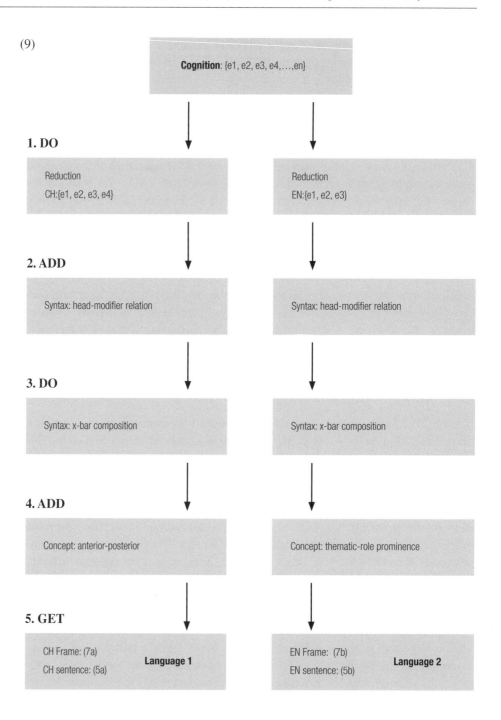

Mapping from cognition onto language: Step 1 is reduction; step 2 acquires syntactic relation; step 3 performs syntactic composition; step 4 obtains conceptual relation; step 5 is frame formation, producing sentences in specific languages.

5.   Conclusion

As Wang has repeatedly reminded linguists working on Chinese, team work on various levels of the linguistic research and exploration is important for achieving a fruitful result. Jim Tai has proposed his PTS emphasizing its iconicity. But iconicity is not as crucial as cultural values or inclinations in determining the structure of a Chinese sentence. Many years later Jim Huang proposed a theory of macro-principles and macro-parameters. That convincing theory provides the inspiration that I need to try to recast Tai's PTS as the anterior-posterior conceptual relation, against which the English thematic-role prominence relation is a contrastive conceptual relation. These two culturally determined relations are like Huang's two macro-parameters, but they operate on the process of mapping cognition to language, and not just on the syntax of a language, as Huang has originally envisioned. Jonah Lin (2001) and Audrey Li (2010) have also suggested that there is a conceptual aspect in addition to a syntactic aspect of the Chinese function of subject, providing me with further encouragement. And these scholars jointly inspired me to propose my preliminary view here. Wang is right. Chinese may be in some respects similar to English, but in other respects, it is different from English. And it is worthwhile, and indeed an exciting challenge, for Chinese linguists to try to build an indigenous Chinese grammar. From the perspective of globalization, a world in which different regions are interacting to generate innovation and diversity for the growth of the world is a more effective approach than a world in which a leading region sets a standard and other regions follow to consolidate the single standard. Focus has its short-term advantage, but diversification should have its long-term effect. If someday, there are indigenous grammars of all kinds, the discipline of linguistic investigation could become much more interesting, challenging, and rewarding.

Eastward Flows the Great River: Festschrift in Honor of Professor William S-Y. Wang on his 80th Birthday

REFERENCES

Boroditsky, L. 2010. Remembrances of times east: Absolute spatial representations of time in an Australian aboriginal community. *Psychological Science* 21:1635–1639.

Boroditsky, L. 2011. How does language shape thought. *Scientific American,* February 2011.

Chomsky, N. 1995. *The Minimalist Program.* Cambridge, MA: MIT Press.

Her, One-soon. 1991. Interaction of syntactic changes. In *Proceedings of the Second International Symposium on Chinese Languages and Linguistics* 238–250. Taipei: Academia Sinica.

Her, One-soon. 1994. Interaction of syntactic changes. In *Chinese Languages and Linguistics II: Historical Linguistics,* 263–293. Taipei: Academia Sinica.

Her, One-soon. 1997. *Interaction and Variation in the Chinese VO Construction.* Taipei: Crane Publishing.

Her, One-soon. 1989. History, structure, and competition. Paper presented at *the Eight International Workshop on Chinese Linguistics, POLA*, University of California at Berkeley, March 20–21, 1989.

Her, One-soon. 1991. Interaction: Some basic concepts. Ms. (Lecture notes, Januray 23, 1991).

Her, One-soon. 2006. Three types of semantic opacity and their challenge to teachers of Chinese. *Journal of Chinese Language Teaching* 3.1:83–115.

Her, One-soon. 2011. On Jim Huang's idea of macro-parameters. MS.

Huang, James C.-T. 1988. Wo pao de kuai and Chinese phrase structure. *Language* 64:274–311.

Huang, James C.-T. 2005. Syntactic analyticity and the other end of the parameter, lecture notes, Harvard University.

Huang, James C.-T. 2006. The macro-history of Chinese syntax and the theory of change. Paper presented at *the Chinese Linguistics Workshop*, University of Chicago. (PowerPoint file)

Huang, James C.-T. 2007. The thematic structure of verbs in Chinese and their syntactic projections. *Linguistic Sciences* 4:3–21. (in Chinese)

Huang, James C.-T. 2013. On syntactic analyticity and parametric theory. To appear in *Handbook of Chinese Linguistics*, eds. by C.-T. James Huang, Andrew Simpson, and Audrey Li. Wiley-Blackwell.

124

Huang, James C.-T., Audrey Y.-H. Li, and Yafei Li. 2009. *The Syntax of Chinese*. Cambridge: Cambridge University Press.

Huang, Chu-ren, and L. Mangione. 1985. A reanalysis of de: Adjuncts and subordinate clauses. In *Proceedings of the Fourth West Coast Conference on Formal Linguistics*, eds. Jeffery Goldberg, Susannah MacKayeand Michael Wescoat, 80–91. (Center for the Study of Language and Information—Lecture Notes).

Kiparsky, P. 1978. Rule ordering. In *Readings in Historical Phonology*, eds. P. Baldi, and R. Werth, 218–235. University Park, Penn.: Penn State University Press.

Li, Audrey. 2010. Deletion, phrase structures and constraints. Keynote speech at the IACL 18-NACCL 22, at Harvard University. May 20–22, 2010.

Lin, Jonah Tzong-Hong. 2001. Light verb syntax and the theory of phrase structure. PhD dissertation, UC Irvine.

Mitchell, M. 2009. *Complexity: A Guided Tour*. USA: Oxford University Press.

Tai, James H.-Y. 1985. Temporal sequence and Chinese word order. In *Iconicity and Syntax*, ed. John Haiman, 49–72. Amsterdam: John Benjamins.

Tai, James H.-Y. 2002. Temporal sequence in Chinese: A rejoinder. In *Form and Function: Linguistic Studies in Honor of Shuanfan Huang*, eds. I-wen Su Lily, Chinfa Lien, and Kawai Chui, 331–351. Taipei: Crane.

Talmy, L. 2000. *Toward a Cognitive Semantics* (2 volumes). Cambridge, MA: MIT Press.

Wang, William S-Y. 1969. Competing changes as a cause of residue. *Language* 45:9–25.

Wang, William S-Y. 1999. Language and people of China. In *Chinese Languages and Linguistics V: Interactions in Language*, eds. Yuen-mei Yin, I-li Yang, and Hui-chen Chan, 1–26. Taipei: Academia Sinica.

Wang, William S-Y., and C.-F. Lien. 1993. Bidirectional diffusion in sound change. In *Historical Linguistics: Problem and Perspectives*, ed. C. Jones, 345–400. London: Longman Group.

8

Arguments for a Construction-Based Approach to the Analysis of Sino-Tibetan Languages*

Randy J. LAPOLLA
Nanyang Technological University

Abstract

One of the things that has always impressed me about Professor William Wang is his amazing ability to draw from many different fields and synthesize what he learned from them into a cohesive discussion of some topic. I have always hoped to learn to do that, as my own influences are many and varied. In this paper I will discuss a few of these influences, to show how and why I have come to support a radically construction-based view of language structure, doing away completely with global categories such as form classes and grammatical relations.

* I would like to present this paper to Prof. William S-Y. Wang as an expression of my respect, gratitude, and affection for his teaching, help, and friendship over the years. An earlier version of this paper was presented first at Nanyang Technological University in April 2011, and at the Workshop on Typological Studies of Languages of China held in conjunction with the Association of Linguistic Typology meeting in July, 2011. I'd like to thank all those who gave me useful feedback after those presentations, in particular K. K. Luke.

1.   My Personal Path to a Construction-Based Approach

In the early 1980s, having just returned from several years in China, I was searching for a grammatical framework that would help me understand how the Chinese language works. I studied all the major theories of that period, such as Relational Grammar (RG), Government and Binding (GB), Lexical Functional Grammar (LFG), Generalized Phrase Structure Grammar (GPSG), and Categorial Grammar (CG). One major point about these theories was that all assumed that "subject" is a global category, and is manifested in all languages (i.e., is universal), and yet analyses of natural Mandarin discourse and computational implementations of Chinese structures always seemed to point to problems with "subject" in Chinese.

Discussions of "subject" at that time saw "subject" as a single "thing" (e.g., Keenan 1976 and other papers from Li 1976). Li and Thompson's (1976, 1981) approach to Chinese was helpful but not the whole picture.

In the late 1980s I found Role and Reference Grammar (RRG; Foley and Van Valin 1984), which did not assume "subject" as a universal, or even as a global category within a single language (see also Van Valin and LaPolla 1997, Chap. 6; Dryer 1997). It saw what we thought of as "subject" not as a single "thing" or category, but as a set of pivot constructions, that is, constructions where one NP is singled out for special prominence and treatment, and there is a restricted neutralization of semantic roles in that pivot position. It is therefore not a single category, and languages are seen to differ in terms of which constructions, if any, had grammaticalised pivots in the language.

An important point about this construction-based approach is that the meaning of the construction is not just the sum of the parts, but forces a particular interpretation (i.e., the construction itself has a meaning). For example, the "Cross-clause co-reference constraint" in English forces a particular co-reference interpretation on the overall construction, as in (1), which must mean the man burst.

(1)   The man$_i$ dropped the melon and Ø$_i$ burst. (Comrie 1988, 191)

In languages where this type of pivot has not grammaticalised (including languages said to have "subject", such as Italian), common sense would lead to the interpretation that the melon burst. An example of such a language is Rawang (Tibeto-Burman, Kachin State, Myanmar), where the following structure could be understood as any of the three translations given:[1]

(2)   əpʰūŋí ədɯsəŋ ədip bɯa nɯ ŋɯa:ʔmì

      əpʰūŋ-í   ədɯ-səŋ   ədip bɯ-a   nɯ Ø ŋɯ-ap-ì

      Apung-AGT Adeu-LOC hit   PFV-TR.PST   PS   cry-TMdys-INTR.PST

      (i)   'Apung hit Adeu and (Apung) cried' or

      (ii)   'Apung hit Adeu and (Adeu) cried', or

      (iii) 'Apung hit Adeu and (someone else) cried'

---

1. Abbreviations used in this paper: AGT agent marker; CL classifier; CSM change of state marker; INTR. PST intransitive past tense marker; LOC locative marker; NEG negative marker; PFV perfective marker; PS predicate sequencer; TR.PST transitive past tense marker.

At that time I also read Dwight Bolinger and others arguing that much of language use involves recall of complete forms, including sentences, from memory rather than generation of totally new forms, as these remembered forms are what become fixed syntactic patterns (constructional schemata). Bolinger (1961, 1976) argued for something like constructions, what he called 'idioms', and combinations of constructions, what he called 'syntactic blends' to form new syntactic structures, and pointed out 'the permeation of the entire grammatical structure by threads of idiom' (1961, 366). (See also Pawley 1985; Grace 1987; Langacker 1987; Matisoff 1979; Nunberg, Sag, and Wasow 1994; and Fillmore (e.g., 1982) on Frame Semantics.)

In 1984–85, when I took the Syntax course at UC Berkeley, it was co-taught by Charles Fillmore and Paul Kay, and they began developing Construction Grammar as the material for the course. This led to Fillmore, Kay and O'Connor's 1988 paper on the idiom *let alone* and other work on constructions. Cognitive Grammar (e.g., Langacker 1987) was also developing at the time. There was (and is) a close relationship between Construction Grammar and Cognitive Grammar, and there was much discussion between all of these more functionally oriented approaches (Construction Grammar, RRG, Cognitive Linguistics, and what came to be the "Santa Barbara approach", which began with Wallace Chafe at UC Berkeley in the late 1970s and early 1980s before he moved to UC Santa Barbara).

When I looked at Chinese from the RRG construction-based perspective of syntactic relations, I found that none of the relevant constructions manifested a syntactic pivot, so I talked about Chinese as not having "subject" or "direct object" (e.g., LaPolla 1988a, 1988b, 1990, 1993; for alternative explanations for word order patterns, see LaPolla 1995, 2009a; LaPolla and Poa 2005, 2006).

Interest in grammaticalization theory took off with the publication in 1984 of Heine and Reh's book *Grammaticalization and Reanalysis in African Languages* and Lehmann's 1982 book and 1985 article on grammaticalization. This led to Elizabeth Traugott and Paul Hopper teaching a class on grammaticalization as part of the 1987 LSA Institute (the course notes became Hopper and Traugott, 1993). Having taken that class as well as an earlier class at UC Berkeley on diachronic syntax, I moved more into looking at that aspect of the languages I was interested in.

Working with natural language led me to begin questioning the componential view of language (and linguistic theory). The componential view assumes that there are three components: the phonological component, the syntactic component, and the semantic component. The lexicon crosses all three, but the components must be linked by "linking", "interface", or "realization" rules. All non-constructional grammars are basically variants of the componential model. The constructionist approach appealed to me because it avoids the unnaturalness of the componential model, as the construction includes all these aspects at the same time.

Sperber and Wilson's *Relevance* was published in 1986, and it made a big splash, and greatly influenced my way of thinking about communication, allowing me to tie together the different strands of research I was doing: historical morphosyntax (grammaticalization), pragmatics, and morphosyntactic typology. The breakthrough came from my work on syntactic relations in Chinese. Once in 1996, after presenting my ideas about Chinese lacking "subject" in a seminar at City University of Hong Kong, I was told that while my data and analysis were correct, the idea that Chinese didn't have a "subject" could not be accepted. I then said

"What if instead I said that Chinese doesn't constrain the interpretation of the roles of referents in discourse the way English does?" They said, "That would be fine." So the direction of my research since then has been talking about grammatical structures as constraining the interpretation in particular ways, e.g., LaPolla and Poa 2002, LaPolla 2003, 2005a. (LaPolla 2006a and 2006b discuss this view specifically relative to grammatical relations, and LaPolla 2005b, 2009b are applications to language learning and language contact, respectively.)

This view also entails that each language is unique, and each structure which conventionalizes in a language does so in a particular type of situation, so each construction is unique.

In the late 1990s I also became familiar with Michael Halliday's work (esp. 1994), which is the most holistic of all approaches to linguistics, further confirming in my mind the problems of the componential and "interfaces" model. His work also reflects an understanding of constructions, where the whole is more than the sum of the parts.

In the 2000s I got involved in debates about form classes in Chinese and Tagalog (e.g., LaPolla 2008, 2010). I argued against universal form classes cross-linguistically and against global classes within a single language, and also argued (LaPolla and Poa 2006) against the use of assumed universal categories (e.g., SOV) in discussions of word order. When publishing this work, comments from reviewers of my publications often involved reference to William Croft's work, generally mentioning that we were saying similar things, so I made myself familiar with his work, in print and in person during his visit to the Research Centre for Linguistic Typology in 2010. Later in 2010 I also attended his ten-lecture workshop as part of the 8th China International Forum on Cognitive Linguistics in Beijing. From that I came to be convinced in his view that we can extend the same construction-based approach we had in dealing with syntactic relations to other grammatical categories and phenomena, that is, that they can be defined purely in terms of constructions, and so there are no global categories. Most recently I have tried to apply this view to the question of transitivity (LaPolla, Kratochvil and Coupe 2011).

2. The Distributional Method vs. the Constructionist Approach

The standard methodology in linguistics for identifying linguistic categories such as form classes is the distributional method. In this method, one identifies certain constructions as criterial for determining the membership of a word or structure in a particular category. So, for example, a noun is defined structurally as a word that can appear as the head of a noun phrase. The categories so defined, such as word classes, are then seen as the building blocks of larger syntactic structures.

One problem with this is that not all constructions point to the same categories. There is in fact tremendous diversity within each language and across languages. The Structuralists, who developed the distributional method for identifying linguistic categories, for example Bloomfield (1933) and Harris (1946), acknowledged that following the distributional method rigorously would lead to the creation of many small classes and membership of the same word in different classes (Bloomfield's "class cleavage"). They argued that the way to deal with this was to consider particular constructions as more important than others in determining class membership and choose those as the ones they thought defined the class best, while ignoring the others. Croft (2001, 2013) calls such a move "methodological opportunism". Methodological opportunism allows one to invoke any grammatical construction (context) to justify a particular category or distinction. This allows one to assume a universal syntactic element no matter what the diversity of grammatical behavior is.

The facts of languages that lead to the need to resort to methodological opportunism show there is a conflict between the distributional method and the building block model. There is also the problem that we define the categories on the basis of the constructions, yet define the constructions based on the categories defined by the constructions. For example, a noun is defined as a word that can appear as the head of a noun phrase, but a noun phrase is defined as a construction that has a noun as its head. This is completely circular. So we need to either give up our commitment to the distributional method, or we need to give up the idea of the building block model of grammar and just take the constructions as basic (see Croft, 2013).

In construction-based approaches, grammatical knowledge is represented as constructions: pairings of form and meaning/function. The phonological, syntactic, and semantic properties are all within the construction, not different components. In constructions there are only part-whole roles.[2] Constructions can be complex or atomic (single words or morphemes), schematic or substantive (or anything in between), and they can be organized into taxonomic hierarchies. There are no syntactic categories that are independent of the constructions, only the whole-part roles within the individual constructions. The constructions are also language-specific; there are no universal construction types.

As argued in LaPolla and Poa 2002 and LaPolla 2003, in communication, there is no coding or decoding, just ostension by the communicator and (abductive) inference by the addressee to create a context of interpretation in which the communicator's ostensive act can be seen to make sense (be relevant to some purpose). The role of language (as well as gestures and other ostensive acts) is to constrain the interpretation of the communicative intention of the communicator by the addressee. All language structure is the conventionalization of repeated patterns of discourse (cf. Hopper 1987, 1988), that is, repeated patterns of constraining the interpretation in a particular way. Constructions are conventionalized patterns of experience which constrain the interpretation in a particular way.

3.   Constructions in Chinese Grammar

Chinese grammar has traditionally been talked about and taught as constructions, such as the *bǎ* construction, the *bèi* construction, and the *shì . . . de* construction. The *bǎ* construction was given

---

2. This is the view of Radical Construction Grammar (Croft 2001). Some other construction-based approaches also allow for part-part relations within constructions, but as Croft (2001) has shown, these are not necessary and in fact problematic.

by Thompson (1973) as <NP1 *bǎ* NP2 V1 (V2) (NP3)>. The example in (3) is a natural example that fits this template (using Thompson's categories).

(3) 他們計劃明年把共祭活動推廣到陵園和社區。

[Tāmen]	jìhua	míngnian
3pl	plan	next.year
NP1		

bǎ	[gongjì	huódòng]	tuīguǎng	dao	[língyuan hé	shequ]
BA	public.obervance	activity	spread	arrive	cemetery and	community
bǎ	**NP2**		**V1**	**V2**	**NP3**	

'Next year they plan to spread the public observance activities to the cemeteries and communities.'

(http://news.sina.com.cn/c/2011-04-04/100722235984.shtml)

In many works on the *bǎ* construction, *bǎ* is said to be followed by an NP and said to mark the "direct object" of V1 (e.g., Sun and Givon 1985).

Although such constructions were recognized, attempts were still made to define word classes according to the building blocks model using the distributional method. But in Chinese it is notoriously difficult to define word classes. Y. R. Chao (1968) devoted more than 300 pages of his grammar to defining word classes (1968, 498–815), aside from another whole chapter trying to define "word" itself in Chinese, yet was not able to fit words into clear neat categories. Chao, as with the other Structuralists, recognised the problem of overlapping classes:

> In Chinese 怪 *guay* is an adjective in 可是這很怪 *Keesh jeh heen guay* 'But this is odd', an adverb in 怪難看的 *guay nankann de* 'rather ugly', and a transitive verb in 別怪我！*Bye guay woo!* 'Don't find me odd—don't blame me!'... (1968, 498)

By saying this, Chao is in effect saying that there is no global category for 怪 *guay* (Pinyin *guai*); the word gets its function (form class, meaning) from the construction it occurs in. This view was much earlier espoused by Lí Jǐnxī 黎錦熙 (1924, 24): "凡詞，依句辯品，離句無品" 'The class of a word depends on the sentence (it appears in), outside of a sentence it has no class' and "由職顯類" 'through (its) function (its) class becomes manifest' (1953, 10–11). Chao claimed to disagree with this view (1968, 498), but in effect argued for the same position in the quote above. Li Jinxi argued for a sentence-based approach to Chinese grammar ("Sentence-based grammar" "句本位的文法"), which might be seem as an early attempt at a construction-based approach, as "sentence" (句) didn't have a clear definition at that time and could refer to different types of structures.[3]

---

3. K. K. Luke (2006) has argued that many of the problems in the analysis of Chinese have been because of the lack of clear definitions for phrase, clause and sentence. Refining Li Jinxi's "sentence-based" approach, he argues for a "clause-based" approach to Chinese grammar.

Another major problem in Chinese grammar is the question of syntactic relations. Basically three approaches have developed to how to characterise clause structure in Chinese:

Topic-Comment (Y. R. Chao, 1968 / Lu Shuxiang, 1979 / LaPolla, 2009a)

Topic-prominent (Li and Thompson, 1976, 1981)

Subject-Predicate (most of the formalist camp)

For us to identify global form classes in Chinese and also syntactic relations using the distributional method, we would need to use key constructions as "tests" or "criteria" for membership in the category or for particular syntactic relations.

Let us start with the *bǎ* construction. As mentioned above, *bǎ* is said to be followed by an NP and said to mark the "direct object" (e.g., Sun and Givon 1985). Normally the initial NP is said to be the "subject", understood as the agent. Let's look at some examples (4a–d) from Ma 1987, 428–29).

(4) a. 蘿蔔把刀切鈍了。

    Luobo bǎ   dāo   qie   dun   le.

    radish BA   knife   cut   dull   CSM

    'The radish made the knife dull (when I/you/he cut it).'

  b. 他把筆寫禿了。

    Tā   bǎ   bǐ   xiě   tū   le.

    3sg   BA   pencil write blunt CSM

    'He made the pencil blunt from writing with it.'

  c. 這包衣裳把我洗累了。

    Zhe   bǎo   yīshang bǎ   wǒ   xǐ   lèi   le.

    this   package clothes BA   1sg wash tired CSM

    'Washing this pack of clothes has made me tired.'

  d. 這些事把頭發愁白了。

    Zhe   xiē   shì   bǎ   tóufa chóu   bǎi   le.

    this   CL   affair BA   hair   worry white CSM

    'Worrying about these affairs has made (my/yours/his/her) hair turn white.'

In (4a) the knife is an instrument, not the patient of 'cut', so it is difficult to say it is the direct object of the main predicate, 'cut', and the radish is certainly not the agent of 'cut' or 'dull'. In (4b) 'he' can be seen as an agent, but the pencil is an instrument, not the patient of 'write'. In (4c) the clothes are the patient of 'wash', not the agent of 'wash', and in fact the agent of 'wash' appears after bǎ. In (4d) 'these affairs' is not the agent of 'worry', and the hair is not any kind of semantic argument of 'worry'.

From these examples we can see that there is no way we could say that bǎ is marking a particular syntactic function. Let us now look at what sorts of elements can appear after bǎ in the construction. Consider the examples in (5):

(5) a. 不要把吃飯變成一場戰爭。

      bu   yao   bǎ   [chī fàn]   bian   cheng   yī-chǎng zhanzhēng

      NEG   want   BA   eat   rice   change   become   one-CL   war

      'Don't make eating into a war.'

      (http://renyifei.172baby.com/posts/137278.html)

    b. 為甚麼有些人把吃飯睡覺當成最重要的？

      weishenme   yǒu   xiē   rén   bǎ   [chī fàn   shùijiào]

      why   EXIST   CL   people   BA   eat   rice   sleep

      dāng   chéng   zūi   zhòngyào   de

      take.as   become   most   important   NOM

      'Why do some people take eating and sleeping as the most important (things)?'

      (http://zhidao.baidu.com/question/228560628.html)

    c. 為甚麼把吃飯各自付款稱為AA？

      wèishénme   bǎ   [chī fàn   gèzì fùkuan]   cheng   wei   AA

      why   BA   eat   rice   each   pay   call   be   AA

      'Why is eating and each person paying for themselves called "AA"?'

      (http://iask.sina.com.cn/b/17752493.html)

In (5a) a "verb phrase" appears in the post-bǎ slot, in 8.5(b) two "verb phrases" appear in the post-bǎ slot, and in (5c) a whole clause appears in the post-bǎ slot.

Trying to use the bǎ construction to define form classes or grammatical relations, then, will not work. What we can do is say we have a construction that marks a secondary topic that is affected in some way by an action.

Another construction that has been talked about for many years in discussions of form classes in Chinese is what has come to be known as the "這本書的出版 *zhe bèn shū de chūbǎn* construction" since this phrase was first used by Zhu Dexi, Lu Jiawen and Ma Zhen in a famous 1961 article. Zhu et al. argued that even though in this construction *chūbǎn* has a referring function, and is the head of a noun phrase, *chūbǎn* is still a verb. My question is, Why is it necessary to posit global categories such as noun and verb, and assign words to particular classes based on their appearance in certain constructions, when in fact they can appear in other constructions used to define other classes? There is also the problem of circularity mentioned above. Why not just take the constructions as basic and define the functions (referential, modifying, or predicative) of particular words based on those constructions?

Consider the following natural examples. In the construction in (6a), *bōchū* has a predicative function, but in the construction in (6b), *bōchū* has a referring function:

(6) a. CNN循環播出中國國家形像宣傳片。

    CNN xunhuan **bōchū**   Zhōngguó guójiā   xíngxiàng   xuānchuánpiàn

    CNN circulate **broadcast** China   country   image   propaganda.film

    'CNN repeatedly broadcast a propaganda film promoting China's national image.

    (*http://www.sina.com.cn/* 2011年01月19日07:49 新浪播客)

    b. 有沒有看到那天的播出？

    Yǒu   mei   yǒu   kan   dào   nèi   tiān   de   **bōchū**?

    exist   NEG   exist   watch   arrive   that   day   ASSOC   **broadcast**

    'Did (you) see the broadcast of that day?'

    (《明日之星》（電視節目）2011.06.11)

Yet another construction to consider is the basic clause construction, which is a Topic-Comment construction. In (7a) *tóngzhuō chīfàn* appears in the comment position, and has a predicative function, but in (7b) the same phrase appears in the topic position and has a referring function:

(7) a. 書記和我們同桌吃飯。

    Shūjì   hé   wǒmen   **tóng**   **zhuō**   **chī**   **fàn**

    secretary   and   1pl.excl   **same**   **table**   **eat**   **rice**

    '(The Party) secretary ate at the same table as us.'

    (http://d.wanfangdata.com.cn/periodical_ddkg201101023.aspx accessed 2011.07.10)

    b. 同桌吃飯也就具有了表演的性質。

    Tóng **zhuō** **chì** **fàn**   yě   jùyǒu   le   biǎoyǎn   de   xìngzhi

    same **table** **eat** **rice**   also   possess   PFV   perform   ASSOC   nature

    'Eating at the same table also has the nature of a performance.'

    (http://baike.baidu.com/view/13977.htm accessed 2011.07.10)

In (8) we have an example with the word *chī 'eat'* used alone in topic position. In this position of this construction it can only have a referring function.

(8) 在中國及世界的許多國家，吃是一種文化。

    Zài Zhōngguó jí shìjiè de xǔduō guójiā   **chī**   shì   yī   zhǒng   wénhuà.

                                             eat   COP   one   kind   culture

    'In China and many countries of the world, eating is a kind of culture'

    (http://baike.baidu.com/view/13977.htm accessed 2011.07.10)

In (9) and (10) we have the expressions *shīrén* 'poet' and *dàxuéshēng* 'university student' used predicatively. They have this predicative function because they occur in the predicative slot (comment) of the construction.

(9) 這些人都很詩人。

Zhèxiē   rén   hěn   shīrén.

this CL   person   very   poet

'These people are very (much like) poet(s).'

(http://hi.baidu.com/xmfine/blog/item/8c8b804404b6cb84b2b7dcbb.html)

(10) 都大學生了還這麼幼稚？

Dōu   dàxuéshēng   le   hái   zhème   yòuzhi?

all   university.student   CSM   still   this.much   naïve

'(You) are already a university student, (but) still so naïve?'

(http://video.baomihua.com/goodadv/12901470?P3P31)

We can see from all these examples that these constructions cannot be used for determining form classes. The same is true of all other constructions.

4.   Conclusions

There is no need for abstract global categories in individual languages or cross-linguistically. Taking the constructions as basic and avoiding methodological opportunism makes for much more empirically grounded linguistics, and allows us to be open to and appreciate the diversity of structures found in languages.

When we write grammars of individual languages using a construction-based approach, there is no need for chapters on supposed global grammatical categories. Instead we present the constructions used for propositional acts: referring expressions, predicative expressions, attributive expressions, and complex propositional constructions.

In doing language comparison from a construction-based approach, just the same we should not assume any global or universal grammatical categories. In description and comparison we should work inductively, looking to see what constructions are manifested in the languages, approaching the description from the point of view of the following questions:

- Is the interpretation of a particular functional domain constrained?
- If so, to what extent?
- If so, what form does the construction take?

In this way we will have descriptions and comparisons that are empirically based and more fully reflect the diversity of structures found in the languages of the world.

REFERENCES

Bloomfield, L. 1933. *Language.* New York: Holt, Rinehart and Winston.

Bolinger, D. L. 1961. Syntactic blends and other matters. *Language* 37:366–381.

Bolinger, D. L. 1976. Meaning and memory. *Forum Linguisticum* 1 (1): 1–14.

Chao, Yuen Ren. 1968. *A Grammar of Spoken Chinese.* Berkeley: University of California Press.

Comrie, B. 1988. Coreference and conjunction reduction in grammar and discourse. In *Explaining Language Universals,* ed. J. Hawkins, 186–208. Basil Blackwell.

Croft, W. 2001. *Radical Construction Grammar: Syntactic Theory in Typological Perspective.* Oxford: Oxford University Press.

Croft, W. 2013. Radical construction grammar. In *The Oxford Handbook of Construction Grammar,* eds. G. Trousdale and- T. Hoffmann. Oxford University Press.

Dryer, M. S. 1997. Are grammatical relations universal? In *Essays on Language Function and Language Type,* eds. J. Bybee, J. Haiman,s and S. A. Thompson, 115–143. Amsterdam & Philadelphia: Benjamins.

Fillmore, C. J. 1982. Frame semantics. In *Linguistics in the Morning Calm,* ed. The Linguistic Society of Korea, 111–137. Seoul: Hanshin Publishing Co.

Fillmore, C. J., P. Kay, and M. C. O'Connor. 1988. Regularity and idiomaticity in grammatical constructions: The case of let alone. *Language* 64:501–538.

Foley, W. A., and R. D. Van Valin, Jr. 1984. *Functional Syntax and Universal Grammar.* Cambridge: Cambridge University Press.

Grace, G. C. 1987. *The Linguistic Construction of Reality.* London, New York & Sydney: Croom Helm.

Halliday, M. A. K. 1994. *An Introduction to Functional Grammar.* 2nd (revised) edition. London: Edward Arnold.

Harris, Z. 1946. From morpheme to utterance. *Language* 22:161–183.

Heine, B., and R. Mechtild. 1984. *Grammaticalization and Reanalysis in African Languages.* Hamburg: Helmut Buske Verlag.

Hopper, P. 1987. Emergent grammar. *Proceedings of the 13th Annual Meeting of the Berkeley Linguistics Society,* 139–155.

Hopper, P. 1988. Emergent grammar and the a priori grammar postulate. In *Linguistics in Context: Connecting Observation and Understanding*, ed. D. Tannen, 117–134. Norwood, NJ: Ablex.

Hopper, P. J., and E. C. Traugott. 1993. *Grammaticalization*. Cambridge: CUP.

Keenan, E. L. 1976. Towards a universal definition of 'subject'. In *Subject and Topic,* ed. C. N. Li, 305–333.

Langacker, R. W. 1987. *Foundations of Cognitive Grammar,* Vol. I, *Theoretical prerequisites.* Stanford: Stanford University Press.

LaPolla, R. J. 1988a. 'Subject' and referent tracking: Arguments for a discourse-based grammar of Chinese. In *Proceedings of the West Coast Conference on Linguistics,* Vol. I, eds. J. Emonds, P. J. Mistry, V. Samiian, and L. Thornburg, 160–173. Department of Linguistics, California State U., Fresno.

LaPolla, R. J. 1988b. Topicalization and the question of lexical passives in Chinese. *Proceedings of the Third Annual Ohio State University Conference on Chinese Linguistics*, eds. Marjorie K. M. Chan, and T. Ernst, 170–188. Indiana University Linguistics Club.

LaPolla, R. J. 1990. Grammatical relations in Chinese: Synchronic and diachronic considerations. PhD dissertation, University of California, Berkeley.

LaPolla, R. J. 1993. Arguments against 'subject' and 'direct object' as viable concepts in Chinese. *Bulletin of the Institute of History and Philology* 63 (4): 759–813.

LaPolla, R. J. 1995. Pragmatic relations and word order in Chinese. In *Word Order in Discourse*, eds. P. Downing, and M. Noonan, 297–329. Amsterdam & Philadelphia: Benjamins Pub. Co.

LaPolla, R. J. 2003. Why languages differ: Variation in the conventionalization of constraints on inference. In *Language Variation: Papers on Variation and Change in the Sinosphere and in the Indosphere in Honour of James A. Matisoff,* eds. D. Bradley, R. J. LaPolla, B. Michailovsky, and G. Thurgood, 113–144. Canberra: Pacific Linguistics.

LaPolla, R. J. 2005a. Typology and complexity. In *Language Acquisition, Change and Emergence: Essays in Evolutionary Linguistics,* eds. J. W. Minett and William S-Y. Wang, 465–493. Hong Kong: City University of Hong Kong Press.

LaPolla, R. J. (Luo Rendi). 2005b. Di'er yuyan xide dui diyi yuyan de yingxiang (The influence of second language learning on one's first language). *Papers from the 4th International Conference on Bilingual Studies*, eds. Dai Qingxia and Jia Yimin, 50–57. Guangzhou: Jinan University Press.

LaPolla, R. J. 2006a. On grammatical relations as constraints on referent identification. In *Voice and Grammatical Relations: Festschrift for Masayoshi Shibatani* (Typological Studies in Language), eds. Tasaku Tsunoda and Taro Kageyama, 139–151. Amsterdam & Philadelphia: Benjamins.

LaPolla, R. J. 2006b. The how and why of syntactic relations. Invited plenary address and keynote of the Centre for Research on Language Change Workshop on grammatical change at the annual conference of the Australian Linguistics Society, University of Queensland, 7–9 July, 2006. To appear in *Evolution of Syntactic Relations* (Trends in Linguistics Series), eds. C. Lehmann, S. Skopeteas, and C. Marschke. Berlin: Mouton De Gruyter.

LaPolla, R. J. 2008. Constituent structure in a Tagalog text. Plenary presentation to the 10th Philippine Linguistics Congress, University of the Philippines—Diliman, Quezon City, December 10–12, 2008.

LaPolla, R. J. 2009a. Chinese as a Topic-Comment (not Topic-Prominent and not SVO) language. In *Studies of Chinese Linguistics: Functional Approaches*, ed. Janet Xing, 9–22. Hong Kong: Hong Kong University Press.

LaPolla, R. J. 2009b. Causes and effects of substratum, superstratum and adstratum influence, with reference to Tibeto-Burman languages. In *Issues in Tibeto-Burman Historical Linguistics* (Senri Ethnological Studies 75), ed. Yasuhiko Nagano, 227–237. Osaka: National Museum of Ethnology.

LaPolla, R. J. 2010. Feilubin Tagaluo yu (Tagalog) de cilei fanchou (The lexical categories of the Tagalog language of the Philippines). *Yuyanxue Luncong* 41:1–14. Beijing: Peking University.

LaPolla, R. J., F. Kratochvil, and A. R. Coupe. 2011. On transitivity. *Studies in Language* 35 (3): 469–491.

LaPolla, R. J., and D. Poa. 2005. Jiaodian jiegou de leixing ji qi dui Hanyu cixu de yingxiang (The typology of focus structures and their effect on word order in Chinese). In *Jiaodian Jiegou he Yuyi de Yanjiu (Studies on the Structure and Semantics of Focus)*, ed. Liejiong Xu and Haihua Pan, 57–78. Beijing: Beijing Foreign Studies University Press.

LaPolla, R. J., and D. Poa. 2006. On describing word order. In *Catching Language: The Standing Challenge of Grammar Writing*, eds. F. Ameka, A. Dench, and N. Evans, 269–295. Berlin: Mouton de Gruyter.

Lehmann, C. 1982. *Thoughts on Grammaticalization: A Programmatic Sketch. Vol. I.* Köln: Arbeiten des Kölner Universalien-Projekts, Nr. 48.

Lehmann, C. 1985. Grammaticalization: Synchronic variation and diachronic change. *Lingua e Stile* 20:303–318.

Li, C. N., (ed.). 1976. *Subject and Topic*. New York: Academic Press.

Li, C. N., and S. A. Thompson. 1976. Subject and topic: A new typology of language. In *Subject and Topic,* ed. C. N. Li, 459–489. New York: Academic Press.

Li, C. N., and S. A. Thompson. 1981. *Mandarin Chinese: A Functional Reference Grammar.* Berkcley: University of California Press.

Li, Jinxi. 1924 [1992]. *Xin Zhu Guoyu Wenfa* (*New Grammar of Mandarin*). Beijing: Commercial Press.

Li, Jinxi. 1953. Zhongguo yufa de "cifa" yantao (Discussion of the grammar of words in Mandarin Chinese grammar). *Zhongguo Yuwen* 1953, 9:8–12.

Lu, Shuxiang. 1979. *Hanyu Yufa Fenxi Wenti* (*Questions in the Analysis of Chinese Grammar*). Beijing: Commercial Press.

Ma, Xiwen. 1987. Yu dongjieshi dongci youguan de mouxie jushi (Certain syntactic patterns associated with verb-result type verbs). *Zhongguo Yuwen* 1987, 6:424–441.

Matisoff, J. A. 1979. *Blessings, Curses, Hopes, and Fears: Psycho-ostensive Expressions in Yiddish.* Philadelphia: ISHI. Second edition 2000 Stanford, California: Stanford University Press.

Nunberg, S., I. A. Sag, and T. Wasow. 1994. Idioms. *Language* 70:491–538.

Pawley, A. 1985. Lexicalization. In *Language and Linguistics: The Interdependence of Theory, Data, and Application*, eds. D. Tannen and J. E. Alatis, 98–120. Washington DC: Georgetown University Press.

Sun, Chaofen, and T. Givon. 1985. On the so-called SOV word order in Mandarin Chinese: A quantified text study and its implication. *Language* 61:329–351.

Thompson, S. A. 1973. Transitivity and some problems with the *bǎ* construction in Mandarin Chinese. *Journal of Chinese Linguistics* 1 (2): 208–221.

Van Valin Jr., R. D., and R. J. LaPolla. 1997. *Syntax: Structure, Meaning, and Function.* Cambridge: Cambridge University Press.

Zhu Dexi, Jiawen Lu, and Zhen Ma. 1961. Guanyu dongci, xingrongci "mingwuhua" de wenti. *Journal of Beijing University* 1961 (4): 51–64.

9

The Language Niche

Helena H. GAO
Nanyang Technological University

John H. HOLLAND
University of Michigan

Abstract

The term *niche* is widely used, with varying precision, in disciplines ranging from ecology to marketing. Here, "niche" is used to designate a complex flow of signals and interactions between language users. Basic patterns of these interactions persist through time, a bit like the vortices that persist around rocks in a white water stream. Viewed in this way, language and language acquisition depend upon persistent, dynamic social interactions that exploit the language niche.

1. Intoduction

Human language acquisition is in many ways remarkable. The newborn receives an incredible amount of stimulation: In the retina alone there are roughly 1,000,000 light sensitive neurons, each firing dozens of times a second. Inevitable variation in incoming light levels means that no firing pattern ever exactly repeats—there is perpetual novelty in the input. Similar comments apply to other sensory modes. To handle this perpetual novelty the newborn must extract and respond to regularities and patterns, treating similar patterns as "equivalent". Then the infant must learn from social interactions to make utterances that produce predictable reactions in other humans. As time goes on the infant learns to combine these utterances to produce "sentences", allowing increasingly subtle descriptions and, even, conjectures.

There is some wired-in help in this task, supplied by a long evolutionary history. Infants can imitate facial gestures between 12 and 21 days of age, an age much earlier than predicted by stage development theory (e.g., Jean Piaget). Such imitation implies that human neonates equate their own behaviors, which they often cannot see, with gestures they see others perform (Gopnik and Meltzoff 1997; Meltzoff and Borton 1979; Melzoff and Moore 1977; Meltzoff and Williamson 2013). But how does the newborn go on from there to make sense of the torrent of novel input? In particular, how does the newborn travel the long distance from very limited initial abilities to full language acquisition? Though we have large collections of relevant data, we have little theory of the dynamics of this process.

Our objective in this article is to suggest a way to bridge the gap between linguistic data and a theory of the dynamics of language acquisition. There are substantial differences between the suggested bridge and previous attempts to come to a broad understanding of language acquisition. A brief examination of these previous attempts will help explain why we consider these differences important.

1.1 Behavioral theories

Behavioral theories became known in the early and mid 1990s. Chomsky's critique of Skinner's Verbal Behavior (Chomsky 1959) led to behaviorists' approach becoming increasingly known and used as a point of reference. Behaviorists proposed that human verbal behavior is a form of operant conditioning subject to the same controlling variables as any other operant behavior (Skinner 1957). That is to say, children learn language like they learn other complex behavior, through principles of operant conditioning (reinforcement and imitation). The role of parents as models of other complex behavior was emphasized but relatively little attention was paid to children. The fact that children are able to produce perfectly understandable original sentences and phrases without reinforcement and imitation does not seem to support the behaviorist view. This is because there is little evidence that parents use strictly structured techniques to teach their children at home; yet almost all children learn their native language without much effort within their first three years of life. Also, research has shown that parents seldom correct children when they produce any ungrammatical utterances but only focus on the meaningfulness of their spoken messages (Brown and Hanlon 1970) and that new grammatical rules, such as tenses and plurals, are typically used spontaneously with no evidence of imitation before their school age (Bloom et al. 1974).

A post-Skinnerian account of human language and cognition called the Relational Frame theory proposed by Hayes, Barnes-Holmes, and Roche (2001) explains the origin and development of language competence and complexity based on Skinnerian behaviorism and argues that children acquire language through interacting with the environment. Under the concept of functional contextualism in language learning, predicting and influencing psychological events, such as thoughts, feelings, and behaviors are regarded as important variables that can manipulate contextual learning. Their empirical studies show that a learning process which they call "derived relational responding" appears to occur only in humans possessing a capacity for language (Hayes et al. 2002). This suggests that children learn language via a system of inherent reinforcements rather than purely depending on innate abilities.

Findings of various studies make a behavioral theory unlikely adequate to explain some critical features of child language acquisition. Thus, this approach has not been widely accepted in either psychology or linguistics. In the past decade, however, there has been a re-thinking of behaviorists' approach and behaviorist models are used today in empirical studies (Ramscar and Yarlett 2007; Roediger 2004).

1.2   Nativist theories

Nativist theories were started by the work of Chomsky (1957). Chomsky's critique of Skinner's Verbal Behavior (Chomsky 1967) leads to an even more abstract analysis of language acquisition. His Logical Structure of Linguistic Theory (Chomsky 1955, 75) is based on his analysis of a context-free grammar that he extends with transformational rules to account for the productivity or creativity of language. Chomsky emphasized that it is something innate that allows children to acquire language effortlessly. To account for the fact that the language input that children receive is usually too complicated and ambiguous for them to distinguish grammatical rules, Chomsky suggested that besides the surface structure of a language, a second structure of language, the deep structure, exists. It is the underlying meaning of language, a "species-specific characteristic…latent in the nervous system until kindled by actual language use." (Sacks 1989, 81). Chomsky believed that humans possess an innate neural device, the language acquisition device (LAD). It is this device that imposes order on incoming stimuli. This nativist idea of Chomsky has influenced most linguistic theorists' understanding of the nature of child language acquisition. His well-known "universal grammar" (UG) and "language acquisition device" (LAD) have guided much of linguistic research for decades. However, the UG/LAD approach left unexplained the mechanisms whereby an infant actually acquires a language. Later, more empirical approaches along these lines, such as Relational Frame Theory, Functionalist Linguistics, Social Interactionist Theory, and Usage-based Language Acquisition, still relied on an innate, "wired in" grammar.

1.3   Social Interactionist theories

These theorists take an interactive perspective and see the social environment as playing a more important role than innate "wiring". The innate learning mechanisms proposed by the nativist theorists and the domain-general set of learning devices as proposed by the behaviorists are well accepted by the social interactionist theorists, but the aspects of the environment, especially parents, are regarded as being specially important. Jerome Bruner (1983) is the leading theorist who holds this view. He believes that language is presented to children with a selection of the contents for the child's current abilities by the people around them. By doing so, children are provided with the best possible chance of learning. This social-pragmatic view of language acquisition argues that "children's initial skills of linguistic communication are a natural outgrowth of their emerging understanding of other persons as intentional agents" (Carpenter et al. 1998, 126). Tomasello (2003) also argues that language acquisition is based on more primitive social processes, such as shared joint attention. Language thus is considered as a social-cognitive tool, user-based, learned through functional distributional analysis, and used to manipulate other people's attention.

In psychology, Jean Piaget's experimental study of child cognitive development revealed stage-development in children. He found that a child's intellectual skills in the first 2 years of life depend upon sensori-motor experiences, not words and symbols (Piaget 1954, 1962). The wider cognitive system then makes it possible for children to develop a series of rules for language. The constraints of sensori-motor experience lead to similarities in children's progressive acquisition of language. Following Piaget, psychologists, as well as linguists such as Melissa Bowerman (1991, 2004), Elizabeth Bates and her colleagues (Bates 1995, 1999; Bates and Goodman 1997, 1999), and Jean Mandler (1998, 2004), made data-based assumptions that there could be many learning processes involved in language acquisition. For example, empirical studies on child-directed speech have provided ample data to such a nature of children's learning. Child-directed speech, or infant-directed speech, which was originally termed by Snow (1972) as motherese, is found to be a simpler and more redundant speech than the speech that mothers or others use with older children. More specifically, mothers are found to typically use high-pitched tones, exaggerated modulations, simplified forms of adult words, many questions, and many repetitions (Cooper and Aslin 1990, 1994; Fernald 1992; Fernald and Mazzie 1991, Fish and Tokura 1996; Hoff 2001; Karzon 1985; Kitamura et al. 2002; Kuhl et al. 1997; Masataka 1996, 1998; Moor et al. 1997; Stern et al. 1982; Trainor et al. 2000). Some researchers regard this special form of adult speech to young children as a reflection that there is some innate language-transmittal mechanism in adults' brains. For example, Bruner (1983) suggested that adults' brains have a special mechanism that allows them to respond to young children with an automatic change of speech to a more understandable form, which called Language acquisition support system (LASS). These studies show that although infants are biologically prepared to acquire language, social-emotional context provides an equally important foundation for language development. The social interactionist approach thus compromises between "nature" and "nurture" in their theoretical arguments.

Looking at the biologically wired-in and experiential aspects from a neurolinguistic perspective, Locke (1997) proposed a theory of neurolinguistic development involving four overlapping and interactive stages: vocal learning, utterance acquisition, analysis and computation, interaction and elaboration. Experimental studies conducted by other researchers have shown that the early phases of children's development do require social cognition for language development (DeCasper and Spence 1986; Fernald 1992; Locke 1993; Mehler et al. 1988; Spence and Freeman 1996). In addressing the relation between lexical and syntactic development, Elizabeth Bates and her colleagues (Bates and Goodman 1997, 1999) have shown that the relation between vocabulary size and syntactic complexity is stronger than the relation between age and syntactic complexity, indicating that age alone is unlikely the only underlying factor for language development. This finding allowed Bates and her colleagues to be in a good position to argue against Chomsky's LAD hypothesis. Their data show that children may not need a "grammar module". Grammatical rules emerge from a need to organize the vocabulary when it becomes big enough to be sorted, categorized, and used with certain rules. What Bates and her colleagues propose is a connectionist approach in which grammar emerges out of the acquisition and analysis of individual words (Elman et al. 1996). They emphasize the dynamic interaction between a brain with innate processing constraints and a language-speaking world. This is different from the nativist view that different aspects of language development are relatively independent.

More recent approaches emphasize that, with built-in learning mechanisms, child language emerges through imitation and social interaction (Bates 1999; MacWhinney 2004; Snow 1999; Tomasello and Bates 2001; Tomasello 2003). For example, emergentist theories, represented by MacWhinney's competition model (1987), argue that language acquisition emerges from the interaction of biological pressures and the environment through a cognitive process. These theories emphasize that nature and nurture need to be jointly involved to trigger language learning in a child.

1.4   Statistical learning

Based on the experimental findings of connectionist models, statistical learning theories of language acquisition (Creel et al. 2004; Saffran et al. 1996; Saffran et al. 1997;) proposed that statistical learning is a basic mechanism of information processing in the human brain and many of the language aspects, especially for bootstrapping early language skills and competence at a later age, can be explained by statistical properties of the language input. For example, in the phonetic category development children are born with the capability to distinguish any native and non-native phonetic contrasts (Aslin et al. 1981; Best et al. 1988; Eimas et al. 1971; Werker and Tees 1999). They can also discriminate between speech sounds that belong to the same native category but differ in the acoustic domain. However, by the end of the first year, infants' ability is restricted to their own native language sounds, but not the non-native contrasts (Sheldon and Strange 1982; Werker et al. 1981; Werker and Tees 1984). However, infants' acquisition of native phonetic categories is not a simple task. It is found that the development continues at least to the second decade of life (Hazan and Barret 2000). Evidence suggests that the phonetic categories are formed by statistical properties of the speech that the infant is being exposed to (Maye et al. 2002). Empirical studies of children's learning of words and syntax also show the statistical learning principles that contribute largely to infants' language acquisition (Houston and Jusczyk 2000; Johnson and Jusczyk 2001; Maye et al. 2002; Mintz et al. 2002; Mills et al. 2004; Newport and Aslin 2004; Saffran 2001; Saffran et al. 1996; Saffran et al. 2008; Singh et al. 2008; Smith and Yu 2008; White and Morgan 2008; Wonnacot et al. 2008).

Each of these approaches provides a useful perspective on language acquisition, but there is a considerable gap between the observations they explain and the mechanisms that supply the dynamics of language acquisition. An historic example points up the difficulty of relating observations to dynamics: For millennia humans accumulated observations of the movement of inanimate objects, ranging from falling stones and flying arrows to the movement of planets. Fallacious "laws" were common: "a moving object always comes to rest", "heavier objects fall faster", and so on. It took Newton's theory to bring unity to this vast array of observations. It is unlikely that simple laws will encompass language acquisition, but even a rudimentary theory should offer advantages in, say, second language teaching and automatic language translation.

2.   Consciousness

In a newborn, language development certainly depends upon an expanding consciousness, but "consciousness", like "life" or "mind", is difficult to define precisely. Still, for "life" and "mind" there are well-developed sciences, biology and psychology respectively, so we should not be too quick to dismiss an approach centering on "consciousness". Relating consciousness to language is, of course, not new:

> *He gave man speech, and speech created thought, which is the measure of the universe.*
>
> Percy Bysshe Shelley (1792–1822)

> *Speech was given to man to disguise his thoughts. [La parole a ete donnce a l'homme pour deguiser sa pensee.]*
>
> Charles Maurice de Talleyrand-Perigord (1754–1838)

> *Speech was given to the ordinary sort of men, whereby to communicate their mind; but to wise men, whereby to conceal it.*
>
> Robert South (1634–1716)

> *Men use thought only to justify their wrong doings, and employ speech only to conceal their thoughts. [Ils ne se servent de la pensee que pour autoriser leurs injustices, et emploient les paroles que pour deguiser leurs pensees.]*
>
> Francois Marie Arouet Voltaire (1694–1778)

In these quotations, consciousness is implicitly discussed as thought expressed in language. Even further back, in Plato's time, there was a general agreement that one can only speak of what one is consciously aware.

Personal Construct theory (Kelly 1955/1991) defines human consciousness as undergoing both conscious and unconscious processes. It postulates human cognition as starting from unconscious processes, or "low levels of cognitive awareness". These fundamental concepts of consciousness form the basic understanding of how human beings develop as social beings. Nowadays, however, linguistic theories rarely touch upon consciousness. Chomsky's (1965) theory of universal grammar holds that all children are born with an innate grammar based on mental transformational rules, enabling the production of sentences not previously heard. In that theory there is no discussion of what mental activities impel a child to create a novel sentence. A fortiori, the theory makes no provision for consciousness as an activator of transformational rules.

Recent cross-disciplinary research does, however, open a channel for researchers to discuss consciousness in relation to language. Peter Carruthers (1996, 2000), for instance, argues that much of conscious thinking takes place in natural language. On this view, a better understanding of consciousness contributes to a better understanding of language and vice versa. Certainly, consciousness does not exist on its own; its existence becomes observable only when other mental activities are actively involved, such as conscious body movement vs. unconscious body movement, conscious utterance vs. unconscious utterance, and conscious thought vs. unconscious thought. Therefore, consciousness is to a large extent revealed by other types of mental phenomena that together make one's mental life as a whole.

3.   Levels of Consciousness

According to Zelazo's (2004) Levels of Consciousness theory (LoC), the characteristics of children's development of consciousness undergo various levels of what Kelly termed "conscious processes" before the child reaches full linguistic capability. The age-related increases in LoC are related to the quality of experience, the potential for recall, the complexity of children's explicit knowledge structures, and the possibility of the conscious control of thought, emotion, and action. The basic assumption of the LoC model is that children's consciousness has several dissociable levels of consciousness—information can be available at one level but not at others. This differs from models mainly based on adult data that distinguish between consciousness and a meta-level of consciousness (e.g., Moscovitch 1989; Schachter 1989; Schooler 2002). With the LoC model, consciousness is hierarchically arranged, and it is possible to observe the level at which consciousness is operating in specific situations.

The approach we take here examines mechanisms (behavioral traits) that generate the behaviors at different levels of consciousness, relating different levels of consciousness to well-known transitions in physiological and mental control as the newborn develops. Following Braitenberg's (1984) Vehicles, Experiments in Synthetic Psychology, we will select mechanisms at each level that mesh smoothly with the mechanisms adduced for earlier levels. We delimit five levels, starting from capabilities that are pre-primate—a wired-in evolutionary heritage—

and ending with capabilities that characterize human language production—learned through interaction with other language-competent humans. The term "levels" immediately suggests a progression from level to level, and a corresponding dynamics.

We are particularly interested in an approach that moves up levels of consciousness by forming new rules that give the learning infant increasing autonomy—the ability to have ongoing interior activity that is modulated, but not determined, by current stimuli. This developmental approach thus relates language acquisition to a newborn's increasing autonomy as it gains experience through social interactions. Such autonomy gives the ability to plan ahead, anticipating future effects of current actions. In language acquisition, this ability allows the learning agent to determine what future utterances will fit grammatically with current utterances.

An important part of our outlook for generating new rules is the idea that new rules can be formed by combining building blocks extracted from rules already established. This procedure involves operations similar to those used by breeders in crossbreeding to get more sophisticated varieties. The ontogeny of language is reflected, then, in the mechanisms that transform each model into the next model in the sequence. As a bonus, many of the mechanisms, and the resulting changes, can be reinterpreted as relevant to the phylogeny of language. By taking this dynamics into account we hope to arrive at new experiments and, even, new approaches to teaching language.

4. Agent-based Models of LoC

Because this approach concentrates on the social nature of language, the exposition uses agent-based models. Each agent is defined by a set of IF/THEN rules that respond to external and internal signals. As an agent learns, through interactions with its physical environment and other agents, new rules are discovered and extant rules are modified. In effect, the agent's rules amount to hypotheses at different levels of precision, with the rules being confirmed (or disconfirmed) as the agent gains experience. The different levels of precision will be related to different levels of consciousness.

Increasing consciousness in these agent-based models arises from mechanisms that increase the recirculation and feedback of signals within the agent. This increasing recirculation allows responses that are only modulated by exterior stimuli. We claim that such autonomy is a sine qua non for language production. We will illustrate the claim with a series of rule-based models that serve as simple examples of the progressive autonomy that accompanies successive levels of consciousness. One advantage of this agent-based approach is that it lets us employ methods used in the general study of complex adaptive systems (*cas*)—a point we will elaborate later.

Based on the central claim, LoC models make the following assumptions of the age-related changes in executive functions as children develop:

LoC 0   Unconscious activities: Inherited ('wired in') cognitive abilities.

Pre-primate precursors to language acquisition:

(i)   Ability to imitate utterances and gestures.

(ii)   Ability to distinguish between objects and actions.

(iii)   Awareness of a mutually apprehended salient object or action.

(iv)   Basic learning procedures (akin to Hebb's learning rule).

LoC 1   Minimal consciousness: Innate reinforcement of repeatable activities, ranging from repetition of sounds and motions to actions that produce innate rewards.

Example: Directed motion of hand across visual field (a precursor to gesture).

LoC 2   Stimulus-response (conditioned) consciousness: Labeling from semantic long-term memory.

Example: Utterances that cause innate rewards (such as causing T to smile).

LoC 3   Simple recursive consciousness: Use of labels (utterances) to cause others to act (such as causing T to fetch bottle).

Example: Utterances that lead to food acquisition when food visible.

LoC 4   Extended recursive consciousness: Use of labels to cause others to act when object is not present.

Example: Food acquisition when food not visible.

LoC 5   Self-consciousness: Use of labels facilitate planned sequences of action (e.g., sequenced utterances), characterize mental activities of others, to look ahead and explore alternative courses of action.

Example: Distinguish between two similar objects using a sequenced pair of utterances.

Newborn babies are assumed to experience LoC1, the simplest, but still conceptually coherent, consciousness that accounts for the behavioral evidence (cf. Armstrong 1980). LoC1 is unreflective, present-oriented, and makes no reference to a concept of self. So, in LoC1, the infant is conscious of what it sees (the object of experience), but not of seeing what it sees, let alone that its 'self' is seeing what it sees. As a consequence, it cannot recall seeing what it saw. LoC1 infant behavior lasts till the end of the first year.

Numerous new abilities appear within months of birth, such as producing repeatable utterances, using objects in a functional way, pointing proto-declaratively, and searching flexibly for hidden objects. The infant works through conditioned consciousness, LoC2, to a new form of consciousness—recursive consciousness (LoC3), observed in 2-year-olds. LoC3 is marked by two signs: (i) the existence of a perceptual experience and (ii) the ability to label using semantic long-term memory. For instance, if a 1-year-old toddler says 'dog', it is assumed that the infant successfully combines a perceptual experience with a label from semantic long-term memory. The existence of labeling makes the contents of minimal consciousness perceptible and recoverable, and thus provides an enduring trace of the experience of certain content. This trace lasts long enough to be deposited into both long-term memory and working memory. The contents of working memory (e.g., representations of hidden objects) can then serve as goals to trigger action programs indirectly so the toddler is not restricted to responses triggered directly by minimal and conditioned experience of an immediate present stimulus (LoC1 & 2).

When provided with a pair of rules to use in a choice situation, 3-year-olds, in contrast to 2-year-olds, do not perseverate on a single rule. However, there are still limitations on 3-year-olds' executive function, as seen in their perseveration in the Dimensional Change Card Sort (see below), which represents the integration of two incompatible pairs of rules into a single structure. The Dimensional Change Card Sort requires children to adopt an even higher level of consciousness, extended recursive consciousness, LoC4. Evidence indicates that LoC4 first emerges around 4 years of age, together with a range of meta-cognitive skills studied under the rubric of 'theory of mind' (Frye et al. 1995; Perner and Lang 1999; Carlson and Moses 2001).

William James (1901) suggested that an understanding of consciousness would provide the key to intellectual accomplishment. A child's awareness of self, then, is seen as a major developmental transition. It begins at the end of the second year. Linguistically, this transition is marked by a child's first use of personal pronouns; cognitively, it is marked by their self-recognition in mirrors; and emotionally it is marked by their display of self-conscious emotions such as shame (Tracy and Robins 2004). This transition is marked by another level of consciousness, referred to as self-consciousness, LoC5.

According to Zelazo et al. (2007), increases in level of consciousness are brought about by the re-processing of experienced information via neural circuits in prefrontal cortex.

The potential for recall, the complexity of knowledge structures, and the possibility of action control, all increase. Reprocessing adds depth to subjective experience because more details can be integrated into the experience before the contents of consciousness are replaced by new environmental stimulation. Each degree of reprocessing causes information to be processed at a deeper, less superficial level, which increases the likelihood of retrieval (Craik and Tulving 1975). So the more complex knowledge structures increase the scope of cognitive control. This advance, in turn, moves consciousness away from stimuli and responses, making possible more de-contextualized discursive reasoning.

The infant's increasing autonomy shows itself first in conditioning that provides the infant with responses based on experience, then in anticipation and short-term planning and, finally, in internal models that allow planning and lookahead (as in playing a game of chess). Each of stage is closely related to progression in control of utterances and, ultimately, in organized, meaningful sequences of utterances. In short, the approach outlined here claims that this increasing autonomy marks progressive changes in linguistic ability.

5. Experiments

The need for different LoC's for a knowledge/action dissociation is illustrated by experiments done by Zelazo and his group of researchers with different versions of the Dimensional Change Card Sort (DCCS). In a typical experiment, children are shown two target cards (e.g., a blue rabbit and a red car) and asked to sort a series of bivalent test cards (e.g., red rabbits and blue cars) according to one dimension (e.g., color). Then, after sorting several cards, children are told to stop playing the first game and switch to another (e.g., shape), 'Put the rabbits here; put the cars there.'). Regardless of which dimension is presented first, 3-year-olds typically continue to sort by that dimension despite being told the new rules on every trial (e.g., Brooks et al. 2003; Frye et al. 1995; Jacques et al. 1999; Perner and Lang 2002). By contrast, 4-year-olds recognize immediately that there are two sets of rules for the game and a switch of rules is needed regarding shape or color.

The example shows that the two groups of children, 3-year-olds and 4-year-olds, are at different stages of conscious development. For 3-year-olds, understanding one set of rules at a time, doesn't seem to be a problem. But, once a new set of rules is introduced, children at this age are found to be unable to switch back and forth. They seem to be unable to represent the rules at a level of consciousness that allows a deliberate decision to follow either the pre-switch rules or the post-switch rules. For 4-year-olds, the two ways of construing the stimuli are perceived as a reflection of multiple perspectives on the situation. Such understanding allows an integration of the different rules into a more complex rule structure. Zelazo (2004) makes this point clearly.

There are numerous examples of age-related changes in children's ability to disengage from a compelling construal of a situation. For example, children become more likely, over the course of the second year, to perform pretend actions (e.g., talking on the telephone) with pretend objects (e.g., a spoon) that bear little physical resemblance to the real objects. They also become more likely to perform pretend actions without objects altogether (e.g., Ungerer et al. 1981). Similar changes continue into the preschool years (O'Reilly 1995; Overton and Jackson 1973). As these changes occur, there are complementary changes in children's ability to resist responding with actions suggested by the objects (e.g., putting the spoon into the mouth). (Elder and Pederson 1978; Pederson et al. 1981.)

This general development pattern—from stimulus-dependent to cognitively-controlled activity—we identify with changes in level of consciousness. In the A-not-B task (Piaget 1954; Marcovitch and Zelazo 1999), 9-month-old infants watch as an object is hidden conspicuously at one of two locations, and then they retrieve it. When the object is then hidden at a new location, 9-month-olds are likely to search for it at the first location. Older children, rather than responding in a perseverative, stimulus-bound fashion, evidently use an updated representation of the object's location to guide their search.

Gradually, linguistic meaning comes to dominate sensori-motor experience, as described by Vygotsky (e.g., 1978) and Luria (e.g., 1961). A preliminary study of 3- to 5-year-olds' flexible understanding of the adjectives "big" and "little" (Gao and Zelazo, 2008) provides a good example. When shown a medium sized square together with a larger one, 3-year-olds had little difficulty answering the question, "Which one of these two squares is a big one?" However, when the medium square was then paired with a smaller one, and children were asked the same question, only 5-year-olds reliably indicated that the medium square was now the big one. This example shows an age-related increase in children's sensitivity to linguistic meaning when it conflicts with children's immediate experience. It reveals that interpretation becomes progressively decoupled, from perseverative stimulus properties.

Increasing sensitivity to linguistic information is also seen in children's difficulty in interpreting ambiguous adjectives. Preliminary research (Gao et al. in preparation) indicates that 3-year olds shown medium-sized pictures of a rabbit and a bear, have no difficulty identifying the bear as "a big animal." However, when 3-year-olds are shown a big picture of a rabbit and a small picture of a bear typically point to the rabbit as the "big animal". 4-year-olds seem to sense the ambiguity in the questions; they typically hesitate and then reply in an inconsistent fashion. By 5 years of age, however, children often ask, "What do you mean? The animals here in the picture or real animals?", and they are more likely to point to the bear. Older children are increasingly likely to use verbal input to restrict their attention to the appropriate aspects of a situation (Ebeling and Gelman 1988, 1994).

Language plays a causal role in helping a child to attain higher levels of consciousness. Previous research (e.g., using the Dimensional Change Card Sort and measures of children's theory of mind; Frye et al. 1995) suggests that 4-year-olds are capable of considering two incompatible perspectives in contradistinction, even if they do not always do so. In another study, (Jacques, et al. 2005) 4- and 5-year-olds were presented with the Flexible Item Selection Task. On each trial of this task, children were shown sets of three items designed so that one pair matches on one dimension, and a different pair matches on a different dimension (e.g., a small yellow teapot, a large yellow teapot, and a large yellow shoe.)

Children were first told to show the experimenter two things that go together in one way (Selection 1), and then asked to show the experimenter two things that go together in a different way (Selection 2). To respond correctly, children must represent the pivot item (i.e., the large yellow teapot) first according to one dimension (e.g., size) and then according to another (e.g., shape). Four-year-olds generally perform well on Selection 1 but poorly on Selection 2, indicating that they have difficulty thinking about the pivot item in more than one way—they have difficulty disengaging from their initial construal of the item. However, when children were asked to label the basis of their initial selection (e.g., when they were asked, "Why do those two pictures go together?"), their performance on Selection 2 improved substantially. This was true whether children provided the label themselves or whether the experimenter generated it for them.

In terms of the LoC model, children stepped back from the Selection 1 perspective when it was labeled, reflecting on it at a higher level of consciousness. That higher level of consciousness transforms the child's initial perspective (seeing the objects in terms of size) from a subjective frame into an object of consideration. It puts psychological distance between the child and the perspective allowing the child to adopt an alternative perspective (seeing the objects in terms of shape).

Another study done by Gao et al. (under review) examined 3- and 4-year-olds' interpretation of the relative adjectives "big" and "little". In Experiment 2 of the study, children were asked to interpret adjectives pairs with respect to a medium-sized stimulus that was compared either to a smaller stimulus or to a larger one. On each trial, children were presented with three stimuli that varied only in size, and the experimenter pointed to two of the stimuli, asking children to indicate which one was big or little. On interference trials, children were required to interpret the medium stimulus as either big or little despite interference from the presence of a bigger or littler stimulus, respectively. On switch trials, children were required to interpret the medium stimulus

Figure 9.1 A non-interference trial with the question (with the experimenter pointing at the two in the circle): "Which of the two chicks is the big one?"

Figure 9.2 An interference trial with the question (with the experimenter pointing at the two in the circle): "Which of the two chicks is the little one?"

Figure 9.3 A switch trial with the question (with the experimenter pointing at the two in the circle): "Which of the two chicks is the big one?"

in a way that differed from the previous trial (e.g., they were required to interpret it as big on the switch trial when they had interpreted it as little on the previous trial). See Figures 9.1, 9.2 and 9.3.

By examining performance on both interference and switch trials, it was possible to explore whether young children's difficulty was with switching per se, or whether children also had difficulty attending selectively to the interpretive context in the presence of interference from the stimulus display. To examine further (and in a different way) the effect of stimulus support, children were assessed in one of two conditions, one in which there were blue borders around the two stimuli in question, and one in which there were not. It was assumed that children might be easily distracted by multiple stimuli displayed at the same time and thus black borders were used as a condition under which attention was expected to be drawn to particular stimuli. It was also assumed that linguistically explicit cues would further confine children's attention in a physically and perceptually distracted context and thus verbal feedback were to be given spontaneously when a child failed a trial the first time.

Results of this study first verified that even the younger children were able to understand the basic concepts of *big* and *little*. When the ambiguous stimulus (the medium sized one) became the switching target in both the interference and switch conditions, however, children had to interpret this single stimulus as *big* in one sense (e.g., in relation to the small stimulus) and then as *little* in another sense (e.g., in relation to the big stimulus). Results of the interference and switch trials confirm that children's interpretation of adjectives is sensitive to context from a young age, but also reveals an age-related improvement in flexible adjective interpretation during the preschool years.

The major issue addressed is the apparent disparity between prior findings showing that even 2-year-olds can flexibly interpret these words, and a large literature showing young children's difficulty with switching tasks (e.g., the Dimensional Change Card Sort). The experiments provide a resolution to this disparity by showing that children fairly readily switch interpretations when the context clearly signals a shift (e.g., by changing which items are available to compare), but have more difficulty switching when they need to ignore competing cues that are present in the context. Furthermore, switching is more difficult for younger than older children.

Using the LoC model to interpret findings, we can argue that the 3- to 4 year olds performed above the level of the recursive consciousness (LoC3), since they all passed warm-up trials and non-interference trials. The existence of a perceptual experience and the ability to label using semantic long-term memory are obvious. However, the results of the interference and switch trials show that most children were unable to make the switch flexibly. In particular, children's performance was worsened when scaffolding was removed. For example, children performed better when the relevant items were highlighted (e.g., edged with black borders) than when they were not. Children failed to step back from the perspectives of the interference and switch trials when asked to compare only two instead of three items. A higher level of consciousness did not exist that would have allowed the children to transform their initial perspective (seeing the items in comparison in terms of normality) into a flexible or dynamic perspective to interpret the comparison in terms of relativity. This study addresses a rich question about the relation between language processing and cognitive flexibility, and executive functions in general. What is more interesting in this study is that the specific tasks given to the children allowed us to see that the cognitive flexibility in processing both perceptual stimuli and linguistic cues require different levels of consciousness.

These outcomes make us think that a higher level of consciousness allows for both greater influence of thought on language and greater influence of language on thought. On the one hand, it allows for more effective selection and manipulation of rules (i.e., it permits the control of language in the service of thought). On the other hand, it allows for top-down structuring of interpretive frames. Top-down structuring permits children to respond more appropriately to linguistic meaning despite misleading context—it allows language to influence thought. As a result language and thought become increasingly intertwined in a complex, reciprocal relation. This reciprocal relation can be seen in the growing richness of children's semantic understanding and increasing subtlety of their word usage. Consider, for another example, a child's developing understanding of the semantics of the verb "hit". Children first understand "hit" from its use to depict simple accidental actions (e.g., an utterance by a child at 2;4.0: "Table hit head"; Gao 2001, 220). Usage is initially restricted to particular contexts. Eventually, however, reflection on this usage allows children to employ the word in flexible and creative ways (e.g., "I should hit her with a pencil and a stick", uttered metaphorically by the same child at 3; 8.6; Gao 2001, 219). As Tomasello (2000) explains, such restricted productivity requires engagement in the processes of analogy-making and structure-mapping. A child's linguistic constructions depend on a first step of imitative learning, with some understanding of functional roles. A process of analogy-making then takes place to get to first order constructions and then later to get to higher order constructions.

These findings bring forth a central claim of the LoC framework: Increasing linguistic ability is the result of recursive processing, whereby the content of consciousness at one level is compared to other content at that same level.

6.   An Agent-based Model of *LoC*

Now our objective is to incorporate these observations into a theoretical framework that suggests the mechanisms underlying these LoC transitions, opening the way to new experiments. Specifically, we want to examine mechanisms that use social interactions to build new LoC on top of levels already acquired. Thoussgh the model is constrained by facts and observations, it does not try to supply parameters, such as statistical parameters, for prediction of data; it is an exploratory model.

To emphasize the role of social interaction we will use an agent-based model (Holland 1995). In an agent-based model two or more agents interact through an exchange of signals, learning new behaviors as they adapt to each other. Agent-based models have been used to describe interactions in systems as different from each other as the immune system (where the signals are proteins) and markets (where the signals are buy and sell orders).

Here we will use *rule-based, signal-processing* agents (Holland et al. 1986), with rules of the form

IF (signal x is present) THEN (send signal y).

Signals x and y could be utterances, gestures, or visual input. The kinds of signals processed determine a rule's level of performance, so that we can typically associate certain kinds of rule conditions with the LoC involved. In the following examples, T ("teacher", e.g., the mother) stands for a competent adult that regularly interacts with the infant L ("learner"). For example, a simple rule for L might be,

IF (T lifts milk bottle) THEN (say "milk").

Signals can also serve to coordinate internal process, in which case they have no intrinsic meaning, serving much like the un-interpreted bit strings that coordinate instructions in a computer program. Each agent has many rules and, indeed, many rules can be active simultaneously. This simultaneous activity is roughly the counterpart of the simultaneous firing of assemblies of neurons in the central nervous system (Hebb 1949).

In the rules that follow, <action> denotes an overt action caused by a particular signal.

Typical rule at *LoC 0* [Unconscious activities]:

IF (T utterance) **THEN** (<imitate utterance>)

(Note that L will use limited current abilities to attempt match.

E.g., T-utterance "Gloria" can become L-utterance "Do-ee".)

Typical rule at *LoC 1* [Minimal consciousness—innate reinforcement].

IF (hand in vision cone) **THEN** (<move hand right>)

Typical rule at *LoC 2* [Stimulus-response with labeling from long-term memory].

IF (milk bottle present) **THEN** (<utterance "milk">)
(Note that there will often be correlations between recurring patterns in the environment, such as actions and objects. These correlations can be exploited through conditioning.)

Typical rule set at *LoC 3* [Simple recursive consciousness; e.g., using utterances to cause others to act].

IF (milk bottle present) **THEN** (<utterance "milk">)

T fetches milk bottle.

IF (milk bottle at mouth) **THEN** (<consume milk>)

Typical rule set at *LoC 4* [Extended recursive consciousness; e.g., using utterances to cause others to act on objects not present].

IF (hungry & no food visible) **THEN** <"milk">

   T fetches milk bottle.

IF (milk bottle at mouth) **THEN** (<consume milk>)

Typical rule set at *LoC 5* Self-consciousness [Planned sequences of action].

IF (red ball present and blue ball present) THEN (internal signal x)

IF (internal signal x & red ball desired) THEN (internal signal y & <"red">)

IF (internal signal x & internal signal y) THEN (<"ball">)

(Note that this set of rules only allows the object word "ball" to be uttered after the modifier "red"—a simple form of proto-grammar.)

To *learn* in this rule-based context, the agent must have the ability to modify its signal-processing rules. Such rule-modifying, learning abilities are innate capacities supplied by evolution. Learning abilities can also be expressed as rules—think of Hebb's (1949) learning rule in neuro-psychology—so it is important to distinguish these meta-rules for learning from the signal-processing rules that are the grist for the meta-rules. In agent-based models, the meta-rules are unchanging and common to all agents.

The LoC models described here are based on meta-rules that are demonstrably available to pre-primates. That is, the meta-rules are not language specific. There are two general learning tasks the agent must be able to carry out:

(i)   Credit-assignment

As an agent interacts it must be able to decide which of its rules are helpful and which are detrimental. At higher LoC the agent must even be able to determine which early-acting, stage-setting rules make possible later beneficial outcomes. (As an example, consider the sacrifice of a piece in a game like checkers in order to make a triple jump later.) The credit-assignment learning process assigns strengths to the rules. A rule's strength reflects its usefulness to the system, useful rules having high strengths. Rules then compete to control the agent, stronger rules have a better chance of winning the competition. In effect, the rules in this system are treated as hypotheses to be progressively confirmed or disconfirmed. (See Holland 1998, chap. 4).

(ii)   Rule discovery

Once rules have been rated by credit-assignment, it makes sense to replace rules that have little or no strength by generating new rules (hypotheses). Random generation of new rules is not an option here; that would be like trying to improve a computer program by inserting random instructions. Instead, newly generated rules must somehow be plausible hypotheses in terms of experience already accumulated. (See Holland 1995, chap. 2).

Requirement (ii) leads us to the final topic of this section, *building blocks* (Holland 1995, chap. 1, ff). Building blocks (*generators* in mathematics) have a familiar role in the sciences, best exemplified by the building block hierarchy of the physical sciences—the quark / nucleon / atom / molecule / membrane /… hierarchy. Selected combinations of building blocks at one level form the building blocks of the next level. For example, selected nucleons can be combined, much like children's building blocks, to yield the 92 atoms of classical physics. The atoms can in turn be combined to yield a vast array of molecules; the laws that constrain the combination of atoms were originally set out in the periodic table of the elements. Each level of the hierarchy can be understood in the same way. For spoken language there is a similar a phoneme / word / sentence hierarchy. A grammar specifies the laws that determine how words can be combined to yield sentences. As with atoms, a relatively small number of words, under the compact rules supplied by a grammar, can yield a vast array of sentences.

An important advantage of building blocks in the study of LoC is that the building blocks occur as repeated patterns in the ever-changing torrent of sensory input. That is, the building blocks provide repeatable experiences in a perpetually novel environment. The human face provides a clear example of the extraction and combination of building blocks to provide simple descriptions of complex objects. Indeed the highly variable pattern that we call a "face" can be represented by the combination of just a few building blocks, as exemplified by the "smiley face" emoticon ☺. By adding a few more building blocks we can describe an astonishing array of individual faces. To see this possibility, divide the face into 10 "features": "hair style", "forehead shape", "eye shape and so on (see Figure 9.4). Allow 10 alternatives for each feature. There are

Figure 9.4 Building blocks

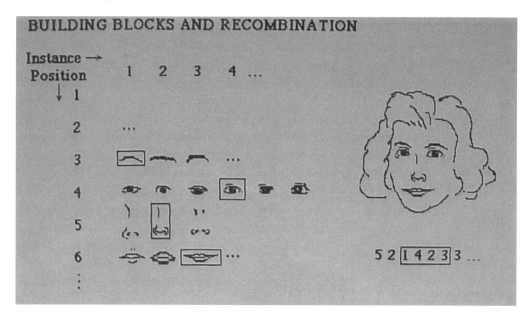

thus 100 building blocks in total. By selecting one alternative for each feature, we can form a complete face. 10 billion distinct faces can be formed in that way. Other important sensory inputs can be treated similarly. Moreover, these building blocks can be arrayed in a LoC hierarchy, similar to the hierarchy in the physical sciences.

When a building block is repeatedly associated with a rewarding event, such as food or a mother's smile, it becomes a sampled regularity that is associated with valuable experience. From the sampling point of view, the building block's reliability is continually tested under the credit assignment procedure. A confirmed building block becomes a plausible hypothesis when combined with other similarly distilled building blocks.

The random variation and imitation that accompany the earliest levels of consciousness provide a random sampling that helps uncover the most primitive building blocks, say phoneme-like utterances. Plausible new conditions and rules are generated by *recombining* building blocks already confirmed. The procedure is much like the crossbreeding of good plants (or animals) to get better plants. There is a substantial literature, centering on genetic algorithms (Holland 1995), that discusses the production of new rules in agent-based models via the crossing of extant rules. There is not space here to discuss genetic algorithms in detail, but it is a well-established procedure.

The meta-rules for credit assignment and rule discovery allow the neonate to achieve a gradual increase in control, corresponding to increasing LoC. The process begins with the acquisition of repeatable sound and gestures. Sounds and gestures reinforced by T become the building blocks for more complex utterances and gestures. For example, various combinations of 2 utterances, 3 utterances, and so on, provide substantial refinements in expression and meaning. The utterance "milk", at the child's single utterance stage, can have a variety of meanings: "give me some milk", "look at the milk bottle over there", and so on. Combining the two utterances "give" and "milk" greatly reduces this ambiguity. In mathematical terms we refine a broad equivalence class into a set of smaller, more informative sub-classes.

In this way, selected combinations of building blocks at one LoC become the building blocks for the next level. Building blocks, like grammars, offer combinatoric possibilities: a large variety of useful or meaningful structures can be constructed from a small number of building blocks. Moving up the LoC hierarchy thus becomes a much more efficient process than trying to "establish" a monolithic rule for each possibility at the highest LoC.

The discussion of credit assignment above pointed up the importance of strengthening "stage-setting" rules. Stage-setting, provided by the self-consciousness of Loc5, is the very essence of planning and autonomy. Autonomy of this kind requires that the agent be able to explore alternatives internally, without taking overt action. Rules so organized constitute an internal model. An agent with an internal model can internally explore possible sequences of action until a sequence leading to a desired outcome is located. Because the agent is dealing with sequences not yet executed, the "stage-setting" act in a sequence may not be obviously related to the last act in the sequence. For instance, in checkers, an agent may give up a piece to accomplish a later triple jump, or, in language, the agent may utter the first word of a sentence in preparation for a later utterance that will clarify the communication. Once the first act in the sequence is executed it causes a change in the environment and constrains what act(s) may be taken next. For instance, the rule set for the LoC5 example exhibits a case where the first rule executed produces an utterance which constrains what kind of utterance may follow. The study of internal models in a rule-based system is presented in Induction (Holland et al. 1986).

7. Summary

This paper is closely related to the manifesto produced by the "The Five Graces Group" at the Santa Fe Institute (Five Graces Group 2010). In particular, it explores the idea "that patterns of use strongly affect how language is acquired, used, and changes over time." Here we explore the effect of perceptual constraints and social motivation upon the newborn's increasing autonomy, described as "levels of consciousness" The resulting interlocked set of models does not try to parametrize the data presented here—the models are exploratory. Nevertheless, the models are constrained by this data and they do suggest how the data might arise. Indeed, the models are meant to suggest further experiments that will clarify both the data and the models.

Because this approach highlights the effects of social interaction on the acquisition of language, the treatment uses a complex adaptive systems (cas) framework, as suggested in the Five Graces manifesto. That is, we consider models in which multiple agents interact and learn from each other. Cas emphasize dynamics, and the agents therein rarely settle down to a static equilibrium. This suggests that each agent will develop its own idiolect and that agents that interact regularly will have many common constructions in their idiolects, a familiar finding of modern linguistics.

It is our intention to build executable versions of these models, testing them and extending human experiments in ways that will suggest improvements to the models. Above all, we would like to provide a strong, testable theoretical base for the "levels of consciousness" approach to language acquisition.

REFERENCES

Armstrong, D. M. 1981. What is consciousness? In *The Nature of Mind and Other Essays*, ed. D. M. Armstrong. Ithaca, New York: Cornell University Press.

Aslin, R. N., D. B. Pisoni, B. L. Hennessy, and A. J. Perey. 1981. Discrimination of voice onset time by human infants: New findings and implications for the effects of early experience. *Child Development* 52:1135–1145.

Bates, E. 1975. Peer relations and the acquisition of language. In *Friendship and Peer Relations: The Origins of Behavior*, eds. M. Lewis and L. Rosenblum, 259–292. New York: John Wiley and Sons.

Bates, E. 1999. Nativism vs. development: Comments on Baillargeon & Smith. *Developmental Science* 2 (2): 148–149.

Bates, E., and J. Goodman. 1997. On the inseparability of grammar and the lexicon: Evidence from acquisition, aphasia and real–time processing. *Language & Cognitive Processes* 12 (5/6): 507–586. [redacted version reprinted in Essential readings in language development, eds. M. Tomasello, and E. Bates. Oxford: Basil Blackwell, 2000].

Bates, E., and J. Goodman. 1999. On the emergence of grammar from the lexicon. In *The Emergence of Language*, ed. B. MacWhinney, 29–79. Mahwah, NJ: Lawrence Erlbaum.

Best, C. T., G. W. McRoberts, and N. M. Sithole. 1988. Examination of the perceptual reorganization for speech contrasts: Zulu click discrimination by English–speaking adults and infants. *Journal of Experimental Psychology: Human Perception and Performance* 14:345–360.

Bloom, L., L. Hood, and P. Lightbown. 1974. Imitation in language development: If, when and why. *Cognitive Psychology* 6:380–420.

Bowerman, M. 2004. From universal to language–specific in early grammatical development [Reprint]. In *The Child Language Reader*, eds. K. Trott, S. Dobbinson, and P. Griffiths, 131–146. London: Routledge.

Bowerman, M. 1990. Mapping thematic roles onto syntactic functions: Are children helped by innate linking rules? *Linguistics* 28:1253–1290.

Braitenberg, V. 1984. *Vehicles: Experiments in Synthetic Psychology*. MIT Press.

Brown, R., and C. Hanlon. 1970. Derivational complexity and order of acquisition in child speech. In *Cognition and the Development of Language*, ed. J. Hayes, 155–207. New York: Wiley.

Bruner, J. 1983. *Child's Talk: Learning to Use Language*. New York: Norton.

Carpenter, M., N. Akhtar, and M. Tomasello. 1998. Fourteen– to 18–month–old infants differentially imitate intentional and accidental actions. *Infant Behavior and Development* 21:S315–330.

Carruthers, P. 1996. *Language, Thought, and Consciousness: An Essay in Philosophical Psychology*. Cambridge University Press.

Carruthers, P. 2000. *Phenomenal Consciousness: A Naturalistic Theory*. Cambridge University Press.

Chomsky, N. 1975. *The Logical Structure of Linguistic Theory*. New York: Plenum Press.

Chomsky, N. 1967. Review of Skinner's verbal behavior. In *Readings in the Psychology of Language*, eds. L. A. Jakobovits, and M. S. Miron, 142–143. Prentice-Hall.

Chomsky, N. 1965. *Aspects of A Theory of Suntax*. MIT Press.

Chomsky, N. 1959. Review of verbal behavior, by B.F. Skinner. *Language* 35:26–57.

Chomsky, N. 1957. *Syntactic Structures*. Mouton.

Chomsky, N. 1955. *Logical Syntax and Semantics. Language*. January–March.

Cooper. 1994. Developmental differences in infant attention to the spectral properties of infant–directed speech. *Child Development* 65:1663–1677.

Cooper, R. P., and R. N. Aslin. 1990. Preference for infant–directed speech in the first month after birth. *Child Development* 61:1584–1595.

Creel S. C., E. L. Newport, and R. N. Aslin. 2004. Distant melodies: Statistical learning of nonadjacent dependencies in tone sequences. *Journal of Experimental Psychology: Learning, Memory, and Cognition* 30:1119–1130.

DeCasper, A. J., and M. J. Spence. 1986. Prenatal maternal speech influences newborns' perception of speech sounds. *Infant Behavior and Development* 9:133–150.

Deloache, J. S. 1995. Early understanding and use of symbols: The model model. *Current Directions in Psychological Science* 4:109–113

Ebeling, K., and S. Gelman. 1994. Children's use of context in interpreting "big" and "little." *Child Development* 65:1178–1192.

Ebeling, K., and S. Gelman. 1988. Coordination of size standards by young children. *Child Development* 59:888–896.

Eimas P. D., E. R. Siqueland, P. Jusczyk, and J. Vigorito. 1971. Speech perception in infants. *Science* 171:303–306.

Elder, J. L., and D. R. Pederson. 1978. Preschool children's use of objects in symbolic play. *Child Development* (49) 2:500–504.

Elman, J. L., E. A. Bates, M. H. Johnson, A. Karmiloff–Smith, D. Parisi, and K. Plunkett. 1996. *Rethinking Innateness: A Connectionist Perspective on Development*. Cambridge, MA: MIT Press.

Fernald, A. 1992. Human maternal vocalizations to infants as biologically relevant signals: An evolutionary perspective. In *The Adapted Mind*, eds. J. H. Barkow, L. Cosmides, and J. Tooby, 391–328. New York: Oxford University Press.

Fernald, A., and C. Mazzie. 1991. Prosody and focus in speech to infants and adults. *Developmental Psychology* 27 (2): 209–221.

Frye, D., P. D. Zelazo, and T. Palfai. 1995. Theory of mind and rule–based reasoning. *Cognitive Development* 10:483–527.

Gao, H. 2001. *The Physical Foundation of the Patterning of Physical Action Verbs: A Study of Chinese Verbs*. Lund, Sweden: Lund University Press.

Gao, H. H., and P. D. Zelazo. 2008. Language and development of consciousness: Degrees of disembodiment. In *Developmental Perspectives on Embodiment and Consciousness*, eds. W. F. Overton, U. Mueller, and J. Newman, 225–246. Mahwah, NJ: Erbaum.

Gao, H. H., P. D. Zelazo, D., Sharpe, and A. Mashari. under review. Beyond early linguistic competence: Development of children's ability to interpret adjectives flexibly.

Gopnik, A., and A. N. Meltzoff. 1997. *Words, Thoughts, and Theories*. Cambridge, Mass.: Bradford, MIT Press.

Hayes, S. C., D. Barnes–Holmes, and B. Roche, eds. 2001. *Relational frame theory A Post–Skinnerian Account of Human Language and Cognition*. New York: Kluwer Academic / Plenum Publishers.

Hazan V., and S. Barret. 2000. The development of phonetic categorization in children aged 6–12. *Journal of Phonetics* 28:377–396.

Hebb, D. O. 1949. *The Organization of Behavior*. Wylie.

Hoff, E. 2001. *Language Development*. 2nd edition. Belmont, CA: Wadsworth.

Holland, J. H. 1998. *Emergence: From Chaos to Order*. Addison–Wesley.

Holland, J. H. 1995. *Hidden Order: How Adaptation Builds Complexity*. Addison–Wesley.

Holland, J. H., K. J. Holyoak, R. E. Nisbett, and P. Thagard. 1986. *Induction: Processes of Inference, Learning, and Discovery*. Cambridge, MA: Bradford Books/ MIT Press.

Houston, D. M., and P. W. Jusczyk. 2000. The role of talker specific information in word segmentation by infants. *Journal of Experimental Psychology: Human Perception and Performance* 26:1570–1582.

Jacques, S., and P. D. Zelazo. 2005. Language and the development of cognitive flexibility: Implications for theory of mind. In *Why Language Matters for Theory of Mind*, eds. J. W. Astington, and J. A. Baird, 144–162. New York: Oxford University Press.

Jacques, S., P. D. Zelazo, N. Z. Kirkham, and T. K. Semcesen. 1999. Rule selection and rule execution in preschoolers: An error–detection approach. *Developmental Psychology* 35:770–780.

Johnson, E. K., and P. W. Jusczyk. 2001. Word segmentation by 8–month–olds: When speech cues count more than statistics. *Journal of Memory and Language* 44:548–567.

Kelly, G. A. 1955/1991. *The Psychology of Personal Constructs Vol.1: A Theory of Personality.* New York, US: Norton. 2nd printing: 1991, Routledge, London, New York

Kitamura, C., C. Thanavisuth, S. Luksaneeyanawin, and D. Burnham. 2002. Universality and specificity in infant–directed speech: Pitch modifications as a function of infant age and sex in a tonal and non–tonal language. *Infant Behavior and Development* 24:372–392.

Kuhl, P. K., J. E. Andruski, I. A. Chistovich, L. A. Chistovich, E. V. Kozhev–nikova, V. L. Ryskina, E. I. Stolyarova, U. Sundberg, and F. Lacerda. 1997. Cross–language analysis of phonetic units in language addressed to infants. *Science* 277 (5326): 684–686.

Locke, J. L. 1997. A theory of neurolinguistic development. *Brain and Language* 58:265–326.

Locke, J. L. 1993. *The Child's Path to Spoken Language*. Cambridge, MA: Harvard University Press.

Luria, A. R. 1961. *Speech and the Regulation of Behaviour*. London: Pergamon Press.

MacWhinney, B. 2004. A multiple process solution to the logical problem of language acquisition. *Journal of Child Language* 31:883–914.

MacWhinney, B. 1987. Toward a psycholinguistically plausible parser. In *Proceedings of the Eastern States Conference on Linguistics (ESCOL 1986)*, S. Thomason ed. Columbus, OH: Ohio State University.

Majid, A., M. Bowerman, S. Kita, D. B. M. Haun, and S. C. Levinson. 2004. Can language restructure cognition? The case for space. *Trends in Cognitive Sciences* 8 (3): 108–114.

Mandler, J. M. 1998. Babies think before they speak. *Human Development* 41:116–126.

Marcovitch, S., and P. D. Zelazo. 1999. The A–not–B error: Results from a logistic meta–analysis. *Child Development* 70:1297–1313.

Masataka, N. 1996. Perception of motherese in a signed language by 6–month–old deaf infants. *Developmental Psychology* 32:874–79.

Masataka, N. 1998. Perception of motherese in Japanese sign language by 6–month–old hearing infants. *Developmental Psychology* 34:241–46.

Maye J., J. F. Werker, and L. Gerken. 2002. Infant sensitivity to distributional information can affect phonetic discrimination. *Cognition* 82:B101–B111.

Mehler, J., P. Jusczyk, G. Lambertz, N. Halsted, J. Bertoncini, and C. Amiel-Tison. 1988. A precursor of language acquisition in young infants. *Cognition* 29:143–178.

Meltzoff, A. N., and M. K. Moore. 1997. Explaining facial imitation: A theoretical model. *Early Development and Parenting* 6:179–192.

Meltzoff, A. N., and M. K. Moore. 1977. Imitation of facial and manual gestures by human neonates. *Science* 198:75–78.

Meltzoff, A. N., and R. A. Williamson. 2013. Imitation: Social, cognitive, and theoretical perspectives. In *Oxford Handbook of Developmental Psychology*, ed. P. R. Zelazo, 651–682. NY: Oxford University Press.

Mills, D. L., C. Prat, R. Zangl, C. L. Stager, and H. J. Neville. 2004. Language experience and the organization of brain activity to phonetically similar words: ERP evidence from 14– and 20–month–olds. *Journal of Cognitive Neuroscience* 16:1452–1464.

Mintz, T. H., E. L. Newport, and T. G. Bever. 2002. The distributional structure of grammatical categories in speech to young. *Cognitive Science* 26:393–424.

Moore, D. S., M. J. Spence, and G. S. Katz. 1997. Six–month–olds' categorization of natural infant–directed utterances. *Developmental Psychology* 33:980–989.

Moscovitch, M. M. 1989. Confabulation and the frontal systems: Strategic versus associative retrieval in neuropsychological theories of memory. In *Varieties of Memory and Consciousness: Essays in Honour of Endel Tulving*, eds. H. L. Roediger, and F. I. M. Craik, 133–160, Erlbaum.

Newport, E. L., and R. N. Aslin. 2004. Learning at a distance I. Statistical learning of nonadjacent dependencies. *Cognitive Psychology* 48:127–162.

O'Reilly, A. W. 1995. Using representations: Comprehension and production of actions with imagined objects. *Child Development* 664:999–1010.

Overton, W. F., and J. Jackson. 1973. The representation of imagined objects in action sequences: A developmental study. *Child Development* 44:309–314.

Pederson, D., A. Rook–Green, and J. Elder. 1981. The role of action in the development of pretend play in young children. *Developmental Psychology* 17:756–95.

Perner, J., and B. Lang. 2002. What causes 3–year–olds' difficulty on the dimensional change card sorting task? *Infant and Child Development* 11:93–105.

Perner, J., and B. Lang. 1999. Development of theory of mind and executive control. *Trends in Cognitive Sciences* 3:337–344.

Piaget, J. 1962. *The Language and Thought of the Child*. London: Routledge & Kegan Paul. (*Le Langage et la Pensée Chez L'enfant*. 1923.)

Piaget, J. 1954. *The Construction of Reality in the Child*. New York: Basic Books. (*La Construction du Réel Chez L'enfant*. 1950, also translated as *The Child's Construction of Reality*. London: Routledge and Kegan Paul, 1955.)

Ramscar, M., and D. Yarlett. 2007. Linguistic self–correction in the absence of feedback: A new approach to the logical problem of language acquisition. *Cognitive Science* 31:927–960.

Roediger, R. 2004. What happened to behaviorism. *American Psychological Society* 17, Presidential Column.

Sacks, O. 1989. *Seeing Voices: A Journey into the World of the Deaf.* New York: Harper Perennial.

Saffran, J. R. 2001. Words in the sea of sounds: the output of infant statistical learning. *Cognition* 81:149–169.

Saffran, J. R., M. Hauser, R. Seibel, J. Kapfhamer, F. Tsao, and F. Cushman. 2008. Grammatical pattern learning by human infants and cotton–top tamarin monkeys. *Cognition* 107:479–500.

Saffran, J. R., E. L. Newport, R. N. Aslin, R. A. Tunick, and S. Barrueco. 1997. Incidental language learning: Listening (and learning) out of the corner of your ear. *Psychological Science* 8:101–105.

Schooler, J. W. 2002. Re–presenting consciousness: Dissociations between experience and metaconsciousness. *Trends Cognitive Science* 6:339–344.

Sheldon, A., and W. Strange. 1982. The acquisition of /r/ and /l/ by Japanese learners of English: Evidence that speech production can precede speech perception. *Applied Psycholinguistics* 3:243–261.

Singh, L., K. S. White, and J. L. Morgan. 2008. Building a word–form lexicon in the face of variable input: Influences of pitch and amplitude on early spoken word recognition. *Language Learning and Development* 4:157–178.

Skinner, B. F. 1957. *Verbal Behavior.* Acton, MA: Copley Publishing Group. ISBN 1–58390–021–7.

Smith, L., and C. Yu. 2008. Infants rapidly learn word–referent mappings via cross–situational statistics. *Cognition* 106:1558–1568.

Snow, C. E. 1999. Social perspectives on the emergence of language. In *The Emergence of Language*, ed. B. MacWhinney, 257–276. Mahwah, New Jersey: Lawrence Erlbaum.

Snow, C. E. 1972. Mothers' speech to children learning language. *Child Development* 43:549–565.

Spence, M. J., and M. S. Freeman. 1996. Newborn infants prefer the maternal low–pass filtered voice, but not the maternal whispered voice. *Infant Behavior and Development* 19:199–212.

Stern, D. N., S. Spieker, and K. McKain. 1982. Intonation contours as signals in maternal speech to prelinguistic infants. *Developmental Psychology* 18:727–735.

The Five Graces Group [C. Beckner, R. Blythe, J. Bybee, M. H. Christiansen, W. Croft, N. C. Ellis, J. H. Holland, J. Ke, D. Larsen–Freeman, and T. Schoenemann]. 2010. Language is a complex adaptive system. *Language Learning*.

The Five Graces Group [C. Beckner, R. Blythe, J. Bybee, M. H. Christiansen, W. Croft, N. C. Ellis, J. Holland, J. Ke, D. Larsen–Freeman, T. Schoenemann]. 2009. Language is a complex adaptive system. Position paper, *Language Learning* 59, Supplement 1:1–27.

Tomasello, M. 2003. *Constructing a Language: A Usage–based Theory of Language Acquisition.* Harvard University Press.

Tomasello, M., and E. Bates, eds. 2001. *Language Development: The Essential Readings.* Oxford: Basil Blackwell.

Tracy, J. L., and R. W. Robins. 2004. Putting the self into self–conscious emotions: A theoretical model. *Psychological Inquiry* 15:103–125.

Trainor, L. J., C. M. Austin, and R. N. Desjardins. 2000. Is infant–directed speech prosody a result of the vocal expression of emotion. *Psychological Science* 11:188–95.

Vygotsky, L .S. 1978. *Mind in Society.* Cambridge, MA: Harvard University Press.

Werker J. F., and R. C. Tees. 1999. Influences on infant speech processing. Toward a new synthesis. *Annual Review of Psychology* 50:509–535.

Werker J. F., and R. C. Tees. 1984. Cross–language speech perception: Evidence from perceptual reorganization during the first year of life. *Infant Behavior and Development* 7:49–63.

Werker, J. F., J. H. Gilbert, K. Humphrey, and R. C. Tees. 1981. Developmental aspects of crosslanguage speech perception. *Child Development* 52:349–355.

Werner, H., and B. Kaplan. 1963. *Symbol Formation: An Organismic—Developmental Approach to Language and the Expression of Thought.* New York: Wiley.

White K. S., and J. L.Morgan. 2008. Sub–segmental detail in early lexical representations. *Journal of Memory and Language* 59:114–132.

Zelazo, P. D. 2004. The development of conscious control in childhood. *Trends in Cognitive Sciences* 8:12–17.

Zelazo, P. D., H. H. Gao, and R. Todd. 2007. Development of consciousness. In *The Cambridge Handbook of Consciousness*, eds. P. D. Zelazo, M. Moscovitch, and E. Thompson, 405–434. New York: Cambridge University Press.

10

Contextual Predictability Facilitates Early Orthographic Processing and Semantic Integration in Visual Word Recognition: An Event-Related Potential Study

Chia-Ying LEE
The Institute of Linguistics, Academia Sinica

Yo-Ning LIU
The Institute of Linguistics, Academia Sinica
Institute of Neuroscience, National Yang-Ming University

Chia-Ju CHOU
Institute of Neuroscience, National Yang-Ming University

Foreword

Sentence comprehension depends on continuous prediction of upcoming words. However, it is largely unknown when and how contextual information affects bottom-up streams of visual word recognition. This study investigates this question by manipulating two variables, include contextual predictability (cloze probability of the sentence's ending word) and orthographic similarity (identical (ID), orthographically similar homophones (O + P+), and orthographically dissimilar homophones (O – P+) for the ending word, in an online sentence comprehension task. The data demonstrate a significant predictability effect at P200; low- predictability words elicited less positive P200 than did high-predictability words. This study finds interaction between predictability and orthographic similarity with different patterns at the anterior N1 and N400. Orthographic similarity only had an effect on anterior N1 with high-predictability sentences, where an identical character elicited greater N1 than both orthographically similar and dissimilar homophones did (ID > O + P+ = O – P+). However, in N400, graded orthographic similarity effects (O – P+ > O + P+ > ID) could be found in both high- and low-predictability sentences. These findings support the interactive account, suggesting that contextual information facilitates visual-feature and orthographic processing in the early stage and semantic integration in the later time window.

1.   Introduction

Most visual word-recognition models assume that recognition of a single presented word begins by extracting the sensory features of the word: the so-called bottom-up process. However, when a word is presented in sentential context, it is possible to anticipate the word based on semantic or syntactic expectations: the so-called top-down process. A substantial body of literature using a variety of measures shows that sentence comprehension depends on continuous prediction of upcoming words, and that processing of a word can be influenced by its preceding context (Dambacher et al. 2006; Duffy, Henderson, and Morris 1989; Federmeier 2007; Van Petten and Kutas 1990). Modular account (Forster 1981; Fodor 1983) and interactive account (McClelland and Rumelhart 1981; Morton 1969) models vary in describing *when* sentential context affects the time course of the bottom-up stream and *what kind* of information the context predicts. Temporal dynamics of integration between bottom-up lexical processing and top-down contextual prediction remain unclear. Event-related potentials (ERPs) effectively address this issue, providing excellent temporal resolution and multiple ERP components, such as N1, P200, N400 and P600, to index different stages of lexical processing (Barber and Kutas 2007). Most research views the N1 and P200 components as indexing visual feature analysis in the very early stage of word recognition (Vogel and Luck 2000; Hsu et al. 2009). The N400 indexes the ease of semantic activation or integration, showing that the poorer the fit of a word with the semantic representation of the context, the larger the N400 (Kutas and Hillyard 1980). This study utilizes ERPs to monitor the precise time course of contextual influence in visual word recognition, and to contrast predictions of modular and interactive views on *when* and *how* context affects lexical processing.

Earlier explanations of how a word is recognized assume that there is a mental lexicon associated with a pool of mentally stored information. Lexical access describes retrieval of such information or access to a discrete lexical entry, either via a search procedure (Forster and Chambers 1973) or by activating some threshold based on features extracted from the stimulus (Morton 1969). These traditional models usually divide visual word recognition into three stages: *pre-lexical*, *lexical* and *post-lexical processing* (Forster 1981; Fodor 1983). These terms describe the processes involved in analyzing the orthographic combinations that make up each word and in retrieving lexicosemantic and morphosyntactic information associated with the word form. Specifically, *pre-lexical processing* refers to any processing that takes place prior to achieving lexical access. It typically processes abstract features of sensory input, such as converting specific font information into an abstract letter code, and combining sublexical orthographic or phonological units to mediate word identification. *Lexical processing* is a fast and automatic stage of processing, matching sensory inputs with an entry in the mental lexicon that associates syntactic and semantic information. Once the match is made, functional characteristics associated with the lexical entry (i.e., its meaning and its grammatical characteristics) become available. Any processing using this information is therefore called post-lexical. *Post-lexical processing* is a slower and controlled stage of processing, combining linguistic information retrieved from the previous stage of lexical processing with contextual and background knowledge to integrate the new word with developing contextual information.

Two major accounts, the modular account (Fodor 1983; Forster 1979) and the interactive account (McClelland and Rumelhart 1981; Morton 1969), hold different assumptions about whether feedback exists from the higher to lower level of lexical processing. The *modular account* assumes that each level of lexical processing is an autonomous module, which operates independently of other processes in the system. The output of one module serves as the input to a second module; however, the internal operations of a given module are blind to the status of other modules. Thus, processing at one level of representation must be completed before its output can combine with information from other processing levels. In contrast, the *interactive account* assumes that information is unrestricted in its flow through the system once the appropriate sensory input initiates lexical processing. Thus, this account allows feedback from higher-level to lower-level representations, whereas modular models deny the existence of such feedback. The modular and interactive accounts hold different predictions on when and how contextual information influences processing of the upcoming word in sentence comprehension. The modular account predicts that contextual engagement can only occur at a post-lexical stage for semantic integration, while the interactive account allows the immediate and mutual contextual influence on processing of the upcoming word at different levels.

Common approaches to this question study how biasing context affects processing of ambiguous words. The modular view predicts that the two meanings of an ambiguous word (e.g., PORT) will be accessed in the same way regardless of any contextual bias (e.g., AFTER DINNER HE DRANK A GLASS OF PORT versus THE SHIP CAME INTO PORT). Since the lexical access mechanism can't 'know' what the context requires, contextual bias suppresses the inappropriate meaning at a postlexical stage, rather than preventing the inappropriate meaning from being accessed at all. In contrast, the interactive view claims that context affects the lexical access level immediately, so that only a single meaning is accessed. Studies using the cross-modal priming paradigm show that, at the immediate test point, both readings of the ambiguous word generate significant levels of priming even in a biasing context. A 200 msec delay permits facilitation only for targets related to a reading of the ambiguous word biased by the context (Swinney 1979; Tanenhaus, Leiman, and Seidenberg 1979). These results demonstrate initial access to all readings of ambiguous words; inappropriate readings are then rapidly suppressed, thus appearing to favor the modular account.

ERP studies usually evaluate the impact of context on reading comprehension by manipulating the degree of fit between the context and its upcoming word as semantic congruency (Kutas and Hillyard 1980, 1980, 1984), predictability (Dambacher and Kliegl 2007; Dambacher et al. 2006; Van Petten and Kutas 1990), or sentential constraint (Federmeier et al. 2007; Hoeks, Stowe, and Doedens 2004). They typically determine contextual influence via the cloze procedure, where participants complete a sentence fragment with the first word that comes to mind. The cloze probability of a word refers to the percentage of people who would complete a sentence frame with that particular word (Taylor 1953). A well-replicated finding shows that N400 amplitudes are inversely proportional to the cloze probability. As a sentence in Kutas and Hillyard's (1984) study: *He liked lemon and sugar in his tea/coffee*, the larger the cloze probability of a word (*tea*) in a context, the more reduced the amplitude of N400 compared to an unexpected word (*coffee*) (Kutas and Hillyard 1984). The stronger the expectation for a specific final word, the smaller the amplitude of the N400 if that word is actually presented. Contradictory, words that make the sentence implausible or semantically anomalous give rise to a larger N400. The N400 thus reflects the influence of contextual information in word recognition. Facilitation of word-processing in a sentence reflects the extent to which the context pre-activates specific properties of those words.

To further examine the interaction between the sentence and word levels, studies not only manipulate the contextual constraint but also the lexical properties of an upcoming word, such as word frequency. Tracking the word-frequency effect across behavioral and electrophysiological paradigms is particularly relevant because its presence is considered a marker for successful lexical access (Embick et al. 2001; Sereno and Rayner 2003). The word-frequency effect represents the difference in responses to high-frequency (HF) words (most commonly used) and low-frequency (LF) words (occurring less frequently). ERP data clearly show that word frequency modulates the N400. With all other factors held constant, N400 amplitude is an inverse function of a word's eliciting frequency (Bentin, McCarthy, and Wood 1985; Rugg 1990). Based on the modular view, contextual integration occurs later, during N400. Van Petten and Kutas (1990) showed that the effect of frequency on N400, in which low-frequency words elicited larger N400 than high-frequency words, was modulated by word position. The effect of frequency on N400 was only evident when the word occurred early in the sentence, but not at a later position in the sentence. Presumably, word position reflects the build-up of context 'online'. The interaction between word frequency and word position implies that the frequency effect of lexical processes can be superseded by the sentence's contextual constraint. Studies have also shown that semantic contextual constraints can override N400 frequency effects (Dambacher et al. 2008; Dambacher et al. 2006; Embick et al. 2001).

Sereno et al. (2003) used ERPs to examine the temporal locus of contextual influence on word frequency and word ambiguity. The contextual effect, coincident with frequency effect, was found in the N1 component from 132 to 192 msec post-stimulus (Sereno, Brewer, and O'Donnell 2003). ERP literature generally considers the N1 to index the visual signal associated with the very early stage of word recognition. Sereno et al's. (2003) findings suggest that the context affects selection of the appropriate meaning of an ambiguous word in the early stage of lexical processing and thus support the interactive view. Penolazzi et al. (2007) found word frequency and probability reflected at 120 and 180 msec after written word onset. Other studies also found frequency by predictability interaction (Hauk, Patterson, et al. 2006; Penolazzi, Hauk, and Pulvermüller 2007; Dambacher et al. 2006, Lee, Liu, and Tsai 2012) and semantic coherence effect (Hauk, Davis, et al. 2006) as early as 130 or so msec in the early stage of lexical processing. These results indicate that semantic context integration may take place at a surprisingly early stage and near simultaneously with the processing of information about the form and lexical properties of a word. That supports the early access theory, which assumes that genuine lexical access, involving retrieval of lexicosemantic properties, occurs at early stage (within 200 msec) of lexical processing.

However, the *late access theory* suggests that the early processing of visually presented word involves bottom-up visual feature analysis of the word form representations, which might consist of sets of bigram, trigram or higher-order combinations of (abstract) letter representations

(Pylkkanen and Marantz 2003; Solomyak and Marantz 2009; Dehaene et al. 2005). The contextual effect in early stage of lexical processing, such as N1 or P200, does not imply that access to lexicosemantic information occurs within the first stages of lexical access. In contrast, contextual information may act in an anticipatory or predictive manner and exert its effect from the early stage of word recognition, such as early perceptual features analysis, to the later stage of lexical activation and selection (Federmeier 2007; Lee et al. 2012).

Solomyak and Marantz (2009) indicated that many studies supporting the early access theory were based on the early effect of lexicality or frequency (Hauk, Patterson, et al. 2006; Penolazzi, Hauk, and Pulvermüller 2007; Dambacher et al. 2006; Sereno, Brewer, and O'Donnell 2003). However, both lexicality and word frequency are highly correlated with the familiarity of a word form. The early effect might be attributed to word form recognition, rather than genuine lexical access. Solomyak and Marantz (2009) tried to distinguish the abstract word-form process from genuine lexical access in the brain by examining the visual recognition of heteronyms. Heteronyms (like 'wind', referring to two different meanings depending on the pronunciation) are phonological and semantically distinct words that share a common orthography. They provide a unique opportunity to distinguish between the processing of lexical property (the frequency ration of one meaning to the other) and word-form properties (open bigram, trigram and whole-word-form frequencies) in the early stages of processing. Solomyak and Marantz (2009) showed a significant effect of heteronym's form properties in left hemisphere M170 and of heteronym frequency ration in M350. The heteronyms' true lexical properties did not affect processing until after 300 msec post-stimulus supports the late access theory. This finding also suggests that the early frequency effect that previous literature reports may only reflect abstract word-form identification rather than genuine lexical access (Solomyak and Marantz 2009).

Taken all together, literature has consistently shown that the N400 is sensitive to the expectancy of a word in a semantic context, while it is still unclear whether early components, such as N1 or P200, would also index the retrieval of lexicosemantic properties of a word in such an early time window across studies. A few studies have shown these early ERP effects under the influence of physical or prelexical variables, such as word length, bigram and trigram frequencies (Hauk, Davis, et al. 2006; Hauk and Pulvermüller 2004). However, frequency usually confounds with word length and the early components are typically focal and short in duration. Mixed usage of words with different lengths or other physical factors may affect or attenuate these short-lived early ERP effects more strongly than widespread long-lasting ERP components, such as N400 or M350. Thus, physical properties of the stimulus must be well-controlled or explicitly taken into account to clarify the functional characteristics of these early ERP effects in sentence comprehension.

The English and Chinese writing systems differ in their orthographic features and in how these features map onto the phonological structure of words. English is an alphabetical language that uses letters and letter combinations to represent the sounds of words. In contrast, the Chinese writing system uses square-shaped characters as the basic reading unit that link directly to monosyllabic sounds but not to phonemes. In modern Chinese, there are approximately 420 syllables (before consideration of tone) mapping onto around 5,000 different characters. On average, 11 characters share a single pronunciation. Moreover, approximately 80% of Chinese characters are phonograms that consist of a semantic and a phonetic radical to provide clues of the meaning and the pronunciation of the character, respectively. Homophonic characters may or may not share graphical forms, such as 罐 (/guan/, means 'a jar'), 灌 (/guan/, means 'to fill') are orthographically similar homophones sharing the same phonetic radical, while 罐 (/guan/, means 'a jar') and 慣 (/guan/, means 'to be accustomed') are orthographically dissimilar homophones which contain no common orthographic structure. These unique characteristics enable us to manipulate orthographic similarity, bypassing possible confusion from phonological similarity, word form frequency, and word length, which are typical confounds in examining orthographic effect in English.

This study takes the advantages of orthographic characteristics in Chinese to further delineate the nature of predictive processing mechanisms in sentence comprehension, especially in the early stage of lexical processing. The effects of contextual predictability (cloze probability) and orthographic similarity (identical, orthographically similar homophone, and orthographically dissimilar homophone) of the ending word in the sentence will be measured in N1, P200 and N400. This allows researchers to examine (i) whether the information brought online by contextual prediction is specific enough to affect processing based on orthographic information and (ii) at what functional stage of word recognition pre-activated information begins to interact with bottom-up processing of visually presented sentence completions.

2.   Methodology

2.1   Participants

Twenty-one right-handed native Chinese speakers (eight males) were paid to participate in this experiment (mean age = 22.4 years, range: 18–29 years), with no history of neurological or psychiatric disorders. All participants were native Chinese speakers with normal or corrected-to-normal vision. Written consent was obtained from all participants.

2.2   Experimental design and materials

The contextual predictability (high versus low) and orthographic similarity of the target word were manipulated in a 2-by-3 factorial design. Two hundred and sixteen sentences, which contain 12 or 16 characters with a two-character target word in the end, were selected for this experiment based on the pilot test using a predictability rating task. All sentences were divided into high- and low-predictability groups, based on the predictability of the final word. Predictability of the final word for each sentence was rated by 32 college students who did not participate in the ERP experiment. In this rating task, participants were presented with sentence fragments preceding the target words and were asked to complete each sentence fragment with the word that first came to their minds. Then, participants were instructed to press the space bar and an assigned two-character target word was presented on the center of screen. Participants were then instructed to perform a five-point predictability rating by pressing the number on the keyboard (1 to 5) based on the following criteria: (1) This is not what I wrote down. There are too many possible answers. The target word can never come to my mind. (2) This is not what I wrote down. There are too many alternatives that can be filled in the sentence. If I think more carefully, the target word may come to my mind. (3) This is not what I wrote down. It will be my next choice, given that there are only a few alternatives which could complete the sentence. (4) This is not what I wrote down. However, they are synonyms or semantically similar words, given there are only a few alternatives that could complete the sentence. (5) This is exactly what I wrote down and there are only a few alternatives that could complete the sentence. One hundred and eight sentences (mean rating score 4.57, mean score for each selected sentence must above 4) were assigned as the high-predictability group and the other 108 sentences (mean rating score 2.95, mean score for each selected sentence must below 2.5) were assigned as the low-predictability group.

Table 10.1 Examples and characteristics of stimuli for each condition

	High Predictability			Low Predictability		
	家裏常見的備用糧食像是鮪魚*罐頭* Tuna *can* is the common reversed food in the family			他認為自己絕對不會*犯錯* He thinks he would never make any *mistakes*		
	Identical 罐頭	O+P+ 灌頭	O−P+ 慣頭	Identical 犯錯	O+P+ 氾錯	O−P+ 泛錯
Predictability	4.52	4.6	4.61	1.93	2.19	2.04
Stroke	12.25	12.62	13.42	12.61	12.97	11.89
Character frequency	812.61	566	608.22	752.44	515.61	800.17
Word frequency	53.33	60.25	40.97	64.31	39.44	45.92
NS	42.5	45.39	44.42	47.19	32.67	38.36
NS1	9.42	14.47	11.53	9.58	7.94	14.11

The two-character target words were embedded in the end of the sentence. The average word frequency was 50.7 per million words. There are three types of identification for the initial character of the target word: (i) identical character (Id), (ii) orthographically similar homophone (sharing the same phonetic radical (O + P+); (iii) orthographically dissimilar homophone (O − P+). The frequency of target word, initial character frequency, and number of strokes of the target characters were not significantly different among the three conditions. Table 10.1 shows these properties and the example of a target with matched previews.

2.3   Procedure

Participants were individually seated at a distance of approximately 70 cm in front of a monitor, in an acoustically shielded room. Each participant received 12 trials for practice and 216 randomized experimental trials in four test blocks. Participants could take a break between test blocks for as long as they needed. For each trial, a cross fixation presented in the left side of the screen indicated that a sentence fragment preceding the target words would appear starting from this position after 800 msec. Participants were instructed to read for comprehension. The sentence would remain on the screen until the participants pressed the space bar to indicate they had finished reading this sentence. The sentence would then be replaced by two short vertical lines presented on the center of the screen for 500 msec. Participants were required to look at the middle point between the two short lines and not to move their eyes or blink once a trial began. The vertical lines would be followed by a blank for a random duration of 200, 250 or 300 msec as jitter. A target word was then presented between the two short lines for 250 msec and replaced by a blank for 450 msec. A question mark '?' was then presented on the screen to instruct participants to perform a five-point predictability rating by pressing the number on the keyboard (1 to 5) based on the same criteria used in the pilot study. The '?' remained on the screen until the participant responded or until an interval of five seconds had passed. Prior to the beginning of the next trial, a capital letter 'B' was presented for 1000 msec as a signal for the participants to blink. The whole experiment last approximately 30 minutes.

2.4   EEG recording and preprocessing

An electroencephalogram (EEG) was recorded from 64 sintered Ag/AgCl electrodes (QuickCap, Neuromedical Supplies, Sterling, Texas, USA) with a common vertex reference located between Cz and CPz. The EEG was continuously recorded and digitized at a rate of 500 Hz. The signal was amplified by SYNAMPS2 (Neuroscan Inc., El Paso, Texas, USA) with a low-pass filter of 100 Hz for off-line analysis. The data were re-referenced off-line to the average of the right and left mastoids for further analysis. Vertical eye movements were recorded by a pair of electrodes placed on the supraorbital and infraorbital ridges of the left eye and horizontal eye movements by electrodes placed lateral to the outer canthus of the right and left eyes. A ground electrode was placed on the forehead anterior to the FZ electrode. Electrode impedance remained below 5 kΩ.

For off-line analysis, the continuous wave was epoched with 100 msec before the onset of the target word and 700 msec post-stimulus intervals. The pre-stimulus interval (-100 msec–0 msec) was used for baseline correction. Trials contaminated by eye movement or with voltage variations larger than 60μV were rejected. The band-pass filter of 0.1 and 30 Hz (zero phase shift mode, 12 dB) was employed. The ERPs were calculated for each participant and each condition for every electrode.

3.   Result

3.1   Behavioral data

Table 2 shows the averaged predictability (plausibility) rating score and reaction time for each condition. These data were subjected to a repeated measures analysis of variance (ANOVA) with two levels of predictability (high and low) and three levels of orthographic similarity (Id, O+P+, and O-P+). For reaction time, results showed significant main effects of predictability ($F_{(1, 20)}$ = 92.77, p < .0001). The reaction time for the high-predictability condition was much faster than that for low predictability condition. Both the main effect of orthographic similarity and the interaction between predictability and orthographic similarity were insignificant (ps > .1). For subjective rating score, results showed significant main effects of predictability ($F_{(1, 20)}$ =18.12, p < .01). The high predictability condition showed higher score than low predictability condition. Both the main effect of orthographic similarity and the interaction between predictability and orthographic similarity were insignificant (ps > .1).

Table 10.2   Mean and standard deviation of plausible rating score for each condition

	High Predictability		Low Predictability	
	RT	score	RT	score
Id	594	4.25	1083	2.78
O+P+	623	4.21	1081	3.02
O-P+	618	4.36	1138	2.99

3.2   ERP data

Figure 10.1 and Figure 10.2 show the grand averaged ERPs at representative electrodes. As the figures show, three major components were identified for further analysis. The first distinct negative peak was N1, which was set around 100 msec at fronto-central sites. The following component was P200, which was a positive-going wave reaching its peak around 220 msec, and was most prominent at the fronto-central electrodes. The N1 and P200 were typical ERP components in visual-stimuli experiments. The third one was N400, a negative deflection following the N1–P200 complex, which peaked around 350 msec with central-parietal distribution. Effects of frequency and predictability were accessed by comparisons of mean amplitudes in these three time windows of interest: N1 (90–140 msec), P200 (200–250 msec), and N400 (250–450 msec).

The repeated measures of ANOVA were performed on these components, with factors of predictability (high or low), orthographic similarity (Id, O + P+ or O – P+), and electrodes in the region of interest. For each ANOVA, the Greenhouse–Geisser adjustment to the degrees of freedom was applied to correct for violations of sphericity associated with repeated measures. Accordingly, for all F tests with more than one degree of freedom in the numerator, the corrected p-value is reported. The post-hoc tests were carried out using Tukey's procedure.

Figure 10.1 The grand average ERPs for the predictability effect at represented electrodes

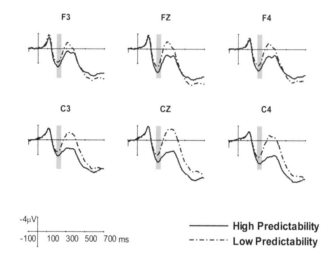

Figure 10.2 The grand average ERPs for all conditions at represented sites
(a) N400 effect in high predictatbility context. (b) N400 effect in low predictatbility context.

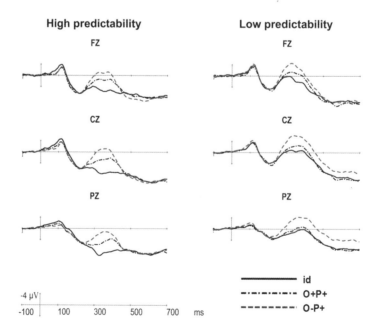

3.3 Anterior N1

The mean amplitude of N1 was analyzed by a three-way ANOVA with predictability (high and low), orthographic similarity (ID, O + P+ and O − P+) and electrode (FZ, FCZ, CZ, F3/4, FC3/4, C3/4) as within-subject factors. The data showed that the main effect of both predictability ($F_{(1,20)}$ = 3.77, p = 0.067) and orthographic similarity ($F_{(2,40)}$ = 1.97, p = .157) was insignificant. The two-way interaction between predictability by orthographic similarity ($F_{(2,40)}$ = 3.64, p=.041) and three-way interaction among predictability, orthographic similarity, and electrode interaction ($F_{(16,320)}$ = 2.58, p =.029) were significant. The post-hoc test showed that the interaction between predictability and orthographic similarity was significant in all electrodes (ps < .0001). Moreover, the orthographic similarity effect was only significant in the reading of high predictability word ($F_{(2,40)}$ = 4.96, p = .011), but not significant in the low predictability word ($F_{(2,40)}$ = 1.93, p = .15). Pairwise comparison revealed that in a high-predictability condition, ID condition showed more negativity N1 than both O + P+ ($F_{(1,40)}$ = 5.71, pv= .021) and O -P+ ($F_{(1,40)}$ = 8.83, p = .005) conditions. However, O + P+ and O − P+ did not significantly differ from each other ($F_{(1,40)}$ = 0.34, p = .563).

3.4 P200

The mean amplitude of P200 was analyzed by a three-way ANOVA with predictability (high and low), orthographic similarity (ID, O + P+ and O − P+) and electrode (FZ, FCZ, CZ, F3/4, FC3/4, C3/4) as within-subject factors. The data reveal a significant main effect of predictability ($F_{(1,20)}$ = 18.43, p < .001) and significant interaction between predictability and electrode ($F_{(8,160)}$ = 5.02, p = .002). The post-hoc test reveals a significant predictability effect in every electrode (ps < .0001). The high- predictability words elicited more positive P200 than low-predictability words did. Both the main effect of orthographic similarity and the interaction between predictability and orthographic similarity failed to reach significant (ps > 0.1).

3.5 N400

The mean amplitude of N400 was conducted separately on the data derived from the midline and lateral sites by the three-way ANOVAs with predictability (high and low), orthographic similarity (ID, O + P+ and O − P+) and electrode in the region of interest as within-subject factors. For midline analysis, five electrodes (FZ, FCZ, CZ, CPZ, and PZ) were selected for midline N400 analysis. For lateral N400, ten electrodes (F3/4, FC3/4, C3/4, CP3/4, and P3/4) were chosen as the electrode variable.

The midline analysis revealed a significant predictability effect ($F_{(1,20)}$ = 133.32, p < .0001). A low-predictability word demonstrated more negativity N400 than a high predictability-word did. In addition, the main effect of orthographic similarity ($F_{(2,40)}$ = 100.53, p < .0001) and the interaction between predictability by orthographic similarity ($F_{(2,40)}$ = 29.02, p = .03) were also significant. Post-hoc tests revealed that the orthographic similarity effects were significant for both high-predictability ($F_{(2,40)}$ = 50.43, p < .0001) and low-predictability words ($F_{(2,40)}$ = 29.02, p < .0001), but with somewhat different patterns.

In high-predictability condition, O-P+ elicited larger negative N400 than ID ($F_{(1,40)}$ = 99.15, p < .0001) and O + P+ ($F_{(1,40)}$ = 14.79, p = .0004). The O + P+ also elicited greater N400 than ID ($F_{(1,40)}$ = 37.75, p < v.0001). In low-predictability condition, O – P+ elicited largest N400 than those form the other two conditions (O – P+ versus ID: $F_{(1,40)}$ = 55.36, p < .0001; O – P+ versus O + vP +: $F_{(1,40)}$ = 26.39, p < .0001).The difference between O + P+ and ID was smaller but remained significant difference (ID versus O + P+: $F_{(1,40)}$ = 5.31, p = .026).

Lateral analysis showed significant main effects of predictability ($F_{(1,20)}$ = 107.57, p < .001) and orthographic similarity ($F_{(4, 80)}$ = 3.90, p = .048). The interaction between predictability and orthographic similarity was also significant ($F_{(2,40)}$ = 3.77, p = .036). Post hoc test revealed that the orthographic effect was significant at both high-predictability ($F_{(2,40)}$ = 47.52, p < .001) and low-predictability conditions ($F_{(2,40)}$ = 27.23, p < .001). The interactions between hemisphere and predictability ($F_{(1,20)}$ = 28.77, p < .0001) and between hemisphere and orthographic similarity ($F_{(2,40)}$ = 3.48, p = .048) were significant. Post-hoc tests revealed that interactions between predictability and orthographic similarity were significant at both right and left hemispheres (ps < .001). Pairwise comparison showed that all three conditions differed significantly from each other in high-predictability condition: O – P+ condition elicited the most negative N400 and the ID condition elicited the less negative one (ID versus O + P+: $F_{(1,40)}$ = 35.36, p < .001; ID versus O - P+:v$F_{(1,40)}$ = 93.39, p < .001; O + P+ versus O – P+: $F_{(1,40)}$ = 13.82, p < .001). For low-predictability condition, a similar pattern was found (ID versus O – P+: $F_{(1,40)}$ = 51.57, p < .001; O + P+ versus O – P+: $F_{(1,40)}$ = 25.62, p < .001), except that the difference between ID and O + P+ (ID versus O + P+: $F_{(1,40)}$ = 4.49, p = 040) was much smaller than that in high-predictability condition.

4.   Discussion

This study investigates how context influences different stages of lexical processing by manipulating the contextual predictability and orthographic similarity of ending words in the sentences. The behavioral data shows the reaction time was only modulated by contextual predictability, and not orthographic similarity. This suggests that participants were still able to retrieve the expected word meaning to give a predictability rating, regardless of whether the target characters were replaced by their orthographically similar or dissimilar homophones. The higher predictability of the target word, the faster reaction time the participant would have.

The ERP data revealed a significant predictability effect at P200, low-predictability words elicited less positive P200 than high-predictability words did. This is congruent with previous findings and suggests the highly-predictable context provides top-down information and facilitates early visual processing of the target word (Federmeier, Mai, and Kutas 2005). The interactions between predictability and orthographic similarity were found at the anterior N1 and N400, but exhibited different patterns. These findings suggest the functional signatures of contextual effect on different stages of lexical processing might be somewhat different.

Previous studies show the contextual effect within 100 msec at anterior or posterior regions (Dambacher et al. 2009; Hauk, Patterson, et al. 2006; Sereno, Brewer, and O'Donnell 2003), suggesting a top-down influence on pre-activated form-based representations. For example, Hauk, et al. (2006) examined the cortical activation elicited by words and pseudo-words that varied in orthographic typicality (the frequency of their component letter pairs (bigrams) and triples (trigrams)). The typicality effect was found within 100 msec after stimulus onset, in which word and pseudo-words with atypical orthography elicited stronger activity in left perisylvian areas (regions extending from Wernicke's area to the posterior/inferior parietal cortex and prefrontal cortex) than those with typical orthographic patterns. Lexicality (words versus pseudo-words) interacts with orthographic typicality around 160 msec. Their data suggest distinct but interactive processing stages in word recognition, from early form-based analysis to the later lexicosemantic processes. This is further supported by Lee and her colleagues's study (2012), which demonstrated the presentability by frequency interaction at anterior N1. With the orthogonal manipulation of contextual predictability and orthographic similarity of the ending word in the sentence, the present study shows the interaction between these two parameters at anterior N1 around 100 msec after the onset of target words. The orthographic similarity effect on anterior N1 only appeared in high-predictability sentences, in which the identical character elicited greater N1 than both orthographically similar and dissimilar homophones did. However, there is no difference between orthographically similar and dissimilar homophones. These findings provide the direct evidence of top-down influence on early orthographic processing, in which the context might afford form-specific predictions for the upcoming words (Lee et al., 2012).

Foxed and Simpson (2002) provided a time frame for the initial trajectory of information flow along the dorsal and ventral visual processing streams (around 56 msec) and on into prefrontal cortex (around 80 msec) of the human (Foxe and Simpson 2002). This early frontal activation might reflect anticipatory responses generated in response to the cue stimulus. The rapid flow of activation through the visual system to parietal and prefrontal cortices (less than 30 msec) provides a context for appreciating the 100–400 msec commonly needed for information processing prior to response output in humans. This supports information processing involving extensive interactions between all levels of cortical systems. Frontal activation can occur early enough (with respect to sensory cortical activation) to be involved in initial alerting functions and subsequent, more fine-tuned top-down influences on sensory processing. In fact, the N1 component, an early visual component, is part of the typical response to visual stimulation. It is widely distributed over the whole scalp, with an earlier peak over frontal than over posterior regions (Mangun and Hillyard 1991; Mangun, Hillyard, and Luck 1993; Ciesielski and French 1989). The anterior N1 often reflects a benefit of correctly-allocated attention resources and is a manifestation of an important sensory gating mechanism of attention. For example, in the visual cueing paradigm, the N1 amplitude is largest for perceptual features in attended (vs. unattended) locations and on attended (vs. unattended) objects, providing evidence that perceptual features are only selected for further perceptual processing if they are in attended locations or on attended objects (Martinez et al. 2006; Anllo-Vento and Hillyard 1996). In this study, the identical character eliciting the largest anterior N1 was only found in high-predictability contexts, suggesting that context plays a role in directing attention to specific sensory features early in the information processing stream. When the expected character is presented, the largest N1 can be evident. This is congruent with the early-selection model of attention, which contends that attention acts as a sensory gain mechanism that enhances perception of the expected stimuli.

The interaction between predictability and orthographic similarity was also evident in the N400 time window; though the pattern is somewhat different from that in the N1. Typical graded orthographic-similarity effects (O-P+ >O+P+ >ID) were found in both high- and low-predictability sentences. The difference of N400 amplitude between expected character (ID) and its orthographic neighbor (O+P+) is smaller in a low-predictability context than that in a high-predictability context. In the literature, the N400 amplitudes are reduced by several factors, such as higher word frequency, repetition, or word-level priming involving orthographic, phonological or semantic feature overlap between prime and target. Such factors also include supportive context information at the sentence or discourse level that might be expected to ease processing for semantic retrieval or integration. The general explanation for how these factors reduce N400 amplitude is that information associated with items that share a high level of overlap with an target stimuli tend to become active in parallel, easing the semantic retrieval of the target word.

The current finding shows that N400 amplitudes for the identical word are markedly reduced than those elicited by the unexpected orthographic neighbor, especially under the highly-predictable context. Nevertheless, the orthographic neighbor of the expected ending word elicited a smaller N400 than the orthographically dissimilar homophone. The findings suggest that, although participants eventually would realize that they were presented with an orthographic neighbor of the expected word rather than the expected completion itself, the orthographic neighbors are to some extent being processed as if they were target characters. It is congruent with previous findings showing that the orthographic neighbors of expected sentence completions elicited smaller N400s than did orthographically unrelated items (Laszlo and Federmeier 2009). The orthographic features provided by the orthographic neighbor of the expected character facilitate the semantic retrieval of the expected word and the semantic integration with the context. The present data shows that contextual predictability modulates how orthographic similarity facilitates the semantic retrieval of the upcoming word in a different way. In the literature, the constraining effect from the message level often overrides the effect from word level, in which the effects from word level (such as frequency or orthographic effects) were mainly found in low-predictability contexts (Coulson et al. 2005; Van Petten et al. 1999). Contradictorily, in this study, the reduction of N400 for expected item (ID) when compared to its orthographic neighbor (O+P+) is larger in high-predictability contexts than in low-predictability ones. It may be due to the expected item receiving greater facilitation from the high-predictability context, which enlarges the difference between N400 amplitude for an expected character (ID) and its orthographic neighbor (O+P+) in the high-predictability context. It further suggests that the later stage of lexical processing, indexed by N400, mainly reflects the interactive effect for ease of semantic integration triggered by information provided from both sentence and word level.

This study's data shows that contextual information affects orthographic similarity in a different way on the early ERP component of anterior N1 than the later component of N400. In the early stage of lexical processing, the N1 reflects the attention-cueing effect predicated on the visual features of the upcoming word. Only under highly-predictable contexts did the presence of the expected word elicit a larger anterior N1. The orthographic neighbor of the expected ending word did not differ significantly from the orthographically dissimilar control. This suggests that contextual information facilitates the visual-feature and orthographic processing in the early stage. While in the later stage of lexical processing, a graded orthographic similarity effect was evident in N400, indexing both the ease of meaning retrieval of the expected word and semantic integration into sentence comprehension. This data supports the interactive view: contextual information facilitates visual-feature and orthographic processing in the early stage, and semantic integration at a later stage.

Acknowledgments

This work was supported by grants from Taiwan National Science Council (NSC 99-2410-H-004-091 -MY2 and NSC 101-2628-H-001-006-MY3).

REFERENCES

Anllo-Vento, L., and S. A. Hillyard. 1996. Selective attention to the color and direction of moving stimuli: Electrophysiological correlates of hierarchical feature selection. *Perception and Psychophysics* 58 (2): 191–206.

Barber, H. A., and M. Kutas. 2007. Interplay between computational models and cognitive electrophysiology in visual word recognition. *Brain Researsh Review* 53 (1): 98–123.

Bentin, S., G. McCarthy, and C. C. Wood. 1985. Event-related potentials, lexical decision and semantic priming. *Electroencephalography and Clinical Neurophysiology* 60 (4): 34–55.

Ciesielski, K. T., and C. N. French. 1989. Event-related potentials before and after training: Chronometry and lateralization of visual N1 and N2. *Biological Psychology* 28 (3): 227–238.

Coulson, S., K. D. Federmeier, C. Van Petten, and M. Kutas. 2005. Right hemisphere sensitivity to word- and sentence-level context: Evidence from event-related brain potentials. *Journal of Experimental Psychology Learning Memory and Cognition* 31 (1): 129–47.

Dambacher, M., K. Goellner, A. Nuthmann, A. Jacobs, and R. Kliegl. 2008. Frequency and predictability effects on event-related potentials and eye-movements. *International Journal of Psychology* 43 (3–4): 46–47.

Dambacher, M., and R. Kliegl. 2007. Synchronizing timelines: Relations between fixation durations and N400 amplitudes during sentence reading. *Brain Research* 1155:147–162.

Dambacher, M., R. Kliegl, M. Hofmann, and A. M. Jacobs. 2006. Frequency and predictability effects on event-related potentials during reading. *Brain Research* 1084 (1): 89–103.

Dambacher, M., M. Rolfs, K. Göllner, R. Kliegl, and A. M. Jacobs. 2009. Event-related potentials reveal rapid verification of predicted visual input. *PLOS ONE* 4.3.

Dehaene, S., L. Cohen, M. Sigman, and F. Vinckier. 2005. The neural code for written words: A proposal. *Trends in Cognitive Sciences* 9 (7): 335–341.

Duffy, S. A., J. M. Henderson, and R. K. Morris. 1989. Semantic facilitation of lexical access during sentence processing. *Journal of Experimental Psychology Learning Memory and Cognition* 15 (5): 791–801.

Embick, D., M. Hackl, J. Schaeffer, M. Kelepir, and A. Marantz. 2001. A magnetoencephalographic component whose latency reflects lexical frequency. *Cognitive Brain Research* 10 (3): 345–348.

Federmeier, K. D. 2007. Thinking ahead: The role and roots of prediction in language comprehension. *Psychophysiology* 44 (4): 491–505.

Federmeier, K. D., H. Mai, and M. Kutas. 2005. Both sides get the point: Hemispheric sensitivities to sentential constraint. *Memory & Cognition* 33 (5): 871–886.

Federmeier, K. D., E. W. Wlotko, E. De Ochoa-Dewald, and M. Kutas. 2007. Multiple effects of sentential constraint on word processing. *Brain Research* 1146:75–84.

Fodor, J. A. 1983. *The Modularity of Mind*. Cambridge, MA: MIT Press.

Forster, K. I. 1979. Levels of processing and the structure of the language processor. In *Sentence Processing: Psycholinguistic Studies Presented to Merrill Garrett*, eds. W. E. Cooper, and E. C. T. Walker, 27–85.

Forster, K. I. 1981. Priming and the effects of sentence and lexical contexts on naming time—Evidence for autonomous lexical processing. *Quarterly Journal of Experimental Psychology Section a—Human Experimental Psychology* 33 (Nov): 465–495.

Forster, K. I., and S. M. Chambers. 1973. Lexical access and naming time. *Journal of Verbal Learning and Verbal Behavior* 12 (6): 627–635.

Foxe, J. J., and G. V. Simpson. 2002. Flow of activation from V1 to frontal cortex in humans. A framework for defining 'early' visual processing. *Experimental Brain Research* 142 (1): 139–150.

Hauk, O., M. H. Davis, M. Ford, F. Pulvermuller, and W. D. Marslen-Wilson. 2006. The time course of visual word recognition as revealed by linear regression analysis of ERP data. *Neuroimage* 30 (4): 1383–1400.

Hauk, O., K. Patterson, A. Woollams, L. Watling, F. Pulvermuller, and T. T. Rogers. 2006. [Q:] When would you prefer a SOSSAGE to a SAUSAGE? [A:] At about 100 msec. ERP correlates of orthographic typicality and lexicality in written word recognition. *Journal of Cognitive Neuroscience* 18 (5): 818–832.

Hauk, O., and F. Pulvermüller. 2004. Effects of word length and frequency on the human event-related potential. *Clinical Neurophysiology* 115 (5): 1090–1103.

Hoeks, J. C., L. A. Stowe, and G. Doedens. 2004. Seeing words in context: The interaction of lexical and sentence level information during reading. *Brain Research Cognitive Brain Research* 19 (1): 59–73.

Hsu, C. H., J. L. Tsai, C. Y. Lee, and O. J. Tzeng. 2009. Orthographic combinability and phonological consistency effects in reading Chinese phonograms: An event-related potential study. *Brain and Language* 108 (1): 56–66.

Kutas, M., and S. A. Hillyard. 1980. Event-related brain potentials to semantically inappropriate and surprisingly large words. *Biological Psychology* 11 (2): 99–116.

Kutas, M., and S. A. Hillyard. 1980. Reading senseless sentences: Brain potentials reflect semantic incongruity. *Science* 207 (4427): 203–205.

Kutas, M., and S. A. Hillyard. 1984. Brain potentials during reading reflect word expectancy and semantic association. *Nature* 307 (5947): 161–163.

Laszlo, S., and K. D. Federmeier. 2009. A beautiful day in the neighborhood: An event-related potential study of lexical relationships and prediction in context. *Journal of Memory and Language* 61 (3): 326–338.

Lee, C. Y., Y. N. Liu, and J. L. Tsai. 2012. The time course of contextual effects on visual word recognition. *Frontiers in Psychology* (3): 285.

Mangun, G. R., and S. A. Hillyard. 1991. Modulations of sensory-evoked brain potentials indicate changes in perceptual processing during visual-spatial priming. *Journal of Experimental Psychology: Human Perception and Performance* 17 (4): 1057–1074.

Mangun, G. R., S. A. Hillyard, and S. J. Luck. 1993. Electrocortical substrates of visual selective attention. *Attention and Performance XIV*, 219–243.

Martinez, A., W. Teder-Salejarvi, M. Vazquez, S. Molholm, J. J. Foxe, D. C. Javitt, F. Di Russo, M. S. Worden, and S. A. Hillyard. 2006. Objects are highlighted by spatial attention. *Journal of Cognitive Neuroscience* 18 (2): 298–310.

McClelland, L. James, and David E. Rumelhart. 1981. An interactive activation model of context effects in letter perception: Part 1. An account of basic findings. *Psychological Review* 88 (5): 375–407.

Morton, J. 1969. Interaction of information in word recognition. *Psychological Review* 76 (2): 165–178.

Penolazzi, B., O. Hauk, and F. Pulvermüller. 2007. Early semantic context integration and lexical access as revealed by event-related brain potentials. *Biological Psychology* 74 (3): 374–388.

Pylkkanen, L., and A. Marantz. 2003. Tracking the time course of word recognition with MEG. *Trends in Cognitive Sciences* 7 (5): 187–189.

Rugg, M. D. 1990. Event-related brain potentials dissociate repetition effects of high- and low-frequency words. *Memory and Cognition* 18 (4): 367–379.

Sereno, S. C., C. C. Brewer, and P. J. O'Donnell. 2003. Context effects in word recognition: Evidence for early interactive processing. *Psychological Science* 14 (4): 328–333.

Sereno, S. C., and K. Rayner. 2003. Measuring word recognition in reading: Eye movements and event-related potentials. *Trends in Cognitive Sciences* 7 (11): 489–493.

Solomyak, O., and A. Marantz. 2009. Lexical access in early stages of visual word processing: A single-trial correlational MEG study of heteronym recognition. *Brain and Language* 108 (3): 191–196.

Swinney, D. A. 1979. Lexical access during sentence comprehension: (Re) Consideration of context effects. *Journal of Verbal Learning and Verbal Behavior* 18 (6): 645–659.

Tanenhaus, M. K., J. M. Leiman, and M. S. Seidenberg. 1979. Evidence for multiple stages in the processing of ambiguous words in syntactic contexts. *Journal of Verbal Learning and Verbal Behavior* 18 (4): 427–440.

Van Petten, C., S. Coulson, S. Rubin, E. Plante, and M. Parks. 1999. Time course of word identification and semantic integration in spoken language. *Journal of Experimental Psychology Learning Memory and Cognition* 25 (2): 394–417.

Van Petten, C., and M. Kutas. 1990. Interactions between sentence context and word frequency in event-related brain potentials. *Memory and Cognition* 18 (4): 380–393.

Vogel, E. K., and S. J. Luck. 2000. The visual N1 component as an index of a discrimination process. *Psychophysiology* 37 (2): 190–203.

11

Larynx Height and Constriction in Mandarin Tones

Scott MOISIK, Hua LIN, John ESLING
University of Victoria

Abstract

We use *simultaneous laryngoscopy and laryngeal ultrasound* (SLLUS) to examine citation form tones in Mandarin. With this methodology, several observations are made concerning the production of Mandarin tone in citation form. We find that the larynx rises continually during level tone production, and this is interpreted as a means to compensate for declining subglottal pressure. We also find that two production strategies are attested for low tone production: (i) larynx lowering and (ii) larynx raising with laryngeal constriction. We conclude that extra-glottal laryngeal mechanisms play important roles in producing or facilitating the production of tone targets and should be integrated into the contemporary articulatory model of tone production.

1.   Introduction

In this paper we employ *simultaneous laryngoscopy and laryngeal ultrasound* (SLLUS; Moisik, Esling, Bird and Lin 2011) to assess laryngeal mechanisms involved in producing Mandarin tones. Electromyographic (EMG) research by Sagart, Halle, Boysson-Bardies and Arabia-Guidet (1986), Erickson (1993) and Hallé (1994) has shown indirectly that changes in larynx height do occur during tone production in Mandarin and Thai, but direct observation of larynx height or larynx state has not been pursued to the same extent. This may be partly due to the lack of techniques available to observe and measure these factors in the execution of tone (concerning larynx height, see Honda 2004). Understanding how glottal pitch can be influenced by larynx height and changes in larynx state provides us with a basis to better model the linguistic role of the connection between the systems governing vocal fold oscillation and the rest of the vocal tract (Honda 1995).

The basic role of larynx height in the execution of tone is complicated by the relationship of larynx height to the state of the larynx: constriction of the supra-glottal laryngeal structures is facilitated by increasing larynx height (Edmondson and Esling 2006) and inhibited by lowering the larynx. Laryngeal constriction can have substantial consequences on the dynamics of the vocal folds by changing their configuration and mechanical relationship to other laryngeal structures such as the ventricular folds (Laver 1980). The connection between larynx height and state, however, has not been fully explored in the context of a tone language and it is the aim of this study to address this by the application of the SLLUS technique to Mandarin.

We present evidence that larynx height and laryngeal constriction are active in Mandarin tone production and serve a facilitating or compensatory role to the primary musculature responsible for pitch regulation. Our findings generally complement those of Sagart et al. (1986) and Hallé (1994) that larynx height positively correlates with F_0 in Mandarin tones; however, we observe that the action of the laryngeal constrictor mechanism and its relation to larynx height complicates this analysis. Beyond the widely attested observation (Honda, Hirai, Masaki and Shimada 1999) that larynx lowering is the *de facto* correlate of pitch lowering, we find that larynx raising in conjunction with laryngeal constriction can also yield low pitch. Furthermore, we observe both larynx raising and lowering mechanisms are employed by a single participant to accomplish different types of tone targets, largely depending on rate of pitch change. Our proposal is that, in addition to cricothyroid joint rotation, laryngeal constriction and larynx height regulate the vertical relationship of the laryngeal structures. The critical effect this has is to change the relationship between the vocal folds and the ventricular folds: we believe this can have an effect on vocal fold dynamics and propose a model for why this would be so.

An important feature of our study is the use of the SLLUS technique to study both larynx height and larynx state at the same time. The two techniques involved, laryngoscopy and laryngeal ultrasound, complement each other: laryngoscopy is ideal for obtaining information about the state of the larynx, but it only provides a limited impression of changes in the vertical position of the larynx, whereas laryngeal ultrasound can be used to quantify changes in larynx height, although it is not an optimal means to study laryngeal state. The simultaneous use of these two techniques provides us with a more complete picture of laryngeal behaviour than one could obtain with either technique independently or with indirect measurements using EMG.

Furthermore, larynx height has been one of the more difficult vocal tract parameters to measure (Honda 2004; Honda et al. 1999, 402), and our approach illustrates how ultrasound can serve as a convenient and robust tool to quantify larynx height.

The quantification of larynx height from the laryngeal ultrasound data involves the use of optical flow analysis (Horn and Schunck 1981). Optical flow analysis creates discrete velocity fields that represent movement between pairs of frames and these can be used to study object kinematics observed in video data. The optical flow algorithm employed in this study is a simple, custom, block-wise cross-correlation based assessment movement tendencies from pixel data in pairs of contiguous frames (discussed at length in Section 3). Very little research has been done which employs optical flow analysis to study video data of speech processes (one example is Barbosa, Yehia and Vatikiotis-Bateson 2008), and optical flow has not previously been applied to ultrasound data in speech research.

2.   Methodology

Modern Standard Mandarin is chosen as the subject of study since its tone system is relatively well understood, it is easy to find fluent speakers, and the set of tones is relatively small and therefore more tractable to describe. We restrict ourselves for this study to just the citation form of the tones in order to focus on canonical effects of larynx height and state and avoiding the complicating factors of intonation and tone sandhi.

The basic tones of Mandarin are high-level (T1), mid-rising (T2), low-rising (T3), and high-falling (T4) (Lin 1998, 2001). Three participants volunteered to take part in the research project. Two of them are native speakers and they will be referred to throughout as Participant M (male) and Participant F (female). We also obtained elicitations from a highly trained phonetician, whom we will refer to as *Participant P*, and his productions were judged by several native Mandarin speakers (including the two other participants in this study) to be highly natural sounding. We consider his data to represent careful phonetic productions of the tones.

2.1   Speech material

Target Mandarin words with [i] vowels were selected to optimize the laryngoscopic view of the larynx, which tends to be obscured by the epiglottis during retracted vowel production. A list of all of the targets used in the study can be found in the Appendix. Both monosyllables and disyllables were elicited. Only the final syllable was used in analysis of the disyllables. The speech material was elicited in list format.

Target forms in Pinyin were presented to Participant P while target forms written in Chinese characters were presented to Participant M and Participant F. Each participant was instructed to repeat the target items three times, although in practice this did not always occur (due to time limitations of the laryngoscopic examination). Table 11.1 provides a summary of the number of tokens for each tone by participant and by context used in the analysis (see Section 4).

Table 11.1 Number of tokens by tone and context

	Participant-P	Participant-M	Participant-F
	Citation	Citation	Citation
T1	10	30	16
T2	9	44	24
T3	8	97	18
T4	8	40	20
Total	35	211	78

2.2 Simultaneous laryngeal ultrasound & laryngoscopy (SLLUS)

For the SLLUS methodology, a standard laryngoscopic examination was performed and the physician in charge was seated in front of the participant while simultaneously the laryngeal ultrasound examination was performed by approaching the subject from the side (see Moisik, Esling, Bird, and Lin 2011).

The ultrasound machine used was a portable LOGIQ e R5.0.1 system (2004, General Electric Corporation) with an 8C-RS probe (also developed by General Electric). The probe pulse frequency was 10 MHz, which allowed for optimal resolution of laryngeal structures. The field of view was consistently set to 120°. A Sennheiser ME66-K6 shotgun microphone was used during the examination to record the audio signal, which was digitized at 44100 Hz (16 bit), using an M-Audio Mobile Pre-Amp as an external sound card. The video of the ultrasound machine was captured using an XtremeRGB video card at 30 fps (uncompressed, 8-bit grey scale, 1024 x 768 pixels) and both signals were integrated using Sony Vegas Pro (version 8.0b).

The laryngoscopy equipment used in this study is an Olympus ENF-P3 flexible fiberoptic nasal laryngoscope fitted with a 28 mm wide-angle lens to a Panasonic KS152 camera. The video signal was recorded using a Sony DCR-T4V17 digital camcorder. The camcorder also recorded an additional audio signal to aid in synchronization of the laryngoscopy data with the laryngeal ultrasound. As with the laryngeal ultrasound video, all laryngoscopy video was post-processed using Sony Vegas Pro for alignment of the video and audio signals.

During each examination, the participants were seated in an examination chair equipped with a head rest to support the head and help provide stabilization. The ultrasound probe was applied manually to each subject's right thyroid lamina near the laryngeal prominence. The probe was held such that the examiner's index finger and thumb were free to anchor on the participant's laryngeal prominence and side of the neck, respectively. This helped to maintain a consistent probe placement during the examination. Before elicitation commenced, the participant was instructed to produce an [i] vowel at a normal pitch so that the vocal folds could be located and centered in the ultrasound view.

Once all data was captured and assembled into Sony Vegas Pro, each token was manually segmented into a pair of files: one for the laryngeal ultrasound and one for the laryngoscopy, each with its own audio track. During the segmentation process, care was taken to ensure that alignment was maintained amongst all of the signals. The two audio signals could be compared at the sample level for precision of global alignment between the laryngoscopy and the laryngeal ultrasound. Alignment between the audio and video of each of these data sources was confirmed through manual inspection.

2.3   Data analysis

Temporal regions of interest (ROIs) were defined over the voiced part of the syllable being analyzed and the STRAIGHT algorithm (Kawahara, de Cheveigné and Patterson 1998) was used to obtain F_0 traces of this region. Larynx state was assessed using laryngoscopic video frames within the ROI. The primary objective of this analysis is to identify the activity of the laryngeal constrictor mechanism (Edmondson and Esling 2006; Esling and Harris 2005). The approach taken is to categorize the images of the larynx using two criteria: whether the larynx is constricted (C) or not (U) and whether the larynx appears to be raised (R), at neutral height (N), or lowered (L). Additionally, a (+) and a (−) are used to add further specificity to the observed larynx height change. Observing changes in larynx height from the laryngoscopic video allows us to corroborate the larynx height change results obtained from the laryngeal ultrasound video.

To track vertical larynx movement, we use a technique called *optical flow analysis* (cf. Horn and Schunck 1981). Optical flow is an image analysis technique that allows movement recorded in a sequence of adjacent video frames to be quantified as a discrete velocity field. The optical flow algorithm employed here is a block-wise, cross-correlation based method developed for this study using MATLAB (version R2009a). Each pair of contiguous frames is decomposed into a grid of equal sized pixel blocks (15 x 15 pixels). (For more details on the implementation of optical flow for ultrasound research we refer the reader to Esling and Moisik (2012)).

Once the optical flow field has been generated, movement is determined by averaging the top 25% of vectors (based on magnitude). Velocity along a particular dimension is determined simply by obtaining the value for the vertical component in the averaged flow vector across time (from one frame pair to the next). The velocity data can then be numerically integrated with a cumulative trapezoidal integrator to obtain an estimate of the evolution of movement along a particular dimension over time. Since no constant of integration can be supplied to the algorithm (because, in the case of the present study, absolute laryngeal height is unknown), the integrator starts at zero displacement. Finally, since the optical flow algorithm measures movement primarily in units of pixels, the output of the algorithm is scaled into units of millimetres. This scaling is possible because the ultrasound machine superimposes a ruler on the side of the ultrasound image it creates, allowing for quantification of movement in familiar units of distance.

The algorithm was validated using a control video of a metal bar sliding along a ruler. The bar velocity was measured manually and with the algorithm. The normalized RMS error of the optical flow estimate of the velocity function (by comparison to the manual measurement) is 12.17%. The estimated displacement value differs from the actual value by 1.8%. We take these results to indicate sufficient accuracy for our present purposes, although we plan on conducting future validation studies to improve the accuracy (and processing speed) of the algorithm.

3.   Results

The results are broken into two sections: Section 3.1 presents time normalized contour data of F_0 and larynx height analyzed Smoothing Spline ANOVA (SS ANOVA). Then, in Section 3.2, we present case studies of noteworthy tokens.

3.1   Analytical overview: SSANOVA of F_0 and larynx height

In this section, time-normalized plots of F_0 and larynx height illustrate the overall movement patterns of the larynx in relation to the tonal F_0 contours for each of the four Mandarin tones by context. Smoothing Spline ANOVAs (SSANOVA; see Davidson 2006) were performed to create each of the time-normalized contour plots. The contour lines show the smoothing spline fit for each of the tones and the gray regions show the 95% Bayesian confidence intervals (based on the ANOVA component of the SSANOVA algorithm). Regions where the intervals overlap are not significantly different. Wider confidence intervals are a product of greater variance in the data (particularly for Participant F 's larynx height data). Tones are labelled on each plot and the line style designates specific tones: T1 is the solid line, T2 is the dash-dotted line, T3 is the dashed line and T4 is the dotted line.

The data for Participant P (male, phonetician) are illustrated in Figure 11.1. We take these productions to represent canonical phonetic forms of the four tones, with T1 level, T2 mid-rising, T3 low-rising, and T4 falling. When these F_0 contours are considered in relation to the larynx height contours, some notable patterns emerge. First, although T1 is produced with a relatively stable F_0, the larynx shows a tendency to gradually rise through the production of the tone; we will show below that this also occurs for the other participants. For T2 and T4, the larynx height contours generally reflect the corresponding F_0 contours. There is, however, a difference in the rate of change between the F_0 contours of T2 and T4 that is not reflected in the larynx height pattern. Finally, T3 first exhibits larynx lowering, with the larynx reaching its nadir roughly halfway through the tone where the F_0 is also low; the larynx then ascends in correspondence with the rising F_0 at this point.

The relationship between F_0 and larynx height for Participant M is illustrated in Figure 11.2. The F_0 contours alone for this participant are characteristic for citation form productions of the tones and are parallel to the canonical forms produced by the phonetician (Participant P). The relationship between larynx height and F_0 for the native speaker is also similar to what we observed for the canonical forms produced by the phonetician. T1 in citation form shows a stable F_0 in correspondence with a gradually rising larynx position. T2 and T4 once again show a strong relationship between F_0 contour and larynx height contour, although the velocity of change is evidently greater for F_0 than for larynx height.

Contour plots for Participant F (female, native) are shown in Figure 11.3. Once again, the expected F_0 contour patterns are observed, and thus all three participants agree in this regard. The larynx height contours for Participant F have broader Bayesian confidence intervals than they do for the other participants: this indicates more variance in the data for this participant.

Figure 11.1   Time-normalized plots of F_0 and larynx height

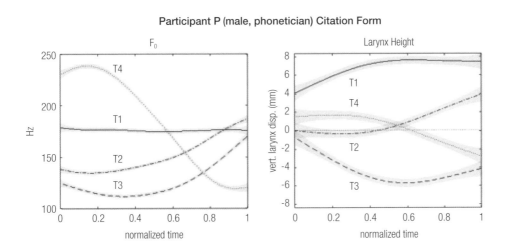

Figure 11.2   Time-normalized plots of F_0 and larynx height

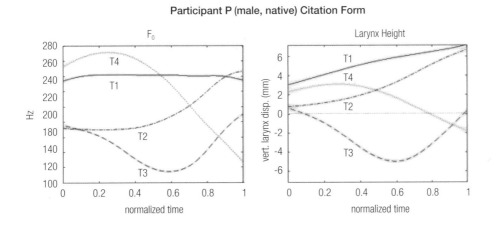

Figure 11.3 Time-normalized plots of F_0 and larynx height

Participant F (female, native) Citation Form

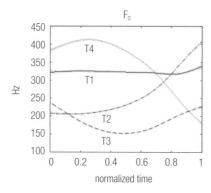
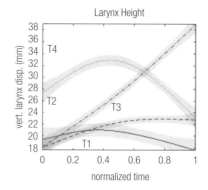

Nevertheless, clearly distinguishable larynx height patterns still emerge from the SSANOVA. T1 shows an initial rise in larynx height and then a slight descent while F_0 is relatively flat. T2 and T4 show larynx height contours that generally correspond with the F_0 movement pattern, but there is some asynchrony. Larynx movement during T2 in citation form is nearly linear with a high rate of change; however, the F_0 for T2 shows a delayed rise. In T4, larynx height reaches peak towards the middle of the production despite F_0 reaching its peak much earlier. For T4, F_0 and larynx height do descend nearly synchronously and with similar slopes. Note that T4 shows the most larynx lowering of any of the tones, although there is no net descent across the tone since the descent follows an initial rise. The persistently high laryngeal position for T3 is unexpected, particularly since this tone has the lowest F_0 of all the tones. This stands in stark contrast to the male participants (P and M), who show the greatest degree of larynx lowering for the low part of T3.

Overall then we have observed the following facts about the nature of larynx height during citation or canonical Mandarin tone production. T1 shows gradual larynx raising. T2 and T4 show a positive relationship between larynx height and F_0, but F_0 exhibits a higher rate of change than larynx height. T3 shows two patterns with regard to the low F_0 part: Participant P and Participant M use larynx lowering and Participant F uses larynx raising. Finally, larynx height generally increases or decreases with F_0 but the change is not always perfectly synchronous.

3.2   Careful phonetic production of Mandarin tones

Several case studies of individual tone tokens for each of the participants are presented in this section to illustrate the full methodology of simultaneous laryngoscopy and laryngeal ultrasound (SLLUS) and to support the observations made in Section 3.1. The reason for selection of the illustrated tones will be made clear in each subsection and, due to space limitations, not all tones are illustrated. In general, the selection is based on the clarity of the laryngoscopy, how well a given token illustrates a participant's canonical production strategy, and how clearly the laryngoscopy corroborates the larynx height data. Each of the case studies shows the acoustic waveform, F_0 contour, larynx height contour (change in larynx height), and four manually selected laryngoscopy frames (the time locations of which are marked on the plots with dashed vertical lines and the corresponding frame number to facilitate identification). Laryngoscopy videos are marked with code letters to indicate the qualitative assessment of the state of the larynx according to whether it is constricted or not (constricted = C; unconstricted = U) and the estimated height of the larynx (L = lowered; N = neutral; R = raised); Plus '+' and minus '−' marks indicate finer detail in terms of raising and lowering, respectively, relative to other frames. No laryngeal ultrasound frames are illustrated because these are not as useful as the larynx height contour itself in interpreting the data patterns.

3.2.1 SLLUS case study of native production of Mandarin tones

We have chosen to exhibit T1 and T3 for both participants (M and F). The other tones, T2 and T4, represent the expected cases where the larynx height correlates positively with F_0. We take T1 as the control case to illustrate the appearance of the individual's larynx. The surprising results appear for T3 when we compare the productions of the two speakers. While Participant M exhibits the canonical larynx lowering pattern to achieve the low F_0 target, Participant F exhibits the opposite laryngeal movement and the laryngoscopy allows us to identify that the raising is associated with activation of the laryngeal constrictor.

First we present two case studies for Participant M. The first case study is of T1 (Figure 11.4), which again exhibits larynx raising on the order of 4 mm despite static F_0. The laryngeal state for this tone is unconstricted. We can confirm this by comparing Frames 21 and 28, which occur during the syllable, with Frames 14 and 35, which occur immediately before and after

Figure 11.4 Case study of Participant M's T1 in /ji⁵⁵/
Traces of the shape of the laryngeal constrictor and glottis are found below. LH = larynx height; Solid outline = epilaryngeal tube; dotted lines = ventricular folds; solid line = glottis.

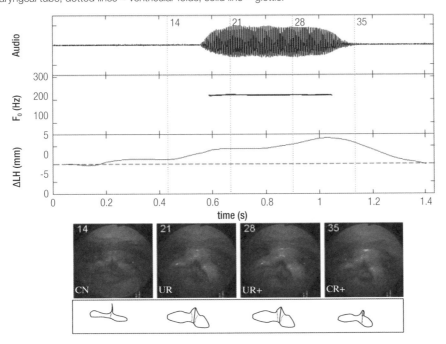

the syllable, respectively. Manual traces of the laryngeal states have been added for clarity. The shape of the larynx in these initial and final example frames is more constricted than what we see for the medial example frames corresponding to the tone, where the larynx assumes its typical state for this speaker associated with modal phonation. Constriction for Participant M is manifest as ventricular incursion and narrowing of the antero-posterior dimension of the epilaryngeal tube, which is particularly evident in Frame 14. The slight rise in larynx height that occurs just prior to this state (between 0.2 and 0.4 s) is likely attributable to this configuration, which favours larynx raising (Edmondson and Esling 2006).

The next case study for Participant M now looks at T3 (Figure 11.5), where we observe larynx lowering in conjunction with F_0 lowering and an overall strong visual correlation between the F_0 and larynx height contours. Critically, we do not observe any form of laryngeal constriction occurring during the low part of the tone visible in Frames 12 and 18. The shape of the epilaryngeal aperture does not undergo significant reduction in the antero-posterior dimension and the relationship between the ventricular folds and vocal folds is consistent from one frame to the next. The laryngoscopy thus provides us with corroborating support for what is observed in the larynx height change data itself. Therefore, but laryngeal state can be considered constant for this example.

The situation is different for Participant F, who employs a larynx raising strategy for low F_0 production during T3. First we demonstrate in Figure 11.6 the appearance of this participant's unconstricted laryngeal state using T1 as an example. The larynx height contour indicates that the larynx rises slightly by about 2 mm during the production of this tone, but we do not observe much change in laryngeal state in the laryngoscopy. Again, the antero-posterior dimension of the larynx is held fixed throughout and the vocal folds are not obstructed by the ventricular folds.

By comparison, the appearance of the larynx during T3 production undergoes a visible change as seen in Figure 11.7: it increases in its degree of constriction during the low F_0 region of the tone illustrated by Frames 18 and 24. The constriction is evident as, once again, reduction of the antero-posterior distance of the epilaryngeal tube and ventricular incursion, although the latter is somewhat difficult to see since the right cuneiform tubercle is obstructing these structures. In fact, the observation that the cuneiform tubercle is in contact with the tubercle of the epiglottis provides an argument that the constriction is particularly strong in this example. It is also important to point out that the auditory quality of phonation becomes increasingly tense and ultimately creaky during the low part of T3 in general. Creakiness is evident in the audio waveform in Figure 11.7, particularly between 0.6 and 0.8 s and in other tokens of this tone for this speaker.

Frames 12 and 30 illustrate the appearance of the larynx during the peripheral parts of this tone where F_0 is relatively high: here we do not observe laryngeal constriction of the same extent as in Frame 18 and 24. It is likely that larynx height is acting in two ways in this example. The larynx is raised during the entire tone and thus can be interpreted as facilitating high tone production, which we have observed in general. The low part of the tone, however, engages a new mode of phonation which is complementary to low F_0 production: creakiness. Since creakiness can be a result of laryngeal constriction (Esling and Harris 2005), and laryngeal constriction is complemented by larynx raising, it stands to reason that the larynx raising is also acting to facilitate or help induce the laryngeal constriction and thus the low tone target.

Figure 11.5   Case study of Participant M's T3 in /ji²¹³/

Traces of the shape of the laryngeal constrictor and glottis are found below. LH = larynx height; Solid outline = epilaryngeal tube; dotted lines = ventricular folds; solid line = glottis.

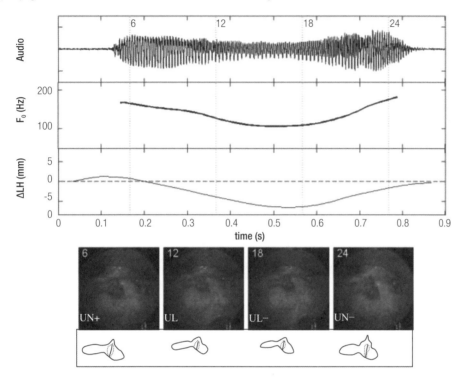

Figure 11.6 Case study of Participant F's T1 in /pi⁵⁵/

LH = larynx height.

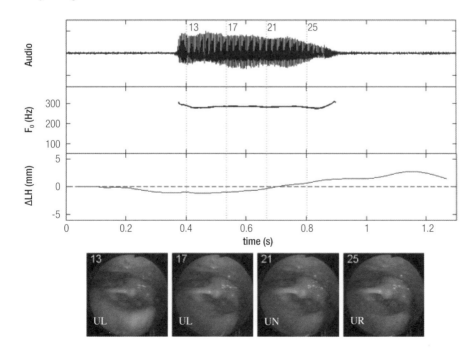

Figure 11.7   Case study of Participant F's T3 in /pi^{213}/

I H = larynx height

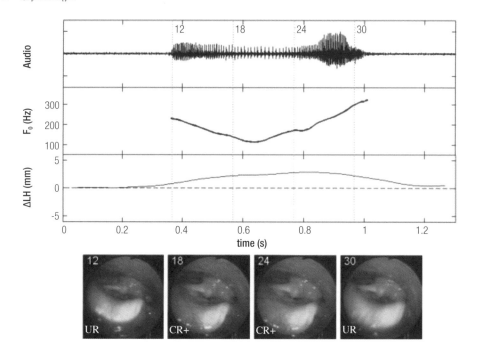

4.   Discussion: Laryngeal Strategies for Tone Production

This section provides discussion of the two key observations emerge from the results. Section 4.1 interprets the general role of larynx height in achieving the citation form tone targets in Mandarin, which pertains to the differing laryngeal behaviour by gender of our participants and the fact that T1 was consistently produced with larynx raising for all speakers. In Section 4.2 we will address the observation that there are two strategies for the production of low F_0 tone targets, which was particularly striking for T3, where the males used larynx lowering and the female used larynx raising in conjunction with laryngeal constriction.

4.1   Overcoming subglottal pressure and vocal fold inertia

The most basic relationship that can be observed in the data arises from the difference in laryngeal behaviour between the male participants (P & M) and the female participant (F). The males exhibited broad larynx height ranges (~20 mm) despite having narrow F_0 ranges (~200 Hz); the female participant exhibited almost entirely the opposite pattern: narrow larynx height range (~5 mm) and broad F_0 range (~400 Hz). Assuming a sexual dimorphism scaling factor of 1.6 (Titze 1989b) between males and females based measurements of the membranous portion of the vocal folds, then the expected F_0 range for the female, based on the male range, would be 320

Hz. The difference between the expected range (320 Hz) and the observed range (400 Hz) may be accounted for by Participant F 's use of creaky phonation to achieve an extra low F_0 and thus expanding her F_0 range overall. The low tonal regions of the males tended to exhibit some slight breathiness but were generally modal.

The concept of *laryngeal inertia* (or perhaps *vocal fold inertia*; see Xu 2002, 6; Xu and Sun 2002, 1405), has currency for the present discussion. Xu and Sun (2002) observed that one of the most important gender differences for F_0 is the rate of acceleration; females were reported to consistently require less time to initiate and halt a change in F_0 than males, which is interpreted as indicative of the fact that female vocal folds are less inertive (i.e., less massive) than male vocal folds, and thus they can more rapidly accelerate and decelerate than male vocal folds.

The results for larynx height in conjunction with the concept of laryngeal inertia indicate an interesting possibility: Individuals with greater vocal fold inertia manipulate larynx height as a compensatory mechanism to increase the acceleration and deceleration of the oscillation of the vocal folds. In general, the difference between the participants in terms of syllable duration was minimal. Assuming that the speakers are all generally under the same time pressure to achieve a given change in F_0, it stands to reason that, if males have greater vocal fold inertia than females, they can compensate by more extensive use of larynx height.

Another argument that larynx height facilitates F_0 change can be formed from Participant F's exceptional use of larynx lowering during T4. This tone is produced under increased time pressure relative to the other tones and competes for possessing the largest F_0 range covered. We interpret the occurrence of larynx lowering during T4 for Participant F and the other participants as a sign that deceleration of vocal fold oscillation cannot meet these phonetic criteria by relying upon the relaxation of the cricothyroid muscles alone. Lowering the larynx will increase the rate of deceleration by actively reducing the tension on the vocal folds by virtue of the cricoid rotation effect described in Honda et al. (1999). The fact that this effect occurs without internal activity of the laryngeal muscles is important since such activity would likely counter-act the reduction in tension that is required to produce the rapid deceleration of the oscillation of the vocal folds.

Another trend observed in the data that supports the view that larynx height facilitates tone production was the tendency for T1 to be produced with gradual larynx raising (see Figure 11.1 to 11.3). We offer the interpretation that the use of larynx raising in this context acts as a compensatory mechanism to mitigate the effect of F_0 decline caused by a declining subglottal pressure (see Titze 1989a; c.f. Collier 1975, 250). Under this hypothesis it is predicted that the effect will be more conspicuous in syllables of longer duration uttered in isolation (as in the citation context). Ultimately it needs to be confirmed that subglottal pressure is indeed dropping at the expected rate such that F_0 remains constant under increased larynx raising and the associated increase in vocal fold tension. It is puzzling why larynx raising is used when increased cricothyroid activity would be enough to achieve the goal of maintaining a stable F_0 level. The answer may lie in the fact that for T1 the activation of the cricothyroid is saturated (Sagart et al. 1986; Hallé 1994) to achieve the high F_0 target. Further contraction may be more taxing on the system than simply engaging the larynx raising mechanism or it might even overcompensate for F_0 decline and result in a non-level F_0 contour. The fact that larynx raising occurs with F_0 raising in general supports this observation, since if CT action were fully sufficient for F_0 regulation, we would not observe a change in larynx height at all. The observations then support the view that larynx height manipulation is a basic component of F_0 control and serves to complement intrinsic factors.

4.2   Two strategies for low tone target production

In the basic model of F_0 regulation (e.g., Hirano, Simada, and Fujimura 1970; Ohala and Hirose 1970; Zemlin 1998; Honda 1995, 2004) the cricothyroid muscles (CT) play the key role in changing the longitudinal tension of the vocal folds—the main factor in determining their fundamental rate of oscillation. But other factors can be significant, for instance, thyroarytenoid activity (Titze, Luschei, and Hirano 1989; Honda 1995), subglottal pressure (Titze 1989a), or—most important for the present discussion—the height of the larynx. Laryngeal raising mechanisms such as the hyomandibular muscle group (mainly the geniohyoid and anterior digastric muscles), genioglossus (Whalen, Gick, Kumada, and Honda 1998) and thyrohyoid muscles can induce tension on the vocal folds by translation or rotation of the thyroid cartilage that favours their elongation (Honda 1995; Vilkman et al. 1996), thus raising F_0. Larynx lowering, which is driven by the infrahyoid strap muscles (sternohyoid and sternothyroid muscles), typically has the opposite effect of reducing vocal fold tension, thus lowering F_0 (Faaborg-Anderson and Sonninen 1960; Ohala and Hirose 1970; Simada and Hirose 1970; Ohala 1972). Based on MRI data, Honda et al. (1999) provide the insight that lowering the larynx causes cricoid rotation favouring vocal fold shortening as the structure moves along the anterior curvature of the cervical spine. Importantly, the body of the vocal folds do not need to contract for this shortening to occur, unlike the situation that occurs for pure isotonic contraction of the thyroarytenoid muscles to lower F_0 (Honda 1995, 221). In the case of Mandarin specifically, Sagart et al. (1986) and Hallé (1994) have both attested using EMG that infrahyoid strap muscle activity was involved in producing mid-low tone targets, supporting the claim that larynx lowering plays a role in low tone production. Erickson (1993) produces similar results for Thai.

We have established that larynx height should correlate positively with F_0, which is what we have observed in the general case in our own data. But we also observed that, in addition to larynx lowering for the low F_0 target of T3, it is possible to raise the larynx and achieve the same effect of low F_0. This seemingly counterintuitive strategy finds its explanation in what can be observed in the laryngoscopy data for Participant F: The larynx constricts. The acoustic product is usually creaky phonation, which indicates that the vocal folds are undergoing a change in mode of vibration during this adjustment. Creaky phonation has been previously observed to occur generally in Mandarin during low F_0 regions of the tones, particularly in citation or terminal form (Davison 1991; Belotel-Grenié and Grenié 1994, 1995; Keating and Esposito 2006, 89).

Since larynx raising can have the effect of reducing the vertical dimension of the epilaryngeal tube (e.g., Fink 1974, 1975; Esling 1996; Esling and Harris 2005; Edmondson and Esling 2006), if all else is held constant, it is plausible that the vocal folds would approach and contact the ventricular folds (see Lindqvist-Gauffin 1972; Hollien and Allen 1972; Laver 1980, 122–126; Edmondson and Esling 2006, 159; Lindblom 2009. This contact is thought to result in a change in mode of vibration towards lower F_0 and irregular period, both characteristic of creaky phonation (e.g., Laver 1980, 122–126). The opposite effect would be anticipated in the case of larynx lowering. Larynx lowering stretches and elongates the vertical dimension of the larynx thereby reducing or counteracting laryngeal constriction; the effect should bias phonation towards breathiness as there is a lateral force on the vocal folds drawing them away from the glottal midline.

If we assume that this model is correct, then we can account for the surprising fact that two types of low tone production strategies are observed in the data. The model holds that, generally, low tone production with larynx lowering should be accompanied by non-constricted phonation (modal or breathy phonation) and with larynx raising it should be accompanied by constricted phonation (tense or creaky). Indeed these two phonation type tendencies were observed in the data. It cannot be strictly determined from the data alone whether this pattern is attributable to sexual dimorphism. It is doubtful, however, since our female participant (F) also uses larynx lowering during T4, where time pressure is increased to achieve the low pitch target. If it is the case, then we predict that the incidence of constricted phonation in conjunction with low tone targets will be greater for female speakers of Mandarin than males. Available evidence (e.g., Belotel-Grenié and Grenié 1994, 1995) does not support such a conclusion, however, since males and females show equal use of creaky phonation. More probable is that the variation in low tone production strategy accidentally corresponds with speaker gender in our study.

5. Conclusion

We have applied *simultaneous laryngoscopy and laryngeal ultrasound* (SLLUS) to the study of canonical forms of Mandarin tones. This technique provides two important types of information: larynx state and change in larynx height. Quantifying change in larynx height relies upon optical flow analysis. This method was quantitatively validated using independent data, and it also receives qualitative validation in the form of visual impression of larynx height changes observed in the laryngoscopy. We have shown that larynx height does indeed positively correlate with F_0 in the production of Mandarin tones, in the general case and in keeping with previous EMG studies (e.g., Sagart et al. 1986; Hallé 1994); however, there is one very important exception to this. Low F_0 tone targets can also be accomplished through larynx raising by employing laryngeal constriction since this state induces phonation types such as creakiness which are biased towards low fundamental frequencies. What is strongly suggested by our work is that the phonetic model of tone production cannot be purely glottal in nature, since it is manifest that larynx height and laryngeal constriction can both influence F_0 and both of these components have an impact on the vocal tract at large in terms of articulation and resonance (see Edmondson and Esling 2006).

Appendix: Elicitation List

Monosyllables			Disyllables		
#	Pinyin	Characters	#	Pinyin	Characters
1	bī	逼	1	dīdī	滴滴
2	bí	鼻	2	dídī	敵滴
3	bǐ	比	3	dǐdī	底滴
4	bì	避	4	dìdī	地滴
5	ī	一	5	dīdí	滴敵
6	í	姨	6	dídí	敵敵
7	ǐ	椅	7	dǐdí	底敵
8	ì	意	8	dìdí	地敵
9	nī	妮	9	dīdǐ	滴底
10	ní	泥	10	dídǐ	敵底
11	nǐ	你	11	dǐdǐ	底底
12	nì	逆	12	dìdǐ	地底
13	mí	迷	13	dīdì	滴地
14	mǐ	米	14	dídì	敵地
15	mì	秘	15	dǐdì	底地
16	lí	离	16	dìdì	地地
17	lǐ	里	17	dīdə	滴的
18	lì	力	18	dídə	敵的
19	dī	低	19	dǐdə	底的
20	dí	笛	20	dìdə	地的
21	dǐ	底	21	lǐmǐ	李米
22	dì	弟	22	límí	厘米
			23	mǐdǐ	米底
			24	mídí	迷底
			25	dǐhuǐ	詆毀
			26	díhuí	敵毀

REFERENCES

Belotel-Grenié, A., and M. Grenié. 1994. Phonation types analysis in Standard Chinese. *Proceedings of International Conference on Spoken Language Processing 1994*, Yokohama, Japan. 343–346.

Belotel-Grenie, A. and M. Grenie. 1995. Consonants and vowels influence on phonation types in isolated words in Standard Chinese. *Proceedings of 13th International Congress of Phonetic Sciences*, Stockholm, Sweden. 400–403.

Belotel-Grenie, A., and M. Grenie. 2004. The creaky voice phonation and the organisation of Chinese discourse. *Proceedings of the International Symposium on Tonal Aspects of Languages: With Emphasis on Tone Languages*. Beijing, China, March 28–31, 2004.

Collier, R. 1975. Physiological correlates of intonation patterns. *Journal of the Acoustical Society of America* 58 (1): 249–255.

Davidson, L. 2006. Comparing tongue shapes from ultrasound imaging using smoothing spline analysis of variance. *Journal of the Acoustical Society of America* 120 (1): 407–415.

Davison, D. S. 1991. An acoustic study of so-called creaky voice in Tianjin Mandarin. *UCLA Working Papers in Phonetics* 78:50–57.

Edmondson, J. A., and J. H. Esling. 2006. The valves of the throat and their functioning in tone, vocal register, and stress: laryngoscopic case studies. *Phonology* 23:157–191.

Erickson, D. 1993. Laryngeal muscle activity in connection with Thai tones. *Annual Bulletin of the Research Institute of Logopedics and Phoniatrics (University of Tokyo)* 27:135–149.

Esling, J. H. 1996. Pharyngeal consonants and the aryepiglottic sphincter. *Journal of the International Phonetic Association* 26:65–88.

Esling, J. H., and J. G. Harris. 2005. States of the glottis: An articulatory phonetic model based on laryngoscopic observations. In *A Figure of Speech: A Festschrift for John Laver,* eds. W. J. Hardcastle, and J. M. Beck, 347–383. Mahwah, NJ: Erlbaum.

Esling, John H., and Scott R. Moisik. 2012. Laryngeal aperture in relation to larynx height change: An analysis using simultaneous laryngoscopy and laryngeal ultrasound. In Dafydd Gibbon, Daniel Hirst and Nick Campbell (eds.), *Rhythm, Melody and Harmony in Speech: Studies in Honour of Wiktor Jassem* [Speech and Language Technology 14/15], 117–128. Poznanå: Polskie Towarzystwo Fonetyczne.

Faaborg-Anderson, K., and A. Sonninen. 1960. The function of the extrinsic laryngeal muscles at different pitch. *Acta Otolaryngologica* 51:89–93.

Fink, B. R. 1974. Folding mechanism of the human larynx. *Acta Oto-laryngologica* 78 (1–6): 124–128.

Fink, B. R. 1975. *The Human Larynx: A Functional Study*. New York, NY: Raven Press.

Hallé, P. A. 1994. Evidence for tone-specific activity of the sternohyoid muscle in modern standard Chinese. *Language and Speech* 37 (2): 103–124.

Hirano, M., Z. Simada, and O. Fujimera. 1970. An electromyographic study of the activity of the laryngeal muscles during speech utterances. *Annual Bulletin of the Research Institute of Logopedics and Phoniatrics (University of Tokyo)* 4:9–25.

Hollien, H., and E. L. Allen. 1972. Laminagraphic investigation of pulse register (vocal fry) phonation (A). *Journal of the Acoustical Society of America* 52 (1A): 124.

Honda, K. 1995. Laryngeal and extra-laryngeal mechanisms of F_0 control. In *Producing Speech: Contemporary Issues—For Katherine Safford Harris,* eds. F. Bell-Berti, and L. Raphael, 215–245. New York: AIP Press.

Honda, K. 2004. Physiological factors causing tonal characteristics of speech: From global to local prosody. Paper presented at Speech Prosody, Nara, Japan. March 23–26, 2004.

Honda, K., H. Hirai, S. Masaki, and Y. Shimada. 1999. Role of vertical larynx movement and cervical lordosis in F_0 control. *Language and Speech* 42:401–411.

Horn, B. K. P., and G. S. Brian. 1981. Determining optical flow. *Artificial Intelligence* 17:185–203.

Kawahara, H., A. de Cheveign, and R. D. Patterson. 1998. An instantaneous-frequency-based pitch extraction method for high quality speech transformation: Revised TEMPO in the STRAIGHT-suite. Paper presented at the International Conference on Spoken Language Processing 1998, Sydney, Australia. December 1998.

Keating, P., and C. Esposito. 2006. Linguistic voice quality. *UCLA Working Papers in Phonetics* 105:85–91.

Laver, J. 1980. *The Phonetic Description of Voice Quality*. Cambridge: Cambridge University Press.

Lin, Hua 1998. Diaosu lun ji Putonghua liandu biandiao ["Tonal elements" and tone sandhi in Putonghua]. *Zhongguo Yuwen* [*Chinese Language*], 1998 (1): 31–39. [林華, 1998, 「調素」論及普通話連讀變調.《中國語文》, 1998 (1): 31–39.

Lin, Hua 2001. *A Grammar of Mandarin Chinese*. Munich, Germany: Lincom Europa.

Lindblom, B. 2009. Laryngeal mechanisms in speech: The contributions of Jan Gauffin. *Logopedics Phoniatrics Vocology* 34 (4): 149–156.

Lindqvist-Gauffin, J. 1969. Laryngeal mechanisms in speech. *Quarterly Progress and Status Report, Speech Transmission Laboratory, Royal Institute of Technology* 2–3:26–31.

Lindqvist-Gauffin, J. 1972. A descriptive model of laryngeal articulation in speech. *Quarterly Progress and Status Report, Speech Transmission Laboratory, Royal Institute of Technology* 13 (2–3): 1–9.

Loveday, E. J. 2003. Ultrasound of the larynx. *Imaging: An International Journal of Clinico-Radiological Practice* 15:109–114.

Moisik, S. R., J. H. Esling, S. Bird, and H. Lin. 2011. Evaluating laryngeal ultrasound to study larynx state and height. In *Proceedings of the 17th International Congress of Phonetic Sciences*. Hong Kong, China.

Ohala, J. J. 1972. How is pitch lowered? *Journal of the Acoustical Society of America* 52:124.

Ohala, J. J., and H. Hirose. 1970. The function of the sternohyoid muscle in speech. *Annual Bulletin of the Research Institute of Logopedics and Phoniatrics* 4:41–44.

Sagart, L., P. Halle, B. de Boysson-Bardies, and C. Arabia-Guidet. 1986. Tone production in modern standard Chinese: An electromygraphic investigation. *Cahiers Linguistique Asie-Orientale* 15:205–221.

Simada, Z., and H. Hirose. 1970. The function of the laryngeal muscles in respect to the word accent distinction. *Annual Bulletin of the Research Institute of Logopedics and Phoniatrics* 4:27–40.

Titze, I. R. 1989a. On the relationship between subglottal pressure and fundamental frequency in phonation. *Journal of the Acoustical Society of America* 85 (2): 901–906.

Titze, I. R. 1989b. Physiologic and acoustic differences between male and female voices. *Journal of the Acoustical Society of America* 85 (4): 1699–1707.

Titze, I. R., E. S. Luschei, and M. Hirano. 1989. Role of the thyroarytenoid muscle in regulation of fundamental frequency. *Journal of Voice* 3:213–224.

Vilkman, E., A. Sonninen, P. Hurme, and P. Körkkö. 1996. External laryngeal frame function in voice production revisited: A review. *Journal of Voice* 10:78–92.

Xu, Y. 2002. Articulatory constraints and tonal alignment. In *Proceedings of Speech Prosody 2002*, Aix-en-Provence, France.

Xu, Y., and X. Sun. 2002. Maximum speed of pitch change and how it may relate to speech. *Journal of the Acoustical Society of America* 111:1399–1413.

Whalen, D. H., B. Gick, M. Kumada, and K. Honda. 1998. Cricothyroid activity in high and low vowels: Exploring the automaticity of intrinsic F_0. *Journal of Phonetics* 27:125–142.

Zemlin, W. R. 1998. *Speech and Hearing Science: Anatomy and Physiology.* 4th Edition. Boston, London, Toronto, Sydney, Tokyo, and Singapore: Allyn and Bacon.

12

Bimanual Coordination and Motor Learning in Pianists and Non-Musicians: A 3T fMRI Study

Shu-Jen KUNG
Institute of Neuroscience, National Yang-Ming University,
Institute of Linguistics, Academia Sinica

Denise H. WU
Institute of Cognitive Neuroscience, National Central University,

Daisy L. HUNG
Institute of Cognitive Neuroscience, National Central University

Ovid J.-L. TZENG
Institute of Linguistics, Academia Sinica

Abstract

In honor of Professor William S-Y. Wang, we presented a research report on bimanual coordination of sequential finger movements, such as playing a piano, within a functional neuro-imaging environment, in order to examine the underlying neuronal bases of learning such an eminent capability of the human motor system. In this study, we utilized functional magnetic resonance imaging to address the plasticity of this system under long-term motor learning and short-term bimanual training in pianists and non-musicians. In each group we compared bimanual parallel movements with mirror movements across four stages of learning: Naïve (new sequence), Intermediate (early learning stage), Automatic (late learning stage), and Novel (another new sequence). The data revealed a parieto-premotor circuit for bimanual coordination in both pianists and nonmusicians, with differential involvements of the two hemispheres across learning stages. The brain activation in non-musicians was left- and right-dominant at the early and late learning stage, respectively. In the Novel stage, the activation pattern in non-musicians became similar to that in pianists, suggesting bilateral involvements of the parieto-premotor circuit in bimanual coordination after substantial training. The observed functional transition reflects the shaping process of the brain from unskilled to skilled via bimanual motor learning. These data provide a basis for understanding short-term functional adaptation and, hopefully, would inspire future studies on bimanual skill acquisition.

Autumn Song

William S-Y. Wang

Sand keeps slipping away	水過殘沙平
Light weakens at close of day	日沉催月明
Fog chills the setting sun	寒霧漫秋光
Life's tangled web is spun	意亂情難停
Gallop on the shore	躍馬岸邊行
Hear the ocean roar	浪高震耳鳴
Watch the eagle soar	極目鷹展翅
Soon there'll be no more	霎時無蹤影

Translated by Ovid Tzeng

2003.11.29

1. Introduction

William S-Y. Wang has been known for his linguistic investigation on the subject of language evolution. Little has been known for his talent in music composition and poetry creation in both English and Chinese. The Autumn Song was hummed by Chuck Fillmore across the campus of the University of California, Berkeley, in the early 1980s and immediately caught the ears and the heart of Ovid Tzeng (one of the authors in this article), who decided to translate the beautiful English poem into Chinese. At the opening ceremony of the "POLA FOREVER" Workshop dedicated to celebrate Professor Wang's 70th birthday, the Autumn Song was sung by Ovid, accompanied by the piano music played by Shu-Jen Kung (the first author of the article). Now, in honor of the great scientific contribution of Professor Wang, to celebrate the coming of his 80th birthday, we report an experiment on bimanual coordination of sequential finger movements, such as playing a piano, within a functional neuro-imaging environment, in order to examine the underlying neuronal bases of learning such an eminent skill of the human motor system.

To achieve a high level of bimanual coordination, as in athletes and musicians, a substantial amount of practice is required. However, little is known about the neuro-anatomical basis of such skill and its acquisition. Neuroimaging studies of the neural correlates of bimanual movements have suggested that the frontal regions are responsible for the change from bimanual mirror movements, which are typically easier to perform, to parallel movements (Chan and Ross 1988). Specifically, when compared to mirror movements (Scholz and Kelso 1990; Mechsner et al. 2001), coordinated bimanual parallel movements are associated with increased activity in the frontal regions (Sadato et al. 1997; Immisch et al. 2001; Ullen et al. 2003). In contrast to these findings, however, evidence from neuropsychological research has pointed to other brain areas that seem to be critical for bimanual coordination. For instance, patients with parietal impairment have been shown to have disrupted bimanual parallel movements while their bimanual mirror movements were intact (Serrien et al. 2001). It remains to be determined whether the parietal regions are involved in bimanual finger movements in healthy participants.

Despite the importance of the frontal regions for bimanual coordination, it is not clear whether they also play a critical role in the acquisition of bimanual movements. In a learning task involving unimanual sequences, performance at the beginning stage was associated with the frontal areas while that at the advanced stages was associated with the parietal regions (Sakai et al. 1998). The same issue was rarely explored for learning bimanual sequences, however. Since the principles guiding bimanual coordination are not mere extrapolations of those underlying unimanual performance (Swinnen 2002), the neural network for unimanual and bimanual movements might be distinct from each other. In the current study, we investigated bimanual movements in different learning stages to examine the neural substrates underlying skilled bimanual finger movements and the processes to acquire such skills.

Bimanual finger movements are a central element of piano playing. Pianists practice parallel scales (a bimanual parallel movement) as well as scales in contrary motion (a bimanual mirror movement) extensively from the beginning of their training. As a result, the expertise of professional pianists offers an ideal model to investigate the effect of long-term practice upon bimanual skill acquisition. In contrast, non-musicians provide an opportunity to reveal functional adaptation during short-term bimanual training. In the current study, we employed a 3T magnetic resonance imaging (MRI) system to identify the neural correlates of bimanual coordination at different stages of motor learning in these two groups. This examination had two specific goals: First, we compared the neural network of bimanual coordination between pianists and non-musicians to reveal the impact of extensive musical (motor) training on the motor system. Second, we addressed functional adaptation under the influence of long-term motor learning and short-term training in pianists and non-musicians, respectively.

2.   Materials and Methods

2.1   Participants

Twenty participants were recruited, and their informed consent was obtained. Each participant was healthy and had no history of neurological or mental disorders. All of them were right-handed, verified by the Edinburgh Handedness Inventory (Oldfield 1971). Ten participants were experienced pianists (6 females and 4 males; mean age 22.1, range 19–27). They were recruited from music conservatories and had piano training for more than one hour per day for at least 15 years. Ten non-musicians were matched with the pianists for age and gender (mean age 23.3, range 20–27). Neither group included any professional typists. Typing speed was measured prior to the study and did not reveal any significant difference between the two groups (36.5 and 37.6 Chinese characters per minute in the pianists and nonmusicians, respectively). The study was approved by the Ethics and Radiation Safety Committees of the Taipei Veterans General Hospital.

2.2   Stimuli and apparatus

There were three types of stimuli (Mirror, Parallel, and Shift), and each type consisted of eight numbers corresponding to the designated finger movements of the right hand (Table 12.1). In the Mirror condition, the finger movements of the left hand mirrored those of the right hand, namely, the index finger of the left hand had to be moved simultaneously with the right index finger and so on. In the Parallel condition, the assignment of the finger movement of the left hand was parallel to that of the right hand, that is, the index finger of the left hand had to be moved simultaneously with the right little finger and so on. In the Shift condition, the participants were instructed to perform the sequence with Mirror and Parallel movements alternately, which emphasized the process of changing from one to the other.

The participants lay supine in the scanner and saw the visually presented stimuli through a mirror. Only the movement sequence of the right hand was presented to the participants. Motor responses were collected via a pair of keypads, with four buttons for each hand, positioned on

Table 12.1   Sequences of bimanual sequential finger movements

	Seq. 1	Seq. 2
Mirror		
Right	31242131, 31242131, ...	42314132, 42314132, ...
Left	31242131, 31242131, ...	42314132, 42314132, ...
Parallel		
Right	31242131, 31242131, ...	42314132, 42314132, ...
Left	24313424, 24313424, ...	13241423, 13241423, ...
Shift		
Right	31242131, 31242131, ...	42314132, 42314132, ...
Left	31242131, 24313424, ...	42314132, 13241423, ...

Abbreviation: 1, index finger; 2, middle finger; 3, ring finger; 4, little finger

the participant's abdomen such that the two hands were roughly parallel to each other. Each finger, excluding the thumb, was positioned over a button. The stimulus presentation and the data collection were controlled by computers.

2.3   Experimental protocol

Each participant was scanned in four stages, each of which was composed of 18 blocks. For each stage, there were nine activation blocks and nine baseline blocks alternating with each other (Figure 12.1a). The first three activation blocks were in the Mirror condition, followed by another three activation blocks of the Parallel condition and then finally another three blocks of the Shift condition. In the activation blocks, the participants were instructed to follow the visually presented sequence and perform eight finger movements bimanually for 19.5 seconds without interruption. After the activation block, the baseline block lasted for 19.5 seconds, in which the participants rested in the same posture and gazed at a cross in the center of the screen (Figure 12.1a).

The MR signals were acquired at four different stages (Figure 12.1b): Naïve, Intermediate, Automatic, and Novel. At the Naïve stage, the participants performed the bimanual finger movements of one sequence (seq. 1) in the Mirror, Parallel, and Shift conditions. After the Naïve stage, they practiced the same sequence for another 20 minutes until they made no errors in 10 successive trials. At this point, they were considered to have achieved the Intermediate stage. The participants then were instructed to practice the sequence 10 successive times in each condition without errors at home every day. After two weeks of this training, the participants were brought back to the lab to evaluate whether they were able to perform the sequence automatically (i.e.,

Figure 12.1 The experimental design

(a)

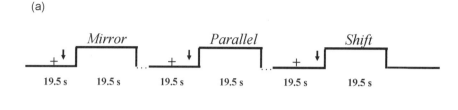

(b)

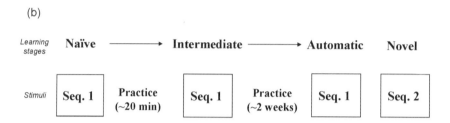

performing the three conditions without errors while orally reporting their basic information, such as home address, mobile phone numbers, etc.). All participants met the criterion and were scanned in this Automatic stage when they performed the three conditions. Following the Automatic stage, the participants were instructed to perform the bimanual movements of a new sequence (seq. 2) in the three conditions. Their brain signals were also acquired at this Novel stage.

The procedures were identical across all stages. The participants were instructed to perform the bimanual movements simultaneously, continuously, and as rapidly and accurately as possible. They were asked to keep the rhythm as stable as possible for the entire duration of the sequence. The accuracy and speed of their motor performance were measured via the keypads during scanning.

In order to ensure that the participants were able to accurately follow the instructions of each condition and were familiar with the experimental demands, they practiced a simple sequence that was not used in the real experiment prior to the scanning of the Naïve stage. The practice session terminated as soon as the participants performed the sequence in the three conditions without errors.

2.4 Imaging acquisition

Images were performed using a 3.0 T Bruker MedSpec S300 system (Bruker, Karlsruhe, Germany) with a quadrature head coil. The participants' heads were immobilized with a vacuum-beam pad in the scanner. Earplugs were used to reduce auditory noise. Global field homogeneity was optimized before data acquisition using both automatic and manual shimming. Functional data were acquired with a T2*-weighted gradient-echo echo planar imaging (EPI) using blood oxygen level dependent (BOLD) contrast, with slice thickness = 5 mm, interslice gap = 1 mm, in-plane resolution = 3.9 x 3.9 mm, and TR/TE/θ= 1950 ms/50 ms/90°. The field-of-view was 250 x 250 mm and the acquisition matrix was 64 x 64. Twenty axial slices were acquired to cover the whole brain. For each learning stage, 185 images were acquired. The first five images of each learning stage were discarded to eliminate non-equilibrium effects of magnetization. Each block was composed of 10 images (19.5 s). The total duration of each learning stage was about 6 minutes. Each participant's anatomical image was acquired using a high-resolution (1.95 x 1.95 x 1.95 mm), T1-weighted, 3D gradient-echo pulse sequence (MDEFT, Modified Driven Equilibrium Fourier Transform; TR/TE/TI = 88.1/4.12/650 ms).

2.5 Data analyses

Reaction time (speed) and accuracy (error rate) of the motor responses were analyzed. In each block, the number of times the sequence was completed and the response time for each button press were recorded. A sequence containing any wrong keystroke in either hand was considered as an error sequence and was excluded from further analysis. The error rate was defined by calculating the number of error sequences divided by the total number of performed sequences in each condition and learning stage. Repeated-measures analyses of variance (ANOVAs) were employed with a 2 (group: pianists and nonmusicians) x 3 (condition: Mirror, Parallel and Shift) x 4 (learning stage: Naïve, Intermediate, Automatic, and Novel) design, with the group as a between-participant variable. Planned comparisons were also performed to demonstrate effects of learning and condition in pianists and nonmusicians separately.

Imaging data were analyzed with Statistical Parametric Mapping (SPM99, Wellcome Department of Cognitive Neurology, London, UK), running under Matlab 6.0 (Mathworks, Sherborn, MA, USA) on a Sun workstation. Scans were time corrected, realigned, normalized (2 x 2 x 2 mm voxel size), and spatially smoothed with a 4 mm full-width half-maximum (FWHM) isotropic Gaussian kernel. The resulting time-series was high-pass filtered with a cut-off time window of 120 sec to remove low-frequency drift in the BOLD signal and temporally smoothed with a hemodynamic response function (HRF). Images of parameter estimates for the canonical and derivative covariant were created using participant-specific contrasts. The t images for each contrast were subsequently transformed into statistical parametric maps of the Z statistics. Two contrasts were tested to examine the process of switching between mirror and parallel coordination, namely, (1) the Parallel versus the Mirror condition, and (2) the Shift condition versus the average of the Parallel and Mirror conditions. Any difference exceeding an uncorrected conservative threshold of $p = 0.005$ with a spatial contrast of the cluster size more than 10 voxels was considered statistically significant. The MNI coordinates (Montreal Neurological Institute) of Z-maxima localized on the normalized SPM99-T1 structural image were converted into Talairach coordinates and then labeled using Talairach nomenclature (Talairach and Tournoux, 1988) with the Talairach Daemon (Research Imaging Center, The University of Texas, USA).

3. Results

3.1 Behavioral results

The mean error rates in the three conditions across the four learning stages are shown separately for the non-musicians and pianists in Figures 12.2a and 12.2b, respectively. Overall, the error rate was lower than 15% in each condition, indicating that the performance of both groups was relatively accurate.

The ANOVA showed fewer errors in the pianists than in the non-musicians ($F_{1,9} = 16.07$, MSE = 0.003, $p < 0.005$). The effect of condition ($F_{2,18} = 6.44$, MSE = 0.001, $p < 0.01$), learning stage ($F_{3,27} = 9.49$, MSE = 0.001, $p < 0.001$), and the interaction between them ($F_{6,108} = 8.44$, MSE = 0.001, $p < 0.001$) were also significant. Although group did not interact with any other variables (both ps > 0.5) and the three-way interaction was not significant ($F_{6,108} = 1.04$, $p > 0.40$), Figure 12.2 suggests that the non-musicians did not improve their Shift performance at the Intermediate stage, whereas the pianists made significant progress (pianists: $F_{3,39} = 8.41$, MSE = 0.000, $p < 0.001$; non-musicians: $F_{3,39} = 1.94$, $p > 0.05$). Apart from that, both groups improved their Mirror and Parallel performances at the Intermediate stage (pianists: $F_{3,39} = 5.80$, MSE = 0.002, $p < 0.005$; non-musicians: $F_{3,39} = 8.00$, MSE = 0.002, $p < 0.001$). These data demonstrated that the Mirror condition was the easiest to perform accurately, followed by the

Figure 12.2 The error rate of keystrokes

(a) Nonmusicians

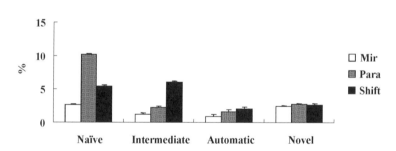

(b) Pianists

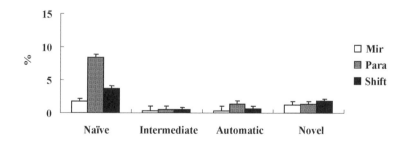

Parallel condition, and the Shift condition was most difficult to perform for the non-musicians. In contrast, the pianists improved their performances of the Parallel and Shift equally, indicating that their long-term intensive training enabled them to switch between mirror and parallel coordination without much difficulty.

The speed of the response revealed different learning patterns in the pianists and non-musicians (Figure 12.3). The ANOVA showed significant differences between groups ($F_{1,18}$ = 197.14, MSE = 9.26, $p < 0.001$), conditions ($F_{2,36}$ = 5.55, MSE = 0.23, $p < 0.01$), and learning stages ($F_{3,54}$ = 36.47, MSE = 0.10, $p < 0.0001$). There was a significant interaction between learning stage and group ($F_{3,54}$ = 4.93, MSE = 0.10, $p < 0.005$). Further analyses demonstrated that the bimanual skill in all three conditions improved from the Naïve stage through the Intermediate to the Automatic stage in non-musicians (for all comparisons, ps < 0.001). In both Parallel and Shift conditions, the performance of non-musicians in the Novel stage was back to the level of the Intermediate stage. Instead of back to the level of the Naïve stage, this finding suggests that learning occurred not only at the execution level but also at a more abstract level. In contrast, their performance of the Mirror condition in the Novel stage was back to the level of the Naïve stage. In addition, performance of non-musicians in the Mirror condition was significantly faster than in the Parallel condition only in the Naïve stage ($F_{2,29}$ = 4.63, MSE = 0.12, $p < 0.05$).

In contrast to the non-musicians, the planned comparison demonstrated that the pianists showed no significant performance difference in the three conditions across all learning stages.

Figure 12.3 The speed of keystrokes

(a) Nonmusicians

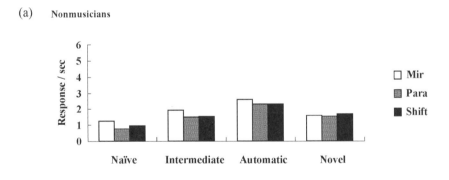

(b) Pianists

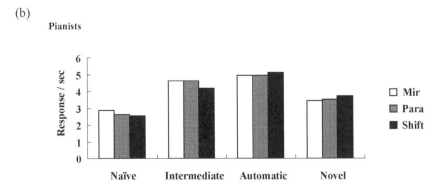

They only showed a significant learning effect ($F_{3,27}$ = 21.54, MSE = 1.46, p < 0.001), mainly caused by the improvement from the Naïve stage to the Intermediate stage (p < 0.005). Contrary to the non-musicians, the performance of the pianists in the Novel stage was not significantly different than that in the Naïve stage (p > 0.24) and was marginally different than that in the Intermediate stage (p = 0.059). The finding that the pianists showed similar performances in the Novel and Naïve stages demonstrates that they had acquired the abstract skill of bimanual coordination through long-term bimanual training.

In summary, both groups performed these tasks accurately and showed the effect of training across different stages. The non-musicians improved their bimanual finger movements across all conditions until the Automatic stage, while the pianists reached nearly optimal performance after about 20 minutes practice, i.e., at the Intermediate stage. The non-musicians were slower in the Parallel than in the Mirror bimanual movements at the Naïve stage. In contrast, the pianists showed equal performance in the Mirror and Parallel conditions at all stages. In addition, the improvement in the Shift condition was slower than that in the Mirror and Parallel conditions in the non-musicians but not in the pianists.

3.2   Imaging results

In order to identify the motor network underlying the Mirror, Parallel, and Shift conditions, the comparison between the activation blocks of each condition and the baseline blocks was performed. Among areas implicated in this comparison, all motor-related regions were activated, including primary sensorimotor cortex extending to bilateral premotor cortex, parietal regions, cerebellum, striatum, thalamus, and the supplementary motor area in all stages, in both pianists and non-musicians.

To identify the neural substrates specific for bimanual coordination required in parallel finger movements, we compared the activation between the Parallel and Mirror conditions in both non-musicians and pianists. The non-musicians showed greater activation in the left premotor area in the Naïve stage (uncorrected, p < 0.005). Interestingly, the activation switched to the homologous regions in the right hemisphere in the Intermediate stage. The difference disappeared in the Automatic stage. However, when the non-musicians performed the new sequence at the Novel stage, the activation in the right premotor area re-appeared (uncorrected, p < 0.001) together with activation in the inferior parietal lobule. In contrast, there was no difference between the Parallel and Mirror conditions across all stages in the pianists (Figure 12.4; Table 12.2). These results are consistent with the behavioral findings showing that the Parallel movement was more difficult than the Mirror movement for the non-musicians but not for the pianists (Figure 12.3).

In the Shift condition, two different kinds of bimanual coordination were performed alternately. The process of switching between mirror and parallel finger movements is believed to be especially challenging for the mechanism of bimanual coordination. In order to determine the neural substrates underlying this transition, a comparison between the Shift condition and

Table 12.2 Activated foci by sequential finger movements: Para>Mir

Threshold for statistical significance p<0.001; *p<0.005, cluster size=10. Voxels indicate overall spatial extents of significant clusters within the activated volume. Stereotaxic coordinates of peak activation are expressed in millimeters and refer to medial-lateral position (x) relative to midline (positive = right), anterior-posterior position (y) relative to the anterior commissure (positive = anterior), and superior-inferior position (z) relative to the commissural line (positive = superior). PM, premotor area; PFC, prefrontal cortex; BG, basal ganglia; IPL, inferior parietal lobule; L, left hemisphere; R, right hemisphere.

Stages	Location		Non-Musicians (NM) Talairach coordinates					Piano Players (PP) Talairach coordinates				
			x	y	z	Zmax	#Voxels	x	y	z	Zmax	#Voxels
Naïve												
	PM											
		L	-30	8	42	3.31*	26					
	PFC											
		R						58	3	19	3.1*	20
								38	20	-4	3.06*	14
Intermediate												
	PM											
		R	30	-9	61	3.2*	14					
	BG											
		L						-14	0	9	3.70	21
		R						12	3	15	3.91	16
	Thalamus											
		R						6	-6	4	3.77	55
Automatic												
Novel												
	PM											
		R	36	2	40	3.63	44					
			26	-9	47	3.61	27					
	IPL											
		L	-59	-43	37	3.35	10					

*p < 0.005

the average of the Parallel and Mirror conditions was performed. The non-musicians showed a switching effect in the parietal regions (Figure 12.5). Specifically, the left parietal regions including precuneus were activated in the Naïve stage while the right homologous regions were activated in the Automatic stage (uncorrected, p < 0.001). No such difference was detected in the Intermediate stage.

Contrary to the non-musicians, the pianists showed higher activation for the Shift condition in bilateral parietal regions in both the Naïve and Intermediate stages. It is noteworthy that, similar to the comparison between the Parallel and Mirror conditions in the non-musicians, the

Figure 12.4   Differential brain responses in comparisons of Parallel and Mirror conditions
Uncorrected p < 0.001 or p < 0.005* with spatial extent more than 10 voxels were considered statistically significant. The color bar denotes the Z value in the (a) nonmusicians and (b) pianists. A, anterior; P, posterior; L, left; R, right.

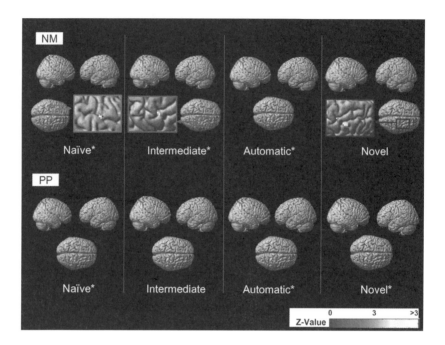

pianists also showed premotor activation in the Naïve and Intermediate stages. They showed bilateral premotor activation with more extent in left hemisphere in the Naïve stage and right hemispheric activation in the Intermediate stage (Table 12.3). There was no difference in the Automatic and Novel stages in the pianists in this comparison. However, after lowering the significance level (uncorrected, p < 0.005), the pianists showed activation in the right premotor area and parietal regions including precuneus in the Automatic and Novel stages as well (Figure 12.5 and Table 12.3).

In sum, the non-musicians showed the neural substrates of bimanual coordination in the left premotor, precuneus, and superior parietal regions in the Naïve stage. After practice, the activation moved to the right homologous areas in the Intermediate and Automatic stages. During the Novel stage, the right premotor area, bilateral precuneus, and bilateral superior parietal lobules were all involved in responding to the new sequence. In the pianists, however, these areas were bilaterally activated in the Naïve and Intermediate stages. In the Automatic and Novel stages they showed activation in these regions in the right hemisphere at a lower significance level.

Table 12.3   Activated foci by sequential finger movements: Shift>Para and Mir

| Stages | Location | | Non-Musicians (NM) | | | | | Piano Players (PP) | | | | |
| | | | Talairach coordinates | | | | | Talairach coordinates | | | | |
			x	y	z	Zmax	Voxels	x	y	z	Zmax	Voxels
Naïve												
	PM											
	·	L						-26	0	44	4	72
		R						32	-1	57	3.5	14
	Precuneus/ SPL											
	·	L	-15	-70	49	3.8	22	-14	-65	51	3.88	83
			-33	-45	51	3.72	27	-42	-56	54	3.53	24
		R						20	-61	56	5.36	245
	IPL											
		L	-38	-50	56	3.85	35	-34	-50	52	3.86	121
	PFC											
		R						57	7	27	3.78	27
Intermediate												
	PM											
		R						22	1	59	4.63	28
	Precuneus/ SPL											
		L						-14	-65	53	4.11	30
		R						18	-63	55	4.19	23
								22	-57	62	3.36	11
Automatic												
	PM							26	-4	43	3.25*	76
	Precuneus/ SPL											
		R	20	-67	57	4.17	84	18	-59	55	3.31*	69
	IPL											
		R	32	-42	52	4.06	45					
Novel												
	Precuneus/ SPL											
		L	-12	-67	51	4.11	47					
		R	18	-67	51	3.62	22	20	-62	51	3.88*	16
	IPL											
		L	-42	-48	48	3.89	55					

PM: premotor area; SPL: superior parietal lobule; IPL: inferior parietal lobule; PFC: prefrontal cortex;

L: left hemisphere; R: right hemisphere

Figure 12.5   Differential brain responses in comparisons of Shift and the average of the Parallel and Mirror conditions

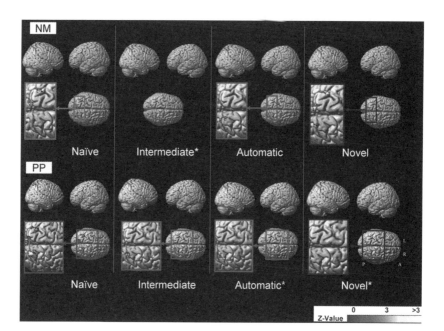

4.   Discussion

The main findings of the current study are: (a) In addition to the premotor area, the parietal regions also participated in bimanual coordination; (b) these regions switched from the left to the right hemisphere after the non-musicians acquired the skill; (c) this switching effect was much less evident in the pianists, who showed bilateral activation in the early learning stages and weak activation in the right hemisphere in the Automatic and Novel stages.

Our study revealed that bimanual movements activated a well-established motor system: the primary sensorimotor cortex, supplementary motor area (SMA), cingulate motor area (CMA), premotor area, parietal regions, basal ganglia, and cerebellum. Within these regions, the Parallel and Shift conditions showed greater activation than the Mirror condition did. We probed the differences between the Parallel and Mirror conditions and also between the Shift and the average of the Parallel and Mirror conditions to elucidate the neural substrates of bimanual coordination. The differences were significant in the premotor area and parietal regions including precuneus (Figures 12.5 and 12.6; Tables 12.3 and 12.4). We discuss the significance and implications of these findings in each motor related area below.

Results of previous animal and patient studies have been interpreted as suggesting that the SMA is responsible for switching motor programs from mirror to parallel movements before execution (Laplane et al. 1977; Brinkman 1981, 1984; Chan and Ross 1988). More recent studies, however, have questioned the major function of the SMA in inter-limb coordination. Reversible inactivation of the SMA (Kermadi et al. 1997) or the SMA including the CMA

(Kazennikov et al. 1998) did not prevent monkeys from performing coordinated bimanual movements but induced a prominent deficit in movement initiation.

Consistent with these findings, we did not observe differential activation in the mirror and parallel bimanual movements in the SMA across all learning stages in both groups. That is, the SMA was activated equally in both mirror and parallel finger movements. Since the patients in previous reports might not have had lesions that were focal enough to determine the function of the SMA, it is possible that this region is related to sequence generation rather than bimanual coordination. This interpretation has been supported by the finding that only the initiation of bimanual movements was impaired after lesions of the SMA (Kazennikov et al. 1998).

Consistent with previous studies, the current data demonstrate that the premotor area is associated with bimanual coordination (Figures 12.4 and 12.5, Table 12.2). The premotor area receives dense corticocortical input from the SMA, which provides the information necessary to generate a motor program, closely reflecting motor aspects of execution (Kurata 1991). It has been demonstrated to have sequence-specific neurons, to be associated with motor set-related activity (Mushiake et al. 1991), and to be implicated in preprogramming sequential motor actions (Kurata 1993). Similarly, patients with premotor lesions showed disintegration of motor acts and skilled movements (Kleist 1907; Kleist 1911; Luria 1966). They also showed a disturbance of unilateral proximal movements, especially in coordination between the two sides (Freund and Hummelsheim 1985). Therefore, the premotor area may be responsible for integrating information from the SMA to coordinate the finger movements between two hands (Sadato et al. 1997).

Although the premotor area has been associated with bimanual coordination in both groups, its involvement was detected in different comparisons in non-musicians and pianists. For the former, this region showed higher activation in the Parallel than the Mirror condition (Figure 12.4; Table 12.2); for the latter, its activation was higher in the Shift than the average of the Parallel and Mirror conditions (Figure 12.5; Table 12.3). This discrepancy might be due to the relative difficulty of the Shift, Parallel, and Mirror conditions to the two groups. As suggested by the behavioral data, the Shift and Parallel conditions were equally difficult for pianists, while the former was more difficult than the latter for the non-musicians. We speculate that the activation of the premotor area had saturated in the non-musicians when they performed the Parallel condition, so that it could not increase in activation in the more difficult Shift condition. As a result, the premotor area only showed activation difference between the Parallel and Mirror conditions. In contrast, the daily practice of the bimanual movements enabled the pianists to perform Parallel and Mirror conditions equally well, hence no difference in brain activation was detected. The comparison between the Shift condition and the average of the Parallel and Mirror conditions thus signifies the mechanism of bimanual coordination.

In addition to the frontal regions, the current data have revealed the participation of the posterior part of the brain in bimanual coordination. Brain activation in the parietal regions has been associated with spatial perception, association of sensory signals, directing attention, visuomotor control, and motor coordination in neuroimaging studies (Fleming and Crosby 1955; De Renzi 1982; Andersen 1987; Husain 1991; Milner and Goodale 1995; Jeannerod 1997). Compared to the frontal areas, however, these areas have rarely been implicated in bimanual coordination regardless of its function in motor programming and motor control. Recent studies have suggested that the parietal region is a prominent site for sensorimotor integration in relation to motor skill (Andersen et al. 1997; Wolpert et al. 1998). Most researchers, however, consider the parietal cortex to be involved only when new patterns of bimanual coordination are needed (Swinnen 2002; Swinnen and Wenderoth 2004).

Differing from neuroimaging studies, neuropsychological research has clearly revealed a link between bimanual coordination and the parietal regions. Bimanual impairments are more commonly seen in patients with parietal lesions than with either frontal or temporal lesions (Wyke 1971). Eliassen et al. (1999) examined a split-brain patient who performed bimanual drawings normally after anterior callosotomy but spatially uncoupled after posterior callosotomy, which disconnected the projection of the parietal lobe through the posterior third of the corpus callosum (see also Franz et al. 1996; Eliassen et al. 2000; Serrien et al. 2001). Echoing these findings, the present study showed that not only the frontal regions but also the parietal areas participate in bimanual coordination. Specifically, the activation in the parietal areas was significantly higher in the Shift conditions than in the average of the Parallel and Mirror condition (Figure 12.5, Table 12.3).

In a recent fMRI study, Wenderoth et al. (2004) showed that the parietal and premotor regions were activated when comparing directionally incompatible versus compatible bimanual movements. It is argued that the directional interference in the incompatible bimanual movements is associated with a parieto-premotor circuit for controlling goal-directed movements (see also De Jong et al. 2002; Ullen et al. 2003; Debaere et al. 2004). The authors further speculated that the parietal region is involved in shifting attention between different locations in space whereas the frontal portion of the circuit has the function of suppressing intrinsically preferred coordination tendencies (Wenderoth et al. 2005).

Our data generally support the framework proposed by Wenderoth et al. (2005). The bimanual movements of the Parallel and Shift conditions may generate directional interference and therefore require more attentional shifting of locations in space than in the Mirror condition. In the parieto-premotor network of bimanually goal-directed movements, the activation in the parietal lobe, specifically at the dorso-anterior precuneus, is involved in the shifting of spatial attention. This section of the precuneus is often activated during the execution or imagination of spatially demanding tasks (Grafton et al. 1992; Connolly et al. 2000; Astafiev et al. 2003; Vanlierde et al. 2003). It has especially high activity when bimanual movements have to be coordinated in a complex spatiotemporal fashion (Christensen et al. 2000; Malouin et al. 2003; Meister et al., 2004). On the other hand, the activation in the premotor area might be correlated with the suppression of mirror tendencies in non-mirror bimanual tasks.

Although the parieto-premotor network for bimanual coordinated movements has received empirical support from previous studies, its laterality is still controversial. Most studies have revealed such a network predominantly in the right hemisphere (Sadato et al. 1997; De Jong et al. 2002; Wenderoth et al. 2004), due to its specialization in processing spatial information. However, a recent report has found bilateral precuneus activation (Wenderoth et al. 2005). Haaland et al. (2004) also reported a similar parieto-premotor network in the left hemisphere when unimanual movements were required, regardless of the performing hand. Specifically, when participants performed complex finger sequences the activation of the left parieto-premotor network was more pronounced than that of the right homologous regions. To explain these data, it is suggested that the left hemisphere is dominantly associated with the cognitive resources required in planning complex sequential movements.

In the present study, we found hemispheric asymmetries in the parieto-premotor network in non-musicians. The left network was more dominant in the early learning stages whereas the right circuit was more pronounced in the late learning stages (Figure 12.4 and 12.5). Following the proposals by Haaland et al. (2004) and Wenderoth et al. (2005), we reason that non-musicians, who are not well-trained in parallel finger movements, plan and organize the sequence in order to perform it without errors in the early learning stages. As a result, the left network is more activated in parallel than mirror movements. After training and being familiar with the motor sequence, people shift their attention towards the spatial aspect of the finger movements, which is related to the right parieto-premotor network.

As in non-musicians, the involvement of parieto-premotor circuit is also demonstrated in pianists (Figure 12.4 and 12.5). The bilateral activation of such a network is consistent with previous studies on unimanual performance of pianists (Jäncke et al. 2000; Krings et al. 2000; Meister et al. 2004). Interestingly, comparing parallel with mirror movements in the Novel stage, in which the strategy for performing the parallel movements has been learned while a new sequence has to be responded to, we found activation in bilateral precuneus and the right premotor area in non-musicians. This pattern is remarkably similar to the brain activation of the pianists in the Naïve stage (Figure 12.5; Table 12.3). Based on these results, we argue that the activation in these regions is associated with the learned strategies of parallel movements through bimanual motor training in the non-musicians and long-term practice in the pianists. A recent report of the involvement of the right anterior region in non-musicians after five weeks of piano practice is consistent with our findings (Bangert and Altenmüller 2003).

Another interesting point to note is that functional adaptation in bimanual coordination can happen quite rapidly. Musical training has been shown to influence the functional organization of the brain in the motor cortex (Krings et al., 2000; Gaser and Schlaug 2003) and the corpus callosum (Schlaug 2003). In the current study, after two weeks of bimanual training, non-musicians demonstrated brain activations similar to those observed in individuals who have received prolonged training of the bimanual skills. Such bilateral activation in pianists and non-musicians after practice might be a consequence of increased interhemispheric communication through the corpus callosum, which is required by complex bimanual motor sequences. This impressive functional adaptability of bimanual coordination is consistent with the recent theory of dynamic motor function (Serrien et al. 2006).

Taken together, the current study demonstrates that the parieto-premotor circuit participates in bimanual coordination in both pianists and non-musicians. Although this network in two hemispheres is differentially involved across different learning stages in non-musicians, it is activated bilaterally in pianists. The transition of the brain activation modulated by short-term and long-term musical training points to the neural substrates subserving the learning process. These data suggest that functional adaptation can operate on relatively short time scales. We hope that our findings will inspire future studies on motor skill acquisition in bimanual coordination.

To conclude and to show our respect to Professor Wang's great life contributions to the scientific investigation of language evolution, we believe that music, motor movements, and creative thinking are all manifestations of coordinated neuronal activities which turn chaos into a synchronized orchestra of harmonious and sensational patterns.

Acknowledgments

This study was supported by grants from the Taipei Veterans General Hospital (90400, 90443, 91361, 91380, 923721, 92348), National Science Council (902314B075124, 902314B075115, 912314B075069, 922314B075095), and Ministry of Education (89BFA221401 and 89BFA221406) of Taiwan.

We extend thanks to Ching-Hung Lin for excellent construction of the MR-compatible keypads. We also thank Jen-Chuen Hsieh, Chou-Ming Cheng, Po-Lei Lee, and Yu-Te Wu for their advice and technical support. Special thanks to Curtis Hardyck, Mary Louise Kean, and Bruno H. Repp for comments on the manuscript and improving the writing quality.

Abbreviations

ANOVA, analysis of variance; BOLD, blood oxygen level dependent; CMA, cingulate motor area; EPI, echo planar imaging; FWHM, full-width half-maximum; HRF, hemodynamic response function; MDEFT, modified driven equilibrium Fourier transform; MNI, Montreal Neurological Institute; MRI, magnetic resonance imaging; SMA, supplementary motor area.

REFERENCES

Andersen, R. A. 1987. Inferior parietal lobule function in spatial perception and visuomotor integration. In *Handbook of Physiology,* eds. F. Plum, and V. B. Mountcastle, 483–518. Bethesda: American Physiological Society.

Andersen, R. A., L. H. Snyder, D. C. Bradley, and J. Xing. 1997. Multimodal representation of space in the posterior parietal cortex and its use in planning movements. *Annu Rev Neurosci* 20:303–330.

Astafiev, S. V., G. L. Shulman, C. M. Stanley, A. Z. Snyder, D. C. Van Essen, and M. Corbetta. 2003. Functional organization of human intraparietal and frontal cortex for attending, looking, and pointing. *J Neurosci* 23:4689–4699.

Bangert, M., and E. O. Altenmüller. 2003. Mapping perception to action in piano practice: A longitudinal DC-EEG study. *BMC Neurosci* 4–26.

Brinkman, C. 1981. Lesions in supplementary motor area interfere with a monkey's performance of a bimanual coordination task. *Neurosci Lett* 27:267–270.

Brinkman, C. 1984. Supplementary motor area of the monkey's cerebral cortex: Short- and long-term deficits after unilateral ablation and the effects of subsequent callosal section. *J Neurosci* 4:918–929.

Chan, J. L., and E. D. Ross. 1988. Left-handed mirror writing following right anterior cerebral artery infarction: Evidence for nonmirror transformation of motor programs by right supplementary motor area. *Neurology* 38:59–63.

Christensen, L. O., P. Johannsen, T. Sinkjaer, N. Petersen, H. S. Pyndt, and J. B.Nielsen. 2000. Cerebral activation during bicycle movements in man. *Exp Brain Res* 135:66–72.

Connolly, J. D., M. A. Goodale, J. F. Desouza, R. S. Menon, and T. Vilis. 2000. A comparison of frontoparietal fMRI activation during anti-saccades and anti-pointing. *J Neurophysiol* 84:1645–1655.

De Jong, B. M., K. L. Leenders, and A. M. Paans. 2002. Right parieto-premotor activation related to limb-independent antiphase movement. *Cereb Cortex* 12:1213–1217.

De Renzi, E. 1982. *Disorders of Space Exploration and Cognition.* Chichester: John Wiley.

Debaere, F., N. Wenderoth, S. Sunaert, P. Van Hecke, and S. P. Swinnen. 2004. Cerebellar and premotor function in bimanual coordination: Parametric neural responses to spatiotemporal complexity and cycling frequency. *Neuroimage* 21:1416–1427.

Eliassen, J. C., K. Baynes, and M. S. Gazzaniga. 1999. Direction information coordinated via the posterior third of the corpus callosum during bimanual movements. *Exp Brain Res* 128:573–577.

Eliassen, J. C., K. Baynes, and M. S. Gazzaniga. 2000. Anterior and posterior callosal contributions to simultaneous bimanual movements of the hands and fingers. *Brain* 123 (Pt 12): 2501–2511.

Fleming, J., and E. Crosby. 1955. The parietal lobe as an additional motor area; the motor effects of electrical stimulation and ablation of cortical area 5 and 7 in monkeys. *J Comp Neurol* 103:485–512.

Franz, E. A., J. C. Eliassen, R. B. Ivry, and M. S. Gazzaniga. 1996. Dissociation of spatial and temporal coulping in the bimanual movements of callosotomy patients. *Psychol Sci* 11: 82–85.

Freund, H. J., and H. Hummelsheim. 1985. Lesions of premotor cortex in man. *Brain* 108 (Pt 3): 697–733.

Gaser, C., and G. Schlaug. 2003. Brain structures differ between musicians and non-musicians. *J Neurosci* 23:9240–9245.

Grafton, S. T., J. C. Mazziotta, R. P.Woods, and M. E. Phelps. 1992. Human functional anatomy of visually guided finger movements. *Brain* 115:565–587.

Husain, M. 1991. In *Vision and Visual Dysfunction*, ed. J. F. Stein, 12–43. UK, Basingstoke: Macmillan.

Immisch, I., D. Waldvogel, P. van Gelderen, and M. Hallett. 2001. The role of the medial wall and its anatomical variations for bimanual antiphase and in-phase movements. *Neuroimage* 14:674–684.

Jäncke, L., N. J. Shah, and M. Peters. 2000. Cortical activations in primary and secondary motor areas for complex bimanual movements in professional pianists. *Brain Res Cogn Brain Res* 10:177–183.

Jeannerod, M. 1997. *The Ccognitive Neuroscience of Action*. Oxford: Blackwell.

Kazennikov, O., B. Hyland, U. Wicki, S. Perrig, E. M. Rouiller, and M. Wiesendanger. 1998. Effects of lesions in the mesial frontal cortex on bimanual co-ordination in monkeys. *Neuroscience* 85:703–716.

Kermadi, I., Y. Liu, A. Tempini, and E. M. Rouiller. 1997. Effects of reversible inactivation of the supplementary motor area (SMA) on unimanual grasp and bimanual pull and grasp performance in monkeys. *Somatosens Mot Res* 14:268–280.

Kleist, K. 1907. Corticale (innervatorische) apraxia. *Jahrbuch Psychiatrie Neurologie* 28:46–112.

Kleist, K. 1911. Der gang und der gegenwartige stand der apraxieforschung. *Neurol Psychiatrie*, 1:342–452.

Krings, T., R. Topper, H. Foltys, S. Erberich, R. Sparing, K. Willmes, and A. Thron. 2000. Cortical activation patterns during complex motor tasks in piano players and control subjects. A functional magnetic resonance imaging study. *Neuroscience Letters* 278:189–193.

Kurata, K. 1991. Corticocortical inputs to the dorsal and ventral aspects of the premotor cortex of macaque monkeys. *Neurosci Res* 12:263–280.

Kurata, K. 1993. Premotor cortex of monkeys: Set- and movement-related activity reflecting amplitude and direction of wrist movements. *J Neurophysiol* 69:187–200.

Laplane, D., J. Talairach, V. Meininger, J. Bancaud, and J. M. Orgogozo. 1977. Clinical consequences of corticectomies involving the supplementary motor area in man. *J Neurol Sci* 34:301–314.

Luria, A. 1966. *Higher Cortical Functions in Man*. New York.

Malouin, F., C. L. Richards, P. L. Jackson, F. Dumas, and J. Doyon. 2003. Brain activations during motor imagery of locomotor-related tasks: A pet study. *Hum Brain Mapp* 19:47–62.

Mechsner, F., D. Kerzel, G. Knoblich, and W. Prinz. 2001. Perceptual basis of bimanual coordination. *Nature* 414:69–73.

Meister, I. G., T. Krings, H. Foltys, B. Boroojerdi, M. Muller, R. Topper, and A. Thron. 2004. Playing piano in the mind—An fMRI study on music imagery and performance in pianists. *Brain Res Cogn Brain Res* 19:219–228.

Milner, A. D., and M. Goodale. 1995. *The Visual Brain in Action*. Oxford: Oxford University Press.

Mushiake, H., M. Inase, and J. Tanji. 1991. Neuronal activity in the primate premotor, supplementary, and precentral motor cortex during visually guided and internally determined sequential movements. *J Neurophysiol* 66:705–718.

Oldfield, R. C. 1971. The assessment and analysis of handedness: The Edinburgh inventory. *Neuropsychologia* 9:97–113.

Sadato, N., Y. Yonekura, A. Waki, H. Yamada, and Y. Ishii. 1997. Role of the supplementary motor area and the right premotor cortex in the coordination of bimanual finger movements. *J Neurosci* 17:9667–9674.

Sakai, K., O. Hikosaka, S. Miyauchi, R. Takino, Y. Sasaki, and B. Putz. 1998. Transition of brain activation from frontal to parietal areas in visuomotor sequence learning. *J Neurosci* 18:1827–1840.

Schlaug, G. 2003. The brain of musicians. In *The Cognitive Neuroscience of Music*, eds. I. Peretz, and R. Zatorre, 366–381. New York: Oxford University Press.

Scholz, J. P., and J. A. Kelso. 1990. Intentional switching between patterns of bimanual coordination depends on the intrinsic dynamics of the patterns. *J Mot Behav* 22:98–124.

Serrien, D. J., R. B. Ivry, and S. P. Swinnen. 2006. Dynamics of hemispheric specialization and integration in the context of motor control. *Nat Rev Neurosci* 7:160–166.

Serrien, D. J., A. C. Nirkko, K. O. Lovblad, and M. Wiesendanger. 2001. Damage to the parietal lobe impairs bimanual coordination. *Neuroreport* 12:2721–2724.

Swinnen, S. P. 2002. Intermanual coordination: From behavioural principles to neural-network interactions. *Nat Rev Neurosci* 3:348–359.

Swinnen, S. P., and N. Wenderoth. 2004. Two hands, one brain: Cognitive neuroscience of bimanual skill. *Trends Cogn Sci* 8:18–25.

Talairach, J., and P. Tournoux. 1988. *Co-planar Sterotactic Altas of the Human Brain.* New York: Theime Medical.

Ullen, F., H. Forssberg, and H. H. Ehrsson. 2003. Neural networks for the coordination of the hands in time. *J Neurophysiol* 89:1126–1135.

Vanlierde, A., A. G. De Volder, M. C. Wanet-Defalque, and C. Veraart. 2003. Occipito-parietal cortex activation during visuo-spatial imagery in early blind humans. *Neuroimage* 19:698–709.

Wenderoth, N., F. Debaere, S. Sunaert, and S. P. Swinnen. 2005. The role of anterior cingulate cortex and precuneus in the coordination of motor behaviour. *Eur J Neurosci* 22:235–246.

Wenderoth, N., F. Debaere, S. Sunaert, P. van Hecke, and S. P. Swinnen. 2004. Parieto-premotor areas mediate directional interference during bimanual movements. *Cereb Cortex* 14:1153–1163.

Wolpert, D. M., S. J. Goodbody, and M. Husain. 1998. Maintaining internal representations: The role of the human superior parietal lobe. *Nat Neurosci* 1:529–533.

Wyke, M. 1971. The effects of brain lesions on the performance of bilateral arm movements. *Neuropsychologia,* 9:33–42.

13

Searching for Language Origins[1]

P. Thomas SCHOENEMANN
Indiana University

Abstract

Because language is one of the defining characteristics of the human condition, exploring the origin of language is important to understanding the evolution of our species. Evolutionary biological principles suggest that evolution proceeds by modifying pre-existing mechanisms whenever possible, rather than by creating whole new mechanisms from scratch, and that non-genetic behavioral change within each generation spurs any later genetic adaptation for that behavior. A model of language origins and evolution consistent with these principles suggests that increasing conceptual complexity of our ancestors—played out in the context of an increasingly socially interactive existence dominated by learned behavior – drove the elaboration of communications systems in our lineage. Attempts to date the origin of language rely on assumptions about how language and material culture are connected, or the relationships between anatomy, brain, and behavior. On the whole, the evidence suggests a very ancient origin of significantly enhanced communication, though exactly when this would have been identifiable to modern linguists as 'language' is unclear. It would appear that some critical components of language date back to the emergence of the genus *Homo*, with other components having an even deeper ancestry.

1. This chapter has benefitted from numerous conversations over the years with Professor William S-Y. Wang. I owe him a great debt of gratitude for his encouragement and support over the years, for the many opportunities he has afforded me to interact with such interesting scholars in a number of conferences and workshops he has organized, and for his keen interest in language evolution. His breadth of interests, his recognition of the many sources of potential knowledge on topics about language evolution, and his deep understanding of the issues, are things I have always admired. This chapter has also benefitted from conversations with Vincent Sarich, Morten Christiansen, Robert Port, Robert Seyfarth, Dorothy Cheney, James Hurford, Tao Gong, JinyunKe, Thomas Lee, Craig Martell, James Minett, Ching Pong Au, Feng Wang, and Reina Wong. I also wish to thank Shi Feng and Peng Gang for organizing this Festschrift for Professor Wang, and for their patience.

1.   Introduction

> The key to the evolution of language also lies far away from us—lost in the dim and remote past of man's earliest developments. When we consider the nature of the challenge, we should, of course, be fully aware of the magnitude of the task. However, it is a key well worth the search, because there is no more critical achievement of the human mind than the invention of language. The more deeply our search takes us into the nature and development of this invention, the more we have come to appreciate the magnificence of this achievement (Wang 1991, 131).

The unique place that humans hold in the evolution of life is in large part the result of the advent of language. The depth and complexity of the types of things about which humans are able to communicate have allowed for a level of coordination, elaboration of shared knowledge, and richness of social life that appear to exceed that of any other species. Reconstructing the origin and evolution of language is therefore one of the most interesting questions not just for linguistics, but for the entire field of evolutionary biology as well.

Professor William Wang has long recognized the importance of this question, and has encouraged many others to this goal through his own thoughtful research and writing. The present author was one of those inspired to pursue this 'holy grail' of evolutionary questions, having first read Professor Wang's essay "Exploration in language evolution" (Wang 1991) as a graduate student. The present essay is an attempt to follow in his footsteps, outlining some of the paths that have been pursued to try to illuminate the natural history of language.

> While it is clear that the capacity for language rests upon biological foundations, it is the fact that it is culturally transmitted that endows it with its immense potential for elaboration and adaptation (Wang 1991, 108–109)

The fact that the phenomenon of human language has both biological and learned cultural dimensions means that an understanding of its origins and evolution requires an integrative, biocultural approach. It is sometimes suggested that the cultural evolution of language may be considered independent of its biological evolution (e.g., Croft 2000). However, the cultural evolution of language is in fact the driving force behind its biological evolution. The recognition that cultural evolution is much faster than biological evolution has led to the suggestion that language adapted to the human brain more often than the human brain adapted to make language possible (Christiansen 1994; Christiansen and Chater 2008; Deacon 1997). Understanding the cultural evolution of language, and especially how it is used by individuals as part of their social existence, is therefore critical to understanding the evolution of language in the broad sense.

2.   Evolutionary Principles

An analysis grounded in an evolutionary perspective makes a set of predictions about how behavioral evolution—of any kind—is likely to proceed. These predictions stem directly from a set of basic principles central to evolutionary biology. The most important of these is that, whenever change occurs, evolution proceeds by modifying pre-existing mechanisms, rather than by creating whole new mechanisms completely from scratch. This is because complex, directional, evolutionary change must in all cases be reproductively adaptive within each and every generation. This in turn rewards individuals who push the limits of their own pre-existing cognitive machinery in order to approximate some behavioral ability. If it were possible to change instantly from completely lacking any of the cognitive machinery necessary for communication, to having full-blown complex natural human language, then it would be possible to take seriously the idea that human language is cognitively unique and shares no common circuitry with any non-human animals. However, it seems very clear that no such single macro-mutation could possibly explain the appearance of language, given the widespread and varied brain resources that are required for language (see e.g., Schoenemann 2009a). Some language theorists have maintained that at least some key aspects of human language are likely to be unique—not deriving from any pre-existing circuitry (Chomsky 1972; Hauser et al. 2002; Pinker 1994). From an evolutionary perspective, however, this is almost surely false, with its likelihood being inversely proportional to the complexity of the supposedly unique features (the more complex, the less likely the features are truly unique). Thus, we must take seriously the idea that meaningful continuities exist between human and non-human communication and cognition.

The ubiquity of preadaptation has a corollary, which is that flexible, non-genetic behavioral change will drive, at each step, later genetic adaptation in the direction of that behavior. If it is beneficial for an individual organism in a particular environment to adapt to new social conditions in some way, this organism must, by definition, do so through the use of behavioral patterns that are not hard-wired. Such a process, repeated generation after generation, will result in evolutionary (genetic) change being driven by behavioral change, and not the other way around. Within evolutionary biology, behavioral change is understood to be the primary driver of many key events in the evolution of life (Lieberman 1984; Mayr 1978). There are numerous examples in human evolution itself, even aside from language, that demonstrate this quite clearly (Schoenemann 2010a). It is now understood that selection favored the evolution of sickle-cell in some African populations because heterozygotes are protected against malaria (Friedman and Trager 1981). It turns out that malaria itself has inadvertently been spread through human behavior, because agriculture creates prime environments for the parasite. Thus, the spread of agriculture (a cultural/behavioral change) drove biological adaptation in the form of sickle-cell (Livingstone 1958).

Another example can be seen in the biological adaptations that allow for the drinking of milk as adults in some European and African populations. Among mammals generally—and the majority of human populations today—adults are actually lactose-intolerant (i.e., unable to digest the major sugar in milk). The few human populations that can drink milk today all have a long history of domestication of animals that were able to produce significant quantities of milk. Because the ancestral condition among humans was to be lactose intolerant as adults, the initial domestication would not have been for milk, but rather for meat and/or hide. It was only after domestication for other reasons that selection could favor genetic changes that allow for adult milk consumption (Durham 1991).

The transition to bipedalism—another critical adaptive shift in human evolution—was also driven by behavioral changes. Hominins did not evolve efficient bipedal anatomy first, only to stumble upon its usefulness later. Instead, there was an adaptive benefit in early hominin niches for bipedalism, if it could somehow be accomplished. Apes today can walk bipedally, though with significantly more difficulty than humans. Thus, individual hominins who could spend longer and longer periods bipedal would have had reproductive benefits over those who could not. The behavioral shifts towards increasing bipedalism would have driven the selection for more efficient bipedal anatomy (see e.g., Hunt 1994).

Exactly the same kind of process would have occurred with respect to language evolution: It must have been beneficial for individuals to communicate with others in their social group, in an increasingly sophisticated manner. Thus, individuals who were able to use whatever pre-existing cognitive mechanisms were available (to themselves and others) to communicate as effectively as possible, would have had the greatest adaptive benefits. Evolutionary changes enhancing language abilities in such a process would have been biased towards modifying these pre-existing abilities at each and every step of the evolutionary process. This does not lead to the evolution of unique modules specific only to language, but rather with obviously modified circuits that show clear evidence of modifications from non-language circuits. We should expect to find minimal biological changes, and should therefore look for ways in which we might explain language in these terms.

Another key part of the story derives from the recognition of the fundamentally interactive nature of communication. As Wang (1991) pointed out, language by definition requires both a sender and a receiver. In order for any new language-relevant mutation to be adaptive for a sender, other individuals in the social group must already have the cognitive circuitry that allowed them to understand the enhanced communication made possible by this mutation. Similarly, in order for a new mutation to be adaptive for a receiver, other individuals must already be producing the types of enhanced signals that could take advantage of such mutations. In both cases, adaptive change would have occurred towards features that either benefited greater understanding of others (given their pre-existing cognitive abilities), or greater understanding to others (Schoenemann 2009b). The types of mutations that would fit these constraints would necessarily be slight modifications of existing cognitive circuitry, not wholly new circuits.

3.   Preadaptations

Language evolution presupposed a rich social existence, thereby making enhanced communication adaptive. Primates are particularly social animals, and are social in a way that is intrinsically interactive and not simply the result of a passive, 'safety-in-numbers' survival strategy. Communication is implicit to this kind of interactive sociality: it is difficult to imagine interactive social interactions devoid of some form of communication. Thus, primate sociality was a critical preadaptation to language. Humans appear to have further elaborated this degree of sociality to an extreme (Dunbar 2003) (see below). All of this further presupposes that there were useful things to learn from others, or useful things to communicate to them, which in turn requires that there be a rich enough internal conceptual world in individuals such that, ultimately, it could be useful to code this information in some manner symbolically. What evidence exists of conceptual understanding in primates? Perhaps the most obvious evidence derives from studies of alarm calls for different predators that have been documented in at least three different monkey species (Cheney and Seyfarth 1990; Zuberbuhler 2000), and at least one gibbon species (Clarke et al. 2006). In order for these primate species to have such calls, they must have separate concepts for each type of predator.

The complexity of their conceptual understanding is not limited to a handful of different predators, however. Baboons at least have been shown to recognize hierarchical relationships both at the level of individuals and families within their social groups (Bergman et al. 2003). This means that individual baboons actually know a great deal of detailed social information about their group (Seyfarth and Cheney 2003). Though there is no evidence that they code this information in some form of productive vocal communication system, they certainly act on this information, indicating that they must have the underlying conceptual understanding of these relationships.

In addition to this, a plethora of ape language studies have demonstrated that, at the very least, apes can learn arbitrary signs for a wide variety of different concepts (Gardner and Gardner 1984; Premack and Premack 1972; Savage-Rumbaugh et al. 1993). This means they must have conceptual categories sufficiently distinct to allow them to mark these reliably with arbitrary symbols. Thus, the conceptual foundations of language would appear to have been set long prior to language evolution. This would, in fact, have to have been the case, because it would not make sense for our ancestors to evolve language if they had nothing to communicate about (Schoenemann 1999).

The use of combinatorial rules (precursors of syntactic rules) in non-human primate communication systems has been much harder to demonstrate, but some intriguing findings have been reported. Campbell's monkeys (*Cercopithecus campbelli*) have been reported to produce the equivalent of a "not" signal in front of their normal predator alarm calls to indicate something akin to: "not a leopard" (Zuberbuhler 2002). In gibbons, their predatory-induced songs apparently differ from their regular songs not in the specific notes used, but rather in how they were specifically organized into songs, and these organizational differences appear to be meaningful to other conspecifics (Clarke et al. 2006). Among ape language studies, Kanzi appears to understand simple grammatical constructions in spoken English, distinguishing commands like: "put the ball on the pine needles" from "put the pine needles on the ball", as well as: "take the ball outside" from "get the ball that's outside" (Savage-Rumbaugh et al. 1993; Savage-Rumbaugh et al. 2009). To do this, he must understand, at least at a rudimentary level, some of the completely arbitrary symbolic features of English grammar—for example that sequential order codes features of argument structure (what gets done to what).

All of this suggests that the following basic components essential to human language were in place long before the human lineage split from the great apes: (i) the existence of distinct cognitive concepts that could be (ii) coded with arbitrary vocalizations, (iii) the incipient ability to use a completely arbitrary device (sequential order) to mark argument relationships between concepts, and (iv) the ability to use these for communicative purposes.

4.   Evidence of Language Origins

The determination of when language began depends entirely on what one means by "language" (Wang 1991). If one imagines language evolution as a continuous progressive development, then there is no specific point in time where language could be said to have appeared. Wang (1991) likens it to asking when a man who has been losing his hair finally becomes bald. Models of language evolution emphasizing distinct intermediate stages, on the other hand (e.g., Bickerton 1995), posit more clear cut transitions between key language developments, which presumably would be more clearly marked in the evolutionary record.

The extent to which language evolution was continuous vs. discontinuous is not actually clear. The spread of new features across languages does appear to occur nonlinearly, following an approximate 'S'-shaped curve (Shen 1997; Wang et al. 2004). Computational models of language change/evolution also often display relatively sharp transitions between states (Gong et al. 2005; Ke and Holland 2006). However, even if we assume individual features of language changed non-linearly, it is still possible that overall language evolution was relatively continuous, if we assume that the change in individual features were independent of each other, and therefore spread over time with different starting points. It is probably most relevant to approach the question of language origins from the perspective of changes in communicative efficacy, rather than the presence or absence of specific grammatical features. From this point of view, language change was arguably continuous.

What direct evidence is there for the origin of language? Because language behavior itself does not fossilize, language evolution must be inferred either from its effects on fossil skeletal anatomy and/or from the material culture left behind by our distant ancestors. A number of theorists have argued that the evidence points to fully modern syntactic language occurring relatively late in human evolution, coincident with—or subsequent to—the origin of our own species, *Homo sapiens* (Bickerton 1995; Klein and Edgar 2002; Tattersall 1998). This would date the origin of language to somewhere under ~150,000 years ago. By contrast, others would prefer to push the date of language origins substantially further back, to more than ~500,000 years ago, and perhaps as far back as the origin of our genus ~2 million years ago (Dunbar 2003; Laitman 1985; Schoenemann 2005; Tobias and Campbell 1981). As will be discussed, it is possible these divergent views are focusing on different parts of the whole story of language evolution, and that neither is actually wrong, but instead both are true but incomplete by themselves. Each may be looking at different parts of a complex evolutionary history.

4.1 Evidence consistent with a recent origin

One of the central arguments offered for a recent development of language is the significant increase in the complexity and range of material culture, particularly in artistic expression, which show a rather dramatic increase in occurrence by ~35,000 years ago. Evidence of even earlier art appears in places in Africa, such as at Blombos Cave in South Africa, where pigment (ochre) processing materials were recently found, dating to ~100,000 years ago (Henshilwood et al. 2011). The connection of representational art specifically to language is tenuous, however. For one thing, representational art is not direct evidence of the type of symbolic activity that is central to language. Linguistic symbols have arbitrary connections with their referents, whereas representational art directly reflects the referent in some obvious way. In the terminology of Pierce (1867), words are true symbols, whereas objects of representational art are just likenesses (he later used the term 'icon'; see also Fetzer 1988). Direct evidence of language would instead require something resembling writing rather than just art. Writing, however, appears to have taken tens of thousands more years to develop. When it does occur, it appears concurrent with very large increases in population, spurred by resource surpluses resulting from the development of agriculture. The first writing systems appear to have been essentially accounting tools (Schmandt-Besserat 1991). Thus, even if we assume that the flowering of representational art marked the origin of language (or at least fully modern syntactic language), actual direct evidence of language would not occur until much later. It is not clear how confident we can be that representational art—as opposed to other possible markers to be discussed below—specifically marks the origin of language. Representational art indicated an enhanced interest in thinking about past events, but its direct connection to language is tenuous.

Henshilwood and Marean (2003) suggest that evidence of non-utilitarian material culture, even if not representational art itself, is nevertheless suggestive of language: "Decoding the meaning of a design engraved on a piece of ochre or understanding why a bone tool is crafted much more carefully than necessary for a utilitarian object is difficult, but objects like these are strongly suggestive of the advanced levels of symbolic thought and language that were necessary for the development of modern behavior" (636). Exactly why language would be required to create engraved designs, or particularly carefully crafted tools, is not clear however. Furthermore, while language may or may not be necessary for such apparently non-utilitarian material culture, it doesn't follow that language must have originated at the same time as the earliest archaeological evidence of such culture. As Glynn Isaac (1976) pointed out, "lack of elaboration does not prove lack of capability." At best, evidence of non-utilitarian material culture would simply suggest that language had fully emerged by ~100,000 years ago.

Another problem with the attempt to tie art to language involves the recognition that there exists among living peoples—all of whom have fully modern language—a huge range of variation in complexity of material culture. The differences between modern cultures in this regard cannot be due to presence or absence of symbolic language, or of specialized evolved circuits in different populations, and are instead a function of population density and accidents of history. As Glynn Isaac (1976) noted when discussing the degree of complexity of stone tool assemblages in the archaeological record:

Few, if any, of the assemblages have ever approached in complexity the limits of capability of their makers. Even the complex material culture of modern times has not presumably reached the extremes of which mankind is capable...If we look at ethnographic information on the artifacts of recent nonagricultural peoples, we find great differences in the degree of elaboration as measured in various ways, in spite of the fact that inherent capabilities are not known to differ. (p. 277)

Complexity in material culture lags behind cognitive evolution. Because the flowering of art in the Upper Paleolithic is also coincident with the development of a wide range of advancements in tools and technology (Schick and Toth 1993), it is entirely possible that the appearance of art simply marks the development of advanced technology (itself likely the result of an earlier increase in population density). The earliest evidence of art is not an unequivocal marker for the origin of language.

Furthermore, there are strong suggestions of artistic endeavors going back much further

Figure 13.1   ~200,000 year old Handaxe from West Tofts, England, containing a beautiful fossil shell in the center
Photo courtesy of the Museum of Archaeology and Anthropology, University of Cambridge.

than even the 100,000 year old date for Blombos Cave material. The collection of fossils by hominins appears to have occurred long before this (Oakley 1973). In a few cases, handaxes dating to ~200,000 years ago have been found with fossil shells prominently centered in their side views, possibly intentionally (Figure 13.1; Oakley 1981). The Paleolithic site of Terra Amata in France, which appears to be even older, revealed several pieces of red ochre that appeared to have been extensively worn through use (de Lumley 1969), presumably as pigment. If the advent of art does indeed signal the origin of language, and if these early examples represent incipient artistic expression, as they appear to, then language origins would predate *Homo sapiens*.

Additional indirect arguments for a recent origin of language have been proposed on the basis of anatomical considerations of fossil specimens. In one case, the narrowness of the thoracic vertebral canal of a particularly complete *Homo erectus* specimen (KNM-WT 15000) has been used to suggest that that species (which predated *Homo sapiens* and even Neanderthal) lacked language (Walker and Shipman 1996). The vertebral canal transmits the spinal cord, and in the thoracic region carries the nerves that innervate the intercostal (rib) muscles of the chest cavity. Since language is partly dependent on the intricate maintenance and manipulation of air pressure through the larynx, and assuming that the size of the vertebral canal accurately predicts the degree of sophistication of muscle control in the chest, Walker and Shipman (1996) argue that narrowness of the vertebral canal could be a marker for language. This conclusion has been called into question, however, by suggestions that KNM-WT 15000 is actually just pathological with respect to its vertebral canal (Latimer and Ohman 2001). This is further supported by that fact that even older *Homo erectus* specimens from the site of Dmanisi in the Republic of Georgia, show normal (for modern humans) vertebral canal dimensions (Meyer 2005). In addition, it is not clear that intercostal muscles actually play a significant role in vocal production to begin with (Meyer 2003).

Another line of fossil anatomical research relevant to language origins has focused on the position of the larynx, which is much lower in the neck in modern humans than it is in apes. Lieberman (1984) argues this allows for a wider range of vowel sounds in humans, and furthermore would not have evolved unless it had some important benefits because it should be expected to increase the likelihood of choking on food. Although death by choking appears to be very rare in modern humans (Clegg and Aiello 2000), very weak selection can still result in very large evolutionary effects (Schoenemann et al. 2000). Fitch and Reby (2001) point out that red-deer also have descended larynges, which they argue is used for sexual-selection purposes, to make themselves appear larger than they really are. They argue that this calls into question the idea that our descended larynx is specifically due to its usefulness for language. However, for this argument to hold, we would have to believe that sexual selection would have been stronger in hominins than all other primate lineages, since only humans have descended larynges among primates. However this is highly questionable: gorillas and orangutans display much greater sexual dimorphism than do humans (Alexander et al. 1979), yet do not show descended larynges.

The extent to which the actual range of sounds is critical to fully modern language is also unclear. Only a handful of distinctive sounds (phonemes) are required to create an infinite number of words, because it is the sequential patterns of sets of sounds that create distinct words, not the individual sounds themselves. The number of phonemes used in specific languages ranges widely (Wang 1976), with Hawaiian making use of only perhaps 15. In addition, the position of the larynx only affects vowel sounds—not consonants—and therefore only influences a relatively small subset of the total phonemes available. Thus, larynx position is likely not a limiting factor with respect to language evolution, though increasing range of vowel repertoire, when it does occur, would presumably say something about the increasing use of vocalizations over time. Larynx position should lag the development of language, not clearly mark its origin.

Estimating the location of the larynx in specific fossil specimens is difficult, because the larynx itself is cartilage and does not fossilize, and the hyoid bone that it hangs on does not have bony attachments to either the cranium or the vertebral column. One method used to infer its location has been to assess the amount of downward flex evident in the posterior part of the bottom of the cranium. The greater the degree of flexion in the cranial base, the lower the larynx is assumed to be. This method has been criticized on anatomical grounds (Arensburg et al. 1990; Burr 1976; Falk 1975), but it does appear that the cranial base is significantly more flexed in modern humans than in modern apes, and this likely has at least some affect on vocalization. Applications of this method suggests that Neanderthal (~130–30 KYA) did not have larynges as low as adult modern humans (Laitman et al. 1979). However, the multivariate analysis actually groups Neanderthal specimens closer to sub-adult modern human children than it does to apes. As an example, one classic Neanderthal specimen from the site of La Ferrassie in France groups most closely with 6–18 year old modern human children (not apes of any age). When talking to a child even as young as 6 years old, it is easy to convince one's self that their phonetic abilities are not meaningfully restricted and that they have the ability to use language. If cranial base flexion is actually telling us something about the location of the larynx, and therefore about the range of linguistic sounds that a fossil specimen was capable of, then we must conclude that even Neanderthal had the ability to make a sufficiently wide range of sounds to approximate that found in modern human children. Unless we have a principled reason to exclude modern human children from possessing modern human language, this research actually supports a much more ancient origin of language. Lieberman (1984) himself, in fact, specifically states he is "...not claiming that Neanderthal hominids lacked language and culture..." (322).

It is important to note here that those who argue for a relatively recent origin for language tend to focus not on language as a whole, but rather only on specific aspects—subcomponents—of modern language that they believe are critical, such as the development of syntax (e.g., Bickerton 1995) and/or the full range of sounds utilized by different modern languages (e.g., Lieberman 1984), rather than thinking about language as a complete package. By focusing on subcomponents they actually implicitly acknowledge that some form of enhanced symbolic communication would have been evident long before the emergence of fully modern language. Exactly what the difference was between earlier and later linguistic forms depends on the theorist. For Bickerton (1995), earlier communication systems—which he refers to as "proto-language"—lacked syntax and grammar entirely. By contrast Lieberman's (1984) emphasis has been on the evolution of phonological abilities. But for both of these models, any proposed tight, functional linkage between modern linguistic abilities and, for example, art, should be seen as tenuous at best. Such ideas seem to be based more on a simplistic desire to tie together in one neat evolutionary package key behaviors thought to be particularly distinctive to modern humans. It is entirely possible that different key types of behavior occurred at different times during human evolution. One well-understood example is the origin of bipedalism in our lineage, which predated the dramatic increase in brain size by at least a million years (and probably more). Why exactly art would require fully syntactic language, and why the appearance of art should indicate something more about language than about important human demographic changes, for example, is not clear. It is likely a mistake to privilege one aspect of language over others as being more crucial to its evolution. By this argument, the roots of language appear to extend very far back, long predating *Homo sapiens* as a species.

4.2 Evidence Consistent with an Ancient Origin

There are a number of lines of evidence that directly hint at a much older origin of language. One source of evidence ironically stems from the same cranial base flexion work discussed above, which had been used to suggest that Neanderthals lacked the same range of sounds as that found in adult modern humans. Laitman (1983) and colleagues' work has shown that Middle Pleistocene hominins from Steinheim and Broken Hill, which predate Neanderthal (and are likely transitional forms deriving from even older *Homo erectus*), actually show the same degree of flexion that is found in modern humans. In fact, Laitman argues his analysis shows that the lowering of the larynx had progressed significantly beyond the ape condition even as far back as *Homo erectus*, which he believes therefore "...had made a quantum step toward the acquisition of the full range of human speech sounds," (Laitman 1983, 83). The oldest hominid specimen examined by Laitman and colleagues that appears to be significantly different from the ancestral ape condition in this regard is OH 24, a *Homo habilis* specimen dating to ~1.8 million years ago (Laitman 1985; Laitman and Heimbuch 1982; Lieberman 1984). Thus, to the extent that cranial base flexion does indicate something about the position of the larynx, and is therefore marking something important about language, it actually suggests that—at a minimum—significantly increased vocal communication goes back to the earliest *Homo* lineages.

A study by Duchin (1990) came to the same conclusion using a different set of anatomical relationships. Duchin (1990) estimated the location of the larynx through its relationship to the hyoid bone, using discriminant function analysis. She was able to predict hyoid location from the length of the mandible and palate in modern chimpanzees (*Pan troglodytes*) and humans. Measurements from both a *Homo erectus* and a Neanderthal specimen, when entered into the discriminant function equation, unequivocally grouped these fossils within the modern human range, and not with chimpanzees

Although the hyoid itself is rare in the fossil record, one Neanderthal specimen has been found, from the site of Kebara in Israel. Analysis suggests that this hyoid is essentially the same as those of modern humans (Arensburg et al. 1990). It is not known, however, how well hyoid shape itself predicts the range of vocal sounds possible for an individual, which makes the relevance of this find to the present discussion unclear.

Other suggestive evidence for a very old origin of language comes from studies of the endocasts (inside surfaces of brain cases) of early hominins. One focus for language evolution has been an area called Broca's cap. This is an indentation on the interior surface of the brain case (resulting in a protrusion of the endocast) at a location that overlays Broca's area of the brain. Broca's area in modern humans plays a key role in language production, including an important role in processing both aspects of syntax and semantics (Bear et al. 2007; Damasio and Damasio 1992; Posner and Raichle 1994). Studies going back to Broca himself (1861) have demonstrated a lateralization of language production to the left hemisphere for most subjects. This functional lateralization also appears to be reflected in actual morphological differences between left and right hemispheres in the size of Broca's area itself (Albanese et al. 1989; Falzi et al. 1982; Foundas et al. 1996). Because homologs of Broca's area have been found in the brains of apes and even monkeys (Striedter 2005), it is reasonable to assume that Broca's caps on hominin endocasts reflect something about the underlying Broca's area region of the individual. However, because apes and monkeys lack human language, the simple presence of Broca's area itself is of course not a reliable marker of the presence of language. There is some evidence that apes have morphological asymmetries in the brain as well in the region of Broca's area favoring the left hemisphere (Cantalupo and Hopkins 2001), however this study only assessed surface area extent in corresponding hemispheres (which would not necessarily be obvious on fossil endocasts). A study of the actual endocranial surfaces of modern apes and humans using non-rigid deformation analysis suggested that humans do have greater asymmetry in the region of Broca's cap (Figure 13.2; Schoenemann et al. 2008). All of this suggests that the endocranial morphology in the region of Broca's cap of fossil hominins is relevant to the origins of language.

Fossil endocasts often, unfortunately, do not retain clear morphological signals of the underlying brain. However, one early *Homo* specimen: KNM-ER 1470 (~1.8 million years old, usually classified as *Homo habilis*), appears to have a more human-like brain surface morphology (pattern of gyri and sulci) in the region of Broca's cap (Falk 1983). This is certainly suggestive of a very early development of language, though does not prove it. Other early *Homo* endocasts generally cannot be assessed in the same way, however, either because of the relevant area is missing or the morphology is unclear in that region.

However, it is possible to at least assess the relative asymmetry in the size of Broca's cap for a fair number of fossil specimens. Holloway et al.'s (2004) compendium of hominin endocasts includes an assessment of Broca's cap asymmetry for all specimens in which both left and right sides are represented. Their assessments show that of the 19 hominin specimens (17 *Homo* and 2 *Australopithecine*) for which Broca's cap asymmetry can be assessed, all but two demonstrated obvious left-biased protrusion of Broca's cap. Figure 13.3 plots these specimens by age and cranial capacity. As can be seen, the only two right-biased specimens are relatively recent, and happen to be Neanderthal specimens. Brain size also appears to be unrelated to degree of hemispheric asymmetry in this region. While these asymmetries do not prove that early hominins had language, they are highly suggestive of neurological changes relevant to language.

An additional attempt to assess the time course of language evolution in fossils involves the assessment of changes in the size of the hypoglpssal canal, which is the opening through the cranium that carries most of the nerves that control the tongue. The relevance to language is that the movement and placement of the tongue plays a critical role in forming the sounds used in speech (Denes and Pinson 1963). Kay et al. (1998) showed that humans average larger hypoglossal canals than do apes, and also that a handful of hominin specimens they were able to

Figure 13.2 Asymmetry in endocranial morphology at Broca's cap

Left hemispheres of: A. Human (*Homo sapiens*), B. Bonobo (*Pan paniscus*), C. Chimpanzee (*Pan troglodytes*). The ovals indicate the approximate region of Broca's cap for each species. Shading indicates degree of difference between the hemispheres, with darker indicating greater protrusion for left vs. right. Greater dark shading within the human oval compared to the other species therefore indicates greater left-biased asymmetry in humans. Analysis from Schoenemann et al. (2008)

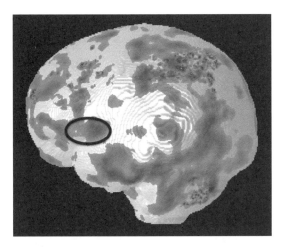

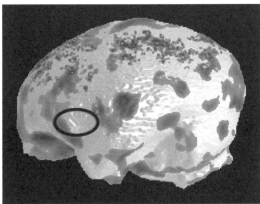

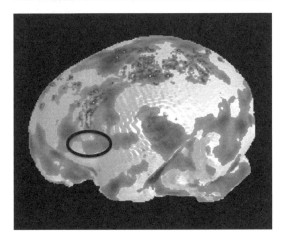

Figure 13.3   Evolution of hominin endocrania over time

A. Asymmetries in Broca's cap in fossil hominins. Specimens are plotted by estimated age and cranial capacity. Circles indicate presumed Homo specimens; squares indicate Australopithecine specimens (more distantly related Hominins). White shading indicates left greater than right; gray shading indicates no obvious difference between hemispheres; black shading indicates right greater than left. Fossil asymmetry assessments for Broca's cap are from Holloway et al. (2004). B. Cranial capacity of all hominin specimens. Specimens are plotted by age and cranial capacity, with presumed fossil species indicated. Modern human and chimpanzee ranges are shown for comparison. Cranial capacity of *Homo* specimens, which date back almost 2 million years, exceed that of modern chimpanzees, whereas Australopithecines overlap. Data sources compiled from the literature by Schoenemann (in press).

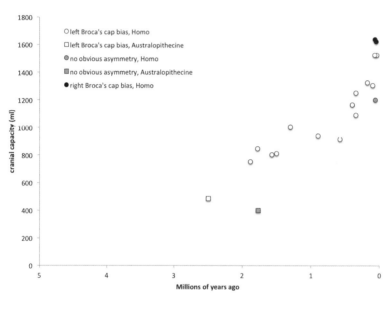

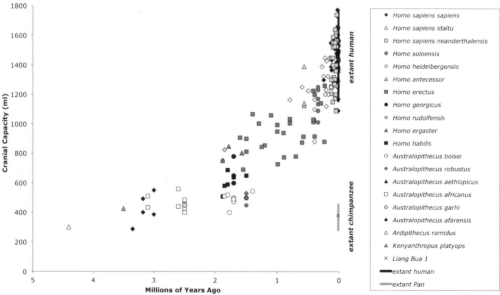

assess fell closer to the human average than ape average. The oldest hominin in their sample was the Kabwe *Homo heidelbergensis* specimen (thought to be ~200,000 years old). This study was questioned by DeGusta et al. (1999) who measured a larger set of human specimens and also included a sample of the small-bodied apes (gibbons) and several other non-ape primates. They reported a much greater overlap with all the apes (which this time included the small-bodied ones). They also presented data from a small study of 5 cadaver specimens suggesting canal size was not unequivocally related to hypoglossal nerve size. From this they argued that hypoglossal canal size was not appropriate for inferring the presence of language. However, even using their broader comparative sample, Kabwe still had a larger hypoglossal canal than any of their ape specimens, and the two Neanderthal specimens in their study were larger than all but the very largest 2 ape specimens (which were likely very large bodied gorillas, though it is not clear from their tables). Thus, though this data is equivocal, it is nevertheless suggestive of increased hypoglossal canal size in hominins, and therefore is consistent with the emergence of increased vocalization at least back to *Homo heidelbergensis* (measurements for older hominins have not been reported to date).

One additional intriguing piece of evidence consistent with an older origin of language is that reconstructed Neanderthal DNA reportedly shows the modern human variant of the FOXP2 gene (Krause et al. 2007). This gene has been implicated in language evolution because mutations of it appear to severely affect language production. Although early claims suggested that FOXP2 might be grammar specific (Gopnik and Crago 1991), individuals with the mutation have a range of impairments, including verbal IQ 19 points lower on average than non-affected family members, pronounced impairment in articulation, and difficulty copying arbitrary or ofacial sequences (Vargha-Khadem et al. 1995). Furthermore, their linguistic deficits with respect to grammar involve a type of morphosyntax that is not universal, and hence cannot be a part of so-called "Universal Grammar" (Schoenemann and Wang 1996). Nevertheless, it has been under apparent selection specifically in the human lineage (Enard et al. 2002), and is likely relevant to language evolution. The finding that the modern human variant was apparently shared with Neanderthal suggests this variant predated the supposed Neanderthal/anatomically-modern-human split. As this has been estimated to be greater than ~300,000 years ago, this would be further evidence of a deep ancestry of important aspects of language.

Lastly, an argument can be made that brain size itself is a reasonable proxy for important parts of language evolution. First, it has been shown that brain size is correlated with a wide variety of markers of increased social complexity, including average group size (Dunbar 2003; Sawaguchi 1988; Sawaguchi 1990; Sawaguchi and Kudo 1990) and the incidence of apparent acts of deception (Byrne and Corp 2004). This therefore suggests that the dramatic increase in brain size in the human lineage, evident by ~2 million years ago (Figure 13.3B), likely involved a significant—and increasing—rise in the extent of social interactivity among hominins. Given that this occurred in the context of the already intensively interactive social existence among primates generally, which is intrinsically communicative in nature to begin with, it is difficult to see how these additional increases could have occurred without involving some form of significantly enhanced communication (c.f., Dunbar 1996). Intriguingly, it has recently been shown that brain size is a significant predictor of the size of the reported vocalization repertoire in primates—even independent of social group size (Hurst 2011).

In addition to this, a major cognitive effect of the brain size increase in hominins was almost surely a very large increase in the complexity of conceptual understanding and awareness (Schoenemann 2005; Schoenemann 2010b). This inference is grounded in the idea that conceptual understanding is instantiated in the brain as networks of interconnectivity between specialized processing regions (Barsalou 2010). Since increasing brain size appears to lead to *decreasing* levels of overall broad connectivity between existing regions (Ringo 1991), larger brains inevitably contain regions that are less directly interconnected than are smaller brains. Because they are less directly interconnected, there is a greater degree of independent and distinct processing within particular regions. In addition, larger brains empirically tend to have larger numbers of distinct anatomical regions (Changizi and Shimojo 2005). Although the specific functions are not always known, these anatomical distinctions are presumed to indicate functional distinctions as well. Thus, larger brains not only have more distinct regions, but these regions are also increasingly distinct with respect to the processing they carry out. Given that concepts are built upon networks of activation among different regions, a larger number of distinct regions will lead to an increasingly rich conceptualization of the world. This means that they would have increasingly interesting things to communicate with others in their social group. This would go hand-in-hand with the increasingly intense, socially-interactive (i.e., communicative) existence of primates, leading inevitably to increasingly complex communication.

Exactly at what point during this process one could label this enhanced communication a true "language" depends, as pointed out before, on exactly what one believes language entails. For many, a language is a communication system that has grammar and syntax (Bickerton 1995; Jackendoff 2002; Pinker 1994). The enhanced communication implied by early hominin brain size increase ~2 million years ago may not have involved syntactic devices sophisticated enough for these theorists to accept the label of "language." However, the degree to which grammar and syntax are truly evolutionarily and cognitively independent of conceptual understanding is highly debatable. There are several models of language that argue grammar and syntax cannot be understood independent of semantics (Haiman 1985; Langacker 1987; O'Grady 1987). To the extent that something like these models is correct, evolutionary elaboration of the conceptual system (as estimated by increasing brain size) would then be a resonable proxy for the development of grammar.

Furthermore, the extent to which there actually are any universals of grammar, and therefore evidence for uniquely evolved separate neural circuitry for grammar, has been seriously questioned (Evans and Levinson 2009). It has been pointed out that grammatical and syntactic features of language that have been claimed to be universal (e.g., Pinker and Bloom 1990) are remarkably general, and instead look very much like simple reflections of our conceptual understanding of the world, rather than rules independent of meaning (Schoenemann 1999). This calls into question the extent to which grammar is really distinct from conceptual understanding, rather than just being an emergent cultural manifestation of it. Savage-Rumbaugh and Rumbaugh (1993) suggest modern human grammatical abilities would likely have been built up in this way, based upon the basic abilities they and others have demonstrated for modern apes. All of this undermines even further the idea of a sharply discontinuous development of language over evolutionary time, and argues that we take a longer view of language evolution.

5.   Future Research

It is almost surely the case that we have not fully mined the available clues for language evolution to date. As examples of intriguing future directions that language evolution research might proceed, three areas that may provide potentially groundbreaking data will be highlighted. First, many new tools have been developed for mathematically describing complex morphological shapes, and these may allow us to extract additional clues from endocasts beyond what we have already. At present, we do not know fully what we can and cannot say about the brains and behaviors of individuals from their endocasts alone. There is clearly a degree of information loss, but we simply don't know how large it is. Using MRI and CT scanning technologies, it is possible to determine how closely different parts of the endocranial surface match the underlying brain of both humans and apes, and this will help clarify this issue. In addition, non-rigid deformation techniques, among others, can be applied to describe in detail species differences in endocranial surfaces (e.g., Schoenemann et al. 2011; Schoenemann et al. 2010). Correlations with behavioral differences can then be assessed at different locations on the endocasts, thereby allowing us to assess whether, for example, the size of Broca's cap predicts something about vocalizations, or other language relevant behaviors. This will then allow us to better understand what these endocranial features might be telling us.

Another intriguing area involves exploring the evolutionary precursors of language areas. Apes and monkeys appear to have homologs of language areas, such as Broca's and Wernicke's (Striedter 2005), but we do not currently fully understand how these areas function in these non-human species. An evolutionary perspective predicts that they process information in ways that —though not part of language *per se*—would be obviously useful for modern human language, perhaps with some minor modifications. One hypothesis that is currently being investigated is that Broca's area in both humans and other primates is involved in extracting and paying attention to sequential patterns of stimuli from the environment. This basic useful function would explain why it has been hijacked for language processing in humans. To explore this, non-linguistic tasks that activate Broca's area in humans (of which implicitly learning basic sequential patterns appears to be one, see e.g.,: Christiansen et al. 2002; Petersson et al. 2010) can be investigated in apes and other non-human primates, to see if these tasks also activate their Broca's area homologs (Schoenemann 2010a). If this turns out to be the case, it would suggest that Broca's area evolved for a more general purpose, but one that would later be very useful for language. This would be a prime example of language (metaphorically) adapting to the human brain, rather than the reverse (e.g., Christiansen and Chater 2008).

Lastly, there is likely much more to be gained from computational approaches that attempt to model the evolution of language. This approach has yielded important insights into the process, showing that a great deal of linguistic structure is basically implicit in socially interactive communication itself, as emergent phenomenon (Gong et al. 2005; Gong et al. 2009; Ke et al. 2002; Kirby 2002; Kirby and Christiansen 2003; Steels 2011). These are surprising results to many theorists, particularly those not well versed in evolutionary theory, but they serve to highlight the pitfalls of relying too heavily on intuition when attempting to explain evolutionary processes. Professor Wang himself realized early on the importance and usefulness of computational studies for studying language evolution, and strongly encouraged their use among his students and colleagues. An application of these methods that might yield clues specifically to the time course of language evolution would be to explore the interplay between increasing conceptual complexity and increasing symbolic conventionalization over time. To the extent that such studies may show the former can drive the latter, we may be able to better anchor the argument that increasing brain size—as a proxy for conceptual complexity—is likely telling us something about language evolution itself. Depending on how tight the linkage might turn out to be between conceptual complexity and symbolic conventionalization in such computational studies, one might be able to use computational data to make fairly good predictions about the development of language itself from the fossil record.

These by no means exhaust the possible future directions language evolution research can proceed, but they are a sample of some intriguing lines of inquiry. There is much work to be done in the area of language evolution.

6.   Conclusions

Language is not a single, unitary behavioral capacity. As such, different components of it will likely have independent—though obviously connected—evolutionary histories. Applying evolutionary principles to language leads to the conclusion that it evolved through the modification of pre-existing cognitive abilities, and not from the evolution of wholly new ones. Several obvious pre-adaptations set the stage for language, including the inherently communicative type of interactive sociality practiced by primates generally, the existence of distinct mental concepts (though presumed to be not as rich as in modern humans), the ability to code these concepts with symbolic behavior, including rudimentary syntax.

Given this, dating the origin of language is problematic, since different components likely evolved at different times, and some cognitive circuits important for language predated the human lineage altogether. While none of the evidence is unequivocal, there are a great many clues pointing to a deeply ancient history for language origins. Evidence used to suggest a very late origin (i.e., either ~150,000 years ago at the appearance of anatomically modern *Homo sapiens*, or ~40,000 years ago at the dramatic increase in material culture that marks the beginning of the Upper Paleolithic) rely on highly questionable assumptions, e.g., that art or other aspects of behavior that is evident archaeologically could only be accomplished if people had language, or that the size of the vertebral column predicts language use, or that language requires a wide phonetic range and that we can reliably detect this in the fossil record. Attempts to estimate phonetic abilities of fossil hominins actually point to important changes dating back to early *Homo*, close to ~1.8 million years ago. Genetic evidence of FOXP2 in Neanderthal ancient DNA also suggests language-relevant changes significantly predated *Homo sapiens*. Finally, a good argument can be made that brain size itself should be seen as a proxy for language evolution. Larger brains suggest both increased interactive—and hence communicative—sociality, as well as increased complexity and subtlety in conceptual thought. Both of these are fundamental to language, and arguably drove language evolution from its simplest beginnings to its current complexity.

The past 50 years have seen a number of creative attempts to extract new information relevant to language evolution out of the fragmentary fossil record. It is almost surely the case that more clues can be extracted, as we learn more and more about the relationships linking skull to brain to behavior. The tools available today to study both morphology and behavior are much more powerful than in the past, and it is likely that much more will be learned about language evolution. Professor Wang's curiosity in language evolution, his extensive interdisciplinary interests and understanding, and his recognition of the fundamental importance of the question, have had a deep and lasting influence in the field. He remains an inspiration to his students.

REFERENCES

Albanese, E., A. Merlo, A. Albanese, and E. Gomez. 1989. Anterior speech region: Asymmetry and weight-surface correlation. *Archives of Neurology* 46 (3): 307–310.

Alexander, R. D, J. L. Hoogland, R. D. Howard, K. M. Noonan, and P. W. Sherman. 1979. Sexual dimorphisms and breeding systems in pinnipeds, ungulates, primates, and humans. In *Evolutionary Biology and Human Social Behavior*, eds. N. A. Chagnon, and W. Irons, 402–433. North Scituate, Massachusetts: Duxbury Press.

Arensburg, B., L. A. Schepartz, A. M. Tillier, B. Vandermeersch, and Y. Rak. 1990. A reappraisal of the anatomical basis for speech in Middle Palaeolithic hominids. *American Journal of Physical Anthropology* 83 (2): 137–146.

Barsalou, L. W. 2010. Grounded cognition: Past, present, and future. *Topics in Cognitive Science* 2 (4): 716–724.

Bear, M. F., B. W. Connors, and M. A. Paradiso. 2007. *Neuroscience: Exploring the Brain.* Baltimore, Philadelphia, PA: Lippincott Williams & Wilkins.

Bergman, T. J., J. C. Beehner, D. L. Cheney, and R. M. Seyfarth. 2003. Hierarchical classification by rank and kinship in baboons. *Science* 302:1234–1236.

Bickerton, D. 1995. *Language and Human Behavior.* Seattle: University of Washington Press.

Broca, P. 1861. Remarques sur le siege de la faculte du langage articule, suivies d'une observation d'aphemie (perte de la parole). *Bulletins de la Societe Anatomique* (Paris), 2e serie 6:330–357.

Burr, D. B. 1976. Neandertal vocal tract reconstructions: A critical appraisal. *Journal of Human Evolution* 5:285–290.

Byrne, R. W., and N. Corp. 2004. Neocortex size predicts deception rate in primates. *Proc Biol Sci* 271 (1549): 1693–1699.

Cantalupo, C., and W. D. Hopkins. 2001. Asymmetric Broca's area in great apes. *Nature* 414 (6863): 505.

Changizi, M. A., and S. Shimojo. 2005. Parcellation and area-area connectivity as a function of neocortex size. *Brain, Behavior and Evolution* 66 (2): 88–98.

Cheney, D. L., and R. M. Seyfarth. 1990. *How Monkeys See the World*. Chicago: University of Chicago Press.

Chomsky, N. 1972. *Language and Mind*. New York: Harcourt Brace Jovanovich, Inc.

Christiansen, M. H. 1994. Infinite languages, finite minds: Connectionism, learning and linguistic structure [Unpublished PhD dissertation]. Edinburgh, Scotland: University of Edinburgh.

Christiansen, M. H., and N. Chater. 2008. Language as shaped by the brain. *Behavioral and Brain Sciences* 31:489–509.

Christiansen, M. H., R. A. Dale, M. R. Ellefson, and C. M. Conway. 2002. The role of sequential learning in language evolution: Computational and experimental studies. In *Simulating the Evolution of Language*, eds. A. Cangelosi, and D. Parisi, 165–187. New York: Springer-Verlag Publishing.

Clarke, E., U. H. Reichard, and K. Zuberbuhler. 2006. The syntax and meaning of wild gibbon songs. *PLOS ONE* 1:e73.

Clegg, M., and L. C. Aiello. 2000. Paying the price of speech? An analysis of mortality statistics for choking on food. *American Journal of Physical Anthropology* S30:126.

Croft, W. 2000. *Explaining Language Change: An Evolutionary Approach*. Harlow, Essex: Longman.

Damasio, A. R, and H. Damasio. 1992. Brain and language. *Scientific American* 267 (3): 89–95.

de Lumley, H. 1969. A Paleolithic camp at Nice. *Scientific American* 220 (5): 42–50.

Deacon, T. W. 1997. *The Symbolic Species: The Co-evolution of Language and the Brain*. New York: W. W. Norton.

DeGusta, D., W. H. Gilbert, and S. P. Turner. 1999. Hypoglossal canal size and hominid speech. *Proceedings of the National Academy of Sciences of the United States of America* 96 (4): 1800–1804.

Denes, P. B., and E. N. Pinson. 1963. *The Speech Chain*. Garden City, New York: Anchor Press/ Doubleday.

Duchin, L. E. 1990. The evolution of articulate speech: Comparative anatomy of the oral cavity in Panand Homo. *Journal of Human Evolution* 19:687–697.

Dunbar, R. 1996. *Grooming, Gossip and the Evolution of Language*. London: Faber and Faber.

Dunbar, RIM. 2003. The social brain: Mind, language, and society in evolutionary perspective. *Annual Review of Anthropology* 32:163–181.

Durham, W. H. 1991. *Coevolution: Genes, Culture, and Human Diversity*. Stanford, Calif.: Stanford University Press.

Enard, W., M. Przeworski, S. E. Fisher, C. S. Lai, V. Wiebe, T. Kitano, A. P. Monaco, and S. Paabo. 2002. Molecular evolution of FOXP2, a gene involved in speech and language. *Nature* 418 (6900): 869–872.

Evans, N., and S. C. Levinson. 2009. The myth of language universals: Language diversity and its importance for cognitive science. *Behavioral and Brain Sciences* 32 (05): 429–448.

Falk, D. 1975. Comparative anatomy of the larynx in man and chimpanzee: Implications for language in Neandertal. *American Journal of Physical Anthropology* 43:123–132.

Falk, D. 1983. Cerebral cortices of East African early hominids. *Science* 221 (4615): 1072–1074.

Falzi, G., P. Perrone, and L. A. Vignolo. 1982. Right-left asymmetry in Anterior speech region. *Archives of Neurology* 39 (4): 239–240.

Fetzer, J. H. 1988. Signs and minds: An introduction to the theory of semiotic systems. In *Aspects of Artificial Intelligence*, ed. J. H. Fetzer, 133–161. Dordrecht, The Netherlands: Kluwer Academic Publishers.

Fitch, W. T., and D. Reby. 2001. The descended larynx is not uniquely human. *Proceedings of the Royal Society of London Series B: Biological Sciences* 268 (1477): 1669–1675.

Foundas, A. L., C. M. Leonard, R. L. Gilmore, E. B. Fennell, and K. M. Heilman. 1996. Pars triangularis asymmetry and language dominance. *Proceedings of the National Academy of Sciences of the United States of America* 93 (2): 719–722.

Friedman, M. J., and W. Trager. 1981. The biochemistry of resistance to malaria. *Scientific American* 244 (3): 154–164.

Gardner, R. A., and B. T. Gardner. 1984. A vocabulary test for chimpanzee (Pan troglodytes). *Journal of Comparative Psychology* 98:381–404.

Gong, T., J. W. Minett, J. Ke, J. H. Holland, and W. S-Y. Wang. 2005. Coevolution of lexicon and syntax from a simulation perspective. *Complexity* 10 (6): 50–62.

Gong, T., J. W. Minett, and W. S-Y. Wang. 2009. A simulation study exploring the role of cultural transmission in language evolution. *Connection Science* 22 (1): 69–85.

Gopnik, M., and M. B. Crago. 1991. Familial aggregation of a developmental language disorder. *Cognition* 39 (1): 1–50.

Haiman, J. 1985. *Natural Syntax: Iconicity and Erosion.* Cambridge: Cambridge University Press.

Hauser, M. D., N. Chomsky, and W. T. Fitch. 2002. The faculty of language: What is it, who has it, and how did it evolve? *Science* 298:1569–1579.

Henshilwood, C. S, F. d'Errico, K. L. van Niekerk, Y. Coquinot, Z. Jacobs, S-E. Lauritzen, M. Menu, and R. García-Moreno. 2011. A 100,000-year-old ochre-processing workshop at Blombos Cave, South Africa. *Science* 334 (6053): 219–222.

Henshilwood, C. S, and C. W. Marean. 2003. The origin of modern human behavior: Critique of the models and their test implications. *Current Anthropology* 44 (5): 627–651.

Holloway, R. L., D. C. Broadfield, and M. S. Yuan. 2004. *The Human Fossil Record, Volume 3. Brain Endocasts—The Paleoneurological Evidence.* Hoboken: John Wiley & Sons.

Hunt, K. D. 1994. The evolution of human bipedality: Ecology and functional morphology. *Journal of Human Evolution* 26 (3): 183–202.

Hurst, D. 2011. Acoustic communities: An amendment to the social brain hypothesis. *American Journal of Physical Anthropology* 144 (Supplement 52): 172.

Isaac, G. L. 1976. Stages of cultural elaboration in the pleistocene: Possible archaeological indicators of the development of language capabilities. *Annals of the New York Academy of Sciences* 280 (1): 275–288.

Jackendoff, R. 2002. *Foundations of Language: Brain, Meaning, Grammar, Evolution.* New York: Oxford University Press.

Kay, R. F., M. Cartmill, and M. Balow. 1998. The hypoglossal canal and the origin of human vocal behavior. *Proceedings of the National Academy of Sciences USA* 95:5417–5419.

Ke, J., and J. H. Holland. 2006. Language origin from an emergentist perspective. *Applied Linguistics* 27 (4): 691–716.

Ke, J., J. Minett, C-P. Au, and W. S-Y. Wang. 2002. Self-organization and selection in the mergence of vocabulary. *Complexity* 7 (3): 41–54.

Kirby, S. 2002. Natural language from artificial life. *Artificial Life* 8 (2): 185–215.

Kirby, S., and M. H. Christiansen. 2003. From language learning to language evolution. In *Language Evolution*, eds. M. H. Christiansen, and S. Kirby, 272–294. Oxford: Oxford University Press.

Klein, R. G., and B. Edgar. 2002. *The Dawn of Human Culture.* New York: John Wiley & Sons.

Krause, J., C. Lalueza-Fox, L. Orlando, W. Enard, R. E. Green, H. A. Burbano, J. J. Hublin, C. Hanni, J. Fortea, M. de la Rasilla et al. 2007. The derived FOXP2 variant of modern humans was shared with Neandertals. *Current Biology* 17 (21): 1908–1912.

Laitman, J. T. 1983. The evolution of the hominid upper repiratory system and implications for the origins of speech. In *Glossogenetics: The Origin and Evolution of Language, Proceedings of the International Transdisciplinary Symposium on Glossogenetics*, ed. E. de Grolier, 63–90. Paris: Harwood Academic Publishers.

Laitman, J. T. 1985. Evolution of the hominid upper respiratory tract: The fossil evidence. In *Hominid Evolution: Past, Present and Future,* eds. P. V. Tobias, V. Strong, and H. White, 281–286. New York: Alan R. Liss.

Laitman, J. T., and R. C. Heimbuch. 1982. The basicranium of Plio-Pleistocene hominids as an indicator of their upper respiratory systems. *American Journal of Physical Anthropology* 59:323–344.

Laitman, J. T., R. C. Heimbuch, and E. S. Crelin. 1979. The basicranium of fossil hominids as an indicator of their upper respiratory systems. *American Journal of Physical Anthropology* 51:15–34.

Langacker, R.W. 1987. *Foundations of Cognitive Grammar.* Stanford: Stanford University Press.

Latimer, B., and J. C Ohman. 2001. Axial dysplasia in Homo erectus. *Journal of Human Evolution* 40 (3): A12.

Lieberman, P. 1984. *The Biology and Evolution of Language.* Cambridge, Massachusetts: Harvard University Press.

Livingstone, F. B. 1958. Anthropological implications of sickle cell gene distribution in West Africa. *American Anthropologist* 60:533–562.

Mayr, E. 1978. Evolution. *Scientific American* 239:47–55.

Meyer, M. R. 2003. Vertebrae and language ability in early hominids. Annual meeting of the Paleo Anthropology Society. Tempe, Arizona.

Meyer, M. R. 2005. Functional biology of the Homo erectus axial skeleton from Dmanisi, Georgia [Dissertation]. Philadelphia: University of Pennsylvania.

O'Grady, W. 1987. *Principles of Grammar and Learning.* Chicago: University of Chicago Press.

Oakley, K. P. 1973. Fossils collected by the earlier palaeolithic men. *Mélanges de Préhistoire, D'archéocivilization et D'ethnologie Offerts à André Varagnac,* 581–584. Paris: Serpen.

Oakley, K. P. 1981. Emergence of higher thought 3.0-0.2 Ma B. P. *Philosophical Transactions of the Royal Society of London* B, *Biological Sciences* 292 (1057): 205–211.

Peirce, C. S. 1867. On a new list of categories. *Proceedings of the American Academy of Arts and Sciences* 7:287–298.

Petersson, K. M., V. Folia, and P. Hagoort. 2010. What artificial grammar learning reveals about the neurobiology of syntax. *Brain and Language.*

Pinker, S. 1994. *The Language Instinct: How the Mind Creates Language.* New York: Harper Collins Publishers, Inc.

Pinker, S., and P. Bloom. 1990. Natural language and natural selection. *Behavioral and Brain Sciences* 13 (4): 707–784.

Posner, M. I., and M. E. Raichle. 1994. *Images of Mind.* New York: W. H. Freeman.

Premack, A. J., and D. Premack. 1972. Teaching language to an ape. *Scientific American* 227 (October): 92–99.

Ringo, J. L. 1991. Neuronal interconnection as a function of brain size. *Brain, Behavior and Evolution* 38:1–6.

Savage-Rumbaugh, E. S., J. Murphy, R. A. Sevcik, K. E. Brakke, S. L. Williams, and D. M. Rumbaugh. 1993. Language comprehension in ape and child. *Monographs of the Society for Research in Child Development* 58 (3–4): 1–222.

Savage-Rumbaugh, E. S., and D. M. Rumbaugh. 1993. The emergence of language. In *Tools, Language and Cognition in Human Evolution,* eds., K. R. Gibson, and T. Ingold, 86–108. Cambridge: Cambridge University Press.

Savage-Rumbaugh, S., D. Rumbaugh, and W. M. Fields. 2009. Empirical kanzi: The ape language controversy revisited. *Skeptic* 15 (1): 25–33.

Sawaguchi, T. 1988. Correlations of cerebral indices for 'extra' cortical parts and ecological variables in primates. *Brain Behavior and Evolution* 32 (1988): 129–140.

Sawaguchi, T. 1990. Relative brain size, stratification, and social structure in Anthropoids. *Primates* 31 (2): 257–272.

Sawaguchi T., and H. Kudo. 1990. Neocortical development and social structure in primates. *Primates* 31 (2): 283–289.

Schick, K. D., and N. Toth. 1993. *Making Silent Stones Speak: Human Evolution and the Dawn of Technology.* Touchstone.

Schmandt-Besserat D. 1991. The earliest precursor of writing. In *The Emergence of Language: Development and Evolution: Readings from Scientific American Magazine,* ed. W. S-Y. Wang. W. H. Freeman.

Schoenemann, P. T. 1999. Syntax as an emergent characteristic of the evolution of semantic complexity. *Minds and Machines* 9:309–346.

Schoenemann, P. T. 2005. Conceptual complexity and the brain: Understanding language origins. In *Language Acquisition, Change and Emergence: Essays in Evolutionary Linguistics,* eds. W. S-Y. Wang, and J. W. Minett, 47–94. Hong Kong: City University of Hong Kong Press.

Schoenemann, P. T. 2009a. Brain evolution relevant to language. In *Language, Evolution, and the Brain,* ed. J. Minett, and W. S-Y. Wang. Hong Kong: City University of Hong Kong Press.

Schoenemann, P. T. 2009b. Evolution of brain and language. *Language Learning* 59 (s1): 162–186.

Schoenemann, P. T. 2010a. The importance of exploring non-linguistic functions of human brain language areas for explaining language evolution. In *The Evolution of Language; Proceedings of the 8th International Conference (EVOLANG8),* eds. A. D. M. Smith, M. Schouwstra, B. de Boer, and K. Smith, 485–486. London: World Scientific Publishing.

Schoenemann, P. T. 2010b. The meaning of brain size: The evolution of conceptual complexity. *Human Brain Evolving: Papers in Honor of Ralph Holloway.* Bloomington, Indiana: Stone Age Institute Press.

Schoenemann, P. T. in press. Brain evolution. In *A Companion to Paleoanthropology,* ed. D. R. Begun. Blackwell.

Schoenemann, P. T., T. F. Budinger, V. M. Sarich, and W. S-Y. Wang. 2000. Brain size does not predict general cognitive ability within families. *Proceedings of the National Academy of Sciences of the United States of America* 97 (9): 4932–4937.

Schoenemann, P. T., R. Holloway, J. Monge, B. Avants, and J. Gee. 2011. Differences in endocranial shape between Homo and Pongids assessed through non-rigid deformation analysis of high-resolution CT images. *American Journal of Physical Anthropology* 144 (Supplement 52): 265–266.

Schoenemann, P. T., R. L. Holloway, B. B. Avants, and J. C. Gee. 2008. Endocast asymmetry in pongids assessed via non-rigid deformation analysis of high-resolution CT images. *American Journal of Physical Anthropology* 135 (Supplement 46): 187–188.

Schoenemann, P. T., J. Monge, B. B. Avants, and J. C. Gee. 2010. Creating statistical atlases of modern primate endocranial morphology using non-rigid deformation analysis of high-resolution CT images. *American Journal of Physical Anthropology* 141 (Supplement 50): 208–209.

Schoenemann, P. T., and W. S-Y. Wang. 1996. Evolutionary principles and the emergence of syntax. *Behavioral and Brain Sciences* 19 (4): 646–647.

Seyfarth, R. M., and D. L. Cheney. 2003. Meaning and Emotion in Animal Vocalizations. *Annals of the New York Academy of Sciences* 1000 (1): 32–55.

Shen, Z-W. 1997. Exploring the dynamics aspect of sound change. *Journal of Chinese Linguistics Monograph* 11.

Steels, L. 2011. Modeling the cultural evolution of language. *Phys Life Rev* 8 (4): 339–356.

Striedter, G. F. 2005. *Principles of Brain Evolution*. Sunderland, MA: Sinauer Associates.

Tattersall, I. 1998. *Becoming Human: Evolution and Human Uniqueness*. New York: Harcourt Brace.

Tobias, P. V., and B. Campbell. 1981. The emergence of man in Africa and beyond [and discussion]. *Philosophical Transactions of the Royal Society of London B, Biological Sciences* 292 (1057): 43–56.

Vargha-Khadem, F., K. Watkins, K. Alcock, P. Fletcher, and R. Passingham. 1995. Praxic and nonverbal cognitive deficits in a large family with a genetically transmitted speech and language disorder. *Proceedings of the National Academy of Sciences of the United States of America* 92 (3): 930–933.

Walker, A., and P. Shipman. 1996. *The Wisdom of the Bones: In Search of Human Origins*. New York: Knopf.

Wang, W. S-Y. 1991. Explorations in language evolution. *Explorations in Language,* 105–131. Taipei, Taiwan: Pyramid Press.

Wang, W. S-Y., J. Ke, and J. W. Minett. 2004. Computational studies of language evolution. In *Computational Linguistics and Beyond,* eds. C. R. Huang, and W. Lenders, 65–106. Academica Sinica: Institute of Linguistics.

Zuberbuhler, K. 2000. Interspecies semantic communication in two forest primates. *Proceedings: Biological Sciences* 267 (1444): 713–718.

Zuberbuhler, K. 2002. A syntactic rule in forest monkey communication. *Animal Behaviour* 63:293–299.

14

Productivity of Mandarin Third Tone Sandhi: A Wug Test

Caicai ZHANG, Gang PENG
The Chinese University of Hong Kong
Shenzhen Institutes of Advanced Technology, Chinese Academy of Sciences

Abstract

Previous studies found that Mandarin Third Tone (T3) sandhi is productive in novel words and Mandarin-English code-mixing phrases. However, it remains unclear whether the application of T3 sandhi is gradient (sandhi T3 remaining distinct from T2) or categorical (sandhi T3 being identical to T2). This study re-confirms the productivity of T3 sandhi via a wug test. In spite of 100% application of T3 sandhi, sandhi T3 exhibits significantly lower F_0 than T2 in pseudo-words, but no significant difference is found in real words. Subtle F_0 differences between T2 and sandhi T3 are likely to be phonetic rather than phonological in nature, which arise due to the impact of factors like coarticulation, elicitation method and speaker difference on the implementation of T3 sandhi rule. In a forced-choice identification test, we found that Mandarin subjects cannot reliably distinguish T2 and sandhi T3 in real and pseudo-words, supporting the 'categorical' viewpoint. Real words are likely to be processed mainly in a top down manner, eliciting similar portions of T2 and T3 responses unselectively to T2 + T3 and T3 + T3 words that are matched in familiarity level; pseudo-words are processed mainly in a bottom up manner, in which case subjects prefer mapping the rising pitch that surfaces in both T2 + T3 and T3 + T3 sequences to T2. To conclude, the categorical application of T3 sandhi is mapped to a fuzzy differentiation in acoustic signals due to speaker difference and other sources of 'noise' in production.

1.   Introduction

In Mandarin Chinese, there are four lexical tones that distinguish semantic meanings (Wang 1967, 1972; Yip 2002). When tones co-occur in an utterance, some tone systematically changes its tonal value depending on neighboring tones (e.g., Chen 2000). In Mandarin Chinese where two third tone[1] (T3 hereafter) syllables co-occur, the first T3 is changed to the second tone (T2) (e.g., Chao 1948; Chen 2000). For example, 耳語 *er3[2] yu3* 'whisper' is a homophone of 兒語 *er2 yu3* 'baby talk'. This phenomenon is known as Mandarin T3 sandhi. The F_0 realization of T3 in the sandhi context is referred to as *sandhi T3* hereafter. The nature of Mandarin T3 sandhi is described as a dissimilating process in which the first one of two low tones is changed to a high tone (Cheng 1966, 1968), which is captured by the following formulation.

(1)   low + low → high-rising + low

The occurrence of Mandarin T3 sandhi is not a recent phenomenon. Mei (1977) traced its origin to the 16th century Mandarin based on philological evidence—Mandarin T3 sandhi rule was clearly documented in the 16th century Chinese textbooks for Koreans. Based on tone correspondence between Mandarin and Middle Korean at that time as well as other evidence, Mei reconstructed the tonal values of the four tones in the 16th century Mandarin. Specifically, T3 was reconstructed as a low tone, or 11 in Chao's tone letters, and T2 was reconstructed as a low rising tone, or 13. This study suggests that T3 sandhi has been in place in the 16th century, and that it bears phonetic similarity to T3 sandhi in Modern Chinese.

In addition to the historical origin of Mandarin T3 sandhi, many other questions have been pursued in previous studies. For example, it has been asked whether there is psycholinguistic evidence to suggest that Mandarin speakers do possess phonological knowledge of T3 sandhi rule (Zhang and Lai 2010). Other studies questioned whether the production of Mandarin T3 sandhi is gradient or categorical (e.g., Zee 1980; Shen 1990a; Peng 2000; Meyers and Tsay 2003). In other words, these studies examined whether the realization of T2 and sandhi T3 is acoustically distinct (gradient) or identical (categorical) in the sandhi context. There are also studies exploring the condition of the application of T3 sandhi, e.g., how syntactic structure interacts with the prosodic domain of a phrase in determining the application of T3 sandhi (e.g., Beattie 1985; Duanmu 2000; Zhang and Lai 2010).

A wealth of knowledge has been accumulated in the literature regarding various perspectives of Mandarin T3 sandhi. Among these interesting questions, the present study focuses on the following two questions: (i) Does T3 sandhi have psychological reality? (ii) Is the application of T3 sandhi gradient or categorical? In the following two subsections, relevant studies were reviewed. After sorting out the empirical findings in previous studies, the aims of the present study were elaborated in subsection 1.3.

---

1. In the literature, the basic value of the third tone (T3) is described either as a low falling tone (21 in Chao's tone letters) or as a low falling-rising tone (214 in Chao's tone letters). Following Mei (1977), this study adopts the former view.

2. In this study, tones are marked as numbers, i.e., 1, 2, 3, and 4, after the pinyin of a syllable. For example, er3, 耳 'ear'.

1.1   Psychological reality of Mandarin T3 sandhi rule

As generative phonology theory gained acceptance in the 1960s, a concern arose among some generative phonologists and other researchers with regard to the psychological reality of phonological rules. Are phonological rules purely descriptive? Or do speakers possess knowledge of phonological rules in a language?

Berko (1958) designed so called wug-test to examine the psychological reality of phonological rules in English. She found that English-speaking children aged between 4 and 7 correctly generalized the allophone of English plural form to novel words, which these children had never learned before. The pioneering work by Berko suggested that children do not learn English plural forms by simply memorizing unanalyzed language materials; instead, children are capable of generalizing rules from reoccurring patterns and productively applying them in the context of novel words. Productivity of a phonological rule in novel words therefore provides critical evidence for its psychological reality.

As far as tone sandhi rule is concerned, however, early work on Taiwanese tones failed to find positive evidence in support of productivity. Hsieh (1970, 1975, 1976) reported great variation associated with individual subjects, lexical items, and tone categories in the application of tone sandhi rules to novel words, which cast doubt on the psychological reality of Taiwanese tone sandhi rules. Moreover, such variability led Hsieh to conclude that the sandhi form and non-sandhi form of a certain tone were listed as morpheme alternants, rather than being computed productively via a phonological rule. Taiwanese tone sandhi rules have been reexamined in a recent study (Zhang, Lai, and Sailor 2011), which attributed the inconsistent application of tone sandhi rules to the combined effects of lexical frequency, phonetic naturalness and phonological opacity. An important implication from these studies is that phonological knowledge cannot be accounted for in isolation from factors of language use such as lexical frequency.

Nevertheless, studies on Mandarin T3 sandhi rule have consistently obtained positive evidence. An early study (Cheng 1968) found that T3 sandhi rule generalized to some novel Chinese-English code-mixing sentences, e.g., 好 professor 不多, 'There are not many good professors'. The rationale was that a word-initial unstressed syllable in English like 'pro' in 'professor' was phonetically similar to a T3 syllable in Mandarin, which triggered the preceding T3 word, i.e., 好 *hao3* 'good' to undergo tone sandhi. Although the application rate of T3 sandhi was not perfect (58.5%, 46.7% and 30% for two-, three- and four-syllable English words respectively[3]), this finding provided initial evidence for its potential productivity.

Xu (1991) provided indirect evidence for the productivity of T3 sandhi rule. He found that subjects made more errors when they recalled visually presented nonsense T3+T3 sequences, presumably because T3 became identical to T2 due to the covert application of T3 sandhi when subjects silently rehearsed these sequences.

With regard to the overt production of T3 sandhi, Xu (1997) found that T3 sandhi applied to a nonsense disyllabic sequence, *ma3 ma3* 馬馬 'horse' 'horse'. Specifically speaking, the first T3

---

3. The application rate was calculated from the number of occurrence of T3 sandhi in Table III of Cheng (1968).

syllable was produced with a rising F_0 contour, acoustically similar to its T2 counterpart in *ma2 ma3* 麻馬 'hemp' 'horse'. However, due to the small sample size (only one disyllabic sequence) there, no conclusive evidence can be drawn to support the productivity of T3 sandhi rule.

Zhang and Lai (2010) provided a scrutiny of the productivity of T3 sandhi in four types of novel disyllabic sequences: (i) *AO-AO (AO=actual occurring), non-occurring sequence of two actual occurring morphemes, e.g., *chi3 sa3*; (ii) AO-AG (AG = accidental gap), an actual occurring morpheme followed by a syllable which is an accidental gap in Mandarin syllabary, e.g., *chuang3 zeng3*; (iii) AG-AO, a syllable which is an accidental gap followed by an actual occurring morpheme, e.g., *ping3 ma3*; and (iv) AG-AG, where both syllables are accidental gaps, e.g., *ping3 zeng3*. These authors found 100% application of T3 sandhi rule to all novel disyllabic sequences, which provided by far the most important evidence for the productivity of T3 sandhi. Despite the 100% application, significant acoustic differences were found between novel words and real words. The F_0 realization of sandhi T3 was influenced by the base tone of T3 to a greater degree in novel words than in real words, a result interpreted as the incomplete application of T3 sandhi in novel words. But it should be noted that the base syllables of T3 (finals in particular) were different between novel words and real words. According to the well established connection between vowel height and fundamental frequency (F_0) (e.g., Lehiste 1970), high vowels like /i/ are associated with high intrinsic F_0 compared to low vowels like /a/. Different finals therefore may have interfered with the F_0 realization of sandhi T3, adding to the acoustic differences between these two conditions. To answer the question whether the application of T3 sandhi is complete or not, it is necessary to directly compare the realization of T2 and sandhi T3 with identical base syllables (such as *er2 and er3*). We now turn to studies seeking to answer this question.

1.2 Application of Mandarin T3 sandhi rule: Gradient or categorical

Studies reviewed in the previous subsection suggested that T3 sandhi applied in both real words and novel disyllabic sequences. A following question is when T3 sandhi applies, and whether the application is gradient or categorical. If sandhi T3 is realized as a F_0 realization distinct from T2, it suggests that the application is gradient. But if T2 and sandhi T3 are indistinguishable, it suggests that the application is categorical. Moreover, this question is relevant for understanding the nature of T3 sandhi rule—if sandhi T3 is systematically realized as a F_0 realization distinct from T2, it may imply that the target of tone sandhi is not T2, but a high-rising tone somewhat different from T2 (Hocket 1947). Previous studies suggested that the relationship between T2 and sandhi T3 is not as clear-cut as it may appear to be. The complication is mainly due to the mismatch between production results and perception results—whereas many production studies found acoustic differences between T2 and sandhi T3, in support of the gradient view, but perception studies suggested that T2 and sandhi T3 are perceptually indistinguishable, in support of the categorical view.

From the production perspective, it has been found that sandhi T3 produced by Beijing Mandarin speakers showed significantly lower average F_0 than T2 (e.g., Zee 1980; Shen 1990a; Xu 1997). This result suggested that sandhi T3 did not completely neutralize with T2 phonetically. But studies using Taiwan Mandarin speakers reported inconsistent results. For example, Chang and Su (1994), Myers and Tsay (2000) failed to find evidence that sandhi T3 was phonetically different from T2. But Peng (2000) reported that sandhi T3 showed significantly lower average F_0 than T2. Moreover, this acoustic difference was maintained across three different speaking rates—slow, mid, and fast.

The above noted studies compared T2 and sandhi T3 in read speech recorded in a laboratory setting. It is likely that the acoustic differences arose as a result of laboratory artifacts, because subjects may exaggerate the lexical contrast of T2 and T3 words when they tried to produce clear tokens. In order to overcome this disadvantage, Yuan and Chen (to appear) conducted a large scale corpus analysis of T2 and sandhi T3 in conversational speech. Acoustic analysis of T3 + T3 words (3938 tokens) and T2 + T3 words (8113 tokens) revealed that sandhi T3 differed significantly from T2 in terms of the magnitude of F_0 rise and the percentage of F_0 rise duration (i.e., the temporal distance from the F_0 minimum to the end of the syllable as the percentage of the syllable duration). These authors reached the conclusion that there were low-level acoustic differences between T2 and sandhi T3 in conversational speech.

This corpus study (Yuan and Chen, to appear) has greatly enriched our understanding of T3 sandhi in natural speech; however, it was not without problems. It did not report the base syllables (intrinsic F_0 of vowels) and the sentential position (intonation effect) of T2 + T3 and T3 + T3 words, which are known to interact with the F_0 realization of a tone. As mentioned earlier, high and low vowels are associated with different intrinsic F_0 (e.g., Lehiste 1970). If the base syllables of T2 and sandhi T3 included different proportions of high and low vowels, the F_0 realization of T2 and sandhi T3 are likely to be biased. Moreover, sentential intonation also interferes with the F_0 realization of tones (e.g., Tseng et al. 2005). Analyzing large amount of T2 and T3 words without fine control in base syllable and sentential position risked introducing greater variability into the data, which may have conflated any subtle acoustic difference between T2 and sandhi T3.

Unlike the inconsistency in production results, perceptual studies have converged to show that sandhi T3 was perceptually indistinguishable from T2. Wang and Li (1967) found that the identification accuracy of T2 + T3 and T3 + T3 words by Beijing Mandarin listeners was close to the chance level (ranging from 49.2% to 54.2%). Moreover, if T2 + T3 and T3 + T3 words were different in frequency (e.g., 友好 *you3 hao3* 'friendly' was more frequent than 油好 *you2 hao3* 'oil good'), listeners tended to identify both words (e.g., *you3 hao3* and *you2 hao3*) as the word with higher frequency (e.g., *you3 hao3*). It suggested that when low level phonetic cues were insufficient for distinguishing T2 + T3 and T3 + T3 words, top down influence (lexical frequency here) determined the perception.

The result that T2 and sandhi T3 were perceptually indistinguishable was replicated in a recent study based on Taiwan Mandarin listeners (Peng 2000). Moreover, Peng (2000) found that the speaking rate (slow, mid and fast) at which the disyllabic sequences were produced did not affect the perception performance—even disyllabic sequences produced at the slowest speaking rate did not significantly elicit more T3 responses.

In summary, most production studies have found acoustic differences between T2 and sandhi T3 in read speech and conversational speech. However, perceptual studies have converged to show that sandhi T3 was perceptually indistinguishable from T2. Such mismatch between production and perception raises serious challenge for interpretation, in that it is difficult to explain why Mandarin speakers produced T2 and sandhi T3 differently while they failed to distinguish them. Moreover, if sandhi T3 was indeed phonetically distinct from T2, it may infer that the target of tone sandhi is not T2, but an intermediate phonetic form distinct from T2. As a result, Mandarin T3 sandhi rule may need to be adjusted to accommodate the findings of production analysis.

In order to provide insight into this question, it requires careful examination of the acoustic differences between T2 and sandhi T3, via fine control of factors that are unrelated to Mandarin T3 sandhi rule. For example, lack of control in base syllable (intrinsic F_0 of vowels) and sentential position (intonation) may have added to the acoustic differences found in some studies. Moreover, small number of word pairs may also influence the F_0 realization of T2 and sandhi T3. For example, only one minimal pair *tu2 gai3* vs. *tu3 gai3* was used in Myers and Tsay (2000). The presence or lack of acoustic differences between T2 and sandhi T3 may arise as random variation due to the small sample size. Furthermore, many previous studies examined T2 and sandhi T3 in read speech, which had the disadvantage of introducing laboratory artifacts into the production because subjects may exaggerate the lexical contrast of T2 and T3 words in order to produce clear tokens. Another concern is individual variation in the production of Mandarin T3 sandhi. Previous studies mainly compared T2 and sandhi T3 at the group level, without analyzing the production of individual subjects. It is likely that group level differences were contributed by only a small portion of subjects, who happened to produce T2 and sandhi T3 distinctly. It is necessary to investigate whether most, if not all Mandarin subjects consistently produced T2 and sandhi T3 differently.

1.3   Research aims

Two questions are pursued in the present study.

(i) Is there psycholinguistic evidence to support that Mandarin speakers do possess knowledge of Mandarin T3 sandhi rule?

In particular, this study aims to replicate the finding of Zhang and Lai (2010) by testing the productivity of T3 sandhi via a wug test (Berko 1958). If Mandarin speakers generalize T3 sandhi rule to pseudo-words, it provides evidence for its psychological reality. In order to expand the previous study (Zhang and Lai 2010), this study includes 30 T3 + T3 pseudo-words with a wide phonetic coverage so as to minimize the influence from base syllables (compared to 8 pseudo-words for each condition in Zhang and Lai (2010)). Moreover, this study uses non-occurring syllables as pseudo-words in order to further control the lexical influence.

(ii) Is the application of T3 sandhi gradient or categorical?

This study compares T2 and sandhi T3 in both production and perception. As discussed above, the debate about the gradient or categorical application of T3 sandhi is centered in production, i.e., whether the acoustic differences between T2 and sandhi T3 are phonetic in nature, or have phonological implication. The present study tries to complement the previous studies by controlling the interference from factors unrelated to the phonological rule in the production test. To avoid the influence of base syllable and small sample size, this study includes 30 minimal pairs of T2 + T3 and T3 + T3 words with identical base syllables. To minimize the artifacts of read speech, this study adopted a repetition paradigm, by asking subjects to repeat two isolated syllables that they heard in the citation form ((e.g., *qi4* 汽 and *che1* 車)) as a disyllabic word (e.g., *qi4 che1* 汽車). More importantly, in addition to group level analysis, individual data are analyzed to investigate whether all subjects produce T2 and sandhi T3 differently.

If significant acoustic differences between T2 and sandhi T3 are systematically attested in the production of each speaker after controlling the confounding factors, it provides more reliable evidence for the gradient application of T3 sandhi. Otherwise, these acoustic differences may merely reflect phonetic variation in the implementation of T3 sandhi rule without bearing any phonological implication.

2. Production Experiment

2.1 Method

2.1.1 Participants

Twelve native Mandarin speakers from Northern China (6F, 6M; mean age = 21.5 yr, s.d. = 3.0) were paid to participate in the production test. No speakers had hearing impairment or long term music training (longer than five years). All participants gave informed consent in compliance with a protocol approved by the Survey and Behavioral Research Ethics Committee of The Chinese University of Hong Kong.

2.1.2 Stimuli

To examine the productivity of T3 sandhi rule, a word list comprising both real words and pseudo-words was designed. The real word condition included 30 minimal pairs of T2 + T3 and T3 + T3 words, e.g., *er2 yu3* 兒語 'baby talk' and *er3 yu3* 耳語 'whisper'. T2 and T3 minimal pairs were matched in familiarity (rated by 10 native Mandarin speakers who did not participate in the production and perception tests) and syntactic structure at the group level. The pseudo-word condition included 30 minimal pairs of T2 + T3 and T3 + T3 tone sequences, e.g., *fia2 sua3* vs. *fia3 sua3*. This study used accidental gaps in Mandarin syllabary as pseudo-words. Non-occurring syllables, which were combinations of Mandarin initials and finals were used, for example, 'fia' is a non-occurring combination of occurring initial 'f' (*f* as in *fei1* 'to fly') and final 'ia' (*ia* as in *jia1* 'home'). Different from the previous study (Zhang and Lai 2010), this study did not use non-occurring combinations of occurring syllables and tones (e.g., *bang2*), for the consideration that non-occurring syllable-tone combinations (e.g., *bang2*) are likely to be assimilated to an occurring morpheme sharing the base syllable (e.g., *bang3* 綁 'to wrap') in perception. Lexical influence can be better controlled by using non-occurring syllables. Details of the word list can be found in Appendices 1 and 2.

In addition to test items, fillers were included to conceal the experiment purpose. The ratio of test items and fillers was 1:1. Fillers included 60 pseudo-words and 60 real words. Real words were disyllabic words of any tone combination other than T2 + T3 and T3 + T3, e.g., *qi4 che1* 汽車 'car'. Pseudo-words were disyllabic tone sequences except for T2 + T3 and T3 + T3 combinations, e.g., *bong2 nia2*.

Full phonetic form of each monosyllable in disyllabic sequences of both test items and fillers (e.g., *qi4* 汽 and *che1* 車) was recorded from a female native speaker of Beijing Mandarin, who did not participate in the production and perception tests. In particular this speaker was instructed to pronounce T3 in its full phonetic form, i.e., 213. Recordings of monosyllables were used as the input stimuli to elicit the production of T3 sandhi.

2.1.3 Procedure

This study adopted a repetition task (e.g., Hsieh 1970; Zhang and Lai 2010). In each trial, recordings of two monosyllables (e.g., *qi4* 汽 and *che1* 車) were presented to the subjects via the earphone. These two monosyllables were separated by a 500 ms silence interval. Subjects were instructed to repeat these two syllables as a disyllabic word (e.g., *qi4 che1* 汽車 'car') as soon as the second syllable was presented. Subjects had to respond within three seconds. Electroglottographic (EGG) recording was obtained simultaneously during the production test. Figure 14.1 illustrates the procedure of the production test.

These 120 test items and 120 fillers were equally divided into four blocks. Each block contained 30 test items and 30 fillers, each with half real words and half pseudo-words. T2 + T3

Figure 14.1 Procedure of the production test. S1 refers to the first syllable, e.g., *qi4,* and S2 refers to the second syllable, e.g., *che1*

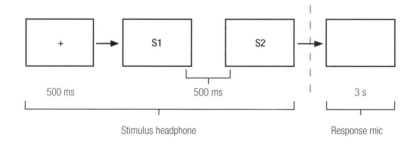

and T3 + T3 sequences in a minimal pair (e.g., *er2 yu3* 'baby talk' and *er3 yu3* 'whisper') never co-occurred in a single block to avoid lexical contrast in production. The order of four test blocks was counterbalanced across the subjects. A practice block containing stimuli not occurring in the test blocks was presented first to familiarize subjects with the procedure.

2.1.4 Analysis

Trials in which a speaker mispronounced the final of a syllable were excluded from the acoustic analysis (e.g., *fia3* mispronounced as *fua3*). This rejection criterion was based on the well established association between vowel height and F_0 discussed above (e.g., Lehiste 1970). If a subject mispronounced one disyllabic sequence, this pair of disyllabic sequences (T2 + T3 and T3 + T3) was discarded altogether. Moreover, this pair of real words, *er2 yu3* 兒語 'baby talk' and *er3 yu3* 耳語 'whisper' was excluded from F_0 analysis for all 12 subjects due to the difficulty in syllabic segmentation.

Duration and F_0 were measured from the rhyme of T2 and T3 syllables for all remaining trials within each speaker. F_0 was measured from 21 sampling points of the rhyme duration (0%, 5%, 10%, ... 95%, and 100%) from the EGG waveform. EGG waveform is a direct trace of the vocal cords vibration, which has the advantage of providing reliable F_0 estimation (e.g., Signol, Barras, and Lienard 2008). Raw F_0 values were then normalized with the log z-score method to minimize between-speaker difference (e.g., Zhu 2005).

For the group level analysis, rhyme duration and normalized F_0 were averaged from all remaining trials for each speaker, and statistical analyses were conducted on the average duration and normalized F_0 of all 12 speakers. Two-way repeated measures ANOVA was carried out on rhyme duration by indicating *lexicality* (pseudo-words and real words) and tone (T2 and sandhi T3) as two within-subjects factors. Three-way repeated measures ANOVA was conducted on normalized F_0 by indicating lexicality (pseudo-words and real words) and *tone* (T2 and sandhi T3) and *point* (21 sampling points) as three within-subjects factors.

In addition to group level analysis, statistical analyses were also conducted within individual speakers in order to find out which speaker produced T2 and sandhi T3 significantly differently. In the speaker analysis, statistical analysis was conducted on all the remaining trials in the pseudo-word and real word conditions separately (due to the unequal number of excluded trials in these two conditions) for each speaker. *Lexicality × tone* repeated measures ANOVA was carried out on normalized F_0 across all trials for each speaker.

2.2 Results

2.2.1 Group level production results

Figure 14.2 displays the rhyme duration of T2 and sandhi T3 in pseudo-words and real words. Statistical analysis of rhyme duration revealed no significant main effects or interaction effects,

Figure 14.2   Rhyme duration of T2 and T3 in pseudo-words (ps) and real words (rl)

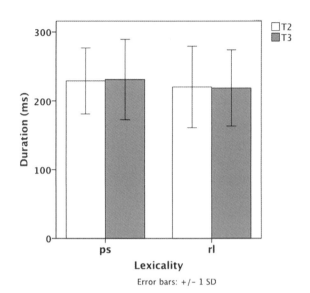

Error bars: +/- 1 SD

suggesting that T2 and sandhi T3 were not different in rhyme duration in both pseudo-words and real words.

Figure 14.3 shows the trajectory of normalized F_0 as a function of normalized duration (i.e., percentage of the rhyme duration). Three-way repeated measures ANOVA on normalized F_0 showed that all main effects and interactions effects reached significance. There were significant main effects of *lexicality* [$F(1, 11) = 24.505$, $p < 0.001$], *tone* [$F(1, 11) = 32.677$, $p < 0.001$], and point [$F(20, 220) = 63.422$, $p < 0.001$], two-way interaction of *lexicality by tone* [$F(1, 11) = 9.584$, $p = 0.01$], tone by point [$F(20, 220) = 10.364$, $p < 0.001$], and lexicality by point [$F(20, 220) = 31.362$, $p < 0.001$], and significant three-way interaction of lexicality by tone by point [$F(20, 220) = 7.467$, $p < 0.001$]. Statistical results indicated unequal effects of pseudo-words and real words on the F_0 realization of T2 and sandhi T3 over time.

Post hoc analyses revealed that T2 and sandhi T3 were significantly different in pseudo-words but not in real words, which account for the unequal effects of pseudo-words and real words. There were significant main effect of *tone* [$F(1, 11) = 65.193$, $p < 0.001$] and interaction of *tone by point* [$F(20, 220) = 12.603$, $p < 0.001$] in pseudo-words. Significant main effect of tone implied that T2 and sandhi T3 were different in *average F_0*; interaction of *tone by point* suggested that T2 and sandhi T3 were different in F_0 *contour* (e.g., Peng 2000; Myers and Tsay 2003). In terms of *average F_0*, sandhi T3 was in average 6.3 Hz lower than T2; in terms of F_0 *contour*, sandhi T3 showed longer portion of falling F_0 at the beginning and reached lower F_0 at the end compared to T2. In real words condition, neither the main effect of tone nor the interaction of *tone by point* reached significance, suggesting that the F_0 trajectory of T2 and sandhi T3 did not differ. Although sandhi T3 was in average 2.9 Hz lower than T2, this subtle

Figure 14.3   Normalized F_0 trajectory of T2 and sandhi T3 in pseudo-words (ps) and real words (rl)

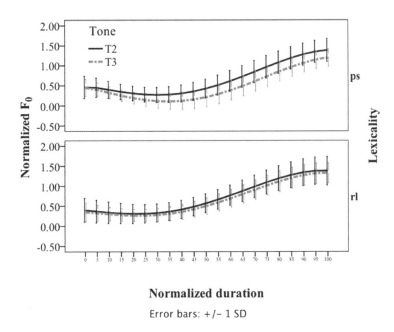

Figure 14.4   Box plot of normalized F_0 of T2 and sandhi T3 in real words

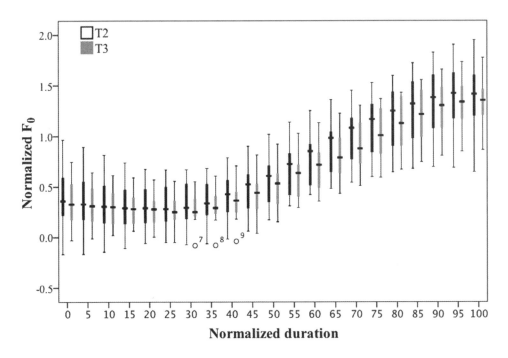

difference did not reach significance.

Although repeated measures ANOVA did not find significant difference between T2 and sandhi T3 in real words, it would be useful to carefully examine the degree of dispersion, which may reveal some differences in the range of variability between T2 and sandhi T3. It is not unlikely that sandhi T3, which is realized as the sandhi form, might show greater degree of variability than T2, which more or less retains its citation form.

Figure 14.4 displays the degree of dispersion of T2 and sandhi T3 across 21 sampling points. From bottom to top, each box plot presents five values—the smallest observation, lower quartile, median, upper quartile, and largest observation of one group of F_0 data at one sampling point. It can be seen that the variability in sandhi T3 do not obviously extend beyond that of T2 either from the point of view of the interquartile range (as indicated by the length of black and grey bars), or from the point of view of the distance between the smallest and largest observation (as indicated by the overall length of each box plot) despite that three outliers, i.e., o^7, o^8, and o^9 lies slightly below the smallest observation of T2 at the corresponding points. The essence of Figure 14.4 is that despite being a sandhi form, sandhi T3 was not obviously produced with greater variability than T2.

2.2.2 Speaker level production result

Group level results may not necessarily hold for the results of each speaker, as shown by the difference between two female speakers in Figure 14.5. Whereas one female speaker (Figure 14.5(a)) produced almost overlapping F_0 trajectory of T2 and sandhi T3 in pseudowords, the other female speaker (Figure 14.5 (b)) produced sandhi T3 consistently lower than T2.

Speaker analysis conducted to investigate the individual variation revealed that in real words five out of twelve speakers (3F, 2M) produced T2 and sandhi T3 significantly differently in either average F_0 or F_0 contour. In pseudo-words, nine out of twelve speakers (4F, 5M) exhibited significant difference in either the average F_0 or F_0 contour of T2 and sandhi T3.

2.3   Discussion

This study found T3 always surfaces as a rising tone rather than a low tone in all pseudo-words. One hundred percent application of T3 sandhi to pseudo-words suggests that T3 sandhi can generalize to novel forms that Mandarin subjects have never learned before. This finding re-confirms the productivity of T3 sandhi rule (Cheng 1968; Xu 1991, 1997; Zhang and Lai 2010), which lends support to the contention that Mandarin speakers have internal knowledge of T3 sandhi rule.

Sandhi T3 is not always acoustically identical to T2. In real words, sandhi T3 is in average 2.9 Hz lower than T2, but this difference does not reach significance. Moreover, sandhi T3 is not produced with greater variability than T2, despite that T3 is a sandhi form. Lack of significant

Figure 14.5   Normalized F_0 trajectory of T2 and sandhi T3 in pseudo-words produced by two female speakers

(a)

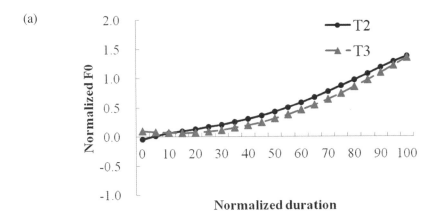

(b)

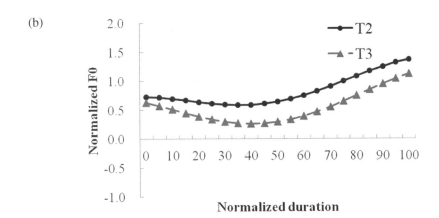

differences together with the analysis of dispersion cast doubt on the claim that sandhi T3 is produced as a phonetic form distinct from T2 in real words.

In pseudo-words, sandhi T3 is significantly different from T2 in both average F_0 (6.3 Hz) and F_0 contour. That sandhi T3 is different from T2 in pseudo-words but not in real words suggests that the implementation of T3 sandhi rule is affected by the lexical status of words (real words and pseudo-words). This finding is consistent with Zhang and Lai (2010), which also reported significant F_0 difference between real words and pseudo-words. The difference between real words and pseudo-words will be discussed in Section 4.

Moreover, there is individual difference in the F_0 realization of sandhi T3. As discussed before, acoustic differences are expected to be systematically attested in all subjects to reach the conclusion that sandhi T3 is realized as a phonetic form distinct from T2. However, individual variability that we found contradicts this expectation. In real words, less than half of the speakers produce T2 and sandhi T3 significantly differently. In pseudo-words, there are more speakers showing significant difference but the result is still not so conclusive as to support the claim that sandhi T3 is realized as a phonetic form distinct from T2.

3.   Perception Experiment

3.1   Method

3.1.1 Participants

The same 12 subjects (6F, 6M; mean age = 21.5 yr, s.d. = 3.0) recruited in the production test participated in the perception test.

3.1.2 Stimuli

Word list in the perception test was the same as in the production test, i.e., 120 test items (60 real words and 60 pseudo-words) and 120 fillers (60 real words and 60 pseudo-words). The difference was that in the production test, subjects listened to recordings of monosyllables, whereas in the perception test they listened to recordings of disyllabic sequences (e.g., *qi4 che1* 汽車). Disyllabic sequences were recorded from the same female speaker who produced the monosyllables, and EGG waveform was obtained simultaneously during the recording.

3.1.3 Procedure

Similar to the production test, all 120 test items and 120 fillers were equally divided into four blocks, with 30 test items and 30 fillers in each block. T2 + T3 and T3 + T3 sequences in a minimal pair (e.g., *er2 yu3* 'baby talk' and *er3 yu3* 'whisper') never co-occurred in a single block. The order of four test blocks was counterbalanced and a practice block was presented

Figure 14.6   Procedure of perception test. S1 + S2 refers to a disyllabic sequence, e.g., *qi4 che1*

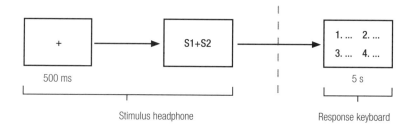

before four test blocks to familiarize subjects with the test procedure.

A four-alternative forced choice identification task was adopted in the perception test. In each trial, recording of a disyllabic sequence (e.g., *qi4 che1* 汽車) was presented to the subjects via the earphone; then four choices were visually displayed on the screen. These four choices were pinyin forms of the presented disyllabic sequence, which included all four logically possible tone combinations of a disyllabic sequence. For example, for the trial qi4 che1 汽車 'car', the four choices were: 1. *qi1 che1*; 2. *qi1 che4*; 3. *qi4 che1*; 4. *qi4 che4*. Choices were displayed in pinyin instead of sinograms in order to maintain identical task condition for pseudo-words (no sinograms) and real words. Subjects were given five seconds to choose the correct pinyin form by pressing labeled buttons on a computer keyboard. Procedure of the perception test is demonstrated in Figure 14.6.

3.1.4 Analysis

For the analysis, the hit rate (i.e., the percentage of correct responses), and false alarm rate (i.e., the percentage that a T2 + T3 response was collected when T3 + T3 sequence was presented and vice versa) were calculated for T2 and T3 in the response of each subject. The sensitivity index, d', which reflects the detection sensitivity of a sound, was computed by subtracting the z-score value of false alarm rate from that of the hit rate (Macmillan and Creelman 1991). d' is an overall indication of how often a subject correctly identified T2 or T3 while refraining from making the same tone response (e.g., T2 + T3 response) when the other tone was actually presented (e.g., T3 + T3 sequence). Two-way repeated measures ANOVA was conducted on d' by indicating lexicality (pseudo-words and real words) and tone (T2 and sandhi T3) as two within-subjects factors.

3.2 Results

3.2.1 Acoustic analysis of the perceptual materials

Before we move on to the perception results, we report the acoustic analysis of T2 and sandhi T3 from disyllabic sequences, which served as the stimuli in the perception test. It has been criticized that previous perception studies (e.g., Wang and Li 1967; Peng 2000) failed to find evidence for the discriminability between T2 and sandhi T3 due to the small acoustic differences in the perceptual materials, rather than due to listeners' insensitivity to the acoustic differences (Myers and Tsay 2003). It therefore merits evaluation of the amount of acoustic differences between T2 and sandhi T3 here.

To this end, F_0 was measured from T2 and sandhi T3 in the perceptual materials. F_0 was obtained at 21 sampling points of the rhyme duration of T2 and sandhi T3 (i.e., 0%, 5%... 95%, and 100%). This pair, *er2 yu3* 兒語 'baby talk' and *er3 yu3* 耳語 'whisper' was again excluded due to the difficulty in segmentation.

Figure 14.7   F$_0$ trajectory of T2 and sandhi T3 in (a) pseudo-words (ps), and (b) real words (rl) produced by a female speaker

(a)

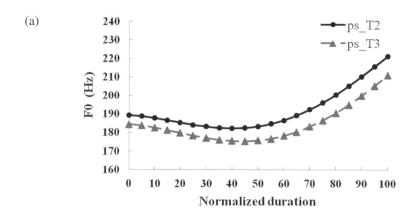

(b)

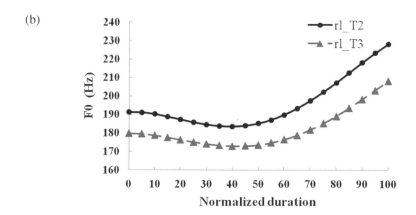

Results revealed that sandhi T3 was in average 7.7 Hz lower than T2 in pseudo-words [t(29) = 6.74, p < 0.001], and 13.9 Hz lower in real words [t(28) = 10.65, p < 0.001] (see Figure 14.7). F$_0$ differences between T2 and sandhi T3 reached significance in both pseudo-words and real words. Moreover, these differences in the perceptual materials were greater than those found in the previous production test (6.3 Hz in pseudo-words and 2.9 Hz in real words; see Figure 14.3 above).

Moreover, a different pattern can be noted between the perceptual materials and the production results. Whereas the amount of F$_0$ difference between T2 and sandhi T3 was greater in real words than that in pseudo-words in the perceptual materials, a reversed pattern was found in the production results. This discrepancy is attributable to the different elicitation methods used (reading a word list vs. repetition task). This effect of elicitation method on the F$_0$ realization of sandhi T3 is discussed in Section 4.

Figure 14.8. d' of T2 and T3 in pseudo-words (ps) and real words (rl)

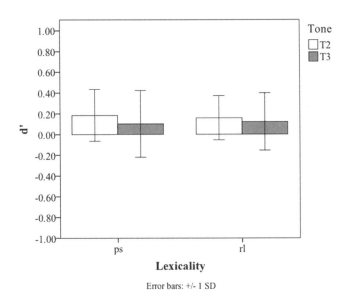

Error bars: +/- 1 SD

3.2.2 *Group level identification result*

Figure 14.8 displays the d' of T2 and sandhi T3 in pseudo-words and real words. d' is an overall indicator of the hit rate and false alarm rate of a sound. In pseudo-words, average d' of T2 was 0.18 (hit rate: 73.89%, false alarm rate: 70%), and average d' of T3 was 0.1 (hit rate: 22.59%, false alarm rate: 19.44%). In real words, average d' of T2 was 0.16 (hit rate: 56.76%, false alarm rate: 51.67%), and average d' of T3 was 0.12 (hit rate: 42.96%, false alarm rate: 38.8%). The closer the d' value is to 1, the more sensitive a subject is in detecting a sound. If d' was close to 0, it means that a subject made random responses to T2 + T3 and T3 + T3 sequences unselectively. For example, a subject may have correctly identified a number of T2 + T3 sequences as T2 (hit rate of T2), but meanwhile this subject also misidentified a number of T3 + T3 sequences as T2 (false alarm rate of T2), which canceled out each other in the calculation of the d'.

Lexicality × tone repeated measures ANOVA on d' found no significant main effects or interaction effects, meaning that the detection sensitivity of T2 and sandhi T3 was not different from each other in pseudo-words and real words.

Two-tailed t-tests were then conducted to compare d' with the baseline (i.e., '0') in each condition. Results revealed that d' of T2 was significantly higher than the baseline in both pseudo-words (t(11) = 2.553, p < 0.05) and real words (t(11) = 2.584, p < 0.05). But d' of T3 was not significantly different from the baseline.

The t-test results should be interpreted with caution. It should be noted that even for T2, d' was not too far away from '0', because subjects very often misidentified sandhi T3 as T2. With this caution in mind, this result indicated that although subjects made a lot of misidentification in both directions, they were less likely to misidentify sandhi T3 as T2 (i.e., false alarm rate of T2) than they were to misidentify T2 as sandhi T3 (i.e., false alarm rate of T3). This asymmetry hints at the possibility that Mandarin subjects may capture some phonetic cue in sandhi T3, presumably the relatively low F_0 (sandhi T3 was in average 7.7 Hz lower than T2 in pseudo-words, and 13.9 Hz lower in real words), which enabled subjects to refrain from misidentifying sandhi T3 as T2. But this phonetic cue is by no means sufficient for Mandarin subjects to reliably distinguish between T2 and sandhi T3, as the misidentification was high in both directions.

3.2.3 Individual variation in responding tendency

Across the board, subjects cannot reliably distinguish between T2 and sandhi T3, as shown by the group level identification result. But individual subjects differed in the way that they tackled the confusion. Some subjects tended to make more T2 responses to most trials (no matter it was T2 + T3 or T3 + T3 sequence) whereas other subjects tended to make more T3 responses.

Examination of Table 14.1 revealed interesting difference between pseudo-words and real words. In the pseudo-word condition most subjects were classified as T2-dominant group, leaving only two T3-dominant subjects, whereas in the real word condition all 12 subjects were evenly classified into T2-dominant and T3-dominant groups. In other words, subjects tended to identify most T2 + T3 and T3 + T3 sequences as T2 in the pseudo-word condition, but they were more likely to randomly make T2 and T3 responses in the real word condition.

3.3   Discussion

Perceptual results in this study replicate the finding that Mandarin speakers cannot reliably distinguish between T2 and sandhi T3 (Wang and Li 1967; Peng 2000). In addition, we found that the lexical status of stimuli (pseudo-words and real words) modulates the responding tendency in a way that subjects tend to make more T2 responses in pseudo-words. Difference in the responding tendency may imply that listeners process real words and pseudo-words via different mechanisms.

In the real word condition, all T2 + T3 and T3 + T3 sequences are real words (e.g., 兒語 er2 yu3 'baby talk' and 耳語 er3 yu3 'whisper') that may have mental representation in the long term memory of subjects. These long term memory traces may be accessed to facilitate the processing of T2 and sandhi T3 in a top down manner, which is revealed by the response tendency in this condition. Subjects show a general tendency to make random T2 and T3 responses, giving rise to similar portions of T2 and T3 responses in average (hit rate of T2: 0.57, hit rate of T3: 0.43; see Table 14.1). This result is expected given that T2 + T3 and T3 + T3 words have matched in subjective familiarity in this study. Top down influence (lexical frequency) has also been discussed in Wang and Li (1967).

In the pseudo-word condition, T2 + T3 and T3 + T3 sequences are sound sequences that Mandarin listeners have never been exposed to before. Without lexical access, T2 + T3 and T3 + T3 sequences are likely to be processed in a mainly bottom up way. When subjects have to rely

Table 14.1 Responding tendency of 12 subjects in pseudo-words and real words

(a) Pseudo-word condition		T2+T3 sequences		T3+T3 sequences	
		hit	false alarm	hit	false alarm
T2-dominant	F03	0.97	0.87	0.07	0.02
	F02	0.97	0.92	0.03	0.02
	M01	0.96	0.94	0.01	0.01
	M06	0.89	0.88	0.01	0.06
	M04	0.88	0.77	0.19	0.10
	F06	0.86	0.80	0.17	0.09
	F01	0.83	0.88	0.10	0.13
	F05	0.66	0.58	0.40	0.27
	M02	0.60	0.56	0.39	0.36
	M05	0.47	0.48	0.14	0.14
T3-dominant	M03	0.50	0.41	0.53	0.48
	F04	0.30	0.32	0.67	0.66
Mean		0.74	0.70	0.23	0.19

(b) Real word condition		T2+T3 sequence		T3+T3 sequence	
		hit	false alarm	hit	false alarm
T2-dominant	M06	0.91	0.89	0.04	0.07
	F03	0.88	0.67	0.32	0.10
	M01	0.88	0.82	0.18	0.10
	M02	0.77	0.80	0.13	0.17
	M04	0.54	0.47	0.51	0.43
	M05	0.52	0.44	0.20	0.24
T3-dominant	F01	0.46	0.40	0.59	0.54
	M03	0.44	0.39	0.59	0.53
	F02	0.40	0.38	0.60	0.56
	F04	0.37	0.34	0.60	0.62
	F05	0.33	0.26	0.74	0.67
	F06	0.31	0.34	0.64	0.62
Mean		0.57	0.52	0.43	0.39

on phonetic cues exclusively in the processing, they tend to make more T2 responses to both T2 + T3 and T3 + T3 sequences (see Table 14.1). But why do subjects prefer T2 responses?

In nonsense disyllabic sequences presented to the subjects, the first syllable in both T2+T3 and T3 + T3 sequences surfaces as a rising pitch. In order to re-analyze this surface rising pitch as T3, subjects have to silently rehearse the T3 + T3 sequence so that T3 sandhi applies in the covert speech. By analyzing the internal synthesis of T3 + T3 sequence, or analysis-by-synthesis, subjects would be able to infer that the rising pitch may be mapped to T3. This analysis also implies that the rising pitch is analyzed interactively with the remaining tone context (i.e., T3), otherwise T3 sandhi would not be triggered in the covert speech. Other factors aside, in analysis-by-synthesis, the likelihood that a rising pitch is mapped to T3 or T2 is equal (50% vs. 50%). Subjects adopting this strategy are expected to make similar number of T2 and T3 responses. Result (see Table 14.1) suggests that two subjects (M03 and $F_0 4$) may have adopted this strategy. Indeed, one subject ($F_0 4$) has gone so far along this process that she over-analyzes most T2 + T3 and T3 + T3 sequences as T3.

Alternatively, subjects may isolate the rising pitch of the first syllable from the remaining tone context and try to match it with the underlying form of a tone. Using this isolation analysis, subjects are far more likely to reanalyze the rising pitch as T2, because T2 is a high rising tone but T3 is underlyingly a low tone. Result suggests that 10 subjects (5F, 5M) may have adopted this analysis.

It is not unlikely that the isolation analysis is relatively straightforward and easy for Mandarin subjects compared to the analysis-by-synthesis method, which may account for the preference for T2 responses in pseudo-words. Different mechanism involved in the processing of sandhi T3 is an interesting direction that merits more research.

4.   General Discussion

At the beginning of this study, two questions are elaborated. These two questions will be discussed with reference to our main findings in the following two subsections.

(i)   Is there psycholinguistic evidence to support that Mandarin speakers possess knowledge of Mandarin T3 sandhi rule?

(ii)   Is the application of T3 sandhi gradient or categorical in terms of both production and perception results?

4.1   Phonological knowledge of Mandarin T3 sandhi rule

In regard to the first question, this study found 100% application of T3 sandhi to pseudo-words, which re-confirms the productivity of T3 sandhi rule (Cheng 1968; Xu 1991, 1997; Zhang and Lai 2010). This study uses non-occurring syllables as pseudo-words to further control the lexical influence. The finding that Mandarin T3 sandhi rule generalizes to non-occurring syllables provides stronger support for the contention that Mandarin subjects have internal knowledge of T3 sandhi rule. Mandarin subjects do not learn the sandhi form of T3 by simply memorizing unanalyzed speech materials; instead, they may have generalized a rule from reoccurring pitch pattern of sandhi T3 in the sandhi context (i.e., T3 + T3) and are capable of productively applying this rule to not only non-occurring combination of occurring morphemes (Cheng 1968; Xu 1991, 1997; Zhang and Lai 2010), but also to non-occurring syllables.

This finding merits further investigation of the neural representation of phonological rule via electrophysiological (EEG) and fMRI experiments. Specifically speaking, EEG studies can detail the time course of the implementation of a phonological rule in online speech production; fMRI studies may shed light on the functional specialization of phonological knowledge in the brain.

4.2   Gradient or categorical application of Mandarin T3 sandhi rule

In perception, previous studies have converged to show that Mandarin listeners cannot reliably distinguish T2 and sandhi T3 (Wang and Li 1967; Peng 2000), a conclusion also supported by the perception results of this study. The controversy regarding the gradient or categorical application of Mandarin T3 sandhi rule is centered in production. Many previous studies reported acoustic differences between T2 and sandhi T3 (e.g., Zee 1980; Shen 1990a; Xu 1997; Peng 2000; Yuan and Chen, to appear), which then motivates the present study to examine the nature of these acoustic differences by controlling confounding factors as much as possible. It is important to determine the nature of the acoustic differences between T2 and sandhi T3, i.e., whether these fine acoustic differences merely reflect phonetic variation or have phonological implication. If sandhi T3 is systematically realized as a F_0 realization distinct from T2 in the production of each speaker, it may infer that the target of tone sandhi is not T2, but a high rising tone somewhat different from T2.

4.2.1 Variability in production

In this study, we find that the implementation of Mandarin T3 sandhi rule is affected by many factors unrelated to the phonological rule *per se*. Firstly, F_0 realization of sandhi T3 is modulated by the lexical status of disyllabic sequences in a way that sandhi T3 differs significantly from T2 in pseudo-words but not in real words. This result is consistent with Zhang and Lai (2010), which also noted significant F_0 difference of sandhi T3 between real words and pseudo-words. Zhang and Lai (2010) interpreted this difference as incomplete application of Mandarin T3 sandhi rule to pseudo-words, but did not spell out exactly what process may have interfered with the application of T3 sandhi. We suspect that the discrepancy between pseudo-words and real words may be due to the influence of *coarticulatory process*, i.e., different degrees of coarticulatory reduction involved in the production of pseudo-words and real words. In particular, due to the unfamiliarity with the pseudo-words (which Mandarin subjects have never heard or produced before), subjects tend to produce pseudo-words relatively slowly (pseudo-words: 229.96 ms; real words: 215.33 ms), in which case less coarticulatory reduction may be involved (e.g., Xu 1997; Peng 2000). It is likely that the low feature in the underlying form of T3 is better preserved in the production of pseudo-words, which gives rise to significant acoustic differences between T2 and sandhi T3 in pseudo-words.

The above discussion touches upon one aspect of variability in the F_0 realization of T3 sandhi—coarticulatory process. Another factor that adds to the variability is the *elicitation method*. The present study finds no significant difference between T2 and sandhi T3 in real words, which deviates from previous studies that reported small but significant acoustic differences (e.g., Zee 1980; Shen 1990a; Xu 1997; Peng 2000; Yuan and Chen, to appear). This deviation can be partly attributed to the elicitation method. In many previous studies, subjects were asked to read aloud a list of words (e.g., Zee 1980; Xu 1997; Peng 2000; Myers and Tsay 2003). It is likely that speakers exaggerate the lexical contrast between T2 + T3 and T3 + T3 words in read speech when they try to produce clear tokens, even without being given explicit instruction in this regard. The present study uses a repetition task by auditorily presenting two monosyllables to the subjects and asking subjects to repeat them as a disyllabic word as quickly as possible. The repetition task may have distracted subjects' attention away from clear production, as subjects have to pay close attention to the phonetic properties of two monosyllables in order to correctly repeat them (especially for pseudo-words). Moreover, T2 + T3 and T3 + T3 sequences in a minimal pair never co-occur in a single block in order to avoid the lexical contrast. In the repetition task, subjects are less likely to focus on the lexical contrast and to exaggerate the pronunciation, thereby considerably reducing the artifacts of read speech.

Some evidence for the effect of elicitation method (reading a word list vs. repetition task) can be drawn here via the comparison of perceptual materials in the perception test and the production results in this study. In order to prepare intelligible perceptual materials for the perception test, a female speaker was given a list of disyllabic words (sinograms for real words, and *pinyin* for pseudo-words), and instructed to read aloud these words at a normal speaking rate. Acoustic analysis of the perceptual materials suggested that sandhi T3 was more different from T2 in *real words* (13.9 Hz) than in *pseudo-words* (7.7 Hz) (see Figure 14.7). However, a reversed pattern was found in the production results using the repetition paradigm, i.e., sandhi T3 was more different from T2 in *pseudo-words* (6.3 Hz) than in *real words* (2.9 Hz) (see Figure 14.3). This comparison implies that F_0 differences between T2 and sandhi T3 may be conflated by the lexical contrast in read speech. But note that the number of speakers is different here (1 speaker vs. 12 speakers). Refined studies are needed to further test the effect of elicitation method.

Individual difference is another dimension of variability. As discussed before, acoustic differences are expected to be systematically attested in all subjects to reach the conclusion that sandhi T3 is realized as a phonetic form distinct from T2. However, findings of this study do not support this expectation. F_0 differences between T2 and sandhi T3 are only found in some speakers, which is insufficient to draw the conclusion that the target of tone sandhi is a high-rising tone somewhat different from T2.

In summary, it is well known that speech production is variable in nature so that repetition of the same sound is never acoustically identical (e.g., Johnson and Mullennix 1997; Liberman 1996; Perkell and Klatt 1986). Variability in the F_0 realization of sandhi T3 presumably reflects the effect of many factors superimposed on the implementation of T3 sandhi rule, such as coarticulatory process, elicitation method, and speaker difference. The essence of the above discussion is that the acoustic differences between T2 and sandhi T3 are likely to be phonetic in nature.

4.2.2 *Other perspectives: Historical development and learnability*

In addition to the variability in speech production, concerns from the historical and learnability perspectives also emphasize the importance of distinguishing acoustic differences that are phonetic in nature from those that have phonological implication.

Labov documented the phenomenon of 'near merger' in sound change, which refers to the situation that speakers consistently differentiate two sounds in production without being able to perceive them (e.g., Labov 1994; Labov, Karen, and Miller 1991). Mandarin T3 sandhi seems to bear some resemblance to the phenomenon of near merger regarding the inconsistency of production and perception results. Let us assume that sandhi T3 and T2 are at the stage of near merger in contemporary Mandarin and consider the possibility of this assumption with reference to the historical development of Mandarin.

According to Mei (1977), the occurrence of Mandarin T3 sandhi can be traced to the 16th century Mandarin. In Chinese textbooks for Koreans at that time, it is mentioned that T3 should be produced as T2 in T2 + T3 words. It means that Mandarin speakers in the 16th century already sensed the phonetic similarity between the sandhi form of T3 and T2. It is not unlikely that T2 and sandhi T3 are also perceptually indistinguishable for speakers of the 16th century Mandarin. Suppose that Mandarin speakers in the 16th century produced sandhi T3 acoustically differently from T2 (if Mandarin speakers in the 16th century do NOT produce sandhi T3 differently whereas Mandarin speakers nowadays do, it would be a different story), acoustic differences that cannot be efficiently captured by the ears of listeners are expected to diminish and disappear through the history of Mandarin. It is doubtful that acoustic differences between T2 and sandhi T3 in the early time have not been offset after a period as long as 500 years. From the historical perspective, therefore, it seems difficult to claim that Mandarin speakers nowadays produce T2 and sandhi T3 distinctly as the consequence of an internalized rule.

Moreover, from the learnability perspective, it also seems paradoxical to suggest that Mandarin speakers 'learn' to produce T2 and sandhi T3 distinctly as a rule while they fail to perceive the difference.

To conclude, acoustic differences between T2 and sandhi T3 are likely to be phonetic in nature. The mapping between a phonological phenomenon and its phonetic realization is complex (e.g., Pierrehumbert 1990, 2000). Due to physiological constraints and other sources of 'noise' in production, categorical implementation of T3 sandhi rule is likely to be mapped to a fuzzy differentiation in acoustic signals. Differentiation in F_0 realizations does not allow us to infer that sandhi T3 is phonologically implemented as a form distinct from T2. Moreover, considerations from the historical and learnability perspectives also cast doubt on the phonological status of the observed acoustic differences. This study concludes that subtle differences between sandhi T3 and T2 are phonetic variation due to the effect of factors unrelated to the phonological rule *per se*.

Appendix 1: Real words list

No.	T2+T3 words			T3+T3 words		
	Pinyin	Sinogram	Gloss	Pinyin	Sinogram	Gloss
1	er2 yu3	兒語	baby talk	er3 yu3	耳語	whisper
2	fan2 xiang3	凡响	ordinary	fan3 xiang3	反响	reaction
3	ren2 zhe3	仁者	benevolent	ren3 zhe3	忍者	ninja
4	tao2 mi3	淘米	to wash rice	tao3 mi3	討米	to ask for rice
5	bai2 ma3	白馬	white horse	bai3 ma3	百馬	one hundred horses
6	bai2 mi3	白米	white rice	bai3 mi3	百米	one hundred meters
7	du2 yin3	毒癮	drug addiction	du3 yin3	賭癮	gambling addition
8	cai2 li3	財禮	dowry	cai3 li3	彩禮	bride price
9	du2 ben3	讀本	reading	du3 ben3	賭本	bookie
10	shi2 guan3	食管	esophagus	shi3 guan3	使館	embassy
11	yang2 jiao3	羊角	horn	yang3 jiao3	仰角	elevation angle
12	zhi2 dao3	執導	to direct	zhi3 dao3	指導	to guide
13	zu2 zhang3	族長	patriarch	zu3 zhang3	組長	team leader
14	lao2 bao3	勞保	labor insurance	lao3 bao3	老鴇	pimps
15	yan2 jian3	鹽鹼	salt	yan3 jian3	眼瞼	eyelid
16	qian2 shui3	潛水	diving	qian3 shui3	淺水	shallow water
17	guo2 jiao3	國脚	football player	guo3 jiao3	裹脚	to wrap one's feet
18	qu2 shui3	渠水	water in a channel	qu3 shui3	取水	to fetch some water
19	tu2 gai3	塗改	to alter	tu3 gai3	土改	land reform
20	hu2 kou3	糊口	to make ends meet	hu3 kou3	虎口	jaws of death
21	mei2 jiu3	梅酒	plum wine	mei3 jiu3	美酒	wine
22	qi2 ma3	騎馬	to ride a horse	qi3 ma3	起碼	at least
23	wu2 bi3	無比	very	wu3 bi3	五筆	a sinogram input method
24	wu2 li3	無禮	rude	wu3 li3	五里	five miles
25	yi2 lao3	遺老	remnant	yi3 lao3	倚老	self-important
26	cai2 zhi3	裁紙	to cut the paper	cai3 zhi3	彩紙	colored paper
27	bai2 shou3	白手	to start from scratch	bai3 shou3	擺手	to wave one's hand
28	qiang2 shou3	強手	strong competitors	qiang3 shou3	搶手	sought-after
29	nian2 mi3	黏米	sticky rice	nian3 mi3	碾米	to grind the rice
30	zhi2 fa3	執法	law enforcement	zhi3 fa3	指法	fingering

Appendix 2: Pseudo-words list

No.	T2 + T3 sequences	T3 + T3 sequences
1	fia2 sua3	fia3 sua3
2	cuang2 rai3	cuang3 rai3
3	fiu2 ra3	fiu3 ra3
4	pe2 dve3	pe3 dve3
5	tei2 bua3	tei3 bua3
6	fai2 dua3	fai3 dua3
7	mia2 zuai3	mia3 zuai3
8	tia2 bv3	tia3 bv3
9	fian2 suang3	fian3 suang3
10	fe2 duang3	fe3 duang3
11	fiang2 zua3	fiang3 zua3
12	dv2 miang3	dv3 miang3
13	piang2 tv3	piang3 tv3
14	tiang2 fua3	tiang3 fua3
15	fiao2 tve3	fiao3 tve3
16	fie2 tuai3	fie3 tuai3
17	lua2 fin3	lua3 fin3
18	biu2 duai3	biu3 duai3
19	mv2 cuai3	mv3 cuai3
20	piu2 zuang3	piu3 zuang3
21	tiu2 ruang3	tiu3 ruang3
22	shong2 muai3	shong3 muai3
23	cua2 luang3	cua3 luang3
24	bou2 ruai3	bou3 ruai3
25	fv2 rua3	fv3 rua3
26	pv2 tua3	pv3 tua3
27	luai2 fao3	luai3 fao3
28	suai2 fi3	suai3 fi3
29	diang2 mua3	diang3 mua3
30	be2 tuang3	be3 tuang3

Acknowledgement

The work described in this paper was partially supported by grants from the National Basic Research Program of China (973 grant: 2012CB720700) and from the Research Grant Council of Hong Kong (GRF: 455911).

REFERENCES

Beattie, D. 1985. Third tone sandhi and the prosodic structure of Mandarin Chinese. *Toronto Working Papers in Linguistics* 6:1–25.

Berko, J. 1958. The child's learning of English morphology. *Word* 14:150–177.

Chang, Yueh-chin, and Yi-ching Su. 1994. La modification tonale du 3ème ton du mandarin parlé à Taiwan [Tone modification of the third tone in Mandarin spoken in Taiwan]. *Cahiers de Linguistique Asie Orientale* 23:39–59.

Chao, Yuen Ren. 1930. A system of tone letters. *Le Maître Phonétique* 45:24–27.

Chao, Yuen Ren. 1948. *Mandarin Primer*. Cambridge: Harvard University Press.

Chen, M. Y. 2000. *Tone Sandhi: Patterns Across Chinese Dialects*. Cambridge: Cambridge University Press.

Cheng, Chin-chuan. 1966. Guanhua fangyan de shengdiao zhengxing gen liandiao bianhua [Tone features and tone sandhi in the Mandarin dialects]. *Dalu Zazhi* 33:102–108.

Cheng, Chin-chuan. 1968. English stresses and Chinese tones in Chinese sentences. *Phonetica* 18:77–88.

Duanmu, S. 2000. *The Phonology of Standard Chinese*. Oxford: Oxford University Press.

Hockett, C. F. 1947. Peiping phonology. *Journal of American Oriental Society* 67:253–267. Reprinted 1964 in *Readings in Linguistics I*, ed. M. Joos, fourth edition, 217–228. University of Chicago Press.

Hsieh, Hsin-I. 1970. The psychological reality of tone sandhi rules in Taiwanese. In *Papers from the 6th Meeting of the Chicago Linguistic Society*, 489–503. Chicago: Chicago Linguistic Society.

Hsieh, Hsin-I. 1975. How generative is phonology? In *The Transformational-Generative Paradigm and Modern Linguistic Theory*, ed. E. F. K. Koerner, 109–144. Amsterdam: John Benjamins.

Hsieh, Hsin-I. 1976. On the unreality of some phonological rules. *Lingua* 38:1–19.

Johnson, K., and J. W. Mullennix. 1997. *Talker Variability in Speech Processing*. San Diego: Academic Press.

Labov, W. 1994. *Principle of Linguistic Change: Social Factors*. Oxford, Cambridge: Blackwell.

Labov, W., M. Karen, and C. Miller. 1991. Near-mergers and the suspension of phonemic contrast. *Language Variation and Change* 3:33–74.

Lehiste, I. 1970. *Suprasegmentals*. Cambridge, Mass.: M.I.T. Press.

Liberman, A. M. 1996. *Speech: A Special Code*. Cambridge, Mass.: MIT Press.

Macmillan, N. A., and C. D. Creelman. 1991. *Detection Theory: A User's Guide*. New York: Cambridge University Press.

Mei, Tsu-Lin. 1977. Tones and tone sandhi in 16th century Mandarin. *Journal of Chinese Linguistics* 5:237–260.

Myers, J., and J. Tsay. 2003. Investigating the phonetics of Mandarin tone sandhi. Taiwan *Journal of Linguistics* 1:29–68.

Peng, Shu-Hui. 2000. Lexical versus 'phonological' representations of Mandarin sandhi tones. In *Papers in Laboratory Phonology V: Acquisition and the Lexicon*, eds. M. B. Broe, and J. Pierrehumbert, 152–167. Cambridge: Cambridge University Press.

Perkell, J. S., and D. H. Klatt. 1986. *Invariance and Variability in Speech Processes*. Hillsdale, N. J.: Lawrence Erlbaum Associates.

Pierrehumbert, J. 1990. Phonological and phonetic representation. *Journal of Phonetics* 18:375–394.

Pierrehumbert, J. 2000. The phonetic grounding of phonology. *Bulletin de la Communication Parlee* 5:7–23.

Shen, Xiao-nan S. 1990a. Tonal coarticulation in Mandarin. *Journal of Phonetics* 18:281–295.

Shen, Xiao-nan S. 1990b. *The Prosody of Mandarin Chinese*. Berkeley: University of California Press.

Signol, F., C. Barras, and J.-S. Lienard. 2008. Evaluation of the pitch estimation algorithms in the monopitch and multipitch cases. *The Journal of the Acoustical Society of America* 123:3077.

Tseng, Chiu-yu., Shao-huang Pin, Yeh-lin Lee, Hsin-min Wang, and Yong-cheng Chen. 2005. Fluent speech prosody: Framework and modeling. *Speech Communication* 46 (3–4): 284–309.

Wang, W. S-Y. 1967. Phonological features of tone. *International Journal of American Linguistics* 33:93–105.

Wang, W. S-Y. 1972. The many uses of F_0. In *Linguistics and Phonetics to the Memory of Pierre Delattre*, ed. A. Valdman, 487–503. The Hague: Mouton.

Wang, W. S-Y. and K.-P. Li. 1967. Tone 3 in Pekinese. *Journal of Speech and Hearing Research* 10:629–636.

Xu, Y. 1991. Depth of phonological recoding in short-term memory. *Memory and Cognition* 19:263–273.

Xu, Y. 1997. Contextual tonal variations in Mandarin. *Journal of Phonetics* 25:61–83.

Yip, M. 2002. *Tone.* Cambridge, U.K.: Cambridge University Press.

Yuan, Jiahong, and Yiya Chen. To appear. Third tone sandhi in Standard Chinese: A corpus approach. To appear in *Journal of Chinese Linguistics*.

Zee, E. 1980. A spectrographic investigation of Mandarin tone sandhi. *UCLA Working Papers in Phonetics* 49:98–116.

Zhang, J., and Yuwen Lai. 2010. Testing the role of phonetic knowledge in Mandarin tone sandhi. *Phonology* 27:153–201.

Zhang, Jie, Yuwen Lai, and Craig Sailor. 2011. Modeling Taiwanese speakers' knowledge of tone sandi in reduplication. *Lingua* 121:181–206.

Zhu, Xiaonong. 2005. *Shanghai Sheng Diao Shi Yan Lu [An Experimental Study in Shanghai Tones]*. Shanghai: Shanghai jiao yu chu ban she.

15

On Modality Effects and Relative Syntactic Uniformity of Sign Languages[1]

James H-Y. TAI
National Chung Cheng University, Taiwan

Abstract

Human language can be expressed in two modalities, visual-gestural modality of signed languages and auditory-vocal modality of spoken languages. These two modalities of human language share several fundamental necessary properties of human language. However, there are also modality effects which contribute to the drastic differences between signed and spoken languages in lexicon, morphology and syntax. Two most important effects are iconic representation of objects and actions and indexic/ostensive identification of referents in signed languages. The two modality effects, on the other hand, render relative uniformity in morphology and syntax across signed languages. At the same time, signed languages share some similarities with creoles because of their similar ambience of language acquisition. The paper attempts to tease apart the syntactic structures due to iconicity vs. structures due to creolization.

1. This paper is a revision of the paper with the same title presented at the Joint Meeting of 14th Annual Conference of the International Association of Chinese Linguistics and 10th International Symposium on Chinese Languages and Linguistics. I take great pleasure in contributing this paper to honor Professor William S-Y. Wang on his 80th birthday. Professor Wang has inspired me to delve into the evolution of human language, of which the study of sign language is a necessary subject. In preparation for this paper, I have benefited from discussions with SU Shiou-fen and CHEN Yi-Chun. I am, however, solely responsible for all possible errors and infelicities herein.

1. Introduction

Research on sign languages in the past three decades has clearly demonstrated that human language can be produced in two modalities, visual-gestural modality of signed languages and auditory-vocal modality of spoken languages. It is therefore not only desirable but also necessary to consider both signed and spoken languages in studying language universals and specifics, and the closely related issue concerning language uniformity and diversity. Relative concepts define each other. Just as language universals and specifics define each other, so does language uniformity and diversity. In this chapter, we hope to approach the issue of language diversity from the point of view of sign languages.

The two modalities of human language share several fundamental necessary properties of human language. They range from fundamental design features of human language, to linguistic forms, to language acquisition, and to hemisphere lateralization. At the same time, there are also modality effects responsible for the structural differences between signed and spoken languages in lexicon, morphology, syntax, and semantics. Two most important effects are iconic representation of objects and actions and indexic/ostensive identification of referents in signed languages (Meier 2002). Furthermore, a more crucial question has been raised by Liddell (2000, 2003) as to whether signed languages also utilize general non-linguistic spatio-cognitive principles to construct meanings.

On the other hand, cross-linguistic comparisons among sign languages that have naturally arisen among the Deaf communities in different parts of the world show striking similarities in morphology and syntax (Newport and Supalla 2000), even though they differ greatly in vocabularies and are unintelligible to each other.[2] In contrast with relative diversity of spoken languages, signed languages exhibit relative uniformity in morphology and syntax. Thus, all natural sign languages reported contain three classes of verbs: plain verbs, agreement verbs, and spatial verbs. Furthermore, most plain verbs are body-anchored across sign languages. Agreement verbs use agreement mechanisms to indicate the subject-object relationship. Spatial verbs do not indicate the subject-object relationship. They use the hand movement to indicate the change of location of a person, animal or object, reflecting the layout of events in the real world (Klima and Bellugi 1979; Sutton-Spence and Woll 1998), Being isomorphic with visual world, spatial verbs across sign languages almost invariably involve classifier predicates in which the classifier systems are based on the same set of object properties underlying the classifier systems in spoken languages (Emmorey 2003). In word order, sign languages show a general tendency towards topic-comment construction, resulting in OSV and SOV orders. In morphology, sign languages tend to use repeated movement to mark temporal aspect or to distinguish nouns from verbs. Sign languages also use facial expressions to indicate sentence types, declaratives, questions and conditionals.

---

2. We do not refer to signed languages patterned after the grammars of spoken languages such as Signed English or Signed Chinese. They are not natural sign languages.

While Meier (2002) attributes the relative uniformity of signed languages to modality effects as well as to their youth.[3] Aronoff, Meir, and Sandler (2005) single out the modality effects as the major factor, especially the iconic motivation in the visual-gestural modality of sign languages. They compare sign languages with creole languages (Bickerton 1975, 1981; Mufwene 2001). They observe that while both types of languages are young languages, young creole languages do not exhibit rich inflectional morphology as sign languages. They thus argue that inflectional morphology in sign languages are due to modality effects rather than the youth of sign languages. The main purpose of this paper is to further explore the modality effects on the structure of sign languages, centering the relative uniformity of signed languages in the setting of the relative diversity of spoken languages.

2.   Sign Language as Natural Language

Systematic research of sign languages has a relatively short history. There was a misconception about sign languages among linguists, and the misconception has remained intact among the general public. The misconception is that sign language is a combination of gestures and pantomimes without grammar. Bloomfield (1933, 39) regarded sign languages as 'gesture languages' developed from ordinary gestures with their complicated structures derived from the conventions of spoken languages. On this view, sign language is merely parasitic upon spoken language, rather than an autonomous system of human communication expressed in visual mode. Spoken language, the auditory mode of human language, was equated to human language. In the same vein, Hockett (1960) compared spoken languages with animal communication systems to identify more than a dozen of design features in human language. To him, the most obvious feature is the auditory-vocal mode of communication. Associated with this mode of communication are design features such as arbitrariness and discreteness of linguistic symbols. We now know that these design features are of very different nature in sign language and deserve further scrutiny. Even Chomsky (1967) characterized language as the correspondence between sound and meaning.[4] This characterization is still prevalent in linguistic literature.

The misconception was first unveiled by William Stokoe and his associates (Stokoe 1960; Stokoe, Casterline, and Croneberg 1965) whose research on American Sign Language demonstrated that signs, like words, are constructed from a small number of elements according

---

3. Along with the youth of sign languages, Meir (2002) has identified their roots in nonlinguistic gesture as a contributing factor to the iconic motivations in sign languages. In this respect, creoles are different from sign languages, even though both types of languages are young languages.

4. Chomsky has since modified his view on the nature of human language by incorporating both signed and spoken languages: "…the language faculty is not tied to specific sensory modalities, contrary to what was assumed not long ago. Thus, the sign language of the deaf is structurally very much like spoken language, and the course of acquisition is very similar." (Chomsky 2000, 121)

to certain formation principles. Thereafter, through several years of study of American Sign Language (hereafter ASL) by a group of dedicated linguists and psychologists led by Klima and Bellugi in 1970s at the Salk Institute for Biological Studies, the structural properties of sign language began to be largely uncovered. Klima and Bellugi (1979) have clearly demonstrated that sign language as exemplified in ASL has a complex structure grammar with the fundamental properties linguists have posited for all human languages. The journal Sign Language Studies was also established in 1970s. The ensuing two decades have witnessed a steady progress in the study of sign language. Some of the representative works include Liddell (1980, 2003), Fischer and Siple (1990), Siple and Fischer (1991), and more recently by Emmorey and Lane (2000), Emmorey (2002) and Meier, Cormier, and Quinto-Pozos (2002). The research on sign languages over the past forty-some years has demonstrated that sign languages are natural languages produced and perceived through gestural-visual means, yet with all necessary properties that distinguish human language from animal communication systems. Like spoken language, sign language is a rule-governed system. It is composed of a set of symbols and rules of concatenation and operation over these symbols. Thus, like spoken language, sign language has elaborated systems of phonology, morphology, syntax, semantics, and pragmatics. Neurolinguistic findings in the past two decades also suggest that the brain's left hemisphere is dominant for signed languages, just as it is for spoken languages (Emmorey 2002). It is now well established that there are two modalities for human language to be produced, namely, auditory-vocal modality of spoken languages and visual-gestural modality of signed languages.[5]

3.   Modality Non-Effects and Effects

The discovery that language can be expressed not only through the vehicle of speech but also through the vehicle of sign has profound implications for linguistics, psychology, anthropology and other disciplines under the umbrella of cognitive science. It should be taken as one of the most crucial research findings in the study of language. No longer can we equate language with speech. Nor can we discuss design features of human language solely based on the data from spoken languages. Language universals as well as language disparities can only be drawn from both signed and spoken languages. Language universals can now be approached from the set of properties shared between signed and spoken languages, or the non-effects of modality. These non-effects of modality as identified in Meier (2002) are: (i) conventionality of pairing between form and meaning; (ii) duality of patterning by menas of which meaningful units are built of meaningless sublexical units; (iii) productivity of new vocabulary through derivational morphology, compounding, and borrowing; (iv) syntactic structure building on syntactic categories such as nouns and verbs and embedded clauses such as relative and complement clauses; (v) similar timetables for acquisition; and (vi) lateralization in left hemisphere.

---

5. As reported in Quinto-Pozos (2002), the tactile-gestural modality, the third modality, is used by deaf-blind signers of American Sign Language.

It appears, however, that these non-effects are only first approximations. Under further scrutiny, these non-effects are likely to exhibit more detailed differences between the two modalities. Let me briefly comment on each of the six non-effects aforementioned. First, although conventionality of pairing between form and meaning holds true to both modalities, iconic motivations are much more pervasive in signed languages at both lexical and syntactic levels. In contrast, arbitrary association is the general rule for spoken languages, although iconicity in syntax (Haiman 1980, 1985) and onomatopoeia and sound symbolism in phonology (Hinton, Nichols, and Ohala 1994) have been documented for spoken languages.

Second, duality of patterning, one of the most important design features of human language, holds true to spoken languages as well as to signed languages. Like spoken languages, signed language use a small limited set of basic elements, i.e., basic handshapes, in conjunction with other parameters such as location of articulation, hand movement, and palm orientation, to form basic vocabulary of the lexicon. However, there is also a difference here. While the phonemic units in spoken languages are meaningless units themselves, the basic handshapes in signed languages are often meaningful by themselves. It is only when they serve as sublexical units, their iconic motivations are submerged. It appears that the preservation of iconic motivation for the whole lexical units forces the sublexical handshapes to function as meaningless units. For instance, in TSL the basic handshape /hand/ by itself stands for hands, but it can be used to form lexical items such as HOUSE and NOW in which it becomes meaningless sublexical units. This difference between the two modalities may have some important implications for the emergence of duality of patterning in the course of evolution of human language (Tai 2005).

Third, like in spoken languages, signed languages create new vocabulary through derivational morphology, compounding, and borrowing. However, derivational morphology appears to be more limited in signed languages than in spoken languages. This may be attributed to the youth of signed languages rather than modality effects (Aronoff, Meir, and Sandler 2005). In contrast, compounding seems to be the most important mechanism in creating new vocabulary in signed language, but not necessary so in spoken languages. As to the mechanism of borrowing, while the borrowed words in spoken languages are subject to phonological regulations of the borrowing language, the whole signs can be borrowed from one sign language to another sign language without much alternation. Thus, the same sign HOUSE are used Chinese Sign Language, Japanese Sign Language, and Taiwan Sign Language.[6] Furthermore, since all these three sign languages use Chinese characters, character spellings are not uncommon in these languages. Both Chinese characters and signs are both visual languages, and they are more compatible with each other than with speech. In alphabet languages, figure spelling is used instead. The use of figure spelling can alter the basic handshape of a sign through initialization (Battison 1978, 2004).

Fourth, the statement that all sign languages have the same parts of speech as in spoken languages needs to be qualified. It seems that prepositions are absent in all sign languages. It is no accident that in their most recent book on sign language and linguistic universals (Sandler

---

6. In terms of language families, Taiwan Sign Language and Japanese Sign Language belong to the same family, but not Chinese Sign Language.

and Lillo-Martin 2006), there is no mention of prepositions at all. It may have to do with the fact that spatial relations as expressed in English prepositions 'in', 'on', 'at', 'from' and 'to' can be expressed in signed languages visually and iconically without explicit morphemes[7]. The category of auxiliaries is in general absent in sign languages. Smith (1989) first found three auxiliaries in TSL and claimed that TSL is the only sign language with auxiliaries. It should be noted that these three auxiliaries all play the role of agreement and are very different in nature from the auxiliaries in spoken languages. Later, Fischer (1996) has shown that something like AUXI in TSL exists in Japanese Sign Language, Sign Language of Netherlands, and Danish Sign Language. As concluded by Fischer (1996, 117) that this something like AUXI sign appears to have the fundamental function of agreement. In sign languages, it is often the case that many nouns are signed by actions associated with the actions. In ASL and other sign languages, these semantically related nouns and verbs by signing the nouns with smaller and restrained but repeated movement (Supalla and Newport 1978). It is, however, not the case in TSL. Thus, the distinction in TSL can only be made in syntactic or discourse contexts. Furthermore, embedding in relative and complement clauses in sign languages are often expressed by nonmanual facial expressions. One of the most difficult tasks in sign language analysis is to identify such expressions and their structural relationship with manual expressions. As to the trade-offs between word order and verb agreement, all the sign languages reported so far have the class of agreement verbs. In addition, all sign languages use the topic-comment structure. With agreement verbs and topic-comment structure, sign languages appear to have relatively freer word order than most of the spoken languages.

Fifth, regarding similar timetable for language acquisition, deaf children acquiring sign language also go through the "babbling" stage when they practice different locations, movements, and handshapes by hands (Lillo-Martin 1999). As a matter of fact, deaf children produce their first words as early as 5-month old, about six to seven months earlier than hearing children who normally produce their first words in spoken language around one-year old (Newport and Meier 1985). Furthermore, according to Siedlecki and Bonvillian (1993), deaf children seem to master locations first, and then movement, and finally handshapes. Thus, the order of phonological acquisition is different from that of spoken languages. It is safe to assume that further studies on the order of acquisition will reveal more differences between these two modalities with respect to the order of acquisition.

Sixth, neurolinguistic findings in the past two decades suggest that the left hemisphere of the brain is dominant for spoken languages as well as signed languages. The left brain has been known to be more important for language and the right is more important for vision and spatial activities. Evidence from brain-damaged deaf people however suggest differences between signs using syntactic space and signs using topographic space (to be discussed in the following

---

7. In TSL and ASL, there is a sign with downward movement of the cup-shape hand which indicates the existence of an object at a certain location. This sign functions like the locative verb 'zai' in Chinese rather than preposition 'at' in English.

section). Syntactic space involves the left hemisphere, whereas the topographic space involves the right hemisphere.

In sign languages, nouns denoting objects can be represented either by shape features or part features of the objects or by actions associated with the objects as we have mentioned earlier. Using fMRI technigue, Chiu et. al. (2005) have found that the neural substrates mediating the representation took different dynamically distributed forms. Modality effects certainly deserve further and deeper study when we developed more sophisticated neurolinguistic techniques.

In sum, it can be expected that the six general statements on the modality non-effects made by Meir (2002) will have to be further qualified with minor but non-trivial differences as we know more about sign languages from different linguistic analysis, facts of language acquisition, and psycholinguistic and neurolinguistic evidence.

At the same time, the possible modality effects, such as the iconicity and non-discreteness in sign languages, need to be reexamined more carefully. We will focus on the iconicity in this paper. In the sections below we will show that the relative uniformity of sign languages in syntax are largely due to the pervasiveness of simultaneous morphology with iconic motivations.

4. Relative Uniformity of Sign Languages

4.1 Three classes of verbs

One very important contributing factor to the relative uniformity of sign languages is that all natural sign languages reported contain three classes of verbs: plain verbs, agreement verbs, and spatial verbs. For example, American Sign Language (Padden 1983) and Taiwan Sign Language (Smith 1989; Chang, Su and Tai 2005) are not related, but they both have these three classes of verbs each of which exhibit similar syntactic behaviors in these two languages. This is true despite that the same concept may be expressed in one language as plain verb and yet as in another language as agreement verb, and vice versa. For instance, LOVE in TSL is an agreement verb, while it is a plain verb in English; LIKE in TSL is a plain verb, while it is an agreement verb in English. The distinction between plain verbs and agreement verbs are not entirely based on the semantics of the verbs as Aronoff, Meir and Sandler (2005, 322) would like to believe. Rather, the distinction is made whether the signs for the verbs are body-anchored nor not. Plain verbs are body-anchored and allows only small local movement of the hand, while agreement verbs are not body-anchored and allows the hand to move from one direction to another in signing space (Tai and Su 2006). Thus, the sign LIKE in TSL is body-anchored but is not in ASL. Conversely, the sign LOVE is body-anchored but is not in TSL. Such contrastive examples aside, most agreement verbs identified in Tai and Su (2006) are also agreement verbs in ASL. Presumably, membership of spatial verbs doesn't vary from one to another sign language. And all spatial verbs in all sign languages exhibit classifier predicates regardless whether they express static spatial relations or dynamic spatial relations involving change of location. What varies from one sign language to another is the use of different classifier handshapes in classifier predicates involving spatial verbs (Emmorey 2003).

Both agreement verbs and spatial verbs move hand from one direction to another, but the hand movement in these two kinds of verbs are of very different nature. While agreement verbs use syntactic space, spatial verbs use topographic space. Topographic space is used to present a schematized layout of the entities and events as they exist in the visual world. For example, to sign "The book is on the table," the topographic space is used to show the spatial relationship "on" between the book and the table. The sign for "book" must be placed above or on top of the sign for "table" in the signing space. For another example, to sign "The car bumped along past the tree", the topographic space is used to show the path trajectory of the moving of the sign for "car" toward, and then past the sign for "tree". Thus, in representing both static and dynamic spatial relationship in sign language, topographic space is able to create a spatial layout which reflects the spatial relationship between the entities involved in the real world.

Spatial verbs in sign language use topographic space. They are thus able to give a visual information about path, trajectory, speed, and even manner and aspect of the movement of action by the verb. They are also able to give information about the location of the action as in signing "The dog is running around in the house." In contrast, syntactic space is used to express abstract concepts and relationships in signing space. Thus, different handshapes can be placed in different areas of the signing space to represent various concepts. For example, in ASL, the sign for "candy" is placed on the chin, the sign for "summer" moving before the forehead, and sign for "train" moving before the dorso (see Klima and Bellugi 1979, 42). In TSL, the sign for "yesterday" is placed above the shoulder, the sign for "now" moving before the stomach, and the sign for "days of the week" moving from the armpit. In all these examples, the location of the sign does not reflect location of entities in the visual world, nor does the moving represent a trajectory in the real world. Syntactic space can also be used to show the contrast between two groups of different people or two different abstract concepts. Thus, in describing people belonging to two opposing political parties, the signer might place a sign referring to one group on the left of his/her signing space, and the other group on the right side. It is also not uncommon for a signer to place the concept of HEALTH in one area of the signing space, and WEALTH in another area to show the relative merits of the two. Furthermore, syntactic space allows the moving in signing space between two defined points to express grammatical relations as in "I sent a book to my friend in Japan." Here the location of "my friend" in the signing space is not the location in the real world, but rather than where the book is directed. In short, plain verbs and agreement verbs in sign languages use mostly syntactic spaces.

Although not all linguists find the distinction between syntactic space and topographic space significant (Liddell 1990; Johnston 1991), we find it is very useful for characterizing three types of verbs in sign languages including TSL. Furthermore, there is evidence from brain-damaged deaf people and experiments on healthy signers that supports the distinction. As mentioned in Section 3, although sign languages are visual languages, they are primarily located in the left hemisphere of the brain. However, the evidence shows that while the use of topographic space in sign languages also engages the right hemisphere of the brain, the use of syntactic space is restricted to the left hemisphere (Poizner, Klima, and Bellugi 1987; Emmorey, Corina and Bellugi 1995).

4.2   Iconicity and simultaneous morphology

The iconicity in the use of topographic space is highly relevant to the theory of signs proposed by Peirce (1932, 2: 247, 277–82) in which a crucial distinction is made between "imagic" and "diagrammatic" iconicity. In imagic iconicity, a sign resembles its referent with respect to some visual or conceptual characteristics. In diagrammatic iconicity, none of the signs necessarily resembles its referent, but their relationships to each other mirror the relationships of their referents in visual or conceptual world. Thus, photographs and statues involve imagic iconicity, but maps and technical diagrams involve diagrammatical iconicity.

The visual-gestural modality allows the abundance of simultaneous morphology for sign languages in both lexicon and syntax. Even Monomorphic signs have a simultaneous appearance. The pioneering phonemic analysis of ASL monomorphic signs by Stokoe (1960) consists of three phonetic parameters (hand configuration, location, and movement) to be simultaneously initiated. Although later Liddell and Johnson (1986) demonstrated the existence of sequential phonology in terms of LML (location-movement-location) in a sign syllable, the same hand configuration spans over the whole LML sequence, yielding an appearance of simultaneity. Signs in sign language tend to be monosyllabic and often preserve iconic motivations, and thus are iconic images. Simultaneous compounds are also abundant in sign languages. For instance, many TSL verbs incorporate the /MAN/ handshape on the weak hand to express actions such as TELL, LOVE, HELP, LEAD, and KILL. Furthermore, moving the /MAN/ handshape and the /WOMEN/ handshape together means MARRY, while moving the two handshapes apart means DIVORCE. Possible examples of simultaneous affixation also exist in TSL, and the clearest case involves both prefix-like and suffix-like negation markers (Myers, ms).

Topographic spatial relationships in sign languages necessarily preserve spatial arrangement of the entities in the real world. They are expressed in sign languages with diagrammatic iconicity which involve simultaneous initiation of more than two monomorphemic signs. This kind of diagrammatic iconicity holds true in the representation of both static and dynamic spatial relationships in sign languages as illustrated by the two examples above, "The book is on the table" and "The car bumped along past the tree." In the second example, in TSL as well as in ASL, not only is the manner of car moving along iconic to the "bumping" in the visual world, but the trajectory of the car moving past the tree is also iconic to the visual world. The iconicity of manner of moving cannot be properly classified either as "imagic iconicity" or "diagrammatic iconicity". Nor can the trajectory of moving be properly so characterized. They are visually iconic, but are neither "iconic images" nor "iconic diagrams" as in Peirce's original taxonomy of signs. They are expressed with simultaneous morphology in the classifier predicate where the classifier hand configuration representing the entity in question, movement of the entity, and the manner and the path of the movement all clustered together along the temporal dimension. In essence, by simultaneous morphology, the classifier predicate represents the static spatial relationship in the three-dimensional world, and the dynamic spatial relationship in four-dimensional world, three-dimensional entities moving along the temporal dimension.

In addition to verb agreement and classifier predicates, all sign languages use simultaneous morphology to indicate various kinds verbal aspects, such as continuative, frequentative, intensive, iterative, and resultative. These aspectual modulations are expressed through the different manners of moving the same hand configuration. These manners consist of different combinations of iconic features such as reduplicated, even, tense, fast, elongated and end-marked (Kilma and Bellugi 1979). These iconic features simultaneously accompany the movement of the hand configuration of signs to indicate verbal aspects.

4.3   Word order freedom

Word order is relatively freer in sign languages than in spoken languages, despite the fact that sign languages vary in their preferred word order as do spoken languages. Three factors seem to contribute to the relative freer word order in sign languages. The first factor has to do with the fact that all sign languages have agreement verbs. One of the most important function of word order is to indicate the subject-object relationship. However, this relationship can also be expressed by verb agreement in both signed languages and spoken languages. Thus there are trade-offs between fixed word order and verb agreement for indicating the subject-object relationship.

The second factor is that sign languages in general are topic-comment languages. Li and Thompson (1976) have proposed a typological distinction between topic-oriented languages like Chinese and subject-oriented languages like English. Sign languages have been described as topic-comment languages like Chinese. For instance, ASL has been described as topic-comment language since Fischer (1976). TSL is also a topic-comment language. In both signed and spoken languages, the topic sets up spatial, temporal, or nominal frameworks for the predications. Sutton-Spence and Woll (1999) characterize topic in BSL as: (1) it comes first (2) it is followed by a pause (3) the eyes are widened during the topic, followed by a pause (4) it can be accompanied by a head nod (5) it may be signed with one hand while producing the comment with the other hand. Based on our limited study, topic in TSL also possesses these syntactic characteristics. In both BSL and TSL, both nouns and verbs can be marked as the topic, resulting in SVO, OSV, and VOS orders. Topic structures as well as verb agreement allows null arguments (Lillo-Martin 1991). While this typological feature holds also true to spoken languages, the prevalence of this feature in sign languages can be attributed to the modality effects.

The third factor is that real world knowledge allows more flexible order in sign languages. Thus, in both BSL and TSL, either MAN NEWSPAPER READ or NEWSPAPER MAN READ, in addition to MAM READ NEWSPAPER. It is because our knowledge of the real world tells us that man can read newspaper but not vice versa. It is only when real world allows both possibility, we have to resort to SVO order or agreement in sign languages. This kind of word order flexibility also exists in spoken languages like Mandarin. But it is very common in sign languages.

4.4   Grammaticalized facial expressions

Facial expressions are used universally to indicate the emotional states of surprise, anger, happiness, fear, sadness, and disgust (Ekman and Friesen 1975). Yet in sign languages, facial expressions are grammaticalized to distinguish sentences types, namely, declaratives, yes-no questions, wh-questions, conditionals. Furthermore, in addition to the marking of topic as mentioned in 4.3. embedding structures such as restrictive relative clauses is also marked by facial expressions as in ASL (Liddell 1980). Facial expressions are also used to express agreement in TSL (Tai and Su 2006). These nonmanual signals in sign languages are based on brow raise, head tilting, lip raising and forward or backward of the head and the body. As they are grammaticalized, their assignment of linguistic functions may vary from one language to another (Kegl, Senghas and Coppola 1999). They present formidable challenges to the analysis of sign languages even for sophisticated sign language researcher.

4.5   Structures shared with young creole languages

Finally, relative syntactic uniformity of sign languages can be further observed from the structural similarities between sign languages and young creole languages. It has been pointed out by previous researchers in ASL (Fischer 1978; Gee & Goodhart 1988) that ASL exhibits striking similarities to young creole languages in grammatical structures. As summarized in Aronoff, Meir, and Sandler (2005), "These commonalities include: no distinction between tensed and infinitival clauses, no tense marking but a rich aspectual system, no pleonastic subjects, no true passives, the occurrence of transitive verbs with agent subjects as intransitives with patient/theme subjects as well, pervasive topic-comment word order; both young creole languages and ASL make extensive use of content words as grammatical markers; neither young creole languages nor ASL use prepositions to introduce oblique cases; both use preverbal free morphemes to express completive aspect; and both rely heavily on prosodic cues like intonation for expressing certain syntactic relations (such as those encoded by relative clauses and conditionals in other languages)." (ibid 307)[8]

---

8. It is worth noting here that most of these structural features also exhibit in Mandarin. While Mandarin definitely is not a young language, one wonders if Mandarin has evolved from a creolized language to begin with.

As pointed out by Aronoff, Meir, and Sandler (2005), there are three factors which likely contribute to these similarities between sign languages and young creole languages: language origin, conditions of acquisition, and age. Let us take a quick look at these factors. Citing the emergence of Nicaragua Sign Language in 1980s, take the position that sign languages, like pidgins, arise spontaneously when people do not share a common language need to communicate. Although the spontaneous emergence of Nicaragua Sign language is recently disputed by Polich (2005), it is true that deaf children use home signs and gesture to communicate with each other before they enter the deaf school for formal education. Even ASL was argued by Woodward (1978) to have resulted from the creolization of French Sign Language which was brought to the United States in 1816. The conditions under which sign languages are acquired also resemble those under which the youngest creole languages are acquired. Less than 10% of the deaf children are born to deaf parents. In other words, more than 90% of the children are born to hearing parents who do not sign. Thus, most deaf children are not exposed to a full-fledged language in early childhood and they have to develop a linguistic system on the basis of impoverished and inconsistent inputs. This situation is no different from the situation in which creole speakers of the first generation develop a language from a pidgin in the mixed environment of other languages. Just as young creole languages evolve from pidgins and other ambient languages, sign languages develop from inconsistent and mixed sources of home signs and gestures. They differ from young creole languages in that each generation of deaf children faces the same conditions of inconsistent and impoverish inputs. In this sense, sign languages are re-creolized with each and every generation of signers (Fischer 1978). The development of full-fledged sign languages depends a lot on the establishment of schools for the deaf. The education system gathers deaf children together to form a stable community with its own cultural and social institutions which in turn sustain the conventionalization of linguistic system. The establishment of schools for the deaf in Europe began in late eighteenth century. ASL can be traced back about two hundred and fifty years old, while TSL can be traced back to early nineteenth century when schools for the deaf were established shortly after Taiwan was colonized by Japan in 1895.

4.6   Sequential morphology

An important distinction can be made in sign languages between simultaneous morphology and sequential morphology. As examined briefly in 4.1, simultaneous morphology in sign languages is largely inflectional and general patterns of agreement, classifier predicates, and aspectual modulations exhibit across different sign languages, notwithstanding their variations from one language to another. Compared with the abundance of simultaneous morphology, sequential morphology appears to be very limited. It is true to ASL and ISL (Aronoff, Meir and Sandler 2005) as well as to TSL (Myers, Ms). Furthermore, sequential morphology is derivational and is specific to individual sign languages. Sign languages allow individual variations more than spoken languages. But, individual variations in sequential morphology are considerably larger than simultaneous morphology. A final point worth mentioning is that while simultaneous morphology is more transparent in iconic motivations, the sequential morphology appears to be arbitrary.

5.   The Young Language Puzzle

We have cited Aronoff, Meir and Sandler (2005) in 4.5 for an enumeration of structural similarities between sign languages and young creole languages. Since they are both young languages with similar language ambience in acquisition. At the same time, these two kinds of young languages differ drastically in that young creole languages normally have little morphology, inflectional or derivational. Aronoff, Meir and Sandler (2005) refer to the rich inflectional morphology in sign languages as the young language puzzle. They solve the puzzle by means of modality effects. They argue that inflectional morphology in sign language is not due to age as in case of spoken languages where inflectional morphology takes longer time to develop than derivational morphology, but rather due to modality effects on sign languages where iconic simultaneous morphology based on spatial cognition are more suitable than arbitrary sequential morphology.

6.   Conclusion

In this paper, we have shown that modality effects can account for fundamental structural differences between signed languages and spoken languages on the one hand and the relative uniformity of signed languages in morphology and syntax on the other hand. Even with respect to each of the six modality non-effects identified by Meier (2002), we have identified further minor differences. It seems to be clear that the surface structure of signed languages are very much shaped by modality effects rather than by modality non-effects, resulting in the appearance that typologically, signed languages are relatively uniform, whereas spoken languages are relatively diverse.

Meier (2002) attributes the relative uniformity of signed languages to modality effects as well as to their youth. However, Aronoff, Meir, and Sandler (2005) take issue with their youth as a contributing factor, arguing for the modality effects, especially the iconic motivation of sign languages, as the major factor. We feel that while the simultaneous morphology (inflectional or derivational) and grammaticalized facial expressions in sign languages can clearly be attributed to modality effects, it would take further research to tease off the modality effects from the youth factor as well as from other typological parameters such as topic-comment structure which may cut across both signed languages and spoken languages. In other words, we propose three major sources for relative uniformity of syntax in sign languages. They are modality effects, the youth factor, and other typological parameters shared by both modalities. Furthermore, the interaction of these three major sources may not so uniform in sign language as we know more about the structure of individual sign languages. For instance, we have noted that word orders in sign languages have resulted from the joint forces from modality effects of agreement and topic-comment typological parameter, which may or may not have anything to do with either age or modality effects.

Whereas sign languages display a more limited range of typological variation than is true of spoken languages, individual signers of a sign language appear to vary much more than individual speakers of a spoken language. This is true not only in syntax but also in vocabulary. Here again, we don't know if this is due to age, acquisition ambience, or modality effects, or all the three factors together. To the best of our knowledge, there is so far no research on this issue. In any case, relative freedom for individual signers to vary their vocabulary and syntax in a deaf community present another puzzle for sign language researchers. It is especially interesting and challenging when we consider relative freedom of individual variations in a deaf community along with relative uniformity of typological variations in sign languages.

REFERENCES

Aronoff, M., I. Meir, and W. Sandler. 2005. The paradox of sign language morphology. *Language* 81 (2): 301–344.

Battison, R. 1978. *Lexical Borrowing in American Sign Language*. Silver Spring, Maryland: Linstok Press.

Bickerton, D. 1975. *Dynamics of A Creole System*. Cambridge: Cambridge University Press.

Bickerton, D. 1981. *Roots of Language*. Ann Arbor: Karoma.

Bloomfield, L. 1933. *Language*. New York: Holt, Rinehart and Winston.

Chang, Jung-hsing, Shiou-fen Su, and J. H.-Y. Tai. 2005. Classifier predicates reanalyzed, with special reference to Taiwan Sign Language. *Language and Linguistics* 6 (2): 247–278.

Chiu, Yi-Hsuan, Jen-Chuen Hsieh, Wen-Jui Kuo, D. L. Hung, and O. J. L. Tzeng. 2005. Vision- and manipulation-based signs in Taiwan Sign Language. *Language and Linguistics* 6 (2): 247–278.

Chomsky, N. 1967. The general properties of language. In *Brain Mechanisms Underlying Speech and Language*, ed. F. Darley. New York: Grune and Stratton.

Chomsky, N. 2000. *New Horizons in the Study of Language and Mind*. Cambridge: Cambridge University Press.

Emmorey, K. 2002. *Language, Cognition, and Brain: Insights from Sign Language Research*. Mahwah, NJ: Lawrence Erlbaum Associates.

Emmorey, K. ed. 2003. *Perspectives on Classifier Constructions in Sign Languages*. Mahwah, NJ: Lawrence Erlbaum Associates.

Emmorey, K., and H. Lane. eds. 2003. *The Signs of Language Revisited: An Anthology to Honor Ursula Bellugi and Edward Klima,* 303–320. Mahwah, NJ: Lawrence Erlbaum Associates.

Emmorey, K., D. Corina, and U. Bellugi. 1995. Differential processing of topographic and referential functions of space. *Paper on Language, Gesture and Space*, eds. K. Emmorey, and J. S. Reilly. Lawrence Erlbaum Associates.

Ekman, P., and W. V. Frisen. 1975. *Unmasking the Face.* Englewood Cliffs. NJ: Prentice-Hall.

Fischer, S. D. 1975. Influences on word order change in American Sign Language. In *Word Order and Word Order Change,* ed. C. N. Li, 1–25. Austin, Texas: University of Texas Press.

Fischer, S. D. 1978. *Sign Language and Creoles.* In Siple, ed., 309–331.

Fischer, S. D. 1996. The role of auxiliaries in sign language. *Lingua* 98:103–119.

Fischer, S. D., and P. Siple. eds. 1990. *Theoretical Issues in Sign Language Research: Linguistics 1.* Chicago: The University of Chicago Press.

Gee, J. P., and W. Goodhart. 1988. American Sign Language and the human biological capacity for language. In *Language Learning and Deafness*, ed. M. Strong, 49–74. Cambridge: Cambridge University Press.

Haiman, J. 1980. The iconicity of grammar: Isomorphism and motivation. *Language* 56 (3): 515–540.

Haiman, J. ed. 1985. *Iconicity in Syntax.* Amsterdam: John Benjamins.

Hinton, L., J. Nichols, and J. J. Ohala. eds. 1994. *Sound Symbolism.* Cambridge: Cambridge University Press.

Hockett, C. 1960. The origin of speech. *Scientific American* 203:88–96.

Johnston, T. 1991. Spatial syntax and spatial semantics in the inflection of signs for the marking of person and location in Auslan. *International Journal of Sign Linguistics* 2 (1): 29–62.

Kegl, J., M. Coppola, and A. Senghas. 1999. Creation through contact: Sign language emergence and sign language change in Nicaragua. In *Language Creation and Language Change: Creolization, Diachrony, and Development*, ed. Michel Degraff. Cambridge, MA: MIT Press.

Klima, E., and U. Bellugi. 1979. *The Signs of Language.* Cambridge. MA: Harvard University Press.

Li, C. N., and S. A. Thompson. 1976. Subject and topic: A new typology of language. In *Subject and Topic*, ed. C. N. Li, 457–489. New York: Academic Press.

Liddell, S. K. 1980. *American Sign Language Syntax.* The Hague: Mouton.

Liddell, S. K. 1990. Four functions of a locus: Reexamining the structure of space in ASL. *Paper on Linguistics of American Sign Language: An Introduction*, ed. C. Lucas, 176–198. Washington: Gallaudet University Press.

Liddell, S. K. 2000. Indicating verbs and pronouns: Pointing away from agreement. In Emmorey, and Lane (eds.) 2003, 303–320.

Liddell, S. K. 2003. *Grammar, Gesture, and Meaning in American Sign Language*. Cambridge: Cambridge University Press.

Liddell, S. K., and R. E. Johnson. 1986. American sign language compound formation processes, lexicalization, and phonological remnants. *Natural Language and Linguistic Theory* 4:445–513.

Liddell, S. K., and R. E. Johnson. 1987. An analysis of spatial-locative predicates in American Sign Language. Paper presented at *the Fourth Internatinal Conference on Sign Language Research*, Lapeenranta, Finland.

Lillo-Martin, D. 1999. Modality effects and modularity in language acquisition: The acquisition of American sign language. In *Hangbook of Child Language Acquisition*, ed. Ritchie and Bhatia, 531–567. Academic Press.

Meier, R. P. 2002. Why Different, why the same? Explaining effects and non-effects of modality upon linguistic structure in sign and speech. In Meier, Cormier, and Quinto-Pozos 2002, 1–25.

Meier, R. P., K. Cormier, and D. Quinto-Pozos. eds. 2002. *Modality and Structure in Signed and Spoken Languages*. Cambridge: Cambridge University Press.

Mufwene, S. S. 2001. *The Ecology of Language Evolution*. Cambridge: Cambridge University Press.

Myers, J. *Morphology of Taiwan Sign Language*. Ms. National Chung Cheng University.

Myers, J., and J. H.-Y. Tai. eds. 2005. *Language and Linguistics* 6 (2). Special Issue on Taiwan Sign Language.

Newport, E. L., and R. P. Meier. 1985. The acquisition of American Sign Language. In *The Cross-Linguistic Study of Language Acquisition*, ed. D. I. Slobin, 881–938. Hillsdale, NJ: Lawrence Erlbaum Associates.

Newport, E. L., and T. Supalla. 2000. Sign language research at the millennium. In Emmorey, and Lane ed. 2003, 103–114.

Padden, C. 1983. *Interaction of Morphology and Syntax in American Sign Language*. San Diego: University of California Ph. D. dissertation.

Peirce, C. S. 1932. *Collected Writings 2: Elements of Logic.* Cambridge, MA: Harvard University Press.

Poizner, H., E. S. Klima, and U. Bellugi. 1987. *What the Hands Reveal About the Brain.* Cambridge, MA: MIT Press.

Polich, L. 2005. *The Emergence of Deaf Coomunity in Nicaragua.* Washington, D.C.: Galllaudet University Press.

Quinto-pozos, D. 2002. Deictic points in the visual-gestural and tactile-gestural modalities. In Meier, Cormier, and Quinto-Pozos 2002, 442–468.

Sandler, W., and D. Lillo-Martin. 2006. *Sign Language and Linguistic Universals.* Cambridge: Cambridge University Press.

Siedlecki, T., and J. D. Bonvillian. 1993. Phonological deletion revisited: Errors in young children's two-handed signs. *Sign Language Studies* 80:223–242.

Siple, P. ed. 1978. *Understanding language Through Sign Language Research.* New York: Academic Press.

Siple, P., and S. D. Fischer. eds. 1991. *Theoretical Issues in Sign Language Research,* Vol. 2, *Psychology.* Chicago: The University of Chicago Press.

Smith, W. H. 1989. *The Morphological Characteristics of Verbs in Taiwan Sign Language.* Bloomington: Indiana University dissertation.

Smith, W. H. 1990. Evidence for auxiliaries in Taiwan Sign Language. In Siple 1978, 211–228.

Stokoe, W. C. 1960. Sign language structure: An outline of the communication systems of the American deaf. *Studies in Linguistics*, Occasional Papers, 8. Silver Spring, MD: Linstok Press.

Stokoe, W. C., D. C. Casterline, and C. G. Croneberg. 1965. *A Dictionary of American Sign Language on Linguistics Principles.* Washington, DC: Gallaudet University Press.

Supalla, T. 1978. Morphology of verbs of motion and location in American sign language. *Proceedings of the Second National Symposium on Sign Language Research and Teaching*, ed. F. Caccamise, Silver Spring. MD: National Association of the Deaf.

Supalla, T. 1982. *Structure and Acquisition of Verbs of Motion and Location in American Sign Language.* San Diego: University of California dissertation.

Supalla, T., and E. L. Newport. 1978. How many seats in a chair? The derivation of nouns and verbs in American sign language. In Siple 1978, 91–132.

Supalla, T., and R. Webb. 1995. The grammar of international sign: A new look at pidgin languages. In *Language, Gesture, and Space*, eds. K. Emmorey, and J. Reilly, 333–352. Mahwah, New Jersey: Lawrence Erlbaum Associates, Inc., Publishers.

Sutton-Spence, R., and B. Woll. 1999. *The Linguistics of British Sign Language: An Introduction.* Cambridge: Cambridge University Press.

Tai, J. H.-Y. 1985. Temporal sequence and Chinese word order. In *Iconicity in Syntax*, ed. J. Haiman, 49–72. Amsterdam: John Benjamins.

Tai, J. H.-Y. 1993. Iconicity: Motivations in Chinese grammar. In *Principles and Prediction: The Analysis of Natural Language,* ed. M. Eid, and G. Iverson, *Current Issues in Linguistic Theory* 98:53–74. Amsterdam: John Benjamins.

Tai, J. H.-Y. 1994. Chinese classifier systems and human categorization. In *Honor of Professor William S-Y. Wang: Interdisciplinary Studies on Language and Language Change*, ed. M. Chen, and O. Tseng, 479–494. Taipei: Pyramid.

Tai, J. H.-Y. 2005. Modality effects: Iconicity in Taiwan sign lnguage. In *POLA FOEVER: Festschrift in Honor of Professor William S-Y. Wang on His 70th Birthday*, ed. Dah-an Ho, and Ovid J. L. Tzeng, 19–36. Institute of Linguistics, Academia Sinica. Taipei.

Tai, J. H.-Y., and Shiou-fen Su. 2006. *Agreement in Taiwan Sign Language.* ms. National Chung Cheng University.

Tai, J. H.-Y., and J. Tsay. eds. 2009. *Taiwan Sign Language and Beyond.*（《台灣手語研究》）。《台灣人文研究叢書》第十冊，國立中正大學台灣人文研究中心。

Talmy, L. 2003. The representation of spatial structure in spoken and signed language: A neural model. *Language and Linguistics* 4 (2): 207–250.

Taub, S. F. 2001. *Language from the Body: Iconicity and Metaphor in American Sign Language.* Cambridge, MA: Cambridge University Press.

Woodward, J. 1978. Historical basis of American sign language. In Siple 1978, 333–348.

戴浩一、蘇秀芬　2006。〈台灣手語的呼應方式〉【百川會海：李壬癸先生七秩壽慶論文集】《語言暨語言學》專刊外篇之五。中央研究院語言學研究所。341–363頁。

16

Visualizing the Architecture and Texture of a Text: A Case Study of Selected Speeches of US President Barack Obama

Jonathan WEBSTER, Joe CHAN, Victor YAN, Kim WONG
City University of Hong Kong

Abstract

In this study of selected speeches of US President Barack Obama, I am interested in how patterning in both lexis and grammar contributes to the meaning of a text, projecting not only a perspective on text as edifice whose rhetorical structure possesses both breadth and depth, but also another perspective on text as tapestry whose texture depends on how cohesive are the threads of discourse.

1. Introduction

The work reported here is part of a larger study in visual semantics whose aim is to develop a framework for visualizing functional-semantic information realized across functionally-significant spans of text ranging from a text's constituent clauses up to the text as a whole.

Figure 16.1 outlines the modularized framework for representing visual semantics information, which includes linguistic data representation, enriched coding using a collaborative visual tagger, and improved visualization for further linguistic analysis.

Immediate and interactive visualization of functional-semantic information facilitates the search for patterning leading to further theorizing about how a text comes to mean what it does.

Figure 16.1 Modularized framework for visualizing functional-semantic information

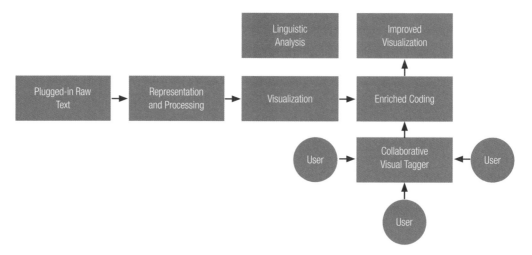

Figure 16.2 3D Visualization in a third-generation AVIE

 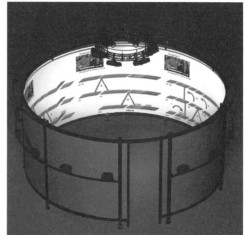

Our aim is to develop a collaborative browser-based Visual Semantics Interface (VSI) which can generate visualizations upon request in a fully automatic and customizable manner. Visualizations may be displayed either as 2D or 3D, depending on the display capability available to users. Figure 16.2 illustrates the 3D visualization in a fully immersive 360-degree browser using a third-generation active stereo AVIE (Advanced Visualization and Interaction Environment), measuring 10 meters in diameter and 3.5 meters in height.

Alternatively, a 2D visualization may be navigated within a web browser :

Figure 16.3   2D Visualization in a web-browser

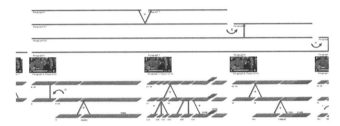

2.   Components of Visualization

There are three main components in the Visual Semantics Interface (VSI) (see Figure 16.4).

First, the text is presented as a segmented video stream. Video segments correspond to the paragraphing found in the original transcript of the speeches being analyzed.

Figure 16.4   Screenshot of Visual Semantics Interface

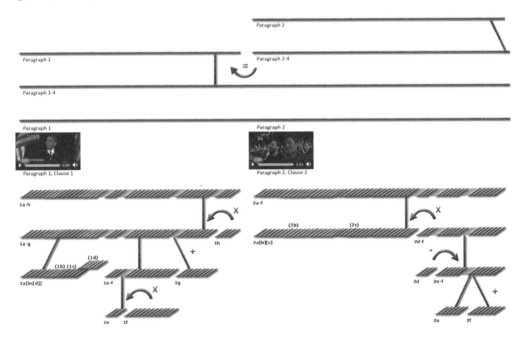

Second, above the segmented video stream is a 2D graphical representation showing the full text at ground level, as it extends, layer by layer, upward through the hierarchical organization of spans of text, all the way to each constituent paragraph at the top.

An overlay map (see Figure 16.5) showing a compressed version of the same 2D graphic is available to facilitate navigation of the full length of the text. Clicking on a particular point in the map takes the user to that same point in the video stream.

Figure 16.5 Navigation map in VSI

Third, below the segmented video stream is a 3D graphical representation showing the analysis from paragraph down to constituent clause. While the representation of logical relations between spans is the same as that described above, the direction is downward from the paragraph at the top down to the clauses at the bottom. The length of each span depends on the number of words/characters in that span. Each word/character is represented by a single bar. The color of the bars changes in response to user's queries designed to interrogate the text for lexico-grammatical patterns occurring in the text.

Figure 16.6, for example, shows the analysis for paragraph 10 of Obama's victory speech:

> <p 10> <c 14a>And while she's no longer with us, <c 14b> I know <c 14c> my grandmother is watching, along with the family [<c 14d> that made me [<c 14e> who I am.]] <c 15a> I miss them tonight, <c 15b> and know <c 15c> that my debt to them is beyond measure. <c 16a> To my sister Maya, my sister Auma, all my other brothers and sisters—thank you so much for all the support <c 16b> you have given me. <c 17> I am grateful to them.

The user queried the occurrence of embedded clauses. Two embedded clauses are highlighted in green color—clauses 14d and 14e. Clause 14e is double embedded in clause 14e, so shown here as raised. The bars are shown as 3D to allow the same bar to be displayed in multiple colors. Suppose, for example, the user queries the occurrence of first person pronouns in embedded clauses, then the bars corresponding to the words 'I' and 'me' would be color coded to indicate both the occurrence of embedding (green) and the first person pronoun (another color).

The representation of words/characters as bars whose color(s) are query-sensitive is intended to facilitate the identification of patterning in the text. At the same time, however, clicking on any line segment either above or below the video stream will display a pop-up window showing the actual text.

Figure 16.6 VSI view of paragraph 10 in Obama's Victory Speech

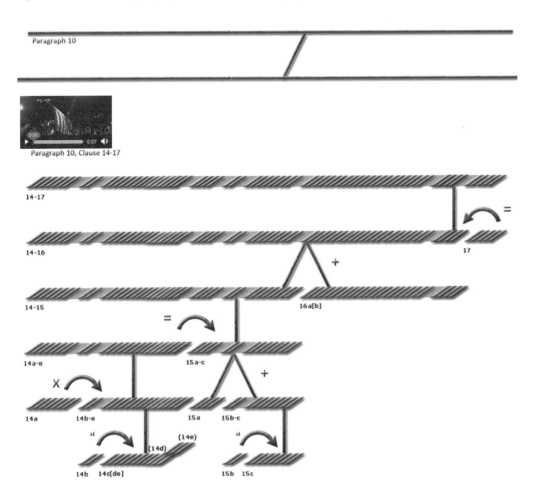

The discovery of lexico-grammatical patterning is essential to our determination of what constitutes a functionally-significant span of text. Repeated occurrence of some structural pattern over a particular span of text uniquely distinguishes that span from its neighbors.

Figure 16.7, for example, displays only a partial picture of Obama's inaugural speech from the text-as-ground up to that point in the speech where the block of paragraphs 6 through 64 divides into seven paratactically joined spans.

The style of representation is borrowed from Rhetorical Structure Theory (RST) (Mann & Thompson 1988)with several modifications. Instead of extending downward from text on top all the way down to constituent clauses on the bottom, we extend upward, showing how the text builds span by span up to each constituent paragraph at the top.

Like RST, hypotaxis between spans is indicated by an arc extending from the dependent span or satellite—as it is referred to in RST—to the main span or nucleus which is linked with

Figure 16.7   Obama's Inaugural—paragraphs 1–70

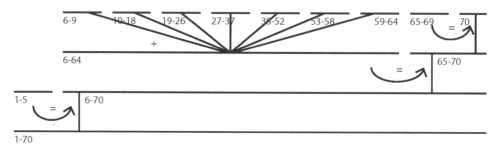

a span on the layer below by a straight line. Parataxis is indicated when two or more spans are linked by straight lines with the same span on the layer below.

Unlike, RST, we do not identify the relations between spans other than to indicate whether the relationship involves elaboration—indicated by an equal sign (=), extension—indicated by a plus sign (+), enhancement—indicated by a multiplication sign (x), or projection—indicated by double quotes ("). Elaboration, extension, enhancement and projection are terms used in systemic-functional grammar.

A span of text is a lexico-grammatically cohesive unit. It contains its own weave, defined by a particular texture consisting of distinctive lexicogrammatical patterns. Each span likewise contributes to the coherent expression to the overall message of the text of which it is part.

Paragraphs 38 through 52, for example, combine to form a single span of text. Throughout these paragraphs, Obama explicitly addresses other than the American people, continually switching between two patterns of address: (i) to so-and-so: know…; (ii) for/to so-and-so, we say/seek/pledge…

> <p 38> <c 65a> And so, **to all the other peoples and governments** [<c 65b>who are watching today], from the grandest capitals to the small village [<c65c> where my father was born:]] **know** …

> <p 44> <c 75a> And **for those** [<c 75b> who seek to advance their aims by inducing terror and slaughtering innocents,] <c 75a> **we say to you now** …

> <p 48> <c 80> **To the Muslim world, we seek** …

> <p 49> <c 81> **To those leaders around the globe** [c 81b>who seek to sow conflict, <c 81c> or blame their society's ills on the West,] <c 81a> **know** …

> <p 50> <c 82> **To those** [<c 82b> who cling to power through corruption and deceit and the silencing of dissent,] <c 82a> **know** …

> <p 51> <c 83a> **To the people of poor nations, we pledge** …

> <p 52> <c 84a> And **to those nations like ours** [<c 84b> that enjoy relative plenty,] <84a> **we say**…

In fact, this same pattern also appeared in John F. Kennedy's inaugural:

> To those old allies whose cultural and spiritual origins we share, we pledge …

> To those new states whom we welcome to the ranks of the free, we pledge …

> To those people in the huts and villages of half the globe struggling to break the bonds of mass misery, we pledge …

> To our sister republics south of our border, we offer a special pledge…

> To that world assembly of sovereign states, the United Nations, our last best hope in an age where the instruments of war have far outpaced the instruments of peace, we renew our pledge of support…

> Finally, to those nations who would make themselves our adversary, we offer not a pledge but a request: …

When identifying spans of text, besides looking for recurring lexico-grammatical patterns, one also expects to find a coherent development of ideas, expressed through parataxis and/or hypotaxis.

3.   VSI as a Tool for Comparing Texts

The Visual Semantics Interface (VSI) is designed to assist in the interrogation of texts leading to the discovery of how and why a text comes to mean what it does to those hearing or reading it.

What is there about a speech that provokes a certain response from its audience? Obama's inaugural address, for example, was criticized by commentators for its lack of eloquence, especially as compared with his earlier speeches, such as the one given on the night he won the presidency, i.e., Obama's victory speech. So why does one speech win acclaim for its eloquence, while another receives only criticism?

Hoping to address this question, I have analyzed both Obama's victory and inaugural speeches in terms of those features which contribute texture and coherence. I will begin by providing some background to the speeches, followed by a look at various approaches to analyzing the speeches, including the use of word clouds and word trees, which have been produced using visualization software developed as part of IBM's Many Eyes Project (www-958. ibm.com/software/data/cognos/manyeyes).

In a word cloud the size of each word is proportional to its word count in the full text. A word tree, on the other hand, shows a selected word in its various contexts of use, and the font size indicates frequency.

For example, the word cloud for President Obama's speech on jobs (delivered 8 September 2011, see Figure 16.8) shows the prominence of the word 'jobs'.

The word tree for the same speech (see Figure 16.9) reveals what some might consider to be the sub-text for the speech: 'pass this jobs bill'.

Figure 16.8   Word cloud for Obama's Jobs Speech (8 September 2011)

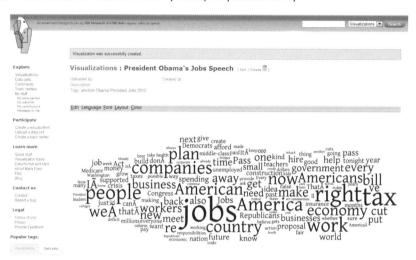

Figure 16.9   Word tree for Obama's Jobs Speech (8 September 2011)

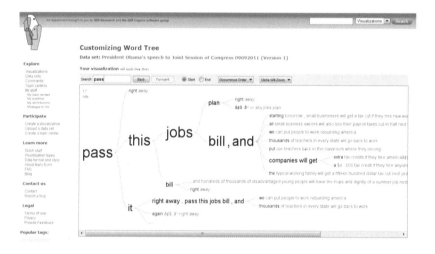

4.   The Speeches of President Barack Obama

The speeches of US President Obama have been described as eloquent and moving. Two speeches that particularly stand out, not just for their style and content, but also for their historical significance, are the victory speech that he gave on the night he won the US presidential election, 4 November 2008, just before midnight in Chicago's Grant Park, and his inaugural address delivered after being sworn in as the 44th President of the United States on 20 January 2009.

Who actually writes Obama's speeches? Obama's chief speechwriter is a thirty-year old named Jon Favreau, who has been ghosting for Obama since 2004. To familiarize himself with

Obama's speech style, Favreau reportedly travels everywhere with a copy of Obama's Dreams From My Father. According to The Guardian, after an hour-long meeting with Obama to discuss Obama's vision for the address, Favreau then went away and, with a team of researchers, spent weeks interviewing historians and speechwriters, studying periods of crisis, and listening to past inaugural speeches, before finally sitting down in a Starbucks in Washington to write the first draft.

5.   Obama's Inaugural

Comparing Obama's inaugural address with those of previous presidents, Jonathan Raban, writing for *The Guardian* ('The golden trumpet', Saturday 24 January 2009), notes that '[i]n no inaugural has a president so completely repudiated the policies of his predecessor as Obama did on Tuesday'; 'none comes close to so categorically rejecting the political philosophy and legislative record of the previous occupant of the White House.' And Obama did so, as Raban puts it, 'by stealth'; 'under the guise of noble platitude'; 'uphold[ing] the stilted linguistic conventions of the form'.

Set in what Raban calls 'the faux-antique dialect of past inaugurals', 'phrased in language as well-worn and conventional as possible', and fully in keeping with the conventional practice of beginning with a nod of thanks to his predecessor, and concluding with a reference to God, Obama announced to the world that 'the Bush era had ended and that America, after a long, unhappy detour in the wilderness, was returning to its better history.'

Referring to it as '[t]he driving theme of the address', Raban notes how it '[makes] its appearance at artfully calculated intervals, with Obama touching on it, departing from it, returning to it, burying it for a while and digging it up again in a way that made some critics call the speech diffuse. But it was not diffuse. It was quietly, courteously insistent on its purpose.'

6.   Obama's Victory Speech

Obama's victory speech was delivered in Grant Park in Chicago on 4 November 2008, the night of his electoral victory over John McCain and his running mate, Sarah Palin.

Aaron Zelinsky, Articles Editor, Yale Law Journal, in his post, 'What We Will Remember: Obama's Victory Speech and McCain's Concession' (5 November 2008, http://www.huffingtonpost.com/politics/) identifies two themes in Obama's victory speech: unity and inspiration; and two historical figures: Abraham Lincoln and Martin Luther King, Jr. Calling for unity, Obama quotes from Lincoln's first inaugural: 'We are not enemies, but friends.'

> <c 51a> As Lincoln said to a nation far more divided than ours: <c 51b> 'We are not enemies, but friends... <c 51c> though passion may have strained <c 51d> it must not break our bonds of affection.'

Obama's reference to 'the arc of history' in the fourth sentence paraphrases Martin Luther King, Jr.'s expression from his August 16, 1967 speech: 'the arc of the moral universe is long, but it bends toward justice.'

> <p 4> <c 4a> It's the answer [<c 4b> that led those [<c 4c> who have been told for so long by so many <c 4d> to be cynical, and fearful, and doubtful [<c 4e> of what we can achieve]] <c 4f> to put their hands on the arc of history <c 4g> and bend it once more toward the hope of a better day.]

James Woods, writing for the *New Yorker*, (17 November 2008, www.newyorker.com/talk/2008/11/17/081117ta_talk_wood#ixzz1KE5MySW1), believes an even more obvious allusion to King is apparent in the following sentence from Obama's speech:

> <p 22> <c 35a> We may not get there in one year or even in one term, <c 35b> but America—I have never been more hopeful <35c> than I am tonight <c 35d> that we will get there. <c 36a> I promise you—<36b> we as a people will get there

Woods writes,

> When the President-elect warned that the road will be long, and that 'we may not get there in one year or even one term, but America . . . I promise you—we as a people will get there,' the word 'promise' surely activated, however unconsciously, the rich narrative of exodus that found a culminating expression in King's last speech, in Memphis: ' And I've seen the promised land. I may not get there with you.'

Quotes and paraphrases aside, Zelinsky identifies 'the most rhetorically elegant part of the speech, and its emotional core' as the series of totally original statements near the close of the speech beginning with the form of address 'to those'

> <p 34> <c 54a> To those [<c 54b> who would tear the world down]—<c 54a> we will defeat you. <c 55a> To those [<c 55b> who seek peace and security]—<c 55a> we support you.

> <p 35> <c 56a> And to all those [<c 56b> who have wondered <c 56c> if America's beacon still burns as bright]—<c 56a> tonight we proved once more <c 56d> that the true strength of our nation comes not from the might of our arms or the scale of our wealth, but from the enduring power of our ideals: democracy, liberty, opportunity and unyielding hope.

7.   Comparing the Speeches

Literary critic, Stanley Fish, writing in the Opinionator, an exclusive online commentary from the *New York Times* (22 January 2009), complemented USA Today for identifying the most frequently used words in the Inaugural, adding, 'This is exactly the right kind of analysis to perform, for it identifies the location of the speech's energy in the repetition of key words and the associations forged among them by virtue of that repetition.'

Below are word clouds for both the Inaugural (Figure 16.10) and Victory (Figure 16.11) speeches.

Figure 16.10   Obama's Inaugural Address word cloud

Figure 16.11   Obama's Victory Speech word cloud

Comparing both word clouds, certain words clearly stand out as more prominent in one than the other; 'nation', 'new', and 'America' in the Inaugural, as compared with 'America', 'tonight' and 'people' in the victory speech.

The word tree visualizations for the pronoun 'I' (see Figures 16.12 (Inaugural) and 16.13 (Victory) below) show that the first person singular pronoun, 'I', occurs only three times in the Inaugural, while as many as 27 times in the Victory speech.

Figure 16.12 'I' in Obama's Inaugural Address

Figure 16.13 'I' in Obama's Victory Speech

In comparing the two speeches, I(naugural) and V(ictory), I have compiled the following statistics showing process type by pronominal (see Table 16.1).

The proportion of process types with a pronominal participant are similar across the speeches, except that there are more mental processes in the Victory speech than the Inaugural.

Table 16.1 Pronouns by process type in Obama's Inaugural and Victory speeches

	I		let us		we		you		he		she		they		Total / %	
	I	V	I	V	I	V	I	V	I	V	I	V	I	V	I	V
material	1	9	1	2	41	34	7	6	1	2		1	6	2	58 / 61%	56 / 55%
mental		8	1	2	7	5		1		1		2	4	2	12 / 13%	21 / 21%
relational		7			9	6	1					4	7		17 / 18%	17 / 17%
verbal	1	2		1	3										4 / 4%	3 / 3%
behavioral	1	1	1		2	2				1		1			4 / 4%	5 / 5%
Total /%	3 / 3%	27 / 27%	3 / 3%	5 / 5%	41 / 43%	47 / 46%	8 / 8%	7 / 6%	1 / 1%	4 / 4%	0	8 / 8%	17 / 18%	4 / 4%	95 / 100%	102 / 100%

Of the 27 occurrences of the pronoun 'I' in the Victory speech, 8 occur as cognizant in connection with a mental process. Without those 8 mental processes, the proportion of mental processes across both speeches would be about the same.

Aside from comparing the two speeches in terms of the frequencies of content words or pronouns, what is there about each speech which contributes to how the listener/reader responds? Trying to understand what it is about the language that produces a particular response from listeners/readers, commentators have offered various, sometimes contradictory, explanations. Consider the following debate between literary critic, Stanley Fish, and linguist, Mark Liberman, over whether the Inaugural was paratactic or hypotactic.

8. Responding to Obama's Speeches

Fish begins by noting how radio and television commentators criticized Obama's inaugural address for its lack of eloquence, especially as compared with his earlier speeches, such as the one given on the night he won the presidency, i.e., Obama's victory speech. Fish goes on to describe the inaugural address as 'a framework on which a succession of verbal ornaments was hung, and we were being invited not to move forward but to stop and ponder significances only hinted at.'

Elaborating on this point, Fish complains, 'There are few transitions and those there are —"for," "nor," "as for," "so," "and so"—seem just stuck in, providing a pause, not a marker of logical progression. Obama doesn't deposit us at a location he has in mind from the beginning; he carries us from meditative bead to meditative bead, and invites us to contemplate.'

Citing the *Oxford English Dictionary* definition for the technical term 'parataxis'—i.e., 'the placing of propositions or clauses one after the other without indicating . . . the relation of co-ordination or subordination between them'—as opposed to 'hypotaxis' where relations between propositions and clauses are marked by 'connectives that point backward or forward', Fish describes Obama's inaugural address as 'surely more paratactic than hypotactic', as 'incantatory rather than progressive; the cadences ask for assent to each proposition ("That we are in the midst of crisis is now well understood") rather than to a developing argument. The power is in discrete moments rather than in a thesis proved by the marshaling of evidence.'

Comparing the two styles, Fish writes,

> One kind of prose is additive—here's this and now here's that; the other asks the reader or hearer to hold in suspension the components of an argument that will not fully emerge until the final word. It is the difference between walking through a museum and stopping as long as you like at each picture, and being hurried along by a guide who wants you to see what you're looking at as a stage in a developmental arc she is eager to trace for you.

Blogging two days later in the Language Log ('Presidential parataxis?', 24 January 2009), Mark Liberman, founder and director of the Linguistic Data Consortium, criticizes Fish's terminology as 'arguably misleading'. 'Hypotaxis,' argues Liberman, 'is not crucially characterized by the use of connectives, but by the use of explicit grammatical embedding, hierarchical structuring that 'places' (= -taxis) some words or phrases 'beneath' (= hypo-) others.'

Comparing Obama's 2009 inaugural address with George W. Bush's 2005 address, Liberman notes that both show a similar rate of sentence-initial connectives—ten out of a hundred sentences in Bush's 2005 inaugural; fourteen out of a hundred and eight sentences in Obama's 2009 inaugural. The use of what Fish refers to as 'connectives that point backward or forward' is admittedly not high in either inaugural.

Comparing Obama's inaugural with his speech on winning the South Carolina Democratic Presidential Primary, otherwise known as the Yes We Can speech, Harris and DiMarco (2009, 51) conclude that 'The high proportion of asyndeton [Gk, "no connectives"] in the Inaugural goes a long way to explaining most interpreter's sense of terseness in the speech and especially Fish's stop-and-ponder opinion. The address has several paratactic passages, but the effect of these are heightened substantially by asyndeton.'

Liberman argues, however, that the relatively low number of connectives by itself indicates neither a lack of logical progression, nor the absence of hypotaxis.

To illustrate how 'logical progression' can be achieved in spite of the absence of any 'explicit connective or adverb indicating the discourse relation', Liberman gives examples illustrating what Halliday refers to as linear thematic progression across sentences, though without labeling it as such.

For example, he notes how the phrase 'the words' at the beginning of the fourth sentence refers back to 'the presidential oath' mentioned at the end of the previous sentence, and how "the oath" is again mentioned at the beginning of the fifth sentence.

<p 3> <c 3> Forty-four Americans have now taken **the presidential oath**.

<p 4> <c 4> **The words** have been spoken during rising tides of prosperity and the still waters of peace. <5> Yet, every so often, **the oath** is taken amidst gathering clouds and raging storms.

Halliday refers to repeated reference to the same entity in sentence-initial position as continuous thematic progression. Both linear and continuous thematic progression play an important role in helping to 'carry the thread of discourse forward' in Obama's inaugural (Liberman).

As for whether Obama's inaugural is more paratactic than hypotactic, Liberman notes that the proportion of hierarchical embedding in Obama's 2009 was similar to that of Lincoln's 1865, and significantly greater than Bush's 2005. In an earlier blog ('Inaugural Embedding', 9 September 2005), Liberman explained how he quantified the distribution of degrees of embedding. He 'marked only subordinate finite clause boundaries, not infinitive clauses or nominalizations of various sorts, and not main clauses strung together by coordinators like "and" and "but".' The following examples illustrate how he annotated each text. The number in the left column indicates the level of embedding of the corresponding clause on the same line.

From George Washington's:

0	In this conflict of emotions all I dare aver is
1	[that it has been my faithful study to collect my duty from a just appreciation of every circumstance
2	[by which it might be affected.]]

From Abraham Lincoln's:

0	It may seem strange
1	[that any men should dare to ask a just God's assistance in wringing their bread from the sweat of other men's faces,]
0	but let us judge not,
1	[that we be not judged.]

The table below shows the number of words at each level of embedding in all four inaugural speeches (see Table 16.2).

On the one hand, I agree with Fish's comment that the Inaugural was indeed more paratactic than hypotactic, and that '[t]he power is in discrete moments rather than in a thesis proved by

Table 16.2   Number of words by levels of embedding

	0	1	2	3	4	Mean Sentence Length
George Washington 1	629 (44%)	554 (39%)	206 (14%)	36 (3%)	5 (<1%)	60
Abraham Lincoln 2	440 (63%)	222 (32%)	38 (5%)	0	0	26
George W Bush 2	1842 (88%)	244 (12%)	4 (<1%)	0	0	22
Barack Obama 1	1493 (62%)	799 (33%)	101 (4%)	0	0	22

the marshaling of evidence.' But, at the same time, I also agree with Liberman that Obama's inaugural is heavily hypotactic, with a substantial amount of what he calls embedding.

However, I disagree with Fish's reasons for saying that the Inaugural is paratactic, and I fault Liberman for confusing what are two distinctive linguistic phenomena occurring between clauses: hypotaxis and embedding.

Unlike Liberman, I take -taxis, whether parataxis or hypotaxis, to indicate a relationship between functionally-significant spans of like or equal grammatical status. Embedded clauses, on the other hand, are rank-shifted units functioning at a rank below clause level, such as when a nominalized clause takes on the role of grammatical Subject in another clause.

Comparing instances of—taxis and embedding across the two Obama speeches, the percentages of clauses with embedding are similar for both, i.e., 17%. While the percentages for parataxis (26%) and hypotaxis (27%) are similar for Obama's Inaugural, in the Victory speech, the percentage of hypotactically joined clauses is less than those paratactically joined (see Table 16.3).

Table 16.3   Percentages of parataxis, hypotaxis and embedding

	Victory	Inaugural
parataxis	21%	26%
hypotaxis	36%	27%
embedding	17%	17%

The following example from Obama's victory speech illustrates parataxis at clause level (see also Figure 16.14):

<p 20>   <c 31a>**There are mothers and fathers** <31b> who will lie awake <31c> after their children fall asleep <31d> and wonder...

        <c 31e> how they'll make the mortgage,

          +

        <c 31f> or pay their doctor's bills,

          +

        <c 31g> or save enough for their child's college education.

<c 32a> There is new energy <c 32b> to harness

+

<c 32c> and (there are) new jobs <c 32d> to be created;

    +

    <c 32e> (and there are) new schools <c 32f> to build

+

<c 32g> and (there are) threats <c 32h> to meet

    +

    <c 32i> and (there are) alliances <c 32j> to repair.

Figure 16.14   Obama's Victory Speech, paragraph 20, sentences 31–32

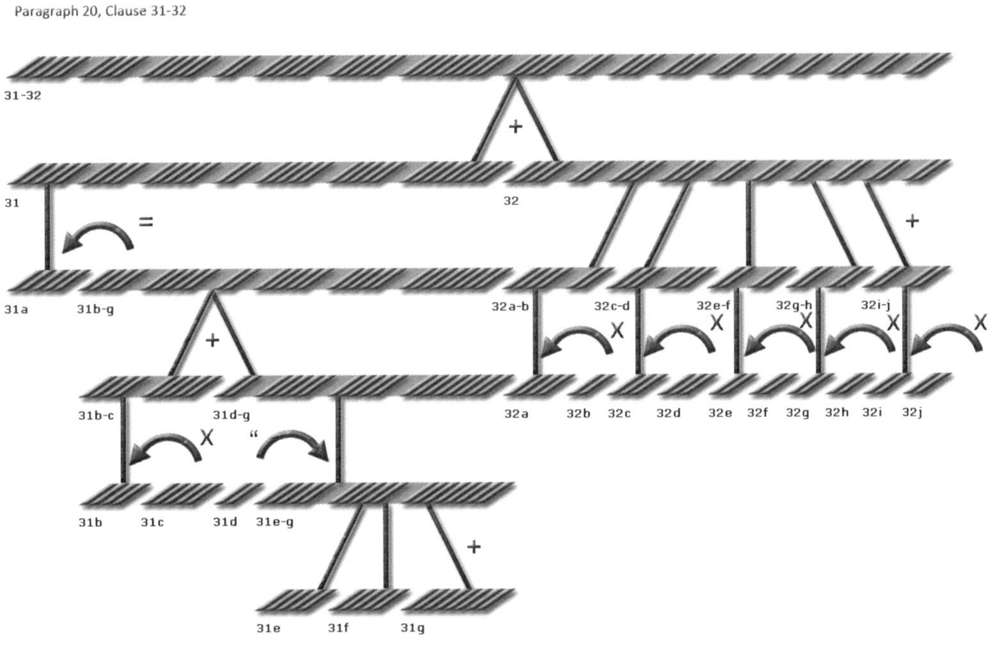

Paragraph 20, Clause 31-32

As we get into clause level analysis, there is frequent parataxis, typically involving pairs or triplets. In clause 31, sleepless parents wonder (i) how they'll make the mortgage, (ii) or pay their doctor bills, (iii) or save enough for their child's education. In clause 32, there is (i) new energy, (ii) and new jobs, new schools, (iii) and threats and alliances.

Threaded throughout both the victory and the inaugural speeches are multi-item (often three-part) lists. Just a few examples from the Victory Speech:

      <p 23>…<c 39a> But I will always be honest with you…

        …<c 40a> I will listen to you…

        …<c 41a> And above all, I will ask you…

      <p 28>…<c 46a> So let us summon…

        …<c 47a> Let us remember…

        …<c 48a> Let us resist..

        …<c 49a> Let us remember…

The span of text from paragraph 36 to the end of the speech demonstrates how paratactic repetition helps to establish a rhythm that gradually builds into the climactic conclusion whose impact was plain to see on the faces of his listeners.

      <p 36>…<c 57b> that America can change.

        <c 58> Our union can be perfected.

        … [<c 59c> what we **can** and must achieve tomorrow.]

      <p 39>…<c 64a> … the heartache and the hope;

        the struggle and the progress;

        the times [<c 64c> we were told <c 64d> that we can't, and the people

        [<c 64e> who pressed on with that American creed:]

      <p 43><c 72a >She was there for **the buses in Montgomery, the hoses in Birmingham,**

        a bridge in Selma, and **a preacher** from Atlanta

      <p 44><c 74a> A man touched down on the Moon,

        <c 74b> a wall came down in Berlin,

        <c 74c> a world was connected by our own science and imagination.

      <p 45><c 77> America, we have come so far.

        <c 78> We have seen so much.

        <c 79> But there is so much more to do.

<p 46>…<c 80b> **if** our children **should live** <c 80c> **to see** the next century;

<c 80d> **if** my daughters **should be** so lucky **to live** as long …

<c 80e> **what change will** they see?

<c 81> **What progress will** we have made?

<p 47><c 82a> **This is our** chance …

<c 83> **This is our** moment.

<p 48><c 84a> **This is our** time –

<c 84b> **to put** our people back to work <c 84c> **and open** doors …

<c 84d> **to restore** prosperity <c 84e> **and promote** …

<c 84f> **to reclaim** the American dream <c 84g> **and reaffirm** …

9.   Text as Edifice

Why critics felt the Inaugural was diffuse may be related to what Fish identifies as parataxis, but not only parataxis at clause level, but also parataxis above clause level.

Each of the seven spans making up the block of paragraphs 6 through 64 returns to what Raban calls '[t]he driving theme of the address', or, in other words, Obama's call to reject the policies of his predecessor, George W. Bush.

In the span made up of paragraphs 6–9, Obama focuses on the crisis at hand, repeating the word 'crisis' three times.

Following applause, Obama again brings listeners' attention back to the day itself, initiating succeeding paragraphs with the same wording

<p 10><c 19a> On this day, we gather….

<p 11><c 20a> On this day, we come…

Tense over the span of paragraphs from 10 to 18 ranges from simple present to present perfect to simple past as Obama recalls those from America's past who 'struggled and sacrificed and worked'.

Over the next span, paragraphs 19 to 26, pronominal references are primarily first person plural—'we' and 'our', and tense goes from simple present to future, as another crescendo builds, repeating 'we will' five times, climaxing with simple parataxis:

<p 26><c 48> All this we can do. <c 49> All this we will do.

Three times in the span from paragraph 27 to 37, the word 'question' is repeated:

<p 27> <c 50> Now, <c 50a> there are some <c 50b> who question the scale of our ambitions, …

<p 29><c 53a> The question [<c 53b> we ask today] is [<c 53c> not …

<p 32><c 57a> Nor is the question before us …

<p 33><c 59a> But this crisis has reminded us <c 59b> that without a watchful eye, the market can spin out of control. <c 60a> The nation cannot prosper long <c 60b> when it favors only the prosperous.

The conjunction 'But' at the beginning of paragraph 33 shifts listeners attention away from wrong-headed questions to what are regarded as some of the most original and memorable lines of the address, including 'The nation cannot prosper long when it favors only the prosperous'; 'we reject as false the choice between our safety and our ideals'; 'Those ideals still light the world, and we will not give them up for expedience sake.'

As noted earlier, over the span of paragraphs 38–52, Obama directs his words to other than the American people, switching between two patterns of address: (1) *to* so-and-so: know… ; (2) *for*/to so-and-so, we *say/seek/pledge*…

In paragraphs 53 through 58, after referring to those serving in the military, whom 'we remember…'; 'we honor…', Obama repeats another pattern beginning with *it is..* that/which, or what we might refer to as cleft sentences or predicated theme.

<p 55> <c 89a> And yet at this moment, a moment [<c 89b> that will define a generation,] **it is** precisely this spirit **that** must inhabit us all.

<p 56> <c 90a> For as much as government can do, <c 90b> and must do, <c 90c> **it is** ultimately the faith and determination of the American people <c 90d> upon **which** this nation relies.

<p 57> <c 91a> **It is** the kindness [<c 91b> to take in a stranger <c 91c> when the levees break,] the selflessness of workers [<c 91d> who would rather cut their hours <c 91e> than see a friend lose their job] <c 91f> **which** sees us through our darkest hours.

<p 58> <c 92a> **It is** the firefighter's courage [<c 92b> to storm a stairway [<c 92c> filled with smoke,]] but also a parent's willingness [<c 92d> to nurture a child] <c 92e> **that** finally decides our fate.

The next span, from paragraphs 59 to 64, employs three repeated patterns. Paragraph 58 ends with, 'These things are old'; the next paragraph begins 'These things are true.' Paragraph 61, following up on the idea of what is true, includes two thematic equatives in succession:

<p 61> <c 98> **What is demanded**, then, **is** a return to these truths. <c 99a> **What is required** of us now **is** a new era of responsibility—a recognition on the

part of every American [<c 99b> that we have duties to ourselves, our nation and the world; duties [<c 99c> that we do not grudgingly accept, <c 99d> but rather seize gladly, firm in the knowledge [<c 99e> that there is nothing so satisfying to the spirit, so defining of our character <c 99f> than giving our all to a difficult task.]]]

Over the next three sentences, the phrase 'This is…' is repeated.

<p 62> <c 100> **This is** the price and the promise of citizenship.

<p 63> <c 101a> **This is** the source of our confidence—the knowledge [<c 101b> that God calls on us to shape an uncertain destiny.]

<p 64}> <c 102a> **This is** the meaning of our liberty and our creed, <c 102b> why men and women and children of every race and every faith can join in celebration across this magnificent mall; <c 102c> and why a man [<c 102d> whose father less than 60 years ago might not have been served in a local restaurant] can now stand before you <c 102e> to take a most sacred oath. (Applause.)

Obama's victory speech is a very different semantic construct. While at clause level, the texture is similar, and the patterning is much the same as his inaugural, still each speech, as a semantic unit, reveals a rather different architecture (see Figure 16.14).

Obama starts out with a span of five sentences (transcribed as paragraphs), introducing the speech. The first sentence ends with 'tonight is your answer', and each of the next three sentences begins 'It's the answer…'

From paragraph 6 through paragraph 11, after referring to his opponent, John McCain, and his running mate, Sarah Palin, Obama proceeds to thank his own running mate, Joe Biden, his wife, Michelle and other family members, as well as his campaign manager for their support and sacrifice.

Each successive span builds on the previous span, culminating in Obama's resounding 'yes, we can.' Between larger spans, the speech is more hypotactic than paratactic. But then as the spans become smaller, relations between spans become more paratactic.

Paragraphs 12 through 15, identify who are the 'you' in '[this victory] belongs to you': they are <p 14> <c 24> working men and women; <p 15> <c 25> young people and not-so-young people. Expanding on this, Obama repeats 'This is your victory' in paragraph 16 (sentence 26), and then goes on to explain why everyone worked so hard to achieve this victory.

<p 16> <c 26> This is your victory.

<p 17> <c 27a> I know <c 27b> you didn't do this <c 27c> just to win an election <c 27d> and I know <c 27e> you didn't do it for me. <c 28a> You did it <c 28b> because you understand the enormity of the task [<c 28c> that lies ahead.]

<p 18> <c 29a> **For even as we celebrate tonight, <c 29b> we know** <c 29c> the challenges [<29d> that tomorrow will bring] <c 29c> are the greatest of our lifetime—two wars, a planet in peril, the worst financial crisis in a century.

<p 19> <c 30a> **Even as we stand here tonight, <c 30b> we know** <30c> **there are brave Americans** waking up in the deserts of Iraq and the mountains of Afghanistan <30d> to risk their lives for us.

<p 20> <c 31a>**There are mothers and fathers** <c 31b> who will lie awake <31c> after their children fall asleep <c 31d> and wonder <c 31e> how they'll make the mortgage, <c 31f> or pay their doctor's bills, <31g> or save enough for their child's college education. <32a> There is new energy [<c 32b> to harness] <c 32c> and new jobs [to be created]; <32e> new schools [<c 32f> to build] <c 32g> and threats [<c 32h> to meet] <c 32i> and alliances [<c 32j> to repair.]

Both paragraphs 18 and 19, or, in other words, successive sentences 29 and 30, begin with much the same pattern: "For even as we celebrate tonight, we know…"; "Even as we stand her tonight, we know…"; another thread emerges in paragraphs 19 and 20: "there are brave Americans…"; "There are mothers and fathers…"

Unlike the flatter, paratactic structure evident in the architecture of the Inaugural, the Victory Speech displays a step-by-step architecture, building upward, through hypotactic links, from one span to another. The span of paragraphs < p 6> to <p 11>, for example, is hypotactically related to the span from <p 12> to <p 48>, followed, in turn, by the span of paragraphs <p 12> to <p 15> which is hypotactically related to the span from <p 16> to <p 48> (see Figure 16.15), and so on, gradually ascending to Obama's powerful conclusion:

<p 47> <c 82a> This is our chance <c 82b> to answer that call. <c 83> This is our moment.

<p 48> <c 84a> This is our time—<c 84b> to put our people back to work <c 84c> and open doors of opportunity for our kids; <c 84d> to restore prosperity <c 84e> and promote the cause of peace; <84f> to reclaim the American dream <c 84g> and reaffirm that fundamental truth—<84h> that out of many, we are one; <c 84i> that while we breathe, <c 84j> we hope, <84k> and where we are met with cynicism and doubt, and those [<c 84l> who tell us <c 84m> that we can't,] <c 84n> we will respond with that timeless creed [<c 84o> that sums up the spirit of a people:] <c 85> yes, we can.

Figure 16.15   Comparison of Obama's speeches at paragraph level

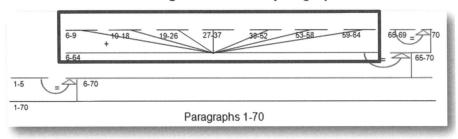

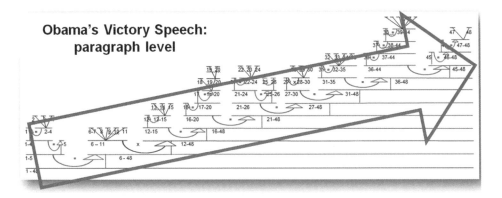

10.   Conclusion

Patterns involving parataxis and hypotaxis play a significant role at both clause level and above in determining the character of the text.

While parataxis and hypotaxis at clause level is largely a grammatical or syntactic phenomenon, above clause level, the relations between spans of text may be less grammatically certain but certainly no less semantically significant.

A text is an instance of meaning created by patterns of choice at both clause level and above. By exploring various ways of visualizing the representation of such patterns, we gain new perspectives on the text as both edifice exhibiting a particular architecture, and the text as tapestry exhibiting a particular texture.

REFERENCES

Harris, R., and C. DiMarco. 2009. Constructing a rhetorical figuration ontology. Persuasive technology and digital behaviour intervention symposium. *AISB 2009 Proceedings.* Heriot-Watt University, Edinburgh, Scotland.

Mann, W. C., and S. A. Thompson. 1988. Rhetorical structure theory: Toward a functional theory of text organization. *Text* 8 (3): 243–281.

Wang, Junling. 2010. A critical discourse analysis of Barack Obama's speeches. *Journal of Language Teaching and Research* 1 (3): 254–261.

Ye Ruijuan. 2010. The interpersonal metafunction analysis of Barack Obama's victory speech. *English Language Teaching* 3 (2) (June).

17

Northern-Min Glottalized Onsets and the Principles of Tonal Split and Tonal Merger

Weera OSTAPIRAT
Mahidol University and Academia Sinica

Abstract

I propose that the so-called 'softened stop/affricate initials' in Proto-Northern-Min (PNM) are glottalized stops and affricates. The principles of tonal split and tonal merger with respect to the onset classes in Min dialects are discussed and formulated.

1.   Introduction

Proto-Min (PM) initial system as having been proposed by Norman (1973, 1974) includes sounds which are not typical to the traditional system of Middle Chinese. These include a series of initials which have been dubbed 'softened stop/affricate initials' (written as *-t, *-d, and so on). The reconstruction of these initial series is based mainly on the distinguished reflexes in the dialects of the Northern-Min (NM) subgroup. Norman (1986a) has later proposed that prenasalization is a source that gave rise to these initials, based on comparison with the related forms in the Miao-Yao languages. The phonetic value of these initials in Proto-Northern-Min (PNM), on the other hand, has been proposed to be voiced breathy sounds (Handel 2003).

In this paper I would like to propose that PNM 'softened stop/affricate initials' are constricted or glottalized. I will write them as *tʔ-, *dʔ-, and so on, contrasting with *t-, *th- and *d-, *dh-, etc. Discussions on tonal split and tonal merger with respect to different classes of onsets will follow.

Tonal categories will be marked with the capital letters A, B, C, and D, which correspond respectively to the traditional categories Píng, Shǎng, Qù, and Rù.

2.   PNM Glottalized Onsets: The Initial Reflexes

For convenience and easy reference, the same eight NM dialects used by Handel (2003) will be first referred to here. They are: Zhenghe (ZH), Zhengqian (ZQ), Jian'ou (JO), Shibei (SB), Jianyang (JY), Chengcun (CC), Chong'an (CA), and Wufu (WF). Other dialects will be further discussed in the last section.

In general, the reflexes of PNM softened stops/affricates are considered to have developed in three different ways. They may have become (I) voiceless stops, (II) voiced stops, or (III) approximants. (Hereafter, alveolars are used to represent stop/affricate initials as a whole).

	I	II	III
*tʔ-, *dʔ-	t-	d-	l-
Dialects	ZH, ZQ, JO	SB	JY, CC, CA, WF

I assume the following main developments from PNM to the daughter dialects.

1. In languages such as ZH, ZQ and JO languages, the onset constriction/glotalization has extended to the rimes (i.e., *tʔ- > t_ʔ, where _ʔ representing the glottalization of the rimes). This feature is still evidenced in a number of modern tone reflexes in these dialects. It is usually marked in the literatures with a glottal stop following the

numeral tonal notation and described as the short and glottalized quality of the tones (cf. Norman 1986a, 378).[1]

$$*t\text{ʔ}- \quad > \quad t\_\text{ʔ}$$

$$*d\text{ʔ}- \quad > \quad d\_\text{ʔ} > t\_\text{ʔ}$$

2. In other dialects, the constricted onsets, both voiceless and voiced, have developed into an intermediate stage of glottalized (or implosive) voiced stops/affricates, namely, *tʔ- and *dʔ- have become *dʔ- (or ɗ-). These glottalized voiced initials have then become voiced in dialects such as SB and lenited into approximants in the so-called 'softening dialects' (JY, CC, CA, WF).[2]

$$*t\text{ʔ}-,\ *d\text{ʔ}- \quad > \quad d\text{ʔ}\ - \quad > \quad d\text{- or l-}$$

Table 17.1 and Table 17.2 illustrate these schemes. JO represents the former type of change and SB and JY represent the subtypes of the latter. The dialect forms are from Norman (1996, 2000), with the phonemic tones being substituted by the phonetic tonal values as provided in Norman (1986a).[3]

Table 17.1 Examples of PNM voiceless glottalized onsets

	JO	SB	JY	PNM	Tones
Reverse	paiŋ 21ʔ	baiŋ 21	waiŋ 21ʔ	*pʔ-	B
Emit	puɛ 21ʔ	buai 21	woi 21ʔ	*pʔ-	D
Wear	tuɛ 21ʔ	duai 31	lue 31	*tʔ-	C
Turn	tyeŋ 21ʔ	dyŋ 21	lyeŋ 21ʔ	*tʔ-	B
Mattress	tsoŋ 21ʔ	dzuiŋ 31	luŋ 31	*tsʔ-	C
Early	tsau 21ʔ	dzɔ 21	lau 21ʔ	*tsʔ-	B
Lard	kau 21ʔ	gɔ 31	au 31	*kʔ-	A
Tie	kai 21ʔ	gai 31	ai 31	*kʔ-	A

---

1   There is evidence that the voiced glottalized onsets (e.g., *dʔ-) may have not yet completely merged with their voiceless counterparts (e.g., *tʔ-) in some dialects. Akitani (2008, 122, 170) describes the reflexes of NM voiced glottalized onsets in tone A in such dialects as Zhenqian and Dikou as partially voiced.

2. Norman (2000, 272) notes the murmured quality accompanying SB voiced stops in some tones and its similarity found in the voiced stops of the Wu dialects. Akitani (2008, 75), on the other hand, describes them as fully voiced but, unlike those in Wu dialects, lacking strong breathy quality. This seems to show variations of how voiced stops may be pronounced in this area, if not simply depending on each speaker. The murmured quality as noted by Norman may be due to the influence of the recent contact with the Wu dialects.

3. The glottal feature -ʔ in JY and SB in some instances is a residue of tonal classes D (stop endings) and B (hypothetically having arisen from early glottal stop ending, cf. Pulleyblank 1962, Mei 1970).

Table 17.2   Examples of PNM voiced glottalized onsets[4]

	JO	SB	JY	PNM	Tones
Thin	pɔ 42ʔ	bɔ 23ʔ	wɔ 43ʔ	*bʔ-	D
Ramie	ty 42ʔ	du 33	lo 21	*dʔ-	B
Long	toŋ 21ʔ	dɔŋ 31	loŋ 31	*dʔ-	A
Itch	tsioŋ 42ʔ	dziaŋ 33	ioŋ 21	*dzʔ-	B
Paste	ku 21ʔ	gu 31	o 31	*gʔ-	A
Stand	kyɛ 42ʔ	gye 33	ue 21	*gʔ-	B

The glottalized stop onsets are also known in such modern languages as Atsi (Burmic branch of Tibeto-Burman, cf. Burling 1967; Yabu 1982) and Chong (Pearic branch of Mon-Khmer, cf. Huffman 1985). In both cases, the vowels become constricted and are sometimes called tense vowels. For Chong, these tense vowels may end with a glottal catch when occur in an open syllable and usually have a low pitch.

The changes from glottalized/implosive voiced stops to voiced stops or sonorants (nasals or approximants) are evidenced in many languages of South China and Southeast Asia, including Vietnamese and Tai. Table 17.3 shows examples of Proto-Tai (PT) glottalized voiced stops and their reflexes in modern dialects. Wuming, spoken in Guangxi (Li 1956), represents dialects which retain the glottalized feature and Dai La, spoken in Yunnan (Liang and Zhang 1996) represents dialects which has changed the onsets into approximants. Siamese is the standard language of Thailand.[5]

Table 17.3   The reflexes of glottalized voiced onsets in some Tai dialects

	Wuming	Siamese	Dai La	PT	Tones
Village	ʔbaːn	baːn	vaːn	*ʔb-	C
Shoulder	ʔbaː	baː	vaː	*ʔb-	B
Obtain, get	ʔdai	dai	lai	*ʔd-	C
Good	ʔdai	diː	liː	*ʔd-	A
Stretch	ʔjiat	jiat	jit	*ʔj-	D
Resin, gum	ʔjiaŋ	jaːŋ	jaːŋ	*ʔj-	A

Proto-Tai does not have a velar glottalized onset *ʔg-, but the following examples from the related Kam-Sui languages may be supplemental. The first Then dialectal forms are from Li (1968), the second Then's are from Liang and Zhang (1996), and the Mak's are from Li (1943b). These forms go back to early complex onsets which include nasal pre-initials in Kam-Sui (cf.

---

4. Norman (1986a, 377) notes that, in another Jianyang dialect he records, the JY zero initial reflex of *gʔ- is generally realized as /ɣ-/.

5. The notations ʔb-, ʔd- and so on follow the convention in Tai linguistics. In dialects such as Siamese, the modern voiced stop reflexes may be pronounced with certain degree of creakiness or slight implosion. The initial /j-/ is now pronounced as a palatal approximant in most dialects, and /v/ may be variantly realized as approximants [w] or [v].

Ostapirat 2006), but the intermediate changes to voiced glottalized stops and approximants in Then dialects illustrate our case at hand.

Table 17.4   Kam-Sui forms showing corresponding voiced stop and approximant reflexes[6]

	Then (1)	Then (2)	Mak	Tones
moss, alga	ʔdau	lau	dou	A
eye	ʔda:	la:	da:	A
shoulder pole	ʔa:n < ʔg-	ɣa:n	ga:n	A
chin	ʔa:ŋ < ʔg-	ɣaŋ	ga:ŋ	A

PT has plain voiced stop and affricate series in its initial inventory. These initials normally become devoiced in modern dialects and the early tones are split—the typical developments that are also known to have occurred in Chinese, including the NM dialects. See Table 17.5.

Table 17.5   Examples of PT voiced stops

	Wuming	Siamese	Dai La	PT	Tones
Father	po:	phɔ:	po	*b-	B
Field	toŋ	thuŋ	tɔŋ	*d-	C
Mouthful	kam	kham	kam	*g-	A

We may note that the developments of voiced stops (Table 17.5) and glottalized stops (Table 17.3) are significantly different. While the early voiced stops are generally devoiced into aspirated or unaspirated stops, the early glottalized stops may retain the voiced quality and become voiced stops or change manner into sonorants. The glottalized voiced stops may also trigger different tonal reflexes from those of early plain voiced or voiceless stops (cf. Li 1943a). These are all likely to be what have occurred in NM.

Alternatively, it is possible to assume that NM 'softened initial' reflexes have developed from prenasalized or intervocalic stops/affricates, as Norman (1986a) has suggested (cf. the development in Kam-Sui languages shown in Table 17.4 and Note 6).[7] Yet, at PNM level at least,

---

6. For the prenasalized stop reflexes in Kam-Sui dialect, see Maonan /ndau/, /nda:/, /ŋga:n/, /ŋga:ŋ/ for the four respective etyma.

7. The following developments of early prenasalized stops in some Miao-Yao dialects can be further illustrative. The Shimen dialect (Wang and Mao 1995) has kept the prenasalized voiceless and voiced stops intact while the Xiaomiaozhai dialect (Chen 1984) has developed the sounds into glottalized stops, with early voicing distinction evidenced in the tones. (Odd-number tones and even-number tones indicate early voiceless and voiced onsets respectively).

	Shimen	Xiaomiaozhai
Pig	mpa[5]	ʔpai[5]
Long	nti[3]	ʔtei[3]
Dove	ɴqa[1]	ʔkau[1]
Fish	mbə[4]	ʔpi[4]
Ramie	nda[6]	ʔtu[6]
Diligent	ɴɢa[6]	ʔkau[6]

the distinctive laryngeal setting from that of the other existing plain stops/affricates needs to be realized since it has caused different tonal split behavior from that of the others. And because that stricture has left its trace as the constriction accompanying the tones in certain NM dialects, I thus assume PNM 'softened initials' to be constricted/glottalized, which in turn can also naturally develop into voiced stops or sonorants in the other NM varieties. The patterns of tonal split and mergers, which will be discussed in the following sections, may further support this.

3.   NM Tone Split/Merger and the Principle of Adjacent Onset Classes

The distinctive tonal split patterns are actually the main evidence Norman used to set up PM softened initial classes. As Norman (1973, 1986a) has shown, PM voiceless unaspirated and aspirated stop/affricate initials (e.g., *t- and *th-) trigger the same tonal reflexes in NM and so do the voiced unaspirated and aspirated initials (e.g., *d- and *dh-). The tonal split patterns may vary in NM dialects for the glottalized onsets (e.g., between *tʔ- and *dʔ-). Thus, each original tone (A, B, C, and D) may have maximally split into four modern tones conditioned by these onset classes. The four onset classes are as follows:

Class I	voiceless stops/affricates	e.g., *t-, *th-
Class II	glottalized voiceless stops/affricates	e.g., *tʔ-
Class III	glottalized voiced stops/affricates	e.g., *dʔ-
Class IV	voiced stops/affricates	e.g., *d-, *dh-

The preceding onset classes (I, II, III, IV) are not entirely in the same order as those in Norman (1996) and Handel (2003), but they are not arbitrarily rearranged. We observe that, in the NM dialects known to us, the tonal mergers within each tonal category may occur only between Class I and Class II, Class II and Class III, and Class III and Class IV. In other words, the tonal mergers usually occur only between the adjacent onset classes, if we arrange them the way we do. This further leads to a hypothesis that there must be some phonetic reasons behind these phenomena; the adjacent onset classes must have shared some common features between them. As we can see, Class I and Class II share the voiceless feature, Class II and Class III share the glottalized feature, and Class III and Class IV share the voiced feature.

And this can be revealing. The tone systems of the eight NM dialects can be described in a matrix form with respect to these early onset classes and tonal categories (Table 17.6). In addition to being able to show in a glance any modern NM tonal system in historical perspective, the patterns of tonal mergers revealed by the matrix may also have an implication on dialect subgrouping. I will hereafter refer to each Matrix cell by its tonal and onset classes, namely, A.II refers to tone A, onset class II.

We can immediately see from Table 17.6 that ZH and ZQ share a unique tonal merger between C.II and C.III classes. This confirms the closeness between these two dialects. And all the remaining six dialects appear to have merged C.III/C.IV and B.I/B.II. If we take these as shared innovations, these dialects will belong to the same subgroup. This will be somehow contrary to the usual scheme that divides NM into three groups according to their reflexes of our

Table 17.6   Modern tone reflexes in NM dialects

ZH	A	B	C	D	ZQ	A	B	C	D
I	53	12	31	33	I	53	213	31	213
II	31	21ʔ	21ʔ	21ʔ	II	31	21ʔ	21ʔ	21ʔ
III	21ʔ	31	21ʔ	31	III	21ʔ	31	21ʔ	31
IV	33	45	45	45	IV	33	45	45	45
JO	A	B	C	D	SB	A	B	C	D
I	54	21ʔ	22	35	I	53	21	33	214
II	21ʔ	21ʔ	21ʔ	21ʔ	II	31	21	31	21
III	21ʔ	42ʔ	44	42ʔ	III	31	33	45	23ʔ
IV	22	44	44	44	IV	33	53	45	43ʔ
JY	A	B	C	D	CC	A	B	C	D
I	53	21ʔ	21	35	I	52	21	22	24
II	31	21ʔ	31	21ʔ	II	22	21	22	21
III	31	21	43	43ʔ	III	22	22	44	5ʔ
IV	33	21	43	43ʔ	IV	45	22	44	5ʔ
CA	A	B	C	D	WF	A	B	C	D
I	53	31	22	24	I	53	11	22	24
II	53	31	22	31	II	31	11	31	11
III	22	22	55	53ʔ	III	31	22	43	43ʔ
IV	334	55	55	53ʔ	IV	34	43	43	43ʔ

glottalized onsets as voiceless stops (e.g., t-), voiced stops (e.g., d-), or approximants (e.g., l-). Other kinds of evidences are needed, but such tonal merger clues can be a useful one.

I suspect that the NM dialects which show voiceless stop reflexes may not necessarily belong to the same subgroup. The merger of the voiced and voiceless stop initial series in favor of the latter is so typical and widespread that it may occur independently in different varieties. The change from *tʔ- and *dʔ- into *dʔ- which later becomes d- or l- are, however, more unique and may imply the lower subgroup of such dialects as SB and the 'softening dialects' (JY, CC, CA, WF). We may call them the Upper-NM group.

While linguistic subgroups and geographical distribution are different matters, in this case they seem to co-occur to a significant degree. The northward migration of the Upper-NM groups seem to follow the Nanpu river (SB group) and the Chongyang river (the 'softening dialects'). We may thus call the SB group as the Nanpu group and the 'softening dialects' as the Chongyang group. The Shuiji dialect (Li 2001), situated along the Nanpu river course in Jianyang county, is reported to have voiced stop reflexes of the glotalized onset series as in SB.

4.   The Principle of Adjacent Onset Classes beyond NM

As Norman (1973, 1986) has shown, such dialects as Shaowu (SW) and Jiangle (JL), which he calls Far-Western Min (FWM) dialects, have different tonal reflexes of PM plain and aspirated voiced stops (e.g., *d- and *dh-, which both belong to NM onset class IV). To accommodate the tonal split/merger behavior in such dialects, it is thus necessary to separate, at the stage earlier than PNM, these two types of initials into onset classes IV (e.g., *d-) and V (e.g., *dh-). All Min dialects show identical tonal reflexes for voiceless unaspirated (e.g., *t-) and voiceless aspirated initials (e.g., *th-), thus they remain together as onset class I.

Table 17.7 illustrates this with a list of words from ZQ (a NM dialect) and SW in tonal category A. While ZQ (and NM dialects in general) shows the same tonal reflexes for plain (class IV) and aspirated (class V) voiced stops/affricates, SW instead merges together plain (class IV) and glottalized (class III) voiced initials.

Table 17.7   The ZQ and SW reflexes of tone A in five Min onset classes

	ZQ	SW	Onset Classes	
Bee	phoŋ 53	phiuŋ 11	I	*ph-
Share	pueŋ 53	pən 11	I	*p-
Thin (liquid)	tsaiŋ 31	thən 55	II	*tsʔ-
Long	tauŋ 21ʔ	thoŋ 33	III	*dʔ-
Tea	ta 33	tha 33	IV	*d-
Peach	tho 33	thau 51	V	*dh-

The maximal scheme of five onset classes interacting with four tonal categories can be shown in Table 17.8. (Alveolar onsets are used as representatives of the whole stops/affricates series; Vl. = voiceless, Vd. = voiced).[8]

---

8. A similar scheme is conceived in the historical study of Tai tones. See also Brown (1965) and especially Gedney (1970), who has noted similar mechanisms as those outlined here.

Table 17.8 A maximal scheme for tonal developments in Min dialects

Onset Classes		Tone Classes	A	B	C	D
VI.	*th-	I				
	*t-	I				
	*tʔ-	II				
Vd.	*dʔ-	III				
	*d-	IV				
	*dh-	V				

Now, let us look at the tonal split/mergers in SW under this scheme from Table 17.9. We note that early tone B only yields one tonal reflex. There is a merger of C.II and C.III/IV; this feature is shared by Jiangle, another Far-Western Min dialect.[9] Neither of these violates the principle of adjacent onset classes with respect to tonal mergers. What is interesting is that there are instances in tone C and tone D that SW's tonal reflexes of onset class I and class V, at the opposite ends, are identical and seem to violate the rule of adjacent onset classes.[10]

Table 17.9 SW tonal system in historical perspective

Onset Classes		Tone Classes	A	B	C	D
VI.	*th-	I	11	55	24	51
	*t-	I	11	55	24	51
	*tʔ-	II	55	55	35	55
Vd.	*dʔ-	III	33	55	35	35
	*d-	IV	33	55	35	35
	*dh-	V	51	55	24	51

However, onset classes V and I (e.g., *dh- and *th-) can be said to be linked to each other by the shared aspirated feature. And if we put the onset classes into a pie form as shown in Figure 17.1,

---

9. SW reflex of tonal class C.II is noted as identical with C.I by Norman (1986a), but he further remarks that this may be problematic since it is based on only one example ('drunk') whose initial reflex (ts- for *tsʔ-) is also irregular. The assignment of tone /35/ for this C.II slot here, following Norman 1986b, is also based on only one example, i.e., 'mattress', but in this case the initial reflex is regular (th- for *tsʔ-). For example:

	SW	SB	JY	Tones
Mattress	thon	dzuiŋ	luŋ	C
Early	thau	dzɔ	lau	B
Thin (of gruel)	thən	dzaiŋ	loiŋ	A

10. The similar development occurs for words in tone C in Fuzhou, an Eastern-Min dialect.

we can see that onset class V and Class I are indeed adjacent. This makes the principle even more attractive and complete. In this way, not only the rule is still held true, the phonetic connection between each onset class and the overall continuum and overlapping areas between voicing (the top and bottom halves of the pie) and other strictures are neatly revealed.

In Table 17.10, I have put the modern tones in six dialects from different subgroups into the same matrix, and the principle seems to hold well. Data on Chaozhou (CZ), a Southern Min

Figure 17.1   Min's strictures and onset classes

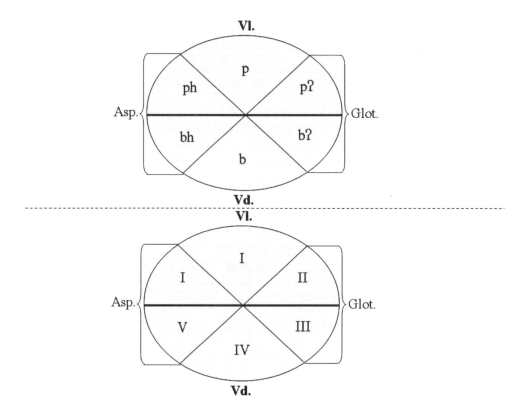

dialect, and Fuzhou (FZ), an Eastern Min dialect, are from Beijing Daxue (1995). The rest of dialects are from Akitani (2008). Fukou (FK) is a Central Min dialect, Taining (TN) is a Far-Western Min dialect, and Dikou (DK) and Xiayang (XY) belong to Northern Min.

It will be interesting to see whether more dialect data would change or support this picture. We do not expect an absolute regularity in all cases since no rule operates without exceptions. Some of the modern tones may have become identical during the course of development beyond the basic principle outlined here. On the other hand, if the picture holds well, and few exceptions are found, the principle may turn out to be useful to our understanding of the complex parameters of tonal split/merger and onset developments in both synchronic and diachronic terms.

Table 17.10   Modern tone reflexes in Min dialects

CZ

CZ	A	B	C	D
I	1	3	5	7
II				
III	2	4	6	8
IV				
V				

FZ

FZ	A	B	C	D
I	1	3	5	7
II				
III	2	6	6	8
IV				
V			5	

FK

FK	A	B	C	D
I	1	3	5	7
II			2	3
III	2	4	5	4
IV				
V				

TN

TN	A	B	C	D
I	1		5	3
II	3			
III	2	3	6	1
IV				
V	5		5	5

DK

DK	A	B	C	D
I	1	3	5	7
II	8	9	9	9
III	9	8	6	8
IV	2	4	7	4
V				

XY

XY	A	B	C	D
I	1	2	5	7
II	9	9	9	9
III				
IV	2	5	6	1
V				

REFERENCES

Akitani, H. 2008. *Minbeiqu San Xianshi Fangyan Yanjiu*. Taipei: Institute of Linguistics, Academia Sinica.

Beijing Daxue. 1995. *Hanyu Fangyan Cihui*. Beijing: Yuwen Chubanshe.

Brown, M. 1965. *From Ancient Thai to Modern Dialects*. Bangkok: The Social Science Association Press of Thailand.

Burling, R. 1967. Proto-Lolo-Burmese. *International Journal of American Linguistics* 33 (2): Part II.

Chen, Qiguang. 1984. Gu Miao-Yao yu biguan seyin shengmu zai xiandai fangyan zhong fanying xingshi de leixing. *Minzu Yuwen* 5:11–22.

Gedney, W. 1970. A spectrum of phonological features in Tai. Paper presented at *the third International Conference on Sino-Tibetan Language and Linguistics*. Cornell University, 9–10 October 1970.

Handel, Z. 2003. Northern Min tone values and the reconstruction of "softened initials". *Language and Linguistics* 4 (1): 47–84.

Huffman, F. 1985. The phonology of Chong. *Southeast Asian Linguistic Studies Presented to Andre-G. Haudricourt*, ed. S. Ratanakul, D. Thomas, and S. Premsrirat, 355–388. Bangkok: Mahidol University.

Li, Fang-kuei. 1943a. The hypothesis of a preglottalized series of consonants in primitive Tai. *Bulletin of the Institute of History and Philology* 11:177–188.

Li, Fang-kuei. 1943b. Notes on the Mak language. *Bulletin of the Institute of History and Philology* 19:1–80.

Li, Fang-kuei. 1956. The Tai dialect of Wuming (texts, translation and glossary). *Bulletin of the Institute of History and Philology monograph series A*(19). Taipei: Institute of History and Philology, Academia Sinica.

Li, Fang-kuei. 1968. Notes on the T'en or Yanghuang language: Glossary. *Bulletin of the Institute of History and Philology* 40 (1): 397–504.

Li, Rulong. 1991. *Minyu Yanjiu*. Beijing: Yuwen Chubanshe.

Li, Rulong. 2001. *Fujian Xianshi Fangyan Shi 12 Zhong*. Fuzhou: Fujian Jiaoyu Chubanshe.

Liang, Min and Junru Zhang. 1996. *Dong-Tai Yuzu Gailun*. Beijing: Zhongguo Shehui Kexue Chubanshe.

Mei, Tsu-lin. 1970. Tones and prosody in Middle Chinese and the origin of the rising tone. *Harvard Journal of Asiatic Studies* 30:86–110.

Norman, J. 1973. Tonal development in Min. *Journal of Chinese Linguistics* 1 (2): 222–238.

Norman, J. 1974. The initials of Proto-Min. *Journal of Chinese Linguistics* 2 (1): 27–36.

Norman, J. 1986a. The origin of the Proto-Min softened stops. Contributions to Sino-Tibetan Studies, *Cornell Linguistic Contributions* 5, eds. J. McCoy, and T. Light, 375–384. Leiden: E. J. Brill.

Norman, J. 1986b. Minbei fanyan de di san tao qing seyin he qing secayin. *Zhongguo Yuwen* 1:38–41.

Norman, J. 1996. Tonal development in the Jennchyan dialect. *Yuen Ren Society Treasury of Chinese Dialect Data* 2:7–41.

Norman, J. 2000. Voiced initials in Shyrbei. In *Memory of Professor Li Fang-kuei: Essays on Linguistic Change and the Chinese Dialects*, eds. A. O. Yue, and Pang-hsin Ting, 271–280. Taipei: Institute of Linguistics (Preparatory Office), Academia Sinica.

Norman, J. 2003. A glossary of the Lianduentsuen dialect. *Yuen Ren Society Treasury of Chinese Dialect Data* 3:339–394.

Ostapirat, W. 2006. Alternation of tonal series and the reconstruction of Proto-Kam-Sui. *Language and Linguistics Monograph Series No. 6* (2): 1077–1121.

Pulleyblank, E. 1962. The consonantal system of Old Chinese. *Asia Major* 9:58–144, 206–265.

Wang Fushi, and Zongwu Mao. 1995. *Miaoyaoyu Guyin Gouni*. Beijing: Zhongguo Shehui Kexue Chubanshe.

Yabu, Shiro. 1982. *A Classified Dictionary of The Atsi or Zaiwa Language (Sadon Dialect)*. Tokyo: Instittute for the Study of Languages and Cultures of Asia and Africa (ILCAA), Tokyo Gaikokugo Daigaku.

18

Different Semantic Nature of Homonym, Metaphor and Polysemy in Mandarin Chinese: Evidence from Behavioral and Functional Magnetic Resonance Imaging Experiments

Fan-pei YANG, Dai-lin WU
National Tsing Hua University, Taiwan

Abstract

The present study aims to study the processing difference of different types of ambiguous Mandarin words during lexical judgment. Forty-six healthy adults (23 males, 23 females, mean age: 22.12, SD = 9.53) enrolled in the behavioral study. Twelve healthy adults (3 males, 9 females, mean age: 21.67, SD = 2.27) participated in the fMRI experiment. In both experiments, subjects were asked to decide whether words in a pair were related, indicating their decision by pressing the right button (related) or the left button (unrelated). Each trial contained the first pair as a probe, the second pair as a target, and a focal point. We had three conditions: consistent, inconsistent, and control. Consistent and inconsistent trials contained the same class of ambiguous words (e.g., metaphors or homonyms) in the second position of both word pairs. Words in pair referred to the same meaning of the ambiguous word. In the inconsistent condition, the second pair referred to a different meaning of the homonym or metaphor. The control condition contained subsequent pairs of words that did not share a common meaning. The behavioral experiment showed a strong priming effect on all types of ambiguous words in both consistent and inconsistent conditions, suggesting that different senses were retrieved early. Among them, homonyms pose the biggest challenge for ambiguity resolution. The fMRI experiment showed an overlap in the medial front gyrus in processing polysemy and metaphor. Polysemy involved additional regions in the parietal and frontal cortices. In sum, the present study suggests that different types of lexical ambiguity do involve different neural networks.

1.   Introduction

Lexical ambiguity is prevalent in daily language use and ambiguity resolution is essential for successful communication. Mandarin words, with long history of grammaticalization and semantic change, are often ambiguous without and sometimes within context. Although this linguistic phenomenon is common and ambiguity resolution happens frequently, little is known about the neural basis for the comprehension of ambiguous words. The purpose of the current research is to investigate the neural underpinnings for Mandarin lexical ambiguity resolution. The most common types of ambiguous words in Mandarin include homonyms, metaphors, and polysemy. Homonyms are words that have the same sound but different meanings. Metaphors are figures of speech that usually use concrete things to represent less tangible things. Polysemy refers to the capacity of a word or words to have multiple meanings. The multiple senses of a polysemous word usually share a central origin and are linked from a semantic network. Previous neuroimaging studies on English word comprehension have established that two general cognitive processes are involved in lexical ambiguity resolution: (i) the activation of various senses of an ambiguous word, and (ii) the selection of a context-relevant meaning (Thompson-Schill et al. 1997). While general activation and selection processes may be involved in lexical comprehension irrespective of semantic nuances, various types of ambiguity may involve distinct sub-processes in understanding words. Given the diverse nature of semantic ambiguity, homonyms, metaphors, and polysemous words might involve different neural activations. Behaviorally, measures of linguistic comprehension such as reaction times and sentence judgment accuracy may also reflect cognitive processing difference. Therefore, it is significant to probe into the subtle neural distinction to provide a better account for ambiguity resolution in the brain.

Grammatical class has also been considered an important organizing principle for linguistic representation, and it may also result in differences in neural processing. Neuropsychological evidence suggests that different grammatical classes are dissociable within the brain, as patients with verb-specific impairments have been reported with lesions in the left ventrolateral PFC (VLPFC), while noun-specific impairments were related with lesions in the lateral temporal cortex (LTC) (Caramazza and Hillis 1991; Damasio and Tranel 1993; Daniele, Giustolisi, Silveri, Colosimo and Gainotti 1994; Silveri and Di Betta 1997). Recent imaging studies have reported verb-specific activation in lVLPFC (Perani et al. 1999; Shapiro et al. 2005; Tyler et al. 2004); however, these results were not supported by other studies (Tyler et al. 2001; Vigliocco and Kita 2006; Vigliocco et al. 2006). We hypothesize that grammatical class may affect processing semantic ambiguity with different classes involving different sub-regions within the semantic memory network.

The present study uses semantic priming paradigm to investigate the behavioral and neural processing differences among different types of lexical ambiguity. Semantic priming has been used as a paradigm in fMRI studies to investigate semantic control in selecting an appropriate meaning from among several competing representations. The standard paradigm involves making a semantic relatedness decision between sequentially presented related or unrelated word pairs. This paradigm is based on the assumption that presence of a related prime may give rise to automatic spreading of activation of features from node to node (J. R. Anderson 1976, 1983a, 1983b), or pre- or direct activation of semantic features in a semantic network (McRae and Ross 2004; Randall et al. 2004; Cree, McRae, and McNorgan 1999; Becker et al. 1997; Bullinaria 1995; Masson 1995; Plaut 1995; Moss et al. 1994; Sharkey and Sharkey 1992; Masson, Besner, and Humphreys 1991). Thus, presence of a related prime (e.g., money bank followed by vault bank) should reduce the level of semantic competition and require lower selection demand, whereas the presence of a related prime with an alternative meaning (e.g., money bank followed by river bank) should trigger a higher level of semantic competition. With this paradigm, we can control the level of selection effort and also manipulate different types of ambiguity that may involve distinct mechanisms of semantic ambiguity resolution.

In this paper, we conduct a behavioral experiment and an fMRI experiment. In the behavioral study, participants will be asked to judge whether words in each word pair were related. Each trial contained the first pair as a probe and the second pair as a target. We have three general conditions: consistent, inconsistent, and control. Consistent and inconsistent trials contain the same class of ambiguous words (e.g., metaphors, polysemous words or homonyms) in the second position of both word pairs. Words in all trials were either nouns or words. In the consistent condition, the first and the second word pair refer to the same meaning of the ambiguous word. In the inconsistent condition, the second pair refers to a different meaning of the homonym, polysemy or metaphor. The control condition contains subsequent pairs of words that did not share a common meaning. We predict that the reaction time of inconsistent pairs will be longer than consistent pairs as the semantic selection demand is higher in resolving inconsistent meanings of a word regardless of relatedness of the meanings. In addition, the priming effect will also be shown in the significantly reduced reaction time in the second word pair relative to the first word pair. In the fMRI experiment, we use the same paradigm but we only include polysemous words and metaphors because the number of homonyms was too small. We anticipate similar behavioral results when participants perform the semantic judgment task in the scanner. We predict that polysemy and metaphor will activate different cortical regions and grammatical class will also modulate the activations.

2.   Experiment 1: Processing Differences in Mandarin Homonyms, Polysemy and Metaphors

2.1   Method

2.1.1 Participants

Forty-six healthy native Mandarin Chinese speakers (23 males, 23 females) participated in the study. Mean age was 22.12 (range: 19–35) years old. They had no history of neurodegenerative diseases, dyslexia, psychiatric disorders or vision problems.

2.1.2 Stimuli

Table 18.1 shows some of the stimuli used in this behavioral experiment. We included three types of semantic ambiguity in our design: homonyms, metaphors and polysemy. Each ambiguous word was presented in both consistent and inconsistent context. Five hundred pairs were presented totally, including 29 consistent homonym noun-noun pairs (condition 1), 29 inconsistent homonym noun-noun pairs (condition 2), 7 consistent homonym noun-verb pairs (condition 3), 7inconsistent homonym noun-verb pairs (condition 4), 37 consistent metaphor noun-noun pairs (condition 5), 37 inconsistent metaphor noun-noun pairs (condition 6), 57 consistent metaphor noun-verb pairs (condition 7), 57 inconsistent metaphor noun-verb pairs (condition 8), 36 consistent polysemy noun-noun pairs (condition 9), 36 inconsistent polysemy noun-noun pairs (condition 10), 23 consistent polysemy noun-verb pairs (condition 11), 23 inconsistent polysemy noun-verb pairs (condition 12), and 122 fillers. Consistent and inconsistent trials contained the same ambiguous words (target word) in the second position of both word pairs. The target words were homonyms, metaphors or polysemy words, and it could be a noun or a verb. The first position in each word pair was always a noun and was an unambiguous word. In each experimental trail, subjects would see two pairs of word. It could be a condition of consistent word pair or in consistent word pair. The first and the second word pair referred to the same meaning of the target word in the consistent condition. For instance, the same literal meaning was referenced in both "鳥類—杜鵑" and "羽毛—杜鵑" pairs (consistent homonym noun-noun condition). It indicated the name of one kind of birds. In contrast, the second pair could refer to a homonym, metaphor or polysemy word though the first pair always had a literal meaning in the inconsistent condition. For example, for the type of homonym ambiguity the first pair "鳥籠—杜鵑"referred to the meaning of one kind of birds whereas the second pair "花朵—杜鵑"was the meaning of one kind of flowers (inconsistent homonym noun-noun condition). The first pair and the second pair made reference to unrelated senses of "杜鵑". The control condition contained subsequent pairs of words that do not share a common meaning. This condition did not have any priming effect from the first pair on the second pair and did not require any selection demand during judgment task. It was important to control the semantic aspects of the words, including the degree of relatedness between words in a pair, the word frequency, the word length and the imageability.

The stimuli of the second section and the questionnaire contained only the target ambiguous words used in the first section of the experiment. In the second section, a total of 189 target words were presented by E-prime to collect the rating of familiarity and imageability of each word.

2.1.3 Procedure

Subjects had to press buttons throughout the computerized experiment presented by the E-prime software on a laptop. There were two test sections the software. In the first section, subjects were asked to decide whether pairs of words displayed on the screen were related in meaning or not. Pairs of words were presented sequentially, one after another.

In the second main section, the subjects were asked to rate the familiarity and imageability of each word is. There were many words in this section. Every word was used to ask subjects

Table 18.1   Behavioral experiment on semantic ambiguity using homonyms, metaphors and polysemy in Mandarin Chinese

	Consistent		Inconsistent	
	Stimuli 1	Stimuli 2	Stimuli 3	Stimuli 4
Homonym Noun—Noun	Condition 1		Condition 2	
	機器　機組	機械　機組	老頭　傢伙	工具　傢伙
	鳥類　杜鵑	羽毛　杜鵑	籠子　杜鵑	花粉　杜鵑
Homonym Noun—Verb	Condition 3		Condition 4	
	目標　鎖定	中心　鎖定	敵機　鎖定	密碼　鎖定
	水庫　放水	浴缸　放水	泳池　放水	作弊　放水
Metaphor Noun—Noun	Condition 5		Condition 6	
	球體　中心	箭靶　中心	花木　園地	小説　園地
	性命　生命	人命　生命	方位　方向	目標　方向
Metaphor Noun—Verb	Condition 7		Condition 8	
	機器　操作	電腦　操作	機器　發動	戰爭　發動
	燈泡　發光	魚類　發光	失眠　頭痛	煩惱　頭痛
Polysemy Noun—Noun	Condition 9		Condition 10	
	玩偶　娃娃	泥土　娃娃	晚輩　小弟	餐廳　小弟
	演講　形式	作文　形式	鼓樂　音節	語音　音節
Polysemy Noun—Verb	Condition 11		Condition 12	
	數學　計算	數目　計算	閒人　進出	款項　進出
	演説　講話	話語　講話	器材　保養	臉蛋　保養
Condition 13 Unrelated	規章　電話	女性　索引	規章　電話	女性　索引

twice in two different questions. First, subjects had to decide whether the words shown by the laptop was familiar to them by scoring from one to seven by pressing the keyboard on the laptop. If they knew the word well, they could give the word a higher score. If they felt the word was unfamiliar, they could give the word a lower score. Second, subjects would decide whether the word was abstract or not. Similarly, if the meaning of the word shown by the laptop was specific, subjects could give a higher score from one to seven. If the meaning of the word was abstract to the subjects, they could give a lower score from one to seven. Each question was presented in black letters against a white background for unlimited time. Subjects had to respond to each question as soon as possible. Their responses were recorded by the E-Prime software.

After the computerized experiment, each participant had to fill in a questionnaire that contained the ambiguous words used in the computerized tests. The questionnaire consisted of 189 three-choice questions. Every question lists two different meanings of an ambiguous word. Subjects were asked to choose which meaning was more common or choose the "equally often" option. Words were randomized in the questionnaire. The purpose of using this questionnaire was to determine whether the ambiguous words used in the experiment were balanced or polar items based on subjects' feedback. A balanced ambiguous word has two senses that are both frequently used, whereas a polar word tends to be used for one sense in preference to the other.

2.1.4 Results

Table 18.2 Reaction Time (RT) and Percent Accuracy (PA) of All Conditions

	PA Stimulus1	PA Stimulus2	RT Stimulus1	RT Stimulus2	RT T-Test (p-value)
Condition1 (Consistent Homonym N- N)	0.913081	0.887675	1527.843	970.2773	<0.001***
Condition2 (Inconsistent Homonym N- N)	0.905473	0.783069	1539.622	1086.179	<0.001***
Condition3 (Consistent Homonym N- V)	0.948413	0.937642	1563.499	978.8953	<0.001***
Condition4 (Inconsistent Homonym N- V)	0.896186	0.700866	1421.742	942.8237	<0.001***
Condition5 (Consistent Metaphor N- N)	0.865007	0.844853	1530.299	962.8773	<0.001***
Condition6 (Inconsistent Metaphor N- N)	0.904922	0.75831	1584.77	975.3441	<0.001***
Condition7 (Consistent Metaphor N- V)	0.896515	0.90302	1492.063	937.2888	<0.001***
Condition8 (Inconsistent Metaphor N- V)	0.852968	0.854883	1455.295	946.9928	<0.001***
Condition9 (Consistent Polysemy N- N)	0.911294	0.904314	1582.07	1027.568	<0.001***
Condition10 (Inconsistent Polysemy N- N)	0.881072	0.86381	1521.281	1070.877	<0.001***
Condition11 (Consistent Polysemy N- V)	0.925584	0.930269	1508.626	939.2441	<0.001***
Condition12 (Inconsistent Polysemy N- V)	0.875396	0.826652	1475.637	1010.653	<0.001***

Table 18.2 shows the Percent Accuracy (PA) and Reaction Time (RT) for all conditions that contain ambiguous words. The filler condition did not have any significant difference in RT and therefore its RT and PA were omitted in the table. All of the second word pair items (stimuli2) that followed a related first word pair (stimulus1) displayed decreased RTs. Note that the RT was significantly reduced even when stimulus1 and stimulus2 referred to two different senses of an ambiguous word. Such decrease in RT was observed in all homonym, metaphor and polysemy conditions. The significant RT difference indicated priming effects. The PA of the inconsistent pairs was always lower than the consistent pairs. Moreover, RTs of the inconsistent stimulus2 were always longer than the consistent conditions. The t-test comparison of PA of stimulus1 and stimulus2 for all conditions did not reach any statistical significance.

We also compared the inconsistent with the consistent condition of the same ambiguity type and grammatical class. Typically the inconsistent conditions required higher demand in semantic selection than consistent conditions after retrieval of the senses associated with a given word. Comparison of inconsistent and consistent conditions for all ambiguous types allows us to determine which type of lexical ambiguity poses the biggest challenge to readers in the face of high selection demand.

Table 18.3 Comparison of RTs for different types of lexical ambiguity

Condition name	P-value Stimulus1 RT	P-value Stimulus2 RT
Homonym (N-N) Incon vs. con	0.71	<0.001**
Homonym (N-V) Incon vs.con	0.06	0.29
Metaphor (N-N) Incon vs.con	0.37	0.68
Metaphor (N-V) Incon vs. con	0.14	0.34
Polysemy (N-N) Incon vs. con	0.03*	0.20
Polysemy (N-V) Incon vs. con	0.42	0.15

*:p-value <0.05, **: p-value<0.001

Table 18.3 shows that disambiguity of homonyms poses greater processing difficulty than metaphors and polysemous words. Specifically, when a meaning of a homonym suggested by the second word pair is different from the first word pair, the RT difference was very significant at the p value of 0.001. The significant difference in RT for inconsistent and consistent polysemy conditions was only observed in stimulus1. But for the stimulus2 of both conditions did no show any significant difference. This may only suggest that certain polysemous words were inherently more difficult to process than other polysemous words even without the conflicting contextual information.

2.1.5 Imageability and familiarity effects

We calculated the imageability and familiarity rating for all ambiguous words during the second section the behavioral experiment to ensure that these two factors do not interfere with ambiguity resolution of the words.

Table 18.4 Imageability and familiarity of ambiguous words

Condition name	Familiarity mean	Familiarity SD	Imageability mean	Imageability SD
Homonym (N-N)	5.947823	0.576502	4.899275	0.934185
Homonym (N-V)	5.966164	0.269855	4.86207	0.89097
Metaphor (N-N)	5.811168	0.481311	4.768603	1.016554
Metaphor (N-V)	5.678209	0.521383	4.740927	0.846614
Polysemy (N-N)	5.97734	0.34472	4.707805	0.916842
Polysemy (N-V)	5.967703	0.444554	4.753177	0.694407

Table 18.4 shows the average ratings of familiarity and imageability of all ambiguous words on a seven-point scale. We examined the ambiguous words in separate grammatical classes. The words fall into one of the categories: a homonymous noun, homonymous verb, metaphoric noun, metaphoric verb, polysemous noun, or polysemous verb. Intuitively, people may conclude that homonyms and polysemous words are more concrete than the metaphors. However, our results indicate that homonyms and polyemy do not receive significantly higher ratings for imageability than metaphors. Furthermore, there was no big difference between nouns and verbs in familiarity and imageability rating for all types of ambiguous words.

The analysis of the questionnaires distributed after the computerized test indicated that all ambiguous words used in the experiment were balanced items. The preference of one sense to another for each word was equal averaged across all subjects. All too often subjects choose the option "equally often" for the words listed in the questionnaire.

2.2   Discussion

Significant difference of RT in Stimulus1 and Stimulus2 for both consistent and inconsistent conditions indicated that semantic priming occurs no matter when contextual clue biases toward a first-selected or different meaning. This suggests that all senses associated with a lexicon were probably retrieved when subjects saw a target word. This finding is significant for investigation of a psycholinguistic model for lexical retrieval. Moreover, homonym, when presented in inconsistent conditions, appeared to be the most difficult for Mandarins to process in comparison with metaphor and polysemy. Lastly, subjects perceived metaphor, homonym and polysemy to be similarly imageable. The familiarity ratings for all three types of ambiguous words were similar. Therefore, imageability and familiarity did not interfere with semantic retrieval and selection in the present study.

3. Experiment 2: Neural Correlates of Polysemy and Metaphor

3.1 Method

3.1.1 Participants

Twelve healthy adults (3 males, 9 females, mean age: 21.67, SD=2.27) participated in the fMRI experiment. They had no history of neurodegenerative diseases, dyslexia, psychiatric disorders or vision problems.

3.1.2 Stimuli

We included two types of lexical ambiguity in our design: metaphor and polysemy. A total of 150 pairs were presented (30 consistent metaphor, 30 inconsistent metaphor, 30 consistent polysemy, 30 inconsistent polysemy, and 30 controls). Consistent and inconsistent trials contained the same ambiguous words in the 2nd position of both word pairs. For half of the critical trials, the repeating word had literal and metaphorical meanings (e.g., 愛情—結晶, 鹽水—結晶), and for the other half the repeating word would be a polysemous word (e.g., 金屬—反射, 膝蓋—反射). The first word in the ambiguous pair was always an unambiguous word and it was always a noun. The ambiguous word could be either a verb or a noun. In the consistent condition, the first and the second word pair referred to the same meaning of the ambiguous word. For example, the same literal meaning was referenced in both "明礬—結晶" and "釉彩—結晶" pairs. In contrast, in the inconsistent condition, the second pair could refer to a polysemy or a metaphor though the first pair always had a literal meaning. For instance, for the metaphor-type ambiguity the first pair "鹽水—結晶" refers to the literal meaning of "crystal" whereas the second pair "愛情—結晶" used the metaphorical meaning. For the polysemy-type ambiguity, the first pair "金屬—反射" and the second pair "膝蓋—反射" made reference to unrelated senses of "反射". The control condition would contain subsequent pairs of words that did not share a common meaning. For example, "宗教—太太" was followed by "果園—觀眾". This condition was intended to prevent any priming effect from the first pair on the second pair. We controlled the semantic aspects of the words, including the degree of relatedness between words in a pair, the mean frequency, the concreteness, the word length and the imageability. In our behavioral experiment, we had collected the ratings for these aspects before we implemented the experiment in the scanner. Examples of words are shown in Table 18.5.

Table 18.5 Semantic aspects of conditions used for the fMRI Experiment

Metaphor Trial type	Condition Name	Pair 1	Pair 2	Demand for semantic selection
Consistent (N-V)	Con_Met_NV	貨品　輸出	肉類　輸出	Low
Inconsistent (N-V)	Inc_Met_ NV	水果　輸出	知識　輸出	High
Consistent (N-N)	Con_Met_NN	明礬　結晶	釉彩　結晶	Low
Inconsistent (N-N)	Inc_Met_NN	鹽水　結晶	愛情　結晶	High
Polysemy Trial type	Condition Name	Pair 1	Pair 2	Demand for semantic selection
Consistent (N-V)	Con_Poly_ NV	藥效　發作	酒力　發作	Low
Inconsistent (N-V)	Inc_Poly_ NV	金屬　反射	膝蓋　反射	High
Consistent (N-N)	Con_Poly_NN	軍隊　前鋒	部隊　前鋒	Low
Inconsistent (N-N)	Inc_Poly_NN	姑娘　小姐	千金　小姐	High
Filler	Condition Name	Pair 1	Pair 2	Demand for semantic selection
Unrelated_Unrelated (N-N)	Unrelated_Unrelated_ NN	宗教　太太	果園　觀眾	N/A
Unrelated_Unrelated (N-V)	Unrelated_Unrelated_ NV	圓環　稱作	琵琶　跨入	N/A

3.1.3 Procedure

Pairs of words were presented sequentially within the scanner, one after another. A trial contained stimulus1 and stimulus2. Subjects were asked to read each pair of words and determine whether the two words were related in meaning, indicating their decision by pressing the keyboard on the laptop corresponding to "Yes" or "No" responses with their right and left thumbs respectively. Subjects were told that related words could be associated in meaning literally (such as "骯髒" and "蒼蠅") or abstractly (such as "黏人" and "蒼蠅"). Each pair was presented in silver-white letters against a black background for 3 seconds. Subjects had respond to each pair within 3 s. Subjects had to respond to each pair within three seconds or the experiment would move on to the next pair and the response was recorded as an error. Subjects' responses and reaction times (RTs) were recorded by the E-prime software. During the inter-trial intervals (ITIs), a fixation cross were displayed on the screen. The experimental procedure is illustrated in Figure 18.1.

Figure 18.1   Experimental procedure

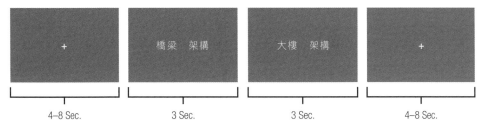

4–8 Sec.	3 Sec.	3 Sec.	4–8 Sec.

3.1.4 *Image acquisition and analysis*

Imaging was performed on a 3T Brucker Scanner. Images were acquired using a custom-built 3-axis balanced-torque 8 channel head gradient coil with end capped birdcage RF coils. The subjects were positioned supine on the gantry of the scanner with the head in a midline location in the coil. Functional images were acquired with an echo-planar image sequence sensitive to BOLD-contrast (TE=30ms, TR=2 s, flip angle=90°). The volume covered the whole brain with a 64 x 64 matrix and 36 transverse slices (4 mm thickness with a 0 mm inter-slice gap); (voxel size 3.44 x 3.44 x 4 mm). 3D T1-weighted scans were acquired for anatomical localization. Raw image data were reconstructed with distortion correction to reduce artifact due to magnetic field inhomogeneity. Data were motion corrected with two iterations of a six-parameter, rigid body realignment technique and the time series of each voxel were normalized by the mean signal value to attenuate between-run scaling differences. Voxel-wise analysis was performed using a general linear model for auto-correlated observations. Included within the model was an empirical estimate of intrinsic temporal autocorrelation, global signal change covariates, and sine and cosine regressors for frequencies below that of the task. Hemodynamic response functions (HRFs) were used to model BOLD responses to trial events using multiple regression. Results from single-subject analyses were entered into second-level t-tests with subjects as a random variable. For these analyses, images of parameter estimates for each contrast of interest (i.e., linear combinations of beta values from the regression analyses) were spatially normalized to the template from the SPM8 package, resliced into 2mm isotropic voxels, and spatially smoothed with an 8mm Gaussian filter using the SPM8 package. These normalized, smoothed subject-specific contrast images are then entered into a second level group analysis—a one-sample t-test—in which the mean value across the group for each voxel were tested against zero. In all analyses, a critical t-value was calculated for each map based on the number of effective degrees of freedom, smoothness, search volume, desired minimum cluster volume, and desired alpha value (α =.05, corrected for multiple comparisons).

3.2   Behavioral results (percent accuracy and reaction time)

We compared the PA and RT of the stimulus2 of inconsistent and consistent conditions to investigate whether inconsistent context would cause more processing difficulty than consistent context. A significantly worse PA or longer RT would reflect more difficulty in selecting a contextually appropriate meaning in reading stimulus2. The PA of inconsistent metaphor NV condition was significantly worse than the consistent metaphor NV condition ($p = 0.004$). The PA of inconsistent polysemy conditions were significantly worse than the consistent polysemy conditions regardless of the grammatical class of the polysemous word ($p = 0.03$ for NN, $p = 0.17$ for NV). Comparison of RTs for inconsistent and consistent conditions revealed no statistical significance.

Table 18.6 Comparison of RTs for inconsistent and consistent conditions

	PA stimulus2	PA SD stimulus2	PA p-value	RT stimulus2	RT SD stimulus2
Condition1 (Consistent Metaphor N- N)	0.783333	0.087004	Consistent vs. Inconsistent Met NN	1092.021	296.0105
Condition2 (Inconsistent Metaphor N- N)	0.754861	0.091379	0.243	1165.06	226.9725
Condition3 (Consistent Metaphor N- V)	0.889646	0.109943	Consistent vs. Inconsistent Met NV	1038.05	296.2031
Condition4 (Inconsistent Metaphor N- V)	0.803704	0.108694	0.004*	1059.325	211.255
Condition5 (Consistent Polysemy N- N)	0.903535	0.132192	Consistent vs. Inconsistent Poly NN	1062.84	235.6587
Condition6 (Inconsistent Polysemy N- N)	0.855556	0.124947	0.03*	1133.552	321.4943
Condition7 (Consistent Polysemy N- V)	0.905556	0.057662	Consistent vs. Inconsistent Poly NV	1028.921	275.1186
Condition8 (Inconsistent Polysemy N- V)	0.809402	0.08663	0.017*	1096.058	230.7385

*:p-value <0.05

3.3   Imaging results

3.3.1 Inconsistent polysemy vs. consistent polysemy (noun-noun +noun-verb)

When consistent polysemy conditions were subtracted from inconsistent polysemy conditions, activations were observed in the superior and medial frontal gyri at p = 0.001, uncorrected.

3.3.2 Inconsistent polysemy vs. consistent polysemy (noun-verb)

When the polyemous words were verbs, the inconsistent condition in contrast to consistent condition revealed activations in the supplementary motor area, the medial frontal gyrus and the superior parietal gyrus.

Figure 18.2a   Inconsistent polysemy vs. consistent polysemy (noun-noun +noun-verb)

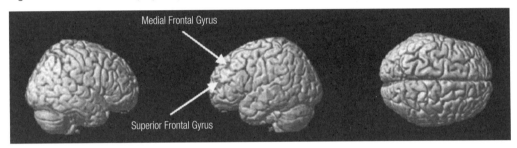

Figure 18.2b   Inconsistent polysemy vs. consistent polysemy (noun-verb)

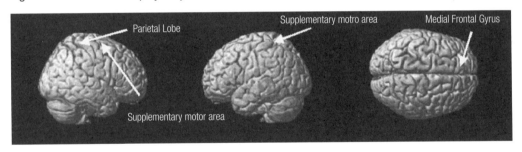

Figure 18.2c.   Inconsistent metaphor vs. consistent metaphor (noun-verb)

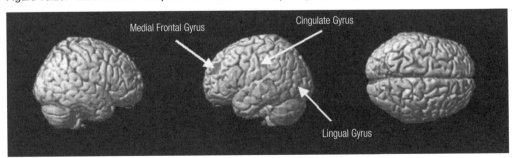

3.3.3 Inconsistent metaphor vs. consistent metaphor (noun-verb)

When the ambiguous metaphoric words were verbs, inconsistent versus consistent conditions showed that activated regions included the medial frontal gyrus, anterior cingulate and the lingual gyrus.

3.4   Discussion

The consistent conditions minus inconsistent conditions for all types of ambiguous words had no voxels survived. Activations were only observed in the inconsistent versus consistent conditions. This suggests that more cognitive resources are required for processing a meaning that is inconsistent with an immediately primed meaning. Resolving ambiguity in polysemy involved activations mostly concentrated in the frontal cortices whereas understanding ambiguity in metaphor recruited additional parietal cortex and anterior cingulate gyrus. The frontal activation is typically associated with semantic selection and increased working memory load. It is possible that understanding a metaphoric word involves other cognitive processes in addition to the general lexical selection process. The parietal involvement may be related with a problem solving process. The anterior cingulate gyrus is part of an error-monitoring system. The involvement of the visual cortex probably suggested a mental visualization process (Yang, Edens, Simpson & Krawczyk 2009). Besides, our results showed that grammatical class indeed affected the ambiguity resolution process in the brain. For metaphors, the inconsistent and consistent N-N conditions did not show significant difference, but the N-V pairs did. This suggested that selecting a context-appropriate meaning of an ambiguous metaphoric verb is more challenging than an ambiguous metaphoric noun.

4.   Conclusion

In this paper, we conducted a behavioral experiment and an fMRI experiment. In the behavioral study, participants were asked to judge whether words in each word pair were related. Each trial contained the first pair as a probe and the second pair as a target. The results of the behavioral experiment presented in the current research suggested two important facts about online processing of Mandarin polysemy, homonym and metaphor. First, multiple senses of an ambiguous word were retrieved when it was first presented to a participant irrespective of the consistency of the ensuing context. This explains why both inconsistent and consistent conditions for all types of ambiguity showed significant priming effect using the subsequent presentation design. Second, homonymous nouns in inconsistent subsequent pairs were harder to process than the other two types of ambiguous words. The imgeability rating of the ambiguous words showed that metaphors were not more imageable than polysemy and homonym. It was probably because in Mandarin Chinese metaphors are so engrained and their original abstract property is not processed during comprehension. The results of the fMRI experiment showed that metaphoric comprehension involved additional activations in the parietal and occipital cortices and the anterior cingulate gyrus. This suggested that understanding ambiguous metaphoric words depended on contribution of the systems of problem-solving, visualization and error-monitoring in addition to the general selection process subserved by the frontal cortices.

REFERENCES

Anderson, J. R. 1976. *Language, Memory, and Thought.* Hillsdale, N.J., New York: L. Erlbaum Associates; distributed by the Halsted Press Division of Wiley.

Anderson, J. R. 1983a. Retrieval of information from long-term memory. *Science* 220:25–30.

Anderson, J. R. 1983b. A spreading activation theory of memory. *Journal of Verbal Learning and Verbal Behavior* 22:261–295.

Caramazza, A., and A. E. Hillis. 1991. Lexical organization of nouns and verbs in the brain. *Nature* 349:788–790.

Damasio, A. R., and D. Tranel. 1993. Nouns and verbs are retrieved with differently distributed neural systems. *Proc Natl Acad Sci USA* 90:4957–4960.

Daniele, A., L. Giustolisi, M. C. Silveri, C. Colosimo, and G. Gainotti. 1994. Evidence for a possible neuroanatomical basis for lexical processing of nouns and verbs. *Neuropsychologia* 32:1325–1341.

Perani, D., S. F. Cappa, T. Schnur, M. Tettamanti, S. Collina, M. M. Rosa, and F. Fazio. 1999. The neural correlates of verb and noun processing. A PET study. *Brain* 122 (Pt 12): 2337–2344.

Shapiro, K. A., F. M. Mottaghy, N. O. Schiller, T. D. Poeppel, M. O. Fluss, H. W. Muller, A. Caramazza, and B. J. Krause. 2005. Dissociating neural correlates for nouns and verbs. *Neuroimage* 24:1058–1067.

Silveri, M. C., and A. M. Di Betta. 1997. Noun-verb dissociations in brain-damaged patients: Further evidence. *Neurocase* 3:477–488.

Thompson-Schill, S. L., M. D'Esposito, G. K. Aguirre, and M. J. Farah. 1997. Role of left inferior prefrontal cortex in retrieval of semantic knowledge: A reevaluation. *Proc Natl Acad Sci USA* 94:14792–14797.

Tyler, L. K., P. Bright, P. Fletcher, and E. A. Stamatakis. 2004. Neural processing of nouns and verbs: The role of inflectional morphology. *Neuropsychologia* 42:512–523.

Tyler, L. K., R. Russell, J. Fadili, and H. E. Moss. 2001. The neural representation of nouns and verbs: PET studies. *Brain* 124:1619–1634.

Vigliocco, G., and S. Kita. 2006. Language-specific properties of the lexicon: Implications for learning and processing. *Language and Cognitive Processes* 21:790–816.

Vigliocco, G., J. Warren, S. Siri, J. Arciuli, S. Scott, and R. Wise. 2006. The role of semantics and grammatical class in the neural representation of words. *Cereb Cortex* 16:1790–1796.

Yang, F. G., J. Edens, C. Simpson, and D. C. Krawczyk. 2009. Differences in task demands influence the hemispheric lateralization and neural correlates of metaphor. *Brain Lang* 111:114–124.

19

A Few Morphological Functions of the Suffix *-s in Shang Chinese#

Ken-ichi TAKASHIMA 高嶋謙一
University of British Columbia

Abstract

This paper discusses some morphological problems in Shang Chinese, the language preceding Early Zhou Chinese. Specifically it aims to show how a few types of noun phrases can be identified which, if correct, will have some clear and substantive morphological implications. Since no such grammatical markers as *zhě* 者, *zhī* 之, and the like are used in Shang Chinese, the types of the noun phrase discussed in this paper could have been either marked or unmarked. After probing into this question, the paper has arrived at a conclusion that they were marked with the suffix *-s* reconstructed for the predecessor of *qùshēng* 去聲 in Middle Chinese and that they are couched in certain syntactic environments. This is analyzed in detail.

\# I would like to thank Professors Mei Guang 梅廣, Yu Suisheng 喻遂生, and Zhu Yongping 朱永平 for their good comments on the paper.

1. Introduction

This paper aims to show how a few types of nominal derivations and noun-phrase formations can be identified while paying particular attention to their meanings. It is hoped that some substantive morphological implications for Shāng Chinese preceding the early stage of Zhōu Chinese[1] will, in the process, become clear.

For the purpose of this paper, I have primarily chosen two OBI (see n. 1) graphs: 𝑘 and 𝑘. The former is a drawing of a kneeling figure under the stylized mouth facing down, and the latter is a drawing of "boat" 舟 as phonetic with two hands one on top and another one at bottom.[2] These graphs are the predecessors of 令/命 *lìng/mìng* 'order, command; law'/'order, cause; decree; life' and 受/授 *shòu* 'receive'/'give', respectively. They correspond to four words in later sources. In such phonological and lexicographical compilations as *Qièyùn* 切韻 and *Guǎngyùn* 廣韻,[3] the first member of the former "doublet" (i.e., 令) has both *píngshēng* 平聲 (in the sense of "cause"; see also n. 8) and *qùshēng* 去聲 (in the sense of "good; order; decree") and the latter member (命) *qùshēng* 去聲 (in the sense of "cause; instruct; mandate; announce; decree; life"), though there are indications that it was also read in *píngshēng* (see infra). As for the 受/授 doublet, the first member (受) is in *shǎngshēng* 上聲 (in the sense of 'receive') and the second member (授) in *qùshēng* 去聲 (in the sense of "give"). For ease of reference, the above-mentioned information is recapitulated as follows:

---

1. In order to arrive at a cogent periodization of pre-Qín Chinese, we can heuristically consider some salient features of the language of oracle-bone inscriptions (abbreviated hereinafter as "OBI", a.k.a. *jiǎgúwén* 甲骨文) and bronze inscriptions (abbreviated as "BRI", a.k.a. *jīnwén* 金文 datable to Period-V OBI). This is Shāng Chinese (ca. 13th c.–11th c. B.C.), the earliest stage, followed by BRI of early Western Zhōu (ca. 11th c.–8th c. B.C.), mid Zhōu (ca. 8th c.–5th c. B.C.) and late Zhōu (ca. 5th c.–3rd c. B.C.). The so-called "Standard Classical Chinese", abbreviated henceforth as "SCC", corresponds roughly to late Zhōu Chinese. "Early Classical Chinese" is abbreviated as "ECC". Given above is a mechanical periodization based on political changes, and whether or not it coincides with of linguistic changes has not yet been worked out.

2. The mouth is normally written like ⊔ which, when turned round, is ⊓. This form is frequently "stylized" to yield ∧ (another example: 吕, 仚 = 合). Underneath ∧ there is a human figure in the kneeling position like 𝑘. I would construe the graphic design of the whole configuration to have been: "person under command (or submission)". As for 𝑘, the phonophoric element 𝑘 (舟) is placed between one hand (𝑘) and another hand (𝑘). I interpret the graphic design of this configuration as "the boat as object is transferred from one hand to another", but since the "boat" is to indicate the pronunciation of the graph 𝑘 (受 or 授), any object is susceptible to the object of receiving or giving. The "boat" graph is nothing but phonophoric.

3. Qièyùn is the *Táng xiěběn* Wáng Rénxù *kānmiù bǔquē qièyùn* 唐寫本王仁昫刊謬補缺切韻 (see Lóng Yǔchún 1968 in Bibliography). The "boat" graph is nothing but phonophoric. This, along with *Guǎngyùn* and others, is conveniently presented in Liú Fù 劉復 *et al.* (1963). It is commonly assumed that the "tones" in Middle Chinese (MC 中古音), excluding *píngshēng* 平聲, can be traced back to some segmental features in Old Chinese (OC 上古音). Such an assumption is similar in nature to the generally practiced projection of SCC lexical and grammatical properties to earlier stages of the language unless we can show that they had undergone changes. OC is used to refer to the phonological reconstructions of late Shāng to late Zhōu Chinese in terms of the mechanical periodization given in n. 1. MC is used to refer to the phonological reconstructions of Chinese of ca. 7th–8th c.

令 {
平聲 "cause"
去聲 "good; order; decree"
}

命 {
平聲? "?"
去聲 "cause; instruct; mandate; announce; decree; life"
}

受　上聲 "to receive"
授　去聲 "to give"

Traditional readings are of course unavailable for the two OBI graphs, but it is possible to infer the existence of some morphological features for the four words represented by the two graphs (a few variants not counted). Schuessler (1985, 347ff.) points out, however, that there are cases to which such a possibility simply does not apply. He cites, for example, the nominal use of *rén* 人 'man' and the verbal use of *rén* 仁 'act like a human being, be humane, kind'. They are cognate, but it is the job of syntax to determine the word class. The former is put in a noun and the latter in a verb "slot", he says, in a SCC sentence. Cikoski (1976, unpublished ms. cited by Schuessler) interpreted this as a derivation of the "abstract" verb 仁 from the "concrete" noun 人. I would agree with them in taking 仁 developed from the noun man, acquiring the class of an independent verb meaning "to be humane, kind" in SCC. This example points to the possibility of a noun used as a verb and vice versa without any morphological change since both 人 and 仁 are *píngshēng* 平聲 words. In this paper, this sort of syntactically dependent lexical differences are excluded from consideration. We will instead focus on the nominal derivations and noun-phrase formations involving the two doublets mentioned above, 令/命, 受/授, and a few other words that have left tonal differences in Middle Chinese (MC): non-*qùshēng* vs. *qùshēng* minimal pairs or doublets. But, as we shall see, the tonal differences are also frequently couched in syntax.

It is widely accepted that the MC *qùshēng* goes back to the segmental **-s* in OC. A number of works on the so-called *qùshēng* derivations have been published. We will make use of them as we see fit, but the main purpose of this paper is to determine what type of *qùshēng* derivations is observable in the two doublets and a few others words, deducing therefrom how such word-formation processes may have expanded the lexicon by adding the suffix **-s*. We will also examine how these processes contribute to the noun-phrase formation and serve as an input to phrasal or syntactic processes.

2.　The Doublet 令 and 命 and Some Related Issues

Although the meaning of 'order, command' associated with both 令 and 命 overlaps in their *qùshēng* reading, the two graphs represent different words. In terms of historical palaeography, however, the addition of the mouth element 口 to 令 to yield 命 seems to have occurred rather late in palaeographical sources (see infra). There are a few theories to explain the addition of the mouth element. They can be phonetic, phonological, prosodic, semantic (both semanticizing and desemanticizing), graphic (including 'ornamental' or *shìbǐ* 飾筆 'decorative writing'), morphological, or even morphophonemic. We cannot critically examine all these possibilities, but it is too simplistic and anachronistic to interpret the OBI graph 𝄃 uniformly as *mìng* 命 as is done by some authors (e.g., JGWB 40/2.7/#90; Shaughnessy 1980-81, 62). In this connection, the theory put forward by Sagart (1999, 79) is interesting and worth further examination:

A prefix *m- has been reconstructed [by a few scholars] on the basis of alternations like *jiū* 摎 MC ljuw 'to tie round, strangle' vs. *miù* 繆 MC mjiw 'to bind round' and *lìng* 令 MC ljengH 'to order, command' vs. *mìng* 命 MC mjængH 'to order, command, appoint'. While these alternations certainly argue for a prefix m-, words like *lìng* 令 and *mìng* 命 are interchangeable in Zhou texts and inscriptions, and it is more likely that they represent iambic and fusing variants of the same prefixed word: *ᵇmə-reŋ-s and *ᵇm-reŋ-s respectively, with regular loss of the prefix in the former, than unprefixed and prefixed members of the same word-family.

The application of Sagart's *ᵇmə- "as a loosely attached verbal prefix' in a "deontic" sense (p. 84) to 令 'order; cause' might work better than what seems at first sight to be a genuine deontic negative *wú* 無 used in a *Shījīng* poem (Ode 235.5) in which *wú*/*ᵇma* 無 (OC form Sagart's 1999) is interpreted as non-negative (the example originally cited in Behr 1994):

(1)   侯服于周，天命靡常，殷士膚敏，祼將于京，厥作祼將，常服黼冔，王
之藎臣，無念爾祖。

(The Yīn 殷) became subservient to the Zhōu; Heaven's mandate is not forever; the officers of Yīn were fine and diligent, but their libations were performed in the (Zhōu) capital; when they made their libations, they (were allowed to) always ware the white and black embroidered robes and ceremonial caps (of Yīn); (oh,) the loyal servants of the king (= Chéng *wáng*), do think of your ancestor.

There are, however, competing interpretations of the last clause: 無念爾祖. If we follow the Máo commentary (Máo *zhuàn* 毛傳), it is possible to take 無 as an instance of Sagart's "iambic prefix" as Máo says 「無念，念也」 (*wúniàn* means *niàn* 'think'). But if we follow the commentary of Zhū Xī 朱熹 (1130–1200), 無 is used rhetorically: 'Should you not think of your ancestor? (Original: 無念，猶言豈得無念也).' Qū Wànlǐ (1983, 453) takes 無念 literally as 勿念 'Don't think of your ancestor [referring to Shāng servants]'. Unless one examines the use of *wú* in the textual and exegetical details of Ode 235, in the whole *Shījīng* corpus, and, in fact, other "reliable" sources,[4] it would be difficult to solve this interpretive problem, if indeed we could do so with any degree of certainty.

But it is quite likely that, whatever the correct interpretation of the *lìng* and *mìng* doublet, it is a question triggered after the period and the source we are concerned with in this paper, Shāng OBI. Sagart's theory of a "loosely attached verbal prefix *[b]mə-" (p. 82) would explain the use of 無 in 無念爾祖, if, **and only if,** we follow the Máo *zhuàn*. But as far as we know the addition of the mouth element to 令 is attested rather late, quite possibly in the mid Zhōu (Gāo Míng and Tú Báikuí 2008, 229, 56; cf. also Liú Zhāo et al. 2009, 507–508; Huáng Dékuān *et al.* 2007, 4, 3529–3542). The mouth element addition happened sometime between ECC and SCC. If we take this palaeographical evidence as is, the use of the mouth element in BRI would probably indicate the notational change in some phonetic or prosodic features of 令 and 命. Since, as mentioned, the OBI graph for 令 (𝑓) already consists of the mouth element, the addition of another mouth element must have been made when the scribe was no longer aware of the fact that the graph 亼 (A) represented the mouth. In general, the further down the time progresses the original graphic import gets forgotten. If we are correct in thinking that this sort of palaeographical evidence is a reflection of some phonetic or prosodic changes, Sagart's 'verbal-prefix' [b]mə- theory[5] is one possibility that could explain the total absence of 命 in OBI.

2.1 The suffix *-s in *lìng*/*rjiŋ-s*/*reŋ(h)*~*rin(s)* 令 :[6] Nominalizer and plain agency marker

Baxter and Sagart (1998, 54–59) provide 32 pairs of doublets in which one member is read in *qùshēng* and another member non-*qùshēng*. They point out that the derivational suffix *-s is the 'easiest to establish for OC', and '[i]n the majority of cases, the suffix *-s is added to adjectives and verbs to make a derived noun' (54). Out of the 32 paired examples, 21 are of this type. They do not, however, include *lìng* 令. As will be made clear, it is one of the issues of this paper to include *lìng* as well on the basis of inscriptional evidence. But what word can *lìng* be paired with

---

4. And, in addition, we need to take the general cultural background of the time into consideration, such as implications of "ancestors" to the Yin survivors among the Zhōu, the conqueror.

5. Also, "loosely attached verbal suffix" seems a strange thing — what in real language could we compare it to? In fact, whether this can be called "verbal-prefix" is also uncertain. Sagart also applies his theory to the alternation of *m-* vs. *p-* initials in the morphology of the deontic negative *wù*/*mut*/*mət* 勿 'don't, should not' and the non-deontic negative *fú*/*put*/*pət* 弗 'do not, did not' (cf. Sagart *op. cit.*: 84), but this seems to me going too far. It is a topic too involved to go into in this paper, but the *m-* vs. *p-* distinction seems to me fundamental in that the former is associated with "existence", while the latter with "identification". More work is needed.

6. Unless otherwise specified, two OC forms are given: the first one is Baxter-Sagart's (2011) followed by Schuessler's (2007, 2009) after the slash.

to form a minimal pair? According to my hypothesis, a good possibility is the word *míng/*C.
meng/*meŋ* 名 'name; to name'. Somewhat different from Schuessler (2007, 387) who takes
mìng 命 as the base verb of 名 'name', it seems equally possible to take 名 functioning both
verbally (to name) and nominally (name).[7] This is similar to *mìng* 命 'to order' and '(order)
decree'. Thus, following the paradigm of Baxter and Sagart, the following minimal pair may be
posited:

(2) a. 名 *míng<*mjeng/*meŋ*   Sagart's OC: *bmeŋ 'to name'

    b. 令 *lìng<*rjiŋ-s/*reŋ(h)~*rin(s)*   Sagart's OC: *bmə-reŋ-s 'to order;
            ordering'[8]

One may of course question the validity of the above *míng* 名 and *lìng* 令 pair because the
available OC reconstructions are not on the surface so encouraging. However, Proto-Tibeto-
Burman (PTB) for *míng* 名 is something like *r-miŋ* (Schuessler 2007, 387) who also notes that
"*lìng* 令 'order' may have preserved a ST or PCH pre-initial *r-, hence *mreŋ<*r-miŋ* which
makes it a homophone of PTB *r-miŋ* 'name' …." Schuessler's 'homophone' idea with PTB
r-miŋ might be correct after all, but as Benedict (1972, 115) has pointed out, 'TB *r-miŋ* 'name'
(also B *mín* 'order, command'); Karen *men* 'name',” there is a contact with *r- in PTB *r-miŋ*
for 名. The issues involved here are rather complicated: the problem of *r-causative, addition
of *-s, 命 rhyming with *píngshēng* words in *Shījīng* (Mattos 1971, 309), Lù Démíng's 陸德明
(556–627) entry under 命 records a tradition of the variant character *míng* 明 (*píngshēng* word)
used for the reading of 命 in *Jīngdiǎn shìwén* 經典釋文, to mention a few issues that require
further examination. So it might still be that in the final analysis 名 in (2a) above should be
replaced, as per Schuessler, with *mìng* 命 'order'. But because the addition of the mouth element
to 令 occurred as late as mid Zhōu, the hypothesis of 名 as the non-*qù* counterpart of 令 is a good
possibility. Also, in terms of meaning, I see a common semantic feature in 'command, order' and
'name' in that both may be considered as 'performative verbs' in that the patient of the former
verb is to respond in action rather than in speech and the patient of the latter just gets named
without the need for any linguistic response. Thus, in actual use of the word 令 whose base is
here suggested to be 名, its patient (direct object) is 'named' to perform a certain course of action
(i.e., the content of 令).

---

7. The use of 名 in OBI is unfortunately rather limited, but it functions both verbally (e.g., *HJ* 19617, *Tunnan*
668) and nominally (but place name in *HJ* 9503, 9505).

8. In OBI *lìng* 令 is often used as the verb "to order". This matches with the *qùshēng* reading in *Guǎngyùn*
where the gloss is "命也" (among others such as 善也 'good', 律也 'decree', etc.). The *Guǎngyùn* also gives
令 under *píngshēng* with the gloss "使也 (to cause)". The verbal meaning of "to name" and the nominal
one of "naming, ordering" are semantically comparable and derivationally meaningful in a certain stage of
derivation. In other stages of the derivational process, it will be shown below that the suffix *-s also indicates
agency (2.3), and "to name" can be put "the one who does the act of 'naming' (noun) or 'namer' (i.e.,
commander)" (more on this to follow) by adding the suffix *s-. As regards the question of the temporal layers
of derivational processes involved in the four "tones", see Mei Tsu-lin (1980). Quite significantly, Mei argues
that this type of *qùshēng* derivation (verb changing to noun) is the earliest.

Let us now look at a few examples of *lìng* 令 which do not appear in the common structure S + V令 + N +VP in the sense of 'S V$_{orders}$ N to VP$_{do\ something}$'. In *HJ* 6155 we find the following three series of inscriptions:

(3)   貞：……于……令。

Tested (the following charge against the spirit of the bone): … from … order.

(4)   ↓勹占方于受令。[9]

(We) beg for [divine aid in our attack against] Gōng *fāng*[10] from **the one who gives orders.**

(5)   ↑貞：于受令勹。

Tested (the following charge against the spirit of the bone): From **the one who gives orders** (we) beg for [divine aid in our attack against Gōng *fāng*].

The first example has some missing graphs, but the second and the third examples are complete. The phrase 受令, which should be interpreted as 授令 'give order', must be a NP because it occurs after the particle *yú* 于 in the directional sense of 'from'. Example (4) is the normal syntactic order (S)VO$_d$ *yú* O$_i$,[11] while (5) has the phrase 于受令 put before the verb *gài* 勹 'to beg', I think, for focussing purposes. It is clear from (4) and (5) that 授令 is an NP. If expressed in SCC, this should be 授令者 '**the one who gives the order**'.[12] Another example of the same structure is found in *HJ* 19563:

(6)   ……酉卜賓貞: 告甼受令于丁三宰𣢠一牛。

Crack making on the …*yǒu day*, Bīn tested (the following charge against the spirit of the bone): (We) will make a ritual announcement about Bi (to) **the one**

---

9. The downwards arrow sign ↓ and the upwards arrow sign ↑, taken together, signify that the charges which follow are to be considered together, often forming a *duìzhēn* 對貞 'a pair of antithetical or contrastive pair of divinatory charges or sentences (命辭)'.

10. 占方 is the direct object of the verb *gài* 勹 'to beg for', but it is a much abridged expression of *(我)伐占方之帝祐 '**divine aid for our attacking** Gōng *fāng*'. If we do not construe the surface phrase 勹占方 in this way (i.e., deletion of the elements in bold face), it does not make sense at all. I assume that to the Shāng the VO compound 勹占方 by itself was sufficient to comprehend what I think it meant. Given their shared understanding that Gōng *fāng* was their enemy, often a target of attack, the meaning of 勹占方 must have been self-evident. Christoph Harbsmeier (何莫邪) thinks that the verb *gài* is lexically specialized to convey such a meaning (private communication, 10 May, 2010). The said deletion may be interpreted as having been motivated by such a shared knowledge.

11. "O$_d$" stands for "O$_{direct}$" and "O$_i$" stands for "O$_{indirect}$".

12. In modern Chinese this may be put: 下達命令者.

who gives orders (and:) as well as to Dīng with three specially reared sheep, (and) cut up (脤=膰) an ox.[13]

While the suffix *-s* in *lìng* 令 in the above examples may be characterized generally as a nominalizer, we should specially note that *lìng* is framed in the VO structure; i.e., (受:) 授令 'to give order'. In (4) and (5) this VO phrase occurs after the particle *yú* 于 in the sense of "from". In (6) it occurs before the same particle and after the VP 告 (授令 being used as an indirect object) and so 于 has the sense of "to". All these suggest that the suffix *-s* has the function of nominalizing the **VO structure as a whole**. This is different from treating the suffix *-s* as the marker for nominal derivatives. Such a function is comparable exactly to *zhě* 者 in SCC. Since 令 in the VO phrase is a noun and V is 授 'to give, grant', it would seem better to interpret the noun 令 as meaning literally 'the act of naming/ordering', not 'the person who names/orders'. The NP 受令 cannot be construed as meaning "*give the namer/orderer". Stated differently, it has the function of a 'cross-lexical' or phrasal nominalization. At the same time, however, if considered lexico-internally as opposed to cross-lexically, the same suffix *-s* has the function of referring to 'action'. Since Shāng Chinese has no 者, we should consider 授令 as meaning 'give the act of ordering'. This is tantamount to 'give orders' in plain English. But we cannot deny that 授令 in examples (4), (5), and (6) does mean 'one who gives orders'. Where does this indefinite pronoun 'one' come from? It is clear that 授令 should be treated as a phrasal nominalization. The use of 于 'from' before 授令 also dictates this analysis. Therefore, we would have to recognize that the suffix *-s* is serving as the marker for pronominal agency. This is similar to the function of 者 in SCC as it can nominalize a VP cross lexically and, depending on context, it refers to an indefinite pronoun.

As mentioned in the beginning of this section, Baxter and Sagart (1998, 54–59) provide 32 pairs of examples (64 words) in which one member is read in *qùshēng* and another member in non-*qùshēng*. Out of the 64 words, 42 have the suffix *-s* added to adjectives and verbs to make derived nouns. In the list of their examples, there is only one word, *shuài/*s-rut-s/*sruts* 帥

---

13. The verb *gào* 告 'to report', when used as a ritual verb, i.e., having the lexical feature of [+rituality], is a quadrivalent verb on the underlying level (cf. Takashima 2002). A full specification of such a verb would have an agent-subject (often omitted), a patient-Od, an addressee/recipient-Oi, and an instrumental-Od. The particle *yú* 于 in the sense of "to" with 告, if used, occurs before the addressee/recipient-Oi, and the instrumental-Od is introduced without any marker. (In SCC the instrumental-Od is often preceded by *yǐ* 以 'using X'). *Yú* 于 can also be used as a conjunction (Takashima 1984–85: 284–288), and even though it does not occur before 受令 as it does in (4) and (5), it is used before Dīng 丁 'Ding (ancestor)' possibly referring to the recently deceased Wǔ Dīng 武丁. So here constructional homonymity may have to be recognized, viz., *yú* as a directional and conjunctive particle meaning "and to".

As to the specific interpretation of the graph 钅, I have excluded the 受 'receive' interpretation on the grounds that there is no other example bearing such a meaning as "*make a ritual announcement about Bi receiving an order from Dīng" for 告叀受令于丁. In other words, the Shāng did not seem to have (received:) accepted "orders" from ancestral spirits.

which fits the pattern 'V + -er'.[14] One may characterize this type of suffix *-s as a nominalizing and agency marker. It is simply a nominal derivation. In this regard, it is quite interesting to find two OBI graphs which may be regarded as the forerunners of *shuài* 帥 'to encamp (verb)' written like 𠂤 (自) in OBI, and shuài 帥 'army' (noun) written like 𠂤 (自). The line at the bottom of 𠂤 made the difference of verbal vs. nominal use of the word, the latter plausibly with the suffix *-s and the former without it. However, the neat semantic paradigm presented by Baxter and Sagart (p. 57), 'to lead' (verb) and 'leader' (noun), is not applicable to the OBI context (cf. also S 440.3–442.3). That is, OBI scholars would most probably **not** give such a meaning as 'to lead' for 𠂤, but instead give 'to camp' which works quite well in context. Also, they would assign the nominal meaning 'army' to the graph 𠂤. This also makes good sense in context, though it is hard to know whether 𠂤 refers to an individual or a whole mass. How the verb meaning 'to camp' is related to the noun 'army' is a problem. If we apply the case of the lexico-internal nominalization of 令 'the act of ordering' to the 𠂤 and 𠂤 pair, the latter may be considered, *mutatis mutandis*, as the 'the act of camping', that is, 'army' could be considered as a unit of men who (habitually) do the act of camping. This explanation seems counter intuitive because one would think that 'army' is a unit of men who fight. Nonetheless, it is a hypothesis engendered by the analysis of the 令 in the above paragraph and thus worth testing it further.

Before moving on to yet another type of nominal derivation by the suffix *-s, we should also consider the graph 𠬤. The graph can be transcribed as 受 which is a *shǎngshēng* 上聲 word meaning "to receive". But as mentioned at the end of n. 13, "to receive" is not appropriate to the examples we are considering (4, 5, 6). There is no doubt that the meaning is *shòu/*djuʔ-s/*duh* + s/h-(suffix extrovert) 授 'to give'. Thus, as presented by Baxter and Sagart (58), the 受/授 doublet displays a different *qùshēng* derivation process, one which yields the ditransitive or causative verbs from transitive verbs (Schuessler's "s/h-suffix extrovert"). This type of *qùshēng* derivation is not limited to the 受/授 doublet in OBI. Other examples include: *yǒu/*oʷəʔ/*wəʔ* = 有 'have, there is' and *yòu/*oʷəʔ-s/*wəs* 出 = 侑 '(to cause to have:) offer'; *lái/*rˤək/*rə* 來 'to come' and *lài/*rˤək-s/*rə(k)h* 來/賚 '(to cause … to come:) to deliver (tribute), contribute'. Since 來 'to come' is not a transitive verb, it would seem preferable to construe this sort of derivation as "causativization".

We have so far identified two different functions of the suffix *-s. One is the 'nominalizer and agency marker' which is associated with the VO phrase 授令 nominalized to yield 'the one who gives orders'. This is a nominalization of the cross-lexical or phrasal type comparable to 者 in SCC. Lexico-internally, the same suffix *-s has the function of yielding a derived noun out of a verb. This is a nominal derivation of the type that implies action (V-ing as in 'naming, ordering,

---

14. There is another word, *zhì/*tip-s/*təps* ? 鷙, to which Baxter and Sagart give "(*one who seizes:) bird of prey", but "one who seizes" and "bird of prey" do not match with the majority of their examples which lead to a generalization that the nominal derivative of the verb *zhí/*tip/*təp* 執 'seize, hold, grasp' is "that which is seized, held, grasped". This is expressible as *suǒ* 所 'that which is V_{pp}'. 執 is written like � or 𡉫 (a drawing of the shackled arms of a kneeling figure or of the shackled feet) and, though the *qùshēng* derivative of the word is written the same in OBI, the context can usually determine if the graph is used as the verb *zhí* or the noun *zhì* 摯 or 贄/鷙 'that which is caught'.

etc.'). It should also be mentioned that the important motivation for the noun-phrase analysis is the use of the particle *yú* 于 in the sense of 'from' in (4) and (5) and 'to' in example (6), though the first one is understood (the second one is not). Thus, it is not entirely certain if the suffix *-s* in and of itself is responsible for the noun-phrase formation. More examples are needed (cf. 2.2 below). Another function of the suffix *-s* we have identified is to 'causativize' a verb either transitive or intransitive, and this seems certain as it is based more on contextual evidence. We will have more examples later.

2.2 The Suffix *-s* in *lìng/*riŋ-s/*rin(s)* 令: Nominalizer and Passive Marker

In addition to the 'nominalizer and agency marker' associated with the suffix *-s* in the phrase 于受令 'from the one who (names:) gives orders', we can identify yet another type of noun-phrase formation involving the same word, *lìng/*riŋ-s/*rin(s)* 令. This type is also susceptible to the environment in which it occurs. There is, however, a significant difference between the two in that the word represented by the graph 令 (令) also specifies the agent-subject Dì 帝 on the surface level. For example:

(7)　　↓ 丙辰卜㕥貞帝令隹娥。　　*HJ* 14161

Crack making on the *bǐngchén* day, (Diviner) Dùn (㕥= 盾) tested (the following charge against the spirit of the bone): **The one whom Di** (names:) **orders** will be Lady Mǐng.

(8)　　↑ 貞帝弗令隹娥。　　　　　　*Ibid.*

Tested (the following charge against the spirit of the bone): **The one whom Di does not** (name:) **order** will be Lady Mǐng.

Examples (7) and (8) form a *duìzhēn* 對貞 'paired testing charges', the former in the positive and the latter in the negative. But note that the clauses following the positive and the negative charges are identical: 隹娥 which, if expressed in ECC, may be equivalent to *wéi* Mǐng 維娥 'it is/will be Mǐng'. In SCC this should be 娥也. What precedes this VP (nominal predicate) can thus be construed as a subject. If expressed in SCC, this would be 帝所令者 'the one whom Di (names:) **orders**' for the positive, and 帝所不令者 'the one whom Di does not (name:) **order**' for the negative.[15] If we are correct in interpreting the suffix *-s* in *lìng/*rjiŋ-s/*rin(s)* 令 as nominalizing the VO phrase 授令 and serving at the same time as the agency marker discussed in 2.1, we might also maintain the same interpretation for (7) and (8). But the agency marker it manifestly is not, since it is already expressed: Dì 帝. We cannot assign such a meaning as 'the

---

15. In modern Chinese the former may be put: 帝向其下達命令之人; the latter: 帝不向其下達命令之人.

one who gives orders' to (7) and (8). Instead, we have a kind of built-in **patient** in 帝令 and 帝弗令. If we do not supply a patient of the indefinite kind, the positive 帝令 and the negative 帝弗令 exhibit the plain S + V structure. But because this is followed by the VP 佳娥, the S + V structure gets nominalized. If we do not have any agent-subject on the surface like *令佳娥, it would have meant '*the one who orders is/will be Lady Mǐng' (*令者娥也) and *弗令佳娥 would have meant 'the one who does not order is/will be Lady Mǐng' (*不令者娥也). The fact that we do not actually find such examples is probably due to reasons that are socio-political and cultural rather than linguistic.

In the last paragraph of 2.1, we have mentioned that the important motivation for the noun-phrase analysis of 授令 is the use of the directional particle 于. One naturally wants to ask if this alone is the sufficient reason for the NP analysis or if this syntactic environment is also conditioned by the suffix *-s. In the previous paragraph, we have found the same NP analysis to be applicable to a different syntactic environment. It follows from this that the use of the directional particle 于 alone does not stipulate the NP analysis.

2.3   The Suffix *-s: Causative and Agency Marker

Let us now consider the following inscriptions as another type of noun-phrase formation involving the suffix *-s added to a verb:

(9)   ↓ 癸酉卜岳貞出責自西。   *HJ* 7103

Crack making on the *guǐyǒu* day, (Diviner) Yuè tested (the following charge against the spirit of the bone): There will be **someone bringing** (tribute) from the west.

(10)   ↑ 亡其責自西。   *Ibid.*

There might not be **anyone bringing** (tribute) from the west.

(11)   王固曰其自東出責。   *HJ* 914r

His Majesty, having prognosticated, said: There will be **someone bringing** (tribute) from the east.

These examples have no subject before the main verbs *yǒu* 出 (= 有) 'have; there is' and *wú* (or *wáng*) 亡 'not have; there is not'. Since the structure is different from 帝令 in (7) and 帝弗令 in (8), we cannot paraphrase the above examples in terms of SCC as *S 所 V 者 for the positive and *S所不V者 for the negative. We should instead paraphrase them as: 有責自西者 and 無其責自西者, in which 者 is a pronominal substitute for the head of a NP, 責自西者 'one who pays tribute from the west'.[16] This NP is then used as the object of the main verbs *yǒu* 屮 (= 有) and *wú* (or *wáng*) 亡.

In Takashima (1984) I interpreted the graph 來 in the same inscriptions as an intransitive verb *lái* 來 'to come'. However, it cannot be applied to all cases, and I now think that here the graph stands for the verb *lài* 賫 '(to cause to come:) bring; pay (tribute)'. In the Shāng divination text, what they were concerned is usually some specific matter, and someone coming or going is laden with additional and practical values. The common-sense interpretation would then be to deliver something to the court or to powerful lineage groups rather than the mere act of a person's coming. More pertinently, the following related inscriptions suggest that the interpretation of *lài* 賫 is superior to that of *lái* 來:

(12)　↓屮賫自南以龜。　　　*HJ* 7076o

There will be someone paying (tribute) from the south; (he) will be bringing turtles.

(13)　↑不其以。　　　　*Ibid.*

(He) might not be bringing (turtles).

In (12) the VP is *yí guī* 以龜 which is matched in the negative counterpart of this *duìzhēn* as 不其以, though the O_d *guī*, being understood, is omitted. Also omitted before 不其以 is the NP 賫自南 which, if expressed in terms of SCC, would be 有賫自南者 'there will be someone paying (tribute) from the south' or 'there will be someone who would be paying (tribute) from the south' (desirable to the Shāng including the diviner, the speaker). In our translation of (13) we have simply supplied 'He' in its place. The idea of this charge is that, even though it is predicted that

---

16. Some may paraphrase 屮賫自西 as "*有賫者自西", arguing that *zìxī* 自西 is the VP in the sense of "to start from the west". In OBI, however, the *zì* phrase generally functions adverbially. There are a few cases which may ostensibly suggest the VP analysis. For example:

　　貞勿詳自上甲至下乙。　　　*HJ* 419o

　　test/should not/(specifically:) necessarily/from/Shàng Jiǎ/to/Xià Yǐ.

But there is an omission of the verb *you* 彭 'to cut, carve (neatly)' before 自 in the positive counterpart of the *duìzhēn* 對貞. Another example:

　　王固曰其自高妣己。　　　*HJ* 438r

　　king/prognosticated/said/MOD/from/High /ancestress/Jǐ.

But this is a prognostication for the *duìzhēn* charges on the obverse:

　　戊辰卜爭貞敯羌自妣己。　　　*HJ* 438o

Crack making on the *wùchén* day, (Diviner) Zhēng tested (the following charge against the spirit of the bone): (We) will disembowel Qiāng tribesmen (as sacrificial offering) starting from Ancestress Jǐ.

　　貞敯羌自高妣己。　　　*Ibid.*

Tested (the following charge against the spirit of the bone): (We) will disembowel Qiāng tribesmen (as sacrificial offering) starting from High Ancestress Jǐ.

Example (11) also illustrates that the adverbial phrase 自東 'from the east' modifies 屮賫.

there may be someone paying tribute, he might not be bringing turtles (undesirable to the Shāng including the diviner, the speaker). If this is correct, the graph 𝑥 must have stood for *lài/*rˤək-s/*rə(k)h* 賚 'to pay/give/deliver (tribute)'. The suffix *-s* can then be interpreted as the causative and agency marker. Here *-s* does not extend to the verb 出 cross-lexically as it does in the VO phrase 授令 in the sense of 授令者 'one who gives orders (sc. naming/ordering)' discussed in 2.1, as well as the SV phrase 帝令/帝弗令 in the sense of 帝所令者 'the one whom Di orders' and 帝所不令者 'the one whom Di does not order' discussed in 2.2. The verbs that occur before 賚 are *yǒu* 出 (= 有) and *wú* (or *wáng*) 亡. It would be strange to nominalize the VO phrase 有賚 (one who has occasions to bring) and the negative VO phrase 亡其賚 (one who has no occasion to bring) because, if we do, we would have to take 自西 as VP in examples (9) and (10). This is an interpretation we have already rejected (cf. n. 16). Example (11) clearly shows that 賚 is a VP. Thus, the suffix *-s* in 賚 has only lexico-internal effects, yielding a derived noun out of a verb. This is a nominal derivation, and in this case it indicates agency (V-er as in "contributor, leader, giver, etc.") rather than action (V-ing as in 'naming, ordering, etc.'). But there is no ambiguity that 賚 is a noun causatively derived from 來. As such 賚 as a VP should mean "There will be someone paying (tribute)."

If the *-s* in the word 賚 has the causative and agency marking function, why didn't the Shāng say *出自西賚 for (9) and *亡其自西賚 for (10)? Indeed we do have 其自東出賚 in (11). This is a difficult question to answer. The possible answer I can think of is that the scope of nominalization by the *-s* suffix cannot extend more than three syllables (whereas that by 者 in SCC can). If this can be acceptable,[17] the NP 授令 'one who gives orders', another NP 帝令 'the one whom Dì orders', and yet another NP 帝弗令 'the one whom Dì does not order' do not come under such a syllabic constraint, but * 自西賚 does. As for *亡其自西賚 and 其自東出賚, however, they require different explanations. To start with the latter first, we have already analyzed 出賚 as VP and 自東 as an adverbial phrase modifying the VP. But here we have *qí* 其 which is basically the genitive pronominal demonstrative (Takashima 1996; Deng Lin 2011). This 其 embeds 自東, resulting in what should be analyzed as an NP literally meaning 'its (being) from the east'. One can construe this functionally as a **topic** expressible as 'As for from the east'. The 其 here is clearly anticipative and cataphoric. This then goes with the VP 賚. As regards *亡其自西賚, the VP shifts to the main verb 亡 and its configuration *其自西賚. Since 賚 has already been analyzed as a nominally derived noun, *其自西賚 contains no verb. It is syntactically incomplete.

The last example I should like to discuss is also a *duìzhēn* in which the graph 𝑓 is used. The graph depicts a hand holding a weapon-container like object (perhaps a symbol of 𝑓, a functionary).[18] It is the predecessor of both *shǐ* 史/使 'envoy (sc. the meaning of 'scribe' is inappropriate in OBI); to send' and *lì* 吏 '(military) officer', appearing, e.g., as follows:

---

17. Independent justification would be desirable, but unfortunately I do not have any. While keeping such desirability in mind, let it be treated as a constraint for the time being.

18. Palaeographers have many different suggestions for the graphic interpretation of 𝑓 / 𝑓. Some interpretations seem quite forced or inferior to some others, but there is none that is superior to others. See *GL* 4.2933/2947–2961.

(14) ↓ 貞在北吏/史出獲羌。   *HJ* 914o

Tested (the following charge against the spirit of the bone): The military officers/envoys in the north will in fact capture Qiāng tribesmen.[19]

(15) ↑ 貞在北吏/史亡其獲羌。   *Ibid.*

Tested (the following charge against the spirit of the bone): The military officers/envoys in the north might not (have occasions to >) in fact capture Qiāng tribesmen.

There is no question that 在北吏/史 is a NP (see below for its structural analysis) functioning as the subject of the positive VP 出獲羌 in (14) and that of the negative VP 亡其獲羌 in (15). The question is: exactly how should we understand ⼽ (吏/史) ? There are two possibilities. One is to construe it basically as a **verb** (*shǐ* 使 written in OBI as ⼽ / ⼽ [史]) which is nominalized [one who has been sent, i.e., 所使者]; another is to construe the same as nominally derived, a noun in and of itself [*lì/*rə?-s/*rəh* 吏 or *shì/*s-rə?-s/*srəh* 使 (cf. Schuessler 2007, 350)]. In this connection, Baxter and Sagart (1998, 53) have suggested the following minimal pair:

(16) a. 吏 *lì <*rə?-s/*rəh*   'clerk, minor official' (Glosses as given by Baxter and Sagart)
      b. 使 *shǐ <*s-rə?-s/*srəh*   '(*cause to be an emissary:) send' (Ditto above)

Even though *lì* 吏 is a *qùshēng* word, Baxter and Sagart did not include it among the 64 words (of which 42 have the suffix *-s* added to adjectives and verbs to make derived nouns, as mentioned earlier). This is probably influenced by their view that these words are of Tibeto-Burman stock in which the prefix *s-* is used in 'causative constructions'.[20] That is, the prefix *s-* is added to the word *lì* 吏 to derive *shǐ* 使 'to send'. Schuessler (2007, 350) also thinks similarly.[21] This is not impossible, but since the word *shǐ* 使 (written typically as ⼽ , ⼽ , ⼽ , ⼽) is already used in the sense of 'to send' in OBI,[22] an alternative interpretation I would postulate is the following derivational prototype:

---

19. For a study of the 出 (= 有)/亡 + V construction with an emphatic import (i.e., giving prominence to the valents associated mainly with the agent-subject of the main verb 出 or 亡), the reader is referred to Takashima (1988).

20. They (*ibid.*) state: "There are traces of other likely prefixes in early Chinese. Alternations of Middle Chinese *s-* or *sr-* with other initial consonants are reminiscent of causative constructions with prefixed *s-* which are widespread in Tibeto-Burman."

21. He says: "'Ambassador' [Zuo] (Downer 1959: 285). The verb 'to send on a mission' [Liji] has later been derived from 'ambassador'." Here "later" is questionable as the meaning of "to send on a mission" is already attested in OBI.

22. Typical examples appear in the charge: *shǐ rén yú* X 使人于X (where X = place name). The graph used for *shǐ* is written ⼽ /⼽ or ⼽/⼽. There is no problem of interpreting numerous *shǐ rén yú* X inscriptions as meaning "send men to X" (mainly, though perhaps not exclusively, for military activities). The negative used for the verb *shǐ* is *wù/*mut/*mət* 勿 'don't, should not' which negates the humanly controllable (or thought of controllable) action verbs.

(17) a. 理 *lǐ* < **rəʔ/*rəʔ* 'to regulate; put … in order'
b. 吏 *lì* <**rəʔ-s/*rəh* 'military (regulator:) officer'

Although we have not been able to identify in OBI the use of 理 in the sense given above, its nominal derivative *lì* 吏 cannot be ruled out. Etymologically, if *lì* 'military officer' is paired with *lǐ* 理 'to regulate; put … in order', it seems to have an edge over *shǐ* 史 'envoy, emissary'.[23] The interpretation of (吏/史) basically as a verb (= 使) which then produces a noun (吏) does not get support from OBI. I would construe the same as a **noun** in and of itself, but in terms of derivational morphology it is derived from *lǐ* 理 rather than from *shǐ* 使. This is based in part on the following inscriptions:

(18) ↓庚子卜爭貞西吏召亡禍盬。 *HJ* 5637o
Crack making on the *gēngzǐ* day, (Diviner) Zhēng tested (the following charge against the spirit of the bone): The Western Military Officer, Shào, shall have no misfortunes, and (will be able to successfully) manage [the king's business王事].[24]

23. Most OBI scholars take the original bone graphs (see above n.) as *shǐ* 史 'envoy, emissary', and I have personally followed this interpretation in the past. Hú Hòuxuǎn (1985; GL 4.2933/pp. 2947-2961) has shown that the graph is used to stand for a word meaning "military officer" (武官). Given below are some examples for further consideration:

……卜王其延公吏…… *HJ* 30770
Crack making: His Majesty will continue on (what) the duke's military officer …

Interpreting the expression as 公吏 'Duke's *lì* "military officer"' seems better than 公史 'Duke's *shǐ* "envoy"'. Consider other examples below:

立須為吏其奠。 *HJ* 816r
(If we) set up Xū to act as military officer, (he) may (be able to) stabilize (奠=鎮) (the situation).

貞立明吏。 *HJ* 7075o
Tested (the following charge against the spirit of the bone): (We) should set up Míng as military officer.

↓癸亥卜㱿貞我吏𢦏缶。 *HJ* 6834o
Crack making on the *guǐhài* day, (Diviner) Nan tested (the following charge against the spirit of the bone): Our military officers will (be able to) harm (or: smite) the Táo (缶>陶).

↑癸亥卜㱿貞我吏毋其𢦏缶。 *Ibid.*
Crack making on the *guǐhài* day, (Diviner) Nan tested (the following charge against the spirit of the bone): Our military officers might not (be able to) harm (or: smite) the Táo (缶>陶).

↓癸未卜𡧊 (=盾) 貞黃尹保我吏。 *HJ* 3481
Crack making on the *guǐwèi* day, (Diviner) Dùn tested (the following charge against the spirit of the bone): Huáng Yǐn will protect our military officers.

↑貞黃尹弗保我吏。 *Ibid.*
Tested (the following charge against the spirit of the bone): Huáng Yǐn will protect our military officers.

In fact, Chén Mèngjiā (1956: 520; GL 4.2933/p. 2949) has consistently transcribed the original bone graphs and as *lì* 吏. Some scholars take the expression as Dì shǐ 帝使 'Dì's messenger'. I am not sure if that is what is meant. Further study is needed.

24. The graph / is *gǔ* 古, but as Guō Mòruò (1931: *apud GL* 1.729/p. 699) has pointed out, it stands for the verb *gǔ* 盬 in the VO compound of *gǔ wángshì* 盬王事 'to manage the king's business well' in OBI and in ECC (e.g. *Shījīng*). *Wáng shì* 王事 'king's business' refers to warfare (*róng* 戎) par excellence (one of the two major activities, *róng* and *sì* 祀 'sacrifice', of the kings in ancient China). These interpretations are based on a separate study.

(19)　　↑庚子卜爭貞西吏召其出禍。　　　　　　*Ibid.*

Crack making on the *gēngzǐ* day, (Diviner) Zhēng tested (the following charge against the spirit of the bone): The Western Military Officer, Shào, might have misfortunes.

In the above *duìzhēn*, 西吏召 is an appositive NP which functions as the subject of the VP 亡禍盤 in (18) and 其出禍in (19). Compare this with 在北吏 in (14) and (15). It is self-evident that 在北吏 constitutes a relative construction in which 在北 'to be in the north' is modifying the head *lì* 吏, meaning 'the military officers (stationed) in the north'. Furthermore, we also have 東 吏 'Eastern Military Officer' as in the following inscription:

(20)　　……卜亘貞東吏來。　　　　　　　　　*HJ* 5635

Crack making on the ... day, (Diviner) Xuān tested (the following charge against the spirit of the bone): The Eastern Military Officer will be coming.

In these examples there is no need to causativize 使 *shǐ* < *s-rəʔ-s/ *srəh '(*cause to be an emissary?:) send' and further '(the one who is sent:) emissary, envoy'. The interpretation of the noun 吏 having been derived from the verb 理 takes care of these examples.

3. Conclusion

Assuming that the reconstruction of the MC *qùshēng* is the suffix *-*s* in OC, the paper has identified three major functions of the suffix: (1) the nominalizer and agency marker associated with the VO phrase *shòu lìng* 授令 'the one who gives orders'; (2) the nominalizer and passive marker as in Dì *lìng* 帝令 'the one whom Dì orders' and Dì *fú lìng* 帝弗令 'the one whom Dì does not order'; and (3) the causative and agency marker as in 出賚 and 亡其賚. The paper has also identified *shòu* 受 'to receive' from which *shòu* 授 'to give' is causatively derived, but it has no agency marking function in *-*s*. Similarly, *lài* 賚 '(to cause ... to come:) to bring; to pay [tribute])' is causatively derived from *lái* 來 'to come', and here it has the agency marking function in *-*s*. The word *shuài* 帥 (𢎥) 'army' is possibly derived from 𠂤 (𢎥) 'to camp' (i.e., "army" may have been considered as a unit of men who habitually do the act of camping). The word *lì* 吏 with the same suffix *-*s* in the sense of "military officer" is considered as a nominal derivative of *lǐ* 理 'to regulate; put ... in order' rather than from *shǐ* 使 'to send'. As such it shows an agency marking function. All these findings are based on actual usages in, and inferences made from, the Shāng OBI. These morphological functions of the suffix *-*s* are therefore contemporary with Shāng Chinese of ca. 13th B.C.

REFERENCES

Baxter, W. H. 1992. *A Handbook of Old Chinese Phonology*. The Hague: Mouton de Gruyter.

Baxter, W. H., and L. Sagart. 1998. Word formation in Old Chinese. In *New Approaches to Chinese Word Formations: Morphology, Phonology, and the Lexicon in Modern and Ancient Chinese*, ed. J. L. Packard, 35–76. Berlin: Mouton de Gruyter.

Baxter, W. H., and L. Sagart. 2011. *Baxter-Sagart Old Chinese Reconstruction,* version of 20 February 2011. Online at the following URL: http:crlao.ehess.fr/document.php?id=1217. PDF version downloaded on April 26, 2011.

Behr, W. 1994. "Largo forms" as secondary evidence in the reconstruction of Old Chinese Initial Consonant Clusters. *Paper presented at the 27th International Conference on Sino-Tibetan Languages and Linguistics.* Paris, October. (Apud Sagart 1999: 79.)

Benedict, P. K. 1972. Sino-Tibetan: Conspectus. *Princeton-Cambridge Studies in Chinese Linguistics Series* No. 2. Cambridge: Cambridge University Press.

Chen, Mengjia（陳夢家）. 1956. *Yinxu buci zongshu* 殷虛卜辭綜述. Beijing: Kexue chubanshe 科學出版社.

Deng, Lin（鄧琳）. 2011. *Early Development of Demonstratives in Pre-Qin Chinese*. Ph.D. Dissertation. Seattle: University of Washington.

Gao, Ming（高明）and Baikui Tu（涂白奎）. 2008. *Guwenzi Leibian* (zengdingben 增訂本) 古文字類編. Shanghai: Shanghai Guji Chubanshe 上海古籍出版社.

GL → *Jiaguwenzi Gulin* 甲骨文字詁林. 4 vols. Yu, Xingwu 于省吾, editor in chief. Yao, Xiaosui 姚孝遂 notes (按語). Beijing: Zhonghua shuju 中華書局, 1996.

Guo, Moruo（郭沫若）. 1931. *Jiaguwenzi Yanjiu* 甲骨文字研究. 2 vols. Shanghai: Dadong shuju 大東書局. Relevant portions quoted in GL 1.729/p. 699.

Hu, Houxuan（胡厚宣）. 1985. Yindai de shi wei wuguan shuo 殷代的史為武官説. *Quanguo Shangshi Xueshu Taolunhui Lunwenji* 全國商史學術討論會論文集 *Yindu Xuekan* 殷都學刊, Zengkan 增刊, 183–197.

Huang, Dekuan（黃德寬）, editor in chief. 2007. Authors: Huang, Dekuan 黃德寬, He, Linyi 何琳儀, Xu, Zaiguo 徐在國, Hao, Shihong 郝士宏, Chen, Bingxin 陳秉新, Wang, Yunzhi 王蘊智. *Guwenzi Puxi Shuzheng* 古文字譜系疏証. 4 vols. Beijing: Shangwu Yinshuguan 商務印書館.

JGWB → *Jiaguwen bian* 甲骨文編. Revised and enlarged ed. Kaoguxue zhuankan yizhong di shisi hao 考古學專刊乙種第十四號. Beijing: Zhongguo kexueyuan kaogu yanjiusuo 中國科學院考古研究所, 1965. This is based on the original edition under the same title by Sun, Haibo 孫海波 in 14 juan. Cambridge: Harvard-Yenching Institute, 1934.

Long, Yuchun（龍宇純）. 1968. *Tang xieben Wáng renxu kanmiu buque qieyun jiaojian* 唐寫本王仁昫刊謬補缺切韻. Hong Kong: Chinese University of Hong Kong.

Liu, Fu（劉復）et al. (comp.) 1963. *Shiyun Huibian* 十韻彙編. Taipei: Xuesheng Shuju 學生書局, 1963.

Liu, Zhao（劉釗）, Yang Hong,（洪颺）, and Xinjun Zhang,（張新俊）. 2009. *Xin Jiaguwen Bian* 新甲骨文編. Fuzhou: Fujian renmin chubanshe 福建人民出版社.

Mattos, G. L. 1971. Tonal "anomalies" in the Kuo Feng Odes. *Tsing Hua Journal of Chinese Studies* 9 (Nos. 1 & 2): 306–324.

Mei, Tsu-lin (Mei, Zulin)（梅祖麟）. 1980. Sisheng bieyi zhong de shijian cengci 四聲別義中的時間層次, *Zhongguo Yuwen* 中國語文 6: 427–43.

Qu, Wanli（屈萬里）. 1983. *Shijing Quanshi* 詩經詮釋. Taipei: Lianjing chuban shiye gongsi 聯經出版事業公司.

S → *Inkyo bokuji sōrui* 殷墟卜辭綜類. Compiled by Shima, Kunio 島邦男. Tokyo: Kyūko shoin 汲古書院, 1971.

Sagart, L. 1999. *The Roots of Old Chinese*. Amsterdam and Philadelphia: John Benjamins Publishing Co.

Shaughnessy, E. L. 1980–81. "New" evidence on the Zhou conquest. *Early China* 6: 59–79.

Schuessler, A. 1985. The function of Qusheng in early Zhou Chinese. *Linguistics of the Sino-Tibetan Area: The State of the Art*, ed. G. Thurgood, J. A. Matisoff and D. Bradley, 344–62. Canberra: The Australian National University.

Schuessler, A. 2007. *ABC Etymological Dictionary of Old Chinese*. Honolulu: University of Hawaii Press.

Schuessler, A. 2009. *Minimal Old Chinese and Later Han Chinese: A Companion to Grammata Serica Recensa*. Honolulu: University of Hawaii Press.

Takashima, Ken-ichi（高嶋謙一）. 1984. Nominalization and nominal derivation with particular reference to the language of oracle-bone inscriptions. Papers in *East Asian Languages* 2: 25–74. Honolulu: Department of East Asian Languages and Literatures, University of Hawaii.

Takashima, Ken-ichi. 1984–85. Noun phrases in the oracle-boneinscriptions. *Monumenta Serica* 36: 229–302.

Takashima, Ken-ichi（高嶋謙一）. 1988. An emphatic verb phrase in the oracle-bone inscriptions.*Bulletin of the Institute of History and Philology* 59 (3): 653–694. (In Memory of Dr. Fang, Kuei Li)

Takashima, Ken-ichi（高嶋謙一）. 1996. Toward a new pronominal hypothesis of *Qi* in Shang Chinese. In *Chinese Language, Thought, and Culture: Nivison and His Critics*, ed. P. J. Ivanhoe, 3–38. Chicago and La Salle: Open Court.

Takashima, Ken-ichi（高嶋謙一）. 2002. Some ritual verbs in Shang texts. *Journal of Chinese Linguistics* 30 (1): 97–141.

20

Computer Simulation of Language Convergence

Tao GONG
University of Hong Kong

Lan SHUAI
Johns Hopkins University

Umberto ANSALDO
University of Hong Kong

Abstract

Based on a lexicon-syntax coevolution model, we evaluate the effects of language-internal (e.g., the lexical or syntactic similarity of contacting languages) and language-external (e.g., the frequency of inter-group communications) factors on the convergence of two contacting languages, and reveal a lexical basis of convergence, i.e., sharing lexical items makes convergence easier than sharing syntactic features. This work extends previous simulations that usually treat languages as monolithic wholes and concentrate solely on language competition or bilingualism, instead of language convergence. The discovery of the lexical basis also sheds light on studies of other contact-induced changes, and extends theories of language contact and evolution.

1.   Introduction

Language contact, namely the prolonged interaction between speakers of different languages (Thomason and Kaufman 1988; Thomason 2001), is a topic widely discussed in historical linguistics, sociolinguistics, and language evolution. There are several possible outcomes of contact, such as competition and endangerment (due to competing for speakers, one or more contacting languages may fall out of use, Crystal 2000), e.g., many minority languages in Southwest China, such as Zhuang, Yi, or Naxi, are endangered due to competition with Mandarin (Wang 2003); bilingualism, multilingualism, and code-switching, all of which are common in a society with two or more frequently used languages (Appel and Muysken 2005), e.g., the Cantonese-English bilinguals in Hong Kong; and language convergence (the merging of lexical, morphological, or syntactic features of contacting languages, Matras and Bakker 2003). Processes of convergence can lead to lexical or grammatical borrowing, e.g., the borrowed English words in Chinese and vice versa (Cheng 1987); to pidgin/creoles formation (the creation of varieties to serve a general communicative need between groups having no common languages, Mufwene 2001), e.g., Daohua in Sichuan, China, due to contact between Chinese and Tibetan (Atshogs 2004); and to admixture, e.g., Wutun language in Qinghai, China, as a Chinese-Tibetan-Mongolian mixed language (Lee-Smith and Wurm 1996). Mixed languages tend to have many fluent native speakers and their components have identifiable sources from the original contacting languages. As in Wutun language, most of the lexical items were from Chinese, whereas the syntax was largely affected by Tibetan and Mongolian.

A variety of factors can influence language contact. For example, speakers' attitudes toward languages may cause one or more languages to lose its or their speakers, as in the case of competition between Mandarin and minority languages in China. Linguistic, as well as social, economic or political reasons can lead to these attitudes. Bilingualism and other convergence cases are often caused by communicative pressures. And in many cases of lexical borrowing, due to salience, borrowed forms are preferred by speakers (Cheng 1987). Noting these, studies of language contact aim to reveal the manners in which contact-induced changes take place and to discuss the roles of relevant factors in these processes.

In recent years, new approaches, especially mathematical and behavioral simulations, have been used to study language contact. For example, Abram and Strogatz (2003) design a mathematical model to transform language competition into differential equations that describe the transition probabilities from the state of using one language to the state of using the other. This model predicts that the initial proportions of the speakers of each language and their relative social prestige values can affect competition, which has been shown in some rather well-established generalizations in contact linguistics (see Thomason 2001; Winford 2003; Ansaldo 2009). Minett and Wang (2008) extend this mathematical model by adding the state of bilinguals to the equations, and reveal some language maintenance strategies from a bilingual perspective. Noting that these equations are purely deterministic, Minett and Wang design a multi-agent system, in which each agent refers to these equations to determine their language choices and the neighboring structures among agents are random. This stochastic, agent-based model also verifies their findings. Following this approach, Castelló et al (2006, 2008) compare these two sets of equations with social factors, such as size and multiplexity, and observe that individual volatility (speakers' willingness to shift their current languages to another) is more powerful than social prestige in causing language death, and that bilingualism actually accelerates language death.

Most of these studies focus exclusively on language competition, and individual language choice is solely decided by social prestige or network structure. Meanwhile, these studies usually treat contacting languages as monolithic wholes without internal components, and apply the transition dynamics uniformly to languages with different features. However, apart from social factors, linguistic factors also play important roles in contact, and different linguistic components may exhibit different dynamics under the same social setting (Ansaldo 2009). For example, in the case of Daohua, the Tibetan women who were married to and lived with the Han soldiers were under great communicative pressure. To communicate with their husbands about everyday issues, these women had to learn some Chinese words, since these lexical items were more salient than actual Chinese grammatical features. The Han soldiers were facing similar communicative pressure, but since their wives started to use Chinese words, these soldiers could notice the Tibetan grammar applied by their wives on those Chinese words (Atshogs 2004). This case study illustrates the necessity of examining the effects of different linguistic factors on language contact.

In this chapter, we adopt a lexicon-syntax coevolution model to evaluate the effect of language-internal and language-external factors on the convergence of contacting languages respectively spoken by individuals from two groups. Language-internal factors are introduced by adjusting the lexical items and syntactic features of these two contacting languages. Language-external factors are introduced by adjusting the ratio of inter-group communications in all communications conducted by the two groups of individuals. The simulation results and statistical analysis reveal (i) a correlation between the understandability of the mixed language and the degree of inter-group communications, and (ii) a lexical basis of convergence. In the following sections, we describe the language model and simulation setting (Section 2), report (Section 3) and discuss (Section 4) the simulation results, and finally, conclude the chapter (Section 5).

2. Computer Model and Simulation Setting

The lexicon-syntax coevolution model was designed to study whether a group of interacting individuals (artificial agents) equipped with general learning mechanisms can develop a compositional language out of a holistic signaling system. The emergent language consists of a set of common lexical items and consistent word order(s) to encode meanings with simple predicate-argument structures. Figure 20.1 shows the conceptual framework of the model. In a nutshell, during iterated communications, individuals can (i) acquire lexical items from recurrent patterns in exchanged sentences, (ii) associate lexical items with syntactic categories based on semantic and sequential information of lexical items in exchanged sentences, and (iii) form global word orders based on local orders among categories to regulate lexical items into sentences. The major components of the model, such as language encoding, learning mechanisms, and communication scenario, are introduced in the Appendix. Detailed descriptions of the model can also be found in Gong (2009, 2011).

The model simulates both the lexical and syntactic components of language, and traces the simultaneous acquisition and close interaction of lexicon and syntax during iterated communications among individuals. The model also simulates many instance-based learning mechanisms for acquiring and updating linguistic knowledge, such as pattern extraction for acquiring lexical items and sequential learning for acquiring word orders. Moreover, the model implements a detailed procedure of diadic communications, including production, perception and update of linguistic knowledge, during which both the lexical and syntactic knowledge, as well as the relevant nonlinguistic information, are used to process linguistic materials. Finally, with individuals initially sharing no or limited linguistic knowledge, the model can simulate the origin of a communal language sufficient to encode many semantic expressions; with individuals initially sharing a complete set of linguistic knowledge to encode all semantic expressions, the model can simulate language change; and by adjusting the lexical or syntactic knowledge of some individuals or setting different group identities or social connections among individuals, the model can also simulate the contact of the languages used by individuals from different groups or with different social connections. All these make the model suitable for our study of language convergence.

Based on this model, we set up two 10-individual groups. These individuals conduct inter-group (individuals for communications are chosen randomly and respectively from the two groups) and/or intra-group (individuals for communication are chosen randomly from the same group) communications. In order to examine the effect of inter-group communications on

Figure 20.1 Conceptual framework of the model
The SEMANTICS rectangle denotes the semantic space. The three ovals denote the acquired linguistic knowledge respectively via pattern extraction, sequential learning, and categorization. The EMERGENT GLOBAL ORDERS rectangle denotes the emergent syntactic patterns. Items within " " are semantic items, and syllables within // are utterances. Semantic items and utterance syllables are not necessarily identical in actual simulations.

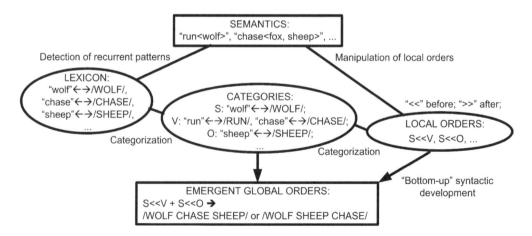

Table 20.1 Parameter setting. Marked parameters are stated in the Appendix.

Parameters	Values
No. of semantic expressions	64
No. of signals*	30
Individual buffer size*	40
Individual rule list size*	60
Utterance exchange per communication*	20
Random creation rate of holistic rules*	0.25
Rule adjustment in competition*	0.1
Rule adjustment in forgetting*	0.01
Forgetting frequency*	10
Number of Communications	6000

language convergence, we define Inter-Rate and Intra-Rate respectively as the proportions of inter-group and intra-group communications, and apply different ratios of Inter-Rate and Intra-Rate to the origin and change simulations. In order to study the effect of lexical or syntactic features on language convergence, in the change simulations, we adjust the initial lexical and syntactic knowledge of the two languages. There are two levels of lexical similarity: similar lexicon (LS), the two languages initially share a large proportion (say, 75%) of lexical rules; different lexicon (LD), these languages share no lexical items. Similarly, there are two levels of syntactic similarity: similar syntax (SS), the two languages initially share 2 out of 3 local order rules; different syntax (SD), these languages share no identical orders. In order to analyze the results, we define the understandability of the mixed language (UR_{mutual}), as the mean percentage of the semantic expressions that individuals from one group can accurately understand based on their linguistic knowledge when individuals from the other group talk to them, and the convergence time (CT_{mutual}), as the number of communications required for UR_{mutual} to be above a threshold, say 0.8.

Table 20.1 lists the parameter setting of the simulations reported in this chapter. The 64 semantic expressions can be encoded by 12 lexical rules and 3 syntactic rules. In the origin simulations, individuals in each group share 8 holistic rules to encode only 8 expressions. This resembles the limited, holistic signaling system before a compositional language. In fact, simulations starting from no linguistic rules report similar results. There are 4 ratios of Inter-Rate and Intra-Rate: 20:80, 40:60, 60:40, and 80:20, and we conduct 20 simulations under each of these ratios. In the change simulations, individuals of each group share 12 lexical rules and 3 syntactic rules. In the case of LS, the two languages share 9 randomly chosen lexical rules. In SS, one language has SV, SO, and VO (SVO), the other has SV, SO, and OV (SOV); whereas in SD, the other has VS, OS, and OV (OVS). Under each ratio, there are 4 sub-conditions: LS_

SS, LS_SD, LD_SS, LD_SD, formed by the two levels of lexical and syntactic similarities. We conduct 20 simulations in each of these sub-conditions. In each simulation, we calculate UR_{mutual} and record shared linguistic knowledge at 100 sampling points evenly distributed along 6000 communications. We also calculate CT_{mutual} based on UR_{mutual}. Note that the simulation results of this model are less dependent on the population size or the number of communications. In a bigger population, simulations report similar results, if more communications are conducted by individuals.

3.   Results and Analysis

The language origin simulations under different values of Inter-Rate and Intra-Rate show a correlation between the proportion of inter-group communications and the mutual understandability among individuals of the two groups. A one-way analysis of covariance (ANCOVA) (dependent variable: mean UR_{mutual} over 20 simulations; fixed factor: 4 ratios of Inter-Rate and Intra-Rate; covariate: number of communications) reveals a significant effect of the ratio of Inter-Rate and Intra-Rate on UR_{mutual} ($F(3,8075) = 2995.79$, $p < .001$, $n_p^2 = .527$). Figure 20.2 shows these results. Besides, covariate also has a significant effect ($F(1,8075) = 10662.342$, $p < .001$, $n_p^2 = .569$).

Figure 20.2(a) shows the marginal mean UR_{mutual} and mean CT_{mutual}. Along with the increase in the proportion of inter-group communications (Inter-Rate), UR_{mutual} increases and CT_{mutual} drops. This indicates that the two groups of individuals start to form a mixed language with good mutual understandability. Figure 20.2(b) shows an example of the shared linguistic knowledge in each group of individuals and the mixed language after 6000 communications, under the ratio of Inter-Rate and Intra-Rate as 20:80. These two groups of individuals independently develop their own languages with good understandabilities, indicated by the high UR of these languages. These two languages also share a word order SVO, formed by SV and VO local orders. However, due to lacking sufficient inter-group communications, these two languages do not share many lexical rules, and individuals using these languages cannot clearly understand each other, as shown by the low UR_{mutual}.

In the change simulations, a three-way analysis of covariance (ANCOVA) (fixed factor: the ratio of Inter-Rate and Intra-Rate, lexical similarity, and syntactic similarity; the other settings are identical to the one-way ANCOVA above) confirms the significant effect of the ratio of Inter-Rate and Intra-Rate ($F(3,32303) = 9796.165$, $p < .001$, $n_p^2 = .476$), and further reveals the significant effects of lexical ($F(1,32303) = 15517.984$, $p < .001$, $n_p^2 = .325$) and syntactic ($F(1,32303) = 281.821$, $p < .001$, $n_p^2 = .009$) similarities and their interactions ($F(1,32303) = 7391.708$, $p < .001$, $n_p^2 = .002$). Figure 20.3 shows these results. Besides, covariate also has a significant effect ($F(1,32303) = 17363.117$, $p < .001$, $n_p^2 = .350$), and there are significant interactions between lexical similarity and ratio ($F(3,32303) = 3041.353$, $p < .001$, $n_p^2 = .220$), between syntactic similarity and ratio ($F(3,32303) = 77.943$, $p < .001$, $n_p^2 = .007$), and among all

Figure 20.2 (a) Marginal mean UR_{mutual} (left y-axis) and mean CT_{mutual} (right y-axis) in the origin simulations. (b) Shared linguistic knowledge in each group of individuals and the mixed language after 6000 communications, under the ratio as 20:80. "S", "O" and "V" are syntactic roles of the categories to which lexical rules belong. As for lexical rules, numbers in ( ) are mean strengths in each group of individuals, those in / / are utterance syllables. As for local orders, numbers in ( ) are percentages of expressions individuals can accurately comprehend using particular orders.

(a)

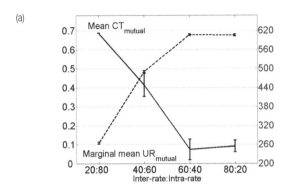

(b) Gen = 6000

Group 1:
UR = 0.898;
Common lexical rules: 10
Rule 1 (V) (0.94): 'run<#>'<->/9 /
Rule 2 (V) (0.94): 'jump<#>'<->/22 /
Rule 3 (V) (0.94): 'yell<#>'<->/24 /
Rule 4 (V) (0.94): 'flee<#>'<->/19 /
Rule 5 (V) (0.94): 'follow<#,#>'<->/5 /
Rule 6 (V) (0.93): 'fight<#,#>'<->/13 /
Rule 7 (V) (0.94): 'attack<#,#>'<->/27 /
Rule 8 (S|O) (0.94): 'wolf '<->/8 /
Rule 9 (S|O) (0.94): 'tiger '<->/3 /
Rule 10 (S|O) (0.94): 'fox '<->/7 /

Local order understandability
SV (0.623); VS (0.0);
VO (0.623); OV (0.0);
SO (0.0); OS(0.0);

Group 2:
UR = 0.98;
Common lexicla rules: 12
Rule 1 (V) (0.95): 'run<#>'<->/9 /
Rule 2 (S|O) (0.95): 'tiger '<->/3 /
Rule 3 (V) (0.95): 'chase<#,#>'<->/17 /
Rule 4 (V) (0.93): 'fight<#,#>'<->/15 /
Rule 5 (V) (0.95): 'follow<#,#>'<->/21 /
Rule 6 (V) (0.95): 'yell<#>'<->/11 /
Rule 7 (V) (0.94): 'jump<#>'<->/22 /
Rule 8 (V) (0.95): 'attack<#,#>'<->/0 /
Rule 9 (V) (0.95): 'flee<#>'<->/27 /
Rule 10 (S|O) (0.95): 'fox '<->/7 /
Rule 11 (S|O) (0.95): 'deer '<->/8 /
Rule 12 (S|O) (0.95): 'wolf '<->/28 /

Local order understandability:
SV (0.713); VS (0.0);
VO (0.713); OV (0.0);
SO (0.072); OS (0.0);

URmutual = 0.07;
Common lexical rules: 4
Rule 1 (V) (0.95): 'run<#>'<->/9 /
Rule 2 (V) (0.94): 'jump<#>'<->/22 /
Rule 3 (S|O) (0.95): 'tiger '<->/3 /
Rule 4 (S|O) (0.95): 'fox '<->/7 /

Local order understandability
SV (0.006); VS (0.0);
VO (0.006); OV (0.0);
SO (0.0); OS (0.0);

fixed factors (F(3,32303) = 61.545, p < .001, n_p^2 = .006). These results are not discussed here, since they are not our foci.

Figure 20.3(a) traces UR_{mutual} under the four ratios of Inter-Rate and Intra-Rate. Consistent with Figure 20.2(a), with the increase in the proportion of inter-group communications, UR_{mutual} increases. Figure 20.3(b) compares the effects of lexical and syntactic similarities. UR_{mutual} in the condition of LS_SS or LS_SD is higher than that in the condition of LS_SS or LD_SS, which indicates that the effect of lexical similarity is more explicit than that of syntactic similarity. Meanwhile, the two lines in Figure 20.3(b) are not parallel, which reflects the interaction between these two types of similarity. Finally, Figure 20.3(c) lists the shared linguistic knowledge in the condition of LS_SD and under the ratio of Inter-Rate and Intra-Rate as 40:60. As shown in

Figure 20.3(c), in simulation 1 (the left panel), the mixed language develops the syntax of OVS, originally from group 2, whereas in simulation 2 (the right panel), the mixed language has the syntax of SVO, originally from group 1.

4. Discussion

As shown in Figures 20.2(a) and 20.3(a), the understandability of the mixed language in our simulations correlates with the frequency of inter-group communications. In this model, learning is via iterated communications among individuals. Given sufficient instances of a language, individuals can acquire or update to this language, using their instance-based, general learning mechanisms and regardless of their available linguistic knowledge. As in the language change LD_SD condition, given sufficient inter-group communications, two initial languages having different lexical items and syntactic rules can still converge to a language having a high UR_{mutual}. These results indicate that inter-group communications are fundamental for contact-induced changes. In real-world situations, there are many ways of inducing inter-group communications, such as migration, colonization, or trade (Thomason 2001), and the degree of mixture of contacting languages can be affected by the frequency or intensity of inter-group contact.

By decomposing a language into lexical and syntactic components and comparing the convergence of languages with similar lexical and/or syntactic features, we identify a lexical basis of language convergence. As shown in Figure 20.3(b), if two contacting languages share some lexical items, they can easily converge to a mixed language with good understandability; however, if they only share some syntactic features, in terms of similar word orders, convergence may not occur easily.

This lexical basis effect is due to the fact that in our model lexical items are more salient in both semantic expressions and utterance syllables. Based on the general pattern extraction ability, individuals may first notice and grasp these surface level recurrent patterns. Only after acquiring some lexical items can individuals start to notice those less explicit recurrent patterns, in terms of similar orders (as in our model) or morphological structures (as in other models, e.g., Steels 2005) among lexical items. At that point, they can develop syntactic rules to record these deep level recurrent patterns. Now, a regular way of organizing lexical items could further help the comprehension and acquisition of new lexical items. In our model, throughout the acquisition process, acquiring lexical items is a prerequisite for acquiring syntax. This "from lexical items to syntax" or "simultaneous" acquisition process has been widely documented in both the first and second language acquisition (see Clark 2003; Bates and Goodman 1997; Fillmore 1979). Apart from normal children, that syntactic development relies upon lexical development has also been observed in atypical populations, such as the early talkers or children with brain damage (Bates et al 1995a, 1995b).

The lexical basis effect also manifests in the comprehension process. In our model, to comprehend the meanings delivered by syntactic structures, e.g., who is the action instigator or who undergoes the action, individuals have to first clarify lexical items, then, identify the

Figure 20.3   (a) Marginal mean UR_{mutual} in the change simulations, these values are the means over UR_{mutual} under four sub-conditions. (b) Marginal mean UR_{mutual} as a function of lexical (Lex) and syntactic (Syn) similarities, these values are calculated as the means over all UR_{mutual} under each ratio of Inter-Rate and Intra-Rate. (c) Two examples of the mixed languages in the condition of LS_SD and the ratio of Inter-Rate and Intra-Rate as 40:60.

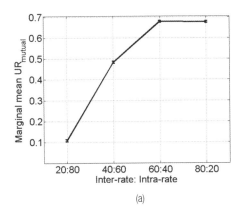

(a)

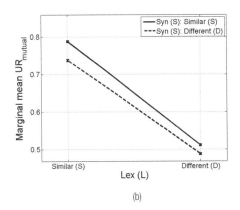

(b)

Gen = 6000

Simulation 1:
URmutual = 0.885;
Common lexical rules: 10
Rule 1 (S|O) (0.94): 'tiger '<->/18 /
Rule 2 (S|O) (0.94): 'fox '<->/27 /
Rule 3 (V) (0.93): 'flee<#>'<->/17 2 /
Rule 4 (V) (0.94): 'run<#>'<->/29 10 /
Rule 5 (V) (0.94): 'chase<#,#>'<->/13 /
Rule 6 (V) (0.94): 'fight<#,#>'<->/2 15 /
Rule 7 (S|O) (0.94): 'wolf '<->/12 /
Rule 8 (V) (0.94): 'follow<#,#> '<->/6 /
Rule 9 (V) (0.94): 'attack<#,#>'<->/22 /
Rule 10 (S|O) (0.94): 'deer '<->/0 /

Local order understandability
SV (0.0); VS (0.699);
VO (0.02); OV (0.699);
SO (0.0); OS (0.0);

Simulation 2:
URmutual = 0.932;
Common lexical rules: 12
Rule 1 (S|O) (0.94): 'tiger '<->/13 10 /
Rule 2 (S|O) (0.94): 'fox '<->/6 25 /
Rule 3 (S|O) (0.95): 'wolf '<->/2 13 /
Rule 4 (V) (0.94): 'run<#>'<->/15 12 /
Rule 5 (V) (0.94): 'jump<#>'<->/2 21/
Rule 6 (V) (0.94): 'yell<#>'<->/9 /
Rule 7 (V) (0.94): 'chase<#,#>'<->/24 2/
Rule 8 (V) (0.94): 'attack<#,#>'<->/26 /
Rule 9 (V) (0.94): 'fight<#,#>'<->/23 /
Rule 10 (V) (0.94): 'follow<#,#>'<->/22 21 /
Rule 11 (V) (0.94): 'flee<#>'<->/20 /
Rule 12 (S|O) (0.94): 'deer '<->/12 /

Local order understandability
SV (0.629); VS (0.0);
VO (0.291); OV (0.0);
SO (0.382); OS (0.0);

(c)

syntactic roles of these lexical items in utterances, and finally, notice the semantic roles of those items. Such comprehension process has also been traced in online comprehension tasks using different languages (e.g., Italian, Bates et al 1996). In many languages, lexical items are actually the carriers of linguistic knowledge, and syntax has to be applied on and reflected by lexical items, since what is needed for sentence processing, such as probabilistic, semantic, and syntactic knowledge, is all coded in lexical items (MacDonald 1994).

Although these simulations focus narrowly on the convergence of two contacting languages and the fact that sharing lexical items accelerates convergence may not be clearly traced in the limited number of case studies of language convergence, the notion of lexical basis may shed some light on studies of other contact-induced changes.

On the one hand, the lexical basis indicates that lexical items are more salient than syntactic features to speakers of different languages. During convergence or other contact-induced changes, lexical items are usually adapted first, whereas syntactic features may be adapted only under intensive contact. This is supported by the evidence that (i) many cases of language convergence start from borrowing, switching, or exchanging lexical items (Thomason and Kaufman 1988); (ii) lexical borrowing is more frequent than grammatical borrowing (Thomason 2001); and (iii) grammatical borrowing tends to occur after lexical borrowing, and can be mediated by borrowed lexical items, as in the case of French in the Prince Edward Island, which was under a great influence from English (King 2000).

On the other hand, the lexical basis could affect the emergence of pidgin/creoles. In the case of Daohua (Atshog 2004), the grammatical development took place after many Chinese lexical items were borrowed and fused in Daohua. If social prestige is involved, lexical items from a more prestigious language tend to be more salient than those from other languages. This will make the pidgin/creole between this language and other(s) preserve more lexical items from this language. The case studies of many competition-caused pidgin/creoles or thoroughly mixed languages have confirmed this prediction. For example, in Daohua and Wutun languages, lexical items were mainly from Chinese, which was more prestigious than Tibetan or Mongolian.

5. Conclusions

This chapter, based on a simulation study, discusses the effects of both language-external and language-internal factors on language convergence. It is impossible to discuss the effect of language-internal factors in some previous simulations that treat languages as monolithic wholes, but such discussion is necessary to better understand the process of contact-induced changes. In addition, the discovery of the lexical basis is insightful for studies of borrowing, switching, pidgin/creoles and thorough mixture. Furthermore, compared with the traditional linguistics means, the simulation study as evident in this chapter provides both the qualitative and quantitative results to support our conclusions. The future development in studies of language contact, change, and evolution will benefit greatly from this multi-disciplinary approach.

Acknowledgement

The work is dedicated to Prof. William S-Y. Wang on the occasion of his 80th birthday. We thank Prof. SHI Feng and Dr. PENG Gang for inviting us to contribute to this anthology.

Appendix: Lexicon-Syntax Coevolution Model

A1: Language and individuals

The model encodes language as a set of meaning-utterance mappings (M-U mappings). All individuals share a semantic space that contains a number of integrated meanings, each denoted by a predicate-argument structure, such as "*predicate<agent>*" or "*predicate<agent, patient>*". *Predicates* here denote actions that individuals can conceptualize (e.g., "run" or "chase"), and *arguments* on or by which those actions are performed (e.g., "fox" or "tiger"). Some predicates take one argument, e.g., "run<tiger>" ("a tiger is running"); others take two, e.g., "chase<tiger, fox>" ("a tiger is chasing a fox"), in which "tiger" denotes *agent* (the action instigator) of the predicate "chase", and "fox" *patient* (the entity that undergoes the action). Meanings with identical agent and patient constituents (e.g., "fight<wolf, wolf>") are excluded.

These integrated meanings are encoded by utterances. An utterance comprises a string of syllables chosen from a signaling space. An utterance that encodes an integrated meaning can be segmented into subparts, each mapping one or two semantic constituents; and subparts that map constituents can combine to encode an integrated meaning. Using predicate-argument structures to denote semantics and using combinable syllables to form utterances have been widely adopted in many structured simulations (Wagner et al. 2003).

Individuals in this model are *artificial agents*. By equipped learning mechanisms, they can acquire linguistic knowledge from M-U mappings obtained in previous communications (see A2), produce utterances to encode integrated meanings, and comprehend heard utterances in communications (see A3).

A2: Linguistic knowledge and acquisition mechanisms

Using compositional rules requires these rules to be regulated in order to form a meaningful sentence. A *syntactic rule* (see Figure A1) specifies an order between two lexical items, for example, "tiger" << "fox" denotes that the constituent "tiger" lies in an utterance *before*— but not necessarily immediately before—"fox". Based on one local order, "predicate<agent>" meanings can be expressed; based on two or three local orders, "predicate<agent, patient>" meanings can be expressed.

Syntactic categories are formed in order for syntactic rules acquired from some lexical items to be applied productively to other lexical items with the same thematic notation. A *syntactic category* (see Figure A1) comprises a set of lexical rules and a set of syntactic rules that regulate the orders between these lexical rules and those from other categories. In this model, we simply simulate a nominative-accusative language and exclude the passive voice. A category that associates lexical rules encoding the thematic notation of agent can be denoted as a *subject* (S) category, since that notation corresponds to the syntactic role of subject. Similarly, patient corresponds to *object* (O), and predicate to *verb* (V). A local order between two categories can

Figure A1 Examples of lexical rules, syntactic rules, and syntactic categories

"#" denotes unspecified semantic item, and "*" unspecified syllable(s). "S", "V", and "O" are syntactic roles of categories. Numbers within ( ) are rule strengths, and those by [ ] association weights. "<<" denotes the order before, and ">>" after. Lexical rules are itemized by letters. Compositional rules can combine, if specifying each constituent in an integrated meaning exactly once. For example, rules (c) and (d) can combine to form "chase<wolf, bear>", and the corresponding utterance is <ehfg>.

Lexical rules

Holistic rules:

(a) "chase<wolf, bear>"←→/a b/ (0.5)

(b) "hop<deer>"←→/c/ (0.4)

Compositional rules:

(c) "wolf"←→/f/ (0.6)

(d) "chase<#, bear>"←→/e h * g/ (0.7)

Syntactic rules

(1) Category 1 (S) << Category 2 (V) (SV) (0.8)

(2) Category 3 (O) >> Category 2 (V) (VO) (0.4)

Categories

Category 1 (S): *List of lexical rules:*

{"wolf"←→/b c/ (0.7)} [0.5]

List of syntactic rules:

Category 1 (S) << Category 2 (V) (0.8)

Category 3 (O) >> Category 1 (S) (0.4)

Category 2 (V): *List of lexical rules:*

{"fight<#,#>"←→/e/ (0.6)} [0.5]

List of syntactic rules:

Category 1 (S) << Category 2 (V) (0.8)

Category 3 (O): *List of lexical rules:*

{"fox"←→/a/ (0.5)} [0.7]

List of syntactic rules:

Category 3 (O) >> Category 1 (S) (0.4)

be denoted by their syntactic roles, e.g., a *before* order between an S and a V category can be denoted by S<<V, or simply SV.

Lexical and syntactic knowledge collectively help encode integrated meanings. As shown in Figure A1, to express "fight<wolf, fox>" using the lexical rules respectively from the three categories and the orders SV and SO, the created sentence should be /bcea/ or /bcae/, following SVO or SOV.

Every lexical or syntactic rule has a strength, indicating the probability of successfully using its M-U mapping or local order. A lexical rule has an association weight to the category to which it belongs, indicating the probability of successfully applying the syntactic rules of this category to the utterance of that lexical rule. Strengths and association weights lie in [0.0 1.0]. A newly-acquired rule has strength 0.5, the same as the association weight of a new association of a lexical rule to a category. These numeral parameters make possible a gradual forgetting of linguistic knowledge, which occurs regularly after a number (scaled to the population size)

Figure A2   Examples of acquisition of linguistic knowledge

(a) acquisition of lexical rules; (b) acquisition of syntactic categories and syntactic rules. M-U mappings are itemized by Arabic numbers, and lexical rules by Roman numbers.

	Available M-U mappings	**Newly acquired lexical rules**
	(1) "hop<*fox*>"←→/a b/	"fox"←→/a/ (0.5)
	(2) "run<*fox*>"←→/a c d/	

(a)   **Available M-U mappings**   **Available lexical rules**

                                                       (i) "fox"←→/d/ (0.5)

(1) "run<fox>"←→/d m/   (ii) "run<#>"←→/m/ (0.6)

(2) "run<wolf>"←→/a c m/   (iii) "wolf"←→/a c/ (0.8)

(3) "fight<fox, deer>"←→/d f k b/   (iv) "fight<#, #>"←→/b/ (0.3)

(b)   **Acquired syntactic categories and syntactic rules**

Category 1 (S): *List of lexical rules:* {"fox"←→/d/ (0.5)} [0.5]

                                             {"wolf"←→/a c/ (0.8)} [0.5]

          List of syntactic rules: Category 1 (S) << {"run<#>"←→/m/ (0.6)} (0.5)

                            ⇒ Category 1 (S) << Category 2 (V) (0.5)

Category 2 (V): *List of lexical rules:* {"run<#>"←→/m/ (0.6)} [0.5]

                                             {"fight<#,#>"←→/b/ (0.3)} [0.5]

          List of syntactic rules: Category 2 (V) >> {"fox"←→/d/ (0.5)} (0.5)

                            ⇒ Category 1 (S) << Category 2 (V) (0.5)

of communications. During forgetting, all individuals deduct a fixed amount from each of their rules' strengths and association weights. Then, the lexical or syntactic rules with negative strengths are discarded; the lexical rules with negative association weights to some categories are removed from those categories; and the categories having no lexical members are discarded, together with their syntactic members. In addition to forgetting, those numeral parameters also make possible a strength-based competition during communications (see A3).

Individuals use some general learning mechanisms to acquire linguistic knowledge. Lexical rules are acquired by detecting recurrent patterns (meanings and syllables appearing recurrently in at least two M-U mappings). Each individual has a buffer storing M-U mappings obtained from previous communications, and a rule list storing linguistic rules. New mappings, before being inserted into the buffer, are compared with those in the buffer. As shown in Figure A2(a), by comparing "hop<fox>"↔/ab/ with "run<fox>"↔/acd/, an individual can detect the recurrent patterns "fox" and /a/, and map them as a lexical rule "fox"↔/a/ with initial strength 0.5, if such a rule is not in the individual's rule list.

Syntactic categories and syntactic rules are acquired according to the thematic notations of lexical rules and the local order relations of their utterances in M-U mappings. As in Figure A2(b), evident in M-U mappings (1) and (2), syllables /d/ of rule (i) and /ac/ of rule (iii) precede /m/ of rule (ii). Since "wolf" and "fox" are both agents in these meanings, rules (i) and (iii) are associated into an S category (Category 1), and the order before between rules (i) and (iii) and rule (ii) is acquired as a syntactic rule. Similarly, in M-U mappings (1) and (3), /m/ of rule (ii) and /b/ of rule (iv) follow /d/ of rule (i), thus leading to a V category (Category 2) that associates rules (ii) and (iv) and the syntactic rule after. Now, since Categories 1 and 2 respectively associate rules (i) and (iii), and (ii) and (iv), the two syntactic rules are updated as "Category 1 (S) << Category 2 (V)", indicating that the syllables of lexical rules in the S category should precede those of lexical rules in the V category.

These learning mechanisms are traced in empirical studies (e.g., Mellow 2008), and the categorization process resembles what is described in the verb-island hypothesis (Tomasello 2003). This hypothesis states that individuals can gradually form categories to associate available and novel lexical items that encode constituents having identical thematic notations and similarly used in utterances.

A3   Communication

A communication act involves two individuals (a speaker and a listener), who perform a number of utterance exchanges, each proceeding as follows (see Figure A3).

Figure A3   Diagram of an utterance exchange
The dotted block indicates that cues are not reliable.

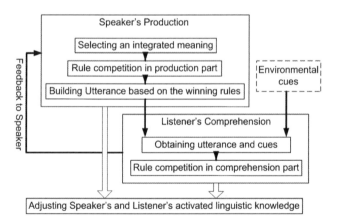

In production, the speaker (hereafter as "she") randomly selects an integrated meaning from the semantic space. Then, she activates (i) the lexical rules encoding some (compositional rules) or all (holistic rules) constituents in this meaning, (ii) the categories associating those lexical rules and having the appropriate syntactic roles, and (iii) the syntactic rules in those categories that regulate those lexical rules in sentences. These rules form the candidate sets for production. Following Equation A1 (where Avg means taking average, aso taking association weights, and str taking rule strengths), she calculates the combined strength ($CS_{production}$) of each set.

$$CS_{production} = Avg\ (str\ (LexRule\ (s))) + Avg\ (aso\ (Cats) \times str\ (SynRule\ (s)))\qquad (A1)$$

$CS_{production}$ is the sum of two parts: the lexical contribution, which is the average strength of the lexical rules in this set; and the syntactic contribution, which is the average product of the strengths of the syntactic rules regulating the lexical rules and the association weights of those lexical rules to the categories in this set. As in Figure A1, the three categories, three lexical rules "wolf", "fight" and "fox", and two syntactic rules SV and SO form a candidate set to encode "fight<wolf, fox>". $CS_{production}$ of this set is 0.98, in which the lexical contribution is 0.6 {(0.7 + 0.6 + 0.5)/3} and the syntactic contribution is 0.38 {(0.8 × (0.7 + 0.6)/2 + 0.4 × (0.7 + 0.5)/2)/2)}.

After calculation, the speaker identifies the set of winning rules that has the highest $CS_{production}$, builds up the sentence accordingly, and transmits the sentence to the listener. If lacking sufficient rules to encode the meaning, she may occasionally (based on a random creation rate) create a holistic rule to encode the meaning.

In comprehension, the listener (hereafter as "he") receives the sentence from the speaker and an environmental cue. The integrated meaning in the cue is set according to the *reliability of cue* (*RC*). For example, if RC is 0.6, there is a 60% chance that the cue contains the speaker's intended meaning; otherwise, the cue contains an integrated meaning that is distinct from the speaker's intended one and randomly chosen from the semantic space. This way of setting avoids mind-reading. After iterated communications, mutual understanding based on linguistic knowledge can be achieved. After receiving these inputs, based on his linguistic knowledge, the listener activates (i) the lexical rules whose syllables fully or partially match the heard sentence, (ii) the categories that associate these lexical rules, and (iii) the syntactic rules in those categories whose orders match those of the lexical rules in the heard sentence. These rules form the candidate sets for comprehension.

Here, the cue may assist comprehension. For example, if the cue's meaning matches exactly the one comprehended by some linguistic rules, the cue is combined with those rules to form a candidate set. If the available rules fail to provide a complete integrated meaning, but the constituent(s) specified by these rules matches that (those) in the cue's meaning, the cue is combined with those rules to form a candidate set, and its meaning becomes the meaning of this set. For example, if the available rules interpret the heard utterance as "chase<tiger, #>", with unspecified patient, and the cue's meaning is "chase<tiger, sheep>", then, the cue is combined with those rules, and "chase<tiger, sheep>" becomes the meaning of this set. Finally, if there are no rules, or the available ones fail to provide an integrated meaning and the constituent(s) specified by these rules contradicts with that (those) in the cue's meaning, the cue itself forms a candidate set.

Following Equation A2, the listener calculates the combined strength of each set. As for a set without a cue, $CS_{comprehension}$ is identical to $CS_{production}$; as for a set with a cue, $CS_{comprehension}$ includes the cue strength; and as for a set with only a cue, the cue strength becomes $CS_{comprehension}$.

$$CS_{comprehension} = Avg\ (str\ (LexRule\ (s))) + Avg\ (aso\ (Cats) \times str\ (SynRule\ (s))) + str\ (Cue)$$

$$(A2)$$

After calculation, the listener selects the set of winning rules that has the highest $CS_{comprehension}$ and interprets the heard sentence accordingly. If $CS_{comprehension}$ of the winning rules exceeds a confidence threshold, the listener adds the perceived M-U mapping to his buffer, and transmits a positive feedback to the speaker. Then, both individuals reward their winning rules by adding a fixed amount to their strengths and association weights, and penalize other competing ones by deducting the same amount from their strengths and association weights. Otherwise, without adding the perceived mapping to the buffer, the listener sends a negative feedback, and both individuals penalize their winning rules. Such linear inhibition mechanism has been adopted in many other models (e.g., Steels et al 2007). For activated rules having initial values of strength and association weight, the linguistic (lexical and syntactic) contribution is 0.75 $\{0.5 + 0.5 \times 0.5\}$. In order to equally treat linguistic and non-linguistic information, we set both the cue strength and confidence threshold as 0.75.

Throughout the utterance exchange, there is no check whether the speaker's encoded meaning matches the listener's decoded one. Equations A1 and A2 exemplify a multi-level selection among lexical, syntactic, and nonlinguistic information (Steels et al 2007), and illustrate how nonlinguistic information assists linguistic comprehension, by clarifying constituent(s) unspecified by linguistic rules and strengthening rules contributing to similar interpretations. Competition and forgetting collectively lead to conventionalization (Burling 2005) of linguistic knowledge among individuals. This model simulates the detailed processing of lexical and syntactic information during communications, and implements a realistic communication scenario avoiding direct meaning transfer (Smith 2001).

REFERENCES

Abram, D. M., and S. H. Strogatz. 2003. Modeling the dynamics of language death. *Nature* 424:900.

Ansaldo, U. 2009. *Contact Languages: Ecology and Evolution in Asia*. Cambridge: Cambridge University Press.

Appel, R., and P. Muysken. 2005. *Language Contact and Bilingualism*. London: Edward Arnold.

Atshogs, Y. V. 2004. *Research on Daohua*. Beijing: Ethnic Publishing House.

Bates, E., P. Dale, and D. Thal. 1995a. Individual differences and their implications for theories of language development. In *Handbook of Child Language*, eds. P. Fletcher, and B. MacWhinney, 96–151. Oxford: Basil Blackwell.

Bates, E., V. Marchman, C. Harris, B. Wulfeck, and M. Kritchevshy. 1995b. Production of complex syntax in normal ageing and Alzheimer's disease. *Language and Cognitive Processes* 10 (5): 487–539.

Bates, E., A. Devescovi, A. Hernandez, and L. Pizzamiglio. 1996. Gender priming in Italian. *Perception and Psychophysics* 58 (7): 992–1004.

Bates, E., and J. C. Goodman. 1997. On the inseparability of grammar and the lexicon: Evidence from acquisition, aphasia and real-time processing. *Language and Cognitive Processes* 12 (5–6): 507–584.

Castello, X., V. M. Eguíluz, and M. S. Miguel. 2006. Ording dynamics with two non-excluding options: Bilingualism in language competition. *New Journal of Physics* 8:308–322.

Castello, X., V. M. Eguíluz, M. S. Miguel, L. Loureiro-Porto, R. Toivonen, J. Saramäki, and K. Kaski. 2008. Modelling language competition: Bilingualism and complex social networks. In *The Evolution of Language: Proceedings of the 7th International Conference (EVOLANG7)*, eds. A. Smith, K. Smith, and R. Ferrer i Cancho, 59–66. Singapore: World Scientific Publishing Co.

Cheng, R. L. 1987. Borrowing and internal development in lexical change. *Journal of Chinese Linguistics* 15:105–131.

Clark, E. V. 2003. *First Language Acquisition*. Cambridge: Cambridge University Press.

Crystal, D. 2000. *Language Death*. Cambridge: Cambridge University Press.

Fillmore, L. W. 1979. Individual differences in second language acquisition. In *Individual Differences in Language Ability and Language Behavior*, eds. C. J. Fillmore, D. Kempler, and W. S-Y. Wang, 203–228. New York: Academic Press.

Gong, T. 2009. *Computational Simulation in Evolutionary Linguistics: A Study on Language Emergence*. Taipei: Institute of Linguistics, Academia Sinica.

Gong, T. 2011. Simulating the coevolution of compositionality and word order regularity. *Interaction Studies* 12 (1): 63–106.

King, R. E. 2000. *The Lexical Basis of Grammatical Borrowing: A Prince Edward Island French Case Study*. Amsterdam: Benjamins.

Lee-Smith, M. W., and S. A. Wurm. 1996. The Wutun language. In *Atlas of Languages of Intercultural Communication in the Pacific, Asia, and the Americas*, eds. S. A. Wurm, P. Mühlhäusler, and D. T. Tyron, 883–898. Berlin: Mouton de Gruyter.

Macdonald, M. C. 1994. Probabilistic constraints and syntactic ambiguity resolution. *Language and Cognitive Processes* 9 (2): 157–201.

Matras, Y., and P. Bakker, eds. 2003. *The Mixed Language Debate: Theoretical and Empirical Advances*. Berlin: Mouton de Gruyter.

Mellow, J. D. 2008. The emergence of complex syntax: A longitudinal case study of the ESL development of dependency resolution. *Lingua* 118 (4): 499–521.

Minett, J. W., and W. S-Y. Wang. 2008. Modeling endangered languages: The effects of bilingualism and social structure. *Lingua* 118 (1): 19–45.

Smith, A. D. M. 2001. Establishing communication systems without explicit meaning transmission. In *Advances in Artificial Life*, eds. J. Kelemen, and P. Sosik, 381–390. London: Springer-Verlag.

Steels, L. 2005. The emergence and evolution of linguistic structure: From lexical to grammatical communication systems. *Connection Science* 17 (3–4): 213–230.

Steels, L., R. van Trijp, and R. Wellens. 2007. Multi-level selection in the emergence of language systematicity. In *Proceedings of 9th European Conference on Artificial Life*, eds. F. Almeida e Costa, L. M. Rocha, and I. Harvey, 425–434. Berlin: Springer-Verlag.

Thomason, S. G., and T. Kaufman. 1988. *Language Contact, Creolization, and Genetic Linguistics*. Berkeley, CA: University of California Press.

Thomason, S. G. 2011. *Language Contact: An Introduction*. Edinburgh, UK: Edinburgh University Press.

Tomasello, M. 2003. *Constructing A Language: A Usage-Based Theory of Language Acquisition*. Cambridge, MA: Harvard University Press.

Wagner, K., J. A. Reggia, J. Uriagereka, and G. S. Wilkinson. 2003. Progress in the simulation of emergent communication and language. *Adaptive Behavior* 11 (1): 37–69.

Wang, William. S-Y. 2003. Yunnan and her cultural treasures. *International Association of Chinese Linguistics Newsletter* 11:3–5.

Winford, D. 2003. *An Introduction to Contact Linguistics*. Malden, MA: Blackwell.

Mufwene, S. S. 2001. *The Ecology of Language Evolution*. Cambridge, MA: Cambridge University Press.

21

On the Evolution of Language and Brain*

Sydney LAMB
Rice University

Abstract

This chapter looks into the controversial question of whether the evolution of language was a gradual long-range process or one that occurred over a relatively short time span.* I intend to show that putting the debate in terms of these two alternatives is misleading, as the situation is more complex than they allow for. Thus the question cannot be given either of these two simple answers. This issue is related to the relationship between language evolution and the evolution of the brain. It has been proposed (Deacon 1992; Schoenemann 2009) that the gradual evolution of language contributed to the evolution of the brain and vice-versa——the co-evolution theory. While attractive at first glance, this theory has serious problems. The real explanation for the great increase in brain capacity of humans lies elsewhere, in an altogether unsuspected non-linguistic realm.

---

*   It is gratifying to me to be able to add these remarks to the impressive collection of contributions that have been made to this topic over the years by Professor Wang.

"Nothing in biology makes sense except in the light of evolution"

Theodosius Dobzhansky

1.   Humans and Chimpanzees

As is well known, humans have much larger brains than chimpanzees, our closest relatives. We also differ from them in communicating with very complex linguistic structures. The idea that these two properties are interrelated has led to the theory of co-evolution of language and brain (Deacon 1992; Schoenemann 2009), at first glance very appealing. Since the evolution of the brain was surely a gradual process, the co-evolution hypothesis is consistent with the doctrine of gradual evolution of language.

But the contrast between humans and chimpanzees is not just a matter of the differences in brain size and in communicative skills. Humans and chimps also differ greatly in other physical features as well as in behavior. Among the profound physical differences are these: (i) humans have legs that are well suited not only for walking but also for running rapidly and for great distances; (ii) human bodies are adapted for skillful swimming and diving, including a large variety of swimming strokes; (iii) humans have far less complex digestive systems; (iv) our head shapes are markedly different, beyond the difference in cranial size; (v) we have comparatively little body hair but long head hair. We are led to ask how such profound differences could arise from such a small difference in DNA (about 1% or 2%), and what caused or allowed such extensive differences in the short time span that has elapsed since our common ancestors were present (about 6 million years ago). This time span is about the same as that for the genus Equus (horses, zebras, asses). Their physical forms are much closer to one another, such that they all occupy the same genus. By contrast, the line of descent of humans from their common ancestors goes through several genera, such as Australopithecus.

Looking at behavior, we likewise see profound differences. Chimpanzees spend several hours every day chewing food. Humans spend relatively only very little time eating, and most of their time is spent in linguistic activity of one kind or another, including silent speech. We also engage in richly varied activities that are quite foreign to chimp (and other primate) behavior. We make and wear clothing and jewelry; we dance and sing; we produce literature and opera; we build buildings, cities, and transportation systems; we construct and use economic institutions such as banks, corporations, mortgages; we have athletic contests and spectator sports: etc.

It can be argued that these distinctive human behaviors derive from the fact that we have language, but that argument goes only so far. It might help to account for our development of economic institutions, but it can hardly explain our propensity to adorn our bodies with manufactured objects (like jewelry); to dance; to make and enjoy music and manufacture musical instruments; or to engage in such a great variety of physical activities and games. On the other hand, these properties of being human can reasonably be related to our large brains. For example, the great variety of swimming strokes that we are capable of, and other enormously diverse kinds of activities requiring physical dexterity, require highly developed motor and pre-motor cortices. The relevance of these observations may become more apparent as I develop my argument.

2.   The Co-evolution Hypothesis

The idea of co-evolution of brain and language has been put forth by Terrence Deacon (1992, 1997), and by P. Thomas Schoenemann (2009). As mentioned, the hypothesis is compatible with the view that the evolution of language was a long process, taking place over a period of hundreds of thousands, or even millions, of years. The contrasting view may be called, for short, the "brain-first hypothesis". It holds that the brain evolved first, then language. The implication of this hypothesis is that language evolution was a short process: Most of it would have occurred in less than 200,000 years, and possibly far less, since the brain may not have been fully developed until about 200 thousand years ago (hereinafter "kya").

According to Schoenemann, a "critical driving force of the evolution of the human brain must have been language" (2009, 191). He also writes of "a coevolutionary process in which both language and brain evolved to suit each other" (ibid., with reference to Deacon 1992). The argument in favor of co-evolution is straightforward: Greater language skills would confer advantages in social interaction as well as in thinking, and would therefore be selected for. Greater language skills require greater intellectual equipment, and since greater intellectual equipment would likewise be selected for. Further development of linguistic capability would thus have contributed to further development of relevant brain equipment and vice versa.

In his presentation of supporting evidence, Schoenemann points out that human brains are about 3 times larger than ape brains. And although mammal brain size tends to correlate with body size, the human brain exceeds predictions on this basis by 5–7 fold (Schoenemann 2009, 200). Moreover, some parts of the human brain are disproportionally even larger, including portions of the cortex that support language. Of particular importance as areas that support language are the angular gyrus and supramarginal gyrus (in the lower parietal lobe), the upper and posterior portions of the temporal lobe, and parts of the prefrontal lobe, especially in the inferior frontal gyrus (Broca's area).

Now, as a caution to those who, like Schoenemann, may be tempted to make too much of this observation, we have to recognize that the cortical areas that are disproportionally larger in humans are *not just* those that particularly support language. They include the *higher-level cortical areas in general*; that is, the associative areas (mainly in temporal and parietal lobes) and the so-called executive areas in the frontal lobes. To understand the situation clearly, we may observe that the cortex of any mammal can be seen as comprising primary areas—primary visual, primary somatosensory, primary auditory, and primary motor—together with higher level areas. The cortex of a rat is mostly devoted to the primary areas; that of a cat still has a large proportion devoted to the primary areas, but also a moderate amount of associative cortex, so-called because it provides association of the information from more than one sensory modality. The proportion of cortex devoted to such associative structures is even greater in primates, and far greater in humans.

The human cortex is also distinguished in having far more brain tissue in the "executive" areas of the frontal lobe, areas which function at a level higher than the associative areas. The executive areas have connections to the associative areas and so are able to use all of that integrated sensory information, but they also (in keeping with their location near motor structures) have the power to use such integrated sensory information to formulate plans and strategies for behavior. The higher-level cortical structures thus provide not just for language but for integration of sensory information, abstract thinking, planning, imagination, foreseeing the probable outcomes of planned activities, and other higher level intellectual processes. Also, besides being far more highly developed in humans than in any other mammal, the pre-frontal lobes are the latest to reach full physical development. It is not until the early twenties that a human has the full capacity developed for these pre-frontal functions. (When my granddaughter once complained that other members of the family were making decisions that affected her without taking full account of her wishes, I pointed out to her that her pre-frontal lobes were not yet fully developed.)

These considerations tend to weaken the appeal of the co-evolution hypothesis. It is not just the language areas of the cortex that are more highly developed in humans, it is the higher-level areas in general, the areas that support general intelligence, planning abilities, and behavioral complexity and dexterity—all of which would seem to confer advantages on those endowed with them, thus leading to competitive advantages of diverse kinds and thus to gradual spread over time. The argument that gradual evolution of language would promote gradual evolution of the cortical structures that support language leaves unexplained the fact that cortical structures that support all the additional features of human intelligence were also evolving.

Be that as it may (and we shall return to the implications of this thought), it needs to be pointed out here that the human cortex not only has far more gray matter than those of chimps (and all other mammals), particularly in the higher-order cortical areas; it also is considerably richer in white matter. The white matter consists of connections among different cortical areas, in the form of myelinated axons. The myelin provides insulation to avoid "cross-talk" among neighboring axons in a bundle (which are likely to have mutually competitive functions), and it also greatly enhances the speed of conduction of neural impulses. It is also white in color, a property that explains why the white matter is so called. A relatively new imaging technique using MRI, called diffusion tensor imaging, shows that, comparing human and chimpanzee brains, it is not just the case that the human cortex has more gray matter, it also has richer connectivity, branching to more areas (Ghazanfar 2008). Such additional connectivity, while it probably contributes to greater linguistic skills, also contributes to general intelligence.

3.   Reservation about Co-evolution

As mentioned above, the co-evolution hypothesis relies on language to explain the extensive growth of higher-level cortical areas, leaving unsettled the issue of why so much of this added cortical territory is used for extralinguistic abilities of humans. An additional reservation concerns a related question.

The co-evolution hypothesis treats language as one object. But it is not just one thing, represented in one part of the brain. What we call "language" is a composite of several capacities, belonging to the categories of phonology, lexicon, grammar, and semantics. These different types of structure are supported by different cortical areas. In fact, each of them taken separately is represented in multiple cortical areas.

For example, phonology consists of two different systems having three different cortical representations: Articulatory phonology is subserved by the mouth portion of the primary motor cortex together with Broca's area, along with supporting sub-cortical structures like the basal ganglia; and articulation also requires somatosensory monitoring, subserved by the mouth portion of the primary somatosensory cortex along with the supra-marginal gyrus. The second major system is auditory phonology, subserved by the primary auditory cortex and Wernicke's area (along with sub-cortical structures).

Similarly, the higher levels are subserved by several different areas, and these areas also have non-linguistic functions. In short, what we call "Language" is a composite of multiple capacities, supported by multiple areas of the cortex. Therefore, the co-evolution could apply to some parts of linguistic structure but not to others

4. The "Recapitulation Hypothesis"

Thinking about the co-evolution hypothesis and its implication that the evolution of language was very gradual, the next questions are, what were the steps of this long process, and how did it get started? We are of course hampered by the absence of any fossil evidence and we need some basis for proceeding other than by pure speculation. One possibility to explore in this connection is the recapitulation hypothesis.

If the "ontogeny recapitulates phylogeny" principle applies to the evolution of language, it would follow that the evolution of language parallels, to some significant extent, the process of language development in children. We can therefore study language development in children to get evidence for the evolution of language. To the casual observer, the major stages in human linguistic ontogeny include, first, the development of phonological agility, with babbling an important milestone, beginning at around six to seven months; next, the acquisition of words, about 50 by age one and up to 150 or more by age 2. Most of these early words are concrete nouns (object names). Many more are then acquired rapidly from age 2 on. And from about this point we also observe the beginnings and then the growth of grammar, with two-word utterances by age 2–2 ½, consisting mainly of Verb plus Noun and Adjective plus Noun.

At first glance the recapitulation hypothesis appears quite attractive, but we have to be cautious, as there are differences in the contexts of the two processes (phylogeny and ontogeny). Most important, modern children have an already developed adult model to follow. It is provided to them by their mothers and older siblings and other playmates. Early hominins had no such models. One very important aspect of this already developed model is that it incorporates the principle of *duality of patterning*, of which more below. A second advantage of modern children is that they have (though not yet as infants) more fully evolved vocal apparatus than did early hominins, allowing them to make clear distinctions among different vowels and consonants (more on this below).

We have to conclude, with a bit of disappointment, that ontogeny—language development in children—may not recapitulate phylogeny after all, at least not in detail for the overall process. It is nevertheless possible to hold on to the idea that the principle applies to certain early aspects of linguistic evolution (see below).

5.   Duality of Patterning

Charles Hockett used the term *duality of patterning* for one of the design features of language (Hockett and Altmann 1968). This feature is also known by Martinet's term *double articulation*. It is a major part of what Hockett elsewhere (1961), along with Gleason (e.g., 1964) and Lamb (e.g., 1964), called *stratification*. With only one level of patterning, sounds relate directly to meanings, with the consequent limitation that it is possible for the system to have only as many lexemes as it has distinct sounds. Notice that this is not the same as saying that it would be able to express only as many meanings as it has distinct sounds, since a lexeme can express more than one meaning (homonymy). This type of system, used by various non-human animals, has just one level of patterning.

With duality of patterning, we have first phonological patterning, second, lexico-grammatical structure (or lexis for short in Halliday's terminology). So from two or three dozen phonemes we can form (in a typical language) a few thousand different morphemes by using multiple phonemes in different combinations, and tens of thousands of lexemes. From them, because of polysemy, we have the potential to represent any of hundreds of thousands of concepts. We are actually dealing here not just with two but with multiple levels, hence the appropriateness of the more general term *stratification*. So, in a more general view, we get, in a typical language, a few dozen phonemes as combinations of about one dozen distinctive features, a few thousand morphemes as combinations of these phonemes, tens of thousands of lexemes, and hundreds of thousands of concepts. And syntactic techniques allow us to freely build representations of indefinitely many new concepts.

The situation may be compared to the structure of matter: From three subatomic particles, proton, electron, and neutron, we get about 90 different elements (not counting those created by atomic physicists); from them are formed thousands of different simple molecular structures, from which can be formed millions of more complex molecules.

All human languages, in contrast to the communication systems of all other primates, have expression systems based on syllables, and it is their diversity of form that allows for a large number of distinct meaningful units. The syllable is a short unit based on a difference between consonant and vowel (a distinction likewise not found in communication systems of other primates). In the simple case it is the open syllable—no final consonant. We can see this simple syllable in development in the babbling stage of modern babies, and we can perhaps apply the recapitulation hypothesis here to reach the supposition that early syllables in linguistic evolution were likewise open. This basic unit—the syllable—tends to be taken for granted by linguists, who generally focus on higher-level structures. But since the ability to produce syllables is beyond the capability of all other primates, it is something that had to evolve before higher linguistic levels could develop.

The syllable provides enormous potential for communication. Even a very primitive phonological system with three vowels /i a u/ and nine initial consonants, / b d g s h m n w y/, provides for 27 different syllables (9 x 3), or 30 if we include syllables with no initial consonant. Since syllables can occur at the rate of about 4 or 5 per second (in adult modern human speech), they can convey information at an enormous rate of speed in comparison with simpler systems.

Such a system is like that of a child approaching one year of age, with the words consisting of one syllable or, more commonly, two identical syllables, as in 'mama', 'dada'. Of course, the maximum potential of thirty different words is never fully utilized, but, on the other hand, it easily expands into (i) much greater syllabic diversity by making use of diphthongs, closed syllables, additional consonants and vowels. and (ii) still greater diversity by using sequences of differing syllables in the word.

6.   Evolution of the Human Vocal Tract

The development of phonological structure was not just a neurological matter. It required changes in the physical structure of the vocal tract. Even a simple system like that sketched above, with its thirty possible syllables, presupposes a degree of vocal dexterity that is altogether lacking in chimpanzees and probably was only partly within the capabilities of Neanderthals, but without clear articulation of the different vowels and consonants (see Figure 21.1).

The vocal tract as a whole has a sub-laryngeal part, consisting of the lungs and trachea, which provides air flow upon which operations are performed to provide diversity of sound. This sub-laryngeal portion is able to produce variations in stress and volume, while the larynx provides voicing (or its absence) by means of its vocal cords, which can also form glottal stops. Their rate of vibration provides the fundamental frequency, which can be varied to provide diversity of pitch. A little further laryngeal variation is also available, like whispering, "creaky voice", and falsetto.

But by far the preponderance of diversity of speech is provided by the supra-laryngeal vocal tract ("SVT"), which in modern humans has two major portions of roughly equal size, situated at about a 90° angle relative to each other, the vertical portion (SVTv), in the pharynx, and the horizontal portion (SVTh), in the oral cavity (Figure 21.1). The SVTh portion and the SVTv portion are almost equal in length. There is a natural discontinuity formed by the intersection of SVTh and SVTv that permits abrupt changes in the cross-sectional area of the human SVT at its midpoint (Lieberman 2007). These differences are shaped by the tongue.

The variations of SVT structure brought about by tongue positioning allow a much greater range of sounds to be produced by humans than by chimpanzees and other primates, all of whom have a relatively much larger horizontal portion and a much smaller vertical portion. In fact their "vertical" portion is not vertical at all but is slanted relative to the mouth cavity at roughly a 45°

Figure 21.1   The adult human supralaryngeal vocal tract

The adult human supralaryngeal vocal tract,showing the almost circular posterior contour of the tongue. The SVTh portion and the SVTv portion are almost equal in length. There is a natural discontinuity formed by the intersection of SVTh and SVTv that permits abrupt changes in the cross-sectional area of the human supralaryngeal vocal tract at its midpoint (from Lieberman 2007).

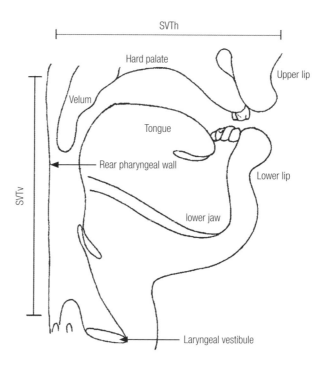

angle (instead of approximately 90°. The tongue is mostly in the mouth in these primates, and they can therefore do very little with the pharyngeal portion of their SVTs, with the consequence that they have very little ability to produce different vowels and consonants.

We think of the tongue as occupying the oral cavity, but it also has a large unseen portion in the pharynx, in which it has an almost circular posterior contour (Lieberman 2007). It can move freely within the SVTv to adjust the size of the passageway, just as it does in the mouth. And since its volume does not change, when it moves to a low position in the mouth (as for [a]) its lower portion moves backward, narrowing the size of the SVTv. And for [i] we get the opposite effect, with a narrow opening in the oral cavity, since the tongue is raised, together with a large opening in the pharynx. For [u] both portions of the SVT are moderately open and the lips are protruded and rounded. These three vowels, [i] [a] [u], have "perceptually salient acoustic properties that can be produced with a certain degree of articulatory sloppiness" (Lieberman 2007). According to Lieberman and McCarthy (2007), "…the vocal tracts of other living primates are physiologically incapable of producing such vowels."

So the evolution of the SVT looms large in what has to have been a long development leading to duality of patterning. In the process of evolution there had to be a change of SVT structure from that observed in chimps, presumably like that of our common ancestors, to that of modern humans. Luckily, it is possible to determine the SVT structure of pre-sapiens hominins from skeletal remains (Lieberman and McCarthy 2007). It turns out that even Neanderthals, the latest in the fossil record leading up to Homo sapiens, did not have the modern human form: "Neanderthal necks were too short to accommodate human vocal tracts" (Lieberman 2007, 47). And Lieberman and McCarthy (2007) even assert that the modern shape of the SVT was not fully developed even in *Homo sapiens* fossils of 100,000 years ago. That is a very recent date within the long period of human evolution from our common ancestry with chimps, and it could have an important bearing on the question of whether the evolution of language was a long gradual process or a short one.

This statement of Lieberman and McCarthy, that the modern form of the SVT was not even present in Homo sapiens fossils of 100,000 years ago, is based upon the examination of a single fossil from the Skhul community dated at about 100 kya. Since this claim is crucial for the concerns of the present paper, it invites careful assessment. There are two reasons for caution in interpreting their evidence: First, mutations spread gradually through populations; second, the Skhul people are just one group of the humans who were alive at the time, and perhaps not truly representative.

First, mutations spread gradually through populations. A mutation starts in one individual (or perhaps a few) and it can then be passed on to succeeding generations if it confers advantages of survival and reproduction, as those who have it will produce more offspring than those without the mutation. It thus spreads through the population during succeeding generations, and in ordinary circumstances the spread is quite gradual. Therefore, there is a period of several or many generations during which some members of a population have it and others do not. The mutation or series of mutations under consideration here resulted in the lowering of the larynx, with concomitant change in the tongue, and thereby enabled its carriers to articulate vowels more clearly than those without it, while also probably enhancing the clarity of production of certain consonants and the contrast between vowel and consonant. As the descended larynx of modern humans is so different from what is found in other primates, even other hominins, there may have been two or more mutations leading step-by-step to the form seen in modern Homo sapiens.

And so we have to ask, with respect to any of those two or three intermediate stage(s), how great was the survival and/or reproductive advantage of being able to articulate vowels (as well as some consonants) with greater ease and clarity? It is probably not the case that those without the modern form of the SVT couldn't articulate vowels at all. Perhaps, like a modern eight-month old, they could produce three unclear but roughly distinct approximations to [i] [a] [u], while those with the mutation were able to produce them clearly and with ease. We can compare the situation to that observed in modern times among people of varying communicative skill. How great is the reproductive advantage of skillful and fluent speakers over those who lack such skills? Probably not so great that the mutation would spread rapidly through the population. The process of spread from the first few individuals to its presence within most of the surviving human population could have taken tens of thousands of years.[1] And so at a time in the middle of that period, about half the population would have had it. In that case a single sample would have a fifty-fifty chance of exhibiting a descended larynx. Therefore, a lone fossil cannot be considered as reliable evidence.

The second reason for skepticism about the claim of Lieberman and McCarthy is that the Skhul people are just one group of the humans who were alive at the time, and not even a representative group, as they were not in Africa, which was still the home of most of the Homo sapiens population of 100,000 years ago. The name Skhul is that of a cave on the slopes of Mount Carmel in Israel, where human fossils were found between 1929 and 1935 (Wikipedia). The remains, which exhibit a mix of archaic and modern traits, have been tentatively dated at about 80,000–120,000 years old using electron spin resonance and thermoluminescence dating techniques (Wikepedia). The brain case is similar to modern humans, but they possess brow ridges and a projecting facial profile, similar to that of the Neanderthals. They were initially regarded as transitional fossils between Neanderthals and modern humans, but they are now regarded as a separate lineage from the Neanderthals, and may represent an early exodus of modern humans from Africa around 125,000 years ago (Wikepedia). It is considered likely that they had died out by 80,000 years ago because of drying conditions (Oppenheimer 2003).

And so the Skhul people are just one group of the humans who were alive at the time in question, and not a representative group, since they were not in Africa. If, as is likely, they died out about 80,000 years ago, we are not descended from them. Modern humans are descended from people who were still in Africa at the time of the Skhul people.

Therefore, even if all the Skhul people lacked the modern form of the SVT, we are not permitted to conclude that it was not present in other human groups, in particular, those who were still in Africa.

We therefore do not have any reliable evidence on the time of emergence of the modern human form of the SVT. The only conclusion we can reach with some assurance is that the first Homo sapiens, of perhaps around 200,000 years ago, may not yet have had a fully descended larynx. We can surmise that the descent of the larynx involved more than one mutation and that the process of spread of each of them through the human population took place over a period of tens of thousands of years (perhaps less under the scenario of note 1). So the whole series of two or three (or more?) steps must have taken correspondingly much longer. Since Neanderthals had evidently not even started the process, the first step must have occurred at some point after the split of the Homo sapiens lineage from that of the Neanderthals, about 500 kya. It may have been well underway by 200 kya, the likely date of the earliest Homo sapiens (cf. Brown and

---

1. Another possibility is a more direct enhancement of reproduction for those having the mutation as a result of their enhanced vocal ability. A young man with good vocal production may have been more attractive to females, just as modern rock stars attract modern girls, or as in an earlier generation Frank Sinatra caused girls to "swoon" at his concerts. Such an early singing sensation would have had a seduction advantage that would allow him to impregnate numerous women, leading to a relatively large number of sons who would carry on his seductive tradition. In this scenario the spread of the mutation would have been considerably faster.

Siegel 2005; O'Neil 1999–2012); and it may have reached completion by around 100 kya, or at latest by about 70 or 60 kya, the latest putative date at which the ancestors of all present non-African humans began to leave Africa. That long time span represents a considerable range of uncertainty, but I think it is the best we can do with presently available evidence.

7.   Phonological Dexterity and Brain Structure

The development of phonological dexterity was not just a matter of physical changes in the SVT. It also required changes in brain structure, both for production and for perception. On the articulatory side, refinement of neurological structures for speaking in syllables with clearly articulated consonants and vowels was needed in the mouth region of the primary motor cortex, Broca's area, and the basal ganglia. On the auditory side, it was probably necessary to enhance the neural structures in the primary auditory cortex and the posterior superior temporal gyrus (Wernicke's area), to allow for the fine discrimination needed, for example, to recognize the differences between stops of different articulatory positions. The clues for recognizing these differences of articulatory position are mainly in the (very rapid) transitions from the consonant to the vowel, and are thus easily missed by hearers lacking highly developed perceptual structure.

A gene, FoxP2, has been identified that seems to have played an important role on the articulatory side. Members of the KE family have a defective variant of FoxP2. It affects basal ganglia and mouth and face areas of frontal lobe. Affected members of the family have impaired phonological production and grammar. They can't position their tongues to enable clear speech. The FoxP2 gene governs embryonic development of neural structures that regulate motor control as well as aspects of cognition and emotion.

It is important to appreciate that while this gene affects phonological production and some features of syntax, it does not deserve the appellation 'language gene' that has been conferred on it by some, since these constitute only parts of linguistic structure: not all of phonology and not all of syntax. It does not affect, for example, phonological recognition (Wernicke's area), lexical information (much of which is in the angular gyrus), and semantics. Moreover, FoxP2 affects oral motor structures generally, not just articulatory phonology. KE family members with the defective variant of FoxP2 have "severe bucco-facial apraxia" (e-mail from Elizabeth Bates). The gene affects aspects of cognition and emotion and even lung structure. In other words, the modern human form of FoxP2 is a prerequisite for modern human speech, but it is not the only prerequisite, and its functions are not limited to language.

FoxP2 is present in different varieties in all mammals. Only 3 mutations separate the human form from the mouse form, and only 2 mutations separate the human form from the chimp form (Lieberman and McCarthy 2007). The modern human form may have appeared only in the last 200,000 years or so and in that case we have another reason for concluding that Neanderthals had very limited phonological abilities and therefore very limited vocabularies. According to Lieberman and McCarthy, "This time frame [i.e., within the last 200,000 years] corresponds with the emergence of anatomically modern humans, suggesting that this genetic variant may have conferred the increased motor control over speech that led to the later evolution of the specialized anatomy that makes modern human speech possible" (Lieberman and McCarthy 2007, 19). On the other hand, it may be that steps toward the descended larynx occurred before the FoxP2 mutation, since if the neurological mutation occurred first, before anatomical change in the SVT, it may not have conferred enough advantages to lead to its survival and spread. And so we may be dealing here with a true case of co-evolution.

8.   The Cost of Phonological Dexterity

Modern human babies (with SVT like those of adult earlier hominins) can suckle and breathe at the same time, as air from the nasal passage goes to the almost adjacent trachea. By contrast, the (adult) human form of the SVT (with much lower larynx) promotes choking, since food can get stuck in the entrance to the trachea. As Lieberman and McCarthy point out (2007), thousands of deaths occur each year from this cause. The value of a lowered larynx had to exceed this cost in order for it to survive and spread through the proto-sapiens population. That value, of course, was phonological dexterity. We are forced to conclude that increased phonological dexterity had some value even back in the days before there was any sizable vocabulary based on syllables. It is therefore likely that some more primitive form of speech, or speech-like vocalization having some survival value, was present before the descent of the larynx, perhaps in Neanderthals and possibly even in *Homo heidelbergensis.*

As Lieberman puts it, "…there would have been no reason for retaining the mutations that resulted in the human vocal tract unless speech was already in place in hominids ancestral to humans" (2007, 45). On the other hand, if several mutations were required to get all the way to the present form, the early forms of vocalization already in place in pre-sapiens hominins may have been quite primitive in comparison to what we call speech today. We shall have to return to the question of the timing of development of phonological dexterity during the period of hominin development.

9.   Alternative to Co-evolution

In its uncritical formulation, the alternative to co-evolution is the hypothesis that the brain developed first, then language. It couldn't be the other way around, since it is clear that the evolution of the brain was a gradual process. This "first brain, then language" hypothesis is consistent with a view that language evolved recently and over a very short time span.

But, as observed above, we are not permitted to treat language as a single object. It is clear at the very least that phonology has to be separated from the higher linguistic levels for a proper understanding of evolution. It is also clear that phonological dexterity as we know it today—a prerequisite for large vocabulary—was not present until quite recently, perhaps in the neighborhood of 100 kya.

Evidently there was a kind of co-evolution of phonological dexterity. But this was not co-evolution in the sense described above: It was not a process that can explain the dramatic growth of higher-level cortical areas. It involved anatomical changes to the SVT as well as to those (temporal and prefrontal) areas concerned with articulation and speech perception. These developments, both neurological and in the structure of the SVT, led to increased phonological dexterity in production and concomitant enhancement of ability to perceive fine phonological distinctions with greater mutual distinctiveness, greater clarity of articulation, and of greater variety.

But co-evolution evidently does not apply for higher-level cortical structures and the higher levels of language. Moreover, as already mentioned, the higher-level cortical structures also have non-linguistic functions. They are useful for a great variety of skills that humans possess, not least of which is our remarkable ability to adapt to new conditions and to learn new skills previously undreamed of. In short, these higher cortical areas contribute to general intelligence. Therefore, they probably developed for extra-linguistic reasons, and were already in place by the time there was enough phonology to make use of them. Consistent with this picture, the higher-levels of language are not as easily localizable as those used for phonological processing.

Since these higher-level cortical areas were not needed for language until large vocabulary was present, presupposing prior development of phonological dexterity, they had to be already in place by the time they became needed. In this connection it may be observed that Neanderthal brains were as large as modern human brains, although the Neanderthal SVT was probably no more proficient at producing distinct consonants and vowels than that of a modern human infant of less than six months. Lieberman asserts (2010a) that "the Neanderthal surpralaryngeal vocal tract resembles that of infants in the newborn to two-month old range when the hyoid bone and larynx are placed in the same positions relative to the vertebral column as adult humans."

It is also relevant that higher-level cortical areas, unlike primary areas, do not have genetically determined functions. Rather, plasticity reigns. They acquire their functions mainly as a result of proximity and experience. Therefore their evolutionary expansion was likely promoted by a variety of benefits.

It is known from neuroanatomy that higher level cortical areas are relatively uniform in structure. In other words, their functions do not depend upon their structures. The various functions of the different areas are determined largely by proximity to areas they are most closely related to. For example, Broca's area is close to primary oral motor cortex, and Wernicke's area is close to primary auditory cortex. In case of damage to the usual area, a neighboring area can take over. Penfield and Roberts (1959) describe a case in which a boy of 18 underwent surgery for removal of a portion of his motor and premotor cortex including (the usual location of) Broca's area and the oral portion of the primary motor cortex. The surgical excision was done in two stages. Following completion of the second stage, no speech-related problems were reported. To understand this outcome, we have to appreciate that this eighteen-year-old boy had suffered from seizures causing an inability to speak from the age of 3 ½. The seizures were probably originating in his Broca's area, and since that area was damaged he had long since recruited a neighboring portion of the cortex, or possibly the corresponding area of the opposite hemisphere, for the functions usually performed by Broca's area. As Penfield and Roberts put it (1959), apparently "the congenital abnormality had caused displacement of function."

And so we have to conclude that

- If more elaborate lexico-grammatical structures could not develop until a large vocabulary was present;

- And if phonological dexterity is a prerequisite for a large vocabulary;

- And if phonological dexterity was not in place until well into the period of Homo sapiens

- Then complex lexico-grammatical structure did not develop until well into the period of Homo sapiens

But the brain of early Homo sapiens was already fully developed (or nearly fully developed). Therefore, the development of the neurological equipment needed for complex grammar and semantics did not depend on language. It follows that the co-evolution hypothesis must be rejected. On the other hand, there was a kind of co-evolution of the development of phonological dexterity.

The beauty of high-level cortical structure is precisely that it is not genetically dedicated to some function (like language). As described above, the functions of higher-level areas are determined by proximity and experience. As a consequence, we are endowed with enormous flexibility—the ability to do any number of things that could not have been foreseen, such as playing Chopin on the piano, driving cars, skate-boarding, space travel to moon, programming computers, building weapons of mass destruction; and, of course, the higher levels of language— lexicon, syntax, and semantics.

And so for lexico-grammar we must accept the alternative theory, first the brain, then language. The implication is that the evolution of complex grammar and rich vocabulary was a recent and short process, which may have begun only after 100 kya.

Since the hypothesis of co-evolution of brain and language does not after all provide an explanation for the evolutionary expansion of the human brain, we need to find another explanation.

10. The Culinary Factor

So, if it was not language development that led to the greatly increased brain size of humans, what was it? As the first step toward an answer, we need to recognize that there is great value in the large cortex that modern humans are endowed with, quite apart from the linguistic abilities it provides. Since our higher-level cortical areas are relatively uniform in structure (until learning occurs) and undedicated in advance to any function, they are flexible and adaptable and are therefore available to take on anything that might come along, activities like playing musical instruments, juggling, operating complex machinery, and building houses and cities. Such flexibility and adaptability must have led to improved survival and reproductive ability from very early days, such as better hunting techniques, better devices for avoiding predators, and more creative wooing techniques. In short, our large brains give us great flexibility and multiple capacities, of which language is just one.

We are thus led to ask, why didn't chimps (not to mention other mammals) also develop larger brains? Why did this development occur only in this one line of primates? We get to the answer by considering the cost factor.

The value of our oversized cortex is offset by a great cost: the huge energy requirement of a large brain. The human brain is only 2% of the weight of the body, but it uses about 20% of the total energy in the body when it is at rest, and even more when thinking (Wrangham 2009). The average power consumption of a typical adult is about 100 W ("Body, Physics of" *Macmillan Encyclopedia of Physics*. New York: Macmillan, 1996). The diets of all other primates are simply unable to provide the necessary energy.

Among all the primates, only humans have a diet that provides energy sufficient to support a large brain. The details are presented in a recent book by Richard Wrangham (professor of physical anthropology at Harvard) *Catching Fire: How Cooking Made us Human* (2009). The diet of a chimpanzee, presumably like that of our common ancestor, consists mainly of fruits and plants, although they also consume insects, eggs, and meat, including carrion. All of their food is raw. Raw plants are hard to digest and they require a large complex digestive system, which consumes considerable energy. Moreover, the chimp has to spend several hours per day simply chewing (Wrangham 2009).

Cooked food is far easier to digest than raw food, with the consequence that far more energy is available to humans than to other animals. Other primates with raw, largely vegetarian, diets simply can't produce enough energy to support larger brains.

And so, as Wrangham explains in detail, what allowed our ancestors to grow larger brains was cooking. Since cooked food is far easier to digest, it not only provides increased energy, it also eliminates the need to expend large amounts of energy for the process of digestion. Less complex digestion means that we have simpler digestive systems, and therefore we don't have to use as much energy for digesting food. Also, more can be eaten in less time. As our ancestors ate less raw vegetable matter, they were able to spend less time chewing, and they thus had time on their hands for other functions.

Wrangham convincingly demonstrates that the transition from Australopithecus to Homo came about after the practice of eating cooked food was adopted, allowing for significant expansion of the cerebral cortex. This step was preceded by the step of eating more meat. Members of the species Australopithecus afarensis (known mainly in the form of the fossil named Lucy) lived about 4 to 2 million years ago (mya). They adopted the practice of eating meat. They were followed by the habilenes, who lived from about 2 mya to 1.5 mya. The habilenes are often assigned to the genus Homo and called Homo habilis, but Wrangham considers them too different from later members of the genus to deserve membership in it. In any case, they are intermediate between Australopithecus and Homo. It was they, according to Wrangham, who adopted the practice of cooking food, and that practice has remained with all succeeding hominins right up to the present.

From about 1.5 mya (or perhaps a little earlier) we have undisputed members of the genus Homo. The earliest was Homo erectus, who lasted until about 400 kya. While that species was still present on the planet, Homo heidelbergensis appeared, sometime around 800 kya, and lasted until around 300 kya. By that time Homo neanderthalensis was present, from around 400 kya. And then we get Homo sapiens, from about 200 kya. The divergence of Neanderthals and Homo sapiens from their common ancestors may have begun about 500 kya. All of these members of the genus Homo had large brains. But apparently none of them had any appreciable language until Homo sapiens.

11. Early Speech

When we look at the information structure of language as a whole, we see an enormous quantity of lexical information along with more or less complicated morphology and syntax, the operation of which requires considerable brain power, along with, quite small by comparison in quantity of information, phonological structure. But though it is relatively much smaller in quantity of neural connections, it is that phonological structure that provides the basis, the sine qua non, for all that vast lexico-grammatical structure.

The higher linguistic levels tend to overwhelm our conception of language, so that when we look at language development in children our tendency is to see the process as starting with the babbling stage, at around six or seven months, and we overlook the essential steps leading up to it. The babbling stage is actually the culmination of a lengthy process leading to the control of syllables (Oller 2000).

The syllable is the key to the remarkable information-bearing power of human speech, giving humans a communicative capacity far beyond what is available for any other known mammalian communication system. Information-bearing power depends on the amount of potential diversity in the speech signal and on the rate of speed at which such diversity-potential can be transmitted. As mentioned above, even with a primitive system having 10 different initials and 3 different vowels and open syllables only, there is a potential for 30 different syllables, and they can occur at a rate of four or five per second. And the power of such a system can be increased by the use of (i) closed syllables, (ii) additional consonantal distinctions (by means of voicing contrast, aspiration, glottalization, etc.), (iii) additional vocalic distinctions (additional vowels, diphthongization, nasalization, tones, etc.).

And so, to understand the evolution of language, it is necessary to focus on the process leading up to the ability to produce and perceive syllables, not just on the stages that follow. For what came later occurred after the human brain was developed, and it made use of all that brain power that was already there by that time, so that progress in vocabulary and grammar could be achieved relatively rapidly.

For the evolution of early speech capability (in contrast to the overall process of language evolution) the recapitulation hypothesis may well be applicable: The stages leading up to mastery of the syllable in human infants may shed light on the corresponding evolutionary stages, which may not have occurred until the period of genus Homo. According to D. Kimbrough Oller (2000), the stages in early language development in modern children are (i) the phonation stage (0–2 months), (ii) the cooing/gooing stage (1–4 months), (iii) the expansion stage (3–8 months), and (iv) the canonical stage (5–10 months). Only at the canonical stage do they have real syllables. The first two of these stages do not provide the basis for much vocabulary, and even the third stage cannot support a sizable vocabulary. As Oller points out, the vocal output of infants in these first three stages is so different from that seen later that it cannot even be represented by the IPA.

Infants in the *phonation stage* (0–2 months) produce not only vegetative and crying sounds but also "brief vocalizations with the same kind of smooth voicing, or phonation, that occurs … in the vowels of speech" (Oller 2000, 63). But they are not actual vowels like those of adults and older children. Oller calls them *quasivowels*. The SVT at this stage has a shape similar to that of earlier hominins.

The second stage, one to four months, is characterized by "gooing" (or "cooing"). Oller terms it the primitive articulation stage. He describes it as follows (2000, 64): "… infants move their vocal tracts while they produce smooth voicing both during solitary bouts of vocalization and during face-to-face conversations with their caretakers … These vocal movements often result in the dorsum … coming into contact with the back the back of the throat or palate, resulting in the protophone we call gooing (sometime also called cooing)." The lips and the front of the tongue are less commonly involved than the dorsum.

The third stage is what Oller calls the expansion stage. It occurs in babies of three to eight months of age, and is characterized by far greater variety of vocal tract posturing, resulting in richer variation in articulation, not only in different vowel-like qualities but also in pitch, amplitude, and duration. Infants at this stage make more use of their lips and tongue in producing articulatory variation, and also experiment with closure of the vocal tract. "In particular, they blow through their tightly-held lips in protophones called *raspberries*" (Oller 2000, 64). They also, during the later phases of this stage, produce sequences of closed articulations plus vowels, i.e., approximations to syllables, but not real syllables, as the "movement between closure and opening is too slow, yielding a protophone type we call *marginal babbling* (Oller 2000, 65).

And then, from five to ten months, we get the *canonical babbling stage*, with well-timed articulation of syllables, usually repetitive (e.g., [ba-ba-ba…]. They exhibit temporal consistency, an aid to speech perception, that is lacking in the marginal babbling of the previous stage. This babbling is obviously speech-like even to the casual untrained observer. Most or all of the syllables produced are similar to those that will be present in the fully developed linguistic systems they will be using for the rest of their lives, although the vowels are not as clearly articulated, as the SVT has not yet reached its adult form. In this stage and the previous one, the infant is not only gaining articulatory skill, he/she is doubtless also building corresponding perceptual connections in the temporal lobe. For example, while saying [babababa] the child is also hearing [babababa] and thus learning the articulatory-auditory correspondences that will aid in the process of perceiving the speech of others.

According to Lieberman and McCarthy (2007), the modern form of the SVT is not reached in children until the age of six to eight years. Yet it is obvious that children are able to articulate syllables and different vowels while less than one year old, even though the formant frequencies of their vowels do not correspond to those of adults. Accordingly, it was not necessary for our ancestors to have fully achieved the modern form of the SVT before they were able to have large vocabularies. And as sizable vocabularies were achieved, grammar was not far behind.

It may be that the canonical babbling stage, with actual syllables, was not reached in human evolution until the period of Homo sapiens. The basis for this supposition is Lieberman's assertion (2010a) that "the Neanderthal surpralaryngeal vocal tract resembles that of infants in the newborn to two-month old range when the hyoid bone and larynx are placed in the same positions relative to the vertebral column as adult humans. The problem derives from the long Neanderthal oral cavity, which can be determined with certainty from the fossil record."

This finding, if it holds up as new evidence becomes available, suggests that even Neanderthals had not progressed beyond the first of Oller's four stages. In that case it may be that the entire evolution of speech from the second stage onward took place during the period of development leading to Homo sapiens after the split from pre-Neanderthals about 500 kya.

Moreover, if Neanderthals had no vocabulary of appreciable size they would not have had much if any basis for syntax. It follows that the development of grammar occurred only during the Homo sapiens period, and possibly only late in that period. This claim runs counter to that of Lieberman (2010b): "Neanderthals in all likelihood possessed a language that made use of syntax to communicate complex information." Elsewhere his claim has been less bold: "There would have been no reason for retaining the mutations that resulted in the human vocal tract unless speech was already in place in hominids ancestral to humans" (2007, 45; cf. 52, 59). This statement is easier to accept, interpreting 'speech' to cover a primitive form of speech that included a very limited vocabulary with little or no syntax. The survival value of clearer articulation did not have to depend on the presence of syntax. Even proto-speech with very limited vocabulary and no syntax is better than mere phonation like that of modern infants of two months. It would include, for example, enhanced ability to imitate animal noises, which would contribute to hunting prowess and to warning community members of predators and, who knows, may have contributed also to more skillful wooing, with its obvious reproductive advantage.

12.   Conclusion

It is apparent that the title of this chapter may be misleading if it suggests that we can think of language as one thing with respect to evolution. Language is multifaceted and its various structural components, while interconnected, have lives of their own, not even restricted to linguistic activity only. We therefore need to consider different aspects of language separately in relation to evolution. In particular, phonological dexterity, the ability to produce clear syllables (and to perceive them accurately) has to be treated separately from lexicon, grammar, and semantics.

I have argued here (i) that phonological dexterity developed gradually and that it involved physical changes in the structure of the supralaryngeal vocal tract along with changes in brain structure; and (ii) that the higher linguistic levels, lexicon, morphology, syntax, semantics, developed rapidly after phonological dexterity was established and that that development did not involve concomitant evolutionary changes in the brain. Rather, the brain structures needed to support them were already in place by the time they became needed.

Those who may be skeptical about this claim may want to think about other remarkable abilities requiring great brain power that humans have developed rapidly as soon as the basis for them became established, without the need for concomitant brain evolution, since the brain power needed was already there. Many such abilities have developed only in relatively recent times: manufacture and use of electronic devices, development of scientific knowledge in nuclear physics, molecular biology, etc., composition and performance of music of enormous variety, and so forth.

To appreciate the principle it helps to understand the hierarchical organization of cortical structure (see also Lamb 1999). The cortex has primary areas, visual, auditory, motor, somatosensory, in genetically predetermined locations. Adjacent to the primary areas are secondary areas, with ability to make use of the primary structures for higher level operation; and so forth. At still higher layers we are no longer restricted to a single modality, so that in the posterior portion of the cortex we have the so-called associative areas, which integrate information from the different sensory modalities, very important among which is the angular gyrus. Similarly, in the frontal lobe we have, moving anteriorly from the primary motor area, successively higher-level structures, which perform more complex operations, using the lower levels. And as the higher-level motor activities involve objects, the more anterior pre-frontal areas have access not only to lower level motor structures but also to information about objects, registered in posterior brain areas. Such access is made possible by longitudinal fibers, including those of the arcuate fasciculus.

Unlike the primary levels, the higher levels do not have predetermined functions. This principle applies increasingly for higher levels of cortical hierarchy. As a result of this structural principle, the highest levels of our brains have the capacity to take on anything that might come along. They acquire their functions mainly as a result of experience, by virtue of their enormous plasticity.

There was a kind of co-evolution of phonological dexterity, involving changes to SVT and to certain brain structures, but this is far from the notion of co-evolution considered at the outset of this chapter. The great cortical expansion that occurred in hominin evolution was therefore not caused by evolution of language. The brain was already fully developed by the time of early Homo sapiens, therefore already fully developed before the phonological basis for modern complex language was laid down. Even Neanderthals had brains as large as modern humans, and they evidently didn't have language.

What brought about the spectacular growth of the brain during hominin evolution can be seen as a combination of two factors: (i) multiple advantages conferred by increased brain power and (ii) an increase in availability of energy needed to fuel a large brain, provided by cooked food. Factor (i) would bring about an increase in brain size for any primate, but it was unable to operate without a means of obtaining the increased energy required by larger brains. As Wrangham puts it, "cooking made us human."

And so we are forced to conclude that the evolution of complex grammar and rich vocabulary was a recent and short process. It may have begun as recently as 100 kya or even later, but progress in expanding vocabulary and adding syntactic constructions, one by one, could have been quite rapid in comparison with the changes that led up to that point, since no further advances in brain power or SVT structure were needed.

Finally, we now have a plausible answer to question of why, among all the species of genus Homo, our ancestors survived while the others died out. What was the competitive advantage of our ancestors? Surely, a major factor must have been that our forebears had language while the Neanderthals and others did not. In this part of the story of mankind, the competition with Neanderthals, long after the expansion of the brain, it's here that language has a leading role.

REFERENCES

Brown, F., and S. Lee. 2005. The oldest Homo sapiens: Fossils push human emergence back to 195,000 years ago. http://www.eurekalert.org/pub_releases/2005-02/uou-toh021105.php#.

Deacon, T. W. 1992. Brain-language co-evolution. In *The Evolution of Human Languages*, eds. J. A. Hawkins, and M. Gell-Man, 49–83. Redwood City: Addison Wesley.

Deacon, T. W. 1997. *The Symbolic Species: The Co-evolution of Language and The Brain*. New York & London: Norton.

Asif G. 2008. Language evolution: Neural differences that make a difference. *Nature Neuroscience* 11 (4): 382–384.

Gleason, H. A, Jr. 1964. The organization of language. *Georgetown University Round Table on Languages and Linguistics* 17:75–95.

Hockett, C. F. 1961. Linguistic elements and their relations. *Language* 27:29–53.

Hockett, C. F., and S. Altmann. 1968. A note on design features. In *Animal Communication: Techniques of Study and Results of Research*, ed. T. A. Sebeok, 61–72. Bloomington: Indiana University Press.

Lamb, S. M. 1964. On alternation, transformation, realization, and stratification. *Georgetown University Round Table on Languages and Linguistics* 17:105–122.

Lamb, S. M. 1999. *Pathways of the Brain: The Neurocognitive Basis of Language*. Amsterdam and New York: John Benjamins.

Lieberman, P. 2007. The evolution of human speech: Its anatomical and neural bases. *Current Anthropology* 48 (1) February.

Lieberman, P. 2010a. E-mail to MTLR@yahoogroups.com, 2 July.

Lieberman, P. 2010b. E-mail to MTLR@yahoogroups.com, 3 July.

Lieberman, P., and R. McCarthy. 2007. Tracking the evolution of language and speech. http://www.museum.upenn.edu/expedition; http://www.cog.brown.edu/people/lieberman/ pdfFiles/Lieberman, P. & McCarthy, R. 2007. Tracking the evolution of.pdf.

Oller, D. K. 2000. *The Emergence of the Speech Capacity*. Mahwah, New Jersey: Lawrence Erlbaum.

O'Neil, D. 1999–2012. Early Modern Homo sapiens. http://anthro.palomar.edu/homo2/mod_ homo_4.htm.

Oppenheimer, S. 2003. *Out of Eden: The Peopling of the World*. London: Constable & Robinson.

Penfield, W., and L. Roberts. 1959. *Speech and Brain Mechanisms*. New York: Atheneum.

Schoenemann, P. T. 2009. Brain evolution relevant to language. In *Language, Evolution, and the Brain*, eds. J. W. Minett, and William S-Y. Wang. Hong Kong: City University of Hong Kong Press.

Wrangham, R. 2009. *Catching Fire: How Cooking Made Us Human*. Harvard University Press.

22

On the History of Chinese Directionals

Alain PEYRAUBE
Paris, France
National Center for Scientific Research
School for Advanced Studies in the Social Sciences

Abstract

This paper develops Peyraube's earlier hypothesis (2006) that Chinese must be considered a satellite-framed language, as suggested by Talmy (1985, 2000), and not an equipollently-framed language, as proposed by Slobin (2004). An analysis of the directional verbs and complements in Chinese leads to the conclusion that Contemporary Mandarin Chinese codes path by means of "satellites" known as directional complements. However, Classical Chinese (5th–3rd centuries BC) was a verb-framed language, since it typically conveyed path information by encoding it in the main verb of the clause (that is, the lexicalization of 'path' was in the main verb). It is consequently argued that Chinese has undergone, some ten centuries ago, a typological shift from a verb-framed language to a satellite-framed language.

1. Introduction

The expression of a basic motion event in natural languages involves several semantic components:

- Figure (or target): the object to be located
- Ground (or landmark): the reference object
- Path
- Manner
- Cause

Three of these are major components across languages: the manner of motion, the path of motion, and the ground (landmark). Examples in English and Mandarin Chinese are:

(1) Greg (figure) climbed (manner of motion) down (path of motion) from the tree (ground-1) to the floor (ground-2).

(2) 他跑進屋裏來了

ta paojin wu li lai le

he run+into room in come aspectual-marker

He ran into the room.

[*ta* 他= figure; *pao* 跑 = manner of motion ; *jin* 進 = path of motion ; *wu* 屋 = ground]

Talmy (1985, 1991, 2000) suggested that languages can be divided into two groups in terms of the way they encode the core feature of a motion event, i.e., a motion along a path: verb-framed languages (V-languages) and satellite-framed languages (S-languages). V-languages typically convey path information by encoding it in the main verb of the clause (the lexicalization of the path is in the main verb) while S-languages encode path using various particles, prefixes or prepositions, called satellites, associated to the main verb.

Examples: *entrer, sortir, monter, descendre* in French, which is a typical V-language; *go in, go out, go up, go down* in English, which is a typical S-language.

Romance languages (French, Spanish, Italian, Portuguese, etc.), but also Semitic languages (like Hebrew), Turkic languages (Turkish), Japanese or Korean are considered as V-languages. Germanic languages (English, German, Dutch, Swedish, Icelandic, etc.), Slavic languages (Russian, Polish, Serbo-Croatian, etc.) are considered as S-languages. Mandarin and many other Sino-Tibetan languages are also claimed by Talmy to be S-languages. Some further examples in Mandarin are:

(3) *Jinlai* 進來 / *jinqu* 進去 'come in, go in'; *chulai* 出來 / *chuqu* 出去 'come out, go out'; *shanglai* 上來 / *shangqu* 上去 'come up, go up'; *xialai* 下來 / *xiaqu* 下去 'come down, go down'.

This dichotomy allows the main verb of the clause in S-languages to be available to encode other dimensions of a motion event, for instance, the manner of motion. Thus, unlike V-languages, S-languages typically conflate motion information with manner information in the main verb of the clause. Compare the following three sets of verbs in English, French and Mandarin: run in, run out in English; entrer en courant, sortir en courant in French; paojinlai跑進來 (run + into + come) / paojinqu 跑進去 (run + into + go) 'run in'; paochulai 跑出來 (run + out + come) / paochuqu 跑出去 (run + out + go) 'run out' in Chinese.

In fact, if one takes the manner of motion as a starting point, instead of taking the path, it also appears that languages vary considerably with regard to this dimension, with V-languages paying much less attention to manner than S-languages. This is evident in the following examples from Spanish and French, both V-languages: Sale un hubo (Spanish); D'un trou de l'arbre sort un hibou (French).

By contrast, many S-languages use a manner verb together with a path satellite, as in Chinese:

(4) 飛出一隻貓頭鷹

Feichu yi zhi maotouying

Fly+out one Classifier owl

An owl flew out.

According to Talmy (2000, 222–3), Chinese is clearly a S-language like most of the Indo-European languages apart from Romance. He noticed that Mandarin is a serial-verb language in which each verb in the series is morphologically unmarked. He then considers the manner verb to be the main verb and the path verb to be the satellite, because paths verbs often do not function as full verbs and because there is a small closed set of path verbs. He also suggests that paths verbs in serial-verb languages often show evidence of grammaticalizing into path satellites, that is, losing some of their features of independent verbs.

Many studies have been undertaken to show that Talmy's dichotomy is not fully comprehensive (Ibarretxe-Antuñano 2003 on basque; Ohara 2003 on Japanese; Kopecka 2003 on French; Rice 2003 on Althapascan; Lamarre 2003 on Chinese). Several revisions of Talmy's typological model have then been proposed, especially by Slobin (2000, 2003, 2004) who has taken into consideration the manner of motion and showed that it is probably more useful to rank languages along a cline of manner salience than to allocate them to one or the other of Talmy's typological categories.

Slobin has also observed that in Chinese and other serial-verb languages both path and manner receive equal weight. The proposal has then been made, first, to treat such languages as "complex verb-framed languages" (Slobin and Hoitin 1994). At present, Slobin holds that it may be appropriate to have a third typological category, following the suggestion of Zlatev and Yang Klang (2003) who showed that languages like Thai cannot be labelled verb-framed or satellite-framed languages (see also Zlatev 2003). He then proposes a "equipollently-framed languages" category to include serial-verb languages (most of East Asian and Southeast Asian languages like

Sino-Tibetan, Tai-Kadai, Austro-Asiatic, Hmong-Mien, Austronesian, but also some African and Amerindian languages) in which both manner and path are expressed by "equipollent" elements, that is elements that appear to be equal in force and significance (Slobin 2004).

The following trichotomy has thus been proposed:

(i)   Verb-framed languages

The preferred means of expressing path is a verb, with subordinate expression of manner. The typical construction type is PATH VERB + SUBORDINATE MANNER VERB. Languages such as Romance, Semitic, Turkic, Japanese, Korean are V-languages.

(ii)   Satellite-framed languages

The preferred means of expressing path is a nonverbal element associated with a verb. The typical construction is: MANNER VERB + PATH SATELLITE. Germanic, Slavic, Finno-Ugric languages are S-languages.

(iii)   Equipollently-framed languages

Path and manner are expressed by equivalent grammatical forms. The typical construction types depend on the language:

–   MANNER VERB + PATH VERB for serial-verb languages (Niger-Congo, Hmong-Mien, Sino-Tibetan, Tai-Kadai, Austronesian);

–   [MANNER + PATH] VERB: bipartite languages (Algonquian, Althabaskan, Hokan, Klamath-Takelman);

–   MANNER PREVERB + PATH PREVERB + VERB: Jaminjungan languages.

Is Chinese a satellite framed-language, a complex-verb framed-language, or an equipollently-framed language? To answer this question fully, an analysis of the historical development of this construction is necessary, but let us first briefly outline what is the situation in Contemporary Chinese.

2.   Contemporary Chinese

There are two types of directional complements in Contemporary Chinese: simple and complex.

First, simple directional complements involve the two DIRECTIONAL verbs: *lai* 來 'come, hither' and *qu* 去 'go, thither, away'. They fill the V2 position in V1 + V2 compounds such as in *zoulai* 走來 (walk + come) 'walk to my direction', *zouqu* (walk + go) 走去 'walk away', *nalai* 拿 來 (take + come) 'bring', *naqu* 拿去 (take + go) 'take away'. The V1 are verbs of MOVEMENT (Va) or other verbs signalling manner of motion ('walk', 'run', 'fly', etc.) or simple transitive verbs that inherently imply a change of location of their direct objects ('take', 'send', 'throw', etc.).

The verbs of movement (Va) belong to a closed list, limited to the following seven verbs: *shang* 上 'go up, ascend', *xia* 下 'go down, descend', *jin* 進 'enter, go in', *chu* 出 'exit, go out', *hui* 回 'return, come back', *guo* 過 'pass, go through', *qi* 起 'rise, go up'.

Second, complex directional complements are formed by a combination of a verb of movement (Va) followed by one of the two directional verbs, *lai* 來 or *qu* 去. They are also involved in V1 + V2 compounds, filling in the V2 position. The V1 are still verbs of motion or simple transitive verbs implying a moving of their objects, BUT NOT the verbs of movement Va, already present in the V2.

The V2 of the complex directional constructions are: *shanglai* 上來, *shangqu* 上去, *xialai* 下來, *xiaqu* 下去, *jinlai* 進來, *jinqu* 進去, *chulai* 出來, *chuqu* 出去, *huilai* 回來, *huiqu* 回去, *guolai* 過來, *guoqu* 過去, *qilai* 起來 (interestingly there is no *qiqu* 起去 in contemporary Chinese). Some examples follow to illustrate this type:

(5) 爬上來 *pa-shanglai* (climb + up + come) 'climb up'; 跑出去 *pao-chuqu* (run + out + go) 'run away'; 走進來 *zou-jinlai* (walk + into + come) 'walk in'; 拿回來 *na-huilai* (take + back + come) 'take back, bring back'.

Finally, there are 'motion resultative constructions', formed by a V1 (the same verbs that fill the V1 position for the complex directional constructions) followed by a V2 which is one of the seven verbs of movement detailed above (Va). As there is no directional verb (*lai* 來 or *qu* 去) in this construction, we will not consider it as a directional construction at all:[1]

(6) 走進 *zou-jin* (walk + into) 'walk in'; 拿回 *na-hui* (take + back) 'take back'.

Is Contemporary Chinese a satellite-framed language as advocated by Talmy, a verb-framed language, or an equipollently-framed language as Slobin claims? The answer to this question depends on the kind of analysis and interpretation that can be provided for the directional complement constructions.

The argumentation would be as follows:

Contemporary Chinese could be considered as a verb-framed (or complex verb-framed) language, if compounds like *paojin* 跑進 (run + enter) or *paochulai* 跑出來 (run + exit + come) are understood as 'enter in running' or 'come running out'. Such an interpretation is given, for instance, by Li and Thompson (1981, 58). This means that the main verb is the last one in the series, implying that there are no satellites in such sentences.

It could be however considered as a satellite-framed language, if the same compounds *paojin* 跑進 (run + into) or *paochulai* 跑出來 (run + out + come) are interpreted as 'run in' or 'run out', as suggested by Chao Yuen-Ren (1968, 458–464). The manner of motion is then expressed

---

1. Hendriks (1998) makes an interesting distinction between motion verbs expressing a deictic path, such as French 'venir' (to come) and 'partir' (to go), and motion verbs expressing a directional path, such as 'monter' (go up) or 'descendre' (go down).

by the main verb (pao 跑) and the path by a satellite (*jin* 進 or *chulai* 出來).

Finally, it could be considered as an equipollently-framed language, if the compounds paojin 跑進 and paochulai 跑出來 are interpreted as 'run and enter' or 'run and exit'. Both the manner of motion and the path of motion are considered in this framework as verbs with their full lexical meaning, the manner verb being the first one, the path verb the second one.

I would like to suggest that the second hypothesis (Contemporary Chinese is a satellite-framed language) is the best one, following Talmy's suggestion. The main reasons are:

The directional verbs *lai* 來 and *qu* 去 are still used as main verbs in Chinese, but besides being main verbs meaning 'come' and 'go', they only indicate, respectively, motion toward or away from the speaker, when used in directional complement constructions.

The same is true for the seven verbs of movement (Va) when they are involved in directional constructions. They are no longer main verbs meaning "go up" (for *shang* 上), 'go down' (for *xia* 下), 'enter' (for *jin* 進), 'exit' (for *chu* 出), 'rise' (for *qi* 起), 'return' (for *hui* 回), 'pass' (for *guo* 過), but complements meaning respectively 'up, on', 'down', 'in(to)', 'out', 'up', 'back', 'over'.

These directional complements (either simple or complex) might still be considered as verbs, but it is obvious that they are no longer fully lexical words (with their original meanings). They have become function words or grammatical elements, after having undergone a process of grammaticalization. The directional complements (simple or complex) form one lexical unit or one word with the preceding verb. This is because the Verb + Directional complement construction expresses only one action.

All these reasons point to the fact that there is no real motivation for denying the status of the directional complements as satellites.

The process of grammaticalization has taken several centuries to be completed, but it can be considered now as finalized. This means of course that Chinese has not always been a satellite-framed language. I would now like to show that it has undergone a typological shift from a verb-framed language to a satellite frame-language. A study of this historical shift will provide more arguments in favour of the hypothesis that Chinese is indeed today a satellite-framed language.

3. Archaic Chinese (Classical Chinese)

The "NP-subject + Verb + Directional Verb" (NP-subject + V + Vd) structure can be traced back to Early Archaic Chinese (11th–6th c. BC), gaining currency in Late Archaic Chinese (the Classical Chinese par excellence 5th–2nd c. BC). For example:

(7) 牛羊下來（詩經）

niu yang xia lai (Shi jing 8th c. BC)

cow sheep go-down come

Cows and sheep are going down (and they) are coming.

In such a sentence, *xia* 下 and *lai* 來 are two separate lexical units, and the construction is typically a serial-verb construction: V1 + V2. *Lai* has its full lexical meaning of 'to come'. As for *qu*, its meaning in Classical Chinese is 'to leave', and not 'to go'.

We also have two separate actions when the V2 of the V1 + V2 serial-verb construction is a verb of movement (Va) instead of being a directional verb, as in:

(8) 走出門（韓非子）

zou chu men (Han Feizi 3rd c. BC)

run go-out gate

(He) ran (and) went out of the gate.

(9) 孔子趨出。（荀子）

Kongzi qu chu

Kongzi hurry-up go-out (Xunzi 3rd c. BC)

Kongzi hurried up (and) went out.

The fact that a coordinate conjunction can be inserted in between the two verbs clearly shows that we are dealing with two separate actions:

(10) 子路趨而出。（荀子）

Zilu qu er chu (Xunzi)

Zilu hurry-up and go-out

Zilu hurried up and went out.

4. Late Han–Six Dynasties (1st–6th c. AD)

Under the Late Han (1st–3rd c. AD) and the Six Dynasties period (3rd–6th c. AD), the following three structures A, B, and C are attested:

A. NP-subject + V + Vd and V + Vd + NP-subject (Vd = directional verb)

B. V + *lai/qu* 來/去 + LP and V + LP + *lai/qu* 來/去 (LP = Locative Phrase)[2]

C. NP1 + Vt + NP2 + *lai/qu* 來/去 > NP2 + NP1 + Vt + *lai/qu* 來/去

---

2. There are some instances in Archaic Chinese where a Locative Phrase (LP) is used with a V1 + V2 serial-verb construction when V2 = *lai* 來 or **qu** 去, but these instances are very few. We thus assume that the V + *lai/qu* 來/去 + LP construction is not a construction typical of Classical Chinese.

4.1   NP-subject + V + Vd and V + Vd + NP-subject

The second of these structures (V + Vd + NP-subject) appeared for the first time at the end of the Late Han period (2nd c. AD). It obviously evolved from the first one, after the NP-subject has been moved from a pre-verbal position to a post-verbal one: NP-subject + V + Vd > V + Vd + NP-subject.

The motivations for such a diachronic word order change are unclear. However, one can assume that they have been mainly pragmatic: the movement probably occurred to put some emphasis on the NP-subject by placing it in a position which is not its normal one. Examples:

(11)   生出此榖 (論衡)

sheng chu ci gu (Lun Heng 2nd c. AD)

give-birth-to come-out this mulberry-tree

That mulberry-tree emerged.

(12)   即便生出二甘蔗 (佛本行集经)

ji bian sheng chu er gan zhe (Fo ben xing ji jing end of 6th century AD)

at-that-moment then give-birth-to come-up two sugarcane

At that moment, two sugarcanes then sprang up.

(13)   飛來雙白鵠 (古辭)

fei lai shuang bai hu (Gu ci)

fly come two white swan

Two white swans flew in.

(14)   忽然自湧出二池水，一冷，一暖 (佛本行集經)

huran zi yong chu er chi-shui, yi leng yi nuan (Fo ben xing ji jing)

suddenly naturally surge come-out two pond-water one cold one warm

Suddenly two ponds surged up, one cold one warm.

In all these examples, we are still dealing with two separate lexical entities, one V and one Vd, but we can assume that this is just the beginning of the process of grammaticalization which will cause the two verbs to merge into one lexical unit (see Li Fengxiang 1997).

4.2.   V + lai/qu 來/去+ LP and V + LP + lai/qu 來/去

At the end of Pre-medieval (Han times), we find many instances of either V + *lai/qu* 來/去 + LP or V + LP + *lai/qu* 來/去. At the beginning, the LPs follow *lai* 來 or *qu* 去, but during the Six Dynasties period, most instances are with the LP inserted in between the two verbs. The historical derivation is as follows: V + *lai/qu* 來/去+ LP > V + LP +*lai/qu* 來/去. Examples of V + LP + *qu* 去follow:

(15)　便出宮去（生經）

bian chu gong qu (Sheng jing beginning of 4th c.)

then go-out palace leave

Then (he) went out from the palace (and) left.

Two separate actions are still probably involved in these sentences, as there are examples where a coordinative conjunction er "and" can still be inserted between the two verbs, as in:

(16)　出國而去（中本起經）

chu guo er qu (Zhong ben qi jing beginning of 3rd c.)

go-out country and leave

He left the country.

Thus, *qu* 去 cannot yet be considered as a directional complement.

However, in the following example, taken from a Buddhist vernacular text of the end of 6th century, *qu* 去 has probably lost its syntactic autonomy and has already become a function word, a grammatical element.

(17)　移他處去（佛本行集經）

yi ta chu qu (Fo ben xing ji jing end of 6th century)

move he place go

(He) moved to his place.

How did the grammaticalization process of qu 去 occur in the *V + LP + qu* 去 pattern? Probably through a meaning shift. *Qu* 去 has now acquired the meaning of wang 往 'go to' and does not have any longer the original meaning of *li* 離 'to leave'.

In the following example where qu 去 is the sole verb, it also has the meaning of 'to go:

(18)　汝何處去?（百喻經）

ru he chu qu (Bai yu jing end of 5th c.)

you what place go

Where are you going?

In fact, *qu* 去 has probably acquired the meaning of 'to go' when the LP was moved after the V + *qu* 去 constituent. This meaning shift from 'to leave' to 'to go' can very well be explained by cognitive motivations (see Lakoff 1987; Zhang Min 1998; Liang, Wu, and Peyraube 2008).

Besides instances involving the verb qu 去, we also have many examples of both VP + *lai* 來 + LP and VP + LP + *lai* 來:

(19)　入來洛陽（志怪）

ru lai Luoyang (Zhi guai)

enter come Luoyang

We entered Luoyang.

(20)　還入城來（雜寶藏經）

huan ru cheng lai (Za bao cang jing end of 5th c.)

return enter city come

(He) returned and entered the city.

4.3.　NP1 + Vt + NP2 + lai / qu 來/去 > NP2 + NP1 + Vt + lai / qu 來/去

What is interesting to note about this construction is that under the Wei-Jin-Nan-Bei-Chao period (3rd–6th c. AD), the NP patient-object is between the two verbs, i.e. before *lai* 來 or *qu* 去. It is rarely after *lai* 來 or *qu* 去. It may also be moved before the NP subject-agent:

NP1+ Vt + NP2 + *lai* 來 /*qu* 去 > NP2 + NP1 + Vt + *lai* 來 / *qu* 去, where NP1 = agent, NP2 = patient, and Vt = transitive verb. For example:

(21)　舍中財物，賊盡持去（百喻經）

she zhong caiwu zei jin chi qu (Bai yu jing end of 5th c.)

house in belongings thief all hold go

A thief has robbed all (our) belongings in the house.

(22)　好甜美者，汝當買來（百喻經）

hao tian mei zhe ru dang mai lai

good sweet beautiful the-one-that you must buy come

You must buy the ones that are good, sweet and beautiful.

In these last two examples, *lai* 來 and *qu* 去 seem to have lost their full lexical meaning and start to be grammaticalized, to become function words or grammatical elements (see Sun Xixin 1992). In both examples, the NP2-object is in a topic- position.

In fact, as early as the Early Han (2nd c. BC–1st c. AD), the "Verb (transitive) + V of movement (also transitive)" construction can be used in sentences with a patient topic. Example:

(23)　晉人也逐出之（史記）

Jin ren ye zhu chu zhi (Shi ji 1st c. BC)

Jin people particle chase go-out they

(They) chased the people of Jin.

In this example, the NP *Jin ren* 晉人 is the topic. The sentence should be understood as 'As far as the people of Jin are concerned, they chased them', where 'them' and 'people of Jin' are co-referential.

What is new under the Six Dynasties period is that the Vi (intransitive verbs) *lai* 來 and *qu* 去 following Vt (Vt +*lai* 來 or *qu* 去) can also co-occur in the patient-topic construction. This has been probably triggered by analogy with the patient-topic sentences involving a Vt + V as in the movement construction.

In conclusion, three new structures appeared under the Six Dynasties period:

(i)   V + Vd + NP, derived from NP + V + Vd after the NP has been moved into the post-Vd position;

(ii)   V + LP + Vd, derived from V + Vd + LP, after moving the LP between the verb and the Vd;

(iii)   NP2 + NP1 + Vt + *lai / qu* 來/去, derived from NP1 + Vt + NP2 + *lai / qu* 來/去, after the NP2 has been moved into a topic position.

When all these NP movements were complete, a reanalysis of the serial-verb constructions V1 + V2 took effect and the V2 started to be grammaticalized and to become a function word or a grammatical element, to be precise, a directional complement.

The condition for *lai* 來and *qu* 去to become real function morphemes were for the LP to express the resultative point of the action.

5.   Late Medieval (Tang–Song times) 7th–13th c. AD

Beginning in the Late Medieval period, the simple directional complement construction that hesitantly appeared during the Early Medieval period consolidates and becomes quite widespread. New kinds of sentences involving directional complements appear, including ones that were not attested before, such as subject-patient sentences (NP-subject-patient + Vt + *lai* 來 or *qu* 去) or passives. For example:

(24)   米 送 來 （大唐求法巡礼行記）
        mi song lai (Da Tang qiu fa xun li xing ji mid-9th c.)
        rice send come
        Rice has been sent in.

(25)   何不早説，恰被人借去了也？（五燈會元）
        he bu zao shuo qia bei ren jie qu le ye (Wu deng hui yuan 12th c.)
        why not early say just by someone borrow away asp.-marker particle
        Why you did not say it earlier, (it) has just been borrowed by someone?

In these examples, lai 來and qu 去are directional complements without a doubt and do not longer act as full lexical verbs. The possibility for the Vt + *lai / qu* 來/去 to take a subject-patient is in fact one of the main criteria to decide when we do have real directional complement constructions (see Liang Yinfeng 2003; Liang Yinfeng 2006).

Such subject-patient sentences come from topic-patient sentences through a reanalysis of the compound Vt + *lai / qu* 來/去. In topic-patient sentences, a subject-agent can be inserted between the topic and the Vt. The Vd *lai* 來 and *qu* 去 can express the directional movement either of the topic-patient or of the subject-agent. Sentences may have two interpretations. In subject-patient sentences, it is impossible for a subject-agent to appear after the subject-patient. The Vd *lai* 來 and *qu* 去, therefore can only express the direction of the movement of the subject-patient.

The historical evolution has been as follows:

Han-times	WJNBC-period	Tang-times
T + Vt + Vdt	Sp + Vt + Vdt	
	T + Vt + *lai* / *qu*	
		Sp + Vt + *lai* / *qu*

[T = Topic; Vt = transitive verb; Vdt = transitive directional verb; Sp = subject-patient]

Yet another structure appears under the Tang: Vt + lai / qu 來/去+ Object. Although this structure is attested during the Six Dynasties period, it is nonetheless very rare. Beginning in the Tang, however, we begin to find many examples, such as:

(26) 差人送來絹一疋 (大唐求法巡禮行記)

cha ren song lai juan yi pi (Da Tang qiu fa xun li xing ji)

send people offer come silk one classifier

(He) sent people to offer (us) one piece of silk.

(27) 我已取來三日香稻 (白衣金幢二婆羅門緣起經)

wo yi qu lai san ri xiang dao (Bai yi jin chuang er po luo men yuan qi jing beginning of 11th c.)

I already take come three day fragrant rice

I have already taken fragrant rice for three days.

Before the Tang-Song period, the object is between the Vt and *lai* 來and *qu* 去, as in the following example, also from a Buddhist text, but dated at the end of the 4th century:

(28) 我已并取明日米來 (中阿含經)

wo yi bing qu mingri mi lai (Zhong a han jing ca. 397–398)

I already at-the-same-time take to-morrow rice come

I have already taken at the same time the rice for to morrow.

The complex directional complements also appeared at the end of the Tang or during the Five Dynasties period (907–979). Several examples of V + Vd1 + Vd2 can already be found in the Zu tang ji 祖堂集, dated 952. The structure comes directly from the simple directional complement construction. Examples:

(29) 師便打出去 (祖堂集)

shi bian dachuqu (Zu tang ji 10th c.)

Master then hit+out+go

The Master hit (it).

We also find instances of V + NP + Vd1 + Vd2 (derived from V + NP + Vd) or V + Vd1 + NP + Vd2 (also derived from V + NP + Vd) where a NP-object is inserted between V and Vd1 or between Vd1 and Vd2 (see Liang, Wu, and Peyraube 2008). For example:

(30)　我與你扶它起來。（張協狀元）

　　　wo yu ni fu ta qilai (Zhang Xie zhuan yuan before 1310)

　　　I with you straighten-up it get-up

　　　With your (help), we will straighten it up.

Hence, by the 13th century, all the directional constructions used today in Contemporary Chinese are in existence.

6. Conclusion

The study of the historical development of the directional complement constructions allows us to make the following three conclusions:

First, Archaic Chinese (Classical Chinese) encoded the path information of the motion events in the main verb of the clause. It was a verb-framed language.

Second, at the end of the Wei-Jin-Nan-Bei-Chao period, that is, around the 5th century AD, Chinese started to use directional complements and to undergo a shift from a verb-framed language to a satellite-framed language. Chinese became a mixed language using both strategies.

Third, some five centuries later, around the 10th century, the shift from a V-language to a S-language was achieved. Languages can move along a cline over time. The movement of Chinese from a V-language to S-language is not unique. It has been reported that the change for Italian, a V-framed language moving in the direction of a S-framed language, may be stimulated by contact with German, especially in Northern Italy. A similar evolution is reported for Brussels French, under the influence of Dutch (see Slobin 2004).

REFERENCES

Chao, Y. R. 1968. *A Grammar of Spoken Chinese*. Berkeley and Los Angeles: University of California Press.

Hendriks, H. 1998. Comment il monte le chat? En grimpant. *Aile* 11:147–190.

Ibarretxe-Antunano, I. 2003. Path in Basque: Some problems for the verb-framed and satellite-framed language typology. Paper delivered to *the 8th International Cognitive Linguistics Conference (ICCL-8)*, Logroño, Spain, July 20–25.

Kopecka, A. 2003. From spontaneous to caused motion: Different ways of talking about motion in French. Paper delivered to *the 8th International Cognitive Linguistics Conference (ICCL-8)*, Logroño, Spain, July 20–25.

Lakoff, G. 1987. *Women, Fire, and Dangerous Things: What Categories Reaveal About the Mind*. Chicago & London: The University of Chicago Press.

Lamarre, C. 2003. Hanyu kongjian weiyi shijian de yuyan biaoda. Contemporary *Research in Modern Chinese* (Japan) 5:1–18.

Li, C. N., and S. A.Thompson. 1981. Mandarin Chinese. *A Functional Reference Grammar*. Berkeley and Los Angeles: California University Press.

Li, F. X. 1997. Cross-linguistic lexicalization patterns: Diachronic evidence from verb-complement compounds in Chinese. Sprachtypologie und Universalienforschung (STUF). *Berlin* 50 (3): 229–252.

Liang, Y. F. 2003. Lun hanyu quxiang buyu chansheng de jufa dongyin (On the syntactic motivations having generating the directional complements in Chinese). Paper delivered at *the International Conference on Chinese Historical Development*, Hangzhou, December.

Liang, Y. F. 2006. *Hanyu Dongbu Jiegou de Chansheng Yu Yanbian*. Shanghai: Xuelin chubanshe.

Liang, Y. F., F. X. Wu, and Beiluobei (A. Peyraube). 2008. Hanyu quxiang buyu jiegou de chansheng yu yanbian. *Lishi Yuyanxue Yanjiu* 1:164–181.

Ohara, K. H. 2003. Manner of motion in Japanese: Not every verb-framed language is poor in manner. Paper delivered to *the 8th International Cognitive Linguistics Conference (ICCL-8)*, Logroño, Spain, July 20–25.

Peyraube, A. 2006. Motion events in Chinese: A diachronic study of directional complements. In *Space in Languages—Linguistic Systems and Cognitive Categories*, eds. M. Hickmann, and S. Robert, 121–135. Amsterdam: John Benjamins.

Rice, S. 2003. Beyond Talmy's motion event taxonomy: Conflation patterns in the Dene Suline verb. Paper delivered to *the 8th International Cognitive Linguistics Conference (ICCL-8)*, Logroño, Spain, July 20–25.

Slobin, D. I. 2000. Verbalized events: A dynamic approach to linguistic relativity and determinism. In *Evidence for Linguistic Relativity,* eds. S. Niemeier, and R. Driven, 107–138. Amsterdam: John Benjamins.

Slobin, D. I. 2003. The mental representation of manner of movement across languages. Paper delivered to *the 8th International Cognitive Linguistics Conference (ICCL-8)*, Logroño, Spain, July 20–25.

Slobin, D. I. 2004. The many ways to search for a frog: Linguistic typology and the expression of motion events. In *Relating Events in A Narrative: Typological and Contextual Perspectives,* eds. S. Strömqvist, and L. Verhoeven, 219–257. Mahwah, N.J.: Lawrence Erlbaum Associates.

Slobin, D. I., and N. Hoilting. 1994. Reference to movement in spoken and signed languages: Typological considerations. *Proceedings of the Berkeley Linguistics Society* 20:487–505.

Sun, X. X. 1992. *Hanhyu Lishi Yufa Yaolue.* Shanghai: Fudan daxue chubanshe.

Talmy, L. 1985. Lexicalization patterns: Semantic structure in lexical forms. In *Language Typology and Lexical Description: Vol. 3. Grammatical Categories and the Lexicon,* ed., T. Shopen 36–149. Cambridge: Cambridge University Press.

Talmy, L. 1991. Paths to realization: A typology of event conflation. *Proceedings of the Berkeley Linguistics Society* 1:480–519.

Talmy, L. 2000. *Toward a Cognitive Semantics: Vol. II—Typology and Process in Concept Structuring.* Cambridge, MA: The MIT Press.

Zlatev, J. 2003. Serializing languages: Neither 'verb-framed' nor 'satellite-framed. Paper delivered to *the 8th International Cognitive Linguistics Conference (ICCL-8)*, Logroño, Spain, July 20–25.

Zlatev J., and P. Yangklang. 2003. A third way to travel: The place of Thai and serial verb languages in motion event typology. In *Relating Events in A Narrative: Typological and Contextual Perspectives*, eds. S. Strömqvist, and L. Verhoeven, 194–199. Mahwah, N.J.: Lawrence Erlbaum Associates.

Zhang, M. 1998. *Renzhi Yuyanxue Yu Hanyu Mingci Duanyu.* Beijing. Zhongguo shehui kexue chubanshe.

23

A Target Location Cue in a Visual Speller: The N200 ERP Component

James William MINETT, Lin ZHOU, & Manson Cheuk-Man FONG
The Chinese University of Hong Kong

Abstract

Visual spellers are brain–computer interfaces that allow individuals with severe neuromuscular disorders to input text to a computer. Most visual spellers take advantage of modulations of the P300 event-related potential component elicited by rapid intensification of visual stimuli to serve as a control signal for the text input. However, visual spellers have also been found to modulate other components, including N200. The magnitudes of the modulations of these other components may exceed those of P300. In such cases, the performance of the speller (in terms of input speed and accuracy) will depend on the reliability with which these other modulations can be detected and characterized. In this paper, we present a preliminary investigation into the factors that modulate the parietal N200 component elicited by a visual speller paradigm, using Chinese text materials as the experimental stimuli. We observe that, for some participants, non-target column intensifications elicit N200 that peaks contralaterally to the visual hemifield in which the non-target intensification is perceived. In other words, non-target intensifications to the left of the attended target elicit right-lateralized N200, while non-target intensifications to the right of the attended target elicit left-lateralized N200. We relate this observation to N2pc, an event-related potential component that is elicited about 200 ms after onset of certain visual search tasks. N2pc peaks at posterior electrodes that are contralateral to the visual hemifield in which a "pop-out" stimulus (i.e., one that appears to be detected automatically) is presented. This component is believed to index cognitive mechanisms that enhance features of the pop-out target and/ or suppress features of distractors. We hypothesize that N2pc contributes to the parietal N200 component elicited by a visual speller, indexing mechanisms that the user engages to maintain attention to the target while suppressing distractions resulting from non-target intensifications. In order to make a more rigorous assessment of this hypothesis, further studies with more participants should be conducted. If it is indeed confirmed by subsequent studies, the lateralization of N200 may serve as an electrophysiological cue for the location of the target in the stimulus matrix of a visual speller, potentially allowing speller performance to be enhanced.

1. Introduction

The majority of people are able to communicate, whether by speaking, by writing, or by signing. However, a substantial minority of people experience damage to their nervous system that limits their ability to control voluntary muscle movement, in some cases preventing them from communicating with others. For example, cerebromedullospinal disconnection, more commonly known as *locked-in syndrome*, is a neurological disorder in which damage to the ventral pons results in quadriplegia (paralysis of all limbs and torso) and anarthria (loss of ability to speak), but which typically preserves affected individuals' consciousness and vertical eye movement (Smith and Delargy 2005). Various other conditions can also cause a person to become locked-in, such as amyotrophic lateral sclerosis (ALS, Langmore, and Lehman 1994) and other types of motor neuron disease (Kuncl 2002), in which progressive degeneration of upper and/or lower motor neurons results in gradual loss of voluntary muscle control, as well as brain stem stroke (Boyle 1994), Guillain-Barré syndrome (Iannello 2005), Parkinson's disease (Clough et al. 2007), and multiple sclerosis (Raine et al. 2008).

Several types of system have been developed to augment communication by individuals who are locked-in. One approach, which is effective for those who retain fine control of eye movement, is to track direction of eye gaze, allowing them to select text or commands from among a table of alternatives presented on-screen (e.g., *EyeMax* and ERICA, DynaVox Mayer-Johnson, Pittsburgh, PA, U.S.A.; *ECOpoint*, Prentke Romich Co., Wooster, OH, U.S.A.). Residual control of other muscles (e.g., *Tongue Drive System*, Huo and Ghovanloo 2010) has also been used to augment communication.

Recently, much attention has focused on inputting text to a computer with brain–computer interfaces (BCIs), which utilize "neurophysiological signals originating in the brain to activate or deactivate external devices or computers" (Birbaumer and Cohen 2007). BCIs may be either invasive, requiring electrode arrays to be implanted onto or into the patient's cortex (e.g., *BrainGate*, Cyberkinetics Neurotechnology Systems, Inc., Foxburgh, MA, U.S.A.), or non-invasive, using sensors positioned outside the skull (e.g., *intendiX,* Guger Technologies OG, Graz, Austria). Non-invasive BCIs may be fitted, removed, and maintained more easily and safely than invasive BCIs, which require neurosurgical implantation (Wolpaw et al. 2002). Non-invasive BCIs are therefore typically more suitable for implementation as consumer products to assist communication than invasive BCIs.

1.1 Visual spellers

Most non-invasive BCIs for text input are based on Farwell and Donchin's original visual speller (Farwell and Donchin 1988; Mak et al. 2011). Such systems present visual stimuli to the user in the form of a matrix, each cell of the matrix representing one or more characters of text. An example of the stimulus matrix of a visual speller is shown in Figure 23.1 (Donchin et al. 2000). Cells of the matrix are briefly intensified, set-by-set, in pseudo-random order while the user attends to the particular target cell to be selected for input. The stimulus matrix may be

Figure 23.1   Example of the stimulus matrix of a visual speller (figure adapted from Donchin et al. 2000)
The stimulus matrix comprises the twenty-six letters of the Latin alphabet, the digits 0–9, and SPACE.

A	B	C	D	E	F
G	H	I	J	K	L
M	N	O	P	Q	R
S	T	U	V	W	X
Y	Z	1	2	3	4
5	6	7	8	9	SPACE

intensified one cell at a time (Guan et al. 2004), one row or column at a time (Farwell & Donchin 1988), or following a checkerboard paradigm in which no two cells occupying either the same row or the same column of the matrix are intensified simultaneously (Townsend et al. 2010). In all such cases, intensification of the target cell is a rare event among a pseudo-random sequence of events, thus constituting an oddball sequence (Donchin 1981). Intensification of the target therefore tends to elicit a P300 event-related potential (ERP) (Sutton et al. 1965), peaking at parietal electrodes, with greater amplitude than that elicited by intensification of other, non-target cells, allowing the user's intended input to be inferred.

Farwell and Donchin's original row–column speller allowed able-bodied users to input 2.3 alphabetic characters (6-by-6 matrix) per minute at 95% accuracy, corresponding to a mean input rate of about 12 bits per minute (Farwell and Donchin 1988). Using the checkerboard paradigm (Townsend et al. 2010), however, able-bodied users could input 3.6 alphanumeric characters (8-by-9 matrix) per minute at 91.5% accuracy, corresponding to a mean input rate of 23.3 bits per minute (compared to 19.9 bits per minute using a row-column speller with the same matrix size).

Most prior research on developing BCIs to assist text input has focused on languages written with alphabetic script, such as English. Alphabets typically comprise a few tens of characters, allowing all of them to be displayed simultaneously in the stimulus matrix of a visual speller. However, Chinese, which has a logographic script (Wang 1973), consists of thousands of sinograms (Wang and Tsai 2011)—the most commonly used dictionary of Chinese, Xinhua Zidian (2004), for example, comprises more than 11,000 entries—making it is impossible to display them all simultaneously in a single stimulus matrix. A few research teams, including our own team based at the Language Engineering Laboratory, have been working to develop BCIs that allow Chinese text to be input in multiple stages (Wu et al. 2009; Jin et al. 2010; Minett et

Figure 23.2   Grand-averaged ERPs elicited from able-bodied participants using the FLAST Speller (figure adapted from Minett et al. 2012)

The figure shows ERPs for both target intensifications (bold curve) and non-target intensification (thin curve) at sites Pz, P7, P8. The plots indicate two bilateral parietal components: a negative component peaking at about 200 ms (N200); and a positive-going component peaking at about 300 ms (P300).

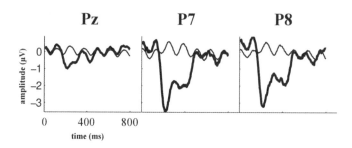

al. 2010, 2012). In our First–Last Speller (FLAST) (Minett et al. 2012), for example, sinogram input is achieved by decomposing each sinogram into two components: the first component, representing the sequence of strokes one would write first when writing that sinogram; and the last component, representing the sequence of strokes one would write last. This decomposition was designed so that a lexicon of more than 7,000 sinograms could be encoded by a set of fifty-six distinct components, all of which could be displayed simultaneously using an eight-by-eight stimulus matrix. The encoding ensures that no more than fifty-six sinograms match any pair of components. Consequently, input of any sinogram by FLAST can be achieved within three stages: selection of first component, followed by selection of final component, and finally selection of the target sinogram itself.

Plots of the grand-averaged event related potentials elicited by both target and non-target intensifications from a group of able-bodied participants using FLAST are shown in Figure 23.2 (Minett et al. 2012) for three parietal electrodes, where P300 is expected to peak. The ERPs elicited by targets are characterized by two main components: a negative bilateral component peaking about 200 ms post target onset, and a positive-going bilateral peak at about 300 ms post target onset. The second, positive-going peak corresponds to the expected P300 component. However, unexpectedly, this component is weaker than the first, negative component, which we shall refer to as N200. Significant modulation of N200 by target intensifications is not unique to FLAST, having been reported in a number of previous BCI studies (e.g., Allison and Pineda 2006; Krusienski et al. 2008; Treder and Blankertz 2010).

No clear explanation has yet been put forward for the cognitive mechanisms that elicit and modulate the parietal N200 component specifically in visual spellers. However, we note that, during operation of a visual speller, the participant is required to locate and maintain attention to a particular target stimulus, enhancing cognitive responses to target intensifications and suppressing cognitive responses to non-target intensifications. We therefore now consider the literature concerning a component, N2pc, that has been shown to index related cognitive mechanisms during visual search tasks, and which might offer an explanation for the visual speller N200.

Figure 23.3 Two examples of visual search tasks

Two examples of visual search tasks involving a single "pop-out" target among an array of distractors: left panel adapted from (Luck and Hillyard, 1994); right panel adapted from (Mazza et al. 2009).

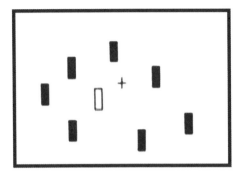 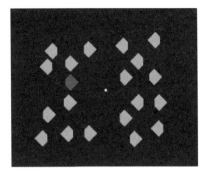

1.2 Visual search tasks and the N2pc component

Different cognitive mechanisms are engaged during visual processing of stimuli in certain visual search tasks. Luck and Hillyard (1994) describe two classes of visual search task: one class in which detection of a target stimulus is effortless and takes place in parallel, another class in which detection of a target stimulus requires an effortful serial search. The former occurs when the target differs from an array of distractors in terms of a simple visual feature (e.g., orientation, color, or size), causing the target to appear to "pop-out" automatically. In contrast, the latter occurs when target and distractors differ in terms of a combination of features that are too complex for such detection to occur in parallel. Figure 23.3 shows two examples of visual search tasks in which a single pop-out target is displayed among an array of distractors that differ from the target uniformly in terms of their color.

Luck and Hillyard (1994) recorded participants' EEG data while viewing stimulus arrays, such as that shown in Figure 23.3 (left panel). In 50% of trials, a homogeneous array of eight identical small, blue, vertically oriented rectangular stimuli were presented on-screen at random, non-overlapping locations. Of the remaining trials, one-third comprised a single green stimulus among an array of seven blue distractors (i.e., color pop-out), one-third comprised a single horizontal stimulus among an array of seven vertical distractors (i.e., orientation pop-out), and one-third comprised a single large (square) stimulus among an array of seven small (rectangular) distractors (i.e., size pop-out). In each block, one pop-out type was selected as target, the participant's task being to respond by button press whenever they observed a target pop-out. Each set of stimuli was displayed for 750 ms, with an inter-trial pause of between 600 and 900 ms. Various ERP components—posterior N2, P2, and P3—were shown to be modulated by the presentation of a target pop-out. Of greatest relevance to the present study was the observation that the posterior N2 component could be decomposed into ipsilateral activity, in which a pop-out target presented to a participant's left visual hemifield elicited a response at left posterior electrodes (and vice versa), and contralateral activity, in which a pop-out target presented to a participant's left visual hemifield elicited a response at right posterior electrodes (and vice versa). The response was found to be greater in magnitude and earlier in latency for the contralateral activity. Based on this, Luck and Hillyard concluded that posterior N2 comprised two distinct ERP components: an earlier contralateral component, which they termed N2pc ('p' for posterior; 'c' for contralateral), followed by a later bilateral component, which they termed N2pb ('b' for bilateral).

Among the various subsequent studies that have investigated the elicitation of N2pc (e.g., Eimer 1996; Woodman & Luck 1999; Eimer & Mazza 2005; Hickey et al. 2006), Mazza et al. (2009) have considered whether N2pc indexes cognitive mechanisms related to distractor suppression—the general interpretation at that time—or cognitive mechanisms related to target enhancement. They presented to participants an array of stimuli consisting of colored diamonds, varying the number, colors, and proximity to the target of a set of distractors of the same shape. An example stimulus array is shown in Figure 23.3 (right panel). The participant's task was to indicate by button press whether the target stimulus appeared to the left or to the right of a central fixation. Stimuli were presented for 150 ms to render eye movements ineffective, with an inter-trial pause of up to 1,500 ms available for the participant to perform a button press. Mazza et al. observed that significantly greater N2pc magnitude was elicited when the number of distractors was large (19) than when the number of distractors was small (3). However, they found that the proximity of distractors to the target stimuli had no impact on N2pc amplitude. Furthermore, a set of distractors sharing a single color elicited stronger N2pc amplitude than another set of distractors of the same number that comprised two distinct colors. Based on this result, they concluded that N2pc indexes cognitive mechanisms that are engaged primarily to enhance targets, rather than to suppress distractors, although they acknowledge that distractor suppression might still contribute to N2pc.

1.3   N200 as a cue for target location

The relevance of the prior research on N2pc to the present study is as follows: During operation of a visual speller, the user is required to locate the target cell containing the text to be input and then to maintain attention to it while the cells of the stimulus matrix are intensified in pseudo-random sequence. We suggest that perception of such intensifications may engage the same cognitive responses as are engaged by perception of pop-out targets during visual search tasks. Whereas a non-target intensification is a distraction to be suppressed, a target intensification allows attention to the target to be maintained (or re-attained), and so is to be enhanced.

By maintaining attention to a particular target cell, no consistent pattern of lateralization of N200 is expected for target intensifications because such intensifications are perceived equally in the two visual hemifields. For non-target intensifications of stimulus matrix columns, however, a contralateral N200 response is expected because such intensifications are perceived differentially in the two visual hemifields. Figure 23.4 illustrates this effect.

In particular, we hypothesize the following: (i) That target intensifications will elicit no consistent pattern of N200 lateralization. (ii) That non-target column intensifications to the left of the attended target will elicit right-lateralized N200 response, and vice versa. (iii) Consistent

Figure 23.4 Schematic illustration showing N200 as a cue for target location

Schematic illustration showing a target stimulus that elicits lateralized N200 Schematic illustration of a target located on the left side of the stimulus matrix, and a non-target column located to the right of the target. For an individual attending to the target, the non-target column is perceived in the right visual hemifield.

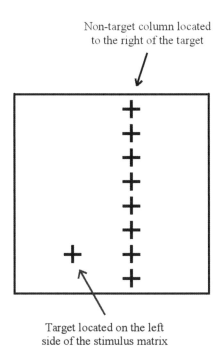

Non-target column located
to the right of the target

Target located on the left
side of the stimulus matrix

with (Luck and Hillyard 1994) and (Mazza et al. 2009), that N200 amplitude will be modulated by the number of cells in the stimulus matrix—with more cells eliciting larger amplitude—but not by the physical size of the matrix.

The following experiment serves as a preliminary investigation into these hypotheses in order to explore the possibility that parietal N200 may act as an electrophysiological cue for target location in a visual speller, potentially allowing speller performance to be enhanced.

2.   Methodology

2.1   Participants

Five students from The Chinese University of Hong Kong (2 female, 3 male), all native Chinese readers, consented to participate in this study. All participants were able-bodied, had normal or corrected-to-normal vision, and reported no history of neurological illness.

2.2   Data acquisition

Each participant was seated in a quiet, dimly lit room about 90 cm before a 15″ LCD monitor that displayed the experimental stimuli. EEG data were acquired using a 32-channel ActiveTwo EEG system (BioSemi B.V., Amsterdam, The Netherlands) with Ag/AgCl active electrodes at positions Fp1, Fp2, AF3, AF4, Fz, F3, F4, F7, F8, FC1, FC2, FC5, FC6, Cz, C3, C4, T7, T8, CP1, CP2, CP5, CP6, Pz, P3, P4, P7, P8, PO3, PO4, Oz, O1, and O2 (Sharbrough et al. 1991). Two additional electrodes, *common mode sense* (CMS) and *driven right leg* (DRL), positioned on either side of vertex, were used to provide a feedback loop to drive the average electrical potential as close as possible to the amplifier reference voltage (Biosemi B.V. 2007). EEG data were recorded at a sampling rate of 256 Hz using ActiView 6.05 (BioSemi B.V., Amsterdam, The Netherlands), and a 0.5 Hz to 30 Hz digital band-pass filter applied. The data were processed using EEGLab 7.2.9.20b (Delorme and Makeig 2004) running in Matlab 7.2.0 (The Mathworks, Natick, MA, U.S.A.). Epochs were extracted from 100 ms before stimulus onset to 600 ms after stimulus onset, the mean voltage in the 100 ms interval prior to stimulus onset being used as the baseline voltage for each epoch. All channels were re-referenced against the average voltage recorded at two electrodes positioned above the left and right mastoid process. Eye artefacts were monitored using electrodes Fp1 and Fp2—trials with eye artefacts (amplitude exceeding 90 μV) were excluded from the subsequent analysis. In total, 90% of target epochs and 94% of non-target epochs were retained for analysis.

2.3   Experimental procedure

Each participant took part in two sessions, which were run on different days. Each session consisted of three blocks, each block following the same experimental procedure except for the contents of the stimulus matrices (described below). Each block consisted of 32 trials, each trial comprising 5 intensification sequences. During an intensification sequence, each row and each column of the stimulus matrix was intensified once in pseudo-random order. Intensifications were implemented by displaying the intensified stimuli more brightly than the unintensified stimuli, and lasted for 80 ms, after which the entire stimulus matrix was displayed unintensified for 80 ms. Before each trial, a target stimulus was displayed on-screen by intensifying the corresponding cell of the stimulus matrix for 2.5 s. Participants were instructed to attend to the target stimulus throughout the subsequent trial, silently counting how many times it was intensified. No behavioural response was required. The location of the target stimulus was counter-balanced across trials, appearing on the left side of the stimulus matrix in half of the trials and on the right side of the stimulus matrix in the remaining trials. There was a 4 s pause between successive trials. Participants were allowed a break after every four trials and between blocks.

Session 1 comprised three blocks, each using a distinct stimulus matrix consisting of sinograms (traditional): 4 by 4 (large), 4 by 4 (small), and 8 by 8. Session 2 also comprised three blocks, the first block using a 6 by 6 stimulus matrix of sinograms, followed by two blocks using

Figure 23.5   The stimulus matrices utilized in this study: (top-left) 4 by 4 (large); (top-right) 4 by 4 (small); (bottom-left) 6 by 6; and (bottom-right) 8 by 8

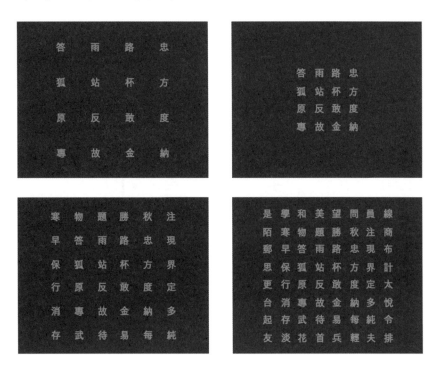

two other stimulus matrices (the results for which are not relevant to the present study). The four stimulus matrices used in the present study are shown in Figure 23.5. The sizes of the stimulus matrices differed in two respects: number of cells and physical size. Stimulus matrices 4 by 4 (large) and 4 by 4 (small) both comprised 16 cells (with identical sinogram content). However, the physical size of the 4-by-4 (large) stimulus matrix was greater than that of 4-by-4 (small). Stimulus matrix 6-by-6 comprised 36 cells (including the 16 sinograms used in the two 4-by-4 matrices, plus 20 others). Stimulus matrix 8 by 8 comprised 64 cells (including the 36 sinograms used in the 6 by 6 matrix, plus 28 others). The physical areas on-screen of the 4 by 4 (large), 6 by 6, and 8 by 8 stimulus matrices were approximately equal.

3.   Results

The purpose of this experiment was to determine what factors modulate the magnitude and lateralization of the parietal N200 component elicited by target and non-target intensifications in a visual speller. In particular, we hypothesized that target intensifications would elicit no consistent lateralization pattern, but that non-target intensifications would elicit a contralateral

Figure 23.6   Schematic illustration of our hypothesis that non-target intensifications of the stimulus matrix of a visual speller elicit contralateral N200

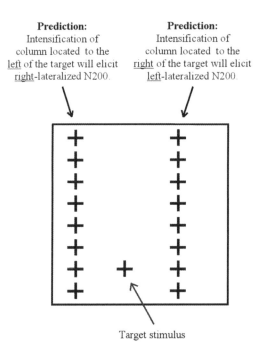

pattern, with intensifications of stimulus matrix columns to the left of target eliciting right-lateralized N200, and intensifications of stimulus matrix columns to the right of target eliciting left-lateralized N200. This hypothesis is illustrated in Figure 23.6. In addition, we predicted that the number of cells in the stimulus matrix would modulate N200 amplitude for target intensifications, with more cells eliciting larger amplitude, but that the physical size of the stimulus matrix would not.

As a first step, we calculated the global field power (see Figure 23.7), averaged across all experimental conditions and participants, to determine the time window from which to extract the N200 component. The optimal time window was found to be 150–250 ms post stimulus onset. Based on our prior research that parietal N200 elicited by a visual speller peaks at electrodes P7 and P8 (Minett et al. 2012), we estimated mean N200 amplitude by averaging the voltage recorded at these two electrodes across this time window, and investigated the lateralization of N200 by comparing the voltage difference between these two electrodes.

3.1   The effect of stimulus matrix

Figure 23.8 displays the grand-averaged ERPs and topological distributions elicited for each stimulus matrix: 4 by 4 (large), 4 by 4 (small), 6 by 6, and 8 by 8. Examining the ERPs, an N200

Figure 23.7 The global field power (GFP)

The GFP averaged across all experimental conditions in this study calculated with respect to common average reference. The figure highlights the time window, 250–350 ms, in which peak GFP was obtained, based on which we selected this window to calculate the mean amplitude of the N200 component. See Figure 23.8 for topological distributions elicited by various experimental conditions.

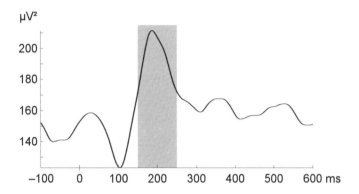

Figure 23.8 Grand-averaged ERPs and topological distribution

Grand-averaged ERPs (mean of P7 and P8; left) and topological distribution (time window of 150–250 ms; right) for each of the four stimulus matrices used in this study: 4-by-4 (large); 4-by-4 (small); 6-by-6; and 8-by-8. The 150–250 ms time window used to estimate mean N200 amplitude is highlighted.

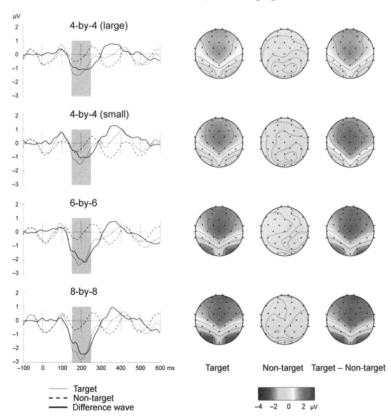

Table 23.1 Results of the analyses of variance for each participant to determine the impact of Stimulus Matrix (4 by 4 (large), 4 by 4 (small), 6 by 6, 8 by 8) and Targetness (Target, Non-target) on mean N200 amplitude

	Stimulus Matrix	Targetness	Interaction
P1	$F_{(1,3)} = 7.20, p = 0.000$	$F_{(1,1)} = 166.6, p = 0.000$	$F_{(1,3)} = 9.86, p = 0.000$
P2	$F_{(1,3)} = 0.31, p = 0.815$	$F_{(1,1)} = 16.13, p = 0.000$	$F_{(1,3)} = 0.13, p = 0.943$
P3	$F_{(1,3)} = 5.78, p = 0.001$	$F_{(1,1)} = 43.77, p = 0.000$	$F_{(1,3)} = 5.61, p = 0.001$
P4	$F_{(1,3)} = 1.72, p = 0.161$	$F_{(1,1)} = 18.83, p = 0.000$	$F_{(1,3)} = 1.04, p = 0.373$
P5	$F_{(1,3)} = 0.44, p = 0.723$	$F_{(1,1)} = 57.20, p = 0.000$	$F_{(1,3)} = 1.54, p = 0.202$

component is evident for target intensifications with all stimulus matrices. The amplitude of this component appears to be greater for stimulus matrices comprising more cells. No clear N200 component is observed for non-target intensifications. Examining the topological distributions elicited by targets in the N200 time window (i.e., 150–250 ms), the negative component has an obvious bilateral distribution at parieto-occipital locations for all stimulus matrix sizes. The topological distributions also show the presence within the same time window of a positive fronto-central component peaking along the mid-line.

We conducted separate analyses of variance for each participant to determine the impact of Stimulus Matrix (4 by 4 (large), 4 by 4 (small), 6 by 6, 8 by 8) and Targetness (Target, Non-target) on mean N200 amplitude. The results of these analyses are summarized in Table 23.1. A main effect of Targetness was obtained for all participants. Only two participants (P1 and P3) exhibited a significant main effect of Stimulus Matrix, these same two participants also exhibiting a significant interaction effect. Consequently, we ran post hoc analyses for P1 and P3 as summarized in Table 23.2 and Figure 23.9. For both participants, significantly greater N200 target amplitudes were elicited by stimulus matrices with a large number of cells (6-by-6 and 8-by-8) than by stimulus matrices with a small number of cells (either 4-by-4 (large) or 4-by-4 (small)), partially confirming our prediction that stimulus matrices with more cells elicit larger amplitude N200 for target intensifications. No significant difference in N200 target amplitude was observed for the 4-by-4 (large) and 4-by-4 (small) stimulus matrices, consistent with our prediction that the physical size of the stimulus matrix does not modulate N200 amplitude for target intensifications. N200 amplitude for non-target intensifications was not significantly modulated by either the number of cells or the physical size of the stimulus matrix.

3.2 Lateralization of N200

Recall our prediction that target intensifications would elicit no consistent N200 lateralization pattern, but that non-target intensifications would elicit contralateral N200. We therefore considered the lateralization of N200 separately for target and non-target column intensifications.

Table 23.2   Results of the post hoc analysis using Tukey's HSD for two participants, P1 and P3 , to determine the effect of Stimulus Matrix on mean N200 amplitude for both target intensifications and non-target intensifications. (4L: 4 by 4 (large); 4S: 4 by 4 (small); 6: 6 by 6; 8: 8 by 8)

Comparison		P1		P3	
		Target	Non-target	Target	Non-target
4L	4S	$t(580) = 1.106$, $p = 0.769$	$t(1780) = 1.497$, $p = 0.561$	$t(481) = 0.309$, $p = 0.990$	$t(1513) = 0.791$, $p = 0.885$
4L	6	$t(583) = 2.132$, $p = 0.115$	$t(2375) = 0.400$, $p = 0.975$	$t(489) = 2.679$, $p = 0.026$	$t(2072) = 0.118$, $p = 0.999$
4L	8	$t(588) = 4.475$, $p = 0.000$	$t(2966) = 0.458$, $p = 0.975$	$t(519) = 4.227$, $p = 0.000$	$t(2732) = 0.407$, $p = 0.978$
4S	6	$t(573) = 2.982$, $p = 0.008$	$t(2343) = 1.703$, $p = 0.244$	$t(460) = 2.370$, $p = 0.072$	$t(1967) = 0.669$, $p = 0.903$
4S	8	$t(578) = 5.376$, $p = 0.000$	$t(2943) = 1.173$, $p = 0.680$	$t(490) = 3.890$, $p = 0.001$	$t(2627) = 0.480$, $p = 0.965$
6	8	$t(581) = 1.722$, $p = 0.222$	$t(3529) = 0.957$, $p = 0.741$	$t(498) = 1.164$, $p = 0.622$	$t(3186) = 0.303$, $p = 0.989$

Figure 23.9   Summary of the results of the post hoc analysis carried out for two participants, P1 (left) and P3 (right), to determine the effect of Stimulus Matrix on mean N200 amplitude

N200 amplitudes are shown for both target intensifications (top row) and non-target intensifications (bottom row). Stimulus Matrix pairs for which a significant difference in mean N200 amplitude was obtained are marked on the figure by "*" ($p < 0.05$) or by "**" ($p < 0.005$). Pairs with no significant difference in mean N200 amplitude are unmarked ($p \geq 0.05$).

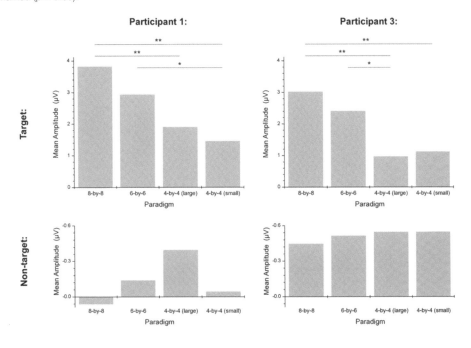

Figure 23.10   Grand-averaged ERPs and topological distributions for left-side targets

Grand-averaged ERPs (left) and topological distributions (right) for left-side targets, i.e., trials in which the target was located in the left side of the stimulus matrix, for three stimulus matrices: 4-by-4 (large); 6-by-6; and 8-by-8. The data for non-targets comprises column flashes to the right of target, only. The ERP plots highlight the N200 time window, 250–350 ms.

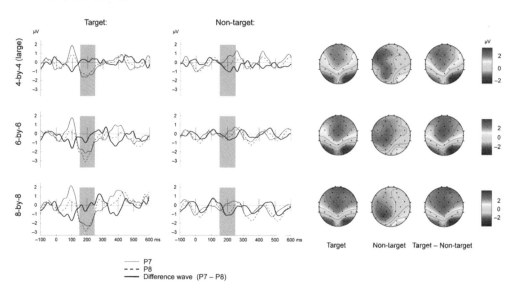

Figure 23.11   Grand-averaged ERPs and topological distributions for right-side targets

Grand-averaged ERPs (left) and topological distributions (right) for right-side targets, i.e., trials in which the target was located in the right side of the stimulus matrix, for three stimulus matrices: 4-by-4 (large); 6-by-6; and 8-by-8. The data for non-targets comprises column flashes to the left of target, only. The ERP plots highlight the N200 time window, 250–350 ms.

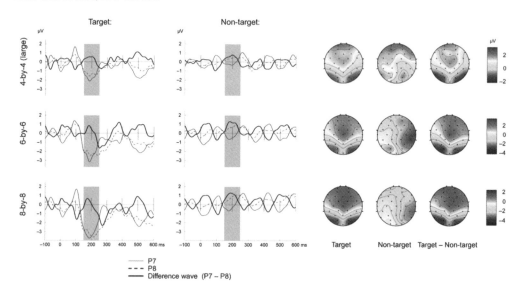

Figures 23.10 and 23.11 show the grand-averaged ERPs and topological distributions elicited by both target intensifications and non-target intensification for three different matrix sizes: 4 by 4 (large), 6 by 6, and 8 by 8. Similarly to Mazza et al. (2009), we distinguish between the ERP responses for targets located on the left side of the stimulus matrix (Figure 23.10) and the ERP responses for targets located on the right side of the stimulus matrix (Figure 23.11). The non-target intensifications used to prepare Figure 23.10 comprise non-target column intensifications to the right of the target, only. In contrast, the non-target intensifications used to prepare Figure 23.11 comprise non-target column intensifications to the left of the target, only. A bilateral N200 component is evident for all target intensifications. The amplitude of this component appears to be greater for stimulus matrices comprising more cells. However, for non-target intensifications, a contralateral centro-parietal N200 is now observed—that is, non-target column intensifications to the right of target elicit left-lateralized N200, while non-target column intensifications to the left of target elicit right-lateralized N200.

To assess these phenomena statistically, we conducted separate analyses of variance for each participant to determine the impact of Stimulus Matrix (4 by 4 (large), 6 by 6, 8 by 8) and Target Side (left, right) on N200 lateralization, calculated as the amplitude difference P7–P8, both for target intensifications and for non-target intensifications.

We consider first the analyses for target intensifications (summarized in Table 23.3): A significant main effect of Stimulus Matrix was observed for a single participant (P5), only. However, Target Side had a significant effect ($p < 0.05$) on N200 lateralization for all three participants (P2, P4, and P5), with a marginal trend observed for a fourth participant (P3). However, no consistent pattern of lateralization was observed for target intensifications across these four subject, with contralateral patterns and ipsilateral patterns each evident across participants in 50% of experimental conditions.

Table 23.3 Results of the analyses of variance for each participant to determine the impact of Stimulus Matrix (4 by 4 (large), 6 by 6, 8 by 8) and Target Side (left, right) on N200 lateralization for target intensifications

	Stimulus Matrix	Target Side Field	Interaction
P1	$F(1,2) = 0.10, p = 0.909$	$F(1,1) = 0.01, p = 0.913$	$F(1,2) = 2.03, p = 0.132$
P2	$F(1,2) = 0.49, p = 0.614$	$F(1,1) = 4.10, p = 0.043$	$F(1,2) = 0.39, p = 0.678$
P3	$F(1,2) = 0.96, p = 0.382$	$F(1,1) = 3.67, p = 0.056$	$F(1,2) = 0.85, p = 0.429$
P4	$F(1,2) = 0.94, p = 0.392$	$F(1,1) = 10.9, p = 0.001$	$F(1,2) = 0.07, p = 0.929$
P5	$F(1,2) = 6.01, p = 0.003$	$F(1,1) = 5.23, p = 0.023$	$F(1,2) = 1.34, p = 0.262$

Table 23.4 Results of the analyses of variance for each participant to determine the impact of Stimulus Matrix (4 by 4 (large), 6 by 6, 8 by 8) and Target Side (left, right) on N200 lateralization for non-target intensifications

	Stimulus Matrix	Target Side	Interaction
P1	$F(1,2) = 0.49, p = 0.610$	$F(1,1) = 8.55, p = 0.004$	$F(1,2) = 0.33, p = 0.716$
P2	$F(1,2) = 0.29, p = 0.746$	$F(1,1) = 20.13, p = 0.000$	$F(1,2) = 2.61, p = 0.074$
P3	$F(1,2) = 2.29, p = 0.102$	$F(1,1) = 50.79, p = 0.000$	$F(1,2) = 0.14, p = 0.872$
P4	$F(1,2) = 0.60, p = 0.547$	$F(1,1) = 14.43, p = 0.000$	$F(1,2) = 0.14, p = 0.867$
P5	$F(1,2) = 1.40, p = 0.248$	$F(1,1) = 27.72, p = 0.000$	$F(1,2) = 1.79, p = 0.167$

Turning now to the analyses for non-target intensifications (summarized in Table 23.4): Target Side had a strongly significant effect ($p < 0.005$) on N200 lateralization for all participants. Furthermore, the pattern of lateralization was quite consistent, with contralateral patterns observed across participants in 80% of experimental conditions, and ipsilateral patterns observed across participants in only 20% of experimental conditions. These findings are broadly consistent with our hypothesis that non-target column intensifications elicit a contralateral N200 lateralization pattern, but that target intensifications do not.

4.   Discussion

The statistical analysis of the ERP data elicited in this study lends preliminary support to our hypothesis that non-target column intensifications of a visual speller elicit contralateral N200. The benefit of making use of brain signals that lateralize in order to predict a user's intentions to control a BCI system has already been well demonstrated. In particular, speech imagery-based BCIs, such as the Berlin Brain-Computer Interface (BBCI) (e.g., Blankertz et al. 1996), make extensive use of lateralized brain signals to perform continuous control (e.g., cursor movement). When an individual plans and performs, or imagines performing, a body movement, neurons in the primary motor cortex and other motor circuits activate contralaterally to the side of the body moved. Particular regions of primary motor cortex are associated with movement of particular parts of the body (Penfield & Rasmussen 1950). The motor-related signals that are elicited during motor imagery include the lateralized readiness potential (LRP) (Coles 1989) and event-related desynchronization (ERD) (Pfurtscheller and da Silva 1999), both of which lateralize according to side of the imagined movement. By localizing measurements of such signals to different electrodes positioned above motor cortex, multiple channels of BCI control can be achieved (e.g., Royer et al. 2010), each linked to imagined movement of a distinct body part.

More recently, Zhao et al. (2011) have investigated the N2pc component elicited by color pop-outs presented among a ring of eleven similarly shaped distractors. This paradigm resembles the presentation paradigm of Hex-o-Spell (e.g., Treder & Blankertz 2010), a multi-stage visual speller for alphabetic text input that organizes text stimuli into a ring of six disks, the disks being intensified one-by-one in pseudo-random sequence. Zhao et al. demonstrated significant modulation of N2pc magnitude at posterior-lateral electrodes (P7/P8, PO7/PO8, and O1/O2) across the 210–290 ms time window (slightly later than the 150–250 ms window that we obtained in the present study). They put forward the hypothesis that N2pc amplitude might be modulated by the degree of color difference between a target and distracters. This raises the possibility that different cells in the stimulus matrix of a visual speller could be intensified using different colors (or other visual features, such as size or orientation) in order to elicit different magnitudes of N2pc. It is not clear whether such an approach can work in practice. Nevertheless, it does encourage us to examine in more detail the potential utility of N2pc and other lateralized components in BCI applications.

We plan to follow up the present study by exploring how to enhance the contralateral N200 component elicited by visual speller intensifications. In addition to manipulating the color of intensification (Zhao et al. 2011; cf. Mazza et al. 2009), other manipulations, such as of size and orientation, are known to modulate N2pc (Luck and Hillyard 1994). It is probable that such manipulations will also modulate the visual speller N200 component. If such modulations are confirmed to be robust, lateralization of N200 may serve as a cue for the location of the target cell, information which may be used to enhance speller accuracy and input speed.

REFERENCES

Allison, B. Z., and J. A. Pineda. 2006. Effects of SOA and flash pattern manipulations on ERPs, performance, and preference: Implications for a BCI system. *International Journal of Psychophysiology* 59 (2): 27–140.

Biosemi, B. V. 2007. *Active Two User Manual* (Version 3.2, July 3, 2007). Amsterdam.

Birbaumer, N., and L. G. Cohen. 2007. Brain–computer interfaces: Communication and restoration of movement in paralysis. *The Journal of Physiology* 579 (3): 621–636.

Blankertz, B., G. Krauledat, M. Müller, K. R. Kunzmann, V. F. Losch, and G. Curio. 2006. The Berlin Brain-Computer Interface: EEG-based communication without subject training. *IEEE Transactions on Neural Systems and Rehabilitation Engineering* 14 (2): 147–152.

Boyle, M. 1994. The effects of brain stem stroke on communication and swallowing. *Topics in Stroke Rehabilitation* 1 (2): 76–86.

Clough, C. G., K. R. Chaudhuri, K. D. Sethi, and S. Muzerengi. 2007. *Parkinson's Disease.* Abingdon, Oxford: Health Press.

Coles, M. G. H. 1989. Modern mind-brain reading: Psychophysiology, physiology and cognition. *Psychophysiology* 26:251–269.

Delorme, A., and S. Makeig. 2004. EEGLAB: An open source toolbox for analysis of single-trial EEG dynamics. *Journal of Neuroscience Methods* 134:9–21.

Donchin, E. 1981. Presidential address. 1980. Surprise! … Surprise? *Psychophysiology* 18 (5): 493–513.

Donchin, E., K. M. Spencer, and R. Wijesinghe. 2000. The mental prosthesis: Assessing the speed of a P300-based brain-computer interface. *IEEE Transactions on Rehabilitation Engineering* 8:174–179.

Eimer, M. 1996. The N2pc component as an indicator of attentional selectivity. *Electroencephalography and Clinical Neurophysiology* 99:225–234.

Eimer, M., and V. Mazza. 2005. Electrophysiological correlates of change detection. *Psychophysiology* 42:328–342.

Farwell, L. A., and E. Donchin. 1988. Talking off the top of your head: Toward a mental prosthesis utilizing event-related brain potentials. *Electroencephalography and Clinical Neurophysiology* 70:510–523.

Guan, C., M. Thulasidas, and J. Wu. 2004. High performance P300 speller for brain–computer interface. *Proceedings of the 2004 IEEE Workshop on Biomedical Circuits and Systems,* S3–5.INV–13–16 (4 pages).

Hickey, C., J. J. McDonald, and J. Theeuwes. 2006. Electrophysiological evidence of the capture of visual attention. *Journal of Cognitive Neuroscience* 18:604–613.

Huo, X., and M. Ghonvaloo. 2010. Evaluation of a wireless wearable tongue–computer interface by individuals with high-level spinal cord injuries. *Journal of Neural Engineering* 7:026008 (12 pages).

Iannello, S. 2005. *Guillain-Barré Syndrome: Pathological, Clinical, and Therapeutical Aspects.* New York: Nova Science Publishers.

Jin, J., B. Z. Allison, C. Brunner, B. Wang, X. Wang, J. Zhang, C. Neuper, and G. Pfurtscheller. 2010. P300 Chinese input system based on Bayesian LDA. *Biomedizinische Technik: Biomedical Engineering* 55 (1): 5–18.

Krusienski, D. J., E. W. Sellers, D. J. MacFarland, T. M. Vaughan, and J. R. Wolpaw. 2008. Toward enhanced P300 speller performance. *Journal of Neuroscience Methods* 167 (1): 15–21.

Kuncl, R., ed. 2002. *Motor Neuron Disease*. London: W. B. Saunders.

Langmore, S. E., and M. E. Lehman. 1994. Physiological deficits in the orofacial system underlying dysarthria in amyotrophic lateral sclerosis. *Journal of Speech and Hearing Research* 37 (1): 28–37.

Luck, S. J., and S. A. Hillyard. 1994. Electrophysiological correlates of feature analysis during visual search. *Psychophysiology*, 291–308.

Mak, J. N., Y. Arbel, J. W. Minett, L. M. McCane, B. Yuksel, D. Ryan, D. Thompson, L. Bianchi, and D. Erdogmus. 2011. Optimizing the P300-based brain–computer interface: Current status, limitations and future directions. *Journal of Neural Engineering* 8:025003 (7 pages).

Mazza, V., M. Turatto, and A. Caramazza. 2009. Attention selection, distraction suppression and N2pc. *Cortex* 45: 879–890.

Minett, J. W., G. Peng, L. Zhou, H.-Y. Zheng, and W. S-Y. Wang. 2010. An assistive communication brain–computer interface for Chinese text input. *Proceedings of the 4th International Conference on Bioinformatics and Biomedical Engineering* (iCBBE 2010). Paper ID 41183 (4 pages).

Minett, J. W., H.-Y. Zheng, M. C.-M. Fong, L. Zhou, G. Peng, and W. S-Y. Wang. 2012. A Chinese text input brain–computer interface based on the P300 Speller. *International Journal of Human–Computer Interaction* 28 (7): 472–483.

Penfield, W., and T. Rasmussen. 1950. *The Cerebral Cortex of Man*. New York: Macmillan.

Pfurtscheller, G., and F. H. L. da Silva. 1999. Event-related EEG/MEG synchronization and desynchronization: Basic principles. *Clinical Neurophysiology* 110 (11): 1842–1857.

Raine, C. S., H. F. MacFarland, and R. Hohlfeld, eds. 2008. *Multiple sclerosis: A Comprehensive Text*. Edinburgh, New York: Saunders/Elsevier.

Sharbrough, F. C. G., R. P. Lesser, H. Lüders, M. Nuwer, and W. Picton. 1991. AEEGS guidelines for standard electrode position nomenclature. *Clinical Neurophysiology* 8:202–204.

Smith, E., and M. Delargy. 2005. Locked-in syndrome. *British Medical Journal* 330: 406–409.

Sutton, S., M. Braren, J. Zubin, and E. R. John. 1965. Information delivery and the sensory evoked potential. *Science* 155:1436–1439.

Townsend, G., B. K. LaPallo, C. B. Boulay, D. J. Krusienski, G. E. Frye, C. K. Hauser, N. E. Schwartz, T. M. Vaughan, J. R. Wolpaw, and E. W. Sellers. 2010. A novel P300-based brain–computer interface stimulus presentation paradigm: Moving beyond rows and columns. *Clinical Neurophysiology* 121:1109–1120.

Treder, M., and B. Blankertz. 2010. (C) Overt attention and visual speller design in an ERP-based brain–computer interface. *Behavioral and Brain Functions* 6 (1): 28.

Wang, W. S-Y., and Y. Tsai. 2011. The alphabet and the sinogram: Setting the stage for a look across orthographies. In *Dyslexia Across Cultures*, eds. P. McCardle, J. R. Lee, B. Miller, and O. Tzeng, 1–16. Brookes Publishing.

Wang, W. S-Y. 1973. The Chinese language. *Scientific American* 228 (2): 50–60.

Wolpaw, J. R., N. Birbaumer, D. McFarland, G. Pfurtscheller, and T. Vaughan. 2002. Brain–computer interfaces for communication and control. *Clinical Neurophysiology* 113:767–791.

Woodman, G. F., and S. J. Luck. 1999. Electrophysiological measurement of rapid shifts of attention during visual search. *Nature* 400:867–869.

Wu, B., Y. Su, J-H. Zhang, X. Li, J-C. Zhang, W.-D. Cheng, and X. X. Zheng. A virtual Chinese keyboard BCI system based on P300 potentials. *Acta Electronica Sinica* 37 (8): 1733–1745. [In Chinese]

Xinhua Zidian, 10th edition. 2004. Beijing: Shang wu yin shu guan. [In Chinese]

Zhao, G., Q. Liu, Y. Zhang, J. Jiao, Q. Zhang, H. Sun, and H. Li. 2011. The amplitude of N2pc reflects the physical disparity between target item and distracters. *Neuroscience Letters* 491:68–72.

24

Consensus in Language Dynamics: Naming, Categorizing and Blending

Vittorio LORETO
Sapienza University of Rome and ISI Foundation

Francesca TRIA
ISI Foundation

Abstract

Understanding the origins and evolution of language and meaning is currently one of the most promising areas of research in cognitive science. New theoretical and computational tools, and synthetic modelling approaches have now reached sufficient maturity to contribute significantly to the ongoing debate in this area. Unprecedented advances in information and communications technologies are enabling, for the first time, the possibility of precisely mapping the interactions of large numbers of actors, whether embodied and/or symbolic, as well as the dynamics and transmission of information along social ties. The combination of these two elements is opening promising new avenues for studying the emergence and evolution of languages, new communication and semiotic systems, triggering a significant boost in the ongoing transition of linguistics into an experimental discipline.

In this paper we shall review some of the progress made in the last few years and highlight potential future directions of research in this area. In particular, the emergence of a common lexicon, a shared set of linguistic categories and the emergence of duality of patterning will be discussed, as examples corresponding to the early stages of a language. We shall emphasize the cultural route to the emergence and evolution of language, i.e., the idea that a community of language users can be seen as a complex dynamical system, which collectively solves the problem of developing a shared communication framework through the back-and-forth signalling between individuals. We shall illustrate a few examples where the predictions of synthetic modelling have been successfully compared with real data. Finally we shall discuss how new technologies and computational facilities are making available a huge amount of resources both as novel tools and data to be analyzed, allowing quantitative and large-scale analysis of the processes underlying the emergence of a collective information and language dynamics.

1.   Introduction and the Theoretical Background

Language dynamics is a rapidly growing field that focuses on all processes related to the emergence, evolution, change and extinction of languages. Recently, the study of self-organization and evolution of language and meaning has led to the idea that a community of language users can be seen as a complex dynamical system (Steels 2000), which collectively solves the problem of developing a shared communication framework through the back-and-forth signalling between individuals. From this perspective, language is thus seen as an evolving and self-organizing system, whose components are thus constantly being (re) shaped by language users in order to maximise communicative success and expressive power, while at the same time minimising effort. In this picture new words and grammatical constructions may be invented or acquired, new meanings may arise, the relation between language and meaning may shift (e.g., if a word adopts a new meaning), the relation between meanings and the world may shift (e.g., if new perceptually grounded categories are introduced). All these changes happen at the level of the individual as well as at the group level, the focus being on the interactions among the individuals, with both vertical (teacher-pupil) as well as horizontal (peer to peer) communications. Here communications acts are particular cases of language games, which, as already pointed out by Wittgenstein (Wittgenstein 1953), can be used to describe linguistic behaviour, even though they can include also non linguistic behaviour, such as pointing. Clark (Clark 1996) argues that language and communication are social activities—joint activities—that require people to coordinate with each other as they speak and listen. Language use is more than the sum of a speaker speaking and a listener listening. It is the joint action that emerges when speakers and listeners (Garrod and Pickering 2004), writers and readers perform their individual actions in coordination, as ensembles. Again language is not seen as an individual process, but rather as a social process where a continuous alignment of mental representations (Garrod and Pickering 2009) is taking place.

The landscape describing the large set of approaches to the study of language emergence and dynamics is extremely diversified, due to the flagrant complexity of a problem that can be addressed under many respects, with different methodologies, guided by often incompatible conceptual frameworks, and with different goals in mind. A useful way to gain insights into such a variegated world is therefore that of focusing on few dimensions that allow for a coarse categorization of the ongoing research (Haeger et al. 2009). In general it is possible to identify broad paradigms that frame the problem in a particular way, focusing on specific problems and addressing precise fundamental questions through concrete models and experiments (Nolfi and Mirolli 2009). Within each framework, then, the investigation can proceed through computational models, experiments with embodied agents, psychological experiments with human subjects and finally exploiting data made available by large information systems like the Web.

In this chapter we shall mainly focus on the mathematical modelling of social phenomena. Statistical physics has proven to be a very fruitful framework to describe phenomena outside the realm of traditional physics (Loreto and Steels 2007). The last years have witnessed the attempt by physicists to study collective phenomena emerging from the interactions of individuals as elementary units in social structures (Castellano, Fortunato, and Loreto 2009). This is the paradigm of the complex systems: an assembly of many interacting (and simple) units whose collective (i.e., large scale) behaviour is not trivially deducible from the knowledge of the rules that govern their mutual interactions. This scenario is also true for problems related to the emergence of language.

From this new perspective, complex systems science turns out to be a natural ally in the quest for general mechanisms to understand the collective dynamics whereby conventions can spread in a population. In particular we shall focus on how conceptual and linguistic coherence may arise through self-organization or evolution, and how concept formation and expression may interact to co-ordinate semiotic systems of individuals. One of the key methodological aspects of the modelling activity in the domains of complex systems is the tendency to seek simplified models to clearly pin down the assumptions and, in many cases, to make the models tractable from a mathematical point of view.

A crucial step in the modelling activity is represented by the comparison with empirical data. This comparison could help in checking whether the trends seen in real data are already compatible with plausible microscopic modelling of the individuals, or require additional ingredients. From this point of view the Web may be of great help, both as a platform to perform controlled online social experiments, and as a repository of empirical data on large-scale phenomena. In this way a virtuous cycle involving data collection, data analysis, modelling and predictions can be triggered, giving rise to an ever more rigorous and focused approach to language dynamics.

It is worth stressing how the contribution that physicists, mathematicians and computer scientists could give should not be considered as alternative to more traditional approaches. We rather think that it would be crucial to foster the interactions across the different disciplines cooperating with linguistics, by promoting scientific activities with concrete mutual exchanges among all the interested scientists. This would help both in identifying the problems and sharpening the focus, as well as in devising the most suitable theoretical concepts and tools to approach the research.

While the research field of semiotics may traditionally be considered a conceptual discipline, the cognitive turn has recently brought central semiotic questions and insights into the laboratories and a new discipline, dubbed experimental semiotics (Galantucci and Garrod 2010), is about to be born. A few important examples have already shown the viability of this approach: from coordination game with interconnected computers (Galantucci 2005; Selten and Warglien 2007) to experimental tests for Iterated Learning Models (Kirby, Cornish, and Smith 2008).

But this is only the tip of a potentially huge iceberg. The new Information and Communication Technologies (ICT) are opening terrific opportunities to monitor human actions both symbolic and embodied. This reverberates in the possibility to turn these new technologies in a living lab devoted to language dynamics and more generally to social sciences. In this framework the Web is playing a special role potentially very relevant for studies in language dynamics. Though only a few years old, the growth of the World Wide Web and its effect on the society have been astonishing, spreading from the research in high-energy physics into other scientific disciplines, academe in general, commerce, entertainment, politics and almost anywhere communication serves a purpose. Innovation has widened the possibilities for communication. Social media like blogs, wikis and social bookmarking tools allow the immediacy of conversation, with unprecedented levels of communication speed and community size. Millions of users now participate in managing their personal collection of online resources by enriching them with semantically meaningful information in the form of freely chosen tags and by coordinating the categories they imply. Wikipedia, Yahoo Answers and the ESP Game (Von Ahn and Dabbish 2004) are systems where users volunteer their human computation because they value helping others, participating in a community, or playing a game. These new types of communities are showing a very vital new form of semiotic dynamics. From a scientific point of view, these developments are very exciting because they can be tracked in real time and the tools of complex systems science and cognitive science can be used to study them. The Web is thus revealing yet another skin as a potential platform to run experiments where the cognitive and linguistic skills of humans have to be challenged and tested.

The outline of the chapter is as follows. Sections 1 and 2 will be devoted to describe how a synthetic population of individuals can bootstrap increasing complex linguistics structures. We shall consider in particular how names and early syntactic structures (Sect. 1) and linguistic categories (Sect. 2) emerge. Section 3 will be devoted to challenging the theoretical predictions against real-world data. Section 4 will briefly describe the new opportunities offered by the new Information and Communication Technologies to setup an experimental framework devoted to language dynamics. Finally the last section is devoted to drawing some conclusions.

1.1   Naming

Let us start by considering the problem of Naming objects. This is probably the simplest, though non-trivial, problem when addressing language emergence. The problem we shall be considering can be posed in the following terms. How a population of individuals, without any pre-coordinated and shared linguistic structure, can bootstrap a shared set of names associated to a set of objects? Is this consensus always reached? Under which conditions? It is important to remark as these questions represent one specific instance of a more general question addressed when investigating social dynamics. How do the interactions between social agents create order out of an initial disordered situation? Order is a translation in the language of physics of what is denoted in social sciences as consensus, agreement, uniformity, while disorder stands for fragmentation or disagreement. It is reasonable to assume that without interactions, heterogeneity dominates: left alone, each agent would choose a personal response to a political question, a unique set of cultural features, his own special correspondence between objects and words. Still it is common experience that shared opinions, cultures, and languages do exist. The Naming Game was expressively conceived to explore the role of self-organization in the evolution of language (Steels 1995, 1996) and it has acquired, since then, a paradigmatic role in the entire field of Semiotic Dynamics. The pioneering work (Steels 1995) mainly focused on the formation of vocabularies, i.e., a set of mappings between words and meanings (for instance physical objects). In this context, each agent develops its own vocabulary in a random and private fashion. Nevertheless, agents are forced to align their vocabularies, through successive conversation, in order to obtain the benefit of cooperating through communication. Thus, a globally shared vocabulary emerges, or should emerge, as a result of local adjustments of individual word-meaning associations. The communication evolves through successive conversations, i.e., events that involve a certain number of agents (two, in practical implementations) and meanings. It is worth remarking that conversations are here particular cases of language games, which, as already pointed out by Wittgenstein (Wittgenstein 1953), are used to describe linguistic behaviour but, if needed, can also include non-linguistic behaviour, such as pointing.

This original seminal idea triggered a series of contributions along the same lines and many variants have been proposed along the years. It is worthwhile to mention here the work proposed in (Ke 2002), who focuses on an imitation model which simulates how a common vocabulary is formed by agents imitating each other either using a mere random strategy or a strategy in which imitation follows the majority (which implies non-local information for the agents). A further contribution of the mentioned paper is the introduction of an interaction model that uses a probabilistic representation of the vocabulary. The probabilistic scheme is formally similar to the framework of evolutionary game theory (Nowak et al. 1999; Nowak et al. 1999b), since a production matrix and a comprehension matrix is associated to each agent. Unlike the approach of Evolutionary Language Games, the matrices are here dynamically transformed according to the social learning process and the cultural transmission rule. A similar approach has been proposed in (Lenaerts 2005).

Here we discuss in details a minimal version of the Naming Game that results in a drastic simplification of the model definition, while keeping the same overall phenomenology. This version of the Naming Game is suitable for massive numerical simulations and analytical approaches. Moreover its extreme simplicity allows for a direct comparison with other models introduced in other frameworks of statistical physics as well as in other disciplines.

1.1.1 The Minimal Naming Game

The simplest version of the Naming Game (Baronchelli 2006) is played by a population of N agents trying to bootstrap a common vocabulary for a certain number M of objects present in their environment. The objects can be people, physical objects, relations, web sites, pictures, music files, or any other kind of entity for which a population aims at reaching a consensus as far as their naming is concerned. Each player is characterized by an inventory of word-object associations he/she knows. All the inventories are initially empty (t = 0). At each time step (t = 1, 2, ...) two players are randomly picked and one of them plays as speaker and the other as hearer.

Their interaction obeys the following rules (see Figure 24.1):

- The speaker selects an object from the current context;

- The speaker retrieves a word from its inventory associated with the chosen object, or, if its inventory is empty, invents a new word;

- The speaker transmits the selected word to the hearer;

- If the hearer has the word named by the speaker in its inventory and that word is associated to the object chosen by the speaker, the interaction is a success and both players maintain in their inventories only the winning word, deleting all the others;

- If the hearer does not have the word named by the speaker in its inventory, or the word is associated to a different object, the interaction is a failure and the hearer updates its inventory by adding an association between the new word and the object.

The game is played on a fully connected network, i.e., each player can, in principle, play with all the other players, and makes two basic assumptions. One assumes that the number of possible words is so huge that the probability of a word to be re-invented is practically negligible (this means that homonymy is not taken into account here, though the extension is trivially possible). As a consequence, one can reduce, without loss of generality, the environment as consisting of only one single object (M = 1).

A third assumption of the Naming Game consists in assuming that the speaker and the hearer are able to establish whether a game was successful by subsequent actions performed in a common environment. For example, the speaker may refer to an object in the environment he wants to obtain and the hearer then hands the right object. If the game is a failure, the speaker may point (non-verbal communication) or get the object himself so that it is clear to the hearer which object was intended.

Macroscopic analysis of the Minimal Naming Game reveals that consensus is always reached going through three different phases. Very early, pairs of agents play almost uncorrelated (and unsuccessful) games and both total number of words in all the inventories and the number of distinct words increase linearly over time. In the second phase the success probability is still very small and agents' inventories start correlating, the total number of words presenting a well identified peak. The process evolves with an abrupt increase in the number of successes

Figure 24.1. Naming Game
Examples of the dynamics of the inventories in a failed (top) and successful (bottom) game. The speaker selects the word highlighted. If the hearer does not possess that word he includes it in his inventory (top). Otherwise both agents erase their inventories only keeping the winning word (bottom).

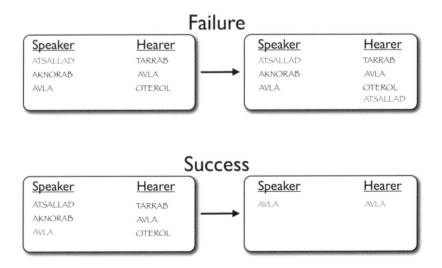

and a further reduction in the numbers of both total and different words. Finally, the dynamics ends when all agents have the same unique word and the system is in the attractive convergence state. It is worth noting that the developed communication system is not only effective (each agent understands all the others), but also efficient (no memory is wasted in the final state). The system undergoes spontaneously a disorder/order transition to an asymptotic state where global coherence emerges, i.e., every agent has the same word for the same object. It is remarkable that this happens starting from completely empty inventories for each agent. The asymptotic state is one where a word invented during the time evolution took over with respect to the other competing words and imposed itself as the leading word. In this sense the system spontaneously selects one of the many possible coherent asymptotic states and the transition can thus be seen as a symmetry breaking transition.

It is important to focus on the scaling behaviour of the relevant quantities, i.e., how they depend on the population size. Let us consider two relevant quantities: the convergence time and the maximal size of all the inventories. The first quantity tells us how long is the convergence process as measured in terms of games per player. It turns out that in a fully connected graph the convergence time scales as:

$$t_{conv} \propto N^{3/2}.$$

The maximal size of all the inventories is a very important quantity to evaluate the typical size of the inventories. In its turn the typical size of an inventory is reflecting the size of the memory required to each individual, i.e., an estimate of his/her cognitive requirements. In a fully connected graph it turns out that the maximal size of all the inventories scales as:

$$N_{word}^{max} \propto N^{3/2},$$

which implies that, at the maximum, the average size of each individual inventory scales as the square root of the population size. This is not a realistic outcome since this implies that the memory size should diverge with the population size. Let us now consider what happens when one considers different interaction topologies with respect to the fully connected graph.

1.1.2 Role of the interaction topology

Social networks play an important role in determining the dynamics and outcome of language change. The first investigation of the role of topology was proposed in 2004 in a seminal paper presented at the 5th Conference on Language evolution, Leipzig (Ke et al. 2008). Since then, many approaches focused on adapting known models on topologies of increasing complexity: regular lattices, random graphs, scale-free graphs, etc.

The Naming Game, as described above, is not well-defined on general networks. When the degree distribution is heterogeneous, it does matter if the first randomly chosen agent is selected as a speaker and one of its the neighbour as the hearer or vice versa: high-degree nodes are in fact more easily chosen as neighbours than low-degree vertices. Several variants of the Naming Game on generic networks can be defined. In the direct Naming Game (reverse Naming Game) a randomly chosen speaker (hearer) selects (again randomly) a hearer (speaker) among its neighbours. In a neutral strategy one selects an edge and assigns the role of speaker and hearer with equal probability to one of the two nodes (Dall'Asta et al. 2006).

On low-dimensional lattices each agent can rapidly interact two or more times with its neighbours, favouring the establishment of a local consensus with a high success rate, i.e. of small sets of neighbouring agents sharing a common unique word. Later on these "clusters" of neighbouring agents with a common unique word undergo a coarsening phenomenon (Baronchelli et al. 2006) with a competition among them driven by the fluctuations of the interfaces (Bray 1994). The coarsening picture can be extended to higher dimensions and the scaling of the convergence time has been conjectured as being $t_{conv} \propto N^{1+1/d}$, where d ≤ 4 is the dimensionality of the space. On the other hand, the maximum total number of words in the system (maximal memory capacity) scales linearly with the system size, i.e., each agent uses only a finite capacity. In summary, low-dimensional lattice systems require more time to reach the consensus compared to mean-field, but a lower use of memory.

Let us now considers what happens on Small-World topologies (Watt and Strogatz 1998). The effect of a small-world topology has been investigated in (Dall'Asta et al. 2006b) in the framework of the Naming Game (Baronchelli et al. 2006) and in (Castelló et al. 2006) for the AB-model (see section below). Two different regimes are observed. For times shorter than a cross-over time, $t_{cross} = O(N / p^2)$, one observes the usual coarsening phenomena as long as the clusters are typically one-dimensional, i.e., as long as the typical cluster size is smaller than $1 / p$. For times much larger than t_{cross}, the dynamics is dominated by the existence of short-cuts and enters a mean-field like behaviour. The convergence time is thus expected to scale as $N^{3/2}$ and not as N^3 (as in d = 1). Small-world topology allows thus to combine advantages from both finite-dimensional lattices and mean-field networks: on the one hand, only a finite memory per node is needed, in opposition to the $O(\sqrt{N})$ in mean-field; on the other hand the convergence time is expected to be much shorter than in finite dimensions. In (Castelló et al. 2006) it has been studied the dynamics of the AB-model on a two-dimensional small world network. Also in this case a dynamical stage of coarsening is observed followed by a fast decay to the A or B absorbing states caused by finite size fluctuations.

We finally conclude this panoramic about different topologies briefly mentioning about the behaviour of the Naming Game on complex networks, and referring to (Dall'Asta et al. 2006) for an extensive discussion. It turns out that the convergence time scales with an exponent compatible with 3/2 both Erdös-Renyi (ER) (Erdös and Renyi 1959, 1960) and Bárabasi-Albert (BA) (Bárabasi and Albert 1999) networks. The scaling laws observed for the convergence time are a general robust feature and they are not affected by further topological details, such as the average degree, the clustering or the particular form of the degree distribution.

1.1.3 Is consensus always reached?

A variant of the Naming Game has been introduced with the aim of mimicking the mechanisms leading to opinion and convention formation in a population of individuals (Baronchelli et al. 2007). In particular a new parameter, β ($\beta = 1$ corresponding to the Naming Game), has been added mimicking an irresolute attitude of the agents in making decisions. β is simply the probability that in a successful interaction both the speaker and the hearer update their memories erasing all opinions except the one involved in the interaction (see Figure 24.1). This negotiation process, as opposed to herding-like or bounded confidence driven processes, displays a non-equilibrium phase transition from an absorbing state in which all agents reach a consensus to an active (not-frozen as in the Axelrod model (Axelrod 1997)) stationary state characterized either by polarization or fragmentation in clusters of agents with different opinions. Figure 24.2 moreover shows that the transition at β_c is only the first of a series of transitions: when decreasing $\beta < \beta_c$, a system starting from empty initial conditions self-organizes into a fragmented state with an increasing number of opinions. At least two different universality classes exist, one for the case with two possible opinions and one for the case with an unlimited number of opinions. Very interestingly, the model displays the non-equilibrium phase transition also on heterogeneous networks, in contrast with other opinion-dynamics models, like for instance the Axelrod model (Klemm et al. 2003), for which the transition disappears for heterogeneous networks in the thermodynamic limit.

Figure 24.2 Phase transitions in the Naming Game

Time t_m required to a population on a fully-connected graph to reach a (fragmented) active stationary state with m different opinions. For every m > 2, the time t_m diverges at some critical value of $\beta_c(m) < \beta_c$.

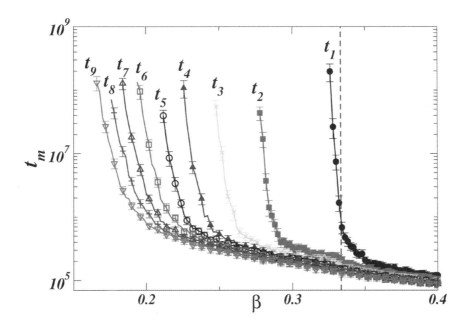

1.1.4 Symmetry breaking: a controlled case

We concentrate now on a simpler case in which there are only two words at the beginning of the process, say A and B. This is a very interesting case since it highlights the close connection with other modelling schemes introduced for opinion dynamics and language competition. In this case the population can be divided into three classes: the fraction of agents with only the word A, n_A, the fraction of those with only the word B, n_B, and finally the fraction of agents with both words, n_{AB}. The description of the time evolution of the three species is straightforward:

$$
\begin{cases}
\dfrac{dn_A}{dt} = -n_A n_B + n_{AB}^2 + n_A n_{AB} \\[2mm]
\dfrac{dn_B}{dt} = -n_A n_B + n_{AB}^2 + n_B n_{AB} \\[2mm]
\dfrac{dn_{AB}}{dt} = 2n_A n_B - 2n_{AB}^2 - (n_A + n_B) n_{AB}
\end{cases}
$$

This system of differential equations is deterministic. It presents three fixed points in which the system can collapse depending on initial conditions. If at time zero $n_A (t=0) > n_B (t=0)$ [$n_B (t=0) > n_A (t=0)$] then at the end of the evolution we will have the stable fixed point $n_A = 1$[$n_B = 1$] and, obviously, $n_B = n_{AB} = 0$[$n_A = n_{AB} = 0$]. If, on the other hand, we start from a perfectly symmetrical situation $n_A (t = 0) = n_B (t = 0)$, then the equations lead to $n_A = n_B = 2n_{AB} = 0.4$. The latter situation is clearly unstable, since any external perturbation would make the system fall in one of the two stable fixed points. Indeed, it is never observed in simulations, due to stochastic fluctuations that in all cases determine a symmetry breaking forcing a single word to prevail.

The system of equations above however, is not only a useful example to clarify the nature of the symmetry breaking process. They also describe the interaction among two different populations that converged separately on two distinct conventions. In this perspective, they predict that the population whose size is larger will impose its conventions. In the absence of fluctuations, this is true even if the difference is very small: B will dominate if $n_B (t = 0) = 0.5 + \varepsilon$ and $n_A (t = 0) = 0.5 - \varepsilon$, for any $0 < \varepsilon \leq 0.5$ and $n_{AB} (t = 0) = 0$. Data from simulations shows that the probability of success of the convention of the minority group n_A, decreases as the system size increases, going to zero in the thermodynamic limit (N → ∞). A similar approach has been proposed to model the competition between two languages in the seminal paper (Abrams and Strogatz 2003). It is worth remarking the formal similarities between modelling the competition between synonyms in a Naming Game framework and the competition between languages: in both cases a synonym or a language are represented by a single feature, e.g., the characters A or B, for instance, in equations above. The similarity has been made more evident by the subsequent variants of the model introduced in (Abrams and Strogatz 2003) to include explicitly the possibility of bilingual individuals. In particular in (Wang and Minett 2005—Minett and Wang 2008) deterministic models for the competition of two languages have been proposed which include bilingual individuals. In (Castelló et al. 2006) a modified version of the Voter model including bilinguals individuals has been proposed, the so-called AB-model. In a fully connected network and in the limit of infinite population size, the AB-model can be described by coupled differential equations for the fractions of individuals speaking language A, B or AB that are, up to a constant normalization factor in the time-scale, identical to corresponding equations for the Naming Game. In (Castelló et al. 2009) it has been shown that the Naming Game and the AB-model are equivalent in the mean field approximation, though the differences at the microscopic level have non-trivial consequences. In particular, the consensus-polarization phase transition taking place in the Naming Game (see section above) is not observed in the AB-model. As for the interface motion in regular lattices, qualitatively, both models show the same behaviour: a diffusive interface motion in a one-dimensional lattice, and a curvature driven dynamics with diffusing stripe-like metastable states in a two-dimensional one. However, in comparison to the Naming Game, the AB-model dynamics is shown to slow down the diffusion of such configurations.

1.1.5 Towards syntax: The case of duality of patterning

Before closing this section we only briefly mention a promising research direction inspired to the Naming Game and devoted to understanding the origin of progressively more complex syntactic structures. The first step has concerned the origin of duality of patterning at the lexicon level. The lexicons of human languages organize their units at two distinct levels (Hockett 1960, 1960b). At a first combinatorial level, meaningless forms (typically referred to as phonemes) are combined into meaningful units (typically referred to as morphemes). Thanks to this, many morphemes can be obtained by relatively simple combinations of a small number of phonemes. At a second compositional level of the lexicon, morphemes are composed into larger lexical units, the meaning of which is related to the individual meanings of the composing morphemes. This duality of patterning is not a necessity for lexicons and the question remains wide open regarding how a population of individuals is able to bootstrap such a structure and the evolutionary advantages of its emergence. In (Tria et al. 2012) this question is addressed in the framework of a multi-agents model, where a population of individuals plays simple naming games in a conceptual environment modeled as a graph. Through an extensive set of simulations we demonstrated the existence of two sufficient conditions for the emergence of duality of patterning in a pure cultural way. The first condition is represented by a noisy communication, i.e., a constraint on the fidelity of message transmission. No predefined relations between objects/ meanings and forms are hypothesized and we adopted a virtually infinite, i.e., open-ended, repertoire of forms. Despite this freedom, the number of different forms that get eventually fixed in the population's lexicon is kept limited by the constraint on transmission fidelity. The second sufficient condition is what we dubbed a blending repair strategy that allows to overcome errors in communication by allowing the creation of new words, crucially exploiting a shared conceptual representation of the environment. New words in the lexicon can be created in two ways. They can be holistically introduced as brand new forms or constructed through a blending strategy that combines and re-uses forms taken from other object's names. At the individual level, the mechanism of blending is thus introduced not as a necessity but as a possibility to exploit when the first communication attempt resulted in a failure. We note that a blending strategy exists in natural languages (e.g., SMOG = SMoke + fOG). The blending strategy we refer to here, however has to be thought as a general mechanism by which different bits of words are put together through blends, compounds or other morphological structures. Interestingly, endowing individuals with a blending ability is necessary but not sufficient in order to observe a lexicon featuring duality of patterning. For instance combinatorial abilities are observed also in nonhuman primates (e.g., monkeys and great apes) though they still appear not having triggered the emergence of duality of patterning (Ottenheimer 2009). Compositional lexicons turn out to be faster to lead to successful communication than purely combinatorial lexicons, suggesting that meaning played a crucial role in the evolution of language.

Two crucial manipulations in the game were (i) the degree of transmission fidelity and (ii) the density of the network representing semantic relations among the objects. Combinatoriality, meant as both forms reusing and economy, is only found when the transmission fidelity is sufficiently low. With a high degree of understanding, the number of distinct forms composing the emerged lexicon turns out to be high with respect to the number of objects to be named (in particular, higher that the number of objects), and the resulting lexicon features an extremely low level of combinatoriality. Conversely, an high degree of noise leads to an high level of compactness and combinatoriality. These results suggest that combinatoriality enhances message transmission in noisy environments (Nowak et al. 1999) and emerges as a result of the need of communicative success. In contrast, the level of compositionality is not strongly affected by the level of noise, but strongly depends on how much the conceptual space is structured. In particular, the lexicons developed by the agents exhibited clear signs of compositionality when the networks representing semantic relations among the objects were neither too sparse nor too dense. This can be understood as follows: compositionality does emerge if we are able on the one hand to find common features in different objects, on the other hand to make distinctions so that not all the objects are equally related to each other. Thus, compositionality emerges as a consequence of the organization of our conceptual space (Gärdenfors 2004; Collins and Loftus 1975).

It is important to stress how this work only considers compositionality in lexicon. In order to properly include syntax, one needs to endow the conceptual space with a more sophisticated structure, where nodes could represent nouns/concepts and links could encode semantic relations or specific actions and roles. From this perspective, the work presented in (Tria et al. 2012) can be thought as a first step of investigation on the emergence of duality of patterning through a pure cultural way. A next step could focus on investigating how a population of individuals can bootstrap a language where categorization and syntax both emerge as a pure outcome of communication efforts. When syntax has to be considered, one cannot forget to link this problem to the emergence of linguistic categories. One has, for instance, to distinguish between nouns and predicates, and if a noun is subject or complement, and more generally one has to be able to express actions and relations. We think there are at least two ways to face the problem in the framework of language games. The simpler way is to consider predefined linguistic categories and look at how a population of individuals is able to bootstrap higher order linguistic structures given for granted the underlying conceptual categorization. Personally, we are however more keen to follow a different route, where categories themselves do emerge as a result of repeated communication acts. In order to do so a richer conceptual space than the one considered in

(Tria et al. 2012) has to be taken into account. For instance, one could consider a more complex conceptual space where nodes represent again nouns/concepts and links encode the semantic relations or specific actions agent/patient. In this framework one could investigate which kind of linguistic structures would emerge and whether holistic or compositional strategies will be eventually successful. A very interesting question would be for instance whether specific structures will emerge to name nodes and links. This would correspond to a first step towards the emergence of linguistic categories, i.e., the onset of syntactic structures.

2. Bootstrapping Linguistic Categories

In this section we shall focus on a more complex consensus problem concerning how a population of individuals, without any pre-coordinated and shared linguistic structure, can bootstrap a shared set of linguistic categories. Categories are fundamental to recognize, differentiate and understand the environment. From Aristotle onwards, the issue of categorization has been subject to strong controversy in which purely cultural negotiation mechanisms (Wittgenstein 1953; Whorf 1956) competed with physiological and cognitive features of the categorizing subjects (Rosch 1973). A recent wave in cognitive science has induced a shift in viewpoint from the object of categorization to the categorizing subjects: categories are culture-dependent conventions shared by a given group. From this perspective, a crucial question is how they come to be accepted at a global level without any central coordination.

Figure 24.3 Basic rules of the category game

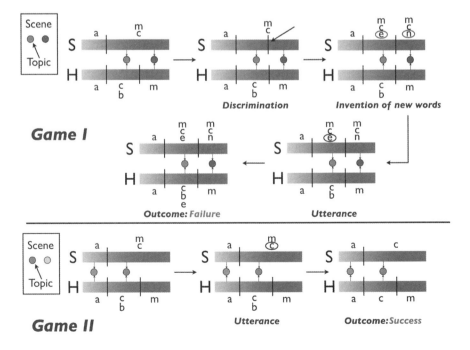

In this chapter we shall focus on the so-called Category Game (Puglisi et al. 2008), a scheme where an assembly of individuals with basic communication rules and without any external supervision may evolve an initially empty set of categories, achieving a non-trivial communication system. Its basic purpose is to examine how a population of interacting individuals can develop, through a series of language games, a shared form-meaning repertoire from scratch and without any pre-existing categorization. The model involves a set of N artificial agents committed to the task of categorizing a single analogical perceptual channel (e.g., the hue dimension of the color spectrum), each stimulus being represented as a real-valued number ranging in the interval [0, 1). We identify categorization as a partition of the [0, 1) interval (representing the perceptual channel of the agents) into discrete sub-intervals which are denoted as perceptual categories. Each individual has a dynamical inventory of form-meaning associations linking perceptual categories (meanings) to words (forms), denoting their linguistic counterpart. The perceptual categories as well as the words associated to them co-evolve dynamically through a sequence of elementary communication interactions, usually referred to as games. In a sense the Category Game concerns the Naming of an unknown and evolving number of objects represented by the different partitions of the perceptual space.

All the players are initialized with only the trivial [0, 1) perceptual category that has no name associated to it. In each step, a pair of individuals (one playing as speaker and the other as hearer) is randomly selected from the population and presented with a new "scene", i.e., a set of M ≥ 2 objects (stimuli) where each object is a real number in the [0, 1) interval. The speaker discriminates the scene and names one object (i.e., the topic) and the hearer tries to guess the topic from the name. A correct guess results in a successful communication. Based on the outcomes of the game, the two individuals update their category boundaries and the inventory of the associated words.

A detailed description of the game is provided in Fig. 24.3, which reports two examples of a failure (Game I) and a success (Game II) game, respectively. In a game, two players (S denoting the speaker and H denoting the hearer) are randomly selected from the population. Both the players are presented with a scene with two objects and the speaker selects the topic for the subsequent communication. In Game I, since the two objects belong to the same perceptual category of the speaker, the speaker has to discriminate her perceptual space by creating a boundary at the middle of the segment containing the two objects (marked by the bold black arrow). The two new categories formed after discrimination inherit the words-inventory of the parent perceptual category (here the words "m" and "c"); in addition, a different brand new word is invented for each of the two categories (words "e" and "n" marked by colored circles). Subsequently, the speaker browses the list of words associated to the perceptual category containing the topic (i.e., "m", "c" and "e" here). At this point, there can be two possibilities: if a previous successful communication has occurred with this category, the last winning word is chosen; alternatively, the last word invented is selected. For the current example, the speaker chooses the word "e" (marked by the black circle here), and transmits it to the hearer. The outcome of the game is a failure since the hearer does not have the word "e" in her inventory associated with the topic. Finally, the speaker unveils the topic, in a non-linguistic way (e.g., by pointing at it), and the hearer adds the new word to the word inventory of the category corresponding to the topic. In Game II, the topic that the speaker chooses is already discriminated. Therefore, the speaker verbalizes it using the word "c" (which, for example, is possibly the winning word in the last successful communication concerning that category). The hearer knows this word and can therefore point to the topic correctly, thereby leading to a successful game. Both the players dispose all competing words for the perceptual category corresponding to the topic except "c". In general, if there are ambiguities (e.g., the hearer finds the word uttered to be linked to multiple categories containing an object), they are resolved by making an unbiased random choice of one of the categories.

The perceptive resolution power of the individuals limits their ability to distinguish between the objects in the scene that are too close to each other in the perceptual space. In order to take this factor into account, no two stimuli appearing in the same scene can be at a distance closer than a given value, denoted as $d_{min}(x)$ where x can be either of the two. This function, usually termed as the Just Noticeable Difference (JND), encodes the finite resolution power of human vision by virtue of which the artificial agents are not required to distinguish between stimuli that a human eye cannot differentiate.

2.1 Dynamical properties of the category game

In the Category Game dynamics it is possible to distinguish two different phases. In the first regime, the number of perceptual categories increases (see dashed lines in Figure 24.4c) due to the pressure of discrimination, and at the same time many different words are used by different agents for naming similar perceptual categories. This kind of synonymy reaches a peak and then dries out (as displayed in Figure 24.4a), in a similar way as in the Naming Game described above. This kind of synonymy reaches a peak and then drops in a fashion similar to the well-known Naming Game. A second phase starts when most of the perceptual categories are associated with only one word. During this phase, words are found to expand their dominion across adjacent perceptual categories (solid lines in Figure 24.4c). In this way, sets of contiguous perceptual categories sharing the same words are formed, giving raise to what we define as "linguistic categories" (see Figure 24.5). The coarsening of these categories becomes slower and slower, with a dynamical arrest analogous to the physical process in which supercooled liquids approach the glass transition (Mézard et al. 1987). In this long-lived almost stable phase, (Mukherjee et al. 2011) usually after games per player, the linguistic categorization pattern has a degree of sharing between 90% and 100%; success is measured by counting in a small time window the rate of successful games (Figure 24.4b), while the degree of sharing of categories is measured by an overlap function, which measure the alignment of category boundaries (both for perceptual or linguistic ones), displayed in Figure 24.4d for a mathematical definition of this function see (Puglisi et al. 2008). The success rate and the overlap both remain stable for 10^5 -10^6 games per player: we consider this pattern as the "final categorization pattern" generated by the model, which is most relevant for comparison with human color categories (see below).

We can thus identify two main outcomes of the Category Game. On the one hand the emergence of a hierarchical category structure made of two distinct levels: a basic layer, responsible for fine discrimination of the environment, and a shared linguistic layer that groups together perceptions to guarantee communicative success. Remarkably, the emergent number of linguistic categories in this phase turns out to be finite and small, as observed in natural languages, even in the limit of an infinitesimally small length scale dmin, as opposed to the number of the underlying perceptual categories which is of order $1/d_{min}(x)$.

Figure 24.4 Time evolution of the category game

We considered here a population of N = 100 individuals a and a flat (constant) JND function $d_{min}(x)=d_{min}$ with different values of d_{min}: a) Synonymy, i.e., average number of words per category; b) Success rate measured as the fraction of successful games in a sliding time windows games long; c) Average number of perceptual (dashed lines) and linguistic (solid lines) categories per individual; d) Averaged overlap, i.e., alignment among players, for perceptual (dashed curves) and linguistic (solid curves) categories.

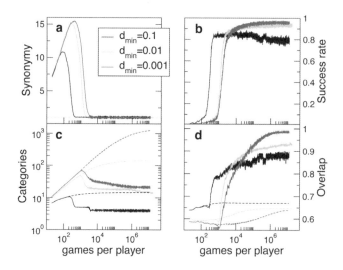

Another important feature of the Category Game concerns its long-time behaviour. Human languages evolve continuously, and a puzzling problem is how to reconcile the apparent robustness of most of the deep linguistic structures we use with the evidence that they undergo possibly slow, yet ceaseless, changes. Is the state in which we observe languages today closer to what would be a dynamical attractor with statistically stationary properties or rather closer to a non-steady state slowly evolving in time? The Category Game allows to address this question in the framework of the emergence of shared linguistic categories in a population of individuals interacting through language games. The observed emerging asymptotic categorization, which we shall see can be successfully tested against experimental data from human languages, corresponds to a metastable state where global shifts are always possible but progressively more unlikely and the response properties depend on the age of the system. This aging mechanism exhibits striking quantitative analogies to what is observed in the statistical mechanics of glassy systems. We argue that this can be a general scenario in language dynamics where shared linguistic conventions would not emerge as attractors, but rather as metastable states.

Figure 24.5 **Typical long-time configuration of five representative agents in the population**
For each agent perceptual and linguistic categories (separated by short and long bars, respectively) are shown. The highlighted portion of two agents illustrates an instance of a successful game in a so-called mismatch region between the linguistic categories of the two agents associated with the words "a" and "b". The hearer—in a previous game—learned the word "a" as a synonym for the perceptual category at the leftmost boundary of the linguistic category "b". During the game the speaker utters "a" for the topic; as a result the hearer deletes "b" from her inventory, keeping "a" as the name for that perceptual category, moving de facto the linguistic boundary.

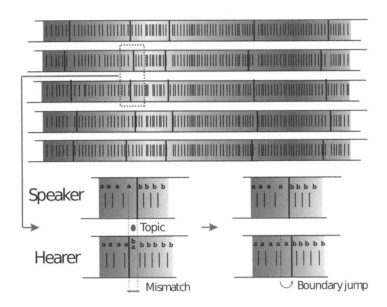

3. Comparison with Real-World Data

An important counterpart of the modelling activity should be the comparison with empirical or experimental data. When theoretical modelling is coupled with a serious data analysis activity devoted to the discovery of emergent features, it can result in a virtuous loop, where measures inspire modelling schemes, model analysis suggests new measures and observations, which in turn allow the evaluation and refinement of models. Traditionally language dynamics suffered for the lack of extensive datasets mainly due to the difficulty of monitoring in a systematic and reproducible way the emergent steps of new linguistic features or new languages altogether. The situation is being radically changing in the last few years, Information and Communication Technologies playing a major role in this revolution. In this section we shall describe a few examples where the predictions of the modelling schemes described above have been tested against experimental data from human languages. Next section will be devoted to illustrate the new perspective to conceive and run synthetic experiments aimed at investigating specific aspects of the emergence and evolution of language.

3.1 Naming syntactic structures in Twitter

Despite a fast growing literature about the emergence of social conventions in online social networks, not many results are available whenever one is interested in the evolution of linguistic conventions. Without the aim of being exhaustive, here we only mention a recent contribution that attracted our attention given the similarity of the dynamics described to that of the Minimal Naming Game described above. In a recent paper (Kooti et al. 2012) investigated the emergence of social conventions in Twitter. Twitter (twitter.com) is an online social networking and microblogging service that enables its users to send and read text-based posts of up to 140 characters, known as "tweets". A specific action on Twitter is the so-called retweet, i.e., the action by which a user makes a post simply re-posting content that has been posted by another user. A retweet is signaled by a specific symbol and what Kooti and collaborators have investigated is the history of the different conventions users adopted for a retweet along the whole Twitter history. The fairly complete dump of the Twitter history allowed the researchers to monitor who first invented each given symbol for a retweet and when each symbol was adopted by which user. It is thus possible to trace the time evolution of each competing convention. They monitored in particular the following conventions (in order of introduction): *via, HT, Retweet, Retweeting, RT, R/T* or the recycle icon. Despite being invented at different times and having different adoption rates, only two variations came to be widely adopted: RT and via. It is important to notice that the most popular convention does not coincide with the first invented. In addition an actual competition of different conventions took place since it is not rare the situation in which users adopted, in their Twitter activity, several conventions at different times and sometimes at the same time. These last two elements make this dynamics quite close to the dynamics of the Naming Game. Also in the Naming Game the winning convention is not always the first invented. In addition each player is adopting, in the Naming Game, several conventions at the same time or in its own lifetime, before converging on a final choice. Finally also the Naming Game predicts the possibility of the coexistence of several conventions in a quasi-stationary state. It would be quite interesting to extend this research in two directions. First, monitoring the time evolution of different conventions and syntactic structures in Twitter in order to test the robustness of the results. Second, perform a thorough quantitative comparison of the Naming Game predictions with the data presented in (Kooti et al. 2012).

3.2 Universality in color naming

A large amount of data on color categorization was gathered in the World Color Survey (Berlin and Kay 1969; Kay and Regier 2003), in which individuals belonging to different cultures had to name a set of colors. The results of the analysis of the categorization patterns obtained in this way have had a huge impact not only on such areas as Cognitive Science and Linguistics, but also Psychology, Philosophy and Anthropology (see for example, Lakoff 1987; Gardner 1985; Deacon 1998). The main finding is that color systems across language are not random, but rather exhibit certain statistical regularities, thus implying that the classical theory of categorization, dating back to the work of Aristotle and claiming the arbitrariness of categorization, had to be reconsidered (Gardner 1985). In this section, we describe how the Category Game model described above can be used to run a Numerical World Color Survey (NWCS) and point out that, remarkably, the synthetic results obtained in this way agree quantitatively with the experimental ones (Baronchelli et al. 2010; Loreto et al. 2012).

3.3   The world color survey

P. Kay and B. Berlin (Berlin and Kay 1969) ran a first survey on 20 languages in 1969. From 1976 to 1980, the enlarged World Color Survey was conducted by the same researchers along with W. Merrifield and the data are public since 2003 on the website http://www.icsi.berkeley. edu/wcs. These data concern the basic color categories in 110 languages without written forms and spoken in small-scale, non-industrialized societies. On average, 24 native speakers of each language were interviewed. Each informant had to name each of 330 color chips produced by the Munsell Color Company that represent 40 gradations of hue and maximal saturation, plus 10 neutral color chips (black-gray-white) at 10 levels of value. The chips were presented in a predefined, fixed random order, to the informant who had to tag each of them with a "basic color term" is her language. Berlin and Kay's established the universal presence of a special subset of color names which they called the "basic color names". These are the most salient and frequently used color words across the majority of the world's languages. They represent the following eleven English color names: black, white, red, green, yellow, blue, brown, orange, purple, pink and gray. Berlin and Kay found that these names have prototype properties which means that there is usually one name that best represents a color while other colors that are progressively more dissimilar with this color become less good examples for the name. They also found that the number of basic color names range from 2 to 11 across the world's languages, of course with exceptions like Russian and Hungarian that have 12 basic names.

A very important result, always due to Berlin and Kay (Kay and Regier 2003), emerged from a quantitative statistical analysis of the World Color Survey, proving that the color naming systems obtained in different cultures and language are in fact not random. Through a suitable transformation Berlin and Kay identified the most representative chip for each color name in each language and projected it into a suitable metric color space (namely, the CIEL*a*b color space). To investigate whether these points are more clustered across languages than would be expected by chance, they defined a dispersion measure on this set of languages L_0 as:

$$D(L_0) = \sum_{l,l^* \in L_0} \sum_{c \in l} min_{c^* \in l^*} \, dist(c,c^*)$$

Where l and l* are two different languages, c and c* are two basic color terms respectively from these two languages, and *dist(c,c*)* is the distance between the points in color space in which the colors are represented. To give a meaning to the measured dispersion $D\,(L_0)$, Kay and Regier created "new" datasets L_i $(i = 1, 2,...,1000)$ by random rotation of the original set L_0, and measured the dispersion of each new set $D\,(L_i)$. The human dispersion appears to be distinct from the histogram of the "random" dispersions with a probability larger than 99.9%. As shown in Figure 3a of (Kay and Regier 2003), the average dispersion of the random datasets, $D_{neutral}$, is 1.14 times larger than the dispersion of human languages. Thus, human languages are more clustered, i.e., less dispersed, than their random counterparts and universality does exist.

A third and a totally unexpected finding of Berlin and Kay concerns the existence of a hierachy of color names. They observed that if a language encodes fewer than eleven names, then there are strict limitations on which names it may encode. The typological regularities observed by them can be summarized by the following implicational hierarchy:

$$\begin{bmatrix} white \\ black \end{bmatrix} < \begin{bmatrix} red \end{bmatrix} < \begin{bmatrix} green \\ yellow \end{bmatrix} < \begin{bmatrix} blue \end{bmatrix} < \begin{bmatrix} brown \end{bmatrix} < \begin{bmatrix} purple \\ pink \\ orange \\ gray \end{bmatrix}$$

Where for distinct color names a and b, the expression a < b signifies that a is present in every language where b is present but not vice versa. Based on the above observation, the authors further theorize that, as languages evolve, they acquire the new basic color names in a fixed chronological sequence of the form.

Stage I: dark-cool and light-warm

Stage II: red (including all shades of violet)

Stage III: either green or yellow

Stage IV: both green and yellow

Stage V: blue

Stage VI: brown

Stage VII: purple, pink, orange, or gray

It is worth noticing that Stage I is not referring to the emergence of the two achromatic colors "black" and "white", rather it refers to a division of the perceptual space that has nothing to do with the chromatic properties of light, being based exclusively on the light intensity. Ratliff writes (Ratliff 1976) that the well-known studies of Dani color terms by Eleanor Heider-Rosch and Donald Olivier (Heider-Rosch and Olivier 1972) "put the question of psychophysiological bases of the two color terms of Stage I into better perspective. These terms appear to be panchromatic, more or less equivalent to the general panchromatic English terms dark and light or dull and brilliant rather than equivalent to the specific achromatic terms black and white. Although the Dani color terms do include chromatic colors, and do have attributes of coolness and warmth, the division between them appears to be based mainly on brightness."

Figure 24.6   The Just Noticeable Difference (JND) function

The wavelength change in a monochromatic stimulus needed to elicit a particular JND in the hue space. For the purpose of the Category Game, $d_{min}(x)$ and topic respectively refers to the JND and the monochromatic stimulus rescaled within the interval [0:1]. The blue circles represent the centers of seven regions (to be used later in the article) that can be together expressed as a vector $\vec{c}$ with entries (c_1, c_2, ... , c_7). The specific values for these entries are $\vec{c}$ = (0.0301, 0.125, 0.250, 0.465, 0.66015, 0.925, 0.970). Each entry, in turn, respectively corresponds to a wavelength (nm) that can be written (approx.) as (445, 475, 500, 545, 585, 635, 645).

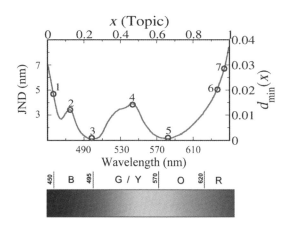

3.4   The numerical world color survey

The key aspect of the statistical analysis described above is the comparison of the clustering properties of a set of true human languages against the ones exhibited by a certain number of randomized sets. In replicating the experiment it is therefore necessary to obtain two sets of synthetic data, one of which must have some human ingredient in its generation. The idea put forth in (Baronchelli et al. 2010) is to act on the d_{min} parameter of the Category Game, describing, as discussed in the previous section, the discrimination power of the individuals to stimuli of a given wavelength. In fact, it turns out that human beings are endowed with a d_{min}, the "Just Noticeable difference" or JND, that is not constant, but rather is a function of the frequency of the incident light (see Figure 24.6).[1] Technically, psychophysiologists define the JND as a function of wavelength to describe the minimum distance at which two stimuli from the same scene can be discriminated (Bedford and Wyszecki 1958; Long et al. 2006). The equivalence with the d_{min} parameter is therefore clear and different artificial sets can be created. On the one hand *human* categorization patterns are obtained from populations whose individuals are endowed with the rescaled human JND (i.e., $d_{min}(x)$). On the other hand neutral categorization patterns are obtained from populations in which the individuals have constant JND d_{min} = 0.0143, which is the average value of the human JND (as it is projected on the [0,1) interval, Figure 24.6).

---

1.   The attention is here on the human Just Noticeable Difference for the hue, see (Baronchelli et al. 2010).

Figure 24.7   Difference of popularity density

Neutral worlds, $D_{neutral}$, (histogram) are significantly more dispersed than human worlds, D_{human}, (black arrow), as also observed in the WCS data (the filled circles extracted from (Kay & Regier 2003) and the black arrow). The abscissa is rescaled so that the human D (WCS) and the average "human worlds" D both equal 1. The histogram has been generated from 1500 neutral worlds, each made of 50 populations of 50 individuals, and M=2 objects per scene. Categorization patterns have been considered after the population had evolved for a time of 10^6 games per agents. The inset figure is the human JND function (adapted from (Long et al. 2006). On the vertical axis: the probability density $p(x_i)$ equals the percentage $f(x_i)$ of the observed measure in a given range $[x_i - \Delta/2, x_i + \Delta/2]$ centring around x_i divided by the width of the bin Δ, i.e., $p(x_i) = f(x_i)/\Delta$. This procedure allows for a comparison between the histogram coming from the NWCS (Baronchelli et al. 2010) and that obtained in the study on the WCS (Kay & Regier 2003), where the bins have a different width.

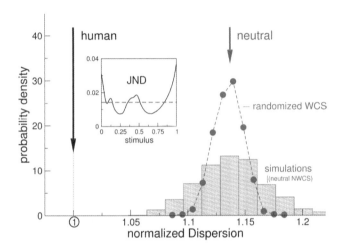

In analogy to the WCS experiment, the randomness hypothesis in the NWCS for the neutral test-cases is supported by symmetry arguments: in neutral simulations there is no breakdown of translational symmetry, which is the main bias in the human simulations.

Thus, the difference between human and neutral data originates from the perceptive architecture of the individuals of the corresponding populations. A collection of human individuals form a human population, and will produce a corresponding human categorization pattern. In a hierarchical fashion, finally, a collection of populations is called a world, which in (Baronchelli et al. 2010) is formed either by all human or by all non-human populations. To each world it corresponds a value of the dispersion D defined above, measuring the amount of dispersion of the languages (or categorization patterns) belonging to it. In the actual WCS there is of course only one human World (i.e., the collection of 110 experimental languages), while in (Baronchelli et al. 2010) several worlds have been generated to gather statistics both for the human and non-human cases.

The main results of the NWCS are presented in Figure 24.7. Since the dispersion D depends on the number of languages, the number of colors, and the space units used, every measure of D in the NWCS is normalized by the average value obtained in the human simulations, and every measure of D from the WCS experiment is divided by the value obtained in the original (non-randomized) WCS analysis (as in Kay and Regier 2003). Thus, both the average of the *human worlds* and the value based on the WCS data are represented by 1 in Figure 24.7. In the same plot, the probability density of observing a value of D in the *neutral world* simulations is also shown by the red histogram bars. Finally, the Figure contains also the data reported in the histogram of the randomized datasets in Figure 3a of (Kay and Regier 2003), whose abscissa is normalized by the value of the non-randomized dataset and frequencies are rescaled by the width of the bins.

Figure 24.7 illustrates the main results. The Category Game Model informed with the human $d_{min}(x)$ (JND) curve produces a class of worlds that has a dispersion lower than and well distinct from that of the class of worlds endowed with a non-human, uniform $d_{min}(x)$. Strikingly, moreover, the ratio observed in the NWCS between the average dispersion of the "neutral worlds" and the average dispersion of the human worlds is $D_{neutral}/D_{human} \cong 1.14$, very similar to the one observed between the randomized datasets and the original experimental dataset in the WCS.

These findings are important for a series of reasons. First of all, it is the first case in which the outcome of a numerical experiment in this field is comparable at any level with true experimental data. Second, as discussed above, the results of the NWCS are not only in qualitative, but also in quantitative agreement with the results of the WCS. Third, the very design of the model suggests a possible mechanisms lying at the roots of the observed universality. Human beings share certain perceptual bias that, even though are not strong enough to deterministically influence the outcome of a categorization, are on the other hand capable of influencing category patterns in a way that becomes evident only through a statistical analysis performed over a large number of languages. This explanation for the observed universality had already been put forth based on theoretical analysis (see for instance Deacon 1998; Christiansen and Chater 2008), but the NWCS represents the first numerical evidence supporting it.

3.5 The hierarchy of color names

We mentioned above the finding about the existence of an implication hierarchy of color names. In the framework of the Category Game it is has been possible to provide a possible explanation of the origin of such a hierarchy. In particular it has been observed (Loreto et al. 2012) that a clear hierarchy for color names is found to naturally emerge, in the framework of the Category Game, through purely cultural negotiations among a population of co-evolving agents, each endowed with the human Just Noticeable Difference (JND) function (Bedford and Wyszecki 1958; Long et al. 2006). In particular, a hierarchy emerges that ranks different color names with respect to the time needed for them to get fixed in a population.

Let us first focus on the frequency of access to higher levels of linguistic categorization as a function of the local value of the JND (see Loreto et al. 2012 for further details). To this end, we computed the extent of the emergent agreement (i.e., match) at different regions of the perceptual space. The notion of match is as follows. A match region *match (i, j)* for a pair of agents i and j is the sum of the lengths of all the regions in their perceptual space where both of them have the same most relevant name. The most relevant name is either the one used in a previous successful communication or the newly invented name in case the category has just been created due to a discrimination event. Note that this is a quantitative measure of the amount of agreement between the agent pair. The match of the whole population is simply:

$$\frac{2\sum_{i=1}^{N}\sum_{j=i+1}^{N} match(i, j)}{N(N-1)}$$

In Figure 24.6, the blue circles indicate the centers c_i of seven such regions (i.e., the points of inflection in the JND function) that we choose to calculate the so-called "regional" agreement. We define a region by the length spanning the interval $[c_i - d_{min}(c_i), c_i + d_{min}(c_i)]$, where $d_{min}(c_i)$ is the y-value corresponding to the x-value (c_i) (see Figure 24.6). In Figure 24.8(a) and (b), we respectively show, for N = 500 and 700, the regional agreement for these seven regions. The plots clearly signal that consensus emerges first in regions corresponding to high values of d_{min} (e.g.,

Figure 24.8 Agreement emergence

Emergence of the agreement in the population. Match for (a) N = 500 and (b) N = 700 in the seven regions marked in Fig. 6. For better visualization, each curve is plotted in a color that best represents the corresponding region in the hue space (see Fig. 6). The time (i.e., t / N) for (c) N = 500 and (d) N = 700 to reach a desired consensus (match = 0.1) versus the value of dmin corresponding to the seven regions. The results present an average over 60 simulation runs. In both the plots the approximate wavelength (nm) associated with each colored data point is mentioned within the parenthesis. Error bars are drawn according to the variance of the distribution of consensus times in the different simulations. The gray lines in both the plots represent a fit of the respective data with an exponential function of the form $Ae^{-\alpha t}$ (see text for more details).

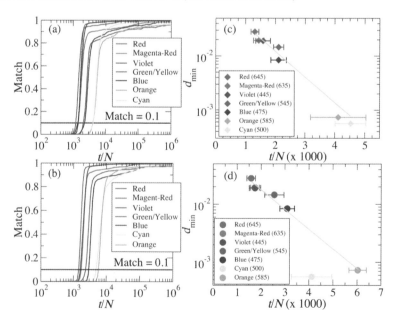

region 6 and 7) while it occurs later in regions corresponding to very low d_{min} (e.g., region 3 and 5). Most strikingly, if the regions are arranged according to the time (i.e., t/N) to reach a desired level of consensus (say a match value of 0.1) then they get organized into a hierarchy (Figure 24.8(c) and (d)) with [red, (magenta)-red], [violet], [green/yellow], [blue], [orange] and [cyan] (or [cyan] and [orange] as is usually observed for secondary basic color names) appearing in this order. This result is strikingly similar to that reported in (Berlin and Kay 1969). Further, the data points for the fixation times are observed to obey a simple functional form, $Ae^{-\alpha t}$, where A and α are non-zero positive constants (gray lines in Figure 24.8(c) and (d)). This amounts to say that the fixation time for specific primary colors at the population level diverges log-arithmically with the resolution power $1/d_{min}$. Though this specific prediction cannot be checked with the currently available data, it is reminiscent of the logarithm law which is typically associated to human perception. Error bars in Figure 24.8(c) and (d), representing the intrinsic variability of fixation times in different simulations, are important to explain the slight fluctuations in the color name hierarchy as observed in the World Color Survey across different cultures.

It is important to observe how the similarity of the ranking of fixation times obtained in the framework of the Category Game with that observed in the framework of the World Color Survey is not the outcome of a pure coincidence. It turns out that only a right choice of JND function, coupled with the language game dynamics, can reproduce the color hierarchy observed across human languages. The Supporting Information of (Loreto et al. 2012) reports the outcomes of two additional experiments performed by substituting the human JND with a flat and an inverse JND. In none of these two cases the hierarchy obtained from the World Color Survey could be reproduced.

In summary these results show that a simple negotiation dynamics, driven by a weak non-language specific bias, namely the frequency dependent resolution power of the human eye, is sufficient to guarantee the emergence of the hierarchy of color names getting so arranged by the times needed for their fixation in a population. The observed hierarchy features an excellent quantitative agreement with the empirical observations, confirming that the theoretical modeling in this area has now attained the required maturity to make significant contributions to the ongoing debates in cognitive science. Our approach suggests a possible route to the emergence of hierarchical color categories: the color spectrum clearly exists at a physical level of wave-lengths, humans tend to react most saliently to certain parts of this spectrum often selecting exemplars for them, and finally comes the process of linguistic color naming, which adheres to universal patterns resulting in a neat hierarchy of the form obtained here. These intuitions are of course not a novelty (see for instance Evans and Levinson 2009); however, we provided a theoretical framework where the origin of the color hierarchy, as well as its quantitative structure, could be explained and reproduced through a purely cultural route driven, on its turn, by a non-language-specific property of human beings.

It should be remarked that, despite the striking universal character of the color hierarchy, fluctuations exist across different languages as for the precise order in which color names got fixed in each language. In the framework of the Category Game this phenomenon is naturally explained as a consequence of the unavoidable stochasticity of the underlying cultural negotiation dynamics (Puglisi et al. 2008). The error bars in the fixation time of each specific color term in Figure 24.8 specifically support this picture.

4.   An Experimental Framework

We already mentioned how the Web is acquiring the status of a platform for social computing, able to coordinate and exploit the cognitive abilities of the users for a given task, and it is likely that the new social platforms appearing on the Web will rapidly become a very interesting laboratory for social sciences in general (Lazer et al. 2009), and for studies on language emergence and evolution in particular. These recent advances are enabling for the first time the possibility of collecting the interactions of large numbers of people at the same time and observing their behaviour in a reproducible way. In particular, the dynamics and transmission of information along social ties can nowadays be the object of a quantitative investigation towards a comprehension of the processes underlying the emergence of a collective information and language dynamics.

A very original example is represented by Amazon's Mechanical Turk (MT) (https://www. mturk.com/mturk/welcome), a crowdsourcing web service that coordinates the supply and the demand of tasks that require human intelligence to complete. It is an online labour market in which users perform tasks, also known as Human Intelligence Tasks, proposed by "employers" and are paid for this. Salaries range from cents for very simple tasks to a dollar or more for more complex ones. Examples of tasks range from categorization of images, the transcription of audio recordings to test websites or games. MT is perhaps one of the clearest examples of the so called crowdsourcing and thousands of projects, each fragmented into small units of Work, are performed every day by thousands of users. MT has opened the door for exploration of processes that outsource computation to humans. These human computation processes hold tremendous potential to solve a variety of problems in novel and interesting ways. Thanks to the possibility of recruiting thousands of subjects in a short time, MT represents a potentially revolutionary source for conducting experiments in social science (Chilton et al. 2009; Paolacci et al. 2010). It could become a tool for rapid development of pilot studies for the experimental application of new ideas. As a starting point for this new idea of experiments, the blog http://experimentalturk. wordpress.com/ already presents a review of the results of a series of classic game theoretical experiments carried out on MT (Suri and Watts 2011).

Despite its versatility (Chilton et al. 2009) MT has not been conceived as a platform for experiments. This is the reason why it is important to develop a versatile platform to implement social games. Here the word game is intended as an interaction protocol among a few players implementing a specific task and it is used as a synonym of experiment. The development of such web games has to take into account the following points: (i) the running applications must be modular, so that they can interact with different services and interfaces and can be interchangeable; they must be event-driven in order to ease the real time interactions between users and have to possibly interact with social networks and cloud services through their own APIs; (ii) the transactions between synchronous (i.e., real time) and asynchronous mode should be the most transparent as possible; (iii) the cross-platform web-based graphical interface, either ajax, flash or java, must be differently designed according to the client platform (e.g., desktops, smart-phones, tablets, etc.); (iv) the hosting infrastructures have to be care- fully designed to manage an expected heavy load and to process and store the relative amount of data. The advantage of this kind of experiments is that every useful piece of information and detail of the evolution will be fully available and leveraged for benchmarking as well as for the modelling activity. Moreover the effects of social interactions can be observed with a larger statistical basis and in a more controlled environment. A first prototype of such a platform is already available and it has been dubbed Experimental Tribe (www.xtribe.eu) (ET) (Cicali et al. 2011). ET is intended as a general-purpose platform that allows the realization of a very large set of possible games. It has a modular structure through which most of the complexity of running an experiment is hidden in a complex Main Server and the experimentalist is left with the only duty of devising the experiment as well as a suitable interface for it. In this way most of the coding difficulties related to the realization of a dynamic web applications are already taken care by the ET Server and the realization of an experiment should be as easy as constructing a webpage with one the main utilities for it (e.g., googlesite).

5.   Short Summary

Before concluding we wish to thank Dr. Peng Gang and Dr. Shi Feng for the kind invitation to contribute to this festschrift devoted to William (Bill) Wang. It is with great joy that we wrote this contribution since Bill has been pioneering the field of language dynamics and most of what we did in the last few years probably wouldn't be there without the initial seed ideas Bill first planted. As a pioneer in evolutionary studies of language Bill always put a special emphasis on a multi-disciplinary perspective with a particular sensibility for pushing forward synthetic modelling approaches as well as for drawing parallels with biological principles. On top of this Bill has always been a friend and a passionate and generous scholar, always ready to guide us with his kind, wise and deep way to transfer his knowledge.

In this chapter we made an attempt to summarize the efforts we made in the last few years to elucidate the processes underlying the emergence of shared linguistic structures in a population of individuals. We presented in particular models of increasing complexity devoted to reproduce in a synthetic way the processes leading to naming objects, bootstrapping a system of linguistic categories and to the emergence of simple syntactic structures such as duality of patterning in lexicons. Along with the theoretical models we presented the results of the comparison of the theoretical predictions with available empirical data. This helps in grounding the hypotheses made against well known facts as well as in triggering a virtuous loop in which new theoretical predictions foster the gathering of new datasets which in turn stimulates further thinking about the underlying mechanisms and so on. We highlighted the need for the field of language dynamics to complete its transformation in an experimental discipline by paying an increasing attention to the comparison with real-world data as well as to the protocols to conceive and run suitable experiments. To this end the Web, and more generally the new Information and Communication Technologies (ICT), could be the new frontier to run linguistics motivated experiments, by leveraging on the possibility to coordinate and exploit the cognitive abilities of the users for a given task. It is very likely that the new social platforms appearing on the Web, could rapidly become a very interesting laboratory for social sciences in general and for studies on language emergence and evolution in particular.

Acknowledgements

The authors are grateful to Andrea Baronchelli, Alain Barrat, Emanuele Caglioti, Luca Dall'Asta, Maddalena Felici, Bruno Galantucci, Tao Gong, Animesh Mukherjee, Andrea Puglisi, Luc Steels with whom most of the work presented in this chapter has been carried out.

REFERENCES

Abrams, D. M., and Steven H. Strogatz. 2003. Modelling the dynamics of language death. *Nature* 424:900.

Axelrod, R. 1997. The Dissemination of culture: A model with local convergence and global polarization. J. *Conflict Resolut* 41 (2): 203–226.

BÁrabasi Albert-László, and A. Reka 1999. Emergence of scaling in random networks. *Science* 286:509.

Baronchelli, A., M. Felici, V. Loreto, E. Caglioti, and L. Steels. 2006. *Sharp Transition Towards Shared Vocabularies in Multi-Agent Systems*. J. Stat. Mech., P06014.

Baronchelli, A., L. Dall'asta, A. Barrat, V. Loreyo. 2006. Topology induced coarsening in language games. *Phys. Rev. E* 73:015102.

Baronchelli, A., L. Dall'asta, A. Barrat, V. Loreyo. 2007. Non-equilibrium phase transition in negotiation dynamics. *Phys. Rev. E* 76:051102.

Baronchelli A., T. Gong, A. Puglisi, and V. Loreto. 2010. Modelling the emergence of universality in colour naming patterns. Proc. Natl. Acad. *Sci. USA (PNAS)* 107:2403–2407.

Bedford, R., and G. Wyszecki. 1958. Wavelength discrimination for point sources. *JOSA* 48 (2): 129–130.

Berlin, B., and P. Kay. 1969. *Basic Color Terms*. Berkeley: University of California Press.

Bray, A. 1994. Theory of phase-ordering kinetics. Adv. *Phys* 43 (3): 357–459.

Castellano, C., S. Fortunato, V. Loreto. 2009. Statistical physics of social dynamics. *Reviews of Modern Physics* 81:591–646.

Castello, X., V. M. Eguiluz, M. San Miguel. 2006. Ordering dynamics with two non-excluding options: Bilingualism in language competition. New J. *Phys* 8 (12): 308.

Castello, X., A. Baronchelli, V. Loreto. 2009. Consensus and ordering in language dynamics. *The European Physical Journal B–Condensed Matter and Complex Systems* 71 (4): 557–564.

Chilton, L. B., and T. Sims Clayton, M. Godman, G. Little, R. C. Miller. 2009. Seaweed: A web application for designing economic games. In *Proceedings of the ACM SIGKDD Workshop on Human Com-putation*, HCOMP '09, 34–35. New York, NY, USA.

Christiansen, M. H., and N. Chater. 2008. Language as shaped by the brain. *Behavioral and Brain Sciences* 31 (5): 489–509.

Cicali, C., P. Gravino, V. Loreto, G. Paolacci, V. D. P. Servedio, F. Tria, and M. Warglien. 2011. Experimental tribe: A general platform for web-gaming and social computation, *Proceedings of the NIPS Workshop on Computational Social Science and the Wisdom of Crowds* (http://people.cs.umass.edu/~wallach/workshops/nips2011css/).

Clark, H. H. 1996. *Using Language*. UK: Cambridge University Press.

Collins, A. M., and E. F. Loftus. 1975. A spreading-activation theory of semantic processing. *Psychological Review* 82 (6): 407–428.

Dall'asta, L., A. Baronchelli, A. Barrat, and V. Loreto. 2006. Nonequilibrium dynamics of language games on complex networks. *Phys. Rev. E* 74 (3): 036105.

Dall'asta, L., A. Baronchelli, A. Barrat, and V. Loreto. 2006b. Agreement dynamics on small-world networks. Europhys. *Lett* 73 (6): 969–975.

Deacon, T. W. 1998. *The Symbolic Species: The Co-evolution of Language and the Brain*. Norton and Company, New York.

Erdos, P., and A. Renyi. 1959. On Random Graphs I. Publ. Math. *Debrecen* 6:290.

Erdos, P., and A. Renyi. 1960. On the evolution of random graphs. Publ. Math. Inst. Hung. Acad. *Sci.* 7:17.

Evans, N., and S. C. Levinson. 2009. The myth of language universals: Language diversity and its importance for cognitive science. *Behavioral and Brain Sciences* 32:429–448.

Haeger, et al. 2009. What can mathematical, computational and robotic models tell us about the origins of syntax? Book chapter in *Biological Foundations and Origin of Syntax*, eds. D. Bickerton, and E. Szathmáry. Strüngmann Forum Reports, Vol. 3. Cambridge, MA: MIT Press.

Galantucci, B., and S. Garrod. 2010. Experimental Semiotics: A new approach for studying the emergence and the evolution of human communication. *Special Issue of Interaction Studies* 11(1).

Galnatucci, B. 2005. An experimental study of the emergence of human communication systems. *Cognitive Science* 29 (5): 737–767.

Gardenfors, P. 2004. Conceptual spaces as a framework for knowledge representation. *Mind and Matter* 2:9–27.

Gardner, H. 1985. *The Mind's New Science: A History of the Cognitive Revolution.* New York: Basic Books.

Garrod, S., and Martin J. Pickering, 2004. Why is conversation so easy? *Trends in Cognitive Sciences* 8 (1): 8–11.

Garrod, S., and Martin J. Pickering. 2009. Joint action, interactive alignment, and dialog. *Topics in Cognitive Science* 1 (2): 292–304.

Heider-Rosch, E., and D. C. Olivier. 1972. The structure of the color space in naming and memory for two languages. *Cognitive Psychology* 3:337–354.

Hockett, C. F. 1960. Logical considerations in the study of animal communication. *Americal Institute of Biological Sciences*, 392–430.

Hockett, C. F. 1960b. The origin of speech. *Scientific American* 203:88–96.

Kay, P., and T. Regier. 2003. Resolving the question of color naming universals. Proc. Natl. Acad. *Sci. USA (PNAS)* 100 (15): 9085–9089.

Ke, J., J. Minett, C-P Au, and W. Wang. 2002. Self-organization and selection in the emergence of vocabulary. *Complexity* 7 (3): 41–54.

Ke, Jinyun, Tao Gong, and W. S-Y. Wang. 2008. Language change and social networks. *Comm. Comput. Phys.* 3 (4): 935–949. Originally presented at the 5th Conference on Language evolution, Leipzig, Germany, March 2004.

Kirby, S., H. H. Cornish, and K. Smith. 2008. Cumulative cultural evolution in the laboratory: An experimental approach to the origins of structure in human language. Proc. Natl. Acad. *Sci. USA (PNAS)* 105 (31): 10681–10686.

Klemm, K., V. M. Eguiluz, R. Toral, and M. San Miguel. 2003. Nonequilibrium transitions in complex networks: A model of social interaction. *Phys. Rev. E* 67(2): 026120.

Kooti, F., M. Cha, K. P. Gummadi, and W. Mason. 2012. The emergence of conventions in online social networks, *Proceedings of the 6th International AAAI Conference on Weblogs and Social Media (ICWSM)*, Dublin, Ireland.

Lakoff, G. 1987. *Women, Fire, and Dangerous Things: What Categories Reveal About the Mind.* University of Chicago Press.

Lazer, D. et al. 2009. Computational social science. *Science* 323:721–723.

Long, F., Z. Yang, and D. Purbes. 2006. Spectral statistics in natural scenes predict hue, saturation, and brightness. Proc. Natl. Acad. *Sci. USA (PNAS)* 103 (15): 6013–6018.

Loreto, V., and L. Steels. 2007. Social dynamics: The emergence of language. *Nature Physics* 3:758–760.

Loreto, V., A. Mukherjee, and F. Tria. 2012. On the origin of the hierarchy of color names. Proc. Natl. Acad. *Sci. USA (PNAS)* 109 (18): 6819–6824.

Lenaerts, T., B. Jansen, K. Tulys, and B. De Vylder. 2005. The evolutionary language game: An orthogonal approach. J. Theor. *Bio* 235 (4): 566–582.

Mezard, M., G. Parisi, and M. A. Virasoro. 1987. Spin glass theory and beyond. *World Scientific Lecture Notes in Physics*. World Scientific New York.

Minett, J. W., and W. S-Y. Wang. 2008. Modeling endangered languages: The effects of bilingualism and social structure. *Lingua* 118 (1): 19–45.

Mukherjee, A., F. Tria, A. Barochelli, and A. Puglisi. 2011. Aging in language dynamics. *PloS ONE* 6 (2): 316677.

Nolfi, S., and M. Mirolli, eds. 2009. *Evolution of Communication and Language in Embodied Agents*. Springer.

Nowak, M., and D. Krakauer. 1999. The evolution of language. Proc. Natl. Acad. *Sci. USA (PNAS)* 96:8028–8033.

Nowak, M., J. B. Plotkin., and D. Krakauer. 1999b. The evolutionary language game. J. Theor. *Bio*. 200 (2): 147–162.

Nowak, M., D. Krakauer, and A. Dress. 1999. An error limit for the evolution of language. *Proceedings of The Royal Society of London Series B, Biological Sciences* 266:2131–2136.

Paolacci, G., J. Chandler, and G. Panagiotis. Ipeirotis. 2010. Running experiments on amazon mechanical turk. *Judgment and Decision Making* 5:411–419.

Puglisi, A., A. Baronchelli, and V. Loreto. 2008. Cultural route to the emergence of linguistic categories. Proc. Natl. Acad. *Sci. USA (PNAS)* 105:7936.

Ratliff, F. 1976. On the psychophysiological bases of universal color terms. *Proceedings of the American Philosophical Society* 120:311–330.

Rosch, E. 1973. Natural categories. *Cognitive Psychology* 4:328–350.

Selten, R., and M. Warglien. 2007. The emergence of simple languages in an experimental coordination game. Proc. Natl. Acad. *Sci. USA (PNAS)* 104 (18): 7361–7366.

Steels, L. 1995. A self-organizing spatial vocabulary. *Artif. Life* 3 (2): 319–332.

Steels, L. 1996. Self-Organizing Vocabularies. *Proceeding of the Fifth International Workshop on the Synthesis and Simulation of Living Systems*, eds. C. Langton, and T. Shimohara. The MIT Press, 179–184.

Steels, L. 2000. Language as a complex adaptive system, in *Proceedings of PPSN VI (Lecture Notes in Computer Science)*, ed. M. Schoenauer. Berlin (Germany).

Suri, S., and D. J. Watts. 2011. Cooperation and contagion in networked public goods experiments. *PLOS ONE* 6(3): e16836.

Tria, F., B. Galantucci, and V. Loreto. 2012. Naming a structured world: A cultural route to duality of patterning. *PLOS ONE* 7(6): e37744 (2012).

von Ahn, L., and L. Dabbish. 2004. Labeling images with a computer game. CHI'04: *Proceedings of the SIGCHI Conference on Human Factors in Computing Systems*, Vienna, Austria, 319–326.

Wang, W. S-Y., and J. W. Minett. 2005. The invasion of language: Emergence, change and death. Trends Ecol. *Evol* 20 (5): 263–269.

Watts, D. J., and S. H. Strogatz. 1998. Collective dynamics of 'small-world' networks. *Nature* 393:440–442.

Whorf, B. L. 1956. *Language, Thought, and Reality: Selected Writings of Benjamin Lee Whorf.* MIT Press.

Wittgenstein, L. 1953. *Philosophical Investigations*. (Translated by Anscombe, G.E.M.) Basil Blackwell, Oxford, UK.

25

Data Acquisition and Prosodic Analysis for Mandarin Attitudinal Speech

Wentao GU

Institute of Linguistic Science and Technology, Nanjing Normal University, China
Graduate School of Information Science and Technology, The University of Tokyo, Japan

Hiroya FUJISAKI
The University of Tokyo, Japan

Abstract

After differentiating attitudes from emotions, the present work proposes a method for collecting attitudinal speech, and investigates prosodic manifestation and perceptual interpretation of Mandarin utterances conveying various attitudes. Using the induction technique, a speech corpus was designed and acquired to incorporate seven classes of behavioral attitudes and two classes of propositional attitudes, among which the speech data of the following five classes have been studied: friendly /hostile, polite / rude, serious /joking, praising /blaming, and confident /uncertain. Perceptual experiment reveals that there are two different confusion patterns between the intended and the perceived attitudes. Statistical analysis of prosodic features shows that speech rate is distinctive in all five classes, while mean F_0 and F_0 range in an utterance are distinctive only for some classes. Moreover, local F_0 features in the words carrying sentential stress are more contrastive for attitudinal expressions than the overall F_0 characteristics in the entire utterance.

1.   Introduction

Expressiveness of speech is an important research topic, not only in the study of phonetics and social psychology, but also in speech technologies, e.g., high-quality speech synthesis. In the last two decades, there have been a great number of studies on expressive/affective speech conveying various emotions, attitudes, and intentions. While psychologists have tried to differentiating between the meanings of these terms precisely, only very few linguists have paid attention to differentiating between 'emotional' and 'attitudinal' speech. Among others, Couper-Kuhlen (1986) defined emotion as a speaker state and attitude as a kind of behavior, while Wichmann (2000) complemented the definition of attitude by incorporating 'propositional attitude' which was a function of opinion, belief, or knowledge. Similarly, Moraes et al (2010) distinguished the involuntary 'basic emotions' from the voluntary 'social affects' (i.e., 'attitudes') which were further divided into two categories, i.e., 'social attitudes' and 'propositional attitudes.'

Fujisaki (1996) classified the information conveyed by speech into linguistic, paralinguistic, and non-linguistic information. Paralinguistic information modifies or supplements the linguistic information of the text and its expression is consciously controlled by the speaker, whereas non-linguistic information concerning the speaker's physical and psychological states is not related to the linguistic information of the text and its expression is not consciously controlled by the speaker, though it can be consciously simulated such as in the case of acting. Along this line of definition, the information concerning speaker's attitude is paralinguistic, whereas the information concerning speaker's emotion is non-linguistic. However, emotion and attitude interact in a complex way in real communication.

In the present study, we propose a conceptual distinction between them in the following way. Emotion is an internal state of the speaker. It is unconsciously conveyed in nature, though it can also be intentionally expressed. Attitude, on the other hand, is an external expression made consciously by the speaker, either associated with intentions to act (named 'behavioral attitude') or related to opinions /beliefs (named 'propositional attitude'); the former is dependent on interaction while the latter is not. In other words, emotion is associated more closely with the physical /physiological state of the speaker, whereas attitude is correlated more tightly with the social relationship between the speaker and the listener, the situation of the conversation, and the cultural background. It is well recognized that external attitude and internal emotion can sometimes be highly related to each other, but they can be dissociated. Namely, attitude is not necessarily a direct reflection of emotion.

There have been a number of studies investigating acoustic correlates and perceptual cues for expressive /affective speech, but in most of them emotions and attitudes are mixed or confounded. Many previous studies on acoustic correlates of emotional speech have shown a high degree of consistency across languages; for example, happy speech tends to have higher pitch level and wider pitch range than sad speech, regardless of the language. This leads us to be usually able to recognize basic emotions of a speaker from his/her speech even if we do not understand the language he /she speaks.

As far as the current authors are aware, rather few studies have dealt exclusively with attitudinal speech as defined here. Among others, Fujisaki and Hirose (1993) compared F_0

contours of confident, interrogative, exhortative, hesitative, as well as neutral speech of Japanese, and examined the accuracy of perceptual recognition. Polite speech has received fairly more studies; e.g., Ofuka et al (2000) made an acoustic comparison on polite and casual speech of Japanese question sentences, showing consistent differences in speech rate and utterance-final F_0 movement. Also, the acoustic and perceptual study by Li and Wang (2004) on friendly speech of Mandarin revealed that pitch was the primary cue for expressing friendliness, while duration was hardly correlated. Notably, a cross-cultural perceptual study by Shochi et al (2009) showed that subjects with different linguistic backgrounds could give different perceptual interpretations to certain attitudinal speech, indicating that some attitudinal expressions were language-specific and dependent on the culture.

Wichmann (2000) argued that the majority of attitudes could only be explained using pragmatic analysis/inference and did not have direct acoustic correlates, because a given prosodic feature could be attitudinally neutral, positive, or negative, depending on a complex interaction between prosody, text, and context. Despite agreeing to this theoretical point of view, we still deem it practically necessary to look into the prosodic correlates of attitudinal speech for the purpose of expressive speech synthesis, in which we believe that there are more demands for conveying attitudinal meanings than for conveying emotions. Although there is no direct prosodic mapping of attitudes without reference to the context, a statistically typical and perceptually recognizable prosody would be helpful for the expressiveness of synthesized attitudinal speech, even if it may be slightly exaggerated.

It is known that both segmental and prosodic features play roles in conveying emotions and attitudes. The latter, however, is generally regarded to be primary. Prosodic features include intonation (voice fundamental frequency, i.e., F_0), duration, intensity, and voice quality. The present study shall be dedicated to investigating the intonational and durational characteristics of attitudinal speech of Mandarin Chinese. Meanwhile, perceptual judgments of the intended attitudinal meanings conveyed in speech will also be examined.

2.   Classification of Attitudes

The studies on attitudinal speech used to compare speech of a certain attitude label with neutral speech, e.g., Ofuka et al (2000) and Li and Wang (2004). However, unlike emotions which usually do not constitute bipolar pairs (e.g. there does not exist a basic emotion 'unsurprised' as the opposite of 'surprised'), attitudes can usually—not necessarily alway—be bipolar, viz. positive on the one end and negative on the other end. Thus, many classes of attitudes can be defined with two opposite poles, or more exactly along a continuum between two poles. A contrastive study between two attitudinal poles would show more distinct patterns.

Instead of giving a systematic and comprehensive classification of attitudes, in the present study we only define the following nine classes of attitudes which are commonly encountered in daily communications.

Behavioral attitudes:

Class 1: Friendly vs. Hostile;

Class 2: Polite vs. Rude;

Class 3: Serious vs. Joking;

Class 4: Praising vs. Blaming;

Class 5: Commanding vs. Suggesting;

Class 6: Sincere vs. Insincere;

Class 7: Willing vs. Reluctant;

Propositional attitudes:

Class 8: Confident vs. Uncertain;

Class 9: Concerned vs. Indifferent.

The first seven classes of attitudes are towards the listener (hence 'behavioral attitudes'), whereas the last two classes are towards the content of speech (hence 'propositional attitudes'). Within each class, we defined two opposite labels (i.e., two poles), though in reality these attitudes can be expressed along a continuum between the two poles. In the present study, the former attitude in each class is labeled as 'positive,' while the latter is labeled as 'negative,' which basically coincides with our common evaluation.

We term the above nine classes of expressions as attitudes rather than emotions, because they are not internal feelings—usually they cannot be embedded in the frame "he /she is feeling …" Being friendly does not necessarily imply whether the speaker is feeling happy or not; being polite does not imply any particular emotion of the speaker, for he/she can behave politely in any emotional state; and apparently, being confident or uncertain is not related to the emotion but to the knowledge. In fact, these expressions are either associated with behaviors (classes 1 to 7), or related to beliefs/opinions (classes 8 and 9). Some of them are highly correlated with the social relationship between the speaker and the listener; e.g., 'commanding' is usually an expression towards a person whose status is lower than the speaker's, whereas 'suggesting' is just the opposite. In short, the above nine classes of expressions are treated as attitudes for they are consciously expressed by the speaker.

3. Attitudinal Speech Corpus

Generally speaking, there are three methods of collecting affective speech: imitated speech without a context, elicited speech in a role-play, and real-world spontaneous speech, as are listed in the ascending order of naturalness yet in the descending order of controllability.

On the one hand, most corpora of affective speech available nowadays are imitated speech without any context; e.g., Mandarin emotional speech corpus such as CASS-ESC (Wang 2004) and CASIA-ESC (Tao et al 2005), and multilingual attitudinal speech corpus built by Shochi et al (2009) and Moraes et al (2010). These corpora of imitated speech can be further divided into two categories. In the one category, different affects use disparate text sentences which are lexically associated with the particular affect; while in the other category, different affects share the same text sentence which is literally neutral and not inherently correlated with any particular affect. Some corpora such as CASS-ESC (Wang 2004) and CASIA-ESC (Tao et al 2005) comprise both categories. The two categories, however, both have intrinsic defects. In the second category, the utterances of different affects share a common linguistic code and hence facilitates a controlled experiment, but the naturalness of utterances is apparently lower than in the first category due to the lack of inherent relevance between text and affect. In any case, imitated speech without a context is easy for design and collection, but it lacks in naturalness or tends to be over-acted, leading it to differ from real affective speech.

On the other hand, more and more spontaneous speech corpora have been built during recent years; e.g., JST/CREST ESP expressive speech corpus of Japanese (Campbell 2004), and Buckeye corpus of English conversational speech (Pitt et al 2005). With innate naturalness and rich expressiveness, spontaneous speech is undoubtedly the ultimate object of speech research. However, it is not suitable for controlled experiment because all factors are varied in spontaneous speech, of which the structure and the content cannot be designed *a priori*. Also, affects conveyed in real-world spontaneous speech can be a mixture of various emotions and attitudes, which poses difficulty on a contrastive study for a given class of attitudes.

Elicited speech in a role-play is a good balance between the above two methods, and has received increasing attention in the research of affective speech, e.g., Yuan et al (2002), though so far no elicited attitudinal speech corpus has been reported. For a tradeoff between naturalness and controllability, the present study chose elicited speech, for which the text is pre-determined and hence comparison can be made on the basis of the same linguistic information. Meanwhile, the naturalness of elicited speech can be guaranteed in a role-play for a given scenario (i.e., the Wizard-of-Oz paradigm). Most important of all, following our conceptual distinction between attitude and emotion, attitudinal speech should in principle be elicited more naturally than emotional speech in a role-play, because attitude is external and consciously expressed in nature. Thus, attitudinal speech can be produced far more naturally by acting than emotional speech, for which acted emotions are inherently different from real emotions and the resulting emotional speech are also perceptually different (Wilting et al 2006).

To ensure the naturalness of elicited speech, in designing scenarios we paid particular attention to having natural contexts and localizing the required attitudes in the target sentences. The scenarios were designed in two different ways. For behavioral attitudes which require interactions, dialogues between two speakers were designed. For propositional attitudes which do not require interactions, only monologues were designed. In both cases, prompting texts were provided to facilitate eliciting the targeted attitudes.

For each of the seven classes of behavioral attitudes (classes 1–7), we designed about 14 target sentences with 6–16 syllables for each. In all classes except class 4 and class 6, the sentences are literally neutral (i.e., not containing any words that lexically imply a specific attitude or emotion) but at the same time can be expressed in opposite attitudes when embedded in two different dialogues. In class 4, some sentences are literally neutral, while the others are literally praising but can pragmatically be blaming in a specific context, viz. 'ironic' due to mismatch between the lexical meaning of the word and the conversational situation. In class 6, most sentences are literally sincere, but the oral expression can be sincere or insincere, depending on the conversational situation.

For each sentence in the seven classes, we designed two dialogues to elicit two opposite attitudes. A dialogue usually comprises 3–5 turns, and the target sentence always constitutes a turn by itself so as to ensure that the intended attitude is exactly located in the target sentence. Prompting texts were also designed to elucidate the relationship between the two speakers and the conversational situation.

For each of the two classes of propositional attitudes (classes 8 and 9), we designed 15 declarative sentences with 6–12 syllables for each. The sentences are literally neutral, without implying whether or not the speaker is certain of or concerned with what he/she is saying. For each sentence, two versions of prompting text were designed to help the speaker produce two opposite attitudes. In these two classes, the scenarios involve both a speaker and a listener, but there is only monologue by the speaker.

For each class of the nine attitudes, a target sentence and two scenarios for the two attitudinal poles are listed below. In all scenarios, the target sentences are spoken by the same role (speaker A). Chinese words in parentheses are not spoken but just used to elicit the intended attitudes.

Class 1: Friendly vs. Hostile

Target sentence: 你大概甚麼時候回來？

(When are you coming back?)

Two scenarios:

【Friendly】 A與B是熱戀中的情侶。B去外地出差了，A忍不住思念，打電話問B甚麼時候回來。

A：親愛的，你在幹嘛呢？

B：我在工作呢。想我了吧？

A：（情意綿綿地）你大概甚麼時候回來？

【Hostile】 A和B感情破裂，約好去民政局辦理離婚手續。約定時間到了，B卻打電話給A說要改天。

A：不是說好今天把手續辦了的嗎？

B：我臨時有事，正在外地出差，回來再說吧。

A：（冷冰冰地）你大概甚麼時候回來？

Class 2: Polite vs. Rude

Target sentence: 現在已經是半價優惠了。

(There is already a half-price discount.)

Two scenarios:

【Polite】 A是精品店的店員，B是VIP客戶，店員A為該客戶提供了熱情周到的
服務。

A：（微笑着接待）您好，本店新到一批精品，而且正在搞促銷活動，包您滿意。

B：那些名牌衣服也能打折嗎？

A：（熱情地推薦）<u>現在已經是半價優惠了</u>。

【Rude】 B到商場買衣服，不小心走進一家精品店。A是店員，看着B的窮酸樣，
估計他買不起，於是十分怠慢。

A：（斜眼打量着B）是想買這件衣服嗎？

B：是啊……哇……這衣服怎麼貴得這麼離譜？不打折嗎？

A：（沒好氣地）<u>現在已經是半價優惠了</u>。

Class 3: Serious vs. Joking

Target sentence: 你應該好好向小劉取取經。

(You should learn from Liu seriously.)

Two scenarios:

【Serious】A是B的班主任老師，B一直學習不認真，A很着急。

A：小劉這次考試又是全年級第一，再看看你呢，有一門課竟然不及格，差距太
大了！

B：他是班長，我哪能跟他比呢？

A：（嚴肅地）<u>你應該好好向小劉取取經</u>。

【Joking】A和B是關系很好的同班同學，小劉是B的舍友。

A：瞧人家小劉，身邊異性朋友不斷，過一陣子換一個，羨煞旁人啊。

B：小劉可真行啊。唉，我怎麼就一個也遇不到呢？

A：（調侃地）<u>你應該好好向小劉取取經</u>。

Class 4: Praising vs. Blaming

Target sentence: 你的演技絕對是一流！

(Your acting skill is absolutely great!)

Two scenarios:

【Praising】B是一名優秀的話劇演員。A十分佩服B的表演功底。

A：聽說你參加全國話劇表演大賽，獲得了青年組一等獎？

B：是啊，我自己也壓根沒想到。

A：（讚嘆地）<u>你的演技絕對是一流</u>！

【Blaming】 A以為B的腿受傷了，很是關心；卻發現B原來是假裝的，頓時不以為然。

A：（疑惑地）你的腿不是受傷了嗎，怎麼這麼快就好了？

B：嗯……其實我腿沒受傷，只是想逃幾天課。

A：（鄙視地）你的演技絕對是一流！

Class 5: Commanding vs. Suggesting

Target sentence: 面試還是安排在周日為好。

(We should better arrange the interview on Sunday.)

Two scenarios:

【Commanding】 學院在討論安排研究生復試的工作。A是主管院長，B是研究生教學秘書。

A：小李，今年研究生復試的日程，都按照學校規定安排好了嗎？

B：其他都確定了，只是面試時間可由各學院自主決定，您看是安排在周日呢，還是安排在下周一？

A：（拍板決定）面試還是安排在周日為好。

B：好，就按您吩咐的。

【Suggesting】 學院在討論安排研究生復試的工作。A是研究生教學秘書，B是主管院長。

A：楊院長，復試名單都已經通知各位導師了，也了解了各位導師對時間安排的意見。

B：面試時間大家傾向於哪一天？

A：（提議）面試還是安排在周日為好。

B：行，就這樣決定了。

Class 6: Sincere vs. Insincere

Target sentence: 單位一直都很重視培養你的。

(Our company has always paid attention to your development.)

Two scenarios:

【Sincere】 A是公司老總，B是公司的青年業務骨干。A對B很器重，將這次去國外著名機構進修的機會給了B。

A：這次出國進修的名額，公司決定給你。機會難得，你要好好鑽研啊。

B：太感謝您了，這麼好的學習機會。我一定不辜負您的厚望！

A：（充滿誠意地）單位一直都很重視培養你的。

【Insincere】 A是公司老總，B是公司的青年業務骨干。今年有一個到國外著名機構進修的名額，大家都以為會給B，結果卻大跌眼鏡，給了老總的秘書小王。B感到不公平，去問老總A。

A：（安撫地）這次名額只有一個，我也很難平衡啊。小王跟了我很久，你也知道的。這次讓他去，下次有機會肯定給你。

B：公司一直強調培養業務骨干，而且這本是一個業務進修的機會，為甚麼反而給了行政人員呢？我覺得單位應該真正重視業務骨干的培養。

A：（尷尬地敷衍）<u>單位一直都很重視培養你的</u>。

Class 7: Willing vs. Reluctant

Target sentence:　我留個電子郵箱給你吧。

　　　　　　　　　（Here is my email address.）

Two scenarios:

【Willing】A與B剛認識，發現原來是同鄉，而且兩人很投緣，於是愉快地交換了聯繫方式。

A：真沒想到原來咱倆是老鄉啊，而且都在南京讀書。

B：是啊，咱倆挺聊得來的。那以後有空多聯繫。

A：（主動爽快地）<u>我留個電子郵箱給你吧</u>。

【Reluctant】A在路上偶遇B做問卷調查，還需要留下聯繫方式。可是A有些猶豫，不太想給。

B：非常感謝您的配合，請留個聯系電話吧，方便以後聯繫回訪。

A：（猶豫地）這……可以不給嗎？我不習慣將聯系方式留給陌生人。

B：請放心，我們不會打擾您的，只是以備急需。

A：（不太情願地）<u>我留個電子郵箱給你吧</u>。

Class 8: Confident vs. Uncertain

Target sentence:　今天劉老師上課。

　　　　　　　　　（Mr. Liu gives a lecture today.）

Two scenarios:

【Confident】A剛剛看到劉老師在隔壁教室上課，因此很肯定地告訴同學B。

A：（確信地）<u>今天劉老師上課</u>！

【Uncertain】　課表上明明寫着是王老師的課，卻看到劉老師走進教室，A很疑惑地向同學B確認。

A：（懷疑地）<u>今天劉老師上課</u>？

Class 9: Concerned vs. Indifferent

Target sentence:　估計又有甚麼項目得金牌了。

　　　　　　　　　（It seems that someone won another gold medal.）

Two scenarios:

【Concerned】 A是體育愛好者。奧運期間，宿舍區響起一片歡呼聲，隔壁宿舍的B
過來打聽有甚麼最新消息。A一邊回應，一邊趕緊打開電腦查看新
聞。

A： （十分關注地） 估計又有甚麼項目得金牌了。

【Indifferent】 A對體育絲毫不感興趣。奧運期間，宿舍區響起一片歡呼聲，隔
壁宿舍的B過來打聽有甚麼最新消息。A繼續全神貫注地玩電腦游
戲，淡淡地回應。

A： （事不關己地） 估計又有甚麼項目得金牌了。

The subjects were 12 native speakers of Mandarin, including 6 males and 6 females around the age of 20. They were undergraduate students majoring in broadcasting and hosting arts at Nanjing Normal University, all excellent at Mandarin pronunciation and skilled in oral expression but *not* professional actors /actresses.

For each target sentence in the nine classes of attitudes, two dialogues (for classes 1–7) or monologues (for classes 8–9) in respective scenarios, together with the isolated sentence in neutral reading, were recorded. In dialogue recording, the current subject played the role of A, while another supporting subject played the role of B. The subjects were allowed to revise the wording of the dialogues slightly in a way they felt most natural and expressive, *except for* the target sentences which must be kept intact. Thus, in each class of attitudes, a target sentence was uttered in three versions, i.e., two opposite attitudes together with the neutral reading.

The recording was conducted in a sound-proof booth after the subjects had got sufficiently familiar with the scenarios. To keep attitudinal expressions consistent, the speech data sharing the same attitude were recorded consecutively in one session.

In the speech corpus, only the utterances of target sentences are investigated. Up to now, we have only analyzed six subjects' (3 males and 3 females) speech data of five classes of attitudes as listed below (viz. 207 utterances for each subject, and thus 1,242 utterances in total). The experimental results reported in next sections are obtained from these data.

Class 1: Friendly vs. Hostile;

Class 2: Polite vs. Rude;

Class 3: Serious vs. Joking;

Class 4: Praising vs. Blaming;

Class 8: Confident vs. Uncertain.

The F_0 values were extracted at 10ms intervals using an accurate autocorrelation analysis provided by the Praat toolkit. After manual correction of gross errors in F_0 extraction, raw F_0 values were smoothed and interpolated (for voiceless intervals) to produce a continuous and smoothed F_0 contour. Syllable segmentation was done manually by visual inspection of waveform and the spectrogram. In analyzing F_0 contours, durational differences were ignored so that F_0 contours of different time spans could be aligned for comparison. Thus, syllable-based time-normalized F_0 contours were obtained by extracting the F_0 values at ten equally-spaced points in each syllable from the continuous and smoothed F_0 contours.

4. Perceptual Experiment

Attitudes may be perceived differently from the intended ones. To test the validity of the attitudinal speech corpus and to investigate the relationship between production and perception of attitudes, we conducted a perceptual experiment, in which six native speakers of Mandarin (including 3 males and 3 females) participated as listening subjects. They were all graduate students majoring in linguistics or literature around the age of 22, with no impairment in hearing or comprehension.

The method of constant stimuli was adopted as the test paradigm. All 1,242 target utterances (stimuli) were re-arranged randomly into 83 sound files, each comprising 14–15 stimuli with 10s inter-stimulus intervals. These sound files were presented to the listening subjects through headphones in a sound-proof booth. Within each 10s inter-stimulus interval, the listeners were forced to give the following two answers for each stimulus on the answer sheet:

Table 25.1 Percentages of perceived attitude labels (%)

Class of attitudes	Intended	Perceived			
		+	0	–	unsure
Friendly /Hostile	friendly (+)	**85.2**	10.7	3.1	0.9
	neutral (0)	10.2	**83.3**	5.6	0.9
	hostile (–)	3.0	4.3	**92.6**	0.2
Polite /Rude	polite (+)	**88.6**	10.8	0.5	0
	neutral (0)	15.8	**81.1**	2.7	0.3
	rude (–)	2.5	4.2	**92.5**	0.8
Serious /Joking	serious (+)	**87.6**	9.0	2.8	0.6
	neutral (0)	22.8	**76.3**	0.7	0.2
	joking (–)	4.3	0.4	**95.4**	0
Praising /Blaming	praising (+)	**81.0**	4.2	14.1	0.8
	neutral (0)	8.7	**86.7**	4.4	0.2
	blaming (–)	16.7	4.6	**78.0**	0.8
Confident /Uncertain	confident (+)	**85.0**	14.4	0.6	0
	neutral (0)	22.0	**77.6**	0.2	0.2
	uncertain (–)	1.5	1.3	**97.2**	0

(1) The perceived attitude (chosen from a list of attitude labels in the given class of attitudes, including 'neutral'; or choosing 'unsure' when failing to make judgment);

(2) The word carrying sentential stress, i.e. the word that is perceptually most prominent in the sentence, if any (to be circled on the sentence text).

Before the experiment, training sessions were repeated until the listening subjects felt confident in giving consistent answers.

Table 25.1 shows the results for the five classes of attitudes. In the table, '+', '−', and '0' represent two attitudinal poles and the neutral speech, respectively. In a given class, for each intended attitude label (including neutral), the percentages of all perceived attitude labels are calculated over all six listening subjects. The values on the diagonal (in bold letters) indicate the rates of recognition, i.e. the rates of coincidence between intended and perceived attitudes.

It is observed that the perceptual patterns are quite different between class 4 and the other four classes:

(1) In all classes except class 4, the rates of recognition are consistently in the order of "negative > positive > neutral." This suggests that these attitudes conveyed in speech are easily interpreted. Negative attitudes are obviously perceived more accurately, indicating that the expression of negative attitudes in these classes is perceptually more recognizable.

Table 25.2 Numbers of perceived sentential stresses

Class of attitudes	Attitude label	Non-final	Final	Total
Friendly /Hostile	friendly (+)	40	44	84
	hostile (−)	53	28	81
	neutral (0)	4	27	31
Polite /Rude	polite (+)	30	18	48
	rude (−)	37	21	58
	neutral (0)	23	9	32
Serious /Joking	serious (+)	38	37	75
	joking (−)	37	45	82
	neutral (0)	24	30	54
Praising /Blaming	praising (+)	23	52	75
	blaming (−)	44	38	82
	neutral (0)	18	35	53
Confident /Uncertain	confident (+)	20	55	75
	uncertain (−)	15	67	82
	neutral (0)	15	36	51

(2)   In class 4, the rates of recognition are in the order of "neutral > positive > negative," exactly reverse to the order in other classes. In particular, the rate of recognition for 'blaming' is much lower than for negative attitudes in other classes.

(3)   In all classes except class 4, perceptual confusion occurs mainly between the positive attitude and the neutral. In particular, the rate of identifying neutral reading as 'serious' or 'confident' is noticeably high (> 22%). This may be because that neutral reading has a placid style which resembles the speaking style in a serious attitude—in fact neutral reading without any affect can be perceived as serious to some extent. Also, neutral reading of declarative sentences is assertive in nature, resulting in a similarity between neutral reading and confident speech.

(4)   In class 4, perceptual confusion occurs mainly between positive and negative attitudes. It is to be noted that many sentences in this class are literally praising but pragmatically blaming (i.e., ironic or sarcastic) when spoken in a specific context. The distinction between praising and blaming can be cued not only by prosody but also by the match/mismatch between word expression and contextual situation. Thus, when an utterance is dissociated from the context, attitudes of this kind may not be inferred reliably.

Table 25.2 lists the numbers of perceived sentential stresses in all target utterances, counting both utterance-final and non-utterance-final positions (henceforth we list '+' and '–' adjacent to each other in the tables, for the contrast between two attitudinal poles is our main concern). A word is deemed to carry sentential stress when more than half of the listening subjects agreed in their judgments. As shown consistently in all five classes of attitudes, more sentential stresses are perceived in attitudinal speech than in neutral speech, suggesting that more stresses are elicited by attitudinal expression. Also, it is observed that the position of sentential stress varies with attitudes. For example, hostile speech and blaming speech tend to introduce more stresses at non-utterance-final positions, while praising speech and uncertain speech tend to introduce more utterance-final stresses.

5.   Acoustic Analysis of Prosody

It is well known that emotions modify prosodic features of utterances. For example, active emotions are usually associated with a wide F_0 range, whereas passive emotions are usually associated with a narrow F_0 range. The results for Mandarin emotional speech have been provided by Zhang et al (2006) and Gu and Lee (2007). The acoustic analysis can also be applied to attitudinal speech here.

Three utterance-level prosodic features were calculated: mean syllabic duration (as an indication of the speech rate), mean F_0 height, and F_0 range over an utterance. The values were then averaged over all target utterances from all six subjects (i.e., over 80–90 samples) for each attitude label. Table 25.3 lists the average measurements for all attitude labels in all five classes

Table 25.3   Mean values of prosodic features

Class of attitudes	Attitude label	Syl.dur (sec.)	F_0 height (Hz)	F_0 range (octave)
Friendly /Hostile	friendly (+)	0.166	184*	1.09
	hostile (−)	0.153	180*	1.29
	neutral (0)	0.173	165	1.19
Polite /Rude	polite (+)	0.165	181*	1.19*
	rude (−)	0.154	180*	1.19*
	neutral (0)	0.178	169	1.25†
Serious /Joking	serious (+)	0.167	172	1.09
	joking (−)	0.178	195	1.38
	neutral (0)	0.179†	172†	1.17†
Praising /Blaming	praising (+)	0.176	195	1.27*
	blaming (−)	0.190	182	1.34*
	neutral (0)	0.180†	171	1.26†
Confident /Uncertain	confident (+)	0.180	190	1.39*
	uncertain (−)	0.199	234	1.30*
	neutral (0)	0.191†	176	1.21†

of attitudes. F_0 height was calculated and averaged in the logarithmic domain, but was then converted back to Hz as presented in the table for the ease of interpretation. F_0 range, measured in octave, was defined as the difference between the maximum F_0 and the minimum F_0 in the log (base 2) scale.

To test the statistical significance of difference, multiple paired *t*-tests with Bonferroni adjustment were conducted between each pair of attitude labels within each class of attitudes. The prosodic features for the two utterances sharing the same text sentence and the same subject but differing in attitude label were paired in the *t*-tests. In Table 25.3, the values with an asterisk (*) indicate that there is *no* significant difference between the two attitudinal poles, while the values with a symbol (†) indicate that neutral speech is at least *not* significantly different from one attitudinal pole in the same class of attitudes. The differences between all others are statistically significant (p < 0.05), and in fact most of them are highly significant (p < 0.001).

The quantitative results in Table 25.3 are summarized below:

(1)   Friendly /Hostile: friendly speech is slower and has a narrower F_0 range than hostile speech; both are faster and have higher F_0 than neutral speech. The results

of comparison between friendly and neutral speech coincide with those reported by Li and Wang (2004).

(2)   Polite /Rude: polite speech is slower than rude speech; both are faster and have higher F_0 than neutral speech.

(3)   Serious /Joking: serious speech is faster and has lower F_0 and narrower F_0 range than joking speech.

(4)   Praising /Blaming: praising speech is faster and has higher F_0 than blaming speech; both have higher F_0 than neutral speech.

(5)   Confident /Uncertain: confident speech is faster and has lower F_0 than uncertain speech; both have higher F_0 than neutral speech.

In summary, speech rate is distinctive in all five classes of attitudes; F_0 height is distinctive only in three classes, i.e., serious/joking, praising/blaming, and confident/uncertain; while F_0 range is distinctive only in two classes, i.e., friendly/hostile and serious/joking.

Until now we have only compared utterance-level (global) prosodic features, which however are not necessarily the only prosodic correlates differentiating various attitudinal expressions. Prosodic details in some critical units are also known to play an important role in conveying emotions. For example, Zhang et al (2006) found that stressed words carried more identifiable acoustic features for emotions than unstressed words. Our perceptual experiment has shown

Table 25.4 Average F_0 features for the words carrying sentential stress consistently in all three attitude labels

Class of attitudes	Attitude label	min F_0 (Hz)	max F_0 (Hz)	mean F_0 (Hz)
	friendly (+)	157	260	214
Friendly /Hostile	hostile (−)	153	243	199
	neutral (0)	139	228	184
	polite (+)	167	254	223
Polite /Rude	rude (−)	177	298	233
	neutral (0)	157	229	197
	serious (+)	152	246	196
Serious /Joking	joking (−)	157	294	219
	neutral (0)	134	215	172
	praising (+)	141	307	219
Praising /Blaming	blaming (−)	146	274	198
	neutral (0)	129	234	181
	confident (+)	141	239	191
Confident /Uncertain	uncertain (−)	161	329	241
	neutral (0)	128	219	170

that attitudinal expressions produce more sentential stresses than neutral speech. We further investigate prosodic differences in these stressed words.

In each class of attitudes, we calculated the following three local F_0 features for each word carrying sentential stress consistently in all three attitude labels: minimum F_0, maximum F_0, and mean F_0. Table 25.4 lists the average measurements for the three features from all stressed words in target utterances of all six subjects. All F_0 values were calculated and averaged in the logarithmic domain, but were then converted back to Hz as presented in the table for the ease of interpretation.

By comparison, the differences in the mean F_0 between attitudinal speech and neutral speech are more conspicuous in stressed words (Table 25.4) than in the entire utterance (Table 25.3). In all five classes of attitudes, F_0 of stressed word in attitudinal speech is consistently higher than in neutral speech. In the classes of friendly/hostile and praising/blaming, F_0 of stressed word is the highest in positive attitudes, while in other three classes F_0 of stressed word is the highest in negative attitudes. Moreover, it is observed that the contrasts in maximum F_0 are more conspicuous, while the differences in minimum F_0 are smaller. This suggests that the top-line F_0 is more characteristic of attitudinal expressions.

6. Conclusions

We differentiated attitudes from emotions by defining the attitude as an external expression imposed consciously by the speaker, in contrast to the emotion as an internal state of the speaker. Along this line of definition, attitudinal speech can be elicited naturally in a role-play, intrinsically involving less acting effect than acted emotional speech. Thus, a corpus of attitudinal speech of Mandarin was designed and acquired, incorporating seven classes of behavioral attitudes and two classes of propositional attitudes, in each of which two attitudinal poles (i.e., positive vs. negative) were defined. Among the corpus, the data of target utterances in four classes of behavioral attitudes and a class of propositional attitudes have been analyzed in detail, both perceptually and acoustically.

Perceptual experiment has shown two different confusion patterns between intended and perceived attitudes. For praising/blaming where irony is involved, the rates of perceptual recognition are in the order of "neutral > positive > negative," where positive and negative tend to be confused with each other. In all four other classes, however, the rates of perceptual recognition are consistently in the order of "negative > positive > neutral," where positive and neutral tend to be confused more easily with each other.

Statistical analysis of utterance-level prosodic features has revealed that speech rate is distinctive in all five classes of attitudes; F_0 height is distinctive only in serious /joking, praising /blaming, and confident /uncertain; while F_0 range is distinctive only in friendly /hostile, and serious /joking. A further comparison on the words carrying sentential stress has revealed that in all five classes the F_0 difference in stressed words is more conspicuous than the average F_0 difference over the entire utterance.

Apparently, the present work is still preliminary and many questions need to be further addressed in our future study. Four other classes of attitudinal speech have been collected but not studied yet, and besides the nine classes we have defined, a more comprehensive classification of real-world attitudes is still required. Prosodic analysis can be conducted on more detailed features, e.g., F_0 can be inspected by looking at lexical tones and sentential intonation separately. In addition to analyzing surface F_0 features, a model-based analysis can also be applied to the entire F_0 contours, as already done for emotional speech of Mandarin (Gu and Lee 2007). Speaker difference in prosodic manifestation of attitudinal expression, cross-linguistic comparison of attitudinal expression, and cross-linguistic perception of attitudes, are also important topics for our future study.

Acknowledgements

This work was supported jointly by the Social Science Foundation of China (10CYY009), the Natural Science Foundation of China (31100814), the Shanghai Social Science Foundation (2011BYY002), the key project from Jiangsu Higher Education Institutions' Key Research Base for Philosophy and Social Sciences (2010JDXM024), the project of Priority Academic Program Development of Jiangsu Higher Education Institutions and the NICT International Exchange Program.

REFERENCES

Campbell, N. 2004. Databases of expressive speech. *Journal of Chinese Language and Computing* 14 (4): 295–304.

Couper-Kuhlen, E. 1986. *English Prosody*. London: Edward Arnold.

Fujisaki, H. 1996. Prosody, models, and spontaneous speech. In *Computing Prosody*, eds. Y. Sagisaka, N. Campbell, and N. Higuchi, 27–42. New York: Springer-Verlag.

Fujisaki, H., and K. Hirose. 1993. Analysis and perception of intonation expressing paralinguistic information in spoken Japanese. *Proceedings of ESCA Workshop on Prosody*, 254–257, Lund, Sweden.

Gu, W., and T. Lee. 2007. Quantitative analysis of F_0 contours of emotional speech of Mandarin. *Proceedings of 6th ISCA Speech Synthesis Workshop*, 228–233, Bonn, Germany.

Li, A., and H. Wang. 2004. Friendly speech analysis and perception in Standard Chinese. *Proceedings of International Conference on Spoken Language Processing*, 897–900, Jeju, Korea.

Moraes, J. A., A. Rilliard, B. A. O. Mota, and T. Shochi. 2010. Multimodal perception and production of attitudinal meaning in Brazilian Portuguese. *Proceedings of 5th International Conference on Speech Prosody*, Chicago, IL.

Ofuka, E., J. D. McKeown, M. G. Waterman, and P. J. Roach. 2000. Prosodic cues for rated politeness in Japanese speech. *Speech Communication* 32 (3): 199–217.

Pitt, M., K. Johnson, E. Hume, S. Kiesling, and W. Raymond. 2005. The Buckeye corpus of conversational speech: Labeling conventions and a test of transcriber reliability. *Speech Communication* 45:90–95.

Shochi, T., A. Rilliard, V. Aubergé, and D. Erickson. 2009. Intercultural perception of English, French and Japanese social affective prosody. In *The Role of Prosody in Affective Speech*, ed. S. Hancil, 31–60. Bern.: Peter Lang AG.

Tao, J., J. Yu, and Y. Kang. 2005. An expressive Mandarin speech corpus. *Proceedings of Oriental COCOSDA*, Bali Island, Indonesia.

Wang, H. 2004. *Acoustic Analysis of Mandarin Affective Speech*. MA thesis, Institute of Linguistics, Chinese Academy of Social Sciences.

Wichmann, A. 2000. The attitudinal effects of prosody and how they relate to emotion. *Proceedings of ISCA Workshop on Speech and Emotion*, 143–148, Newcastle, North Ireland.

Wilting, J., E. Krahmer, and M. Swerts. 2006. Real vs. acted emotional speech. *Proceedings of INTERSPEECH*, 805–808, Pittsburgh, PA.

Yuan, J., L. Shen, and F. Chen. 2002. The acoustic realization of anger, fear, joy and sadness in Chinese. *Proceedings of International Conference on Spoken Language Processing*, 2025–2028, Denver, CO.

Zhang, S., P. C. Ching, and F. Kong. 2006. Acoustic analysis of emotional speech in Mandarin Chinese. *Proceedings of 5th International Symposium on Chinese Spoken Language Processing*, 57–66, Singapore.

Appendix: An Interview with Professor William WANG (26 April 2010)

Interviewers: Professor Virginia Yip
              Professor Stephen Matthews

Yip: We are very happy to have Professor Bill Wang here with us today. First let me give an introduction. Professor William Wang, Wang Shi Yuan is Wei Lun Research Professor at the Department of Electronic Engineering, and is affiliated with the Centre for East Asian Studies, Department of Translation; and Department of Linguistics and Modern Languages at The Chinese University of Hong Kong.

Before joining CUHK, he was Professor of Linguistics at the University of California in Berkeley from 1966–1994, and Chair Professor of Language Engineering at the City University of Hong Kong from 1995–2004. Professor Wang is a distinguished scholar whose influence and contributions are well recognized in the international and regional communities. As a trailblazer, he founded the Division of Linguistics and Division of East Asian languages at Ohio State University, serving as the first chairman of both divisions. He is the founder of the *Journal of Chinese Linguistics* and a central figure in the development of Chinese linguistics. He was elected President of the International Association of Chinese Linguistics when it was first founded in 1992. Professor Wang is also an Academician of the Academia Sinica in Taiwan. At Berkeley, he served as Director of the Chao Yuen Ren Center for Chinese Linguistics and Professor of Graduate School till 2000.

Professor Wang is the recipient of numerous honors and awards, including a Guggenheim Fellowship; two fellowships from the Center for Advanced Studies in the Behavioral Sciences at Stanford; a National Professorship from Sweden; a resident fellowship from the Center for Advanced Studies at Bellagio, Italy; and a fellowship from the International Institute of Advanced Studies in Kyoto. He is an Honorary Professor of Peking University. His publications include numerous articles in technical journals, and several entries in different encyclopedias and general science magazines, including American Scientist, Nature, Proceedings of the National Academy of Sciences, Scientific American and 科學人 in Taiwan. His writings have appeared in Chinese, English, French, German, Italian, and Japanese.

His recent honors include an honorary degree from Beijing University, and the Golden Language Award from Taiwan. In recent years, Professor Wang has collaborated with biologists and computer scientists in a common search for the origin of language and the patterns in language differentiation. At The Chinese University of Hong Kong, he continues his research on language from an interdisciplinary perspective, involving engineering, linguistics, and biological sciences.

Hi Bill. Congratulations on your recent awards. We're so happy for you. Would you like to talk about them?

Wang: Well, this month, I was very lucky. On April 9th, just a couple of weeks ago, I was in Beijing, and was given the title of Honorary Professor of Peking University. I think I have many friends there and I was happy to see them. Just last week, I was in Taiwan. There was an International Conference on Applied Linguistics and the Taiwan University of Science and Technology, which hosted this conference, gave me the Golden Language Award.

Yip: What an honor!

Wang: It was quite a pleasure to be appreciated.

Yip: Yes. We'd like to know about the stories of the *Journal of Chinese Linguistics*. You are the founder of this prestigious international journal. What was it like in the beginning? What inspired you to give birth to this journal?

Wang: It was in the 1970s. In 1973 I had my first opportunity to return to China at the invitation of Peking University and the Academy of Social Science. And when I returned to Berkeley, I recognized that there was a very impressive body of scholarship on the nature of language then in China, with a tradition that stretches back 2000 years. Somehow this tradition of scholarship never merged with international scholarship on language. So I went to the Dean at Berkeley, and he was very enthusiastic about the idea. With a grant from the Dean's office, we started the journal. It was really a rubber-band-paper-clip type of operation at the beginning. We wrote in a lot of Chinese characters by hand because there was no Chinese word processing. It was very much like a garage job but with the support from all quarters, it gradually became stabilized and I was very happy. Two years ago the Chinese University expressed an interest in this journal, and we moved the journal to this campus. So now essentially, it has two headquarters: one at Berkeley, and one here.

Yip: Could you tell us about the early days? Like what problems did you encounter and what was done to overcome all these obstacles?

Wang: In the early days, it was difficult to come to a uniform decision on political alignment. One wouldn't think of such problem for a scholarly journal, but since I felt the bulk of the scholarship, and since most of the scholars in this area were on the mainland, we decided to publish in simplified characters as well as in *pinyin*. This somehow irritated the people in Taiwan, and so the journal was put on the black list in Taiwan. Many of my good friends in Taiwan had no access to the journal, and I myself was put on the black list. For a long time, I was a persona non grata there. But all of this gets washed away by time, and I think right now it enjoys popular support from both sides of the Taiwan Strait.

Yip: So you were a unifying force behind this. You just got this award from Taiwan. I think both Beijing and Taiwan recognize your contributions.

Wang: Yes. I feel that the political divide of the Taiwan Strait is a very artificial one, and a product of the politics of the time has no scholarly validity. So at the very first chance I got, I met the leading scholars from both sides together in Berkeley. At first they were nervous to come into contact with people from the other side, but gradually everybody realized that scholarship is scholarship.

Yip: Could you comment on the major milestones in the evolution of the journal, maybe within the larger field of Chinese linguistics?

Wang: I felt that Professor Chao Yuen Ren was a very strong formative influence on Chinese linguistics, and so when we published the very first issue, I was very proud of it, and took a copy of the first issue to his residence up the hill and presented it to him in person. And right on the first page, it says: "Dedicated to him (Professor Chao)" He was very happy about that.

Yip: Could you tell us what was it like when you were colleagues at Berkeley?

Wang: I have just an infinite amount of admiration for him. He's a very inward person who never talks much. But whenever he opens his mouth, it's usually something very worth-listening. Mrs. Chao, on the other hand, was a very colorful lady who had quite a history of her own. I remember that she would point her finger at her husband and say, "Look, you have written so many papers, so many books, and yet you don't have half the readership that I have with one cookbook," which is *How to Cook and Eat in Chinese*. They lived up the hill, the Berkeley hills, and there was once I was at their house when I first got to know them. I went upstairs, up their three storey house to go to the washroom and I didn't know where the lights were. So I went in to wash my hands in the dark washroom, and then I heard something splashing in the bathtub, and I got really worried. I looked for the lights, found the lights and turned them on. In the bathtub there were three or four big fish, swimming, splashing in there. So Mrs. Chao was fond of cooking. Whenever she had some unexpected guests, she would go up to the bathtub and pull out a fish. Mr. Chao of course spent a lot of time playing the piano so it is a musical household. A piece of clear evidence of this musical influence is their daughter Iris, Pian Chao Ru Lan, who is one of the leading experts on merging Western music with Chinese music. And I just understood from what you just told me, Iris has donated a lot of her musical holdings to Chinese University.

Yip: In fact she has just donated her entire collection of books on music and musical instruments, notes and materials. We're very grateful to her. I mean the entire community of Chinese University is very grateful.

Wang: It must be an amazing donation.

Yip: Her father, Professor Chao Yuen Ren, is known as a musician as well as many other titles like mathematician and linguist. You have a broad range of interests too.

Wang: I think I was influenced by his approach to scholarship. He got his degree in mathematical physics from Harvard, and went on to do lots of things in language and music. One of the songs that I think was most beloved song in the middle twentieth century in China is Jiao Wo Ru He Bu Xiang Ta 《叫我如何不想他》. When *Language* asked me to write a eulogy of Professor Chao, I could think of no better way of ending the eulogy than to put in the song with his music. *Language* told me they don't publish music. However, the editor, Bill Bright, was a good friend of mine, and I asked for an exception to be made for Professor Chao. And he did. They published the line of music in full musical staff at the end of the eulogy.

                 I think language is really interdisciplinary par excellence. Professor Chao is a very good example. But ultimately, I think the whole goal of scholarship is to find out who we are and what a human being is. The most distinguishing feature of a human being is human language. If you look at it from one window, you see some of it; and if you look at it from another window, you see some other parts. It's like the Blind Men and the Elephant. Only by looking at language in many, many different windows can we have a better and deeper idea of what language is. And through that, we understand human nature more deeply.

Yip: So this is one of the motivating forces that drives your work. What are the major discoveries and achievements as far as the origin of language is concerned? What is the relationship between Chinese linguistics, and the more general quest for the origin of language?

Wang: Well the early training that I had in linguistics, especially when I was a graduate student at the University of Michigan, was an offshoot of European neogrammarian view of what languages are, and also very much influenced by Saussure about linguistic systems. At around that time, I was also quite impressed by Darwin's achievements and evolution theory. As I look at language through an evolutionary perspective, I see that there is so much variation and so much flux. The neogrmmarians told us that sounds change, there's no exception; the great Leonard Bloomfield said phonemes change. Nonetheless, I experimented with the idea that maybe it's words that change. Once words which share a phoneme regroup, then it will look like the phoneme changed. Many colleagues call this idea that I worked up as *lexical diffusion*. Since then, I think I have broadened my perspective to think that it's not just sound change, but morphological change, syntactic change, any change in language is actually by changes in words. I think this is probably still a minority view, but nonetheless, it's worth looking at from that perspective.

Matthews: Professor Wang, I understand that you also learned from the late Joseph Greenberg. As he's no longer with us, perhaps you could share some memories of learning from him, maybe like how he had influenced your work.

Wang: Greenberg was another major influence on my thinking. It was quite amusing how I first met him. I was a freshman at Columbia College, and Greenberg was a young lecturer who just returned recently from Africa. You know in Ivy League universities, things are typically a little bit more formal, and instructors come typically with a tie—much more structured than I later found out Berkeley to be. But once I took a course from Greenberg, and first class instead of regular class of 23…30 students, there were maybe five or six of us, and we waited there, we waited there, and 20 minutes past the hour, there's a young man with a very disheveled look came in with a huge batch of handouts, kind of rushed into the room, and that was Greenberg. He had completely overestimated the class, both in size and ability , because the handout was a problem for reconstruction of some African languages, languages that we've never heard of, but it shows how completely absorbed he was in his work, and I enjoyed that class even though I found it very hard because he would wander off into the depth of his own thinking, and lose his students periodically.

Later on, I had the good fortune of being close to him because when I moved to Berkeley, he had already moved to Stanford, and we were only an hour away. I would drive down to visit him. Did you know that Greenberg was a concert quality pianist? And sometimes after dinner, he would sit at the piano and entertain us with some beautiful sonatas, and quite often we would go to the Stanford faculty club, and I think that I really wanted to have his approval of my work. I remember once, I published something in IJAL, International Journal of American Linguistics, about tones, and the last part of the paper dealt with a tone sandhi phenomenon in Chaozhou, which I understand is Virginia's early language. It was a very interesting phonological phenomenon because there are five long tones, two short tones we put aside. The five long tones in the sandhi position chase each other around like in a circle, so this was sometimes called the Min tone circle. And I was very proud in coming up with an elegant, simple rule to describe this tone circle. Bursting with pride, I showed this to Greenberg. I scratched on the napkins at the faculty club at Stanford, and Greenberg listened very patiently, and he said "and then?", and so? I was flabbergasted because it seemed the achievement was right there in front of him. But Greenberg was asking a deeper question. He says "you've shown me a clever trick with a formalism, what do I learn about the nature of language, what do I learn about the nature of Min with this clever trick?" and I went home frustrated, and thought and thought and thought, and I realized how extremely right he was. How excessive abstraction, excessive formalism, removing us from the empirical foundations of language is leading linguistics down the wrong track. On my next trip, I told Greenberg that I understood his question, and he was glad.

Yip: Both Chao Yuen Ren and Joseph Greenberg were two towering figures in linguistics, and I'm interested to hear your view on their lasting legacies. What do you think of their perspectives on language? What have we learned from them?

Wang: I think from both of them, there is a very clear message, that language is not just an autonomous system but it's embedded in culture, it's embedded in human civilization, human cognition. Chao got his degree in mathematical physics. Greenberg got his degree from Northwestern University in anthropology. They both brought to the study of language a very interesting and very useful perspective. Another giant figure that I have the good fortune of being close to is a population geneticist. His name is Luigi Luca Cavalli-Sforza. It took me a long time just to remember that name.

Yip: You said it beautifully.

Wang: Once somebody called a meeting at Berkeley. Somebody who wanted to put together a book and Cavalli was invited up there to write a chapter on human genetics, and my assignment was to write about language. That book never came to fruition but Luca and I became very good friends. We would visit each other, I would drive down, he would drive up, and he made me realize that understanding human prehistory can be very important toward understanding language prehistory. The origin of human behaviors can shed a lot of light on the origin of language and conversely. All these three giants in my life, Luca is still alive and well, and some of us put together a package applying for a honorary academicianship, if there's such a word, and the Academia Sinica, Zhong Yang Yan Jiu Yuan (中央研究院), approved our application, and Luca will probably come to Taiwan this summer to be among the very first batch of honorary academicians of Zhong Yang Yan Jiu Yuan (中央研究院). We're very happy about that.

Matthews: I remember when you came to Hong Kong at a time in your career when many academics would be thinking of retiring, you went off into South China to do field work on minority languages of South China. Could you tell us something about what was motivating that work, and something about what you found?

Wang: Sure. I can't imagine retiring because this work that we do is so interesting. Actually when I was at Berkeley, quite early on, I read about a Chinese anthropologist by the name of Fei Xiao Tong. Fei Xiao Tong, I think in the 1930s or 40s, went to a place in Guangxi called Da Yao Shan to study the Yao people there. And there's a very touching history of him and his young wife going up to Da Yao Shan, finally tracking down these people, and through a series of tragic accidents, he lost his wife on that field trip, so that made a deep impression on me. Later on when I got to know Professor Li Fang Kuei. Li Fang Kuei of course had this master plan of how the languages of China fit together and the Miao-Yao branch was always very controversial. Is it Sinitic? Is it Austro-Asiatic? Is it Austronesian, or is it something of its own?

So Fei Xiao Tong's story, this linguistic controversy, kind of stuck in my mind and I tried to make some trips when I was at Berkeley, but it was just too inconvenient. So when I finally decided to retire from teaching at Berkeley, I thought this would be a much better way of doing it. Just to relocate to Hong Kong and be a lot closer to these endangered languages. One of the first things I did of course was to go to Dao Yao Shan with a bunch of my students and recorded some of the Yao materials with the help of Shi Feng of Nankai University. Since that time, we've also extended our interest to many of the languages in Yunnan and one of my students at the City

University now is a professor at Peking University, by the name of Wang Feng, has studied another such enigma—the Bai language of Yunnan. How is that affiliated?

So I think such languages are of interest in two dimensions. On the one side, we need to solve the scientific problems about language evolution and what is vertical transmission, what is horizontal transmission. On the other hand, I think we ought to call attention to these languages which are disappearing fast. As people tell me there, you pave another road and you lose another language. Because once these villagers smell the success of outside, there's a genuine reluctance to pass on their own heritage. To pass on their own language. And once you lose a language, you lose a culture. So this was one of the reasons that motivated my going to these villages as well as moving across the Pacific in the first place.

Yip: Well, as you know, our department, the Department of Linguistics and Modern Languages is still very young and we'd like to train the next generation of linguistics students. Could you give us some advice, some words of wisdom? How could we train them to be aware of the theoretical interest as well as the applications of Linguistics?

Wang: Well. I think if a person is intellectually alive, they should need not much motivation for them to study language because I think that's the most interesting and most challenging intellectual area towards understanding who human beings are. But I think it is unfortunate that many departments of Linguistics, especially in the United States, have been swept over too much by a conception of Linguistics where there is all too much eagerness to follow the latest fashion, and are expending too much energy and excessive amount of attention on what latest fashionable theory to follow, what latest formula to write. The cleverness that I was talking about earlier, the energy is aside from the way from getting to the real stuff of language.

I was browsing through the wonderful book that you and Steve put out on the bilingual child. I think that's really a beautiful contribution because it's both empirical and theoretical. The two should not be separated. They're two sides of the same coin. As both MacWhinney and O'Grady said in the back cover, this is ground-breaking because people talk about bilingualism from very different perspectives. As I thumbed through your various chapters, every time Sophie makes a comment about Alicia, it's a very insightful and very fresh perspective on how to look at language. So, I think, you know, language acquisition is a fundamental topic towards understanding what language is. The Chinese context is fertile as a laboratory for such studies.

Steve is interested in typology and what we said about endangered languages. That's another very timely and very important topic that we must not neglect. My own curiosity has been led further and further down into the questions about the biological foundations. The child follows … a somewhat uniform time schedule. When does it become more entrenched in its native language, and less able to hear the contrasts in other languages? When do the first words come? When do the first constructions come? And of course this is not accidental. It has to do with the maturation of the brain. So, the more we understand about how the brain actually processes something as complex and intricate as language, the more we'll understand about language. I think all these empirical approaches to language dovetail together very well.

Yip: Yes. This is a very important point, especially when we, say, give promotion talks and orientation talks about linguistics. We want the public and our students to appreciate what interdisciplinary linguistics is. In a way, linguistics is really unique in terms of the humanities, and also sciences. We're known as the most scientific of the humanities.

Wang: Right.

Yip: We have the potential to bridge science and humanities, and we can't think of a better person to embody this interdisciplinarity. You are the quintessential interdisciplinarian because you've done so much work collaborating with engineers, biologists and geneticists, not to mention linguists, in different fields. I think this is really the future of linguistics in order for linguistics to grow and flourish, we have to actively engage in interdisciplinary pursuits.

Wang: I thoroughly agree with that. I think knowledge only progresses when we see new connections. Once we see a new connection and integrate two earlier discipline bodies of knowledge, then we've really made an intellectual revolution. I mean the history of science has followed such examples. When we realized that the movement of the celestial bodies and the falling of the apple are driven by the same force, that was a major breakthrough. When we realized that electricity and magnetism are essentially the same phenomenon working at different frequencies, that's a major breakthrough. When people realized we can study the radioactive decay of isotopes, and apply that to trees and skulls to study human prehistory, that's a major breakthrough. And when Swadesh said, "Oh, maybe we can try something like that with language, and use basic vocabulary to date language", that's a breakthrough, too. But language is much harder than trees and skulls, because it's human behavior and human behavior is always much more variable than the physical phenomenon. Nonetheless, I think it is these interdisciplinary perspectives that connect hitherto unconnected things, that gives us the best chance of advancing knowledge. And I think language is right at the hub of this. I don't believe in departmentalization. This is archeology, this is linguistics, that's psychology. I think knowledge is unity. It's just that we haven't connected certain pieces together yet.

Yip: We know that you're very much interested in language and the brain, and the biological basis of language. So maybe you could comment on that too.

Wang: Well. When somebody goes to the gym and works out, he gets big biceps. Environment or experience is shaping the body. When a pianist plays a lot on the keyboard—now we can image his brain, and we can see that that portion of his motor cortex which controls finger movement is larger. Now a child is born speaking a language, that language has its sound, its words and its constructions. That's a lot of experience, and lots of practice, much more than the pianist of the keyboard. How does this shape his brain? So this is kind of the big question I am struggling with because… How does a language shape the brain that services that language? Chinese is distinctive in many ways, very obviously is distinctive in having tones, is distinctive in having a different writing system than the alphabet. So right now we are looking with primarily EEG techniques, to see how having tones affects one's perception of sounds, such as music. Writing in characters, how does that influence one's perception of graphic patterns? In fact, one of my colleagues, Peng Gang just came back from Guangzhou last weekend. He's been collecting data in the music conservatories in Guangzhou to see whether people who are speakers of tone languages have a better chance of recognizing absolute pitch. This is a question raised by a psychologist at UC San Diego, by the name of Diana Deutsch. She has found this to be true with limited sampling. We want to see whether this is really true and we do it on a much larger scale. So if we can somehow come to some kind of an understanding of how the language we speak shapes our brain, and how in turn our brain shapes our behavior, I think that would be a significant contribution linguistics can make towards understanding humanity.

Yip:　　　It's very exciting. In the next decade or two, we can anticipate a lot of important results coming from research in this direction.

Wang:　　Keeping my fingers crossed. I hope so.

Matthews:　You're also following in the footsteps of and Chao Yuen Ren and Joseph Greenberg, combining language research and what we can learn from being a musician.

Wang:　　Yes, I think we are in a much better position than they were. We have the tools now. Imagine Galileo without a telescope. How can you study the brain without brain imaging? And our telescope into the brain came into being only twenty, thirty years ago. So I think it makes a big difference.

Yip:　　　You have brought us a book. This is a very important book. "永遠的 POLA".

Wang:　　Yes.

Yip:　　　Can you introduce it a little bit?

Wang:　　POLA is a ragged old house. So… Yes, it is. POLA stands for Project On Linguistic Analysis. When we did research in Berkeley, we didn't have a decent place, since the building for the Linguistics Department was all taken up. So they gave us a run-down house called Project On Linguistic Analysis. That's where *Journal of Chinese Linguistics* was started. After we acquired that place, many friends interested in Chinese linguistics would come visit us there. So every half a year or so, we would have a meeting. It was a very relaxing and easygoing meeting. Dr. Ovid J.L. Tzeng was a frequent guest right from the beginning. There were also Zhu De Xi and Ma Xue Liang from Beijing, Mei Tsu Lin from Cornell and Ting Pang Hsin from Taiwan. So the title "POLA forever" was probably suggested by Ovid Tzeng, who felt that that type of…that spirit of informal, in-depth kind of exchange was very productive.

Yip: That's fascinating.

Wang: Indeed it was.

Wang: Ovid said that he would like to cultivate a place like POLA after he returned to Taiwan, to rekindle that spirit. But he hasn't had a chance to do it as yet. He later served as Minister of Education in Taiwan. So he didn't have time.

Yip: There's a music score inside the book. Could you tell us about it?

Wang: Oh yes? Where?

Yip: It's a song called "Autumn Song."

Wang: Yes.

Yip: "Music and lyrics by Prof. William S-Y. Wang." I bet not many people knew you are a composer.

Wang: I don't know much about this stuff actually, but I do like to hum some songs once in a while. When I hummed some music, I thought it might be better to add some words. So I wrote some lyrics in English first. Then Ovid Tzeng said, let me translate them into Chinese. I think he did a better job in the Chinese translation than I did with the English lyrics. So they included this song in the book and some photos as well.

Yip: You have trained many generations of students in Chinese linguistics, many of whom have become influential scholars scattered in different institutions. Maybe you could also say something about this.

Wang: I think what pleases me most is that in the beginning, they were students and I was the teacher. But one year or two later, we became good friends. These friends have all been friends for decades, not just when they were studying. There were some distinguished talents amongst them. When I was at Ohio State, my first PhD student was a Japanese. His name was Mantaro Hashimoto. I was still very young then, so he was two or three years older than me. Although I was his supervisor, I had the impression that he was more knowledgeable than me in many aspects. He studied sinology in Japan, so he learned a lot about the Chinese tradition.

Yip: Thank you, Prof. Wang, for giving us this book. The title of this book is very significant: POLA Forever: Festschrift in Honor of Professor William S-Y. Wang on His 70th Birthday. Inside is a collection of articles written by those distinguished and influential scholars who used to study under Prof. Wang. This is their tribute to Prof. Wang. Let's have Prof. Wang say something about these papers. There are also many nice photos inside.

Wang: This book was edited by two good friends of mine. Ho Dah An was the director of Institute of Linguistics at Academia Sinica. Ovid Tzeng may have been Taiwan's

Minister of Education then. They are both outstanding scholars. Ho Dah An is an authority on the history of Chinese. He has a good knowledge about the dialects, refined discourse, etc., all the essentials of traditional Chinese linguistics. Ovid Tzeng is a psychologist. I think he came to see me at Berkeley in the 1970s. That was the first time I met him. He asked me: why do you linguists study only the spoken language? Why don't you pay the slightest attention to written language? I said: you are a psychologist. So you pay attention to written language. I'll see what I can do. I will give you whatever help I can. At that time, people thought that since Chinese characters are not alphabetical, you can retrieve the semantics directly by looking at the characters, without phonological access. Ovid said: this seems to be a misconception. So he did some very interesting experiments with me. He's an expert at conducting experiments. And I was beside him to give some assistance. Then we wrote a paper together entitled "Speech Recoding in Reading Chinese Characters", published in 1977. That was the first scientific paper about Chinese reading. From then on, many papers have studied this same question: When we look at a character, is phonology involved? Many of the authors here are my good friends, but I can't name them all one by one. For example, Hung Lan is Ovid's wife. She's also an eminent psychologist. Hsieh Hsin-I is a very good friend of mine. He is both a linguist and a poet. He has published many beautiful anthologies of poems at the University of Hawaii. Ting Pang Hsin and I used to have very different views at the beginning. But after much discussion, I found that we shared a lot in common. There are quite a few papers here, so I don't mean to talk about them all. I just mentioned Ting Pang Hsin. I wrote an article with Cheng Chin Chuan at that time on a Min dialect. That Min dialect is Chaozhou. Many tones in Chaozhou were undergoing change then. We thought that change was a kind of lexical diffusion. But P.H. Ting said we haven't considered influence from other dialects. I think what he said made sense. Later on we collected some other data, so we kept on investigating the question. We found that Ting is right in some ways, but we are also right in the paper. Now we have a better understanding of this change in Chaozhou. As for Lien Chin Fa, he is at Tsinghua University in Taiwan. His paper was also a result of my discussion with Ting. Many languages have different strata. Southern Min is such an example. The stratum can be found in each individual syllable. For instance, a dialect may have a literary and a colloquial stratum. In each syllable we can identify three components: tone, initial and final. Some syllables have literary tone but colloquial initial and final. Others have a literary initial but colloquial tone and final. With the binary value of three components, that is, two to the power of three, you get eight. So there are altogether eight possibilities. Lien talked about this in his paper, which I found quite interesting. Matthew Chen is, I think, an authority on tone sandhi. He has studied the phenomenon of sandhi in many dialects. Weera Ostapirat is a Thai name. He's an overseas Chinese from Thailand. I don't know how to pronounce his name in Thai, so I call him by his Chinese name Xu Jia Ping. He studies Kra-Dai, an Austro-Asiatic language. Shen Zhong Wei studies Menggu Ziyun (Mongolian Letters arranged by Rhymes). I saw that there are many pictures here in the book. Two were taken at Tsinghua University, Beijing, which I visited to give a speech in 2004. I learned some good news just a few days ago. After that speech in Beijing, many people felt enthusiastic and inspired. So they will publish a big volume on language evolution and the brain soon, probably toward the end of this year. They compiled forty or fifty-odd papers translated from English into Chinese. I'm helping them take a final look at the book to see if any revision needs to be made. So wherever I go, people tend to say: Here comes Prof. Wang again to sow seeds for us. Indeed it is like sowing seeds. When people reach a certain age, they might not be open-minded enough to accept new ideas. But those young people at twenty or thirty always feel excited when they hear something new. They might say to themselves: it's time for me to work harder. This is one thing that pleases me a lot.

Yip: This is also making us very excited, to hear about your work, and to know that your speech has produced a great impact in such a short time. We hope Prof. Wang will also say something to encourage this young department of ours, the Dept. of Linguistics and Modern Languages, to inspire our young students. If they set their mind on entering this department, how can they prepare themselves to confront different kinds of challenge?

Wang: Well, this is an extremely important question. I'm glad that Prof. Yip cares about this issue. People generally just care about their own business, but I think we have the responsibility to look further. When we look further, Hong Kong is an ideal place. First of all, it carries on the tradition of two thousand years of Chinese linguistics. Secondly, it has easy and full access to various achievements and theories of Western linguistics. Integrating the two approaches of research will be a promising solution. I already talked about this when I launched *Journal of Chinese Linguistics*. Western Linguistics, Chinese Linguistics, let them flow together. I think Hong Kong is a perfect place for the two streams of thought to flow together. It is well known that linguistics can be said to initiate from William Jones' speech in 1786. From then on, most of those brilliant developments in linguistics were found in Europe. Schleicher, Brugmann, Verner, all these prominent linguists worked in Europe. We can thus say that linguistics of the 19th century was essentially in Europe. Europe had the leading role then. The situation was a bit different in the 20th century. For example, there were Leonard Bloomfield and Edward Sapir. And then there was Roman Jakobson from Russia. In Europe there was Hjelmslev from Copenhagen, and J.R. Firth from London. So England and the US led the way in the 20th century. Since Europe led in the 19th century, then Europe and the US in the 20th century, so it is my great hope that the 21st century might be ours to take the lead. Therefore, my advice to these young people is, firstly, they need to work with a direction. They need to have both a historical perspective and a sense of mission. Secondly, when we work together, we should set a common goal. We should let East Asia, China, and Hong Kong become the center of linguistics in the 21st century. This is the greatest dream I wish to fulfill.

Yip: Wow, this is an awe-inspiring vision. I never thought about this before: Prof. Wang's vision. He has such a noble wish in his vision. I do see that now in many fields, whether in economy or elsewhere, China is playing a decisive role. Many world powers and leading countries have turned their eyes on Mainland China now. So our work in linguistics can also play such a role.

Wang: Yes, while working toward that goal, the Childhood Bilingualism Research Centre shoulders a great responsibility.

Yip: Indeed, we have an important mission and a long way to go. Thank you very much. Thank you Prof. Wang.